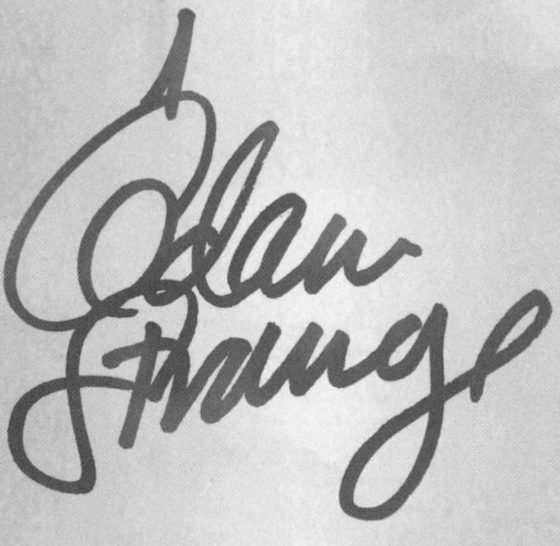

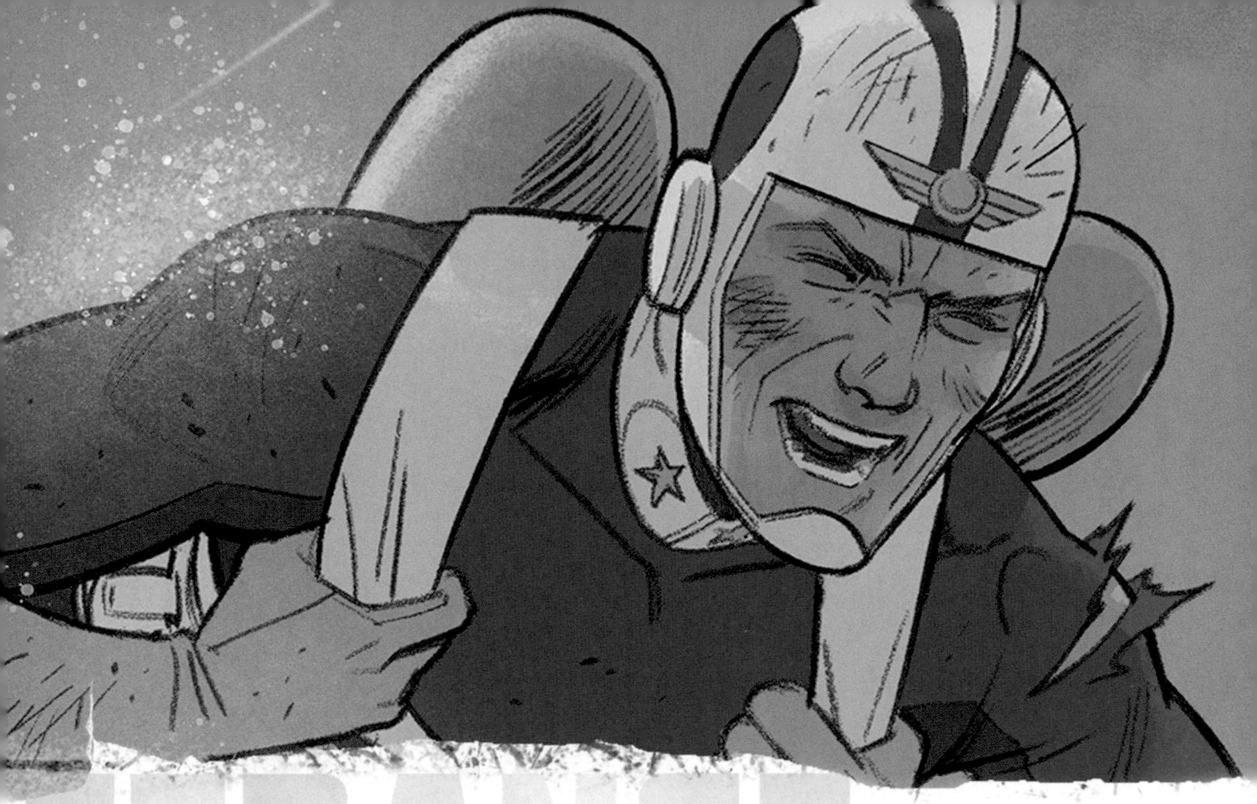

STRANGE ADVENTURES

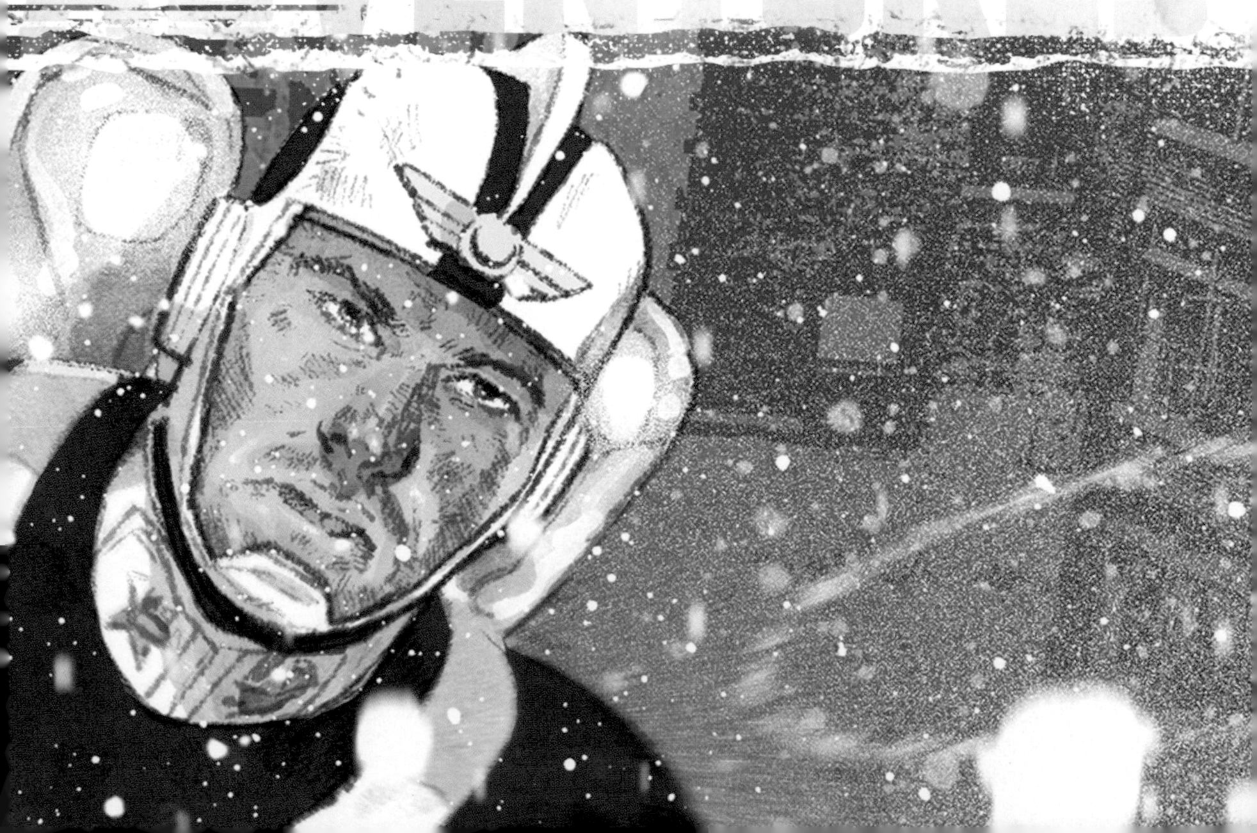

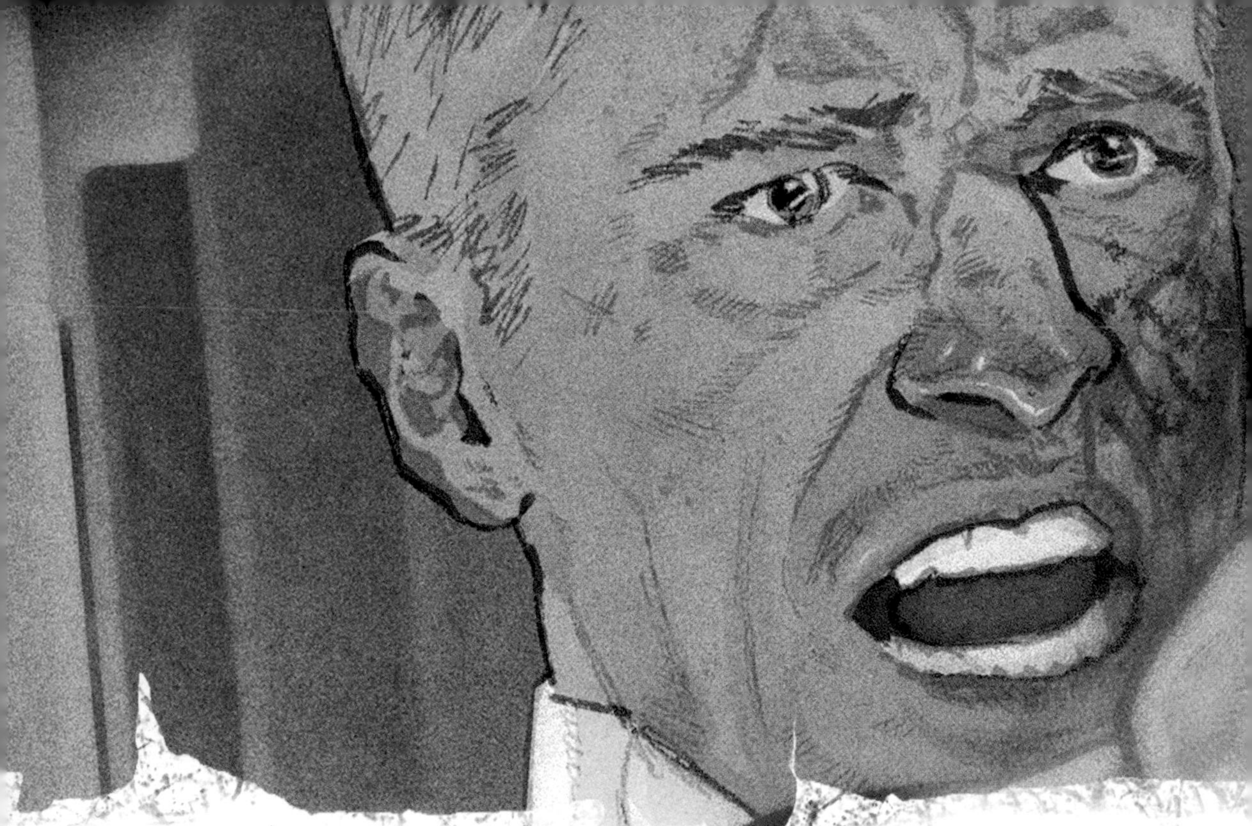

TOM KING WRITER

STRANGE A

MITCH GERADS & **EVAN "DOC" SHANER** ARTISTS

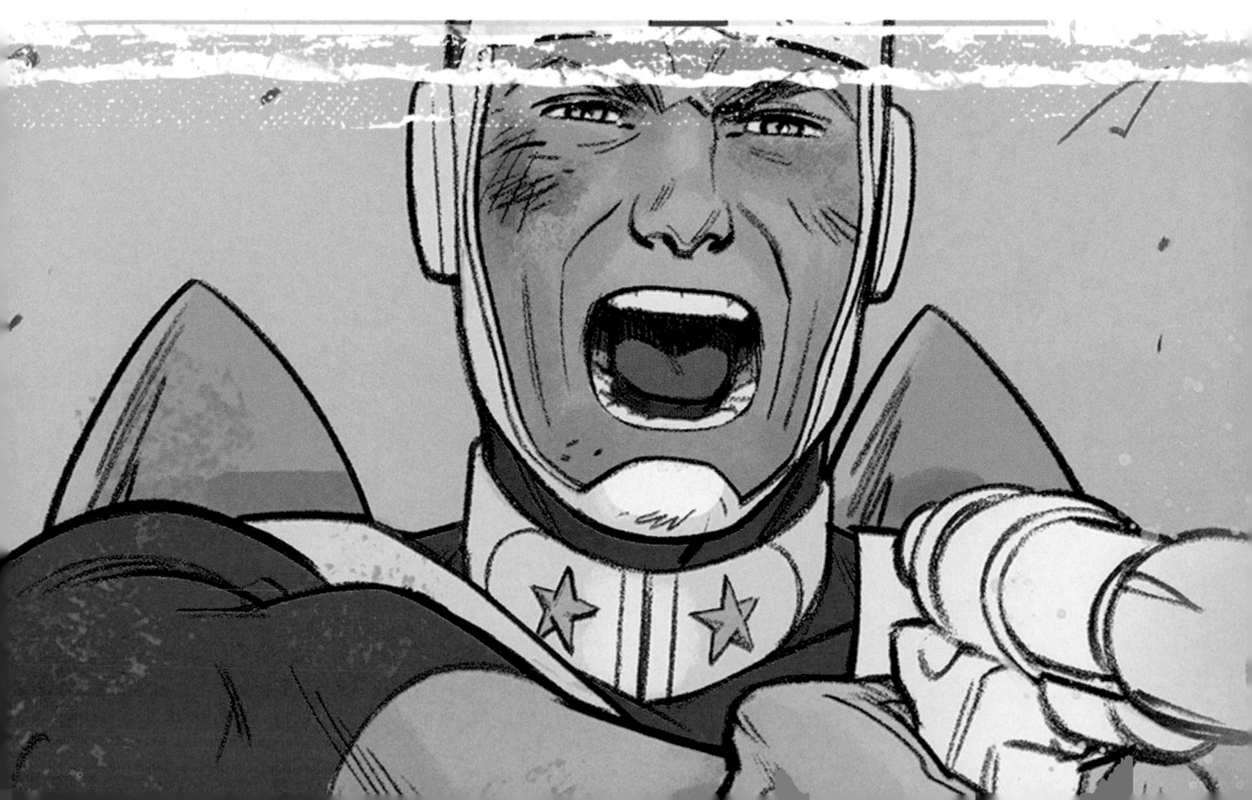

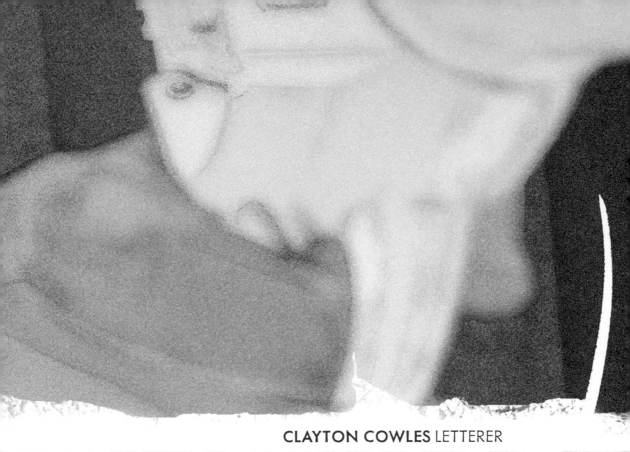

CLAYTON COWLES LETTERER

DVENTURES

MITCH GERADS & **EVAN "DOC" SHANER** COLLECTION COVER ARTISTS

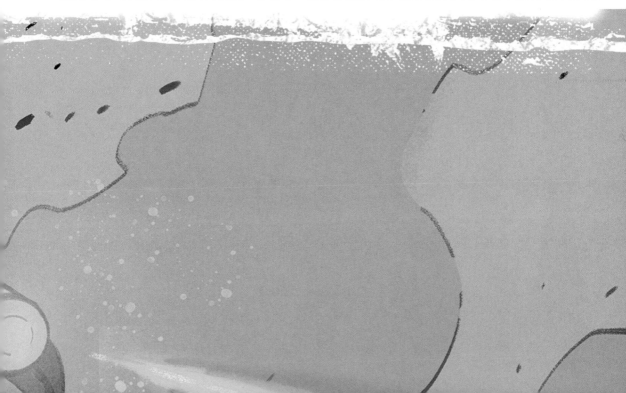

JAMIE S. RICH EDITOR – ORIGINAL SERIES
BRITTANY HOLZHERR ASSOCIATE EDITOR –
ORIGINAL SERIES & EDITOR – COLLECTED EDITION
BIXIE MATHIEU ASSISTANT EDITOR – ORIGINAL SERIES
STEVE COOK DESIGN DIRECTOR – BOOKS
AMIE BROCKWAY-METCALF PUBLICATION DESIGN
CHRISTY SAWYER PUBLICATION PRODUCTION

MARIE JAVINS EDITOR-IN-CHIEF, DC COMICS

DANIEL CHERRY III SENIOR VP – GENERAL MANAGER
JIM LEE PUBLISHER & CHIEF CREATIVE OFFICER
JOEN CHOE VP – GLOBAL BRAND & CREATIVE SERVICES
DON FALLETTI VP – MANUFACTURING OPERATIONS &
WORKFLOW MANAGEMENT
LAWRENCE GANEM VP – TALENT SERVICES
ALISON GILL SENIOR VP – MANUFACTURING & OPERATIONS
NICK J. NAPOLITANO VP – MANUFACTURING
ADMINISTRATION & DESIGN
NANCY SPEARS VP – REVENUE

STRANGE ADVENTURES

DC – A WARNERMEDIA COMPANY.

DC COMICS, 2900 WEST ALAMEDA AVE.,
BURBANK, CA 91505
PRINTED BY TRANSCONTINENTAL INTERGLOBE,
BEAUCEVILLE, QC, CANADA. 11/5/21.
FIRST PRINTING.
ISBN: 978-1-77951-203-1
LIBRARY OF CONGRESS CATALOGING-
IN-PUBLICATION DATA IS AVAILABLE.

PEFC Certified

This product is
from sustainably
managed forests and
controlled sources

PEFC/01-31-106   www.pefc.org

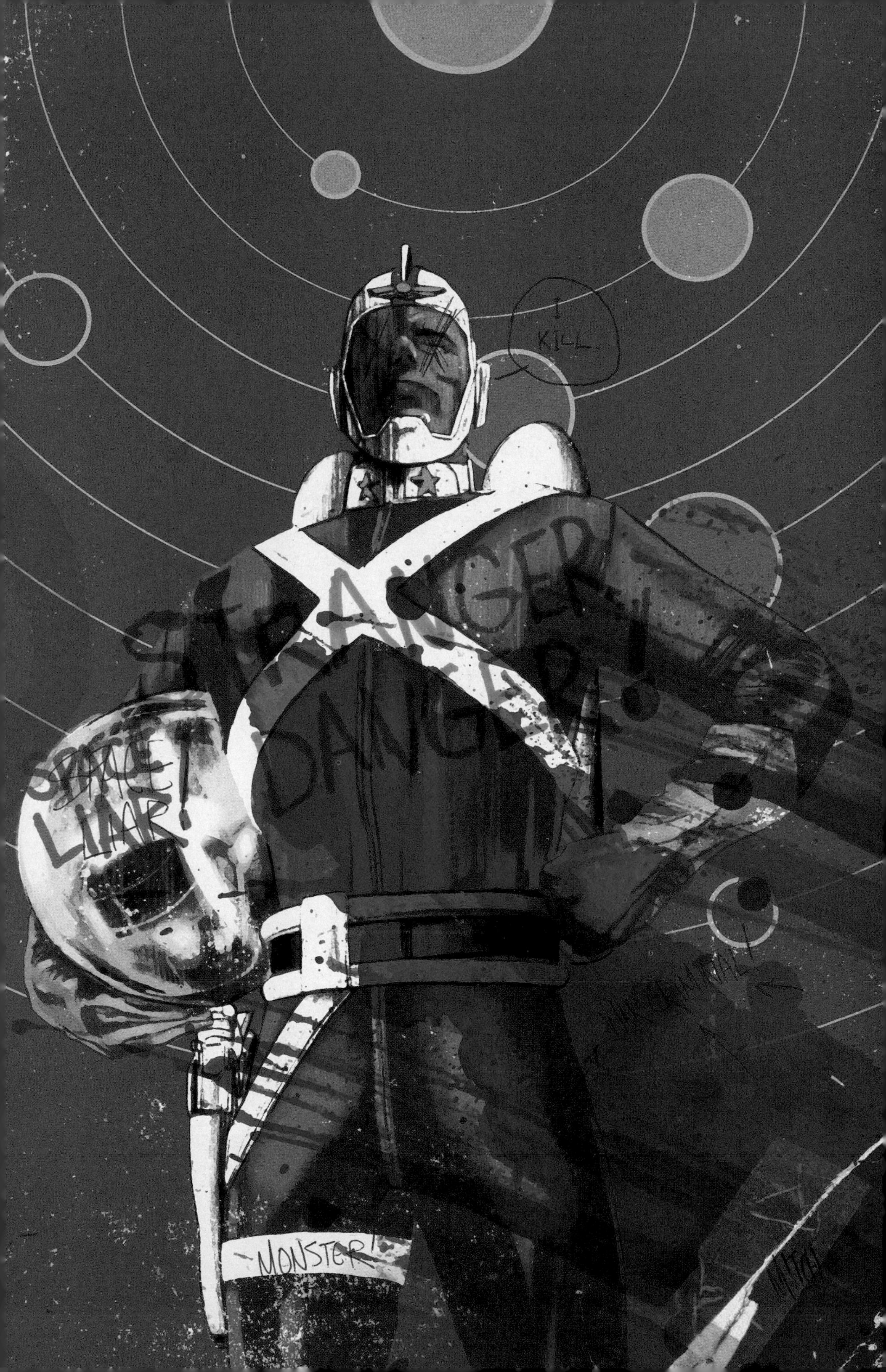
I KILL.
DANGER!
DANGER
SPACE LIAR!
MONSTER!

"YOU'RE A HERO. THEY WANT TO GIVE YOU EVERYTHING."

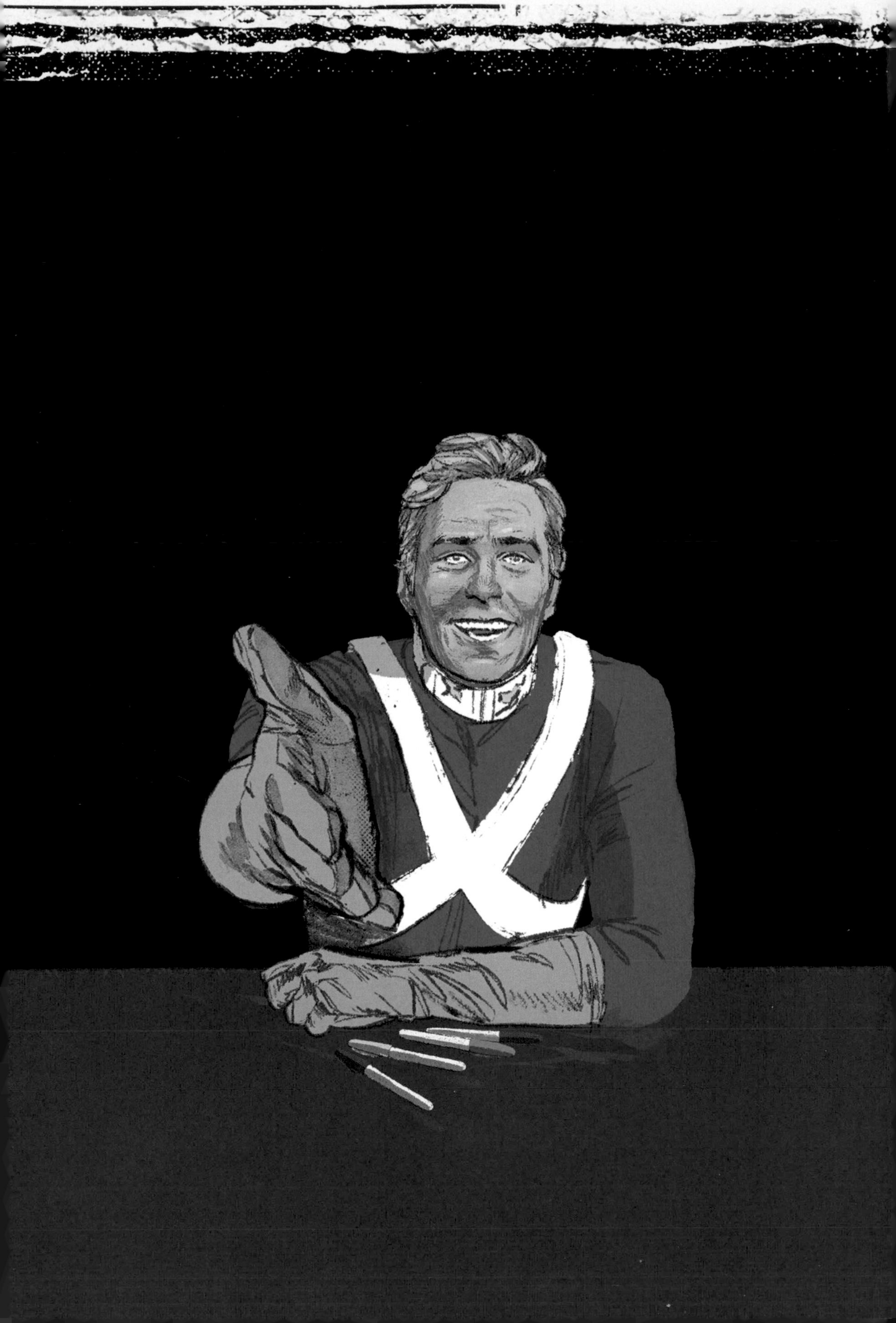

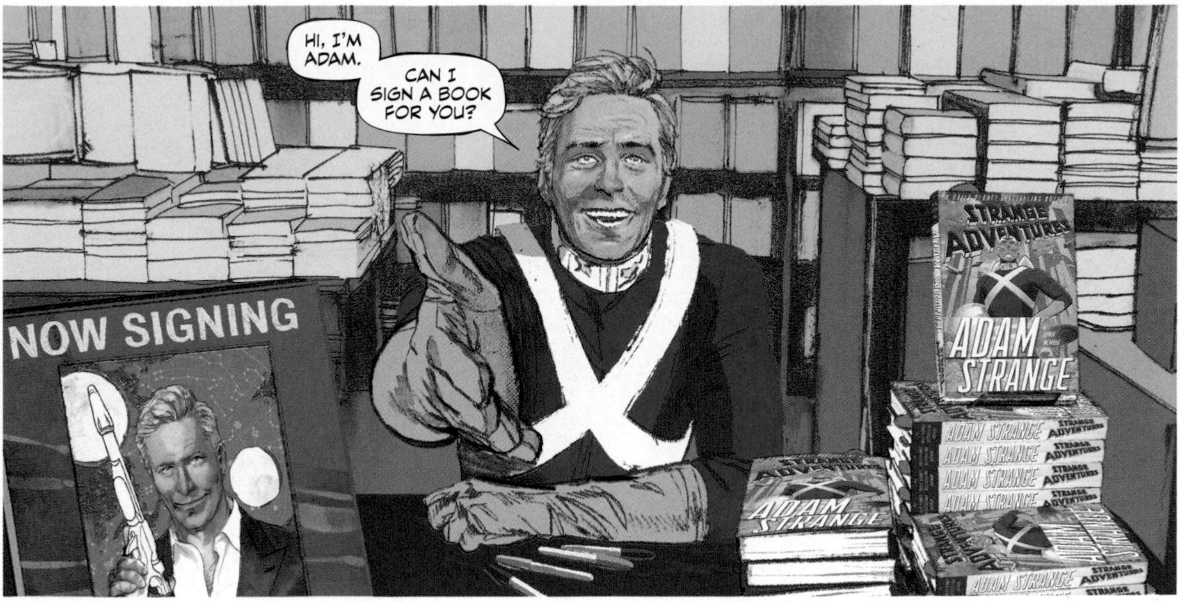
HI, I'M ADAM.
CAN I SIGN A BOOK FOR YOU?
NOW SIGNING
STRANGE ADVENTURES
ADAM STRANGE

Chapter 1

They floated above the ground

TOM KING	...Writer
MITCH GERADS EVAN "DOC" SHANER	...Interior & Cover Artists
CLAYTON COWLES	...Letterer
BRITTANY HOLZHERR	...Associate Editor
JAMIE S. RICH	...Editor

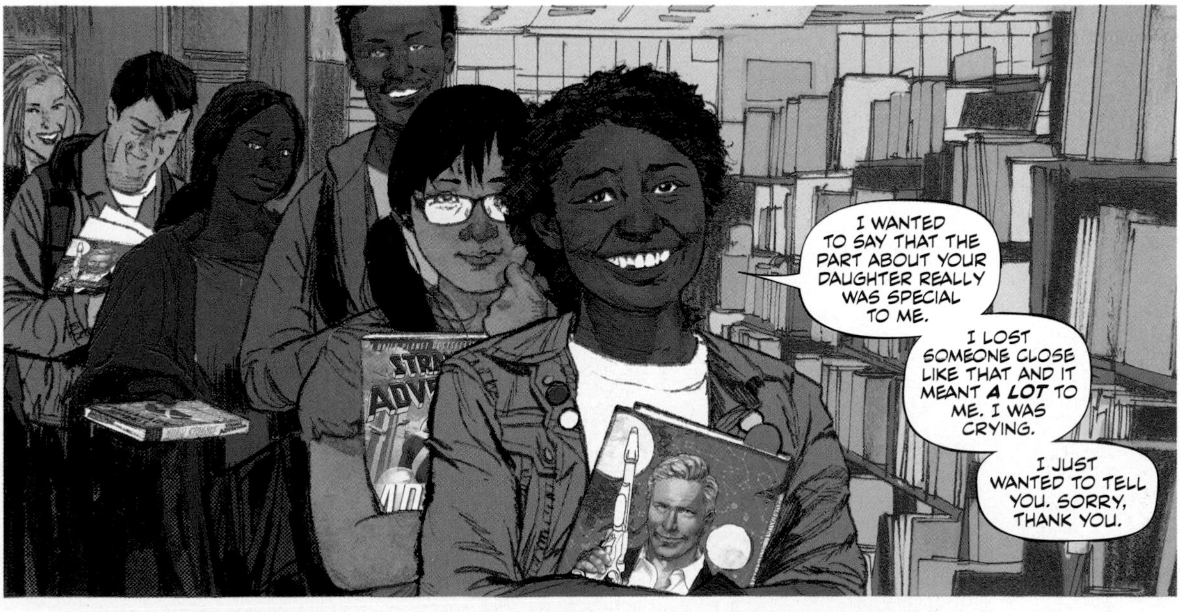
I WANTED TO SAY THAT THE PART ABOUT YOUR DAUGHTER REALLY WAS SPECIAL TO ME.
I LOST SOMEONE CLOSE LIKE THAT AND IT MEANT A LOT TO ME. I WAS CRYING.
I JUST WANTED TO TELL YOU. SORRY, THANK YOU.

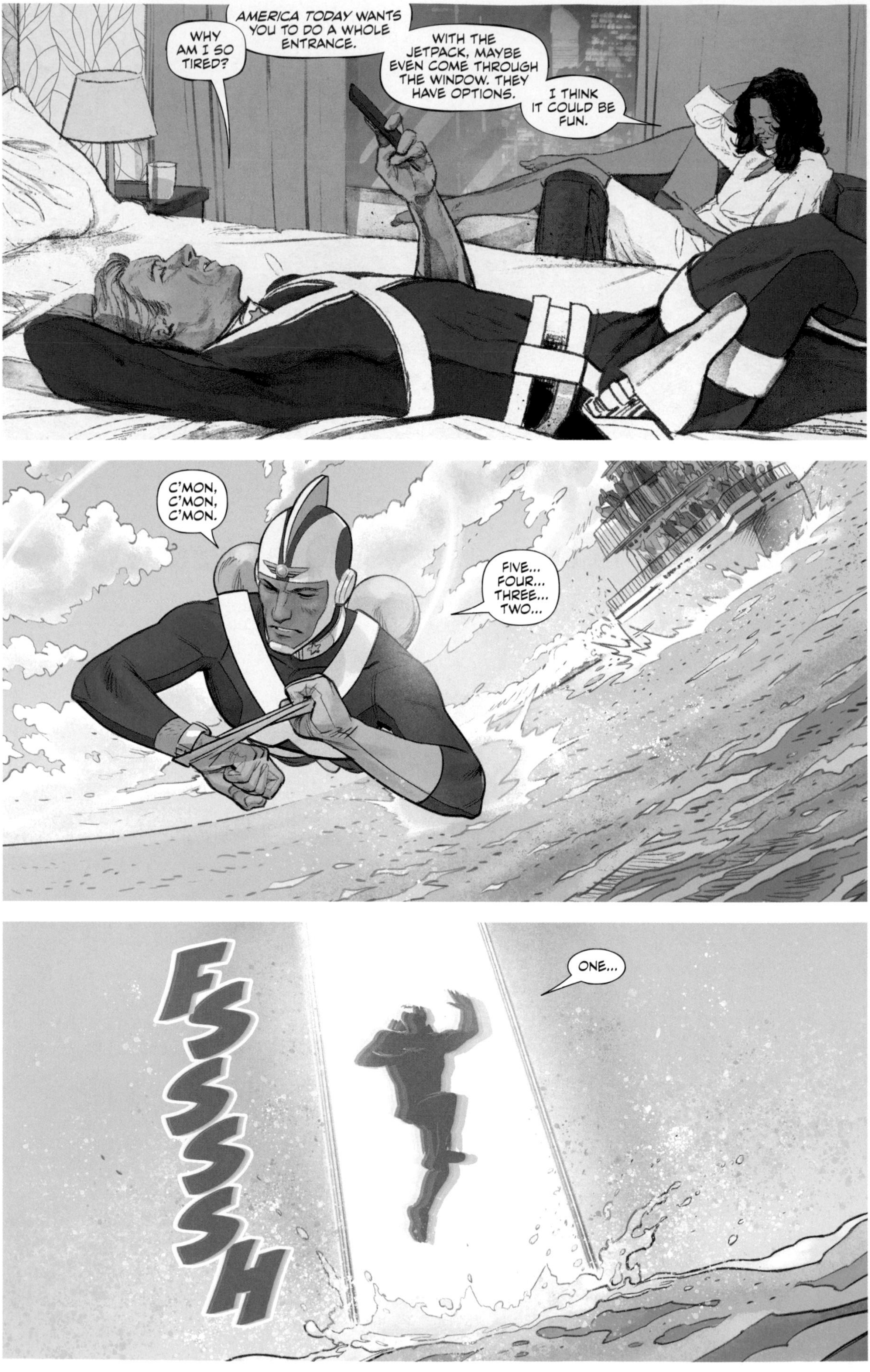
WHY AM I SO TIRED?
AMERICA TODAY WANTS YOU TO DO A WHOLE ENTRANCE.
WITH THE JETPACK, MAYBE EVEN COME THROUGH THE WINDOW. THEY HAVE OPTIONS.
I THINK IT COULD BE FUN.
C'MON, C'MON, C'MON.
FIVE... FOUR... THREE... TWO...
FSSSSH
ONE...

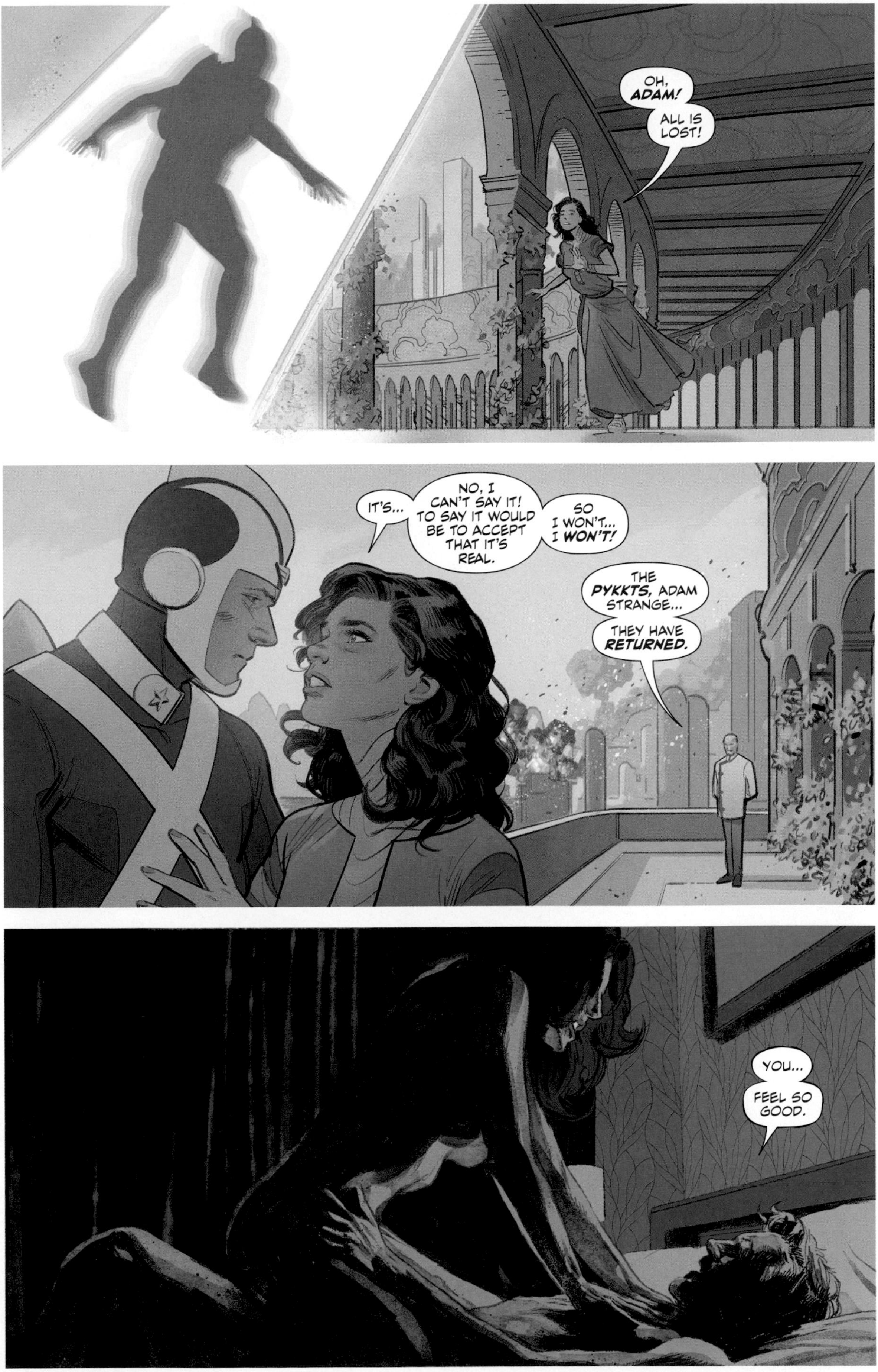
OH, ADAM!
ALL IS LOST!
IT'S...
NO, I CAN'T SAY IT! TO SAY IT WOULD BE TO ACCEPT THAT IT'S REAL.
SO I WON'T... I WON'T!
THE PYKKTS, ADAM STRANGE...
THEY HAVE RETURNED.
YOU...
FEEL SO GOOD.

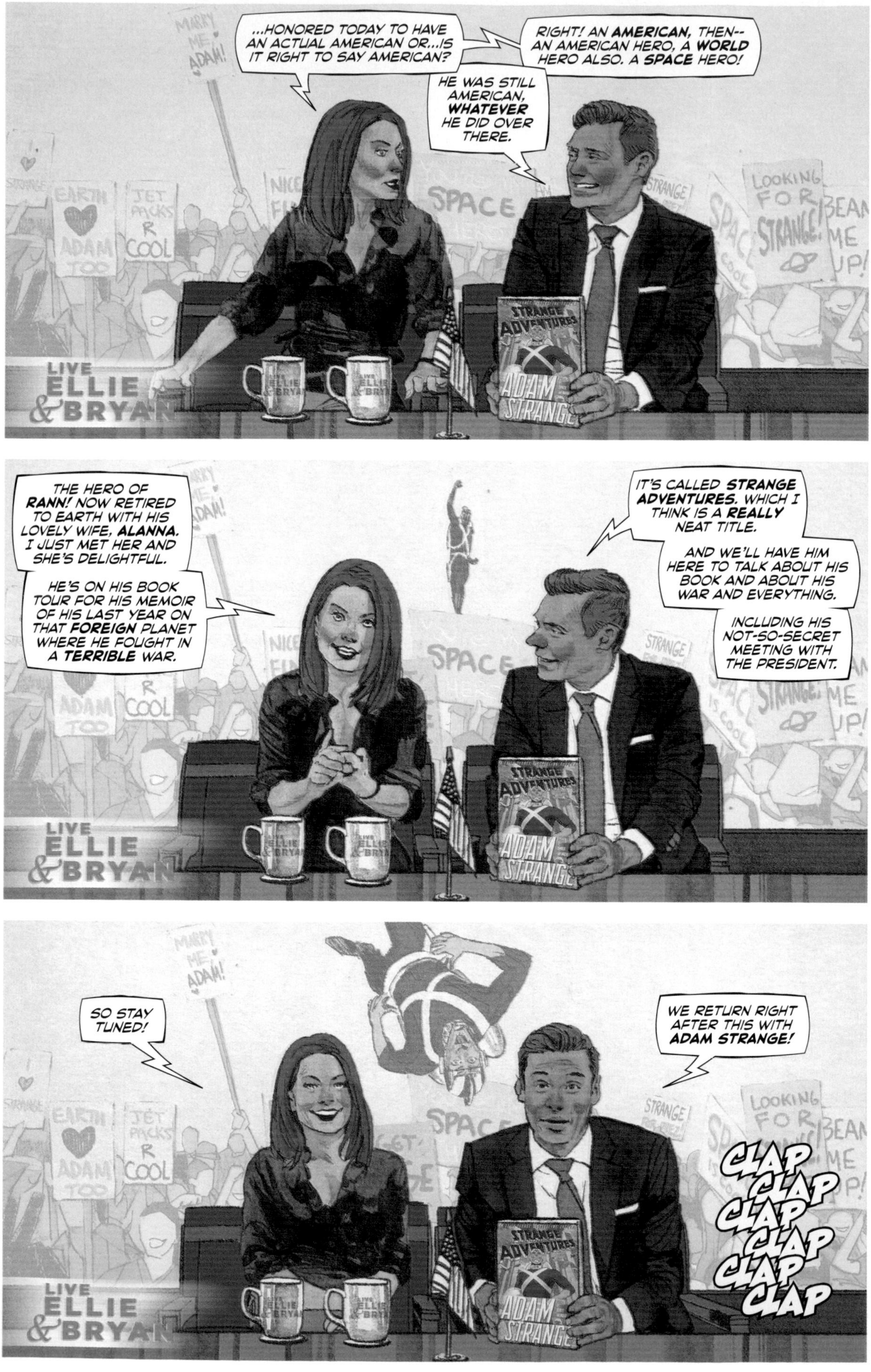
...HONORED TODAY TO HAVE AN ACTUAL AMERICAN OR...IS IT RIGHT TO SAY AMERICAN?
RIGHT! AN **AMERICAN,** THEN-- AN AMERICAN HERO, A **WORLD** HERO ALSO. A **SPACE** HERO!
HE WAS STILL AMERICAN, **WHATEVER** HE DID OVER THERE.
MARRY ME ADAM!
EARTH ♥ ADAM TOO
JET PACKS R COOL
SPACE
LOOKING FOR STRANGE!
BEAM ME UP!
STRANGE ADVENTURES
ADAM STRANGE
LIVE ELLIE & BRYAN
THE HERO OF **RANN!** NOW RETIRED TO EARTH WITH HIS LOVELY WIFE, **ALANNA.** I JUST MET HER AND SHE'S DELIGHTFUL.
HE'S ON HIS BOOK TOUR FOR HIS MEMOIR OF HIS LAST YEAR ON THAT **FOREIGN** PLANET WHERE HE FOUGHT IN A **TERRIBLE** WAR.
IT'S CALLED **STRANGE ADVENTURES.** WHICH I THINK IS A **REALLY** NEAT TITLE.
AND WE'LL HAVE HIM HERE TO TALK ABOUT HIS BOOK AND ABOUT HIS WAR AND EVERYTHING.
INCLUDING HIS NOT-SO-SECRET MEETING WITH THE PRESIDENT.
LIVE ELLIE & BRYAN
SO STAY TUNED!
WE RETURN RIGHT AFTER THIS WITH **ADAM STRANGE!**
CLAP CLAP CLAP CLAP CLAP CLAP
LIVE ELLIE & BRYAN

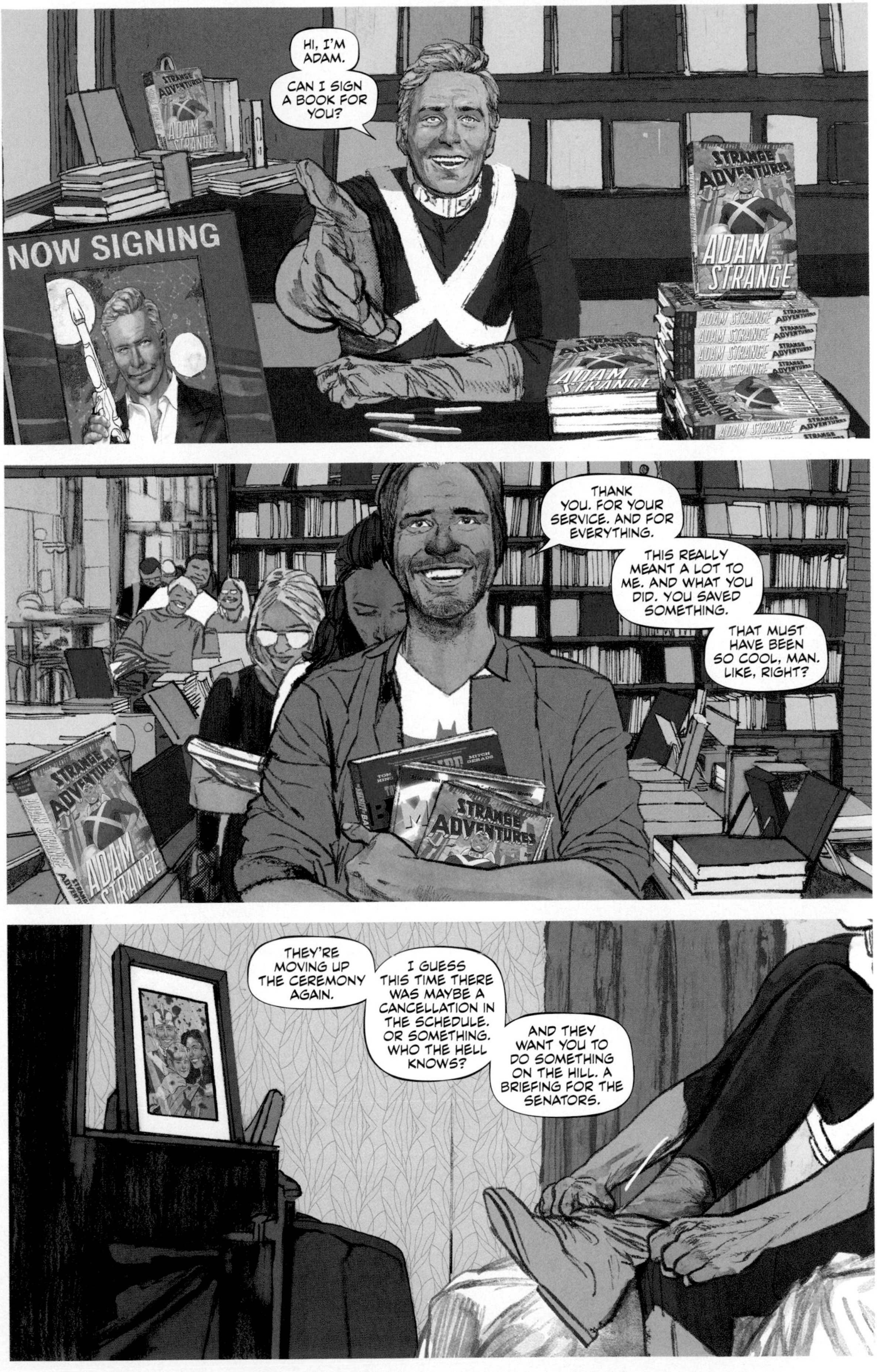
HI, I'M ADAM.
CAN I SIGN A BOOK FOR YOU?
NOW SIGNING
STRANGE ADVENTURES
ADAM STRANGE
THANK YOU. FOR YOUR SERVICE. AND FOR EVERYTHING.
THIS REALLY MEANT A LOT TO ME. AND WHAT YOU DID. YOU SAVED SOMETHING.
THAT MUST HAVE BEEN SO COOL, MAN. LIKE, RIGHT?
THEY'RE MOVING UP THE CEREMONY AGAIN.
I GUESS THIS TIME THERE WAS MAYBE A CANCELLATION IN THE SCHEDULE. OR SOMETHING. WHO THE HELL KNOWS?
AND THEY WANT YOU TO DO SOMETHING ON THE HILL. A BRIEFING FOR THE SENATORS.

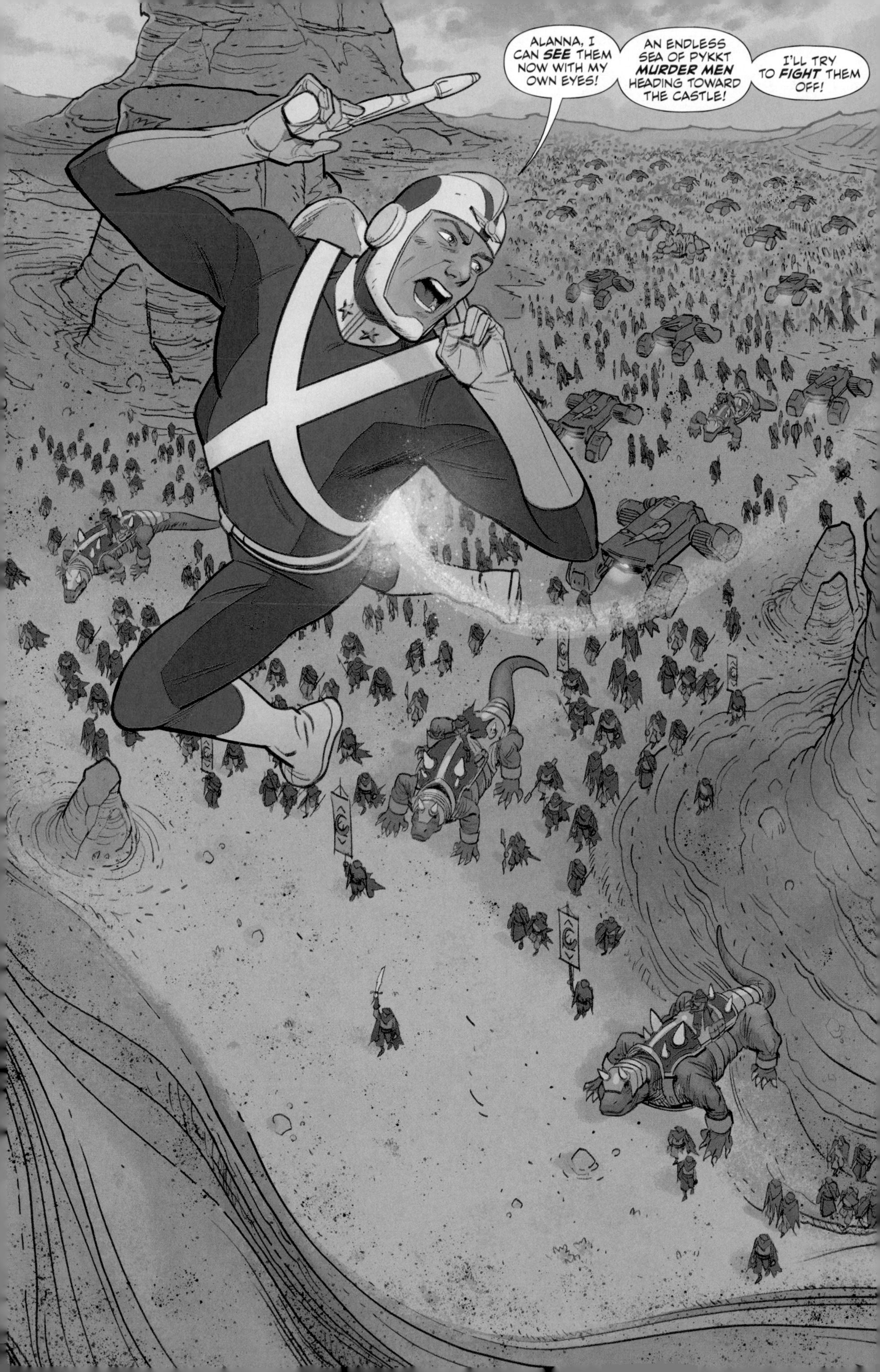
ALANNA, I CAN **SEE** THEM NOW WITH MY OWN EYES!
AN ENDLESS SEA OF PYKKT **MURDER MEN** HEADING TOWARD THE CASTLE!
I'LL TRY TO **FIGHT** THEM OFF!

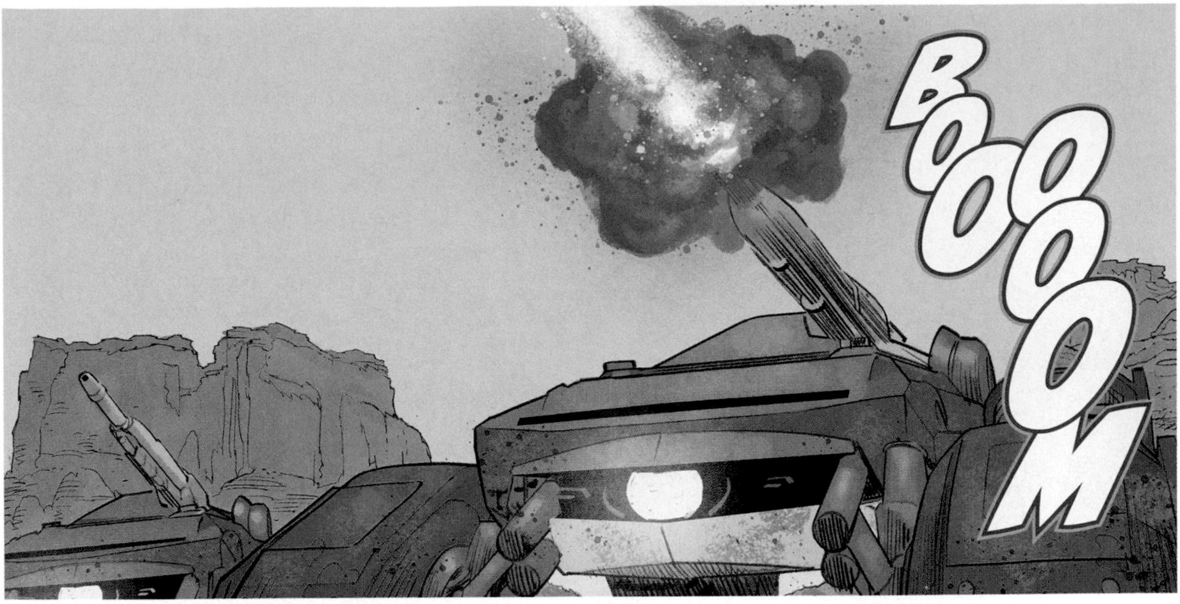
BOOOOOM

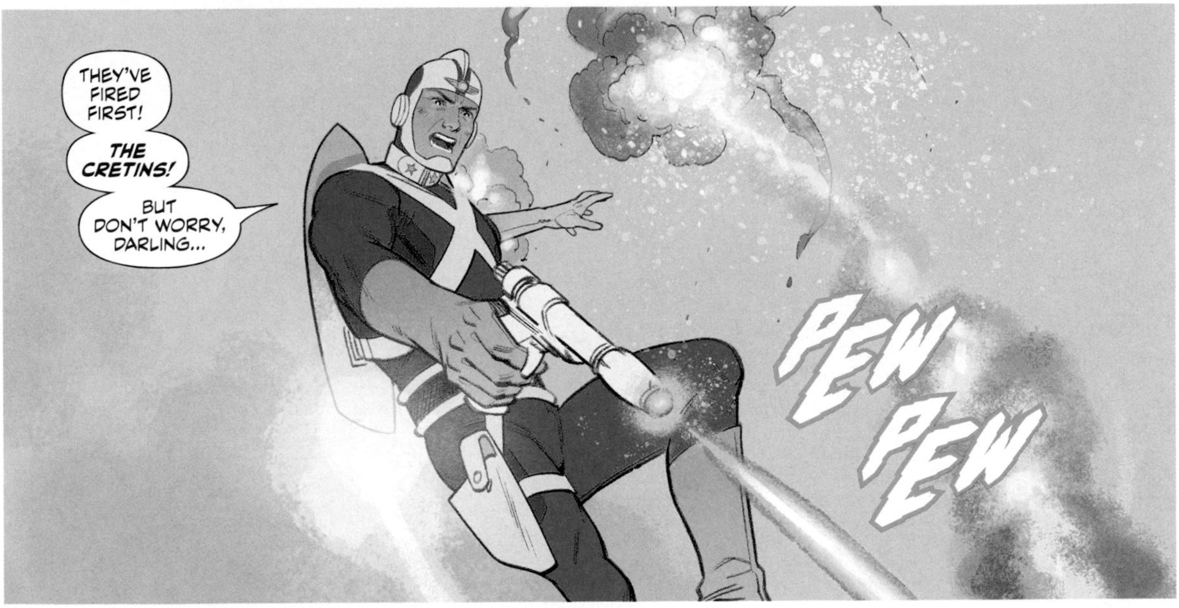
THEY'VE FIRED FIRST!
THE CRETINS!
BUT DON'T WORRY, DARLING...
PEW PEW

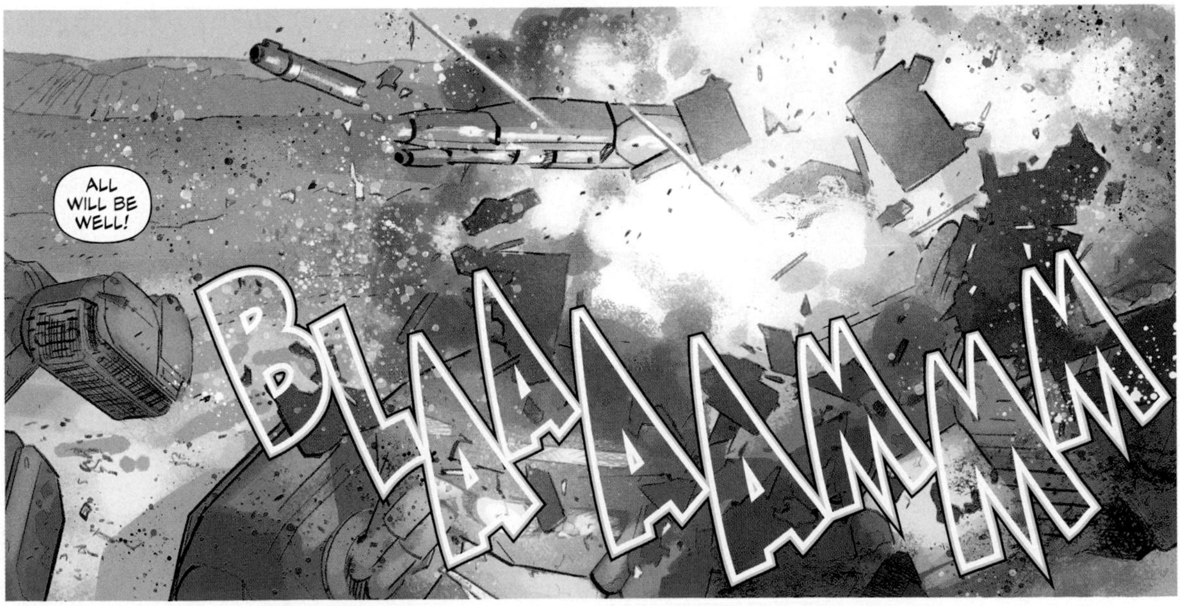
ALL WILL BE WELL!
BLAAAAMMM

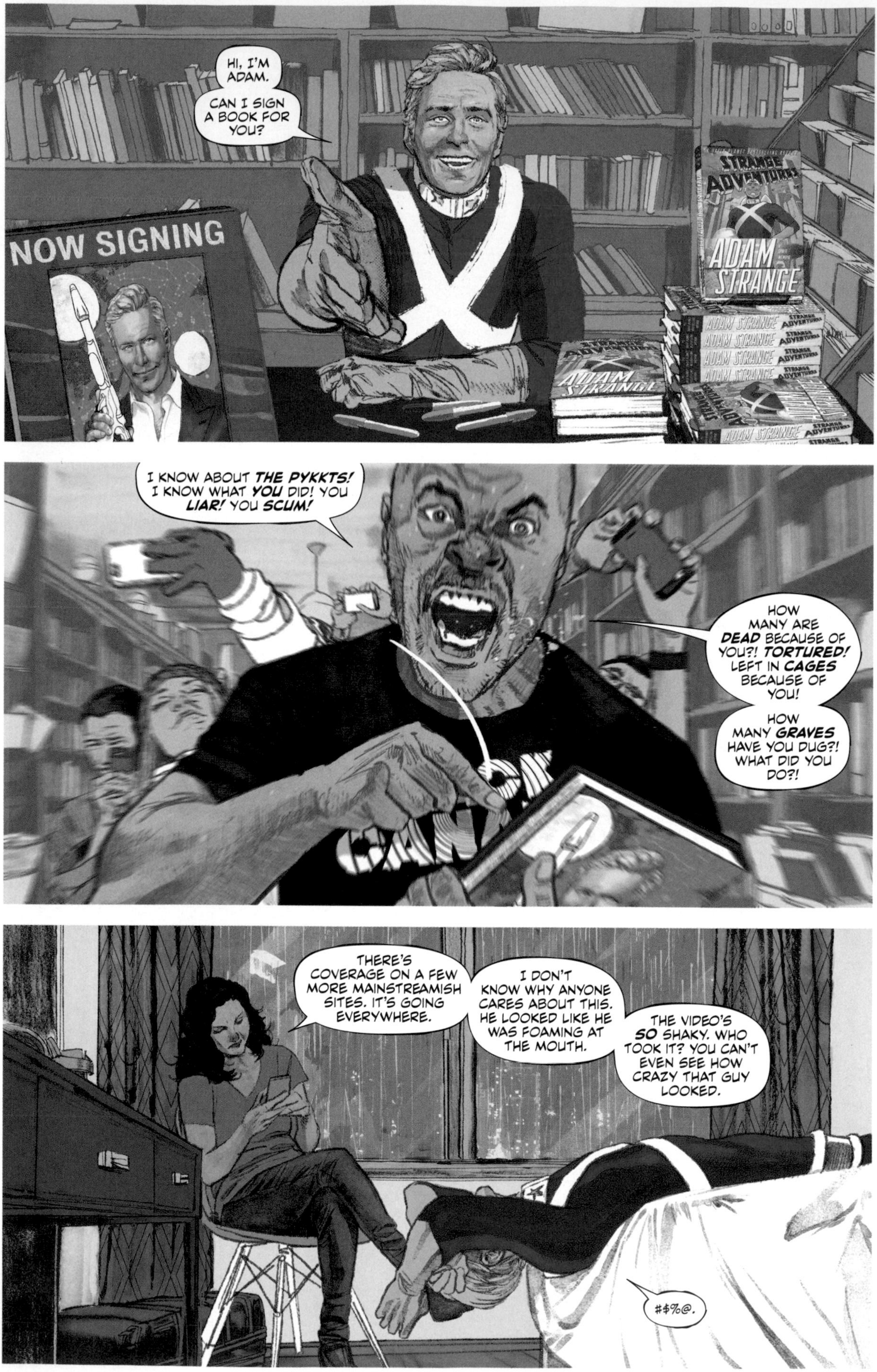
HI, I'M ADAM.
CAN I SIGN A BOOK FOR YOU?
NOW SIGNING
STRANGE ADVENTURES
ADAM STRANGE
I KNOW ABOUT **THE PYKKTS!** I KNOW WHAT **YOU** DID! YOU **LIAR!** YOU **SCUM!**
HOW MANY ARE **DEAD** BECAUSE OF YOU?! **TORTURED!** LEFT IN **CAGES** BECAUSE OF YOU!
HOW MANY **GRAVES** HAVE YOU DUG?! WHAT DID YOU DO?!
THERE'S COVERAGE ON A FEW MORE MAINSTREAMISH SITES. IT'S GOING EVERYWHERE.
I DON'T KNOW WHY ANYONE CARES ABOUT THIS. HE LOOKED LIKE HE WAS FOAMING AT THE MOUTH.
THE VIDEO'S **SO** SHAKY. WHO TOOK IT? YOU CAN'T EVEN SEE HOW CRAZY THAT GUY LOOKED.
#$%@.

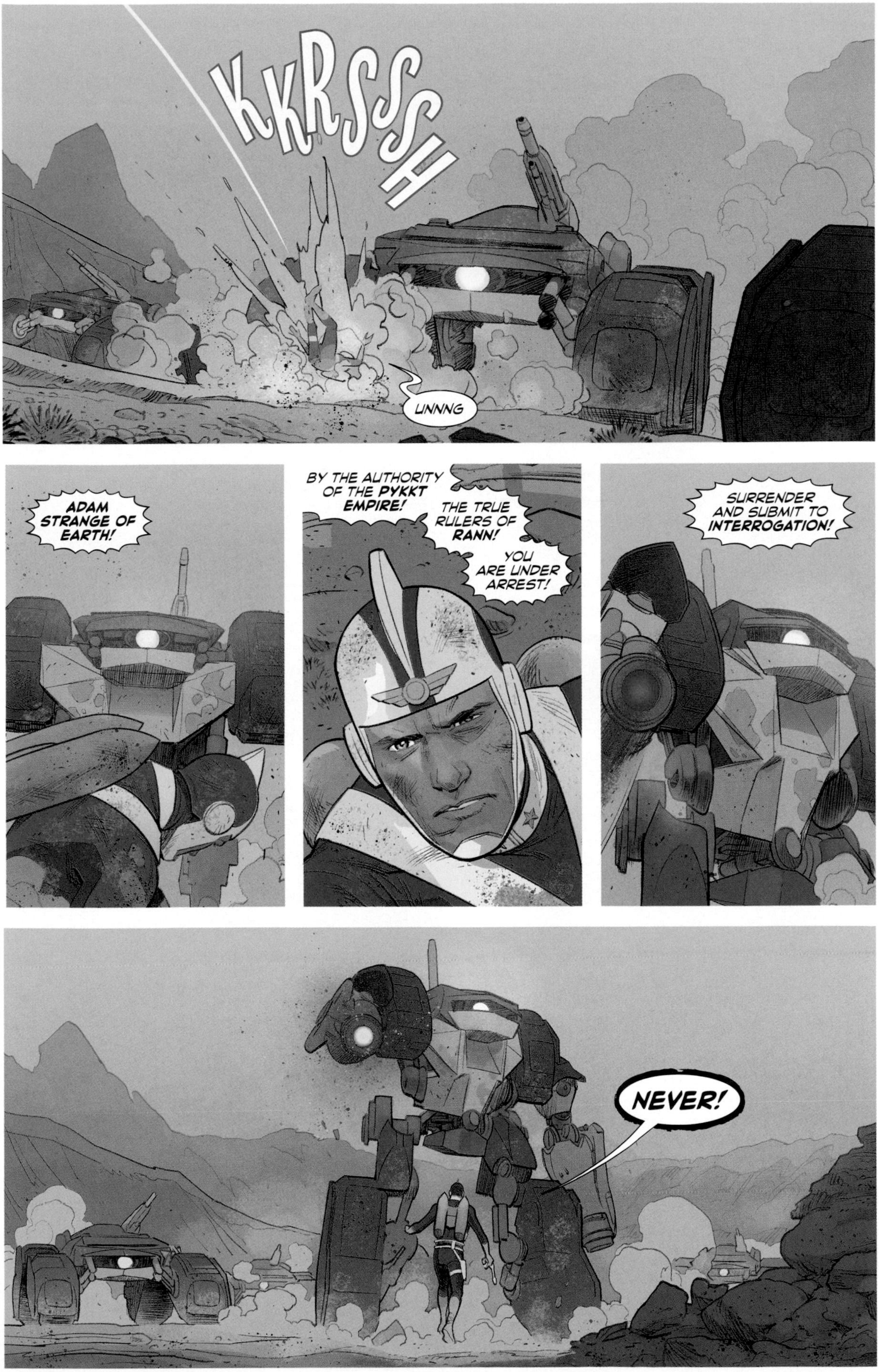
KKRSSSH
UNNNG
ADAM STRANGE OF EARTH!
BY THE AUTHORITY OF THE PYKKT EMPIRE!
THE TRUE RULERS OF RANN!
YOU ARE UNDER ARREST!
SURRENDER AND SUBMIT TO INTERROGATION!
NEVER!

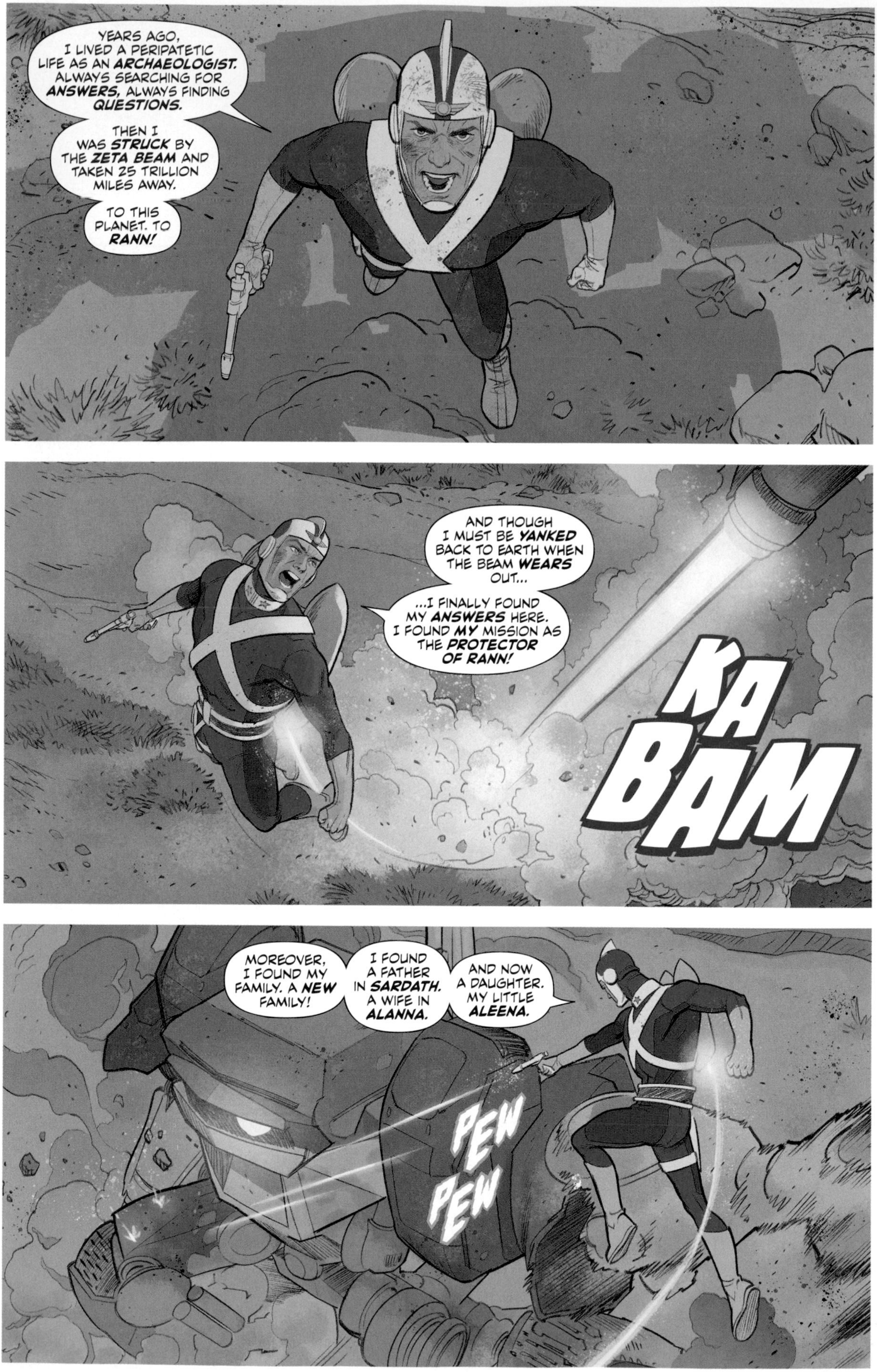
YEARS AGO, I LIVED A PERIPATETIC LIFE AS AN ARCHAEOLOGIST. ALWAYS SEARCHING FOR ANSWERS, ALWAYS FINDING QUESTIONS.
THEN I WAS STRUCK BY THE ZETA BEAM AND TAKEN 25 TRILLION MILES AWAY.
TO THIS PLANET. TO RANN!
AND THOUGH I MUST BE YANKED BACK TO EARTH WHEN THE BEAM WEARS OUT...
...I FINALLY FOUND MY ANSWERS HERE. I FOUND MY MISSION AS THE PROTECTOR OF RANN!
KA BAM
MOREOVER, I FOUND MY FAMILY. A NEW FAMILY!
I FOUND A FATHER IN SARDATH. A WIFE IN ALANNA.
AND NOW A DAUGHTER. MY LITTLE ALEENA.
PEW PEW

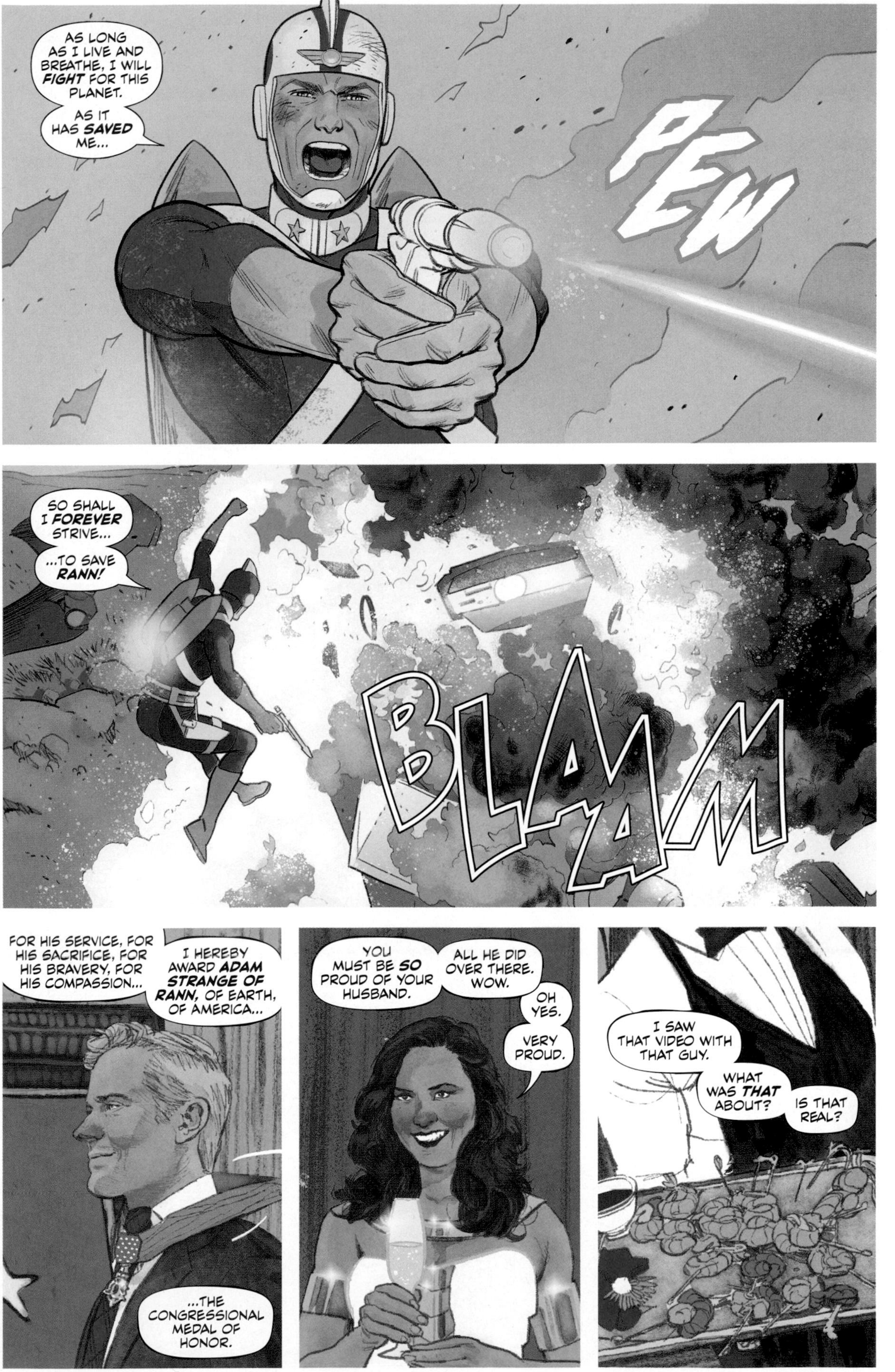
AS LONG AS I LIVE AND BREATHE, I WILL FIGHT FOR THIS PLANET.
AS IT HAS SAVED ME...
PEW
SO SHALL I FOREVER STRIVE...
...TO SAVE RANN!
BLAM
FOR HIS SERVICE, FOR HIS SACRIFICE, FOR HIS BRAVERY, FOR HIS COMPASSION...
I HEREBY AWARD ADAM STRANGE OF RANN, OF EARTH, OF AMERICA...
...THE CONGRESSIONAL MEDAL OF HONOR.
YOU MUST BE SO PROUD OF YOUR HUSBAND.
ALL HE DID OVER THERE. WOW.
OH YES.
VERY PROUD.
I SAW THAT VIDEO WITH THAT GUY.
WHAT WAS THAT ABOUT?
IS THAT REAL?

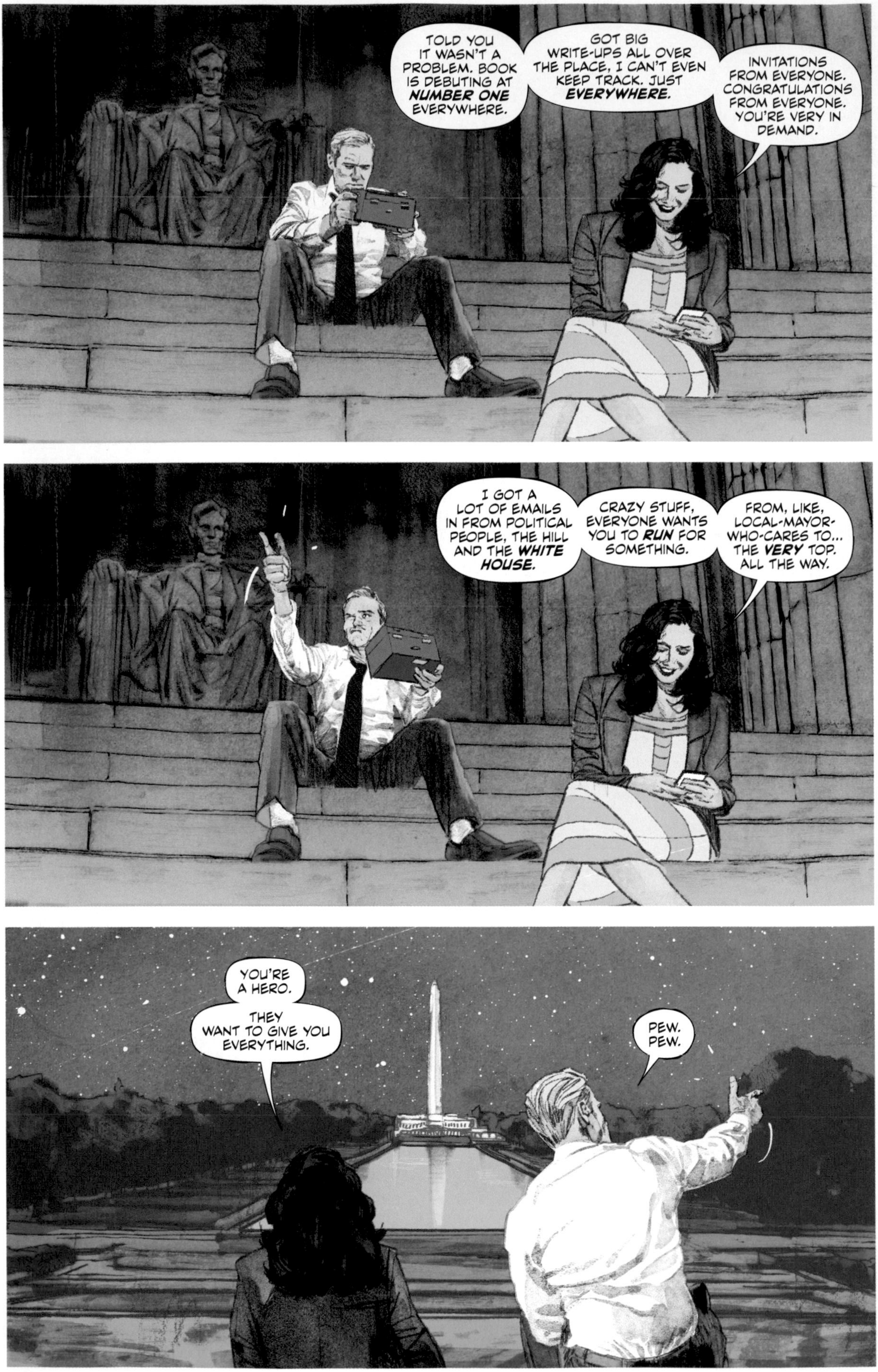
TOLD YOU IT WASN'T A PROBLEM. BOOK IS DEBUTING AT **NUMBER ONE** EVERYWHERE.
GOT BIG WRITE-UPS ALL OVER THE PLACE, I CAN'T EVEN KEEP TRACK. JUST **EVERYWHERE.**
INVITATIONS FROM EVERYONE. CONGRATULATIONS FROM EVERYONE. YOU'RE VERY IN DEMAND.
I GOT A LOT OF EMAILS IN FROM POLITICAL PEOPLE, THE HILL AND THE **WHITE HOUSE.**
CRAZY STUFF, EVERYONE WANTS YOU TO **RUN** FOR SOMETHING.
FROM, LIKE, LOCAL-MAYOR-WHO-CARES TO... THE **VERY** TOP. ALL THE WAY.
YOU'RE A HERO.
THEY WANT TO GIVE YOU EVERYTHING.
PEW. PEW.

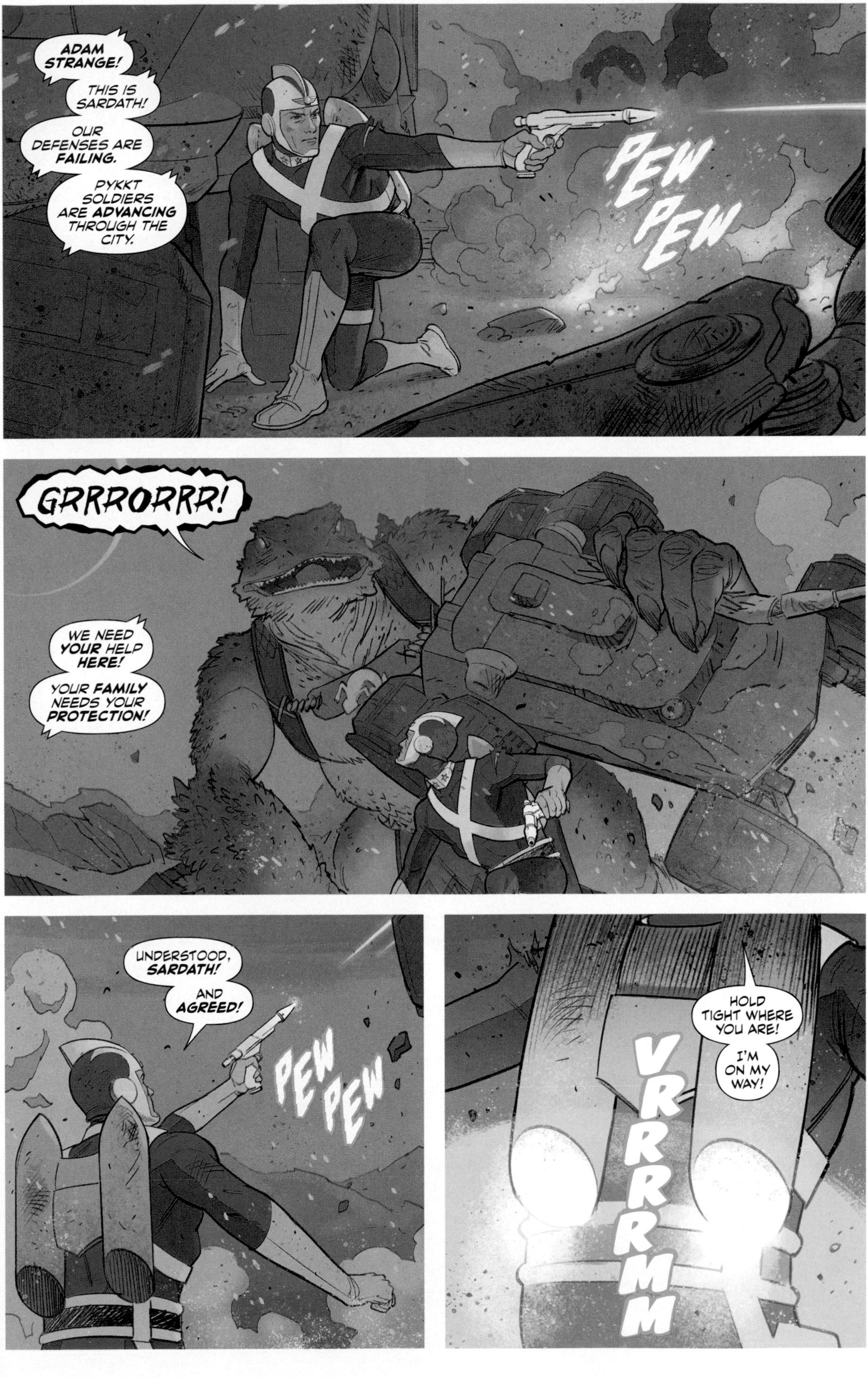
ADAM STRANGE!
THIS IS SARDATH!
OUR DEFENSES ARE FAILING.
PYKKT SOLDIERS ARE ADVANCING THROUGH THE CITY.
PEW PEW
GRRRORRR!
WE NEED YOUR HELP HERE!
YOUR FAMILY NEEDS YOUR PROTECTION!
UNDERSTOOD, SARDATH!
AND AGREED!
PEW PEW
HOLD TIGHT WHERE YOU ARE!
I'M ON MY WAY!
VRRRRMM

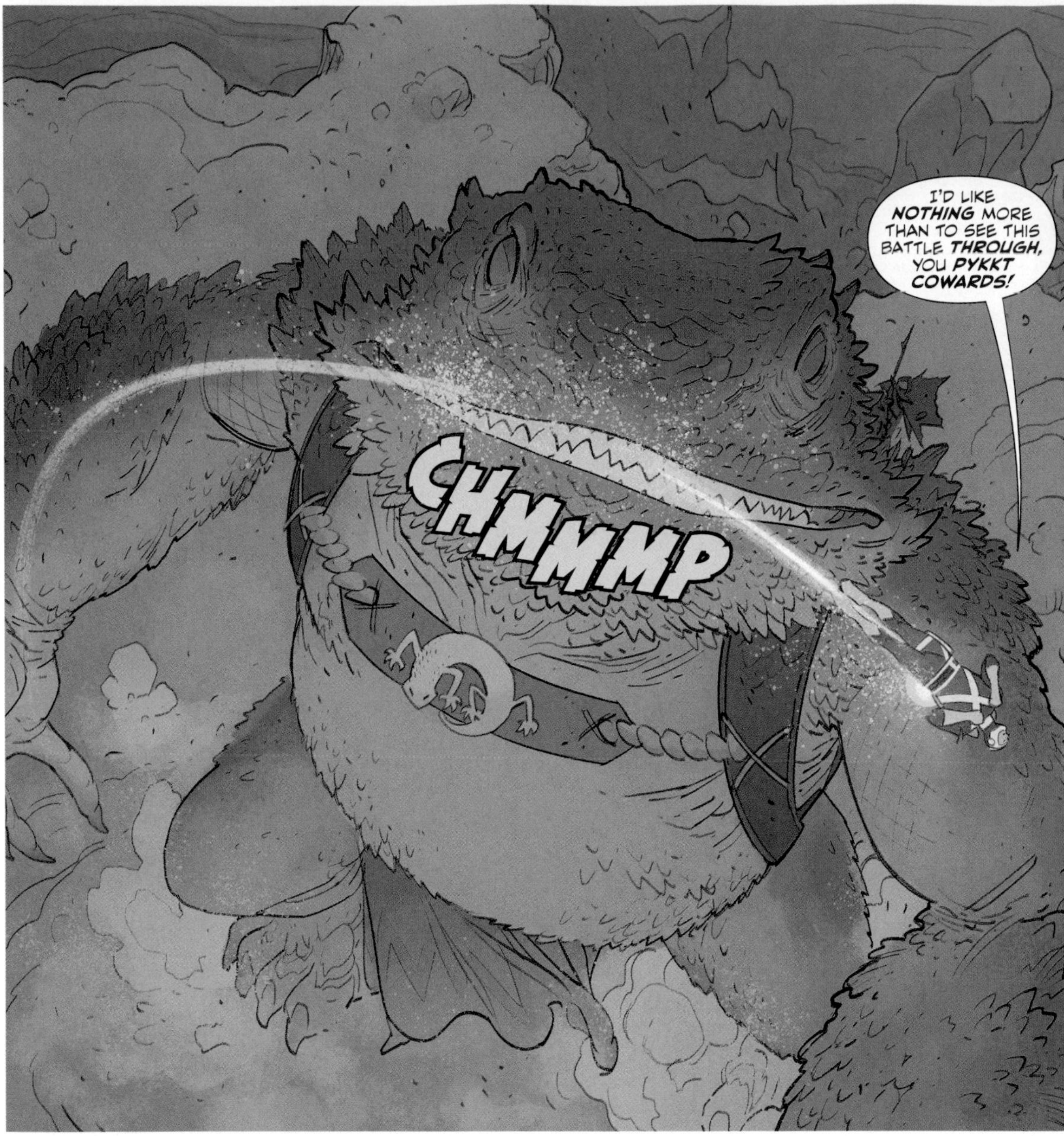
I'D LIKE NOTHING MORE THAN TO SEE THIS BATTLE THROUGH, YOU PYKKT COWARDS!
CHMMMP

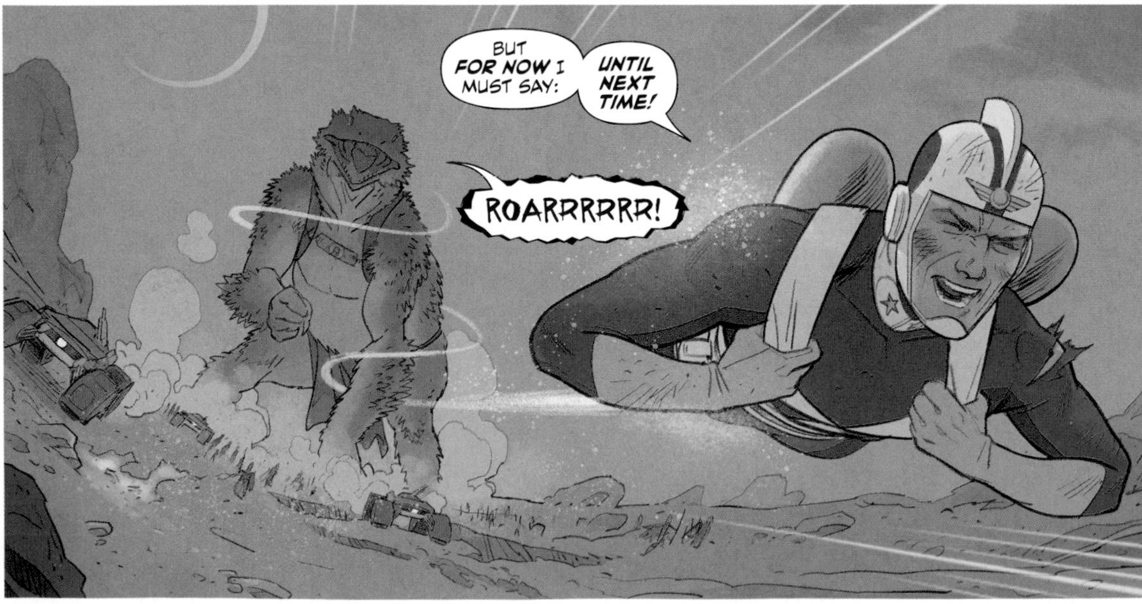
BUT FOR NOW I MUST SAY:
UNTIL NEXT TIME!
ROARRRRRR!

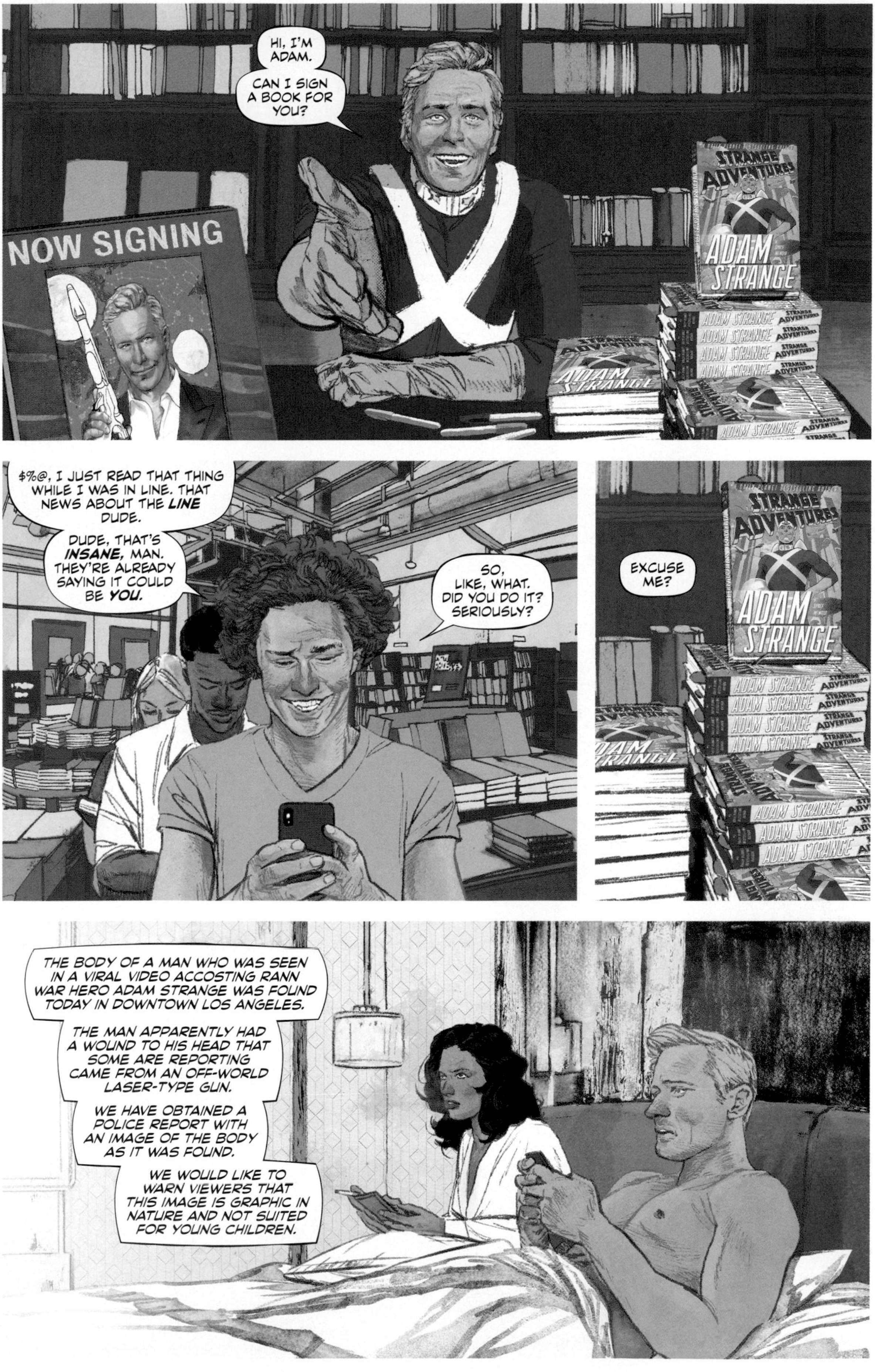
HI, I'M ADAM.
CAN I SIGN A BOOK FOR YOU?
NOW SIGNING
STRANGE ADVENTURES
ADAM STRANGE
$%@, I JUST READ THAT THING WHILE I WAS IN LINE. THAT NEWS ABOUT THE *LINE* DUDE.
DUDE, THAT'S *INSANE,* MAN. THEY'RE ALREADY SAYING IT COULD BE *YOU.*
SO, LIKE, WHAT. DID YOU DO IT? SERIOUSLY?
EXCUSE ME?
THE BODY OF A MAN WHO WAS SEEN IN A VIRAL VIDEO ACCOSTING RANN WAR HERO ADAM STRANGE WAS FOUND TODAY IN DOWNTOWN LOS ANGELES.
THE MAN APPARENTLY HAD A WOUND TO HIS HEAD THAT SOME ARE REPORTING CAME FROM AN OFF-WORLD LASER-TYPE GUN.
WE HAVE OBTAINED A POLICE REPORT WITH AN IMAGE OF THE BODY AS IT WAS FOUND.
WE WOULD LIKE TO WARN VIEWERS THAT THIS IMAGE IS GRAPHIC IN NATURE AND NOT SUITED FOR YOUNG CHILDREN.

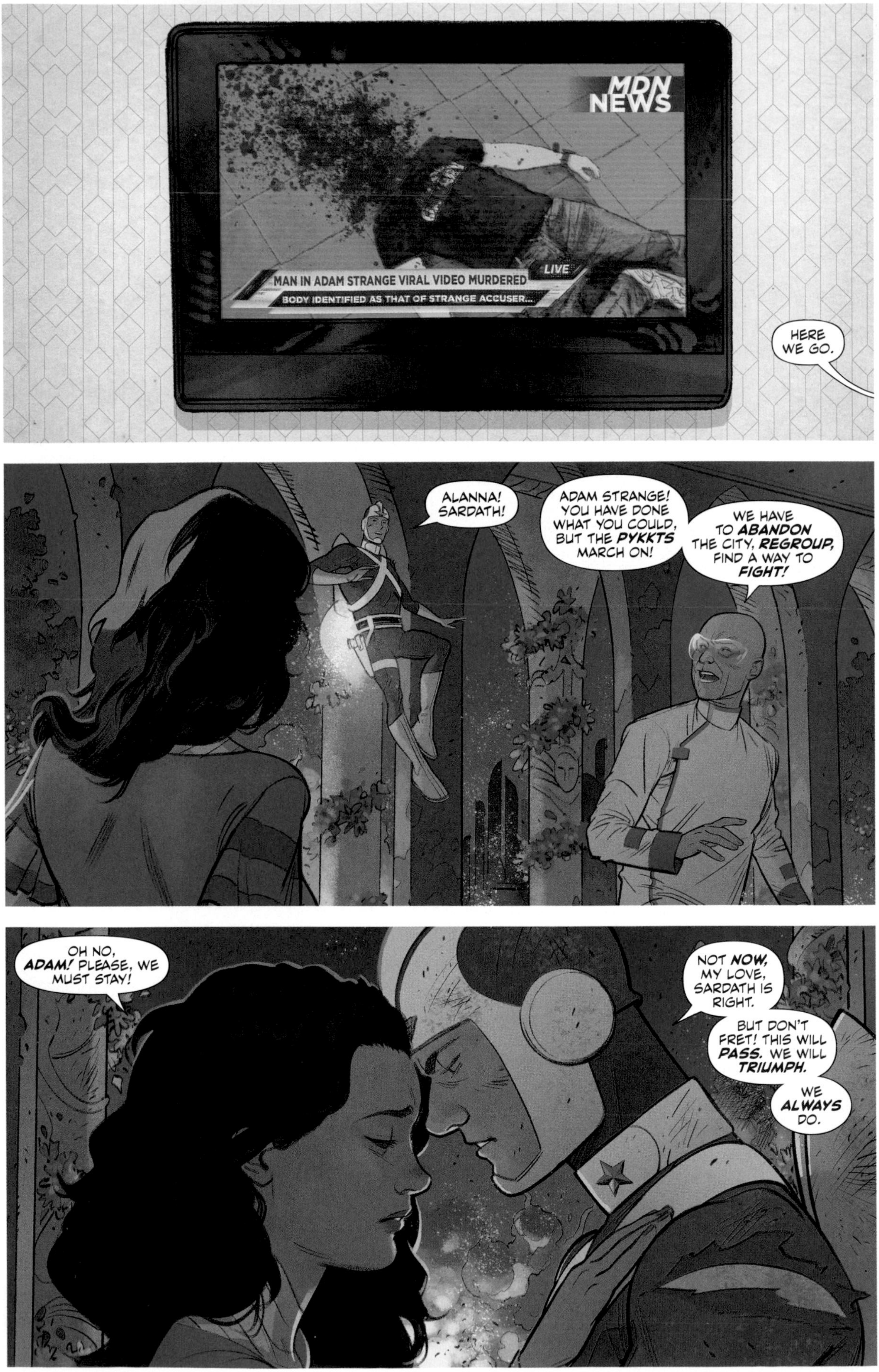
MDN NEWS
LIVE
MAN IN ADAM STRANGE VIRAL VIDEO MURDERED
BODY IDENTIFIED AS THAT OF STRANGE ACCUSER...
HERE WE GO.
ALANNA! SARDATH!
ADAM STRANGE! YOU HAVE DONE WHAT YOU COULD, BUT THE PYKKTS MARCH ON!
WE HAVE TO ABANDON THE CITY, REGROUP, FIND A WAY TO FIGHT!
OH NO, ADAM! PLEASE, WE MUST STAY!
NOT NOW, MY LOVE, SARDATH IS RIGHT.
BUT DON'T FRET! THIS WILL PASS. WE WILL TRIUMPH.
WE ALWAYS DO.

BUT WHAT ABOUT *ALEENA?*

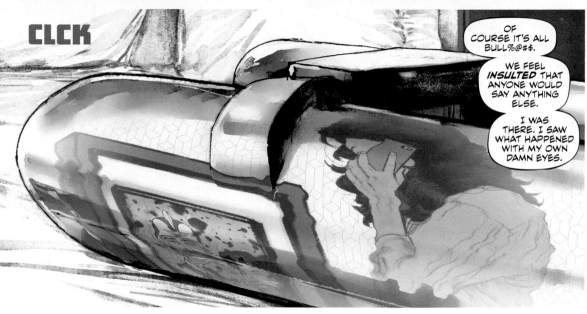

CLCK

OF COURSE IT'S ALL BULL%@#$.

WE FEEL *INSULTED* THAT ANYONE WOULD SAY ANYTHING ELSE.

I WAS THERE. I SAW WHAT HAPPENED WITH MY OWN *DAMN* EYES.

YOU CANNOT *COMPREHEND* WHAT ADAM DID FOR MY PEOPLE.

AND BY STOPPING THE PYKKTS, WHO WOULD'VE COME *HERE* EVENTUALLY...

...WHAT HE DID FOR *YOUR* PEOPLE. FOR *ALL* PEOPLE, REALLY. THE SACRIFICES HE MADE.

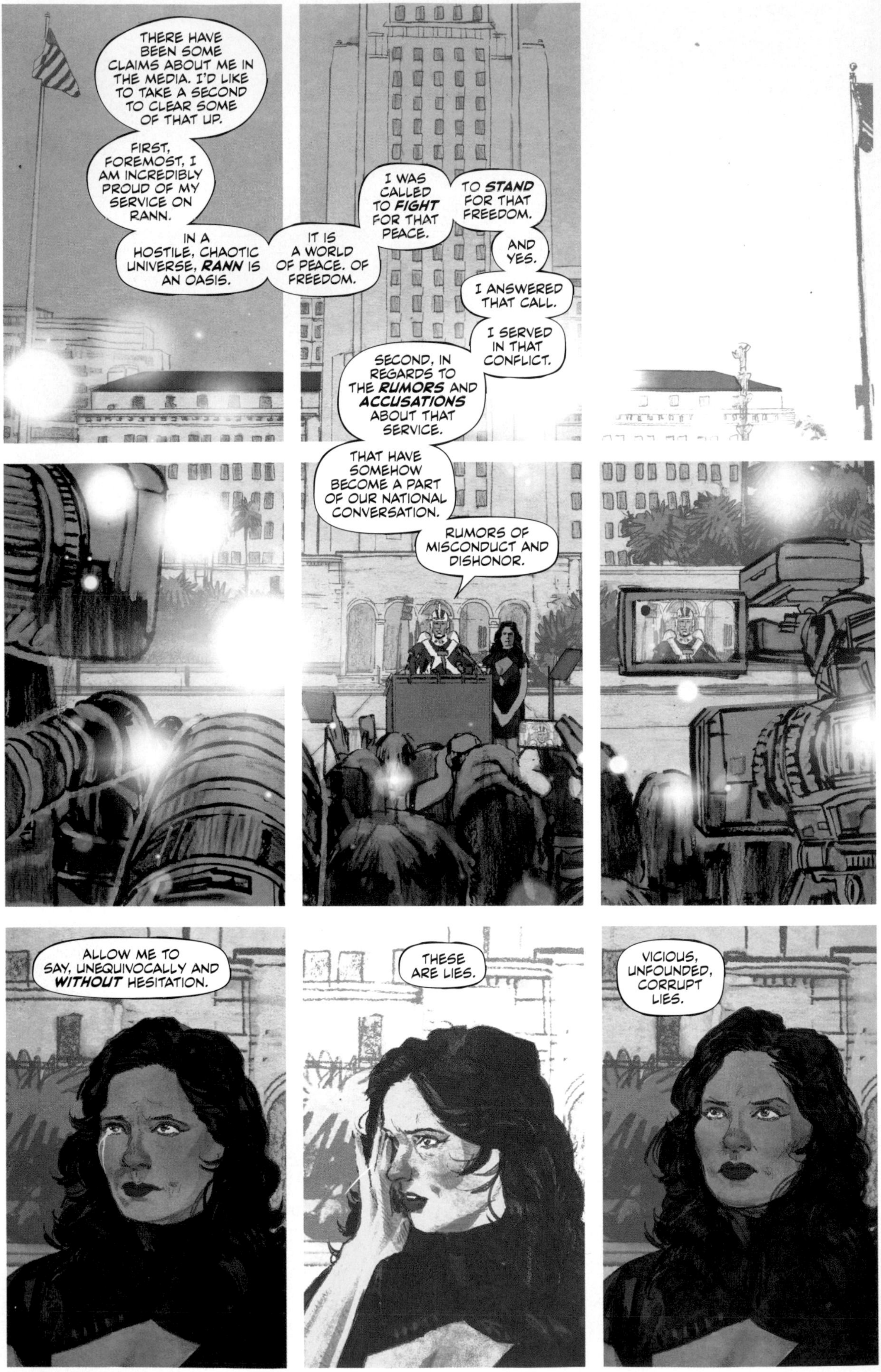
THERE HAVE BEEN SOME CLAIMS ABOUT ME IN THE MEDIA. I'D LIKE TO TAKE A SECOND TO CLEAR SOME OF THAT UP.
FIRST, FOREMOST, I AM INCREDIBLY PROUD OF MY SERVICE ON RANN.
IN A HOSTILE, CHAOTIC UNIVERSE, RANN IS AN OASIS.
IT IS A WORLD OF PEACE. OF FREEDOM.
I WAS CALLED TO FIGHT FOR THAT PEACE.
TO STAND FOR THAT FREEDOM.
AND YES.
I ANSWERED THAT CALL.
I SERVED IN THAT CONFLICT.
SECOND, IN REGARDS TO THE RUMORS AND ACCUSATIONS ABOUT THAT SERVICE.
THAT HAVE SOMEHOW BECOME A PART OF OUR NATIONAL CONVERSATION.
RUMORS OF MISCONDUCT AND DISHONOR.
ALLOW ME TO SAY, UNEQUIVOCALLY AND WITHOUT HESITATION.
THESE ARE LIES.
VICIOUS, UNFOUNDED, CORRUPT LIES.

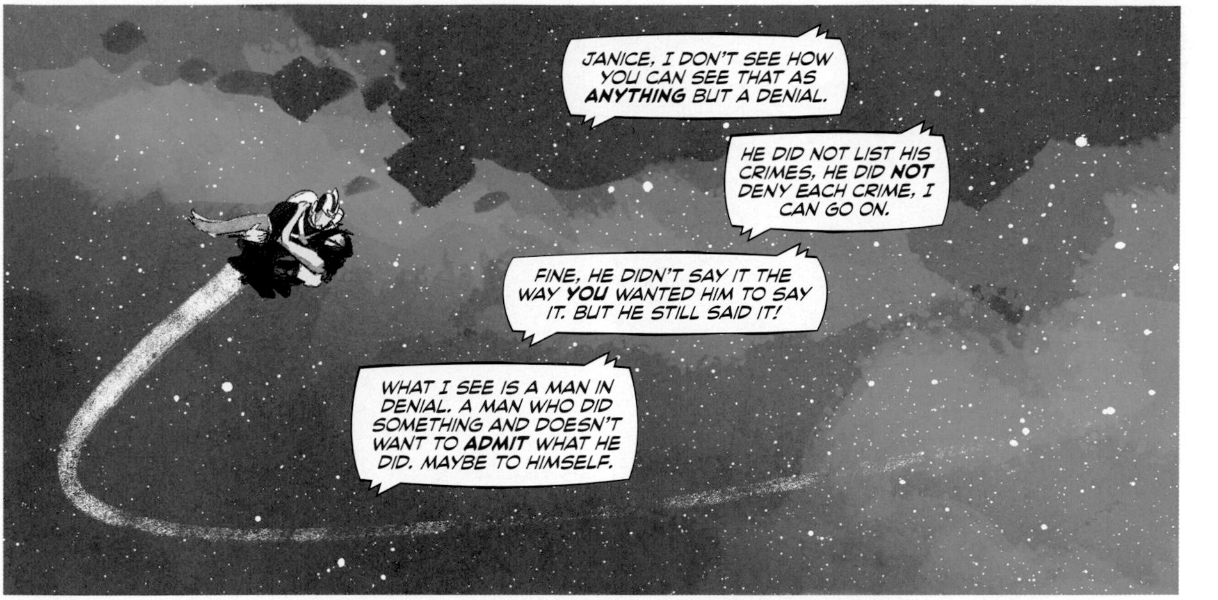
JANICE, I DON'T SEE HOW YOU CAN SEE THAT AS **ANYTHING** BUT A DENIAL.
HE DID NOT LIST HIS CRIMES, HE DID **NOT** DENY EACH CRIME, I CAN GO ON.
FINE, HE DIDN'T SAY IT THE WAY **YOU** WANTED HIM TO SAY IT. BUT HE STILL SAID IT!
WHAT I SEE IS A MAN IN DENIAL. A MAN WHO DID SOMETHING AND DOESN'T WANT TO **ADMIT** WHAT HE DID. MAYBE TO HIMSELF.

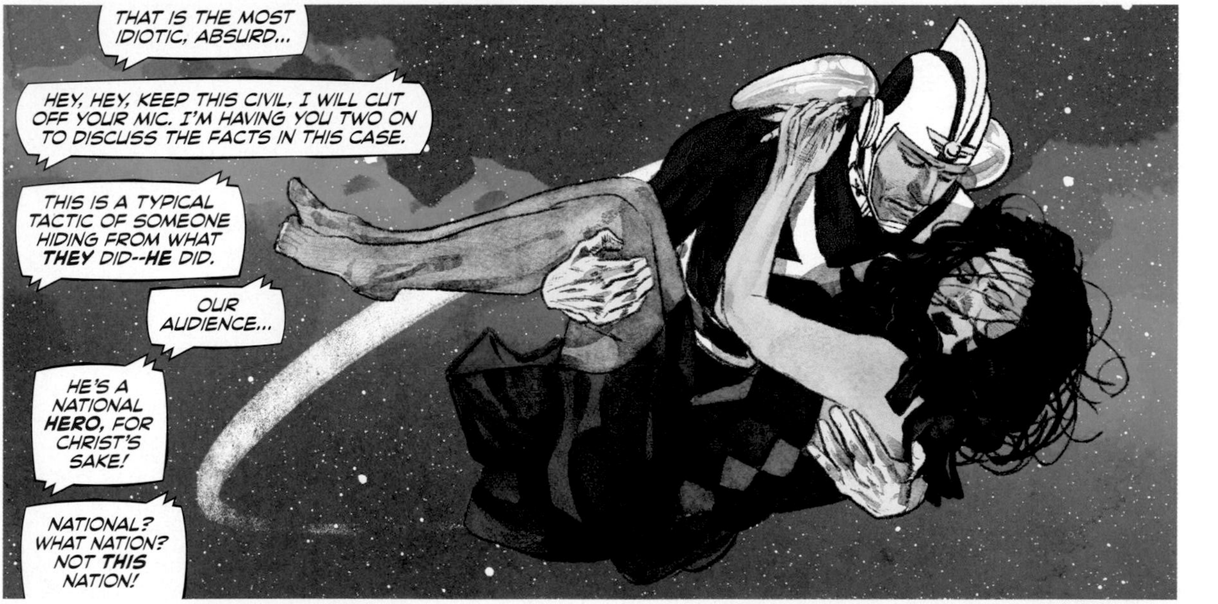
THAT IS THE MOST IDIOTIC, ABSURD...
HEY, HEY, KEEP THIS CIVIL, I WILL CUT OFF YOUR MIC. I'M HAVING YOU TWO ON TO DISCUSS THE FACTS IN THIS CASE.
THIS IS A TYPICAL TACTIC OF SOMEONE HIDING FROM WHAT **THEY** DID--**HE** DID.
OUR AUDIENCE...
HE'S A NATIONAL **HERO,** FOR CHRIST'S SAKE!
NATIONAL? WHAT NATION? NOT **THIS** NATION!

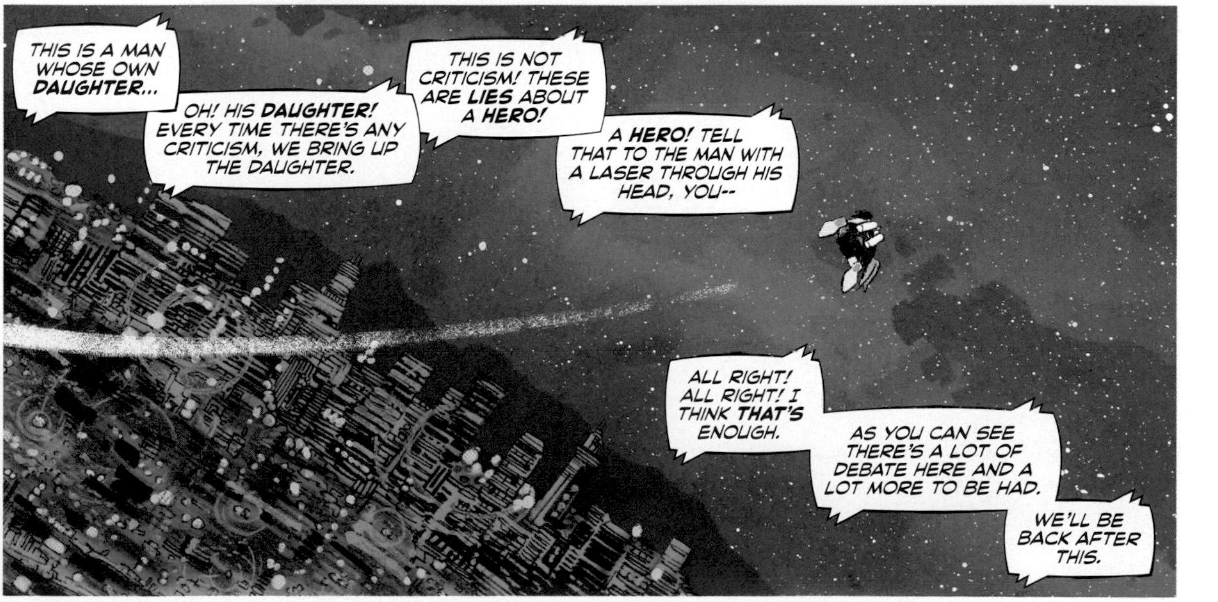
THIS IS A MAN WHOSE OWN **DAUGHTER...**
OH! HIS **DAUGHTER!** EVERY TIME THERE'S ANY CRITICISM, WE BRING UP THE DAUGHTER.
THIS IS NOT CRITICISM! THESE ARE **LIES** ABOUT A **HERO!**
A **HERO!** TELL THAT TO THE MAN WITH A LASER THROUGH HIS HEAD, YOU--
ALL RIGHT! ALL RIGHT! I THINK **THAT'S** ENOUGH.
AS YOU CAN SEE THERE'S A LOT OF DEBATE HERE AND A LOT MORE TO BE HAD.
WE'LL BE BACK AFTER THIS.

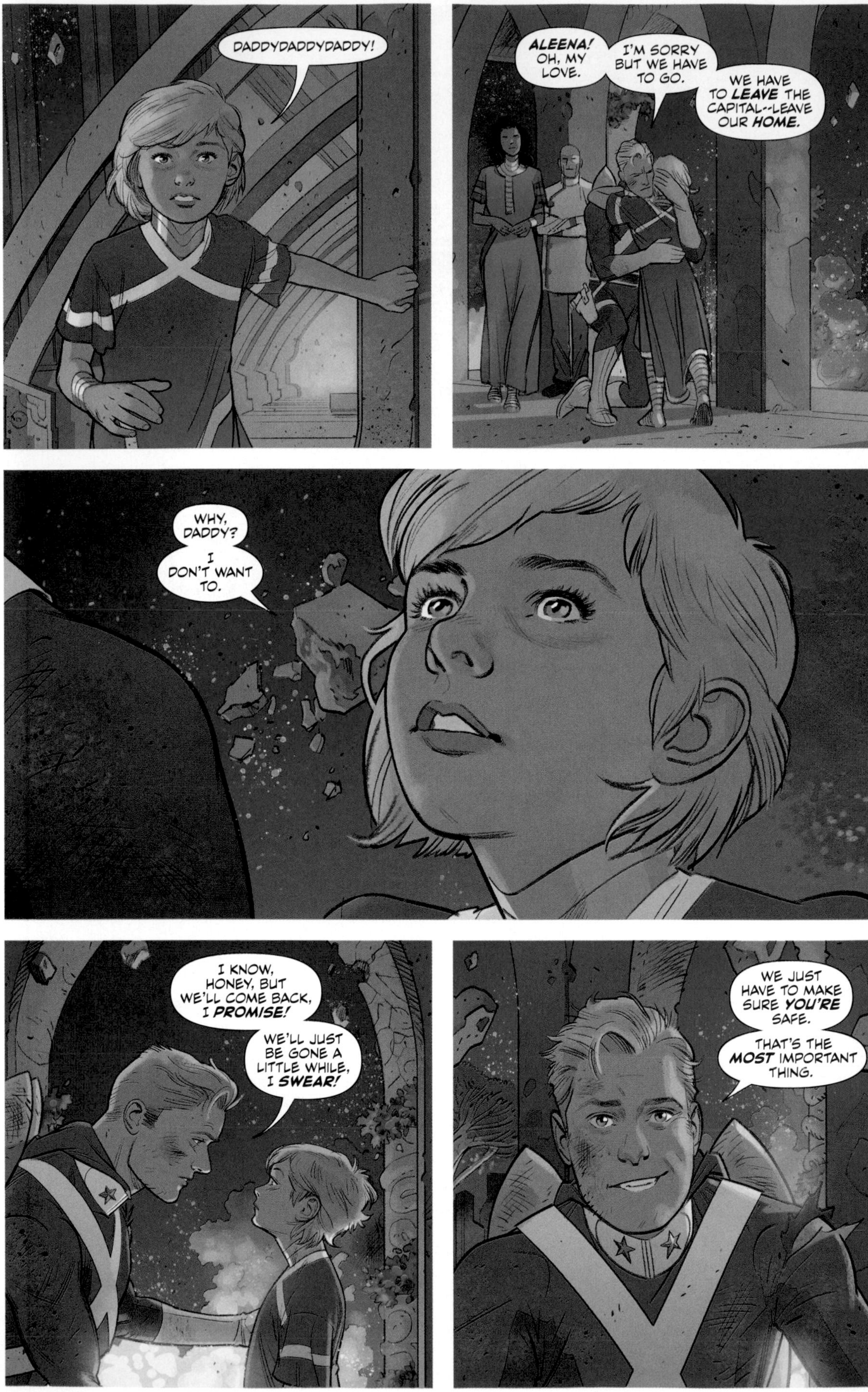
DADDYDADDYDADDY!
ALEENA! OH, MY LOVE.
I'M SORRY BUT WE HAVE TO GO.
WE HAVE TO LEAVE THE CAPITAL--LEAVE OUR HOME.
WHY, DADDY?
I DON'T WANT TO.
I KNOW, HONEY, BUT WE'LL COME BACK, I PROMISE!
WE'LL JUST BE GONE A LITTLE WHILE, I SWEAR!
WE JUST HAVE TO MAKE SURE YOU'RE SAFE.
THAT'S THE MOST IMPORTANT THING.

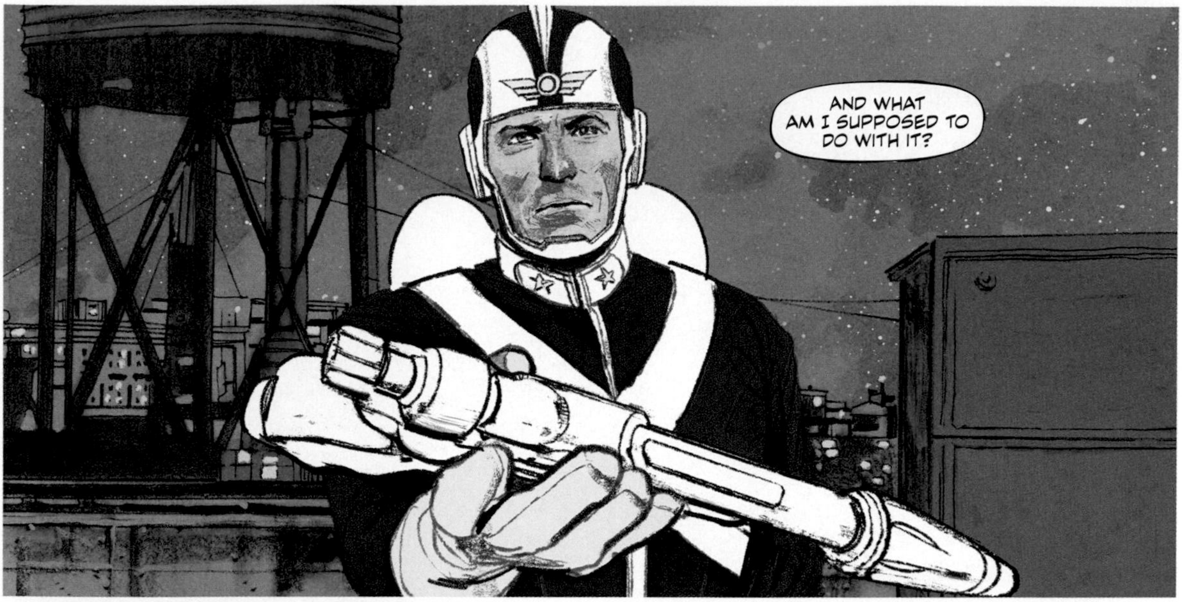
AND WHAT AM I SUPPOSED TO DO WITH IT?

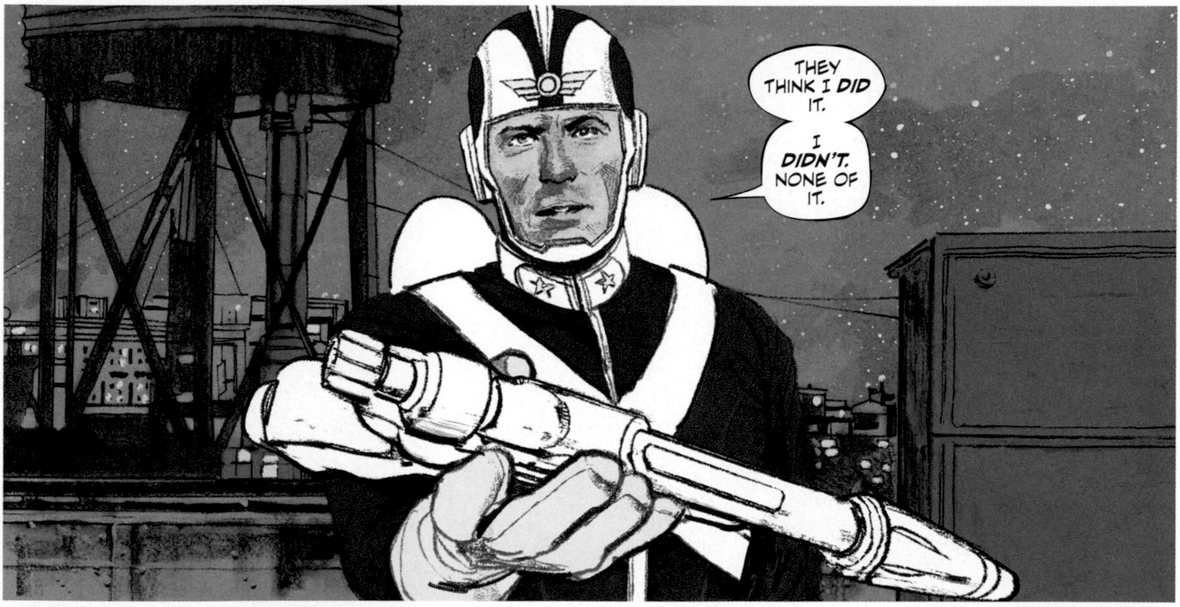
THEY THINK I *DID* IT.
I *DIDN'T.* NONE OF IT.

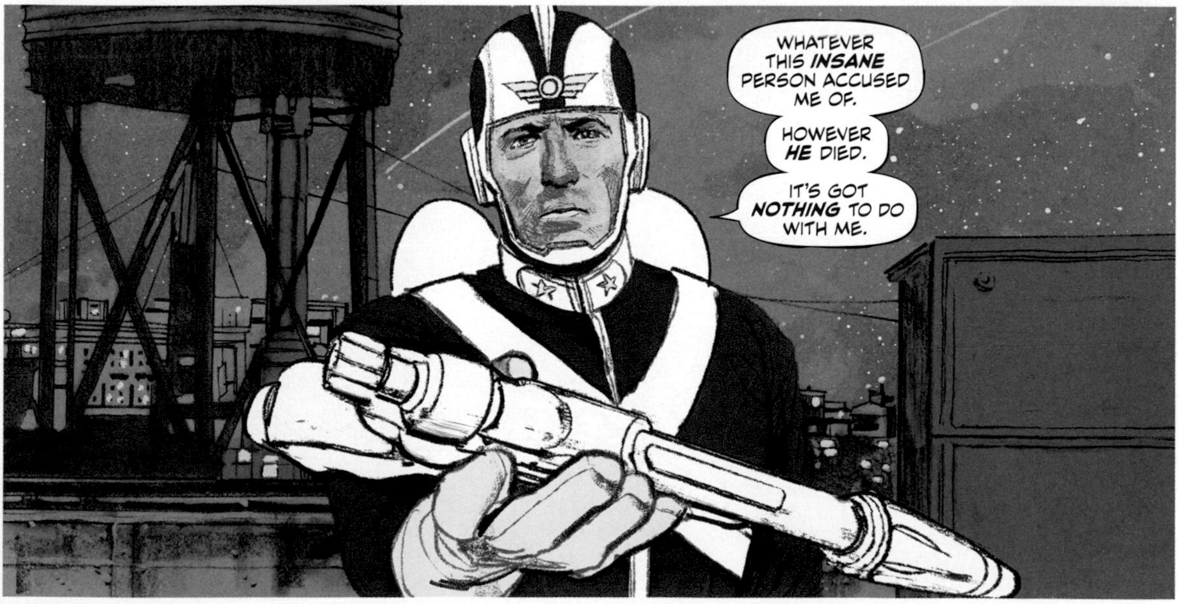
WHATEVER THIS *INSANE* PERSON ACCUSED ME OF.
HOWEVER *HE* DIED.
IT'S GOT *NOTHING* TO DO WITH ME.

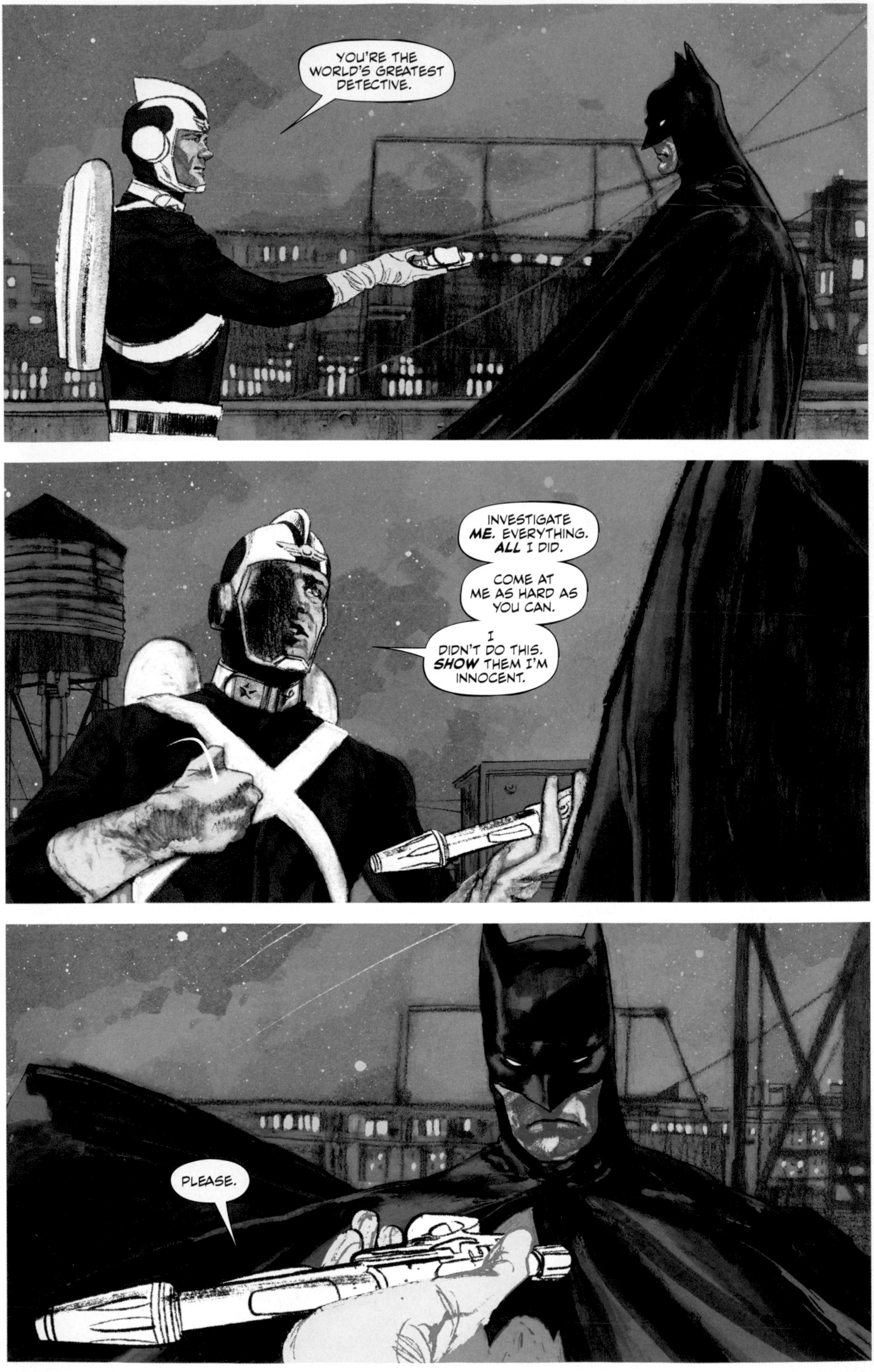
YOU'RE THE WORLD'S GREATEST DETECTIVE.
INVESTIGATE **ME.** EVERYTHING. **ALL** I DID.
COME AT ME AS HARD AS YOU CAN.
I DIDN'T DO THIS. **SHOW** THEM I'M INNOCENT.
PLEASE.

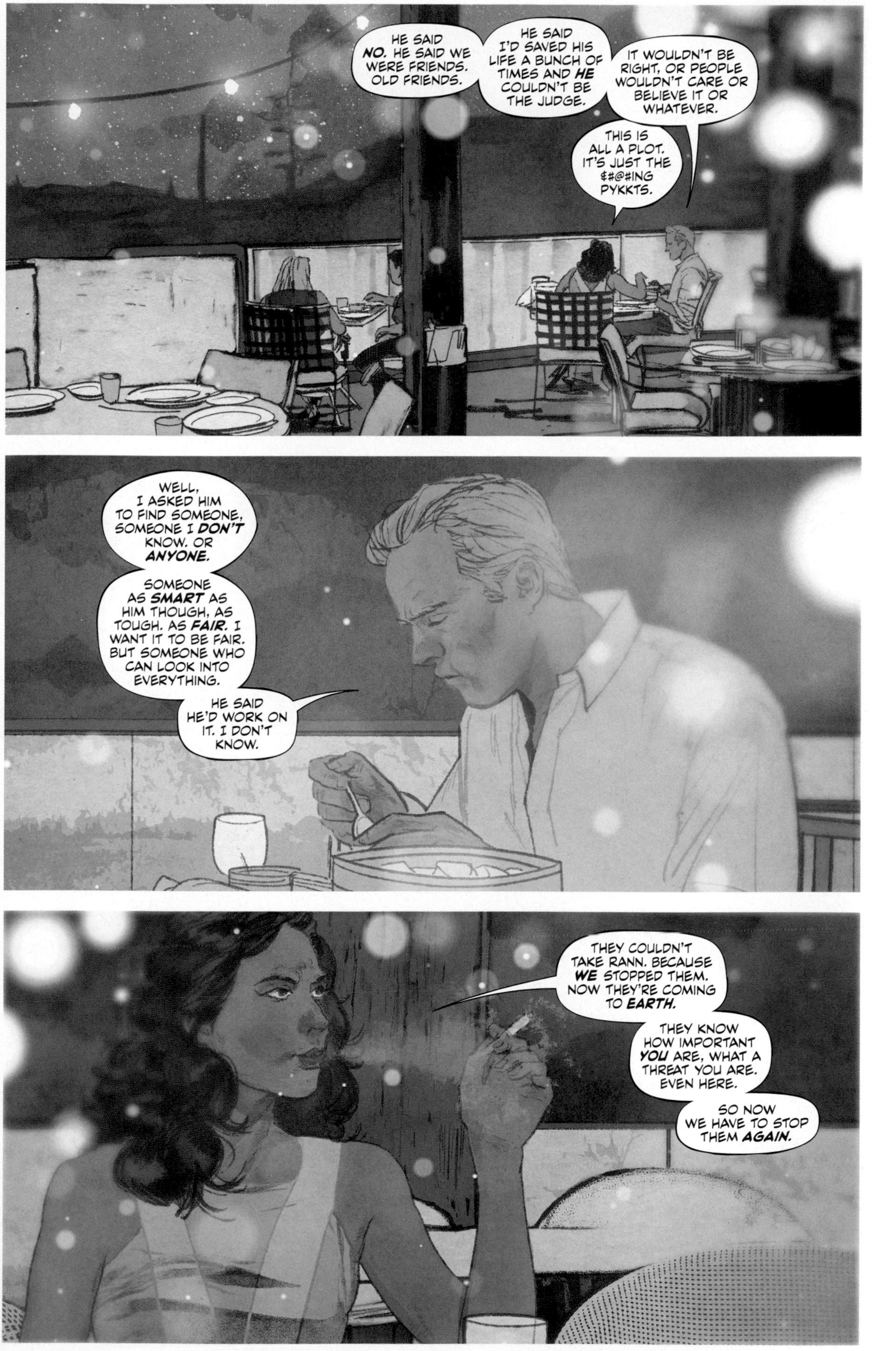
HE SAID NO. HE SAID WE WERE FRIENDS. OLD FRIENDS.
HE SAID I'D SAVED HIS LIFE A BUNCH OF TIMES AND HE COULDN'T BE THE JUDGE.
IT WOULDN'T BE RIGHT, OR PEOPLE WOULDN'T CARE OR BELIEVE IT OR WHATEVER.
THIS IS ALL A PLOT. IT'S JUST THE $#@#ING PYKKTS.
WELL, I ASKED HIM TO FIND SOMEONE, SOMEONE I DON'T KNOW. OR ANYONE.
SOMEONE AS SMART AS HIM THOUGH, AS TOUGH. AS FAIR. I WANT IT TO BE FAIR. BUT SOMEONE WHO CAN LOOK INTO EVERYTHING.
HE SAID HE'D WORK ON IT. I DON'T KNOW.
THEY COULDN'T TAKE RANN. BECAUSE WE STOPPED THEM. NOW THEY'RE COMING TO EARTH.
THEY KNOW HOW IMPORTANT YOU ARE, WHAT A THREAT YOU ARE. EVEN HERE.
SO NOW WE HAVE TO STOP THEM AGAIN.

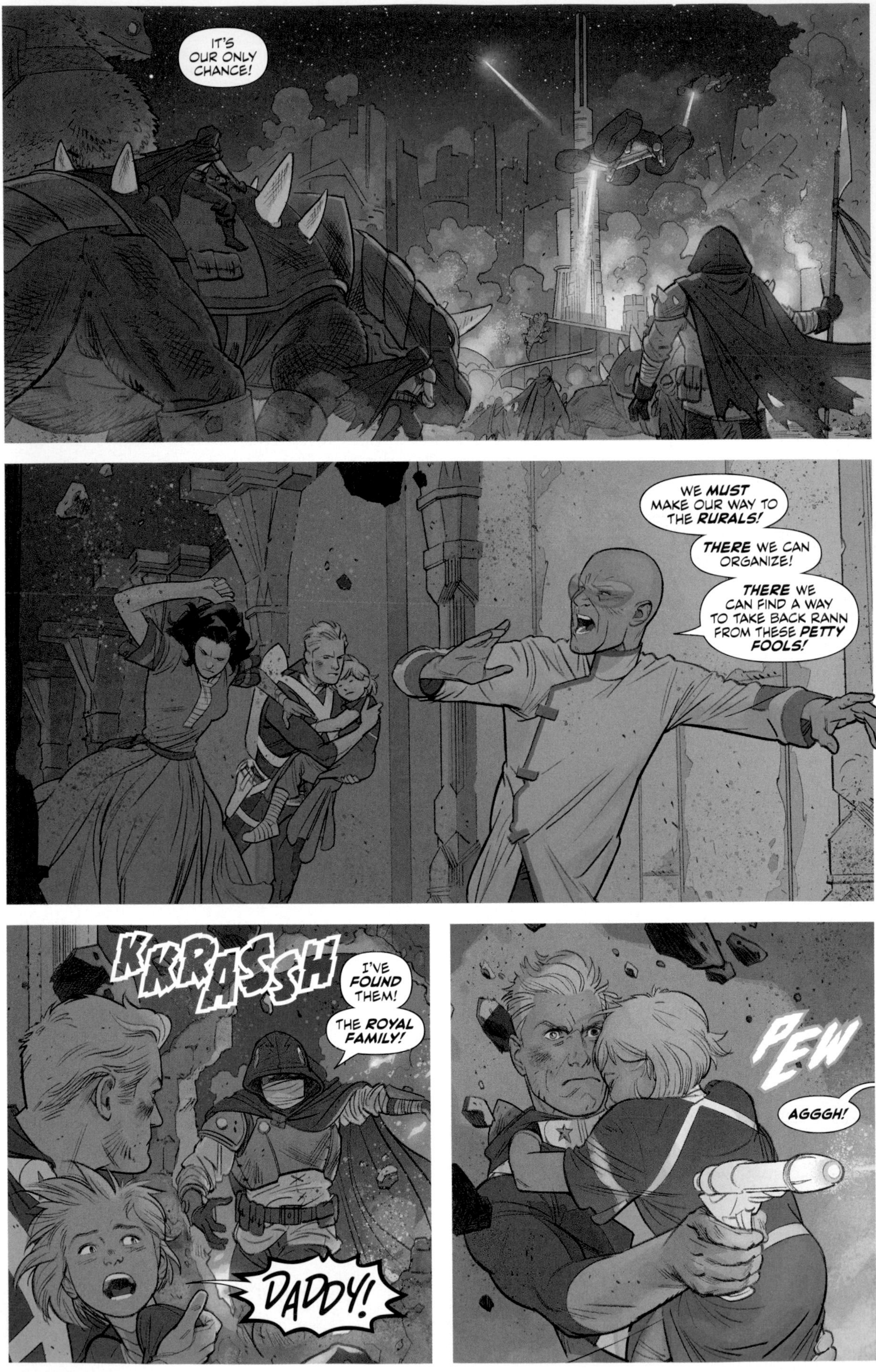
IT'S OUR ONLY CHANCE!
WE MUST MAKE OUR WAY TO THE RURALS!
THERE WE CAN ORGANIZE!
THERE WE CAN FIND A WAY TO TAKE BACK RANN FROM THESE PETTY FOOLS!
KKRASSH
I'VE FOUND THEM!
THE ROYAL FAMILY!
DADDY!
PEW
AGGGH!

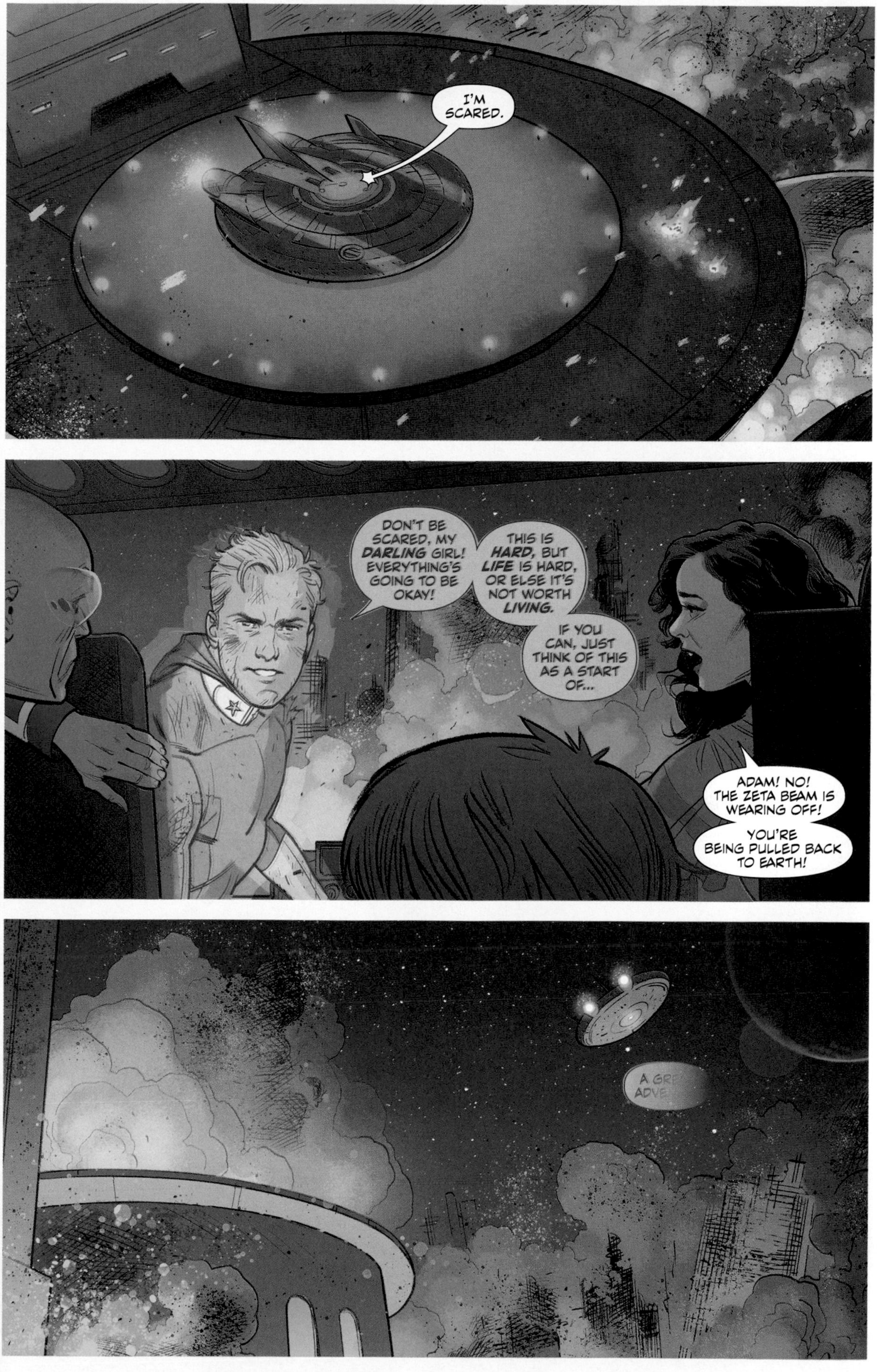
I'M SCARED.
DON'T BE SCARED, MY DARLING GIRL! EVERYTHING'S GOING TO BE OKAY!
THIS IS HARD, BUT LIFE IS HARD, OR ELSE IT'S NOT WORTH LIVING.
IF YOU CAN, JUST THINK OF THIS AS A START OF...
ADAM! NO! THE ZETA BEAM IS WEARING OFF!
YOU'RE BEING PULLED BACK TO EARTH!
A GRE
ADVE

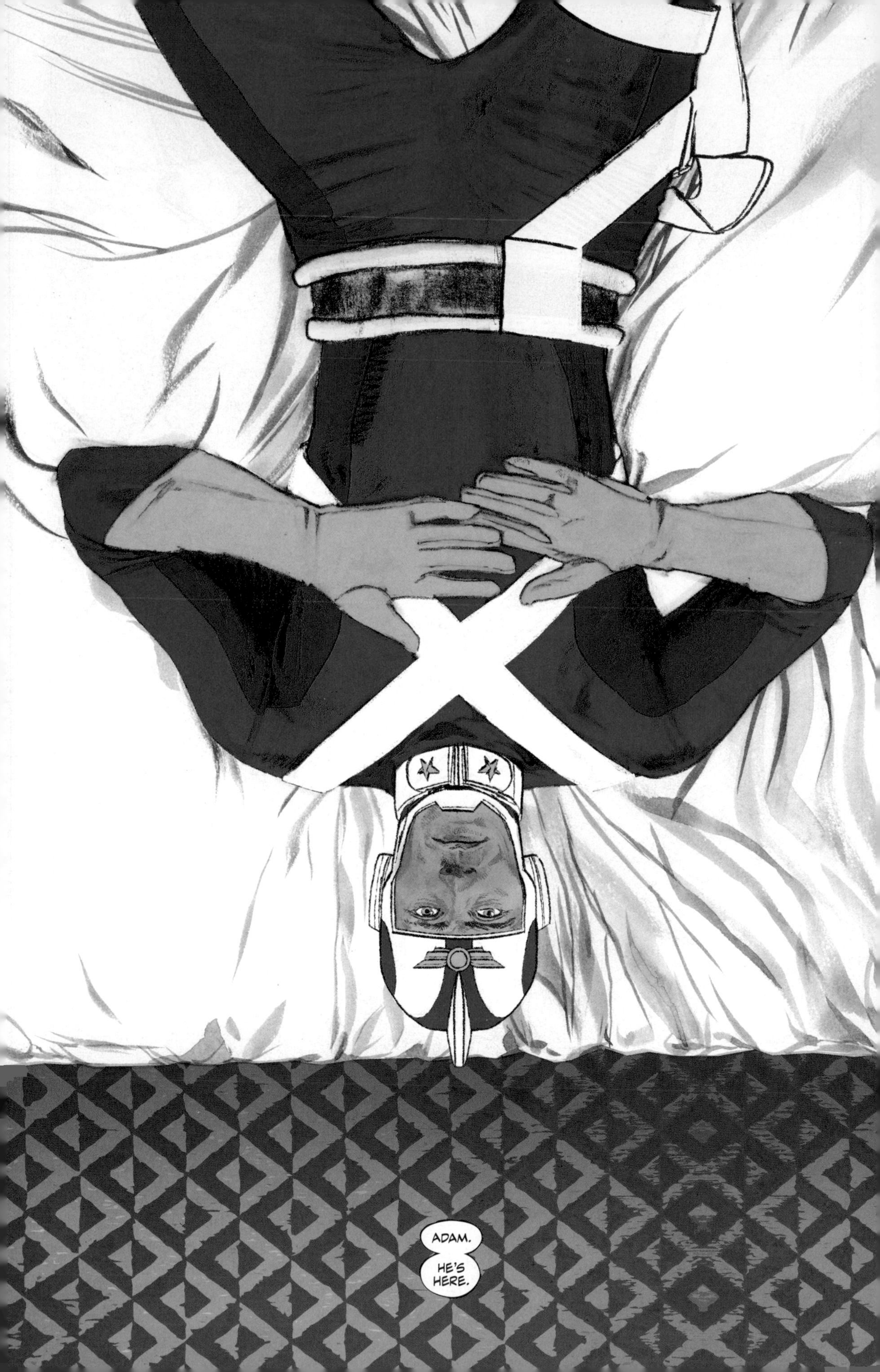
ADAM.
HE'S HERE.

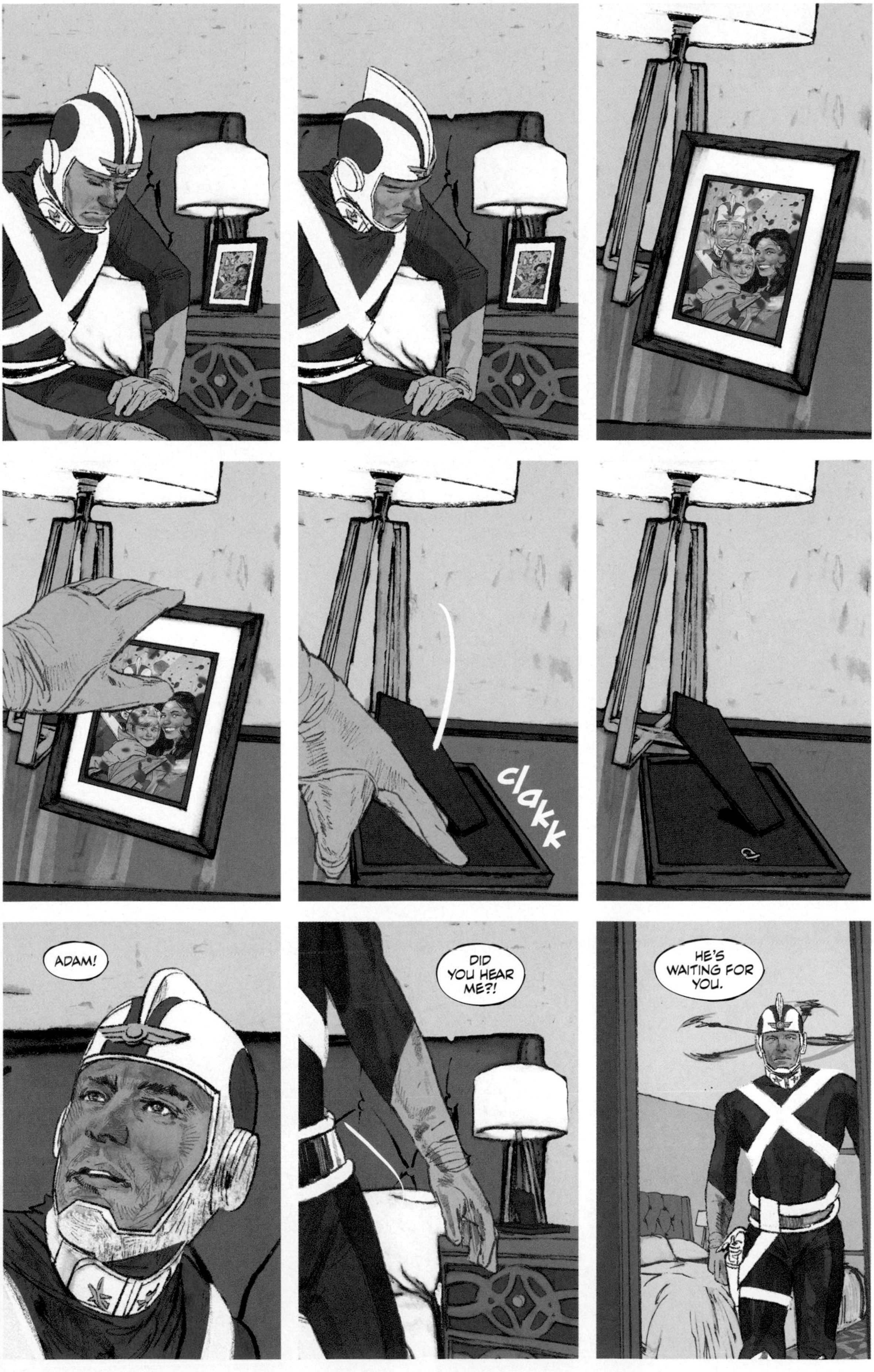
clakk
ADAM!
DID YOU HEAR ME?!
HE'S WAITING FOR YOU.

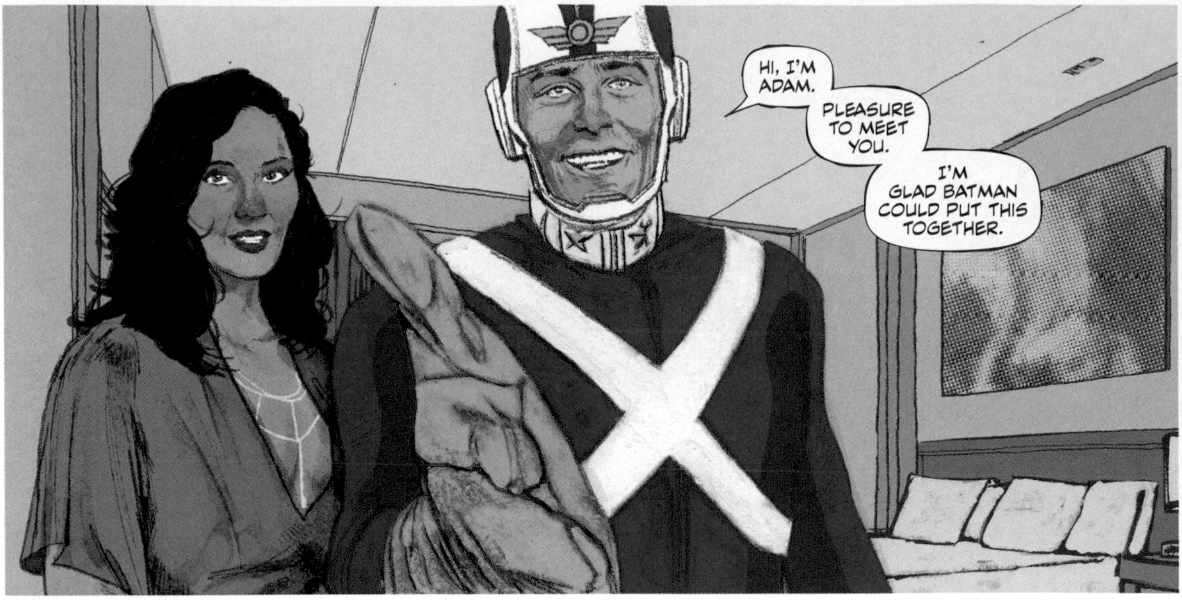
HI, I'M ADAM.
PLEASURE TO MEET YOU.
I'M GLAD BATMAN COULD PUT THIS TOGETHER.

I had three different layers of city where they lived on Rann. The city was built on layers. Of course, the ground was dead. It was gone. It was very interesting, the premise. The scientists of the period said, "We've got to build an area where it's pollution-free, smoke-free." So I built cities in layers, and they got smaller as they went up, and they floated above the ground, which is clever I think.

—Carmine Infantino

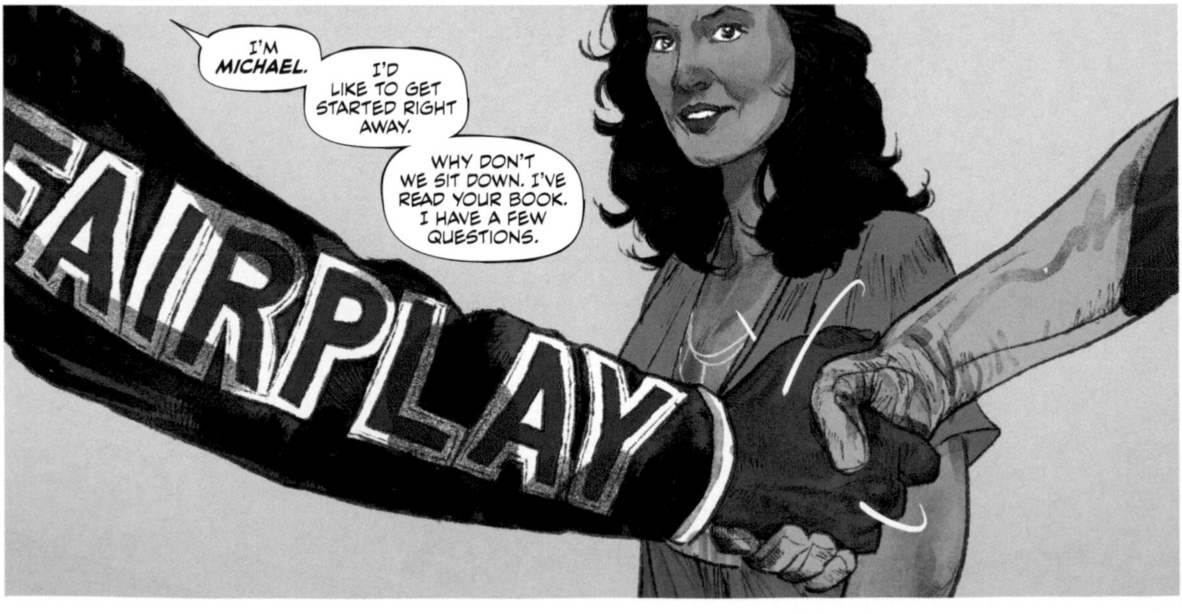
I'M *MICHAEL.*
I'D LIKE TO GET STARTED RIGHT AWAY.
WHY DON'T WE SIT DOWN. I'VE READ YOUR BOOK. I HAVE A FEW QUESTIONS.
FAIRPLAY

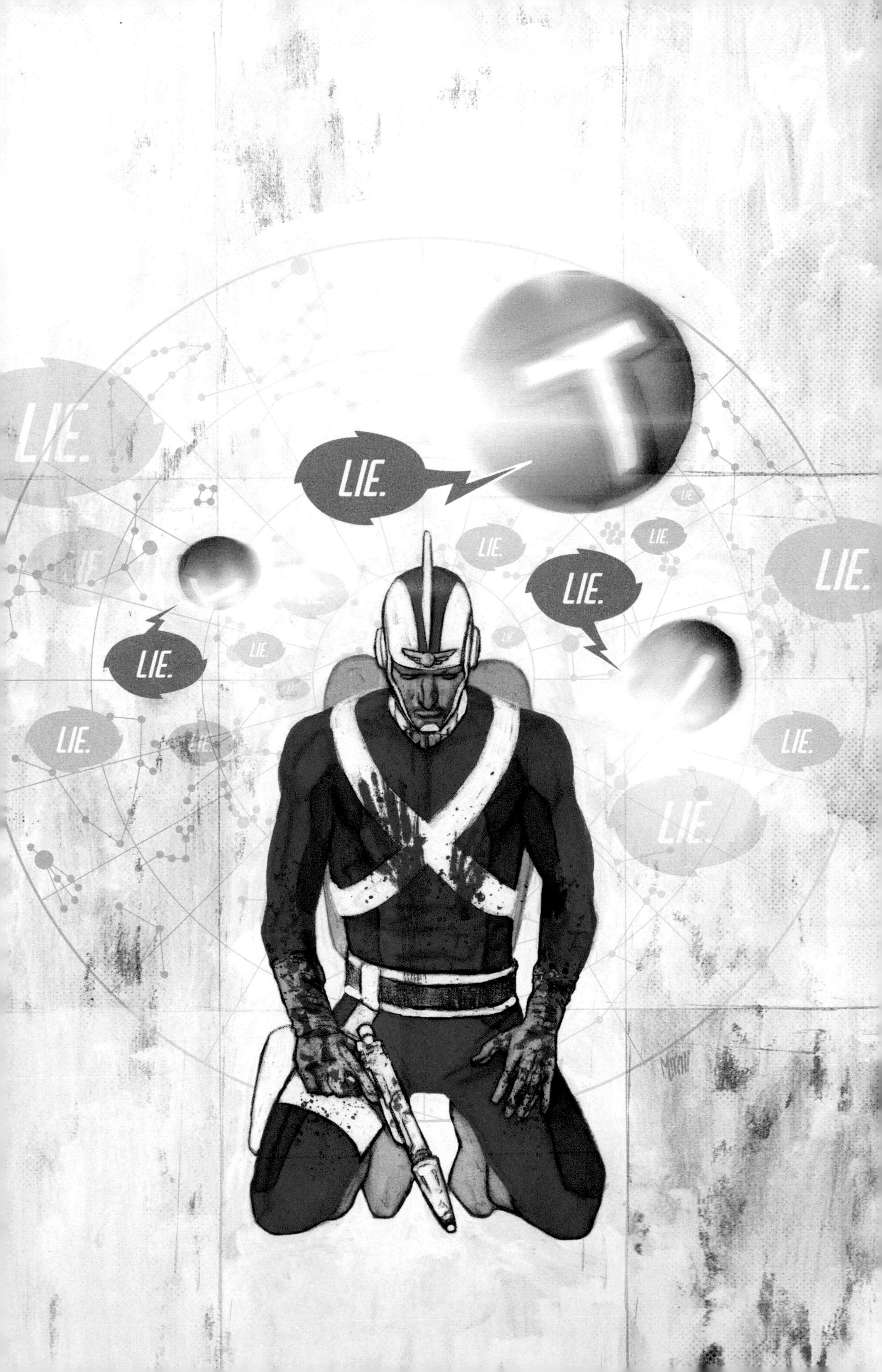

"MY LIFE IS SPENT WITH GRIEF."

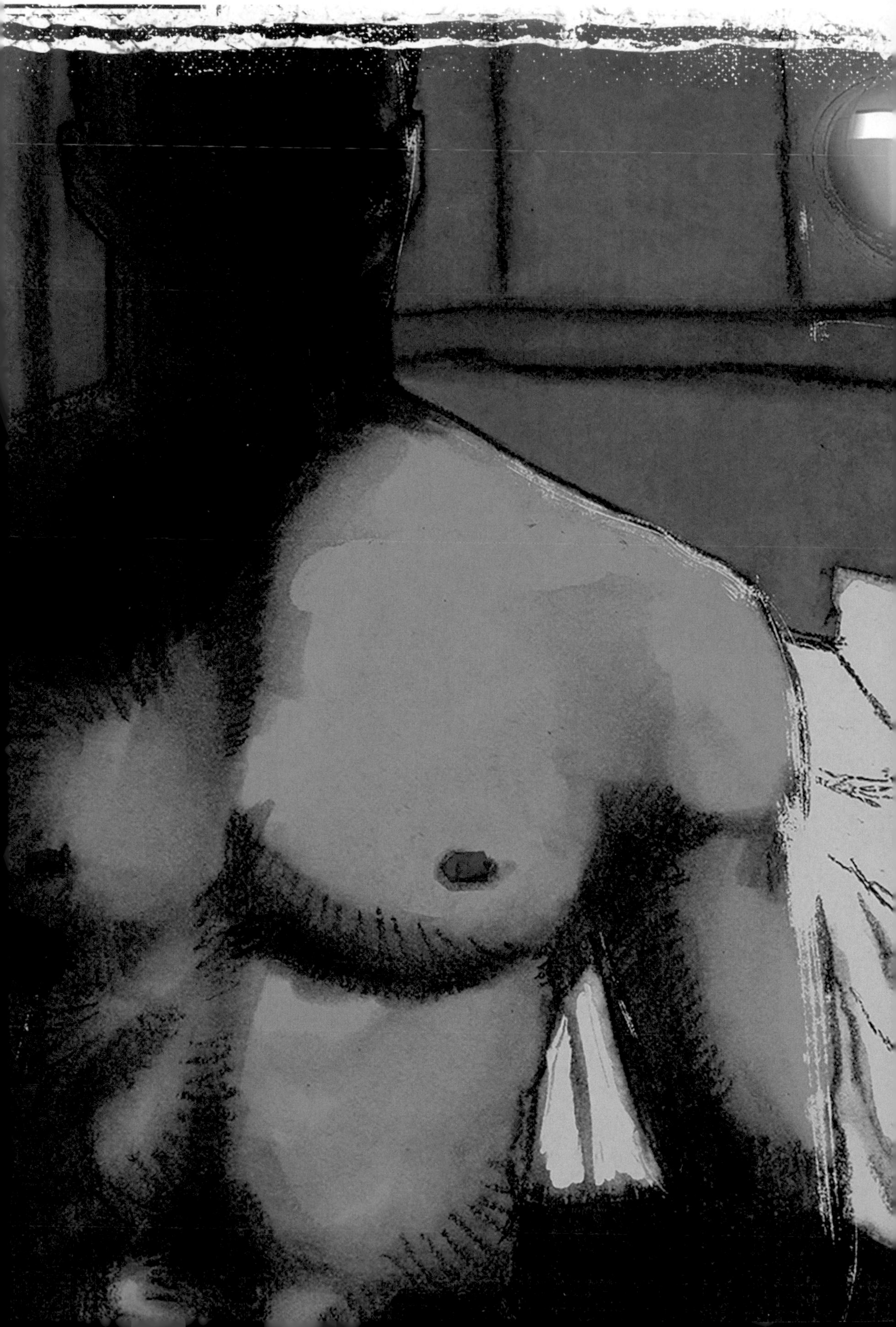

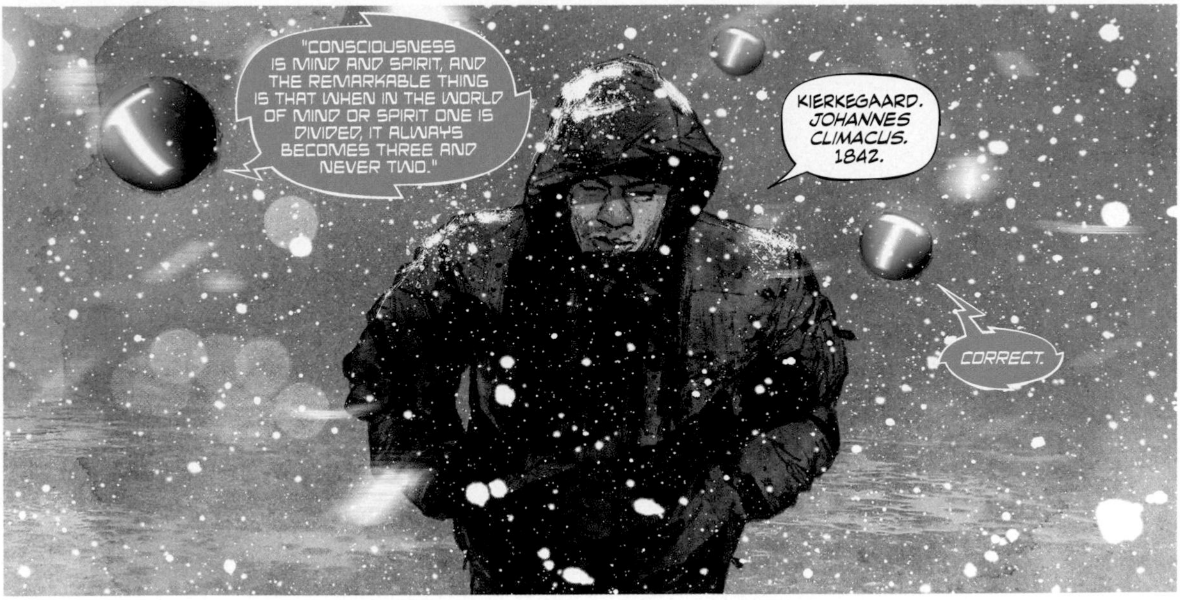
"CONSCIOUSNESS IS MIND AND SPIRIT, AND THE REMARKABLE THING IS THAT WHEN IN THE WORLD OF MIND OR SPIRIT ONE IS DIVIDED, IT ALWAYS BECOMES THREE AND NEVER TWO."
KIERKEGAARD. JOHANNES CLIMACUS. 1842.
CORRECT.

Chapter 2

A little demanding

TOM KING	...Writer
MITCH GERADS EVAN "DOC" SHANER	...Interior & Cover Artists
CLAYTON COWLES	...Letterer
BRITTANY HOLZHERR	...Associate Editor
JAMIE S. RICH	...Editor

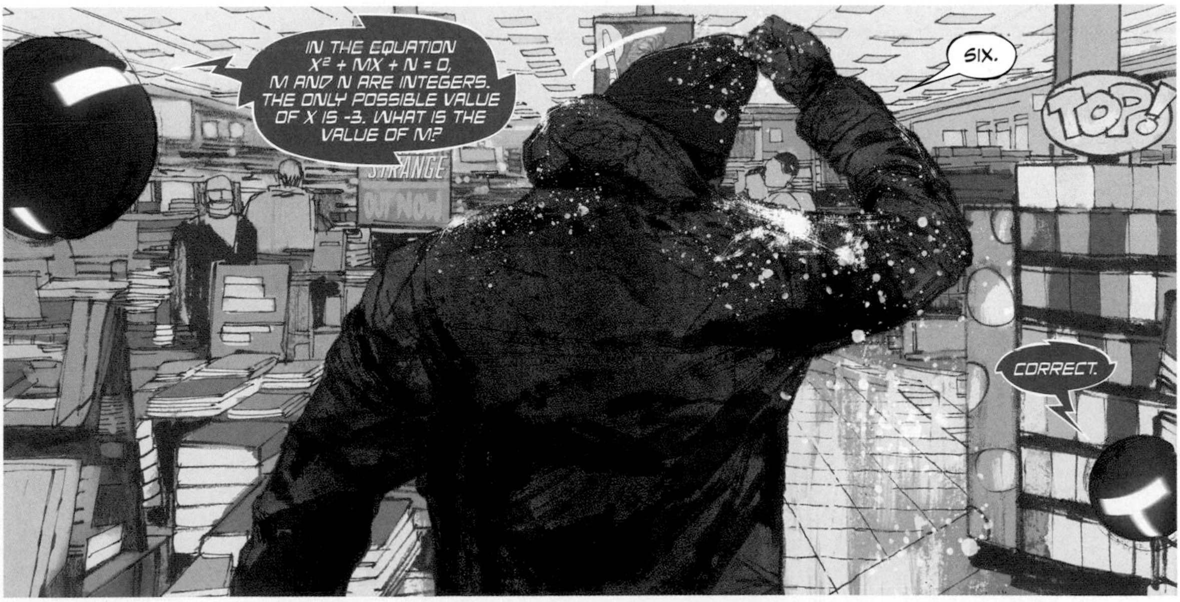
IN THE EQUATION $X^2 + MX + N = 0$, M AND N ARE INTEGERS. THE ONLY POSSIBLE VALUE OF X IS -3. WHAT IS THE VALUE OF M?
SIX.
TOP!
STRANGE
OUT NOW
CORRECT.

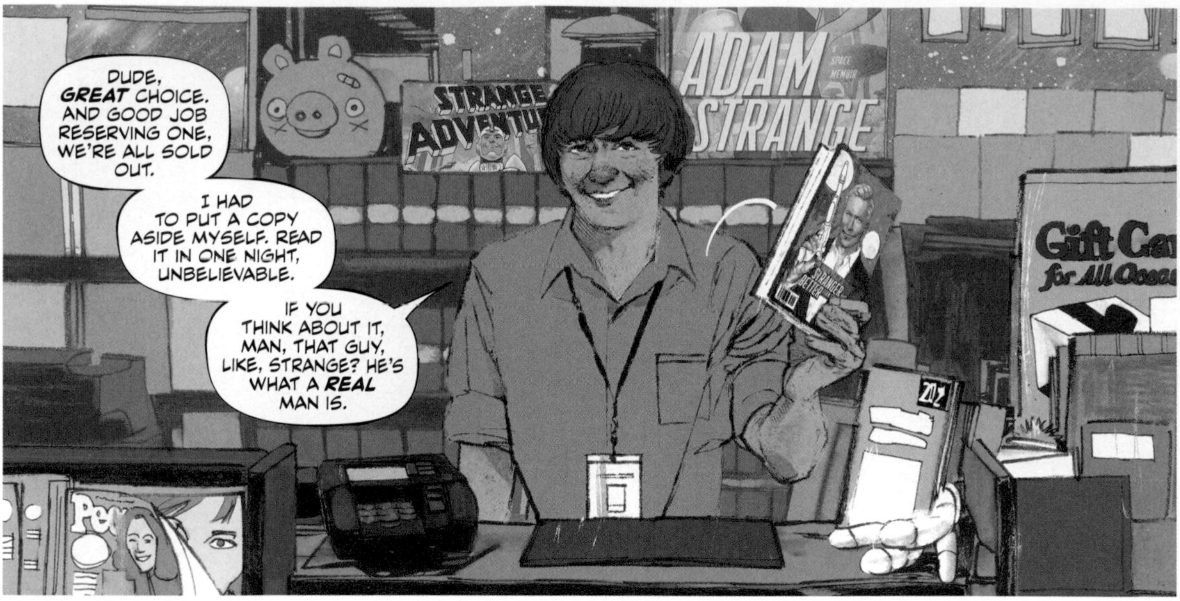
ADAM STRANGE
DUDE, **GREAT** CHOICE. AND GOOD JOB RESERVING ONE, WE'RE ALL SOLD OUT.
I HAD TO PUT A COPY ASIDE MYSELF. READ IT IN ONE NIGHT, UNBELIEVABLE.
IF YOU THINK ABOUT IT, MAN, THAT GUY, LIKE, STRANGE? HE'S WHAT A **REAL** MAN IS.

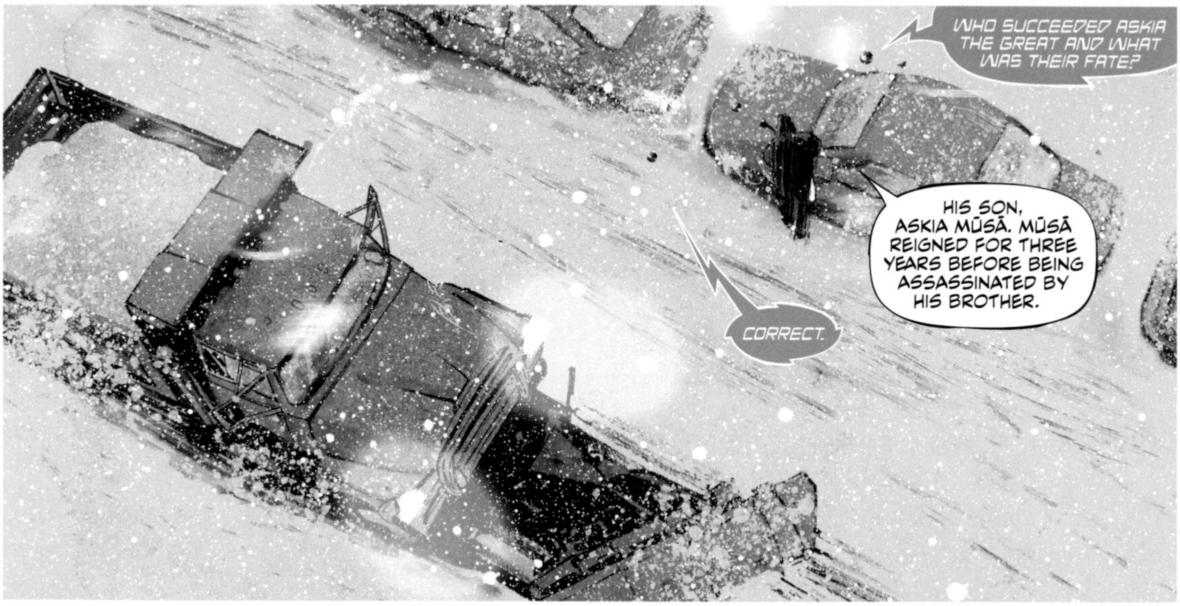
WHO SUCCEEDED ASKIA THE GREAT AND WHAT WAS THEIR FATE?
HIS SON, ASKIA MŪSĀ. MŪSĀ REIGNED FOR THREE YEARS BEFORE BEING ASSASSINATED BY HIS BROTHER.
CORRECT.

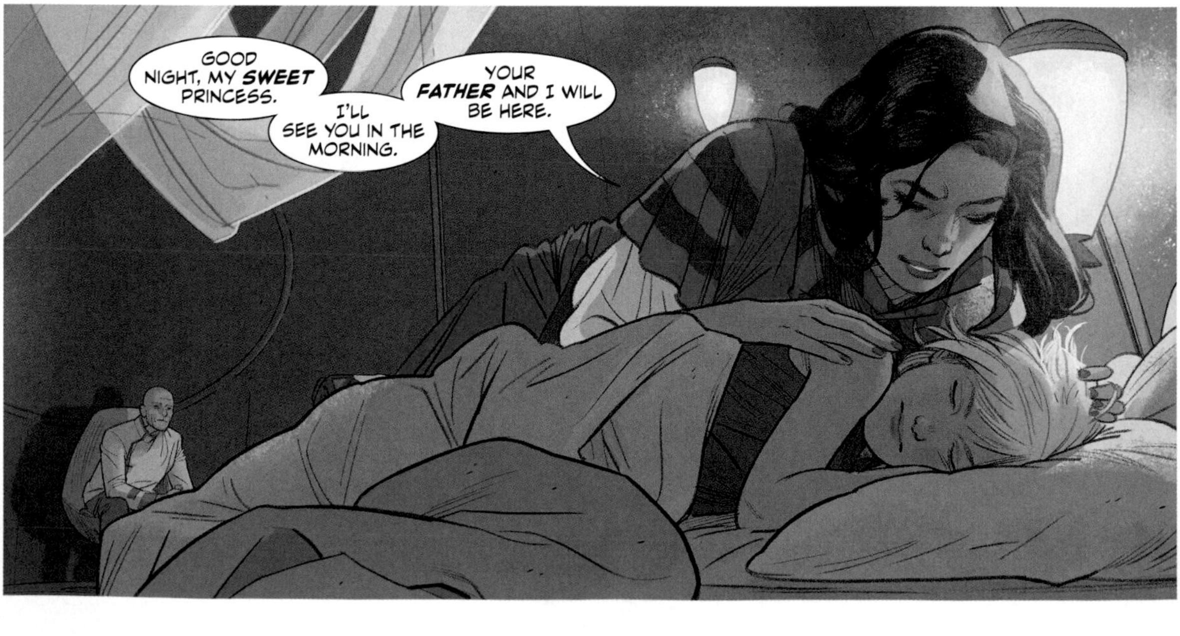
GOOD NIGHT, MY **SWEET** PRINCESS.
I'LL SEE YOU IN THE MORNING.
YOUR **FATHER** AND I WILL BE HERE.

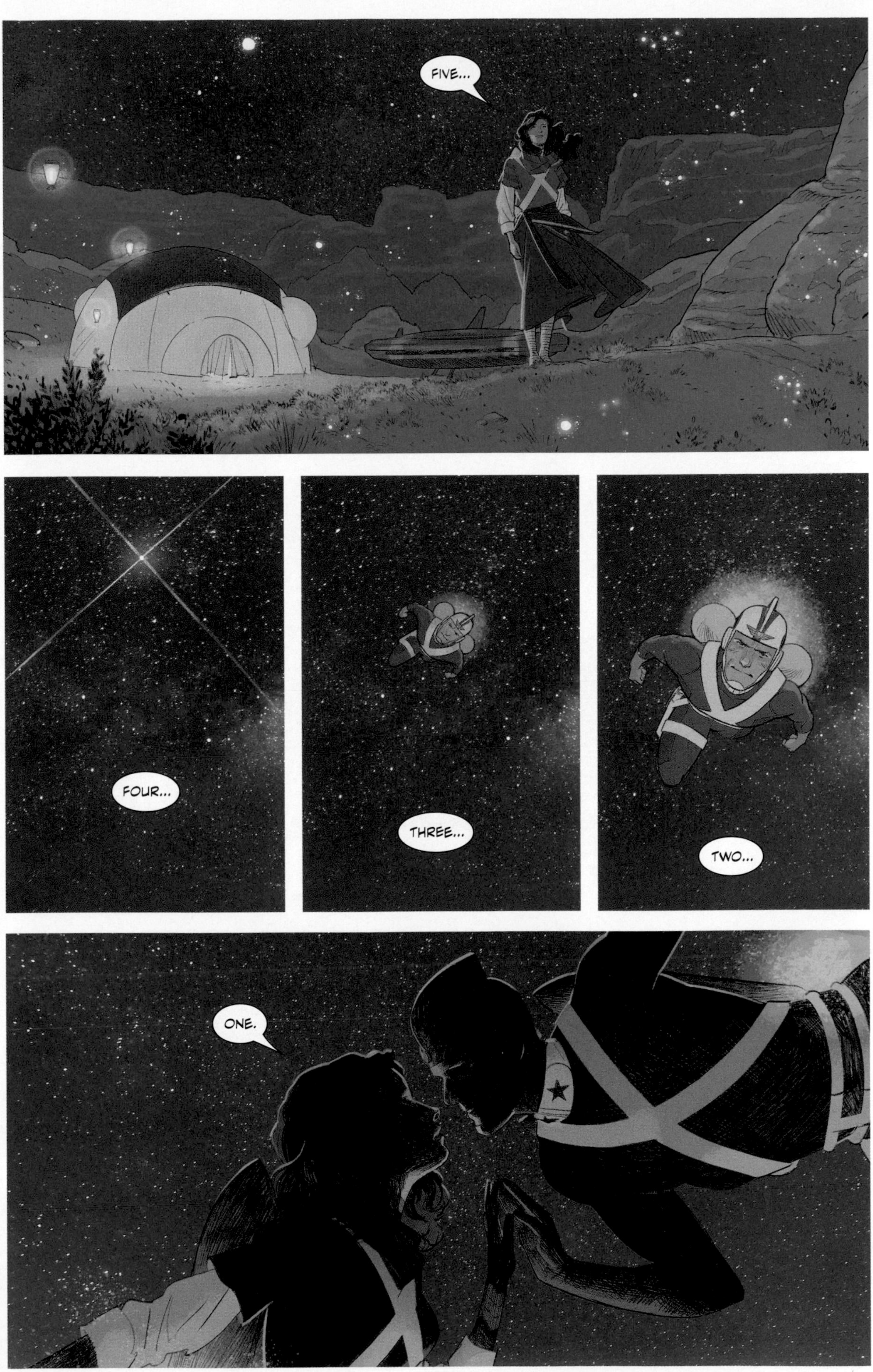
FIVE...
FOUR...
THREE...
TWO...
ONE.

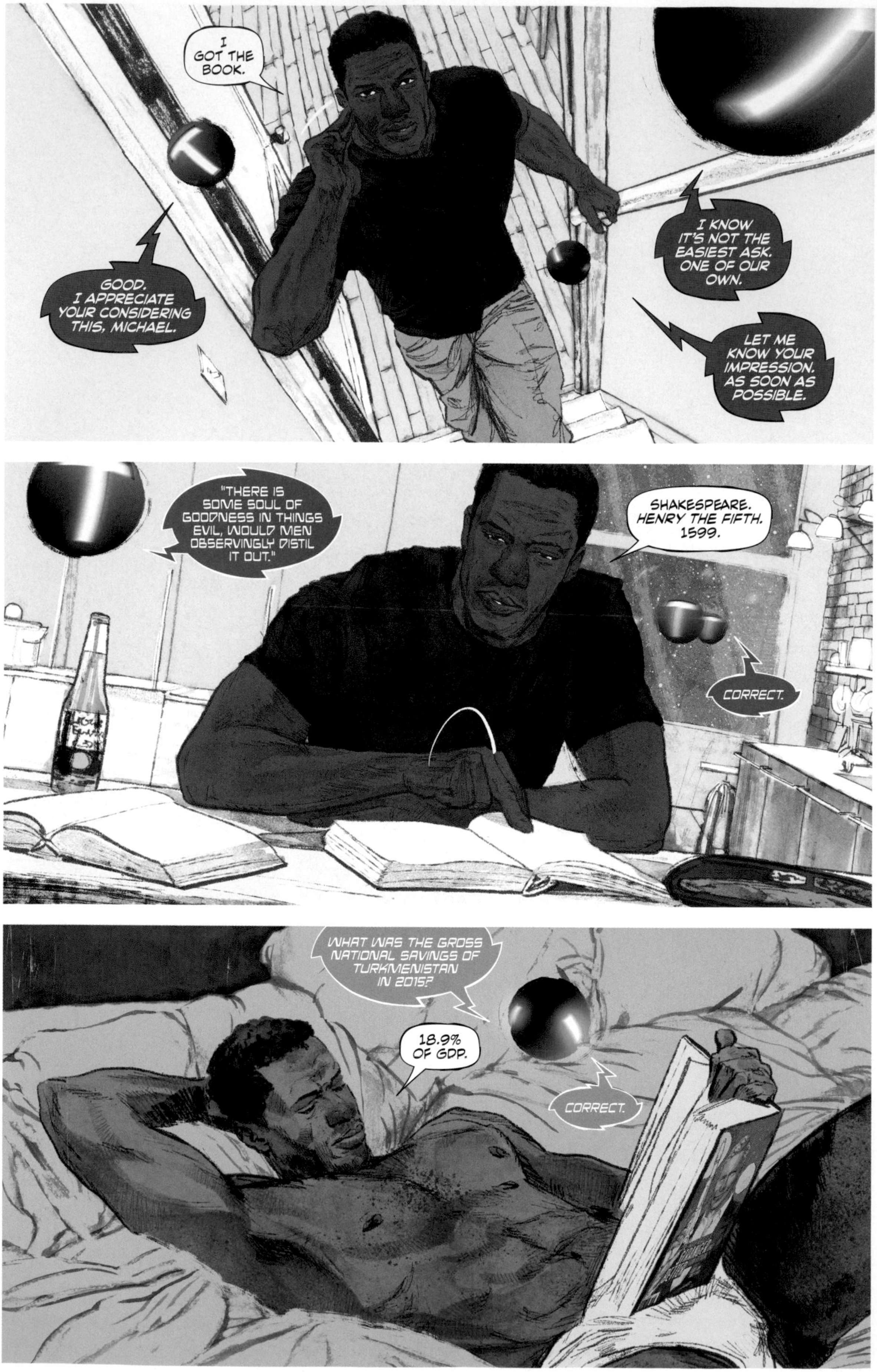
I GOT THE BOOK.
GOOD. I APPRECIATE YOUR CONSIDERING THIS, MICHAEL.
I KNOW IT'S NOT THE EASIEST ASK. ONE OF OUR OWN.
LET ME KNOW YOUR IMPRESSION. AS SOON AS POSSIBLE.
"THERE IS SOME SOUL OF GOODNESS IN THINGS EVIL, WOULD MEN OBSERVINGLY DISTIL IT OUT."
SHAKESPEARE. HENRY THE FIFTH. 1599.
CORRECT.
WHAT WAS THE GROSS NATIONAL SAVINGS OF TURKMENISTAN IN 2015?
18.9% OF GDP.
CORRECT.

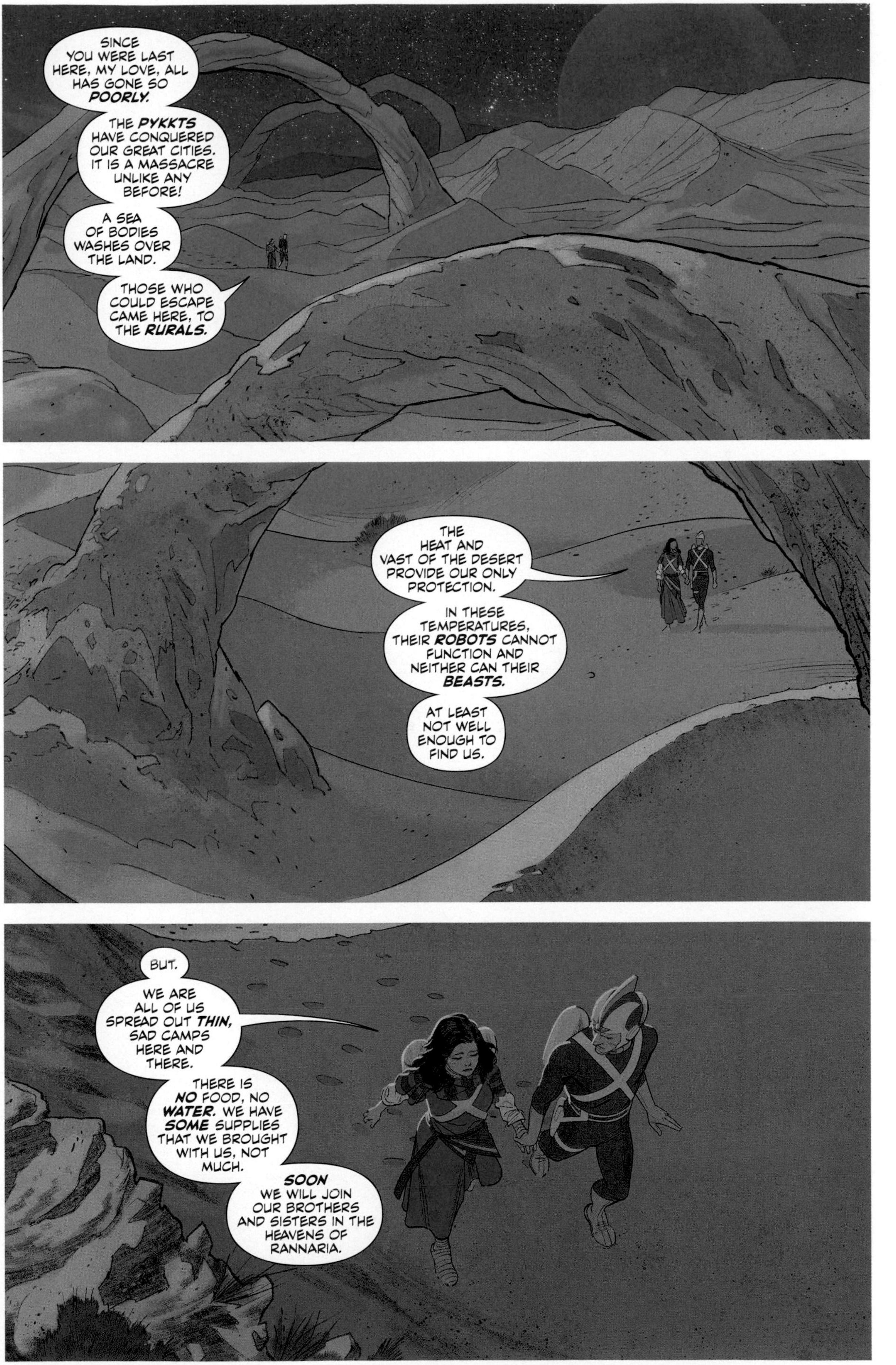

SINCE YOU WERE LAST HERE, MY LOVE, ALL HAS GONE SO ***POORLY.***
THE ***PYKKTS*** HAVE CONQUERED OUR GREAT CITIES. IT IS A MASSACRE UNLIKE ANY BEFORE!
A SEA OF BODIES WASHES OVER THE LAND.
THOSE WHO COULD ESCAPE CAME HERE, TO THE ***RURALS.***
THE HEAT AND VAST OF THE DESERT PROVIDE OUR ONLY PROTECTION.
IN THESE TEMPERATURES, THEIR ***ROBOTS*** CANNOT FUNCTION AND NEITHER CAN THEIR ***BEASTS.***
AT LEAST NOT WELL ENOUGH TO FIND US.
BUT.
WE ARE ALL OF US SPREAD OUT ***THIN,*** SAD CAMPS HERE AND THERE.
THERE IS ***NO*** FOOD, NO ***WATER.*** WE HAVE ***SOME*** SUPPLIES THAT WE BROUGHT WITH US, NOT MUCH.
SOON WE WILL JOIN OUR BROTHERS AND SISTERS IN THE HEAVENS OF RANNARIA.

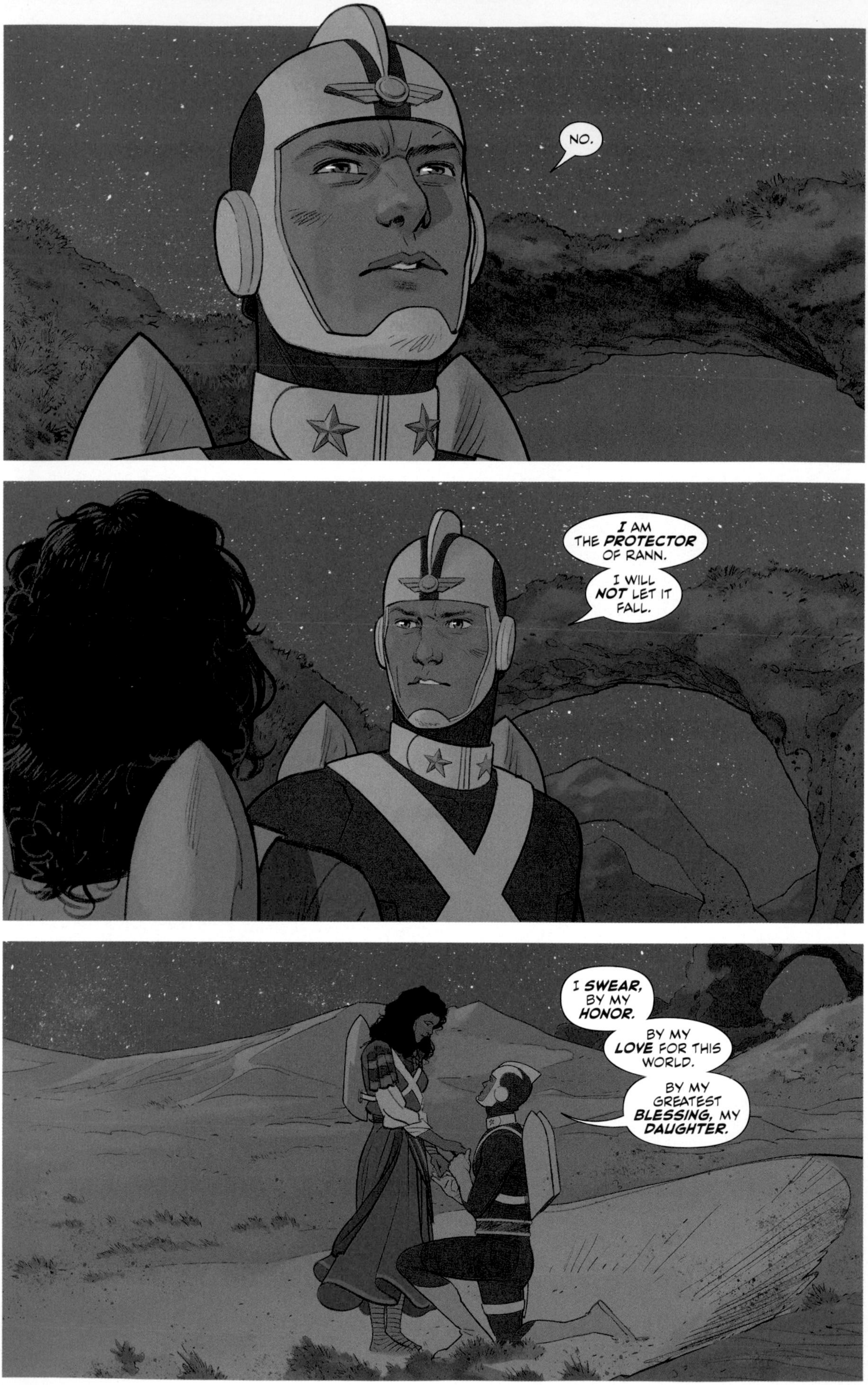
NO.
I AM THE PROTECTOR OF RANN.
I WILL NOT LET IT FALL.
I SWEAR, BY MY HONOR.
BY MY LOVE FOR THIS WORLD.
BY MY GREATEST BLESSING, MY DAUGHTER.

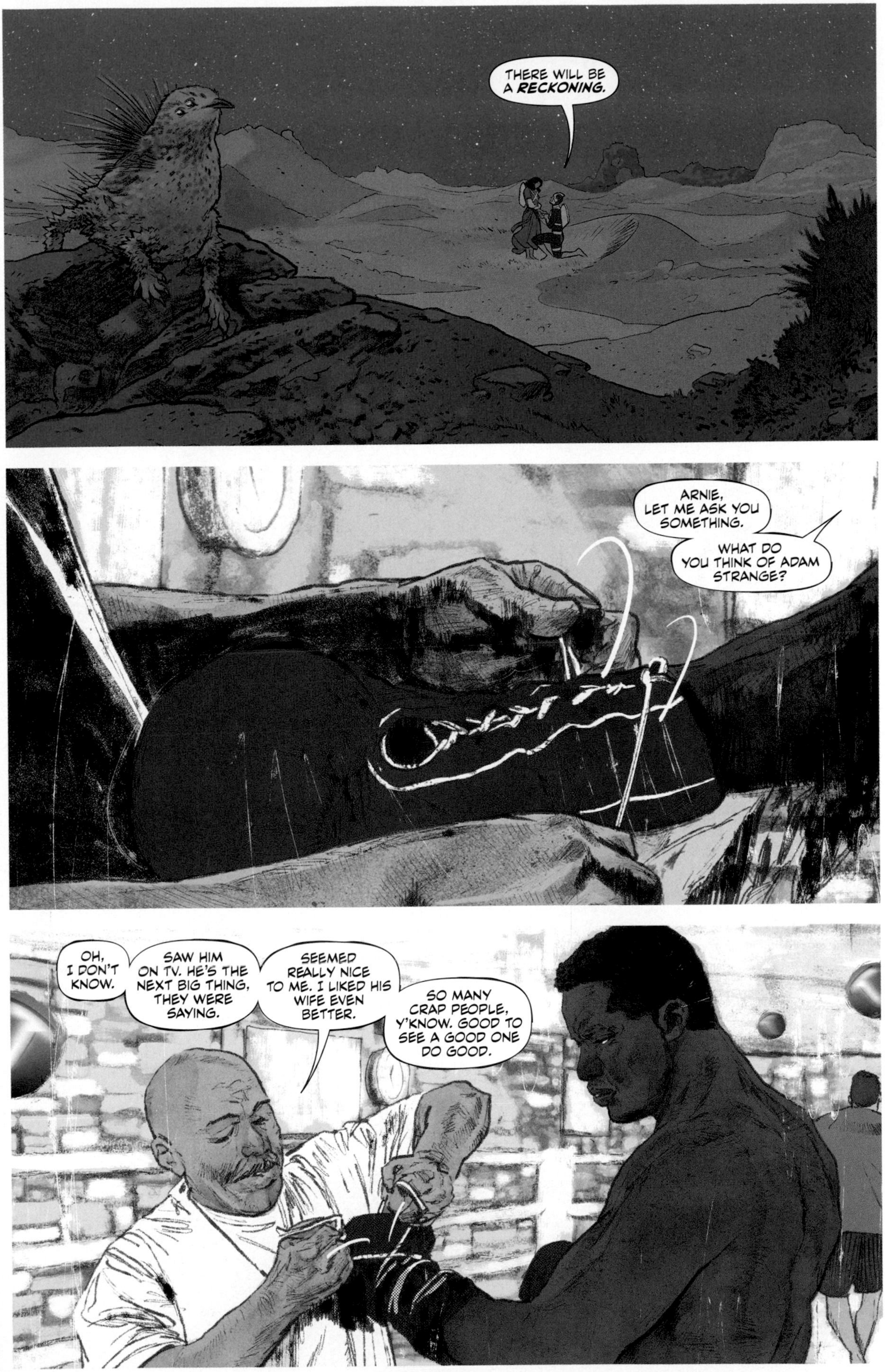
THERE WILL BE A **RECKONING.**
ARNIE, LET ME ASK YOU SOMETHING.
WHAT DO YOU THINK OF ADAM STRANGE?
OH, I DON'T KNOW.
SAW HIM ON TV. HE'S THE NEXT BIG THING, THEY WERE SAYING.
SEEMED REALLY NICE TO ME. I LIKED HIS WIFE EVEN BETTER.
SO MANY CRAP PEOPLE, Y'KNOW. GOOD TO SEE A GOOD ONE DO GOOD.

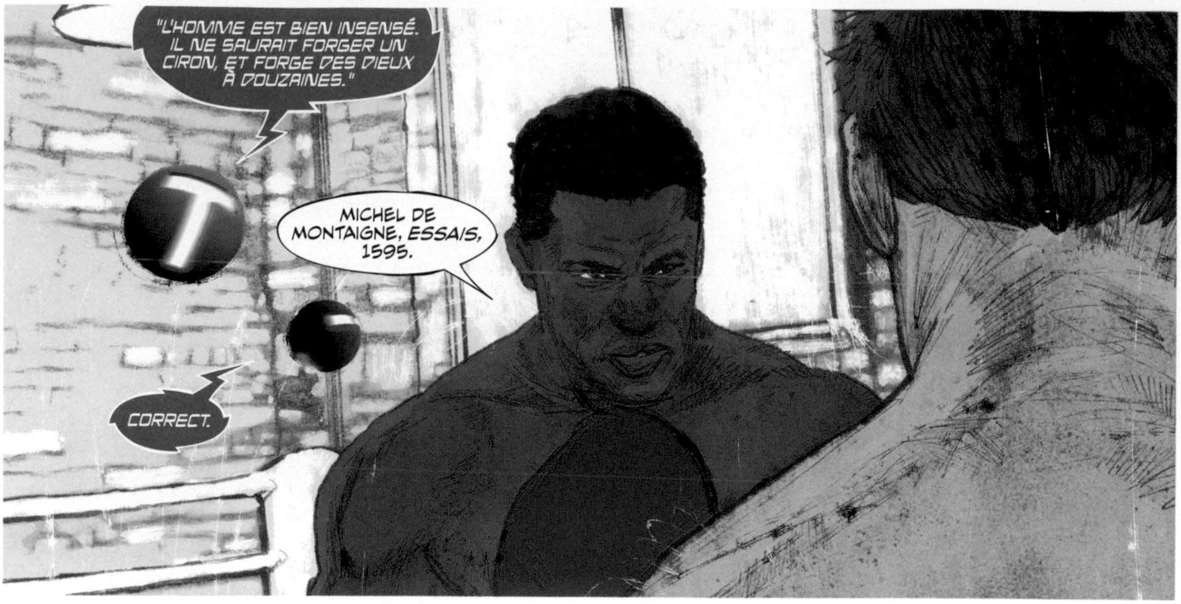
"L'HOMME EST BIEN INSENSÉ. IL NE SAURAIT FORGER UN CIRON, ET FORGE DES DIEUX À DOUZAINES."
MICHEL DE MONTAIGNE, ESSAIS, 1595.
CORRECT.

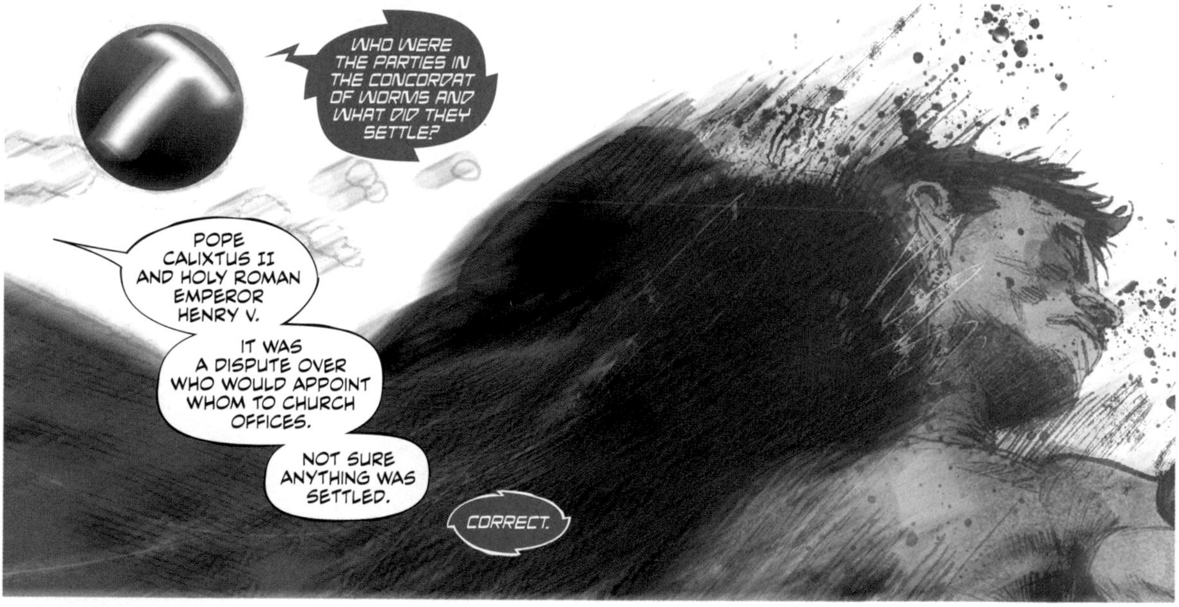
WHO WERE THE PARTIES IN THE CONCORDAT OF WORMS AND WHAT DID THEY SETTLE?
POPE CALIXTUS II AND HOLY ROMAN EMPEROR HENRY V.
IT WAS A DISPUTE OVER WHO WOULD APPOINT WHOM TO CHURCH OFFICES.
NOT SURE ANYTHING WAS SETTLED.
CORRECT.

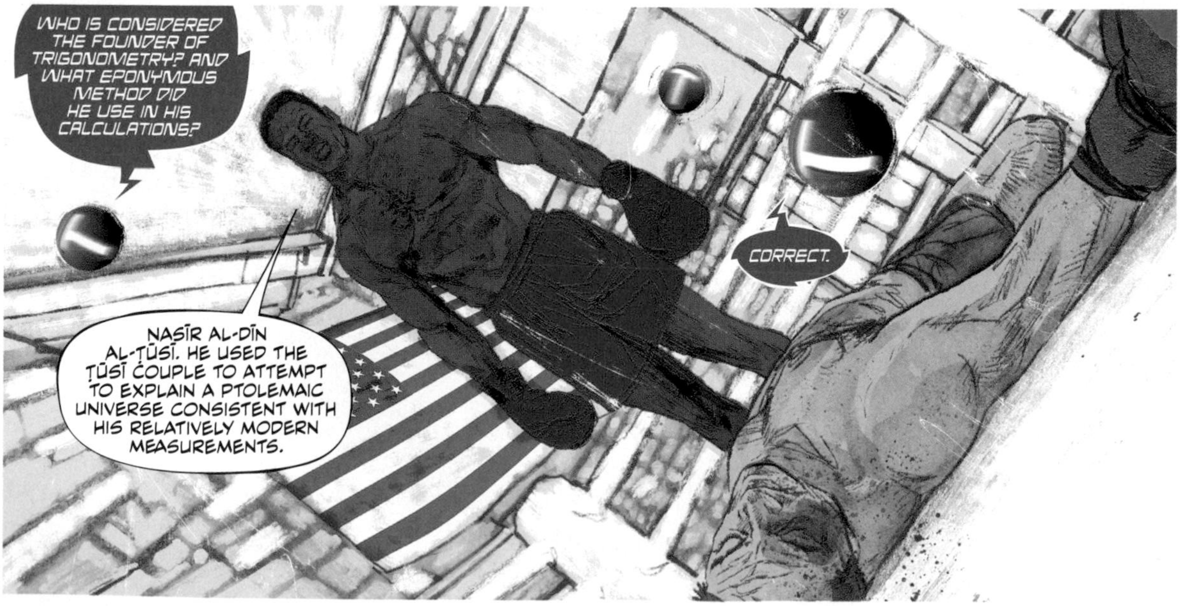
WHO IS CONSIDERED THE FOUNDER OF TRIGONOMETRY? AND WHAT EPONYMOUS METHOD DID HE USE IN HIS CALCULATIONS?
NASĪR AL-DĪN AL-ṬŪSĪ. HE USED THE ṬŪSĪ COUPLE TO ATTEMPT TO EXPLAIN A PTOLEMAIC UNIVERSE CONSISTENT WITH HIS RELATIVELY MODERN MEASUREMENTS.
CORRECT.

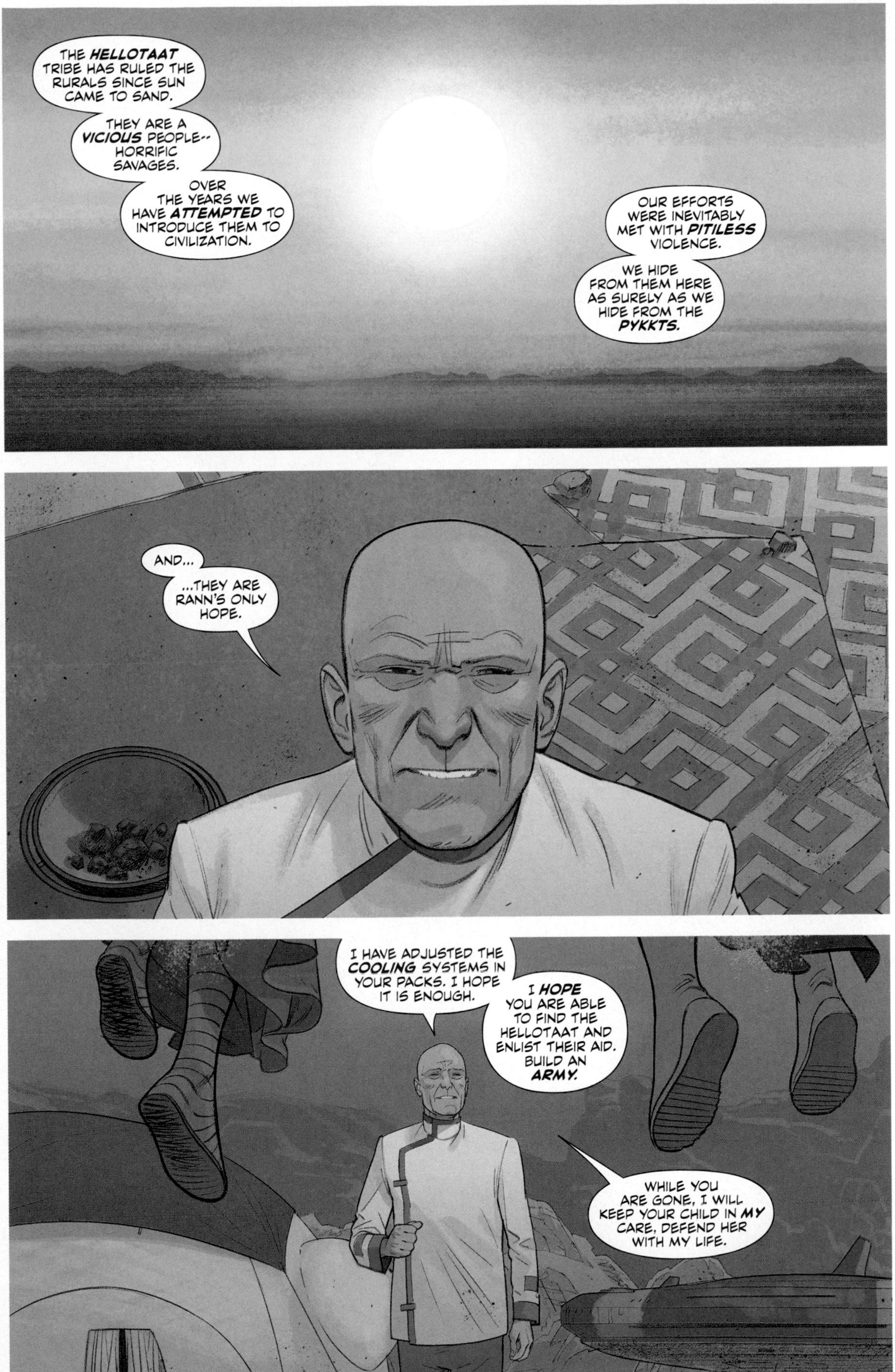
THE HELLOTAAT TRIBE HAS RULED THE RURALS SINCE SUN CAME TO SAND.
THEY ARE A VICIOUS PEOPLE--HORRIFIC SAVAGES.
OVER THE YEARS WE HAVE ATTEMPTED TO INTRODUCE THEM TO CIVILIZATION.
OUR EFFORTS WERE INEVITABLY MET WITH PITILESS VIOLENCE.
WE HIDE FROM THEM HERE AS SURELY AS WE HIDE FROM THE PYKKTS.
AND...
...THEY ARE RANN'S ONLY HOPE.
I HAVE ADJUSTED THE COOLING SYSTEMS IN YOUR PACKS. I HOPE IT IS ENOUGH.
I HOPE YOU ARE ABLE TO FIND THE HELLOTAAT AND ENLIST THEIR AID. BUILD AN ARMY.
WHILE YOU ARE GONE, I WILL KEEP YOUR CHILD IN MY CARE, DEFEND HER WITH MY LIFE.

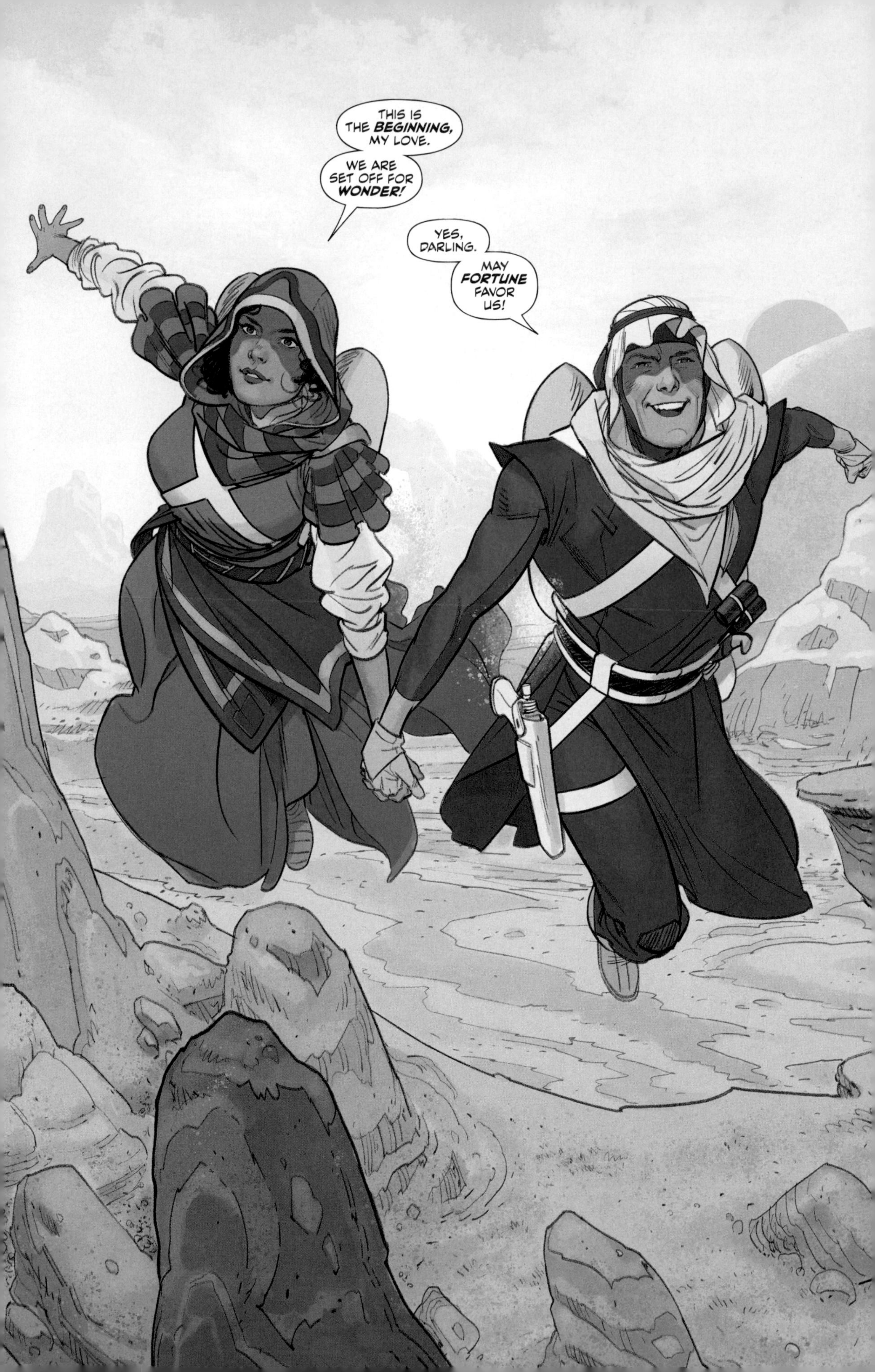
THIS IS THE **BEGINNING,** MY LOVE.
WE ARE SET OFF FOR ***WONDER!***
YES, DARLING.
MAY ***FORTUNE*** FAVOR US!

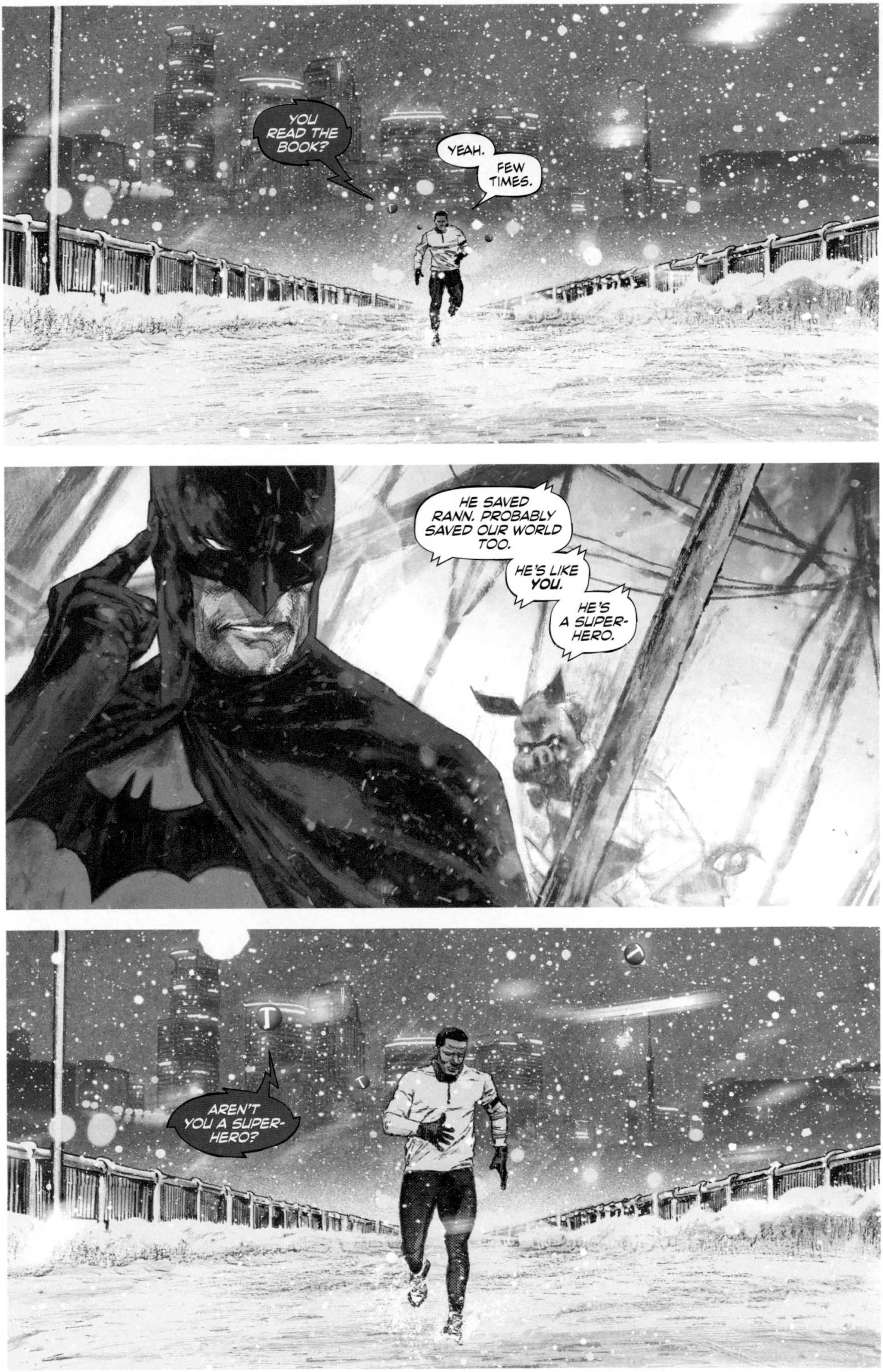
YOU READ THE BOOK?
YEAH.
FEW TIMES.
HE SAVED RANN. PROBABLY SAVED OUR WORLD TOO.
HE'S LIKE **YOU.**
HE'S A SUPER-HERO.
AREN'T YOU A SUPER-HERO?

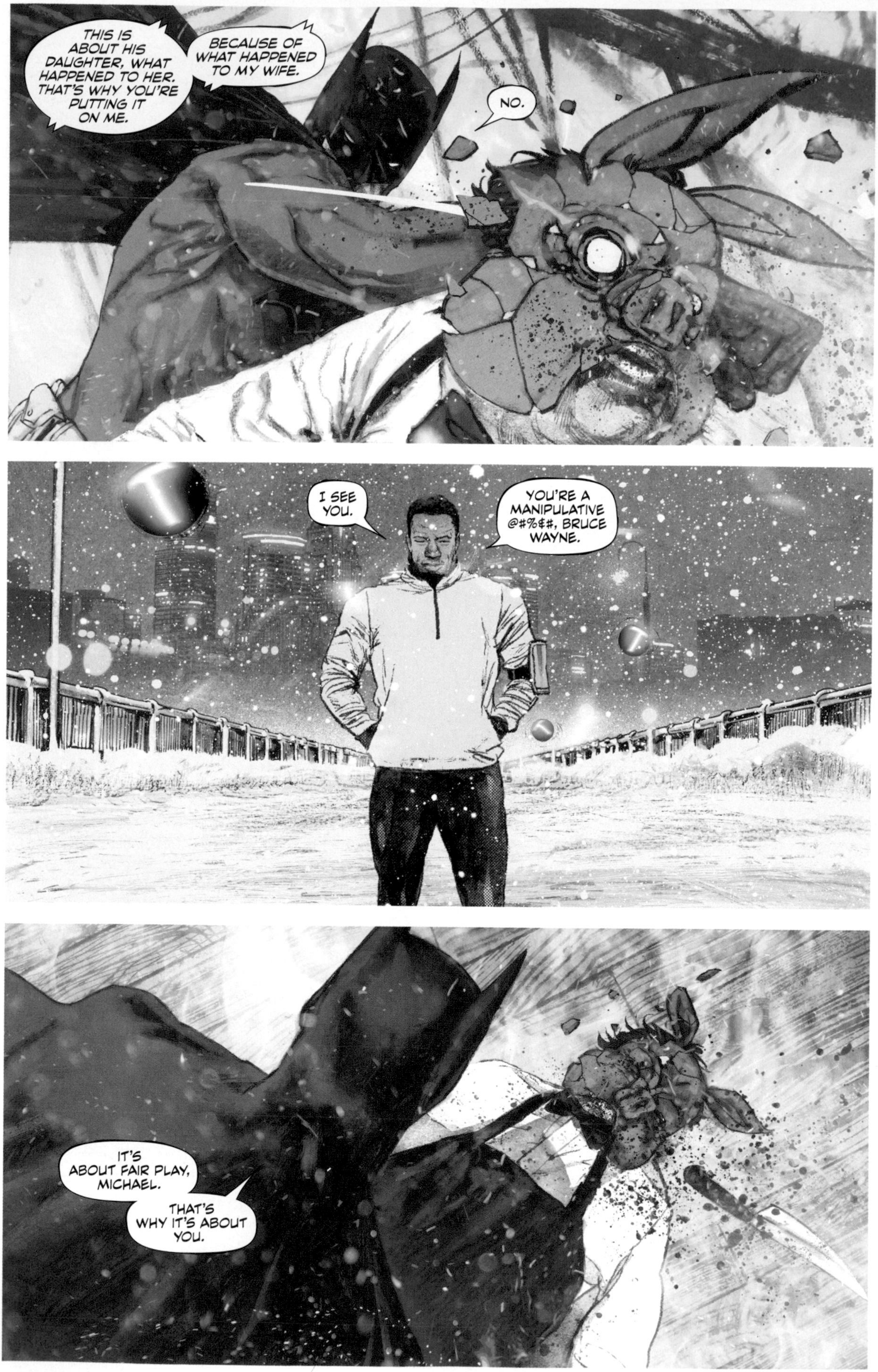
THIS IS ABOUT HIS DAUGHTER, WHAT HAPPENED TO HER. THAT'S WHY YOU'RE PUTTING IT ON ME.
BECAUSE OF WHAT HAPPENED TO MY WIFE.
NO.
I SEE YOU.
YOU'RE A MANIPULATIVE @#%$#, BRUCE WAYNE.
IT'S ABOUT FAIR PLAY, MICHAEL.
THAT'S WHY IT'S ABOUT YOU.

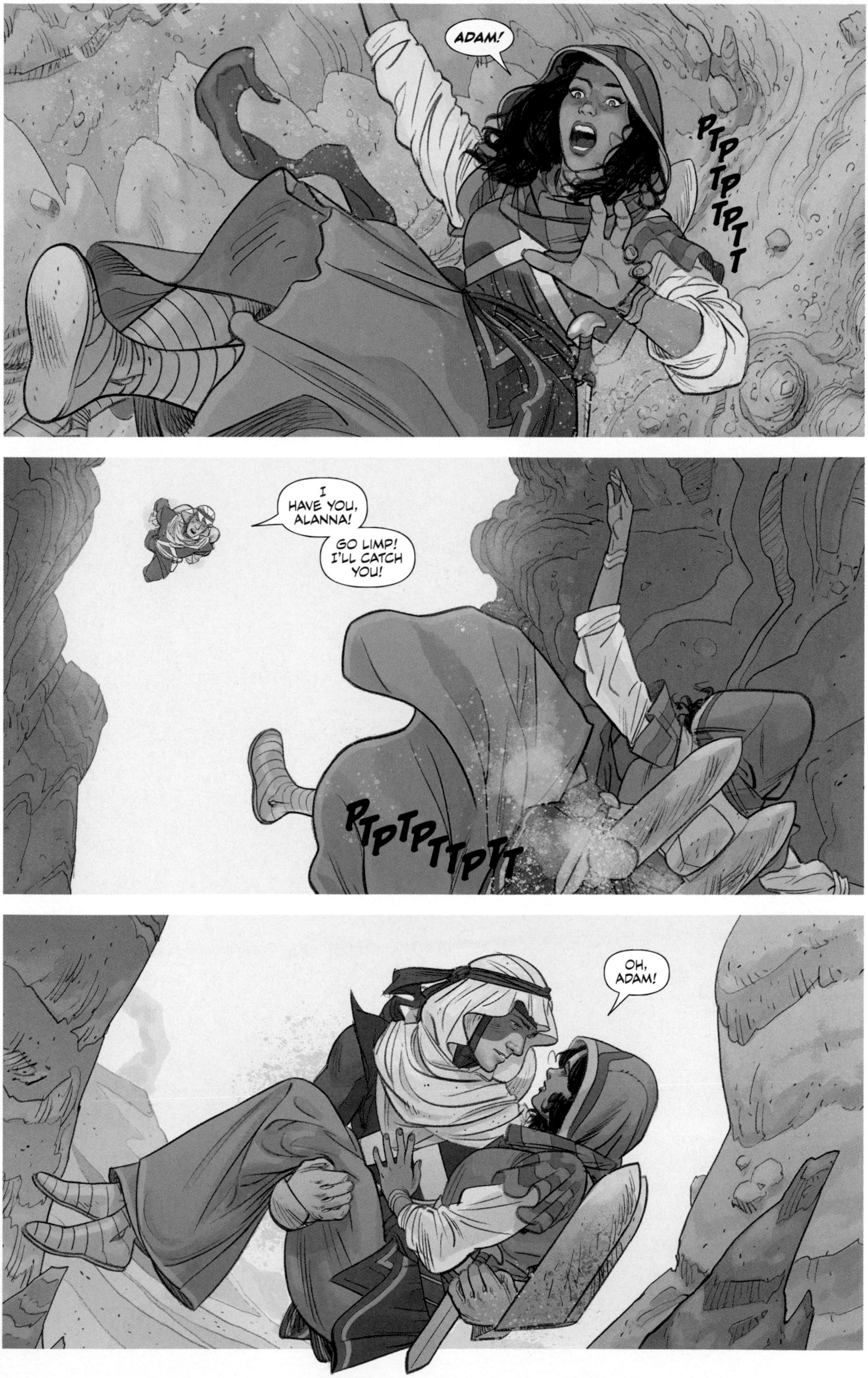
ADAM!
PTPTPTPTT
I HAVE YOU, ALANNA!
GO LIMP! I'LL CATCH YOU!
PTPTPTTTPTT
OH, ADAM!

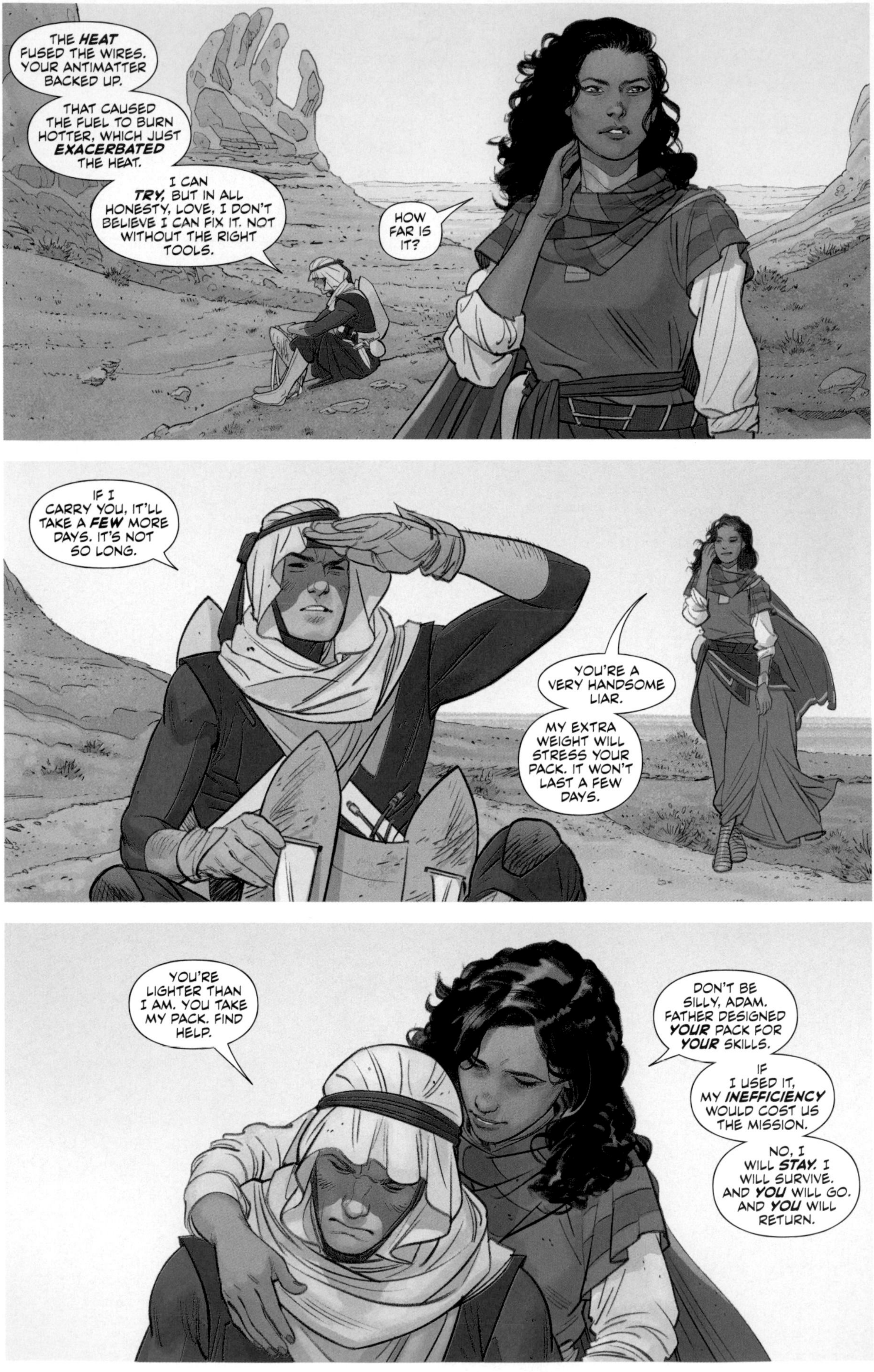
THE HEAT FUSED THE WIRES. YOUR ANTIMATTER BACKED UP.
THAT CAUSED THE FUEL TO BURN HOTTER, WHICH JUST EXACERBATED THE HEAT.
I CAN TRY, BUT IN ALL HONESTY, LOVE, I DON'T BELIEVE I CAN FIX IT. NOT WITHOUT THE RIGHT TOOLS.
HOW FAR IS IT?
IF I CARRY YOU, IT'LL TAKE A FEW MORE DAYS. IT'S NOT SO LONG.
YOU'RE A VERY HANDSOME LIAR.
MY EXTRA WEIGHT WILL STRESS YOUR PACK. IT WON'T LAST A FEW DAYS.
YOU'RE LIGHTER THAN I AM. YOU TAKE MY PACK. FIND HELP.
DON'T BE SILLY, ADAM. FATHER DESIGNED YOUR PACK FOR YOUR SKILLS.
IF I USED IT, MY INEFFICIENCY WOULD COST US THE MISSION.
NO, I WILL STAY. I WILL SURVIVE. AND YOU WILL GO. AND YOU WILL RETURN.

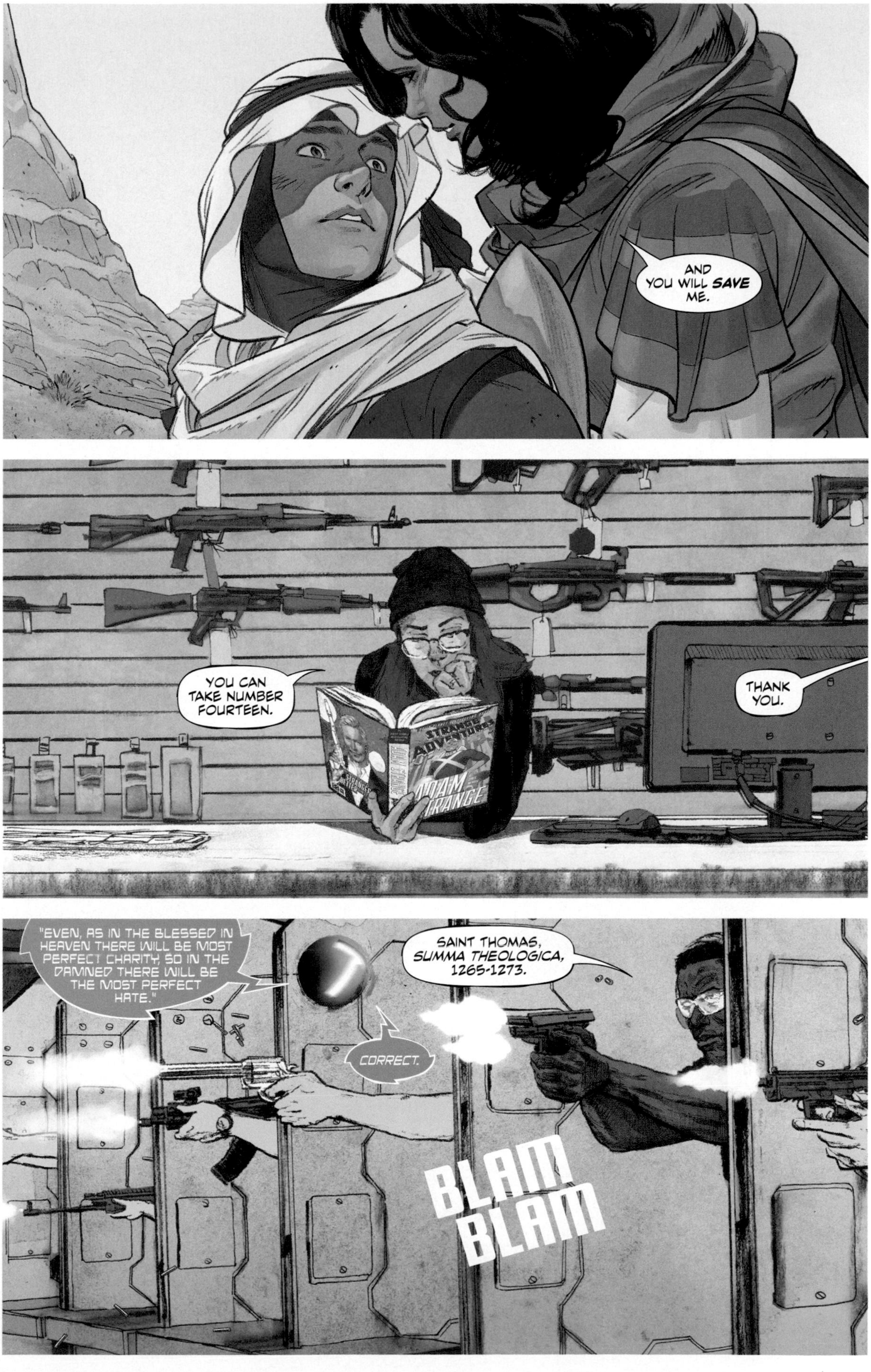
AND YOU WILL SAVE ME.
YOU CAN TAKE NUMBER FOURTEEN.
THANK YOU.
STRANGE ADVENTURES
ADAM STRANGE
"EVEN, AS IN THE BLESSED IN HEAVEN THERE WILL BE MOST PERFECT CHARITY, SO IN THE DAMNED THERE WILL BE THE MOST PERFECT HATE."
SAINT THOMAS, SUMMA THEOLOGICA, 1265-1273.
CORRECT.
BLAM BLAM

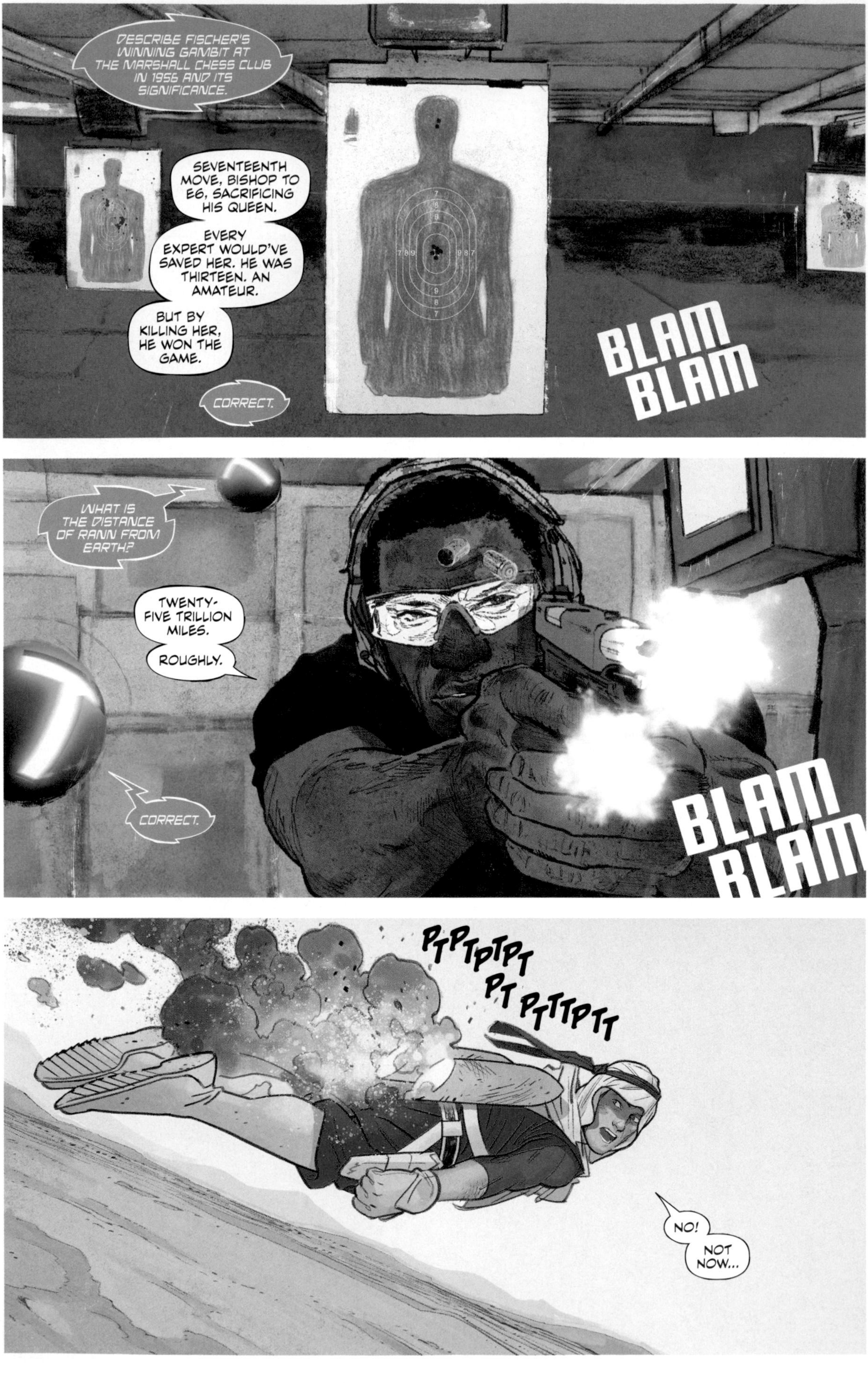
DESCRIBE FISCHER'S WINNING GAMBIT AT THE MARSHALL CHESS CLUB IN 1956 AND ITS SIGNIFICANCE.
SEVENTEENTH MOVE, BISHOP TO E6, SACRIFICING HIS QUEEN.
EVERY EXPERT WOULD'VE SAVED HER. HE WAS THIRTEEN. AN AMATEUR.
BUT BY KILLING HER, HE WON THE GAME.
CORRECT.
BLAM BLAM
WHAT IS THE DISTANCE OF RANN FROM EARTH?
TWENTY-FIVE TRILLION MILES.
ROUGHLY.
CORRECT.
BLAM BLAM
PTPTPTPT PT PTTTPTT
NO!
NOT NOW...

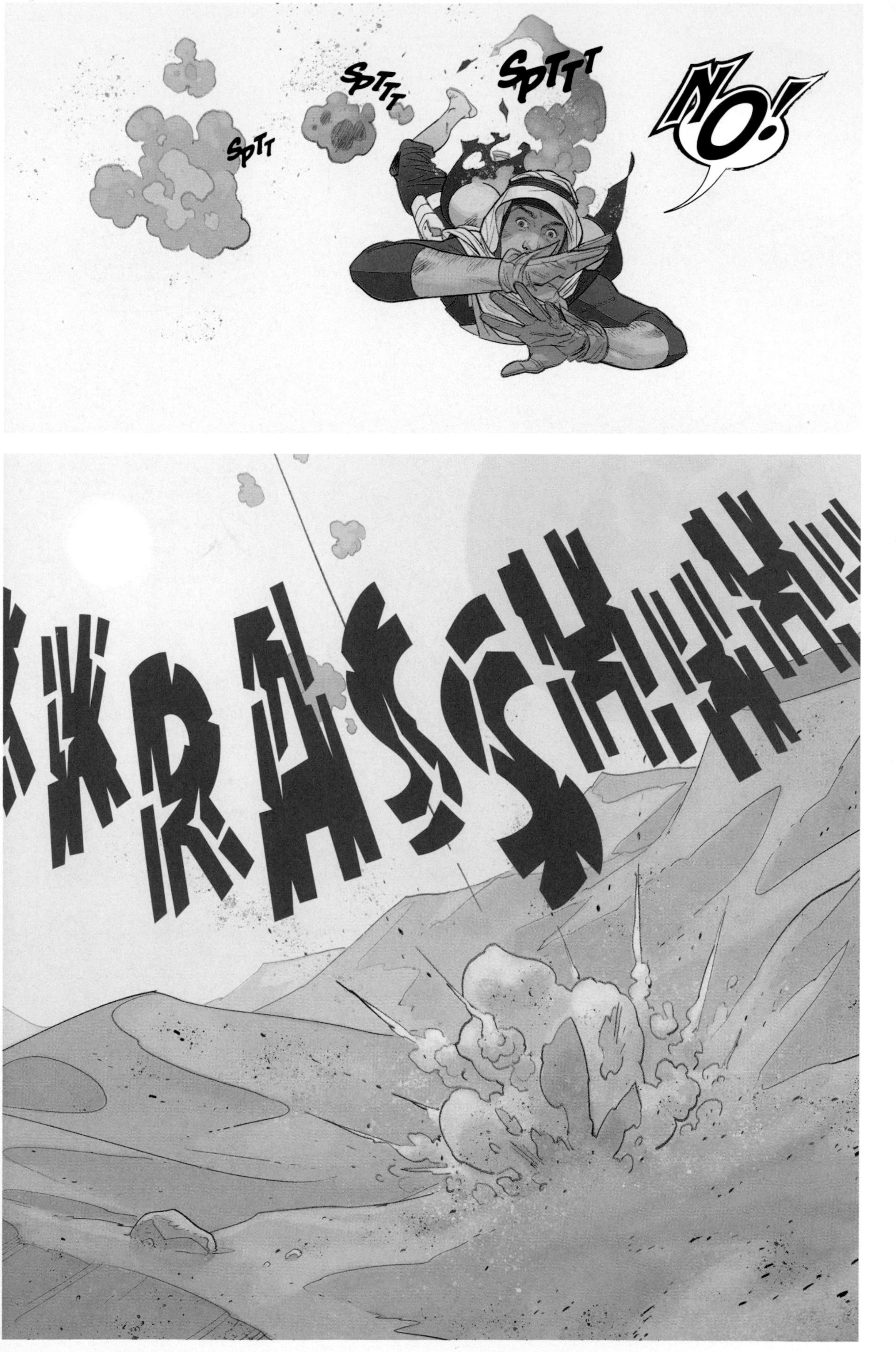
SPTT
SPTTT
SPTTTT
NO!
KKRASSKKK

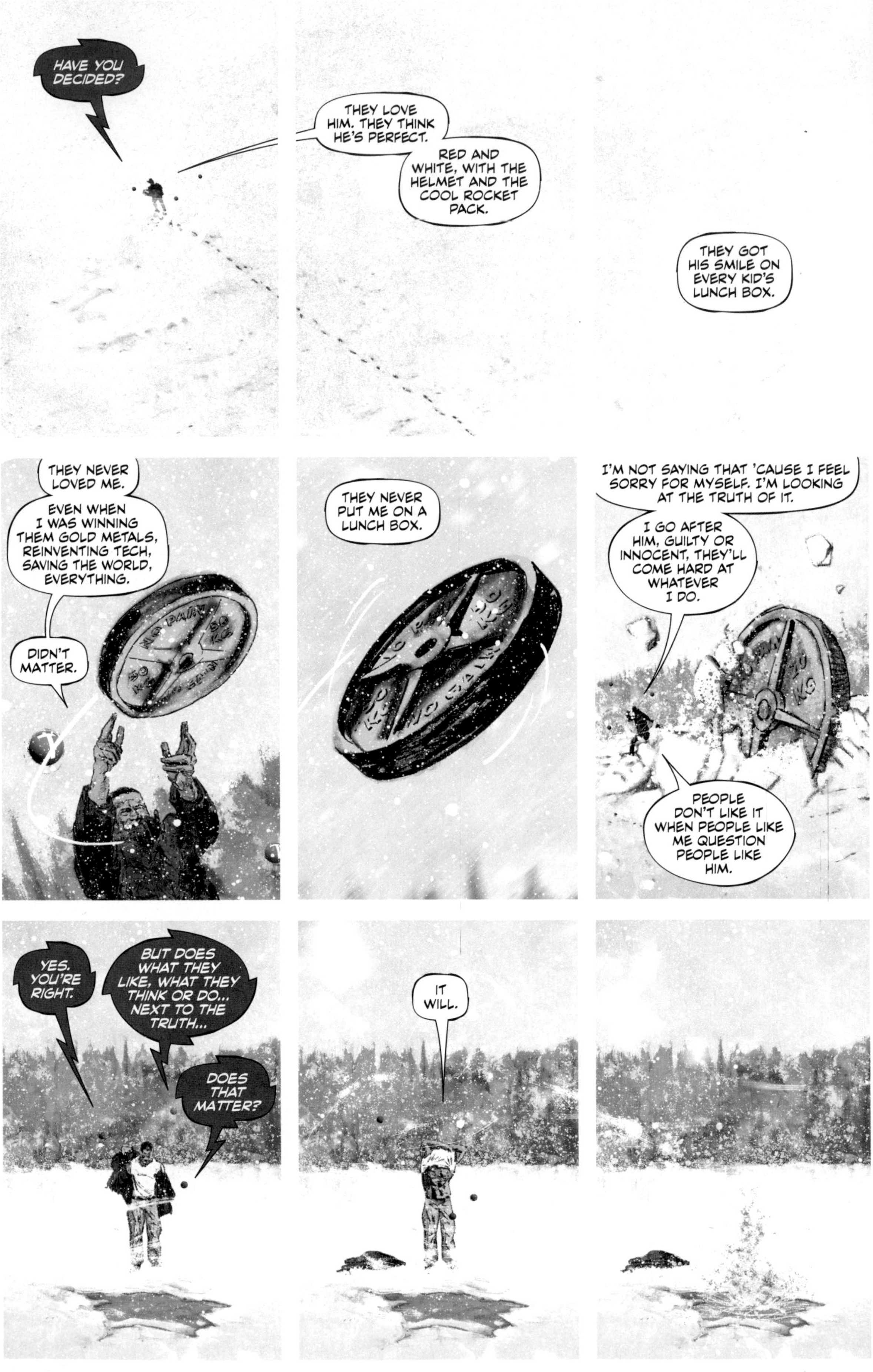
HAVE YOU DECIDED?
THEY LOVE HIM. THEY THINK HE'S PERFECT.
RED AND WHITE, WITH THE HELMET AND THE COOL ROCKET PACK.
THEY GOT HIS SMILE ON EVERY KID'S LUNCH BOX.
THEY NEVER LOVED ME.
EVEN WHEN I WAS WINNING THEM GOLD METALS, REINVENTING TECH, SAVING THE WORLD, EVERYTHING.
DIDN'T MATTER.
THEY NEVER PUT ME ON A LUNCH BOX.
I'M NOT SAYING THAT 'CAUSE I FEEL SORRY FOR MYSELF. I'M LOOKING AT THE TRUTH OF IT.
I GO AFTER HIM, GUILTY OR INNOCENT, THEY'LL COME HARD AT WHATEVER I DO.
PEOPLE DON'T LIKE IT WHEN PEOPLE LIKE ME QUESTION PEOPLE LIKE HIM.
YES. YOU'RE RIGHT.
BUT DOES WHAT THEY LIKE, WHAT THEY THINK OR DO... NEXT TO THE TRUTH...
DOES THAT MATTER?
IT WILL.

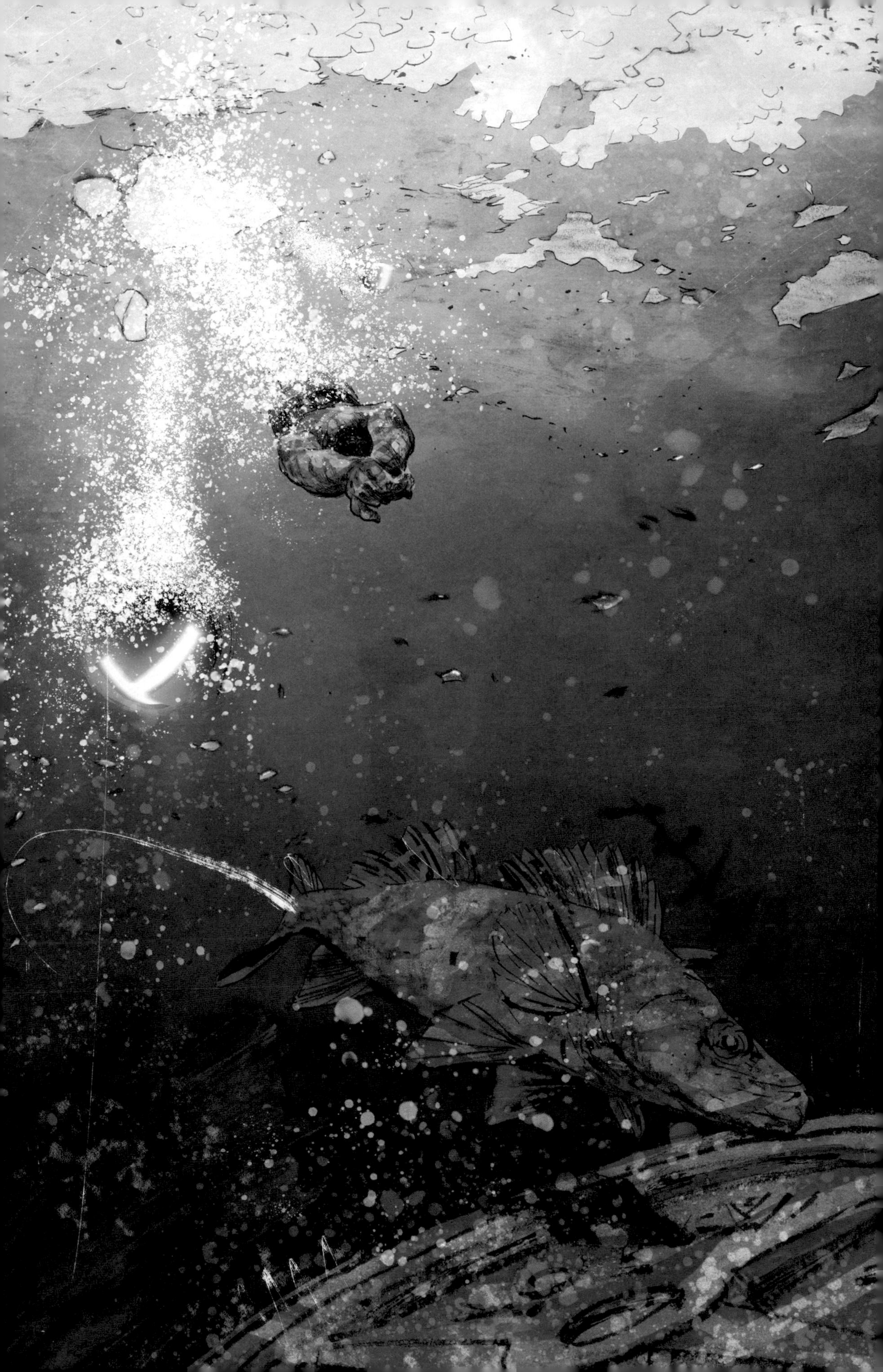

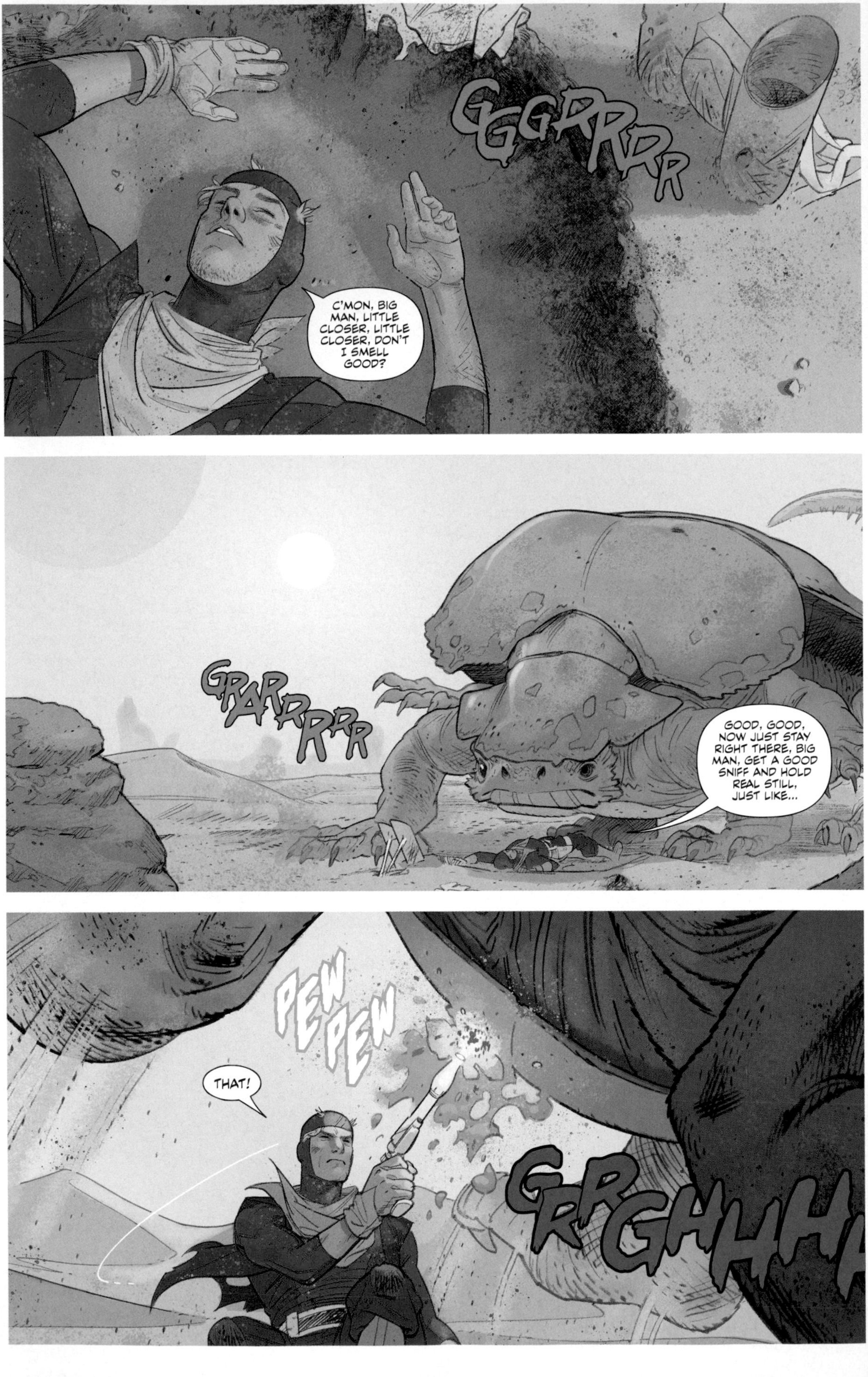
GGGRRRRR
C'MON, BIG MAN, LITTLE CLOSER, LITTLE CLOSER, DON'T I SMELL GOOD?
GRARRRRR
GOOD, GOOD, NOW JUST STAY RIGHT THERE, BIG MAN, GET A GOOD SNIFF AND HOLD REAL STILL, JUST LIKE...
PEW PEW
THAT!
GRRGHHHH

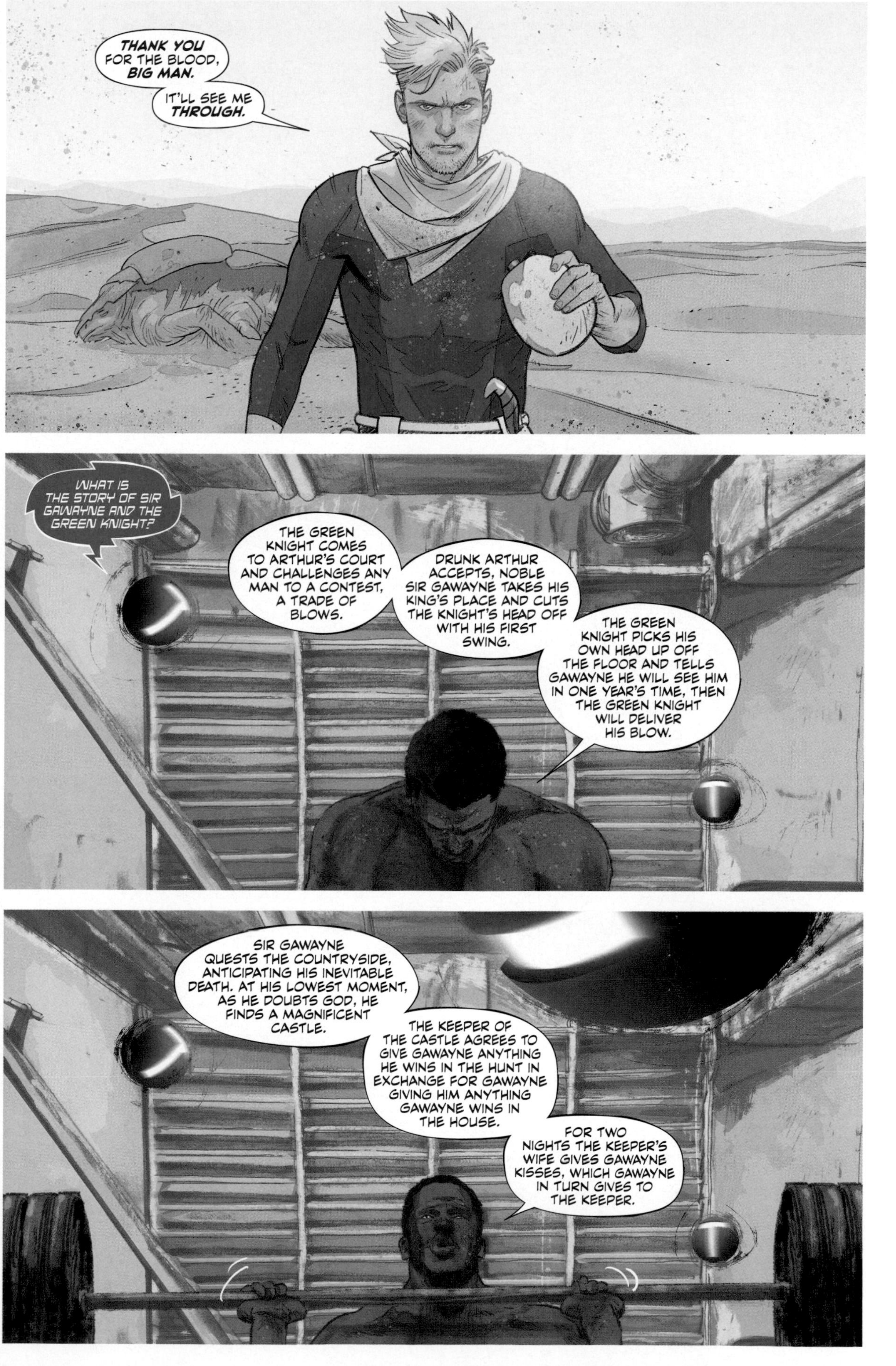
THANK YOU FOR THE BLOOD, BIG MAN.
IT'LL SEE ME THROUGH.
WHAT IS THE STORY OF SIR GAWAYNE AND THE GREEN KNIGHT?
THE GREEN KNIGHT COMES TO ARTHUR'S COURT AND CHALLENGES ANY MAN TO A CONTEST, A TRADE OF BLOWS.
DRUNK ARTHUR ACCEPTS, NOBLE SIR GAWAYNE TAKES HIS KING'S PLACE AND CUTS THE KNIGHT'S HEAD OFF WITH HIS FIRST SWING.
THE GREEN KNIGHT PICKS HIS OWN HEAD UP OFF THE FLOOR AND TELLS GAWAYNE HE WILL SEE HIM IN ONE YEAR'S TIME, THEN THE GREEN KNIGHT WILL DELIVER HIS BLOW.
SIR GAWAYNE QUESTS THE COUNTRYSIDE, ANTICIPATING HIS INEVITABLE DEATH. AT HIS LOWEST MOMENT, AS HE DOUBTS GOD, HE FINDS A MAGNIFICENT CASTLE.
THE KEEPER OF THE CASTLE AGREES TO GIVE GAWAYNE ANYTHING HE WINS IN THE HUNT IN EXCHANGE FOR GAWAYNE GIVING HIM ANYTHING GAWAYNE WINS IN THE HOUSE.
FOR TWO NIGHTS THE KEEPER'S WIFE GIVES GAWAYNE KISSES, WHICH GAWAYNE IN TURN GIVES TO THE KEEPER.

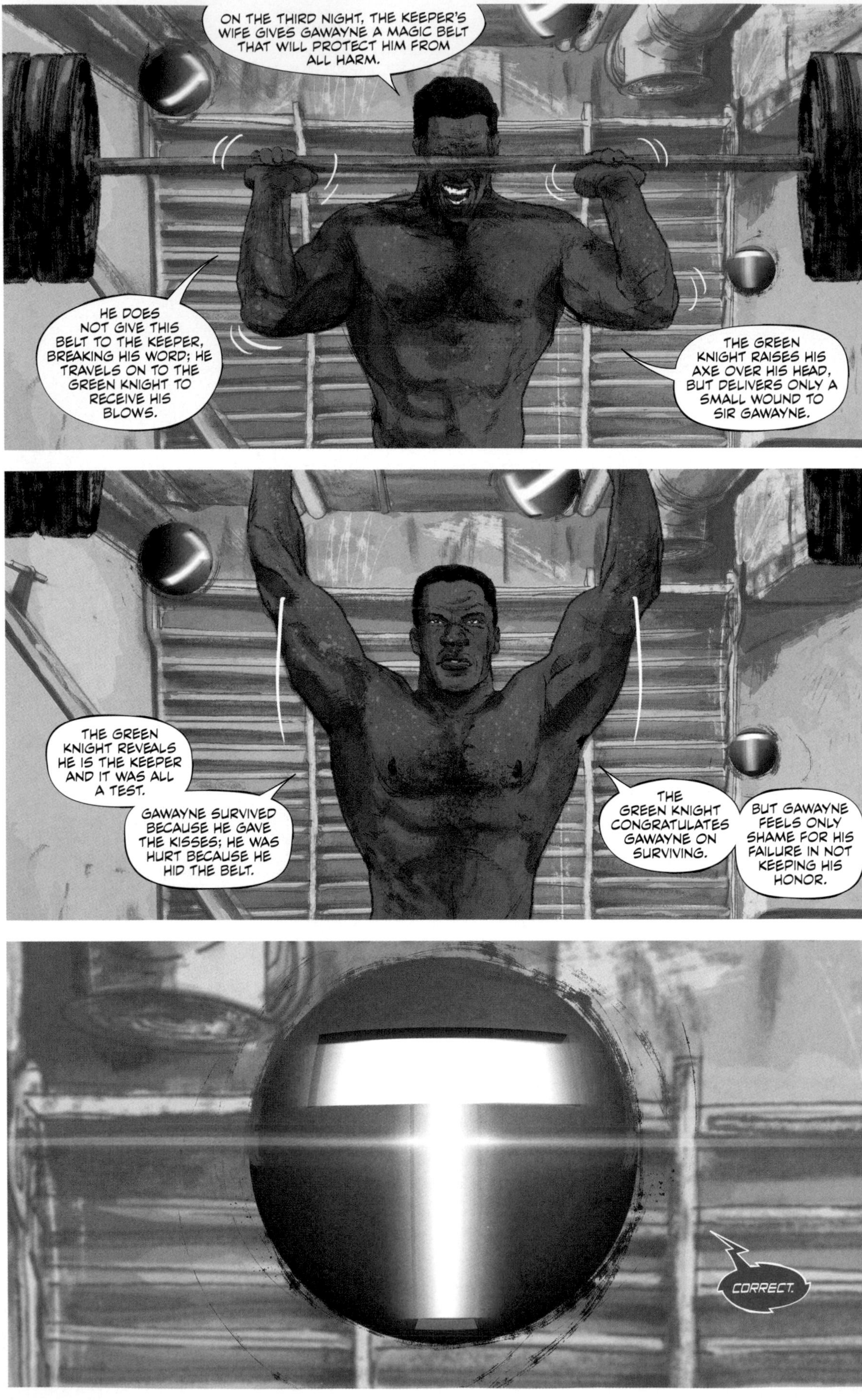
ON THE THIRD NIGHT, THE KEEPER'S WIFE GIVES GAWAYNE A MAGIC BELT THAT WILL PROTECT HIM FROM ALL HARM.
HE DOES NOT GIVE THIS BELT TO THE KEEPER, BREAKING HIS WORD; HE TRAVELS ON TO THE GREEN KNIGHT TO RECEIVE HIS BLOWS.
THE GREEN KNIGHT RAISES HIS AXE OVER HIS HEAD, BUT DELIVERS ONLY A SMALL WOUND TO SIR GAWAYNE.
THE GREEN KNIGHT REVEALS HE IS THE KEEPER AND IT WAS ALL A TEST.
GAWAYNE SURVIVED BECAUSE HE GAVE THE KISSES; HE WAS HURT BECAUSE HE HID THE BELT.
THE GREEN KNIGHT CONGRATULATES GAWAYNE ON SURVIVING.
BUT GAWAYNE FEELS ONLY SHAME FOR HIS FAILURE IN NOT KEEPING HIS HONOR.
CORRECT.

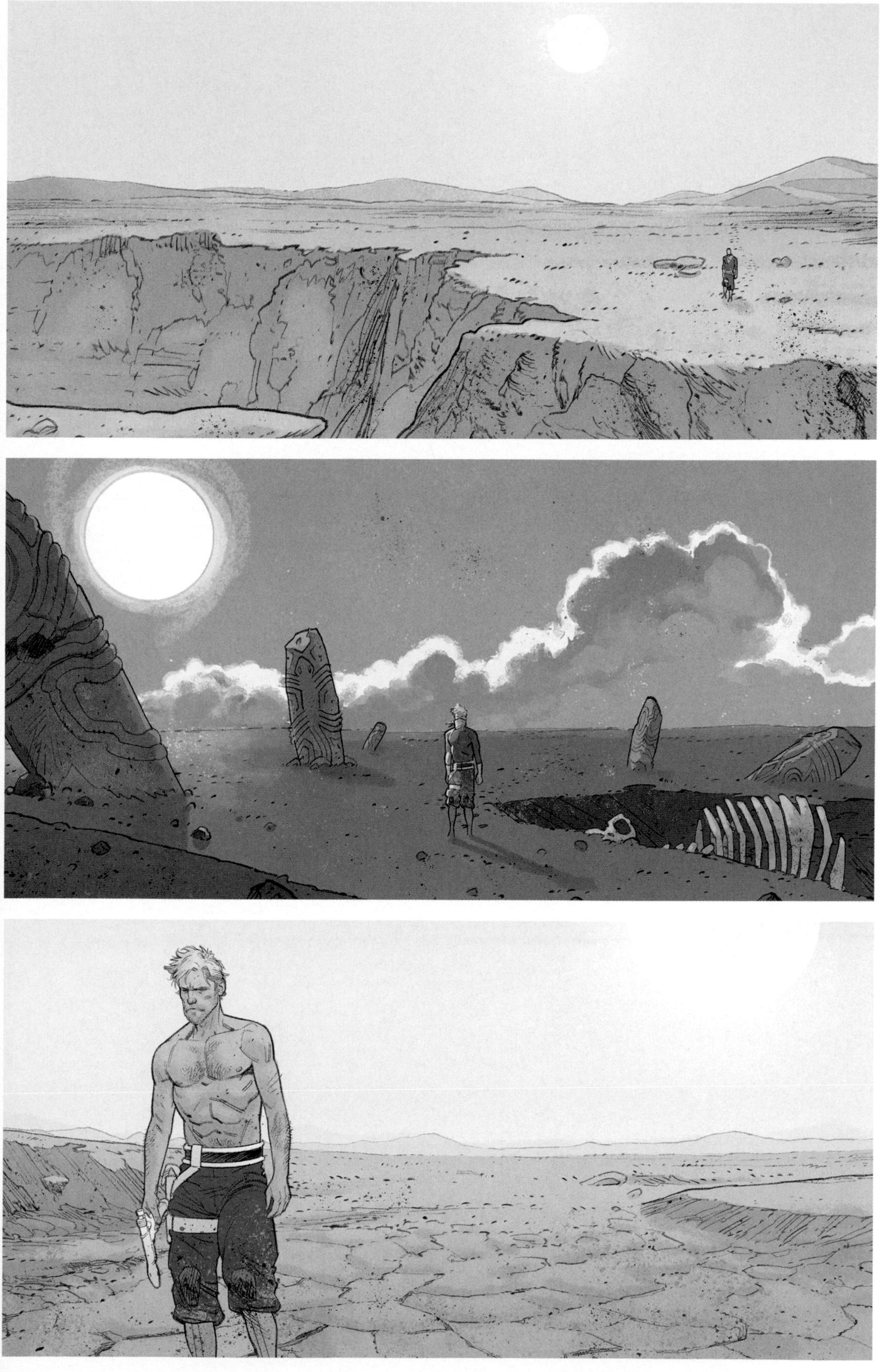

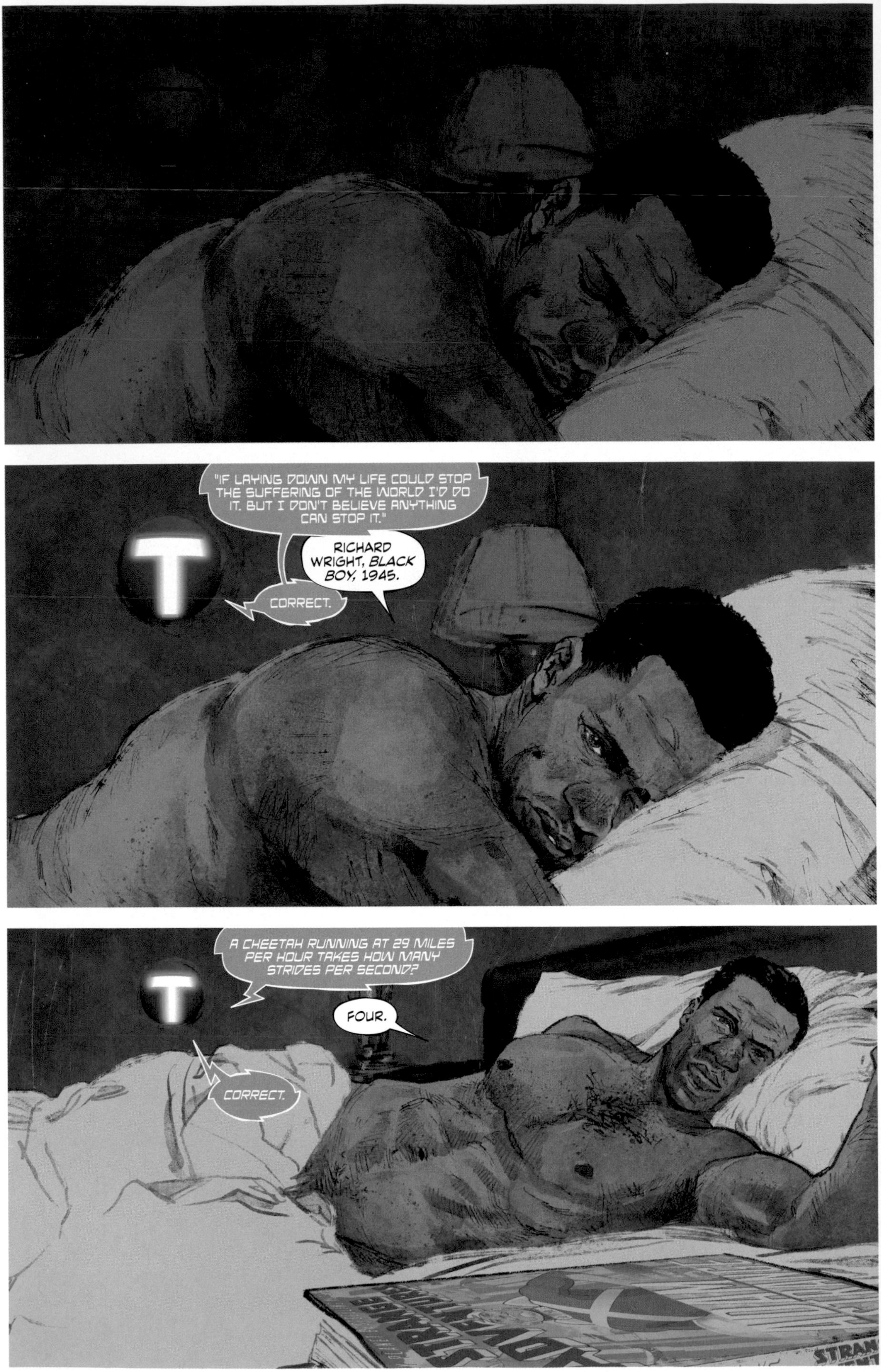
"IF LAYING DOWN MY LIFE COULD STOP THE SUFFERING OF THE WORLD I'D DO IT. BUT I DON'T BELIEVE ANYTHING CAN STOP IT."
RICHARD WRIGHT, *BLACK BOY,* 1945.
CORRECT.
A CHEETAH RUNNING AT 29 MILES PER HOUR TAKES HOW MANY STRIDES PER SECOND?
FOUR.
CORRECT.

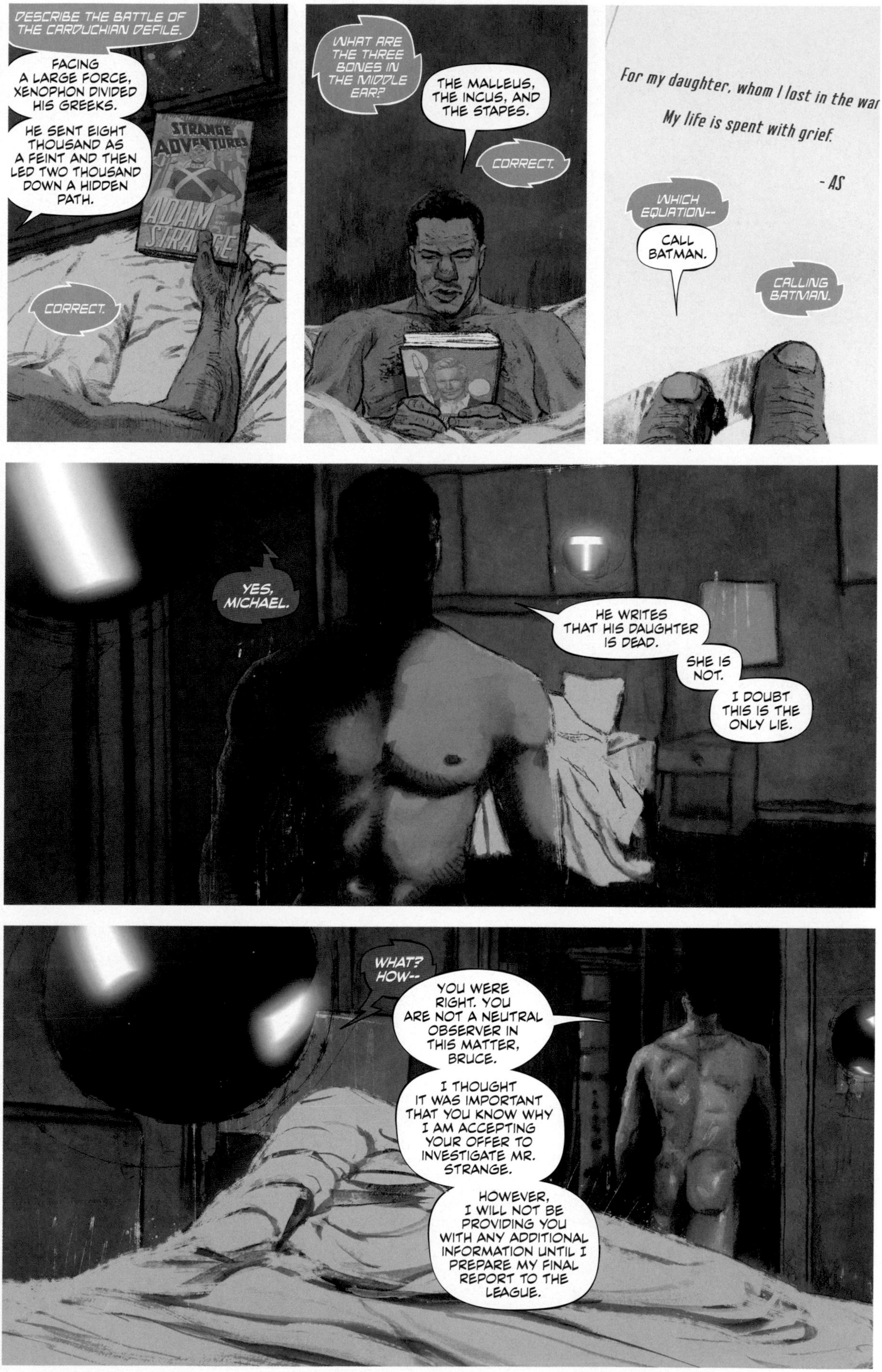
DESCRIBE THE BATTLE OF THE CARDUCHIAN DEFILE.
FACING A LARGE FORCE, XENOPHON DIVIDED HIS GREEKS.
HE SENT EIGHT THOUSAND AS A FEINT AND THEN LED TWO THOUSAND DOWN A HIDDEN PATH.
STRANGE ADVENTURES
ADAM STRANGE
CORRECT.
WHAT ARE THE THREE BONES IN THE MIDDLE EAR?
THE MALLEUS, THE INCUS, AND THE STAPES.
CORRECT.
For my daughter, whom I lost in the war
My life is spent with grief.
- AS
WHICH EQUATION--
CALL BATMAN.
CALLING BATMAN.
YES, MICHAEL.
HE WRITES THAT HIS DAUGHTER IS DEAD.
SHE IS NOT.
I DOUBT THIS IS THE ONLY LIE.
WHAT? HOW--
YOU WERE RIGHT. YOU ARE NOT A NEUTRAL OBSERVER IN THIS MATTER, BRUCE.
I THOUGHT IT WAS IMPORTANT THAT YOU KNOW WHY I AM ACCEPTING YOUR OFFER TO INVESTIGATE MR. STRANGE.
HOWEVER, I WILL NOT BE PROVIDING YOU WITH ANY ADDITIONAL INFORMATION UNTIL I PREPARE MY FINAL REPORT TO THE LEAGUE.

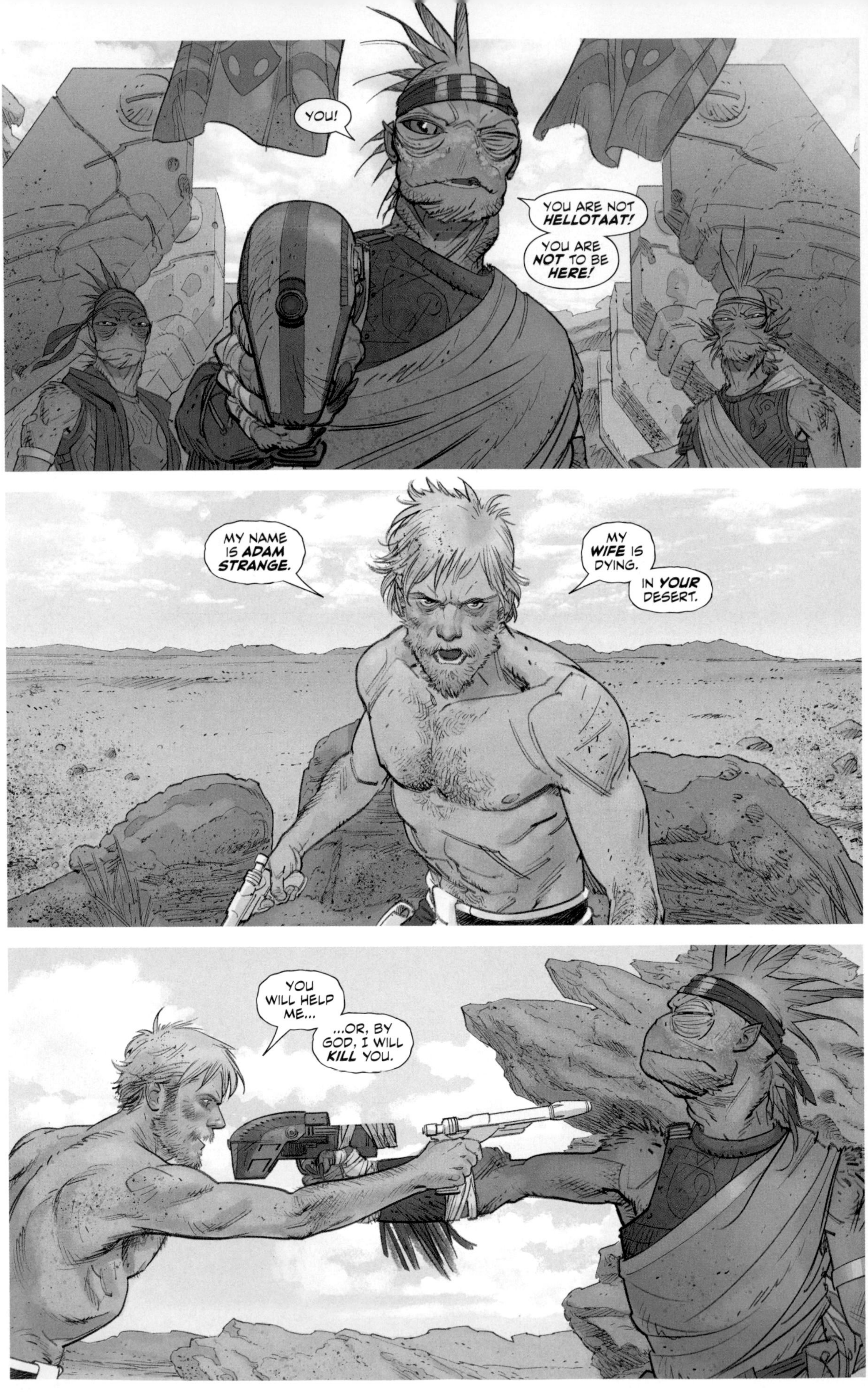
YOU!
YOU ARE NOT HELLOTAAT!
YOU ARE NOT TO BE HERE!
MY NAME IS ADAM STRANGE.
MY WIFE IS DYING.
IN YOUR DESERT.
YOU WILL HELP ME...
...OR, BY GOD, I WILL KILL YOU.

ASK ME SOMETHING I DON'T KNOW.
YOU ARE MR. TERRIFIC.
THE ONLY THING YOU DO NOT KNOW IS THAT WHICH YOU CHOOSE NOT TO KNOW.
ASK ME.
YES.
CALCULATING. CALCULATING. CALCULATING.
WHAT WAS THE SEX OF THE UNBORN CHILD WHO DIED WITH YOUR WIFE?

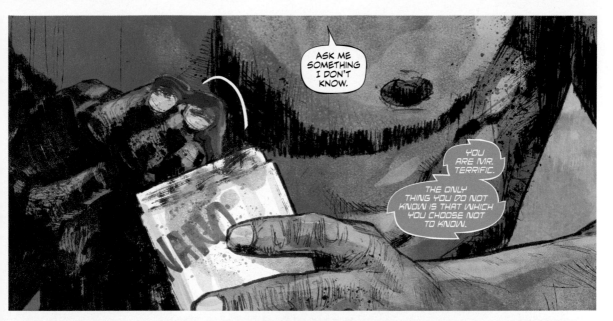

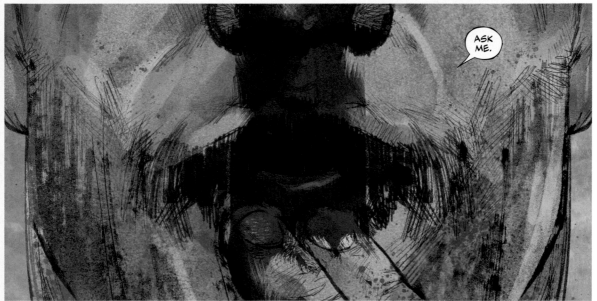

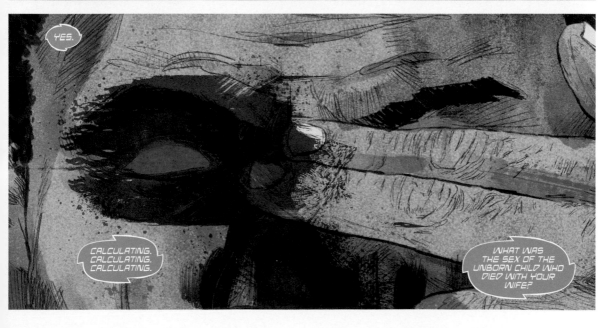

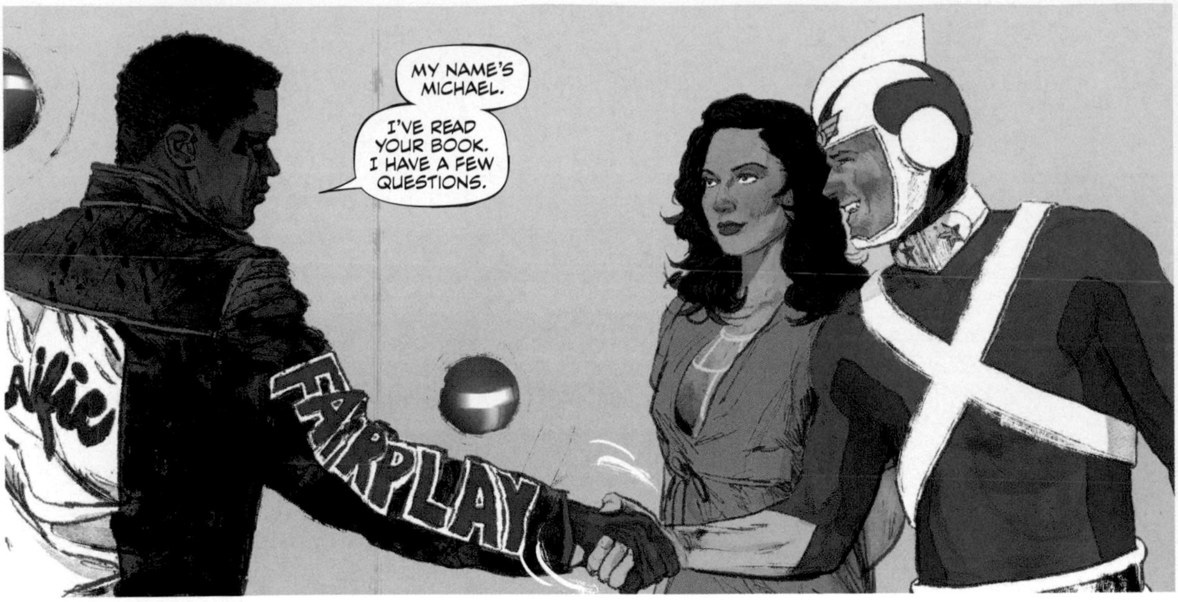
MY NAME'S MICHAEL.
I'VE READ YOUR BOOK. I HAVE A FEW QUESTIONS.
FAIRPLAY

Isn't it a little demanding to insist that an artist remain like that for 30 years?

Being true to your own principles? No.

—Alex Toth, *The Comics Journal* No. 98

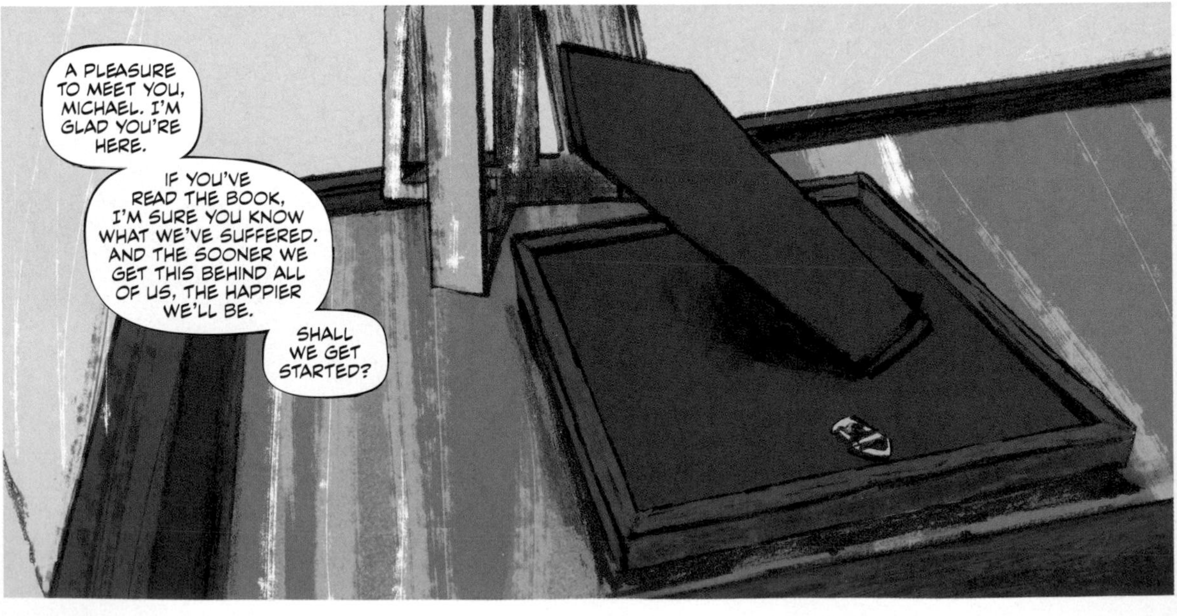
A PLEASURE TO MEET YOU, MICHAEL. I'M GLAD YOU'RE HERE.
IF YOU'VE READ THE BOOK, I'M SURE YOU KNOW WHAT WE'VE SUFFERED. AND THE SOONER WE GET THIS BEHIND ALL OF US, THE HAPPIER WE'LL BE.
SHALL WE GET STARTED?

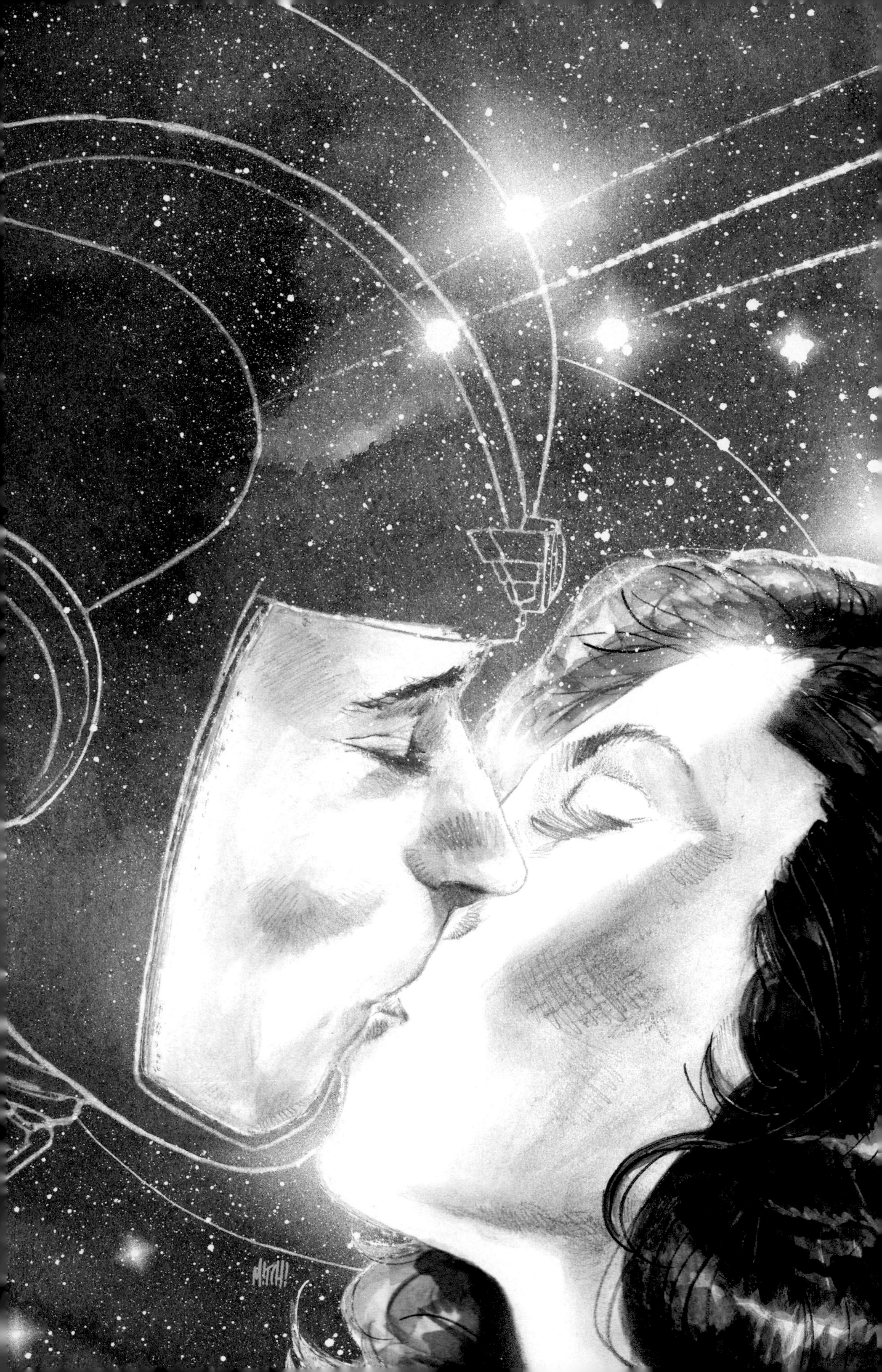

"ISN'T LIFE STRANGE?"

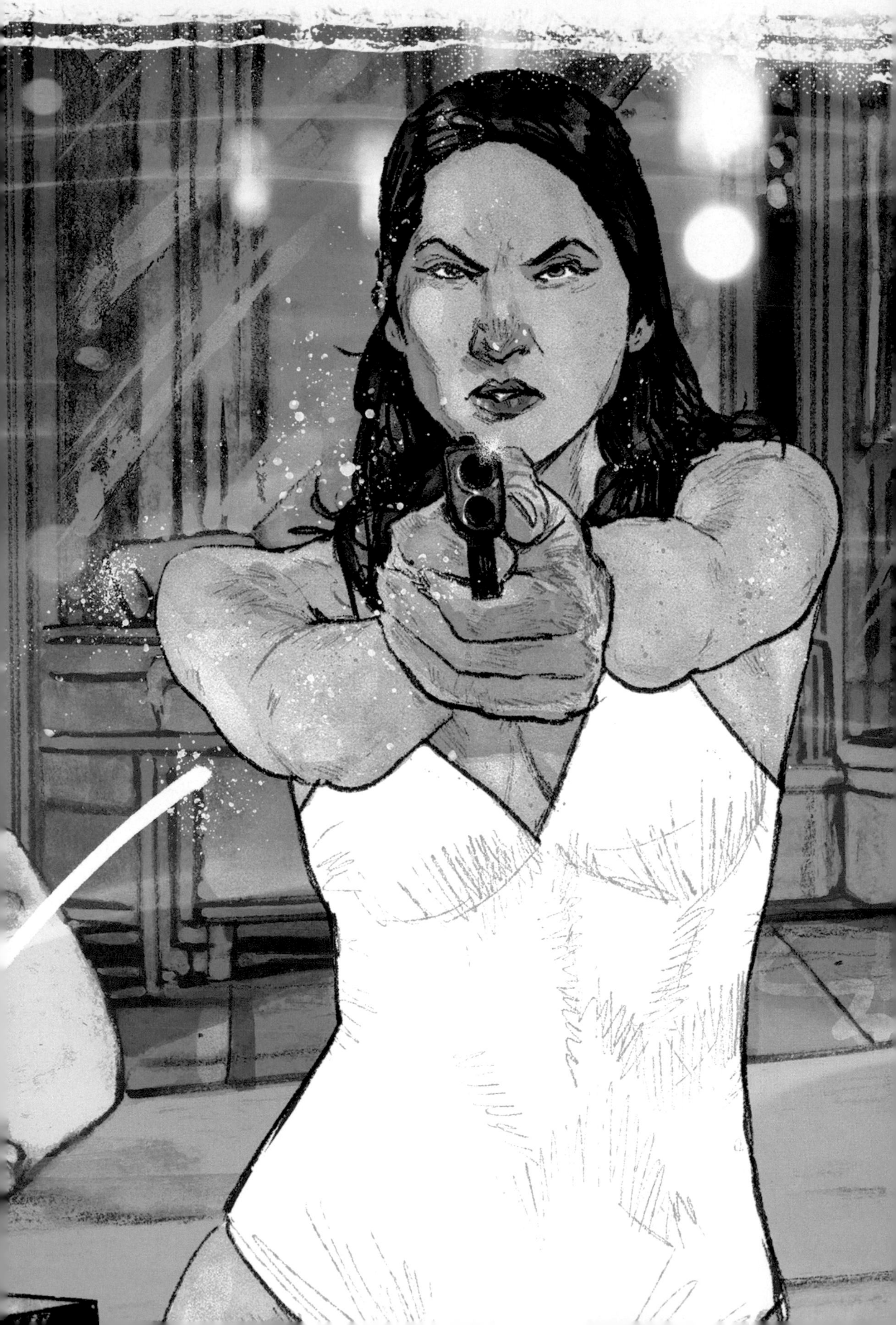

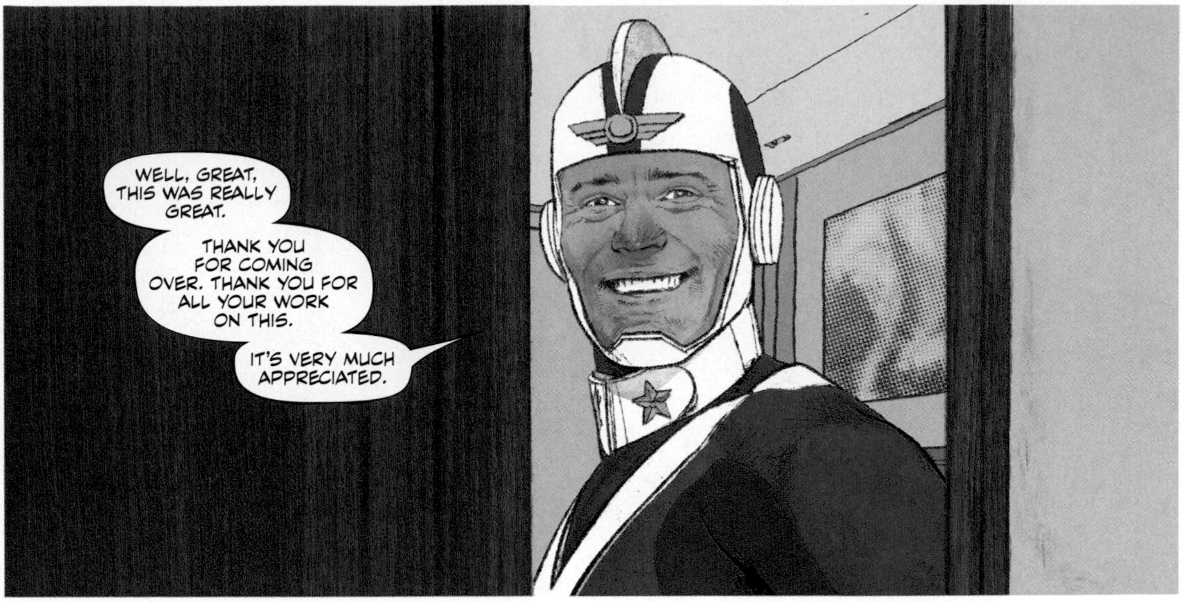
WELL, GREAT, THIS WAS REALLY GREAT.
THANK YOU FOR COMING OVER. THANK YOU FOR ALL YOUR WORK ON THIS.
IT'S VERY MUCH APPRECIATED.

Chapter 3

Good guys and bad guys

TOM KING ...Writer

MITCH GERADS
EVAN "DOC" SHANER ...Interior & Cover Artists

CLAYTON COWLES ...Letterer
BIXIE MATHIEU ...Assistant Editor
BRITTANY HOLZHERR ...Associate Editor
JAMIE S. RICH ...Editor

Superman created by Jerry Siegel and Joe Shuster.
By special arrangement with the Jerry Siegel family.

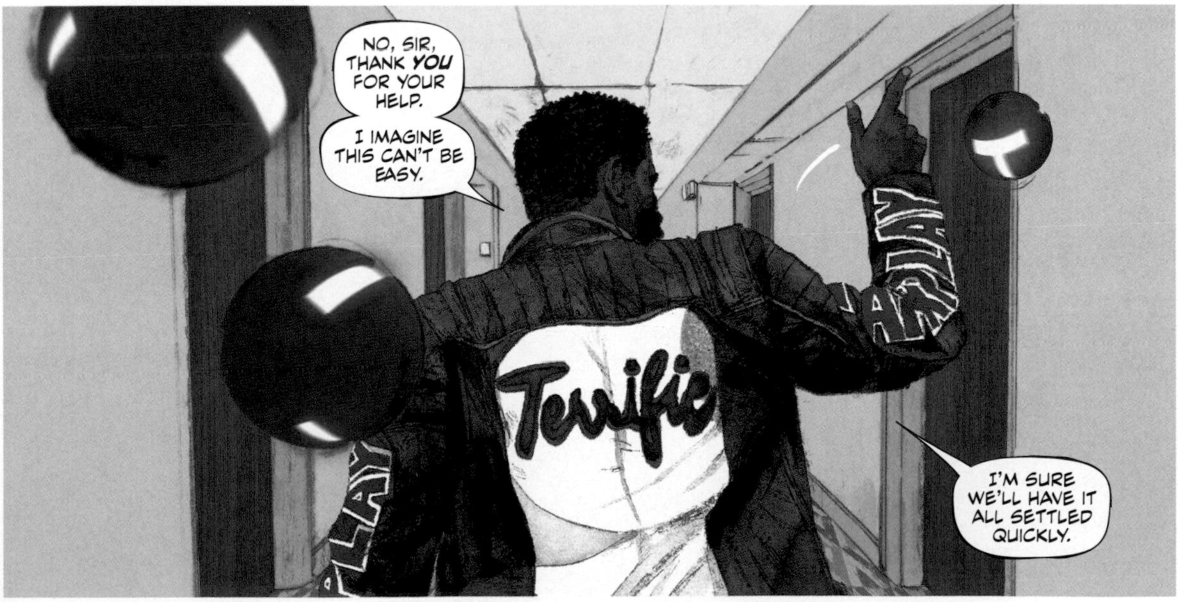
NO, SIR, THANK *YOU* FOR YOUR HELP.
I IMAGINE THIS CAN'T BE EASY.
Terrific
I'M SURE WE'LL HAVE IT ALL SETTLED QUICKLY.

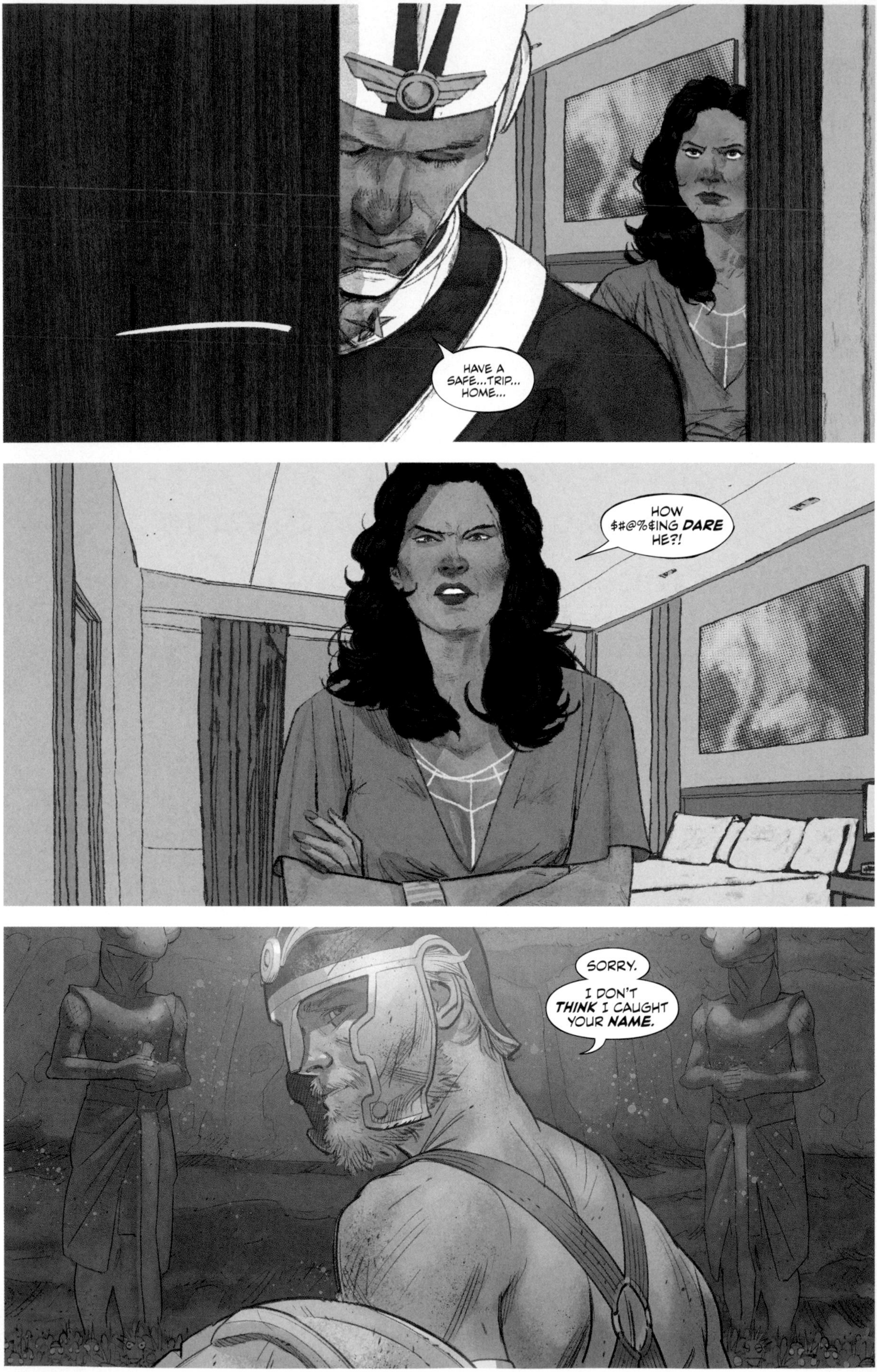
HAVE A SAFE...TRIP... HOME...
HOW $#@%$ING **DARE** HE?!
SORRY.
I DON'T **THINK** I CAUGHT YOUR **NAME.**

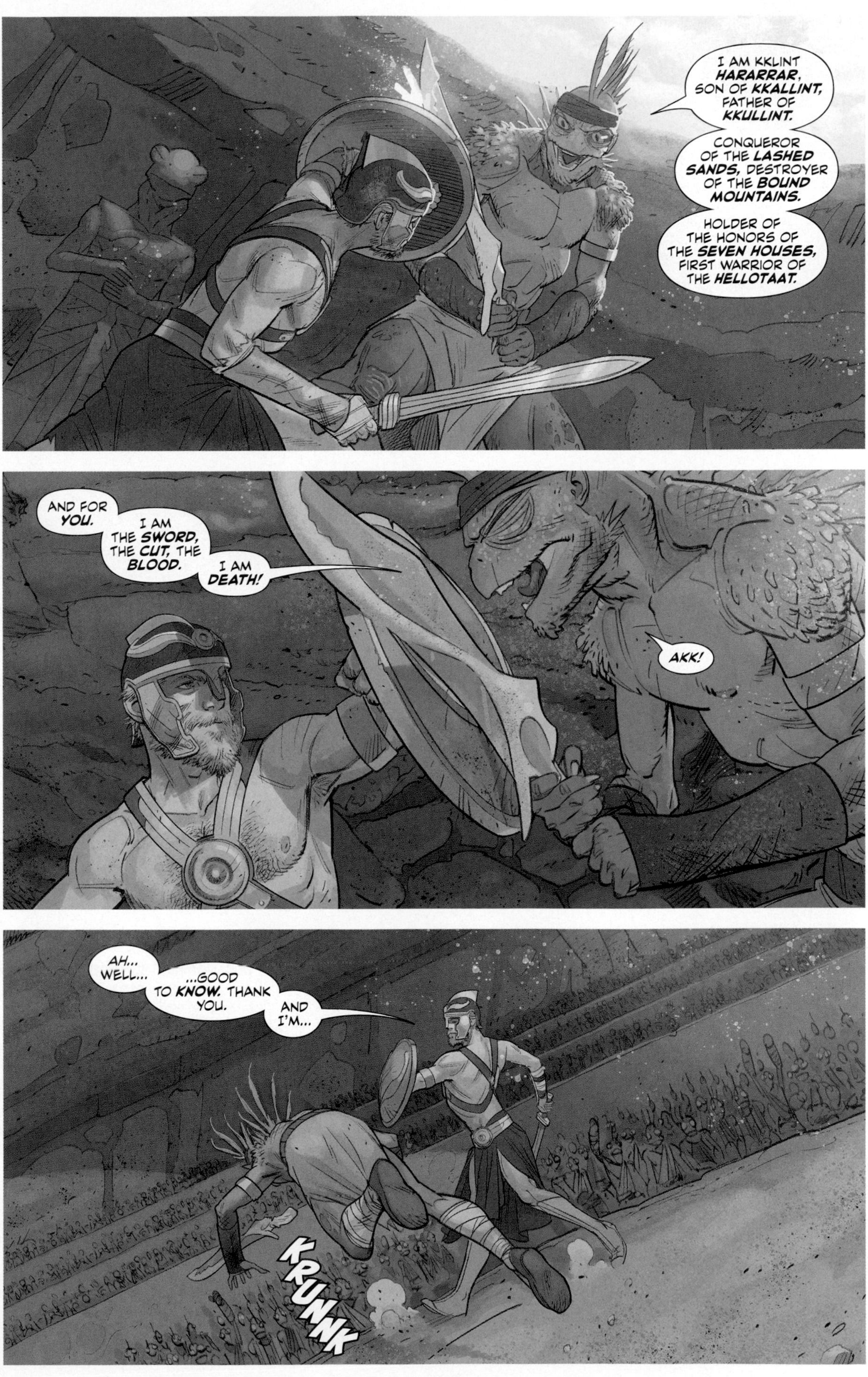
I AM KKLINT HARARRAR, SON OF KKALLINT, FATHER OF KKULLINT.
CONQUEROR OF THE LASHED SANDS, DESTROYER OF THE BOUND MOUNTAINS.
HOLDER OF THE HONORS OF THE SEVEN HOUSES, FIRST WARRIOR OF THE HELLOTAAT.
AND FOR YOU.
I AM THE SWORD, THE CUT, THE BLOOD.
I AM DEATH!
AKK!
AH... WELL...
...GOOD TO KNOW. THANK YOU.
AND I'M...
KRUNNK

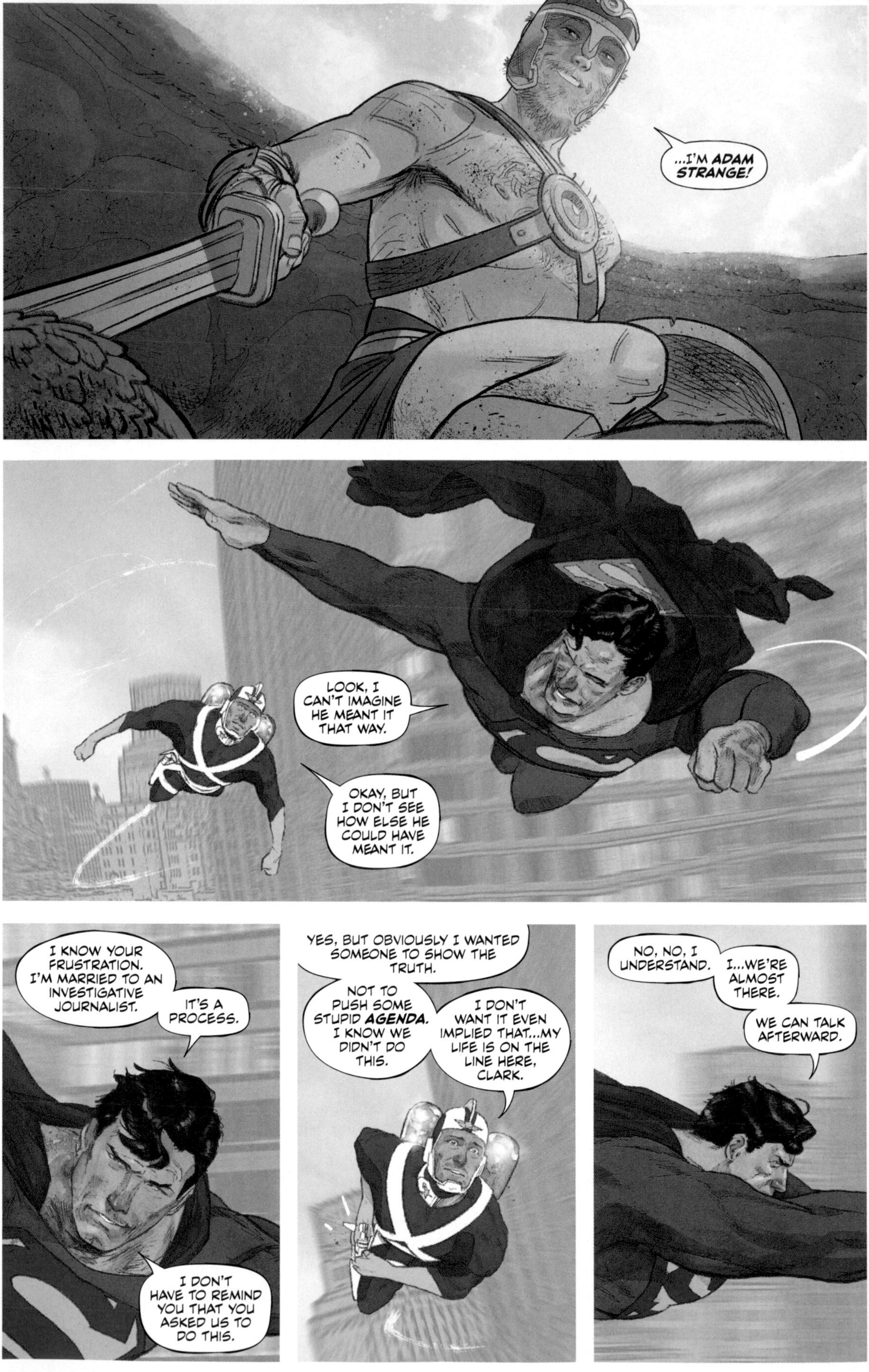

...I'M ADAM STRANGE!
LOOK, I CAN'T IMAGINE HE MEANT IT THAT WAY.
OKAY, BUT I DON'T SEE HOW ELSE HE COULD HAVE MEANT IT.
I KNOW YOUR FRUSTRATION. I'M MARRIED TO AN INVESTIGATIVE JOURNALIST.
IT'S A PROCESS.
I DON'T HAVE TO REMIND YOU THAT YOU ASKED US TO DO THIS.
YES, BUT OBVIOUSLY I WANTED SOMEONE TO SHOW THE TRUTH.
NOT TO PUSH SOME STUPID AGENDA. I KNOW WE DIDN'T DO THIS.
I DON'T WANT IT EVEN IMPLIED THAT...MY LIFE IS ON THE LINE HERE, CLARK.
NO, NO, I UNDERSTAND.
I...WE'RE ALMOST THERE.
WE CAN TALK AFTERWARD.

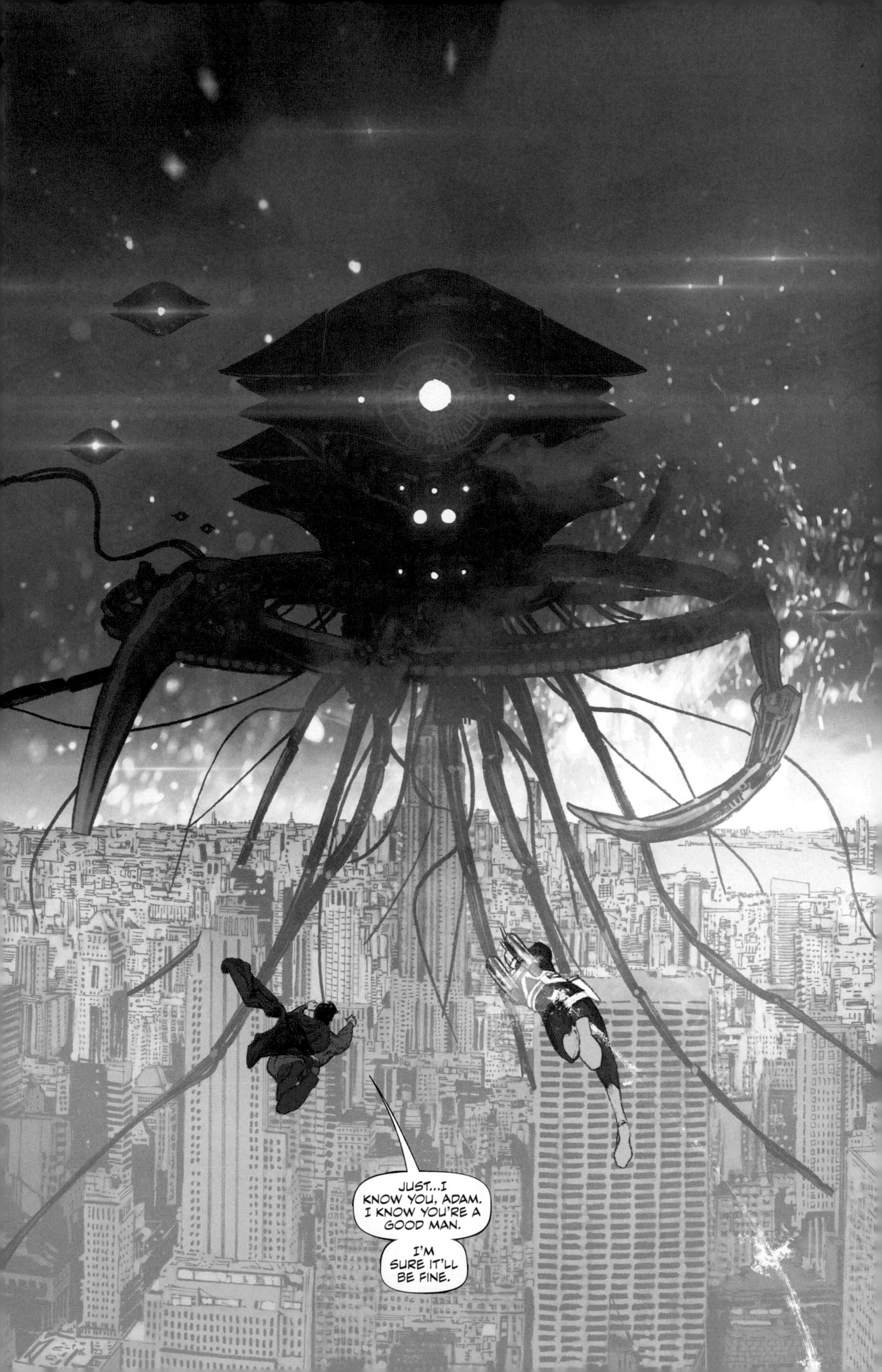
JUST...I KNOW YOU, ADAM. I KNOW YOU'RE A GOOD MAN.
I'M SURE IT'LL BE FINE.

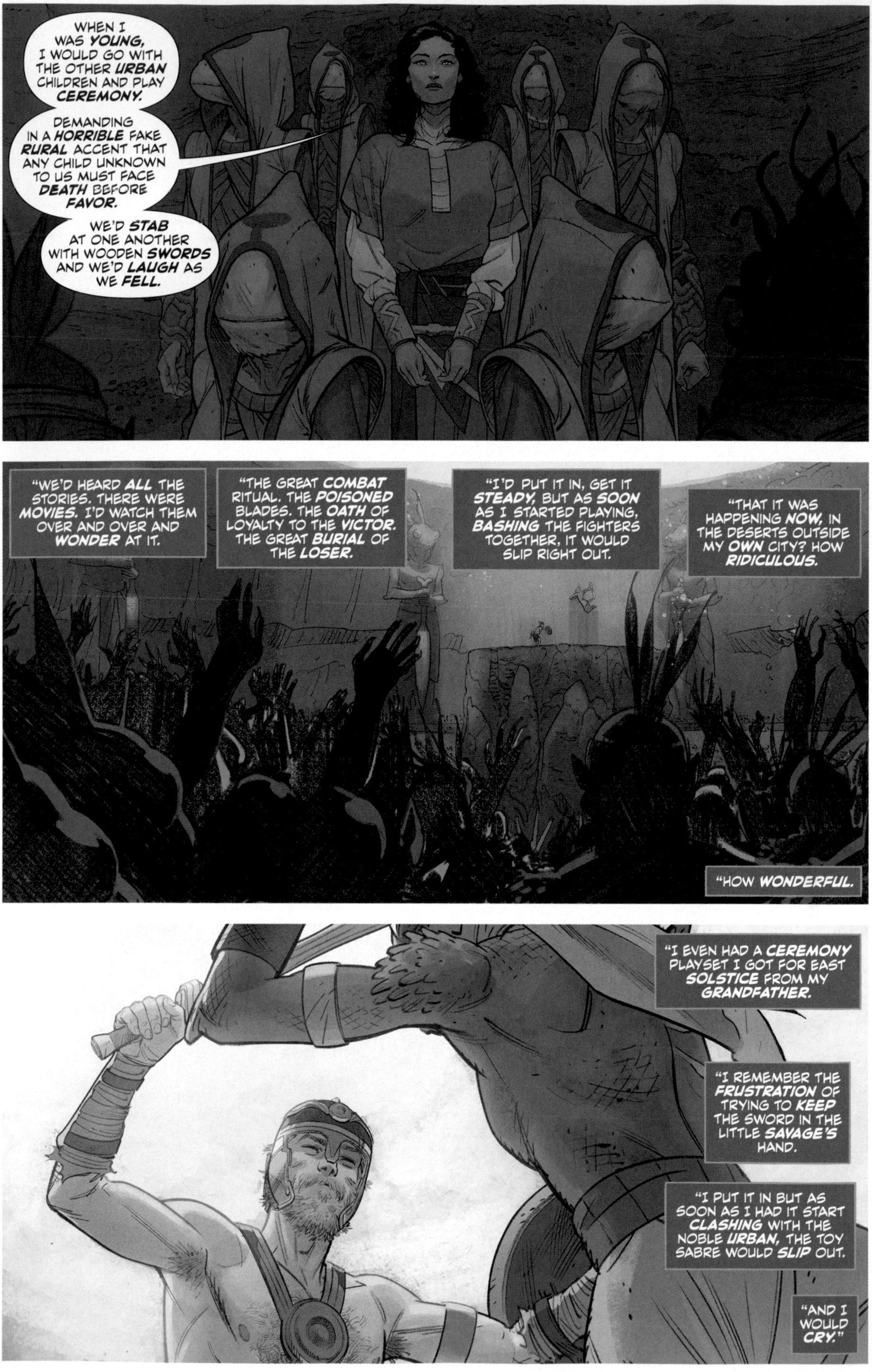
WHEN I WAS YOUNG, I WOULD GO WITH THE OTHER URBAN CHILDREN AND PLAY CEREMONY.
DEMANDING IN A HORRIBLE FAKE RURAL ACCENT THAT ANY CHILD UNKNOWN TO US MUST FACE DEATH BEFORE FAVOR.
WE'D STAB AT ONE ANOTHER WITH WOODEN SWORDS AND WE'D LAUGH AS WE FELL.
"WE'D HEARD ALL THE STORIES. THERE WERE MOVIES. I'D WATCH THEM OVER AND OVER AND WONDER AT IT.
"THE GREAT COMBAT RITUAL. THE POISONED BLADES. THE OATH OF LOYALTY TO THE VICTOR. THE GREAT BURIAL OF THE LOSER.
"THAT IT WAS HAPPENING NOW, IN THE DESERTS OUTSIDE MY OWN CITY? HOW RIDICULOUS.
"HOW WONDERFUL.
"I EVEN HAD A CEREMONY PLAYSET I GOT FOR EAST SOLSTICE FROM MY GRANDFATHER.
"I REMEMBER THE FRUSTRATION OF TRYING TO KEEP THE SWORD IN THE LITTLE SAVAGE'S HAND.
"I'D PUT IT IN, GET IT STEADY, BUT AS SOON AS I STARTED PLAYING, BASHING THE FIGHTERS TOGETHER, IT WOULD SLIP RIGHT OUT.
"I PUT IT IN BUT AS SOON AS I HAD IT START CLASHING WITH THE NOBLE URBAN, THE TOY SABRE WOULD SLIP OUT.
"AND I WOULD CRY."

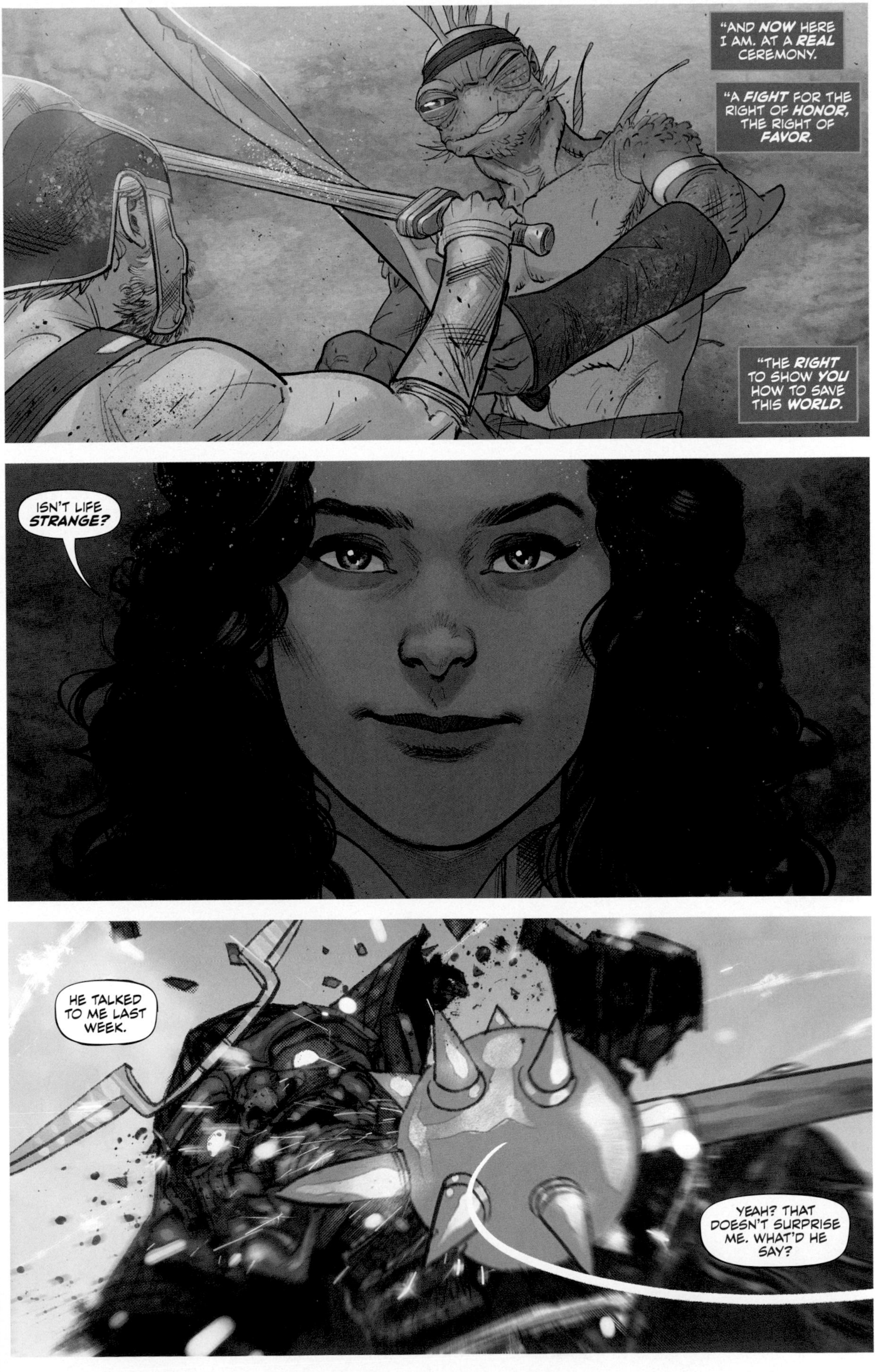
"AND NOW HERE I AM. AT A REAL CEREMONY.
"A FIGHT FOR THE RIGHT OF HONOR, THE RIGHT OF FAVOR.
"THE RIGHT TO SHOW YOU HOW TO SAVE THIS WORLD.
ISN'T LIFE STRANGE?
HE TALKED TO ME LAST WEEK.
YEAH? THAT DOESN'T SURPRISE ME. WHAT'D HE SAY?

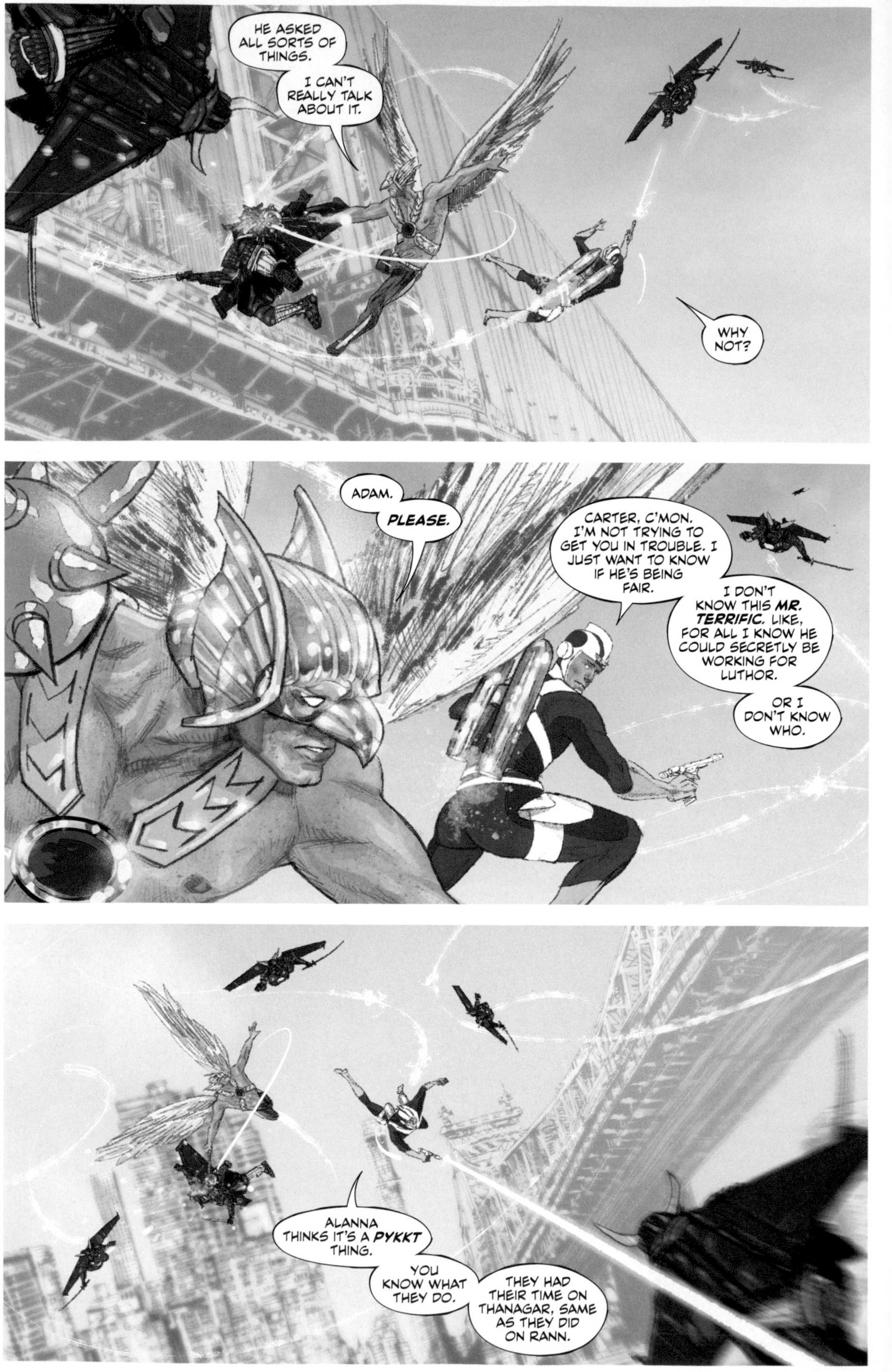
HE ASKED ALL SORTS OF THINGS.
I CAN'T REALLY TALK ABOUT IT.
WHY NOT?
ADAM.
PLEASE.
CARTER, C'MON. I'M NOT TRYING TO GET YOU IN TROUBLE. I JUST WANT TO KNOW IF HE'S BEING FAIR.
I DON'T KNOW THIS **MR. TERRIFIC.** LIKE, FOR ALL I KNOW HE COULD SECRETLY BE WORKING FOR LUTHOR.
OR I DON'T KNOW WHO.
ALANNA THINKS IT'S A **PYKKT** THING.
YOU KNOW WHAT THEY DO.
THEY HAD THEIR TIME ON THANAGAR, SAME AS THEY DID ON RANN.

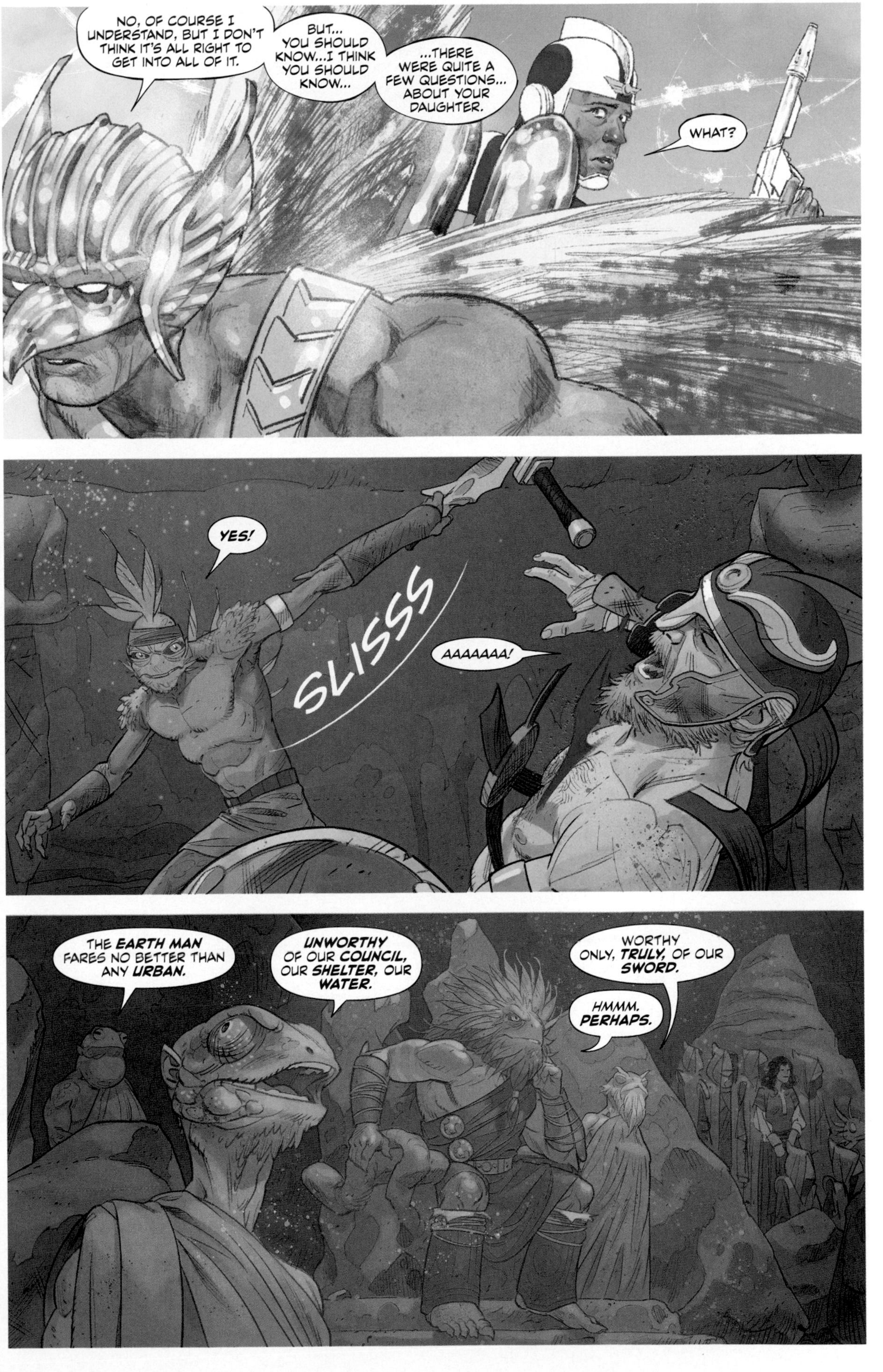
NO, OF COURSE I UNDERSTAND, BUT I DON'T THINK IT'S ALL RIGHT TO GET INTO ALL OF IT.
BUT... YOU SHOULD KNOW...I THINK YOU SHOULD KNOW...
...THERE WERE QUITE A FEW QUESTIONS... ABOUT YOUR DAUGHTER.
WHAT?
YES!
SLISSS
AAAAAAA!
THE EARTH MAN FARES NO BETTER THAN ANY URBAN.
UNWORTHY OF OUR COUNCIL, OUR SHELTER, OUR WATER.
WORTHY ONLY, TRULY, OF OUR SWORD.
HMMM. PERHAPS.

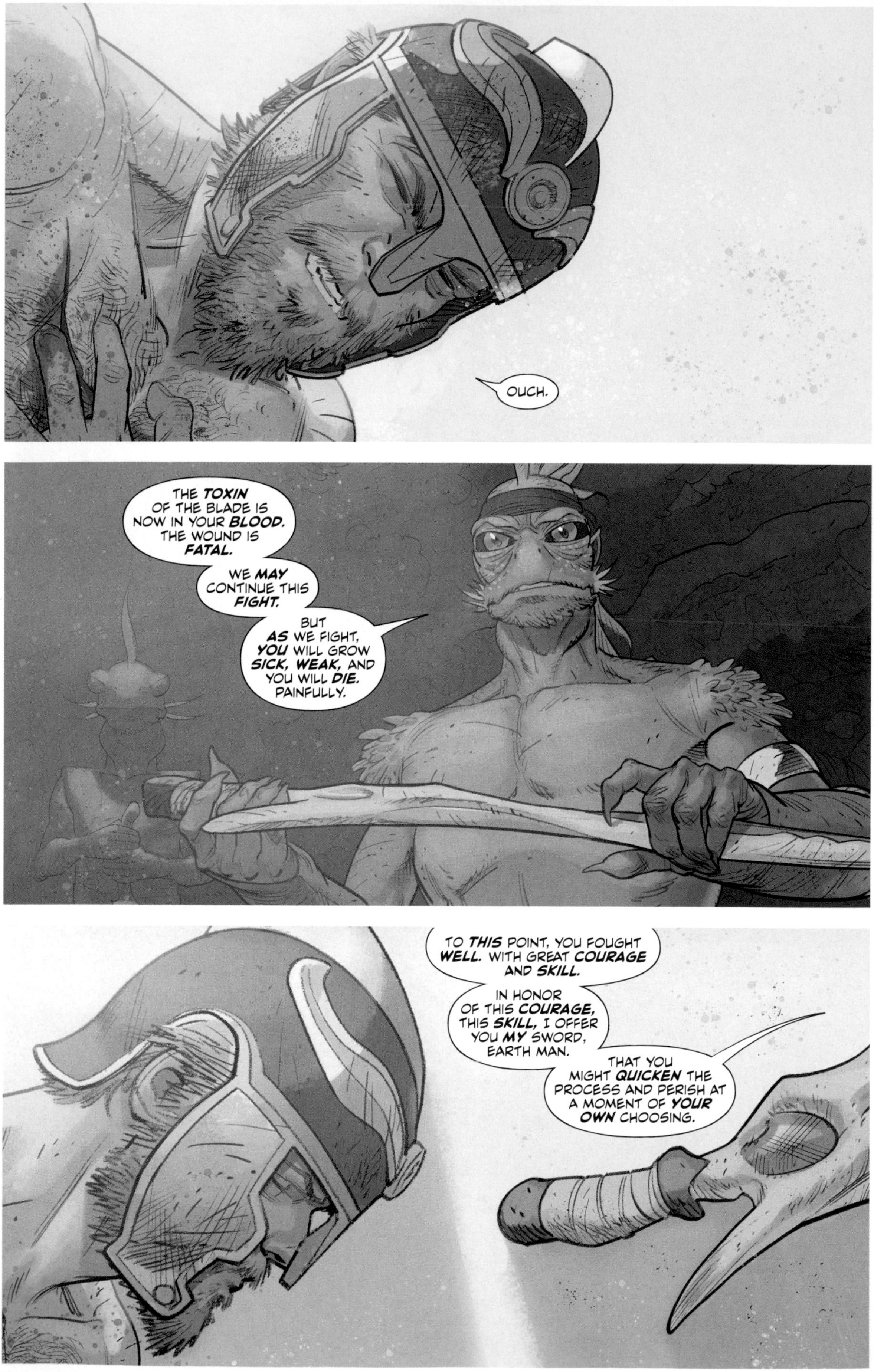
OUCH.
THE TOXIN OF THE BLADE IS NOW IN YOUR BLOOD. THE WOUND IS FATAL.
WE MAY CONTINUE THIS FIGHT.
BUT AS WE FIGHT, YOU WILL GROW SICK, WEAK, AND YOU WILL DIE. PAINFULLY.
TO THIS POINT, YOU FOUGHT WELL. WITH GREAT COURAGE AND SKILL.
IN HONOR OF THIS COURAGE, THIS SKILL, I OFFER YOU MY SWORD, EARTH MAN.
THAT YOU MIGHT QUICKEN THE PROCESS AND PERISH AT A MOMENT OF YOUR OWN CHOOSING.

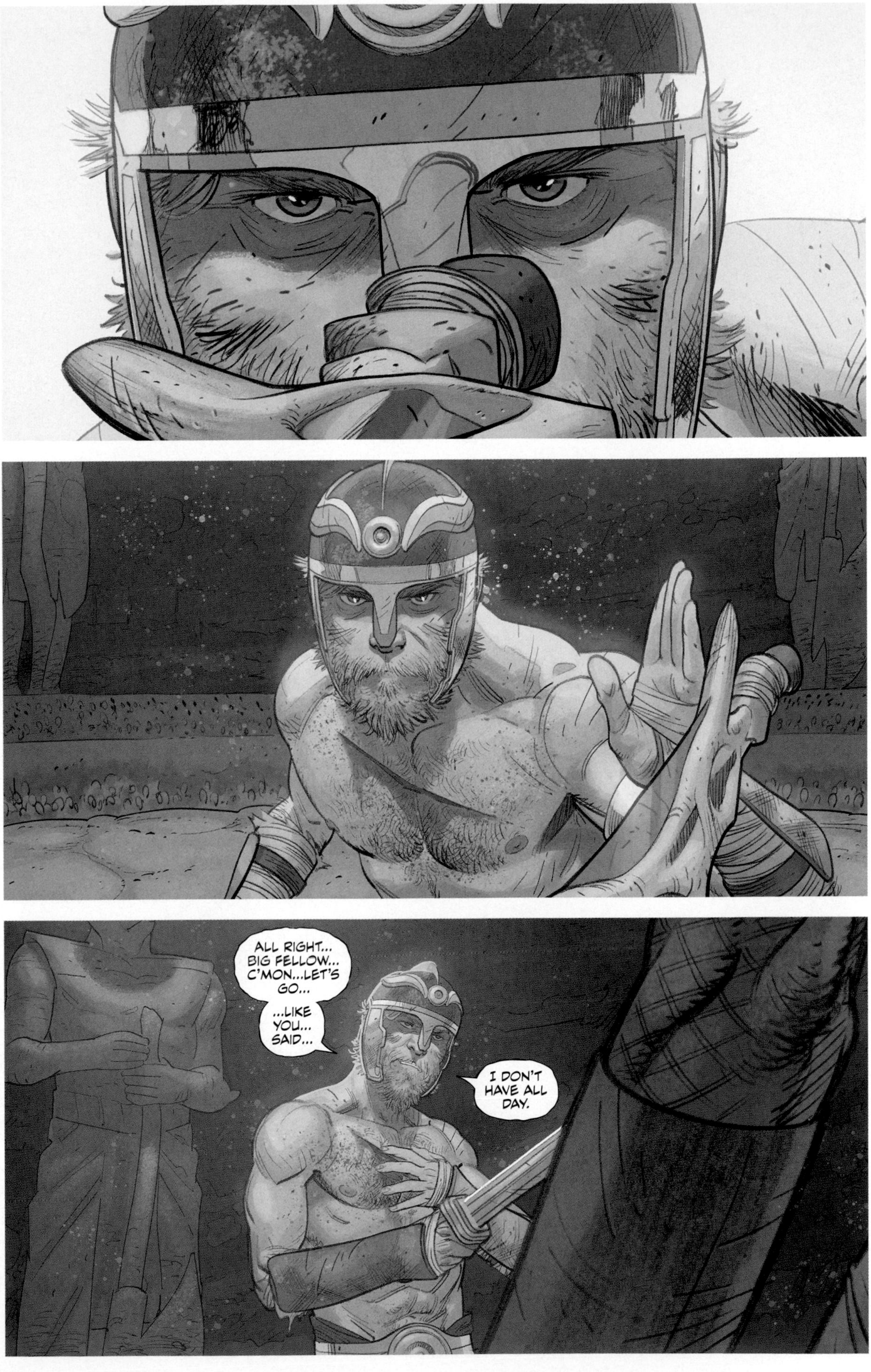
ALL RIGHT... BIG FELLOW... C'MON...LET'S GO...
...LIKE YOU... SAID...
I DON'T HAVE ALL DAY.

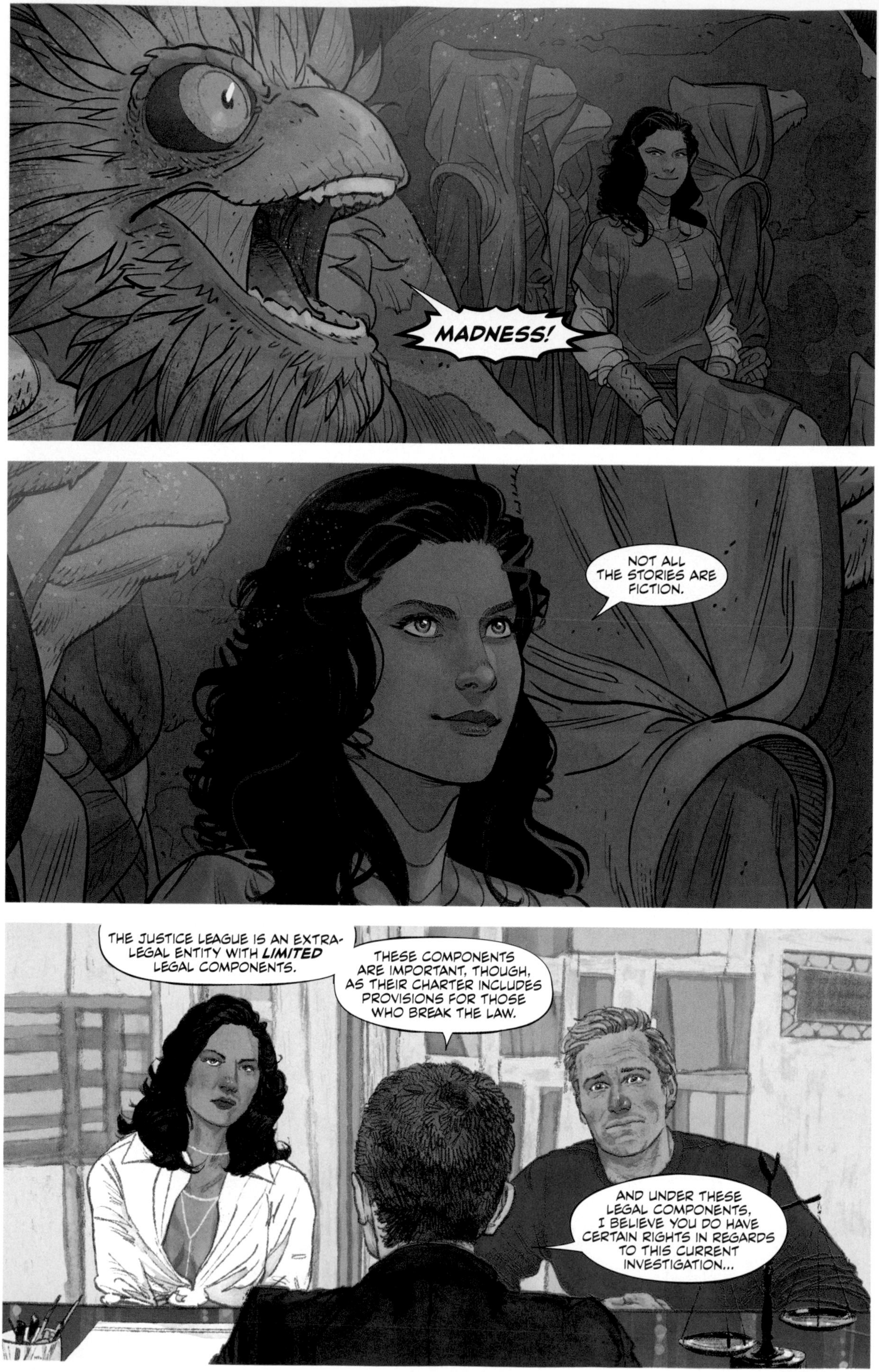
MADNESS!
NOT ALL THE STORIES ARE FICTION.
THE JUSTICE LEAGUE IS AN EXTRA-LEGAL ENTITY WITH LIMITED LEGAL COMPONENTS.
THESE COMPONENTS ARE IMPORTANT, THOUGH, AS THEIR CHARTER INCLUDES PROVISIONS FOR THOSE WHO BREAK THE LAW.
AND UNDER THESE LEGAL COMPONENTS, I BELIEVE YOU DO HAVE CERTAIN RIGHTS IN REGARDS TO THIS CURRENT INVESTIGATION...

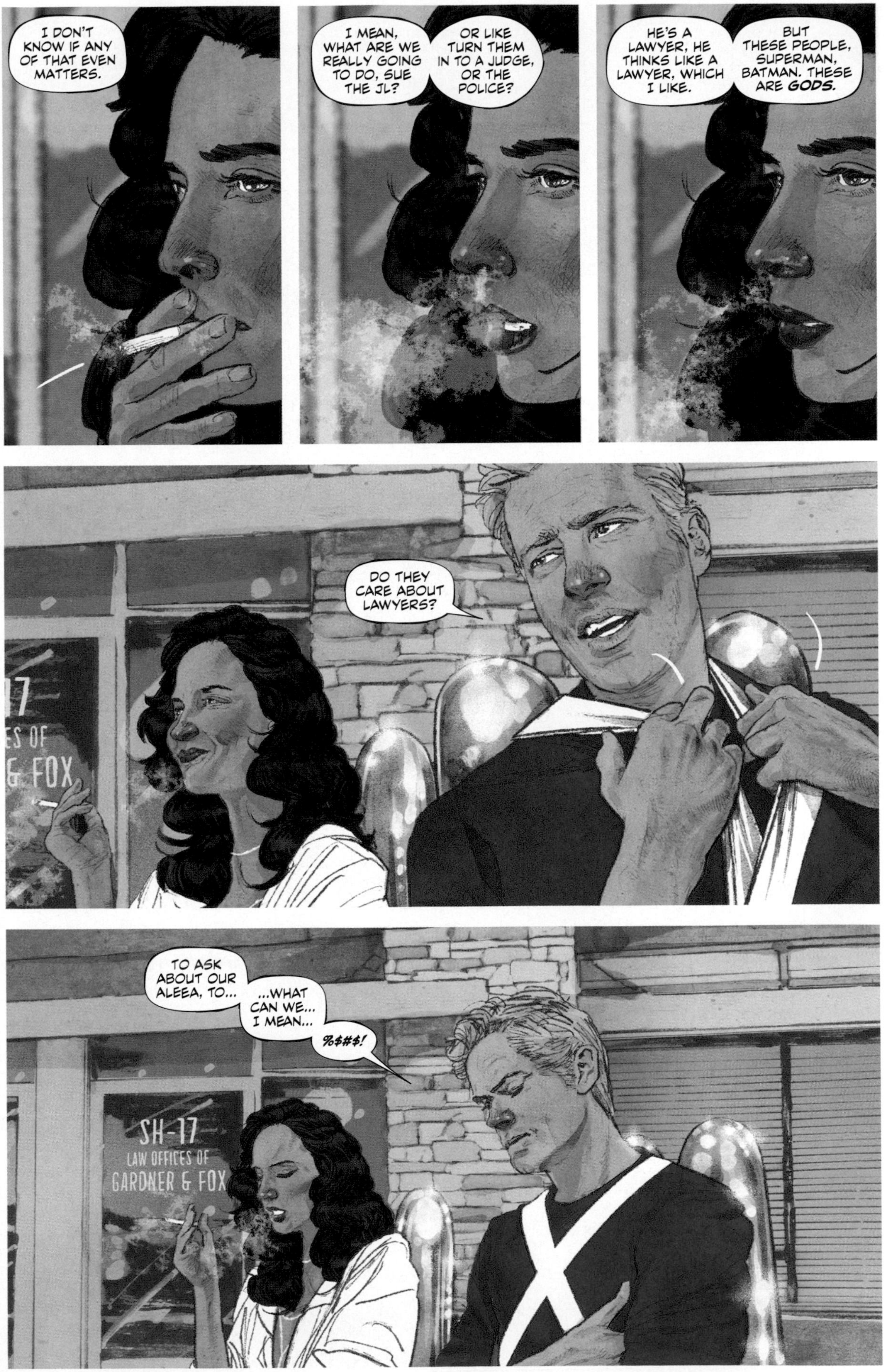
I DON'T KNOW IF ANY OF THAT EVEN MATTERS.
I MEAN, WHAT ARE WE REALLY GOING TO DO, SUE THE JL?
OR LIKE TURN THEM IN TO A JUDGE, OR THE POLICE?
HE'S A LAWYER, HE THINKS LIKE A LAWYER, WHICH I LIKE.
BUT THESE PEOPLE, SUPERMAN, BATMAN. THESE ARE ***GODS.***
DO THEY CARE ABOUT LAWYERS?
TO ASK ABOUT OUR ALEEA, TO...
...WHAT CAN WE... I MEAN...
%$#$!
SH-17
LAW OFFICES OF
GARDNER & FOX

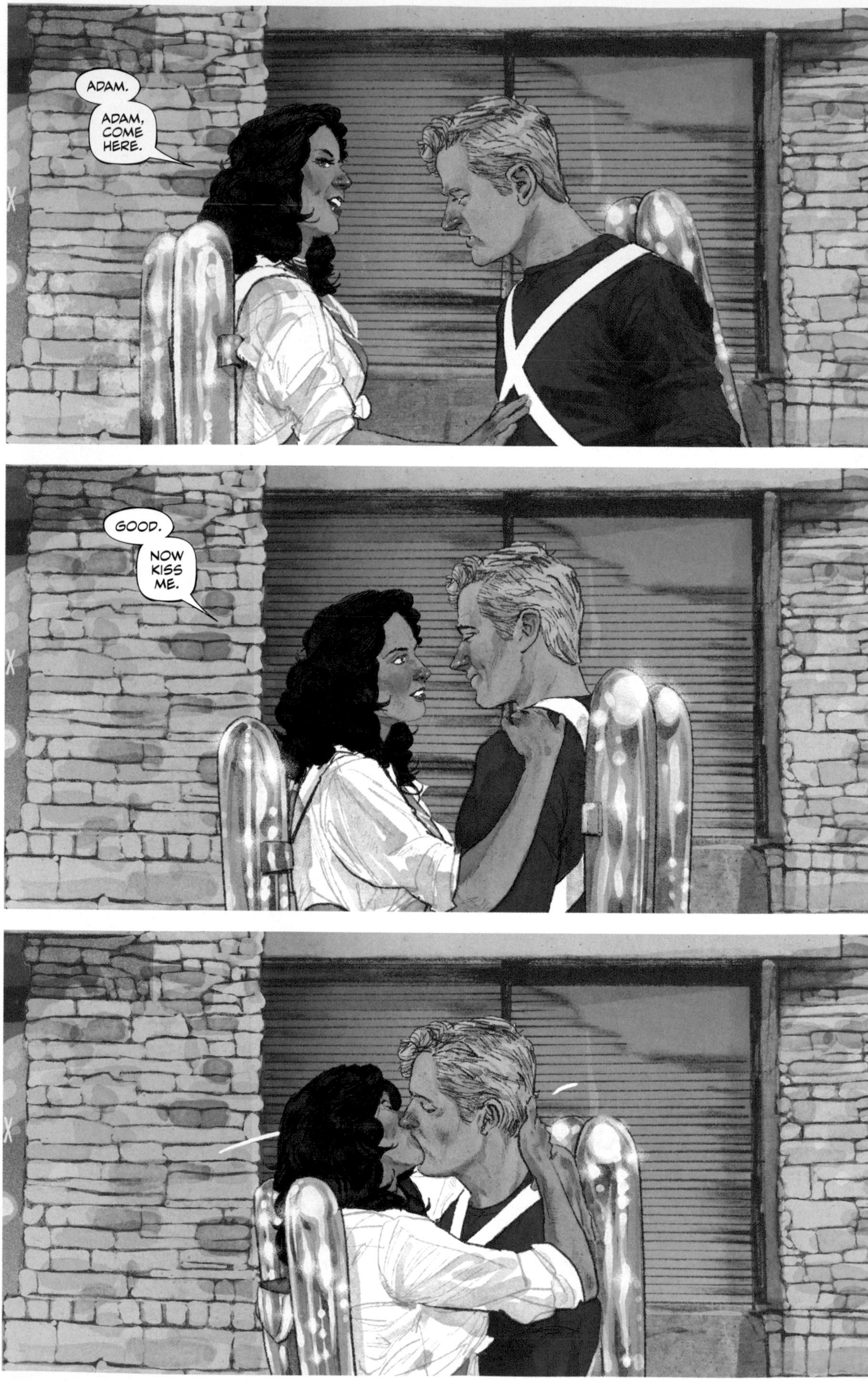
ADAM.
ADAM, COME HERE.
GOOD.
NOW KISS ME.

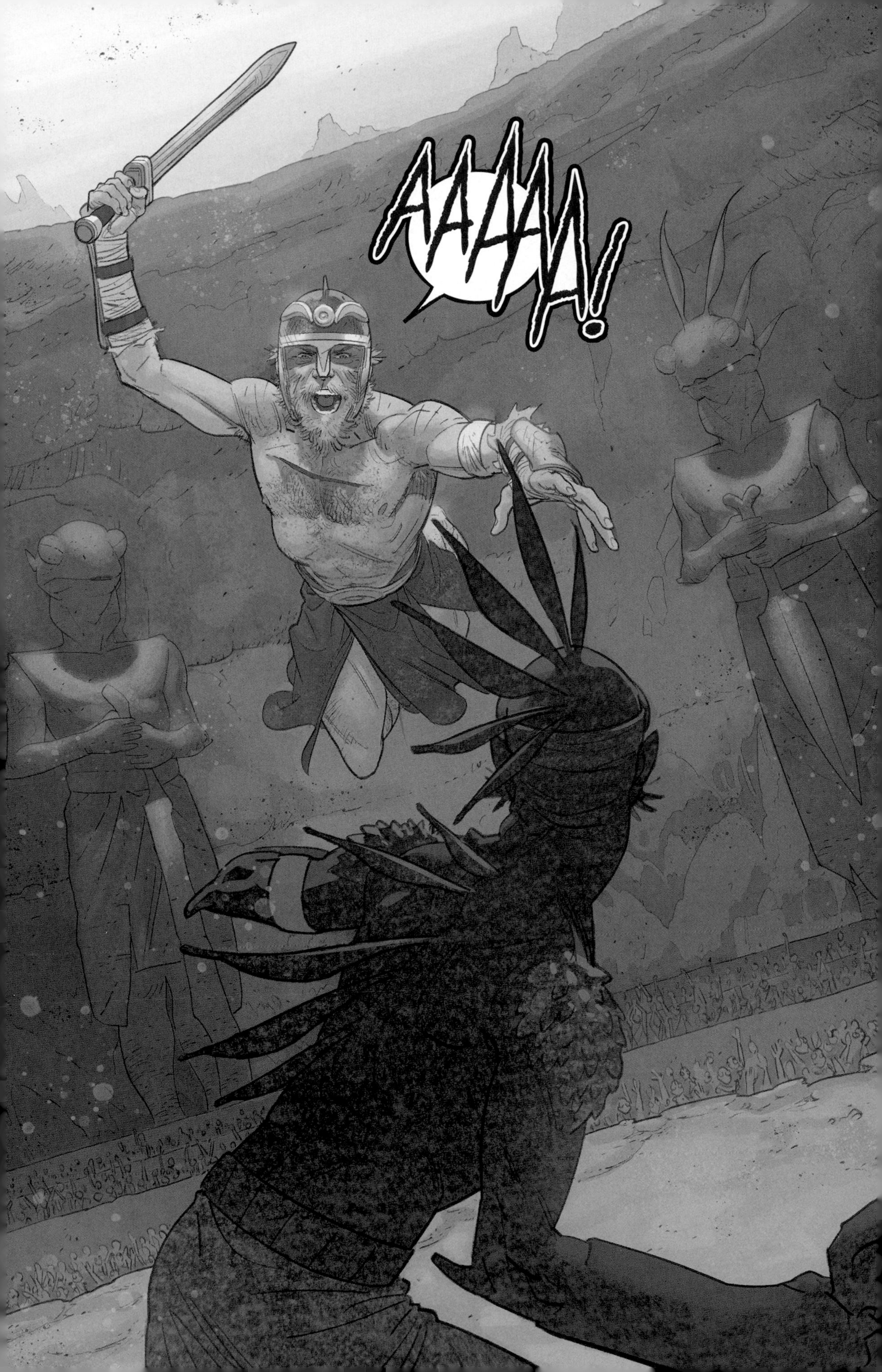
AAAAA!

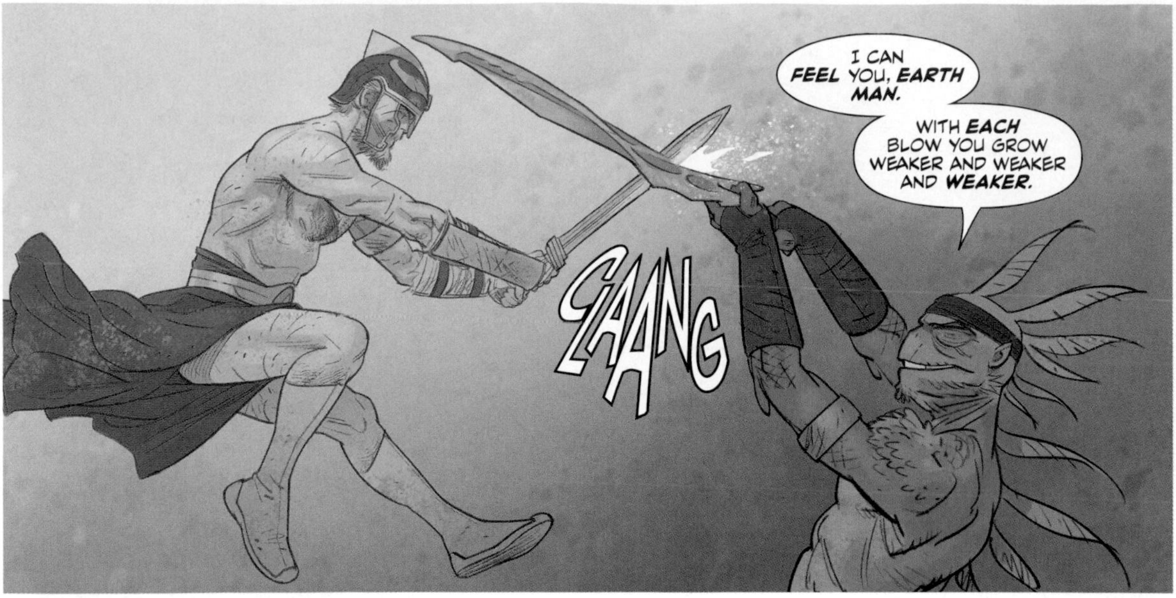
I CAN FEEL YOU, EARTH MAN.
WITH EACH BLOW YOU GROW WEAKER AND WEAKER AND WEAKER.
CLAANG

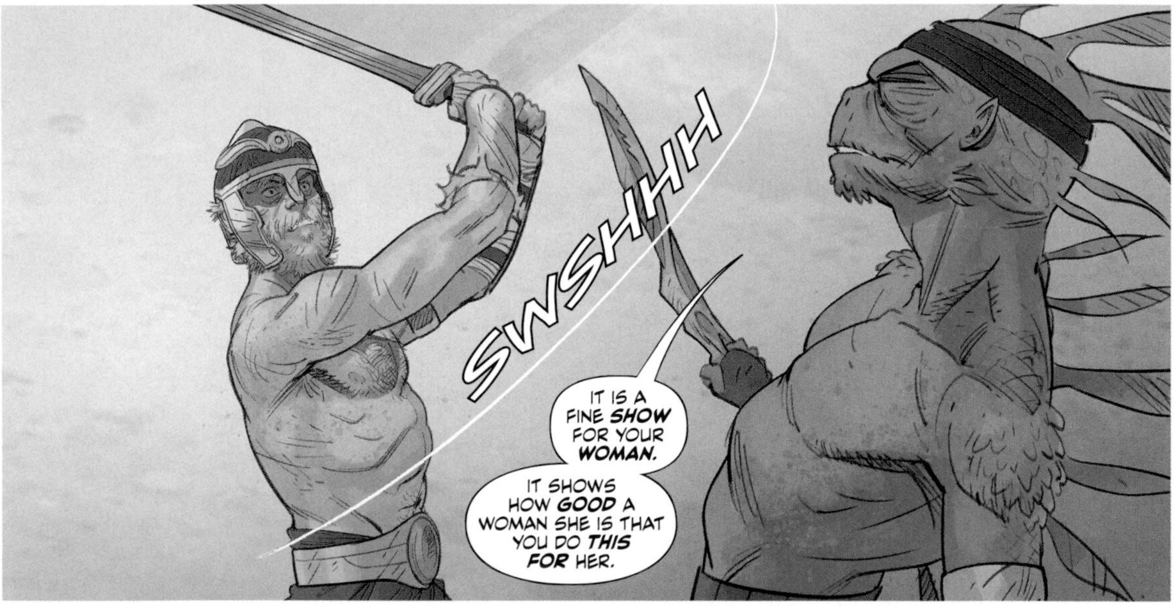
SWSHHH
IT IS A FINE SHOW FOR YOUR WOMAN.
IT SHOWS HOW GOOD A WOMAN SHE IS THAT YOU DO THIS FOR HER.

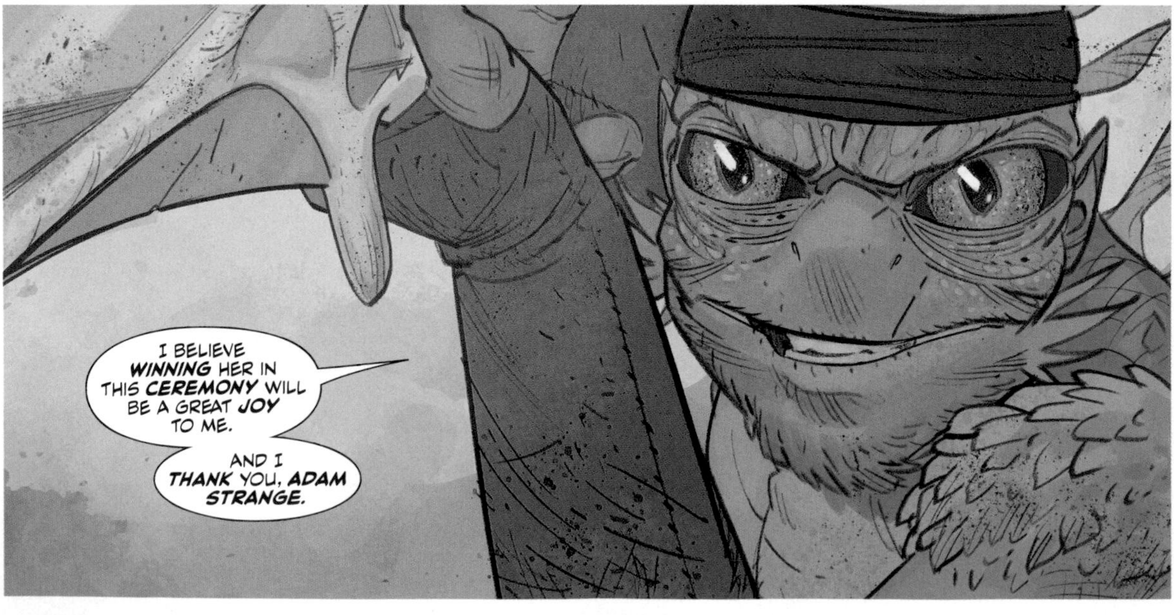
I BELIEVE WINNING HER IN THIS CEREMONY WILL BE A GREAT JOY TO ME.
AND I THANK YOU, ADAM STRANGE.

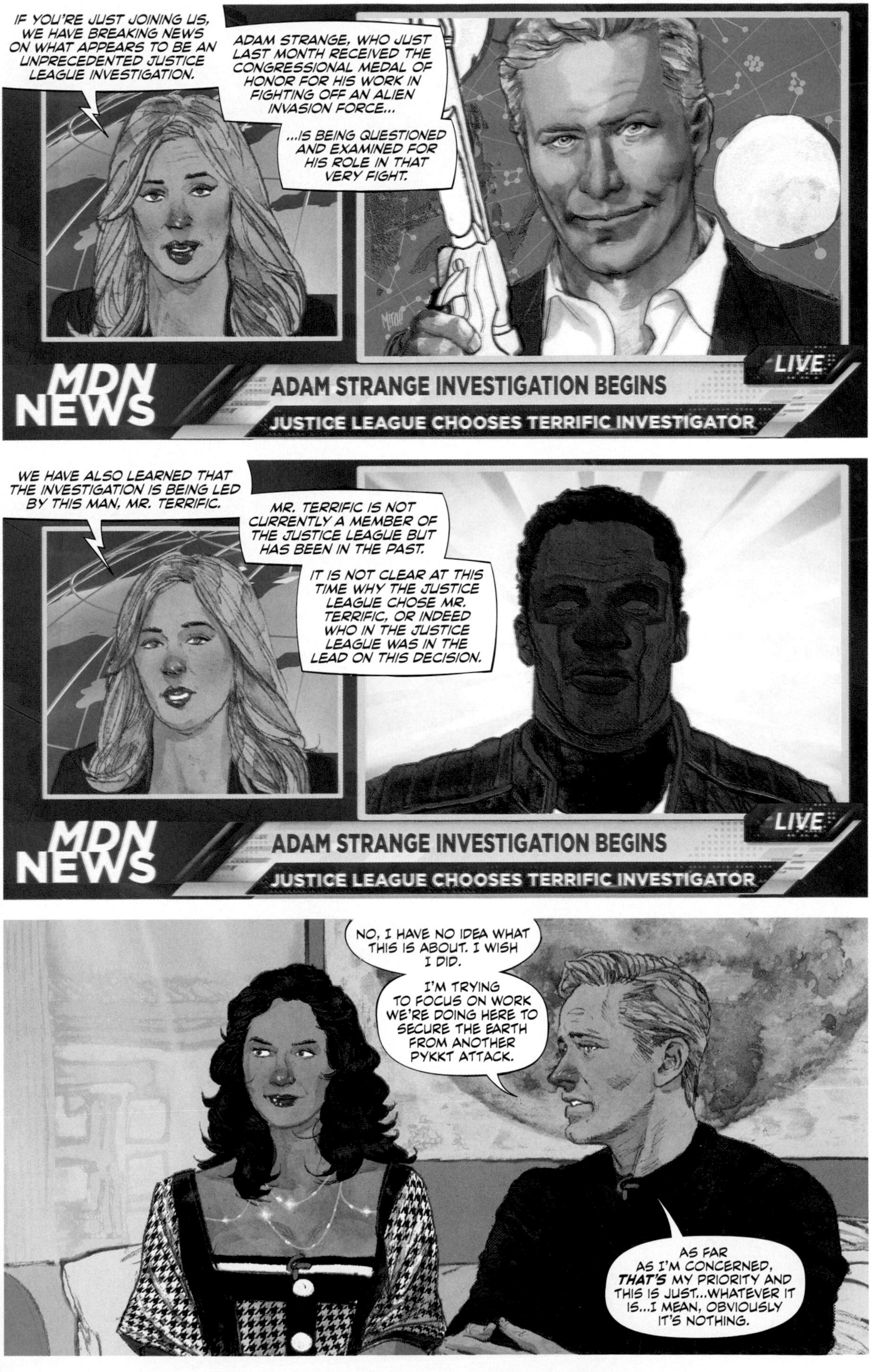
IF YOU'RE JUST JOINING US, WE HAVE BREAKING NEWS ON WHAT APPEARS TO BE AN UNPRECEDENTED JUSTICE LEAGUE INVESTIGATION.
ADAM STRANGE, WHO JUST LAST MONTH RECEIVED THE CONGRESSIONAL MEDAL OF HONOR FOR HIS WORK IN FIGHTING OFF AN ALIEN INVASION FORCE...
...IS BEING QUESTIONED AND EXAMINED FOR HIS ROLE IN THAT VERY FIGHT.
LIVE
MDN NEWS
ADAM STRANGE INVESTIGATION BEGINS
JUSTICE LEAGUE CHOOSES TERRIFIC INVESTIGATOR
WE HAVE ALSO LEARNED THAT THE INVESTIGATION IS BEING LED BY THIS MAN, MR. TERRIFIC.
MR. TERRIFIC IS NOT CURRENTLY A MEMBER OF THE JUSTICE LEAGUE BUT HAS BEEN IN THE PAST.
IT IS NOT CLEAR AT THIS TIME WHY THE JUSTICE LEAGUE CHOSE MR. TERRIFIC, OR INDEED WHO IN THE JUSTICE LEAGUE WAS IN THE LEAD ON THIS DECISION.
LIVE
MDN NEWS
ADAM STRANGE INVESTIGATION BEGINS
JUSTICE LEAGUE CHOOSES TERRIFIC INVESTIGATOR
NO, I HAVE NO IDEA WHAT THIS IS ABOUT. I WISH I DID.
I'M TRYING TO FOCUS ON WORK WE'RE DOING HERE TO SECURE THE EARTH FROM ANOTHER PYKKT ATTACK.
AS FAR AS I'M CONCERNED, *THAT'S* MY PRIORITY AND THIS IS JUST...WHATEVER IT IS...I MEAN, OBVIOUSLY IT'S NOTHING.

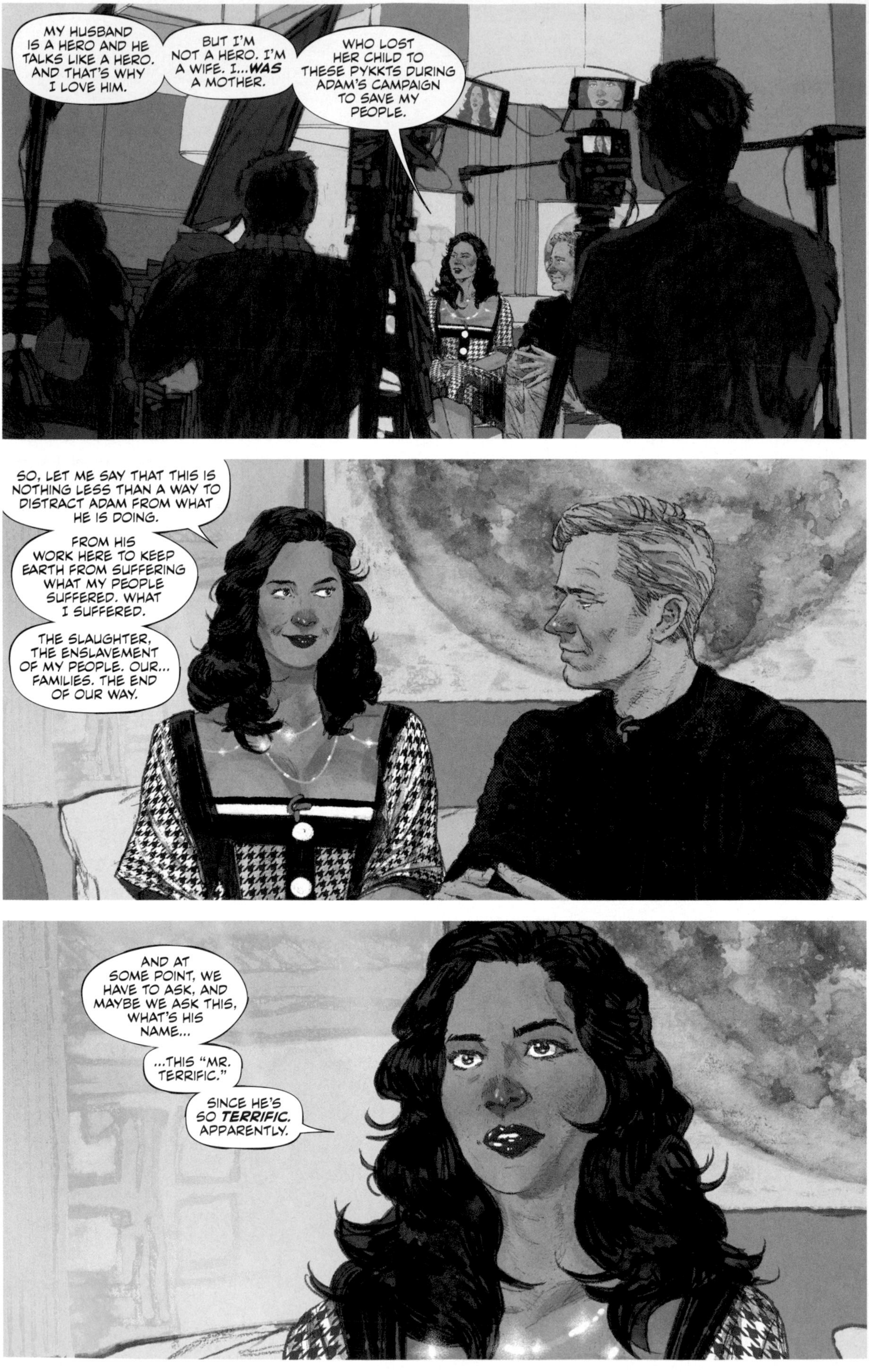

MY HUSBAND IS A HERO AND HE TALKS LIKE A HERO. AND THAT'S WHY I LOVE HIM.
BUT I'M NOT A HERO. I'M A WIFE. I...**WAS** A MOTHER.
WHO LOST HER CHILD TO THESE PYKKTS DURING ADAM'S CAMPAIGN TO SAVE MY PEOPLE.
SO, LET ME SAY THAT THIS IS NOTHING LESS THAN A WAY TO DISTRACT ADAM FROM WHAT HE IS DOING.
FROM HIS WORK HERE TO KEEP EARTH FROM SUFFERING WHAT MY PEOPLE SUFFERED. WHAT I SUFFERED.
THE SLAUGHTER, THE ENSLAVEMENT OF MY PEOPLE. OUR... FAMILIES. THE END OF OUR WAY.
AND AT SOME POINT, WE HAVE TO ASK, AND MAYBE WE ASK THIS, WHAT'S HIS NAME...
...THIS "MR. TERRIFIC."
SINCE HE'S SO ***TERRIFIC.*** APPARENTLY.

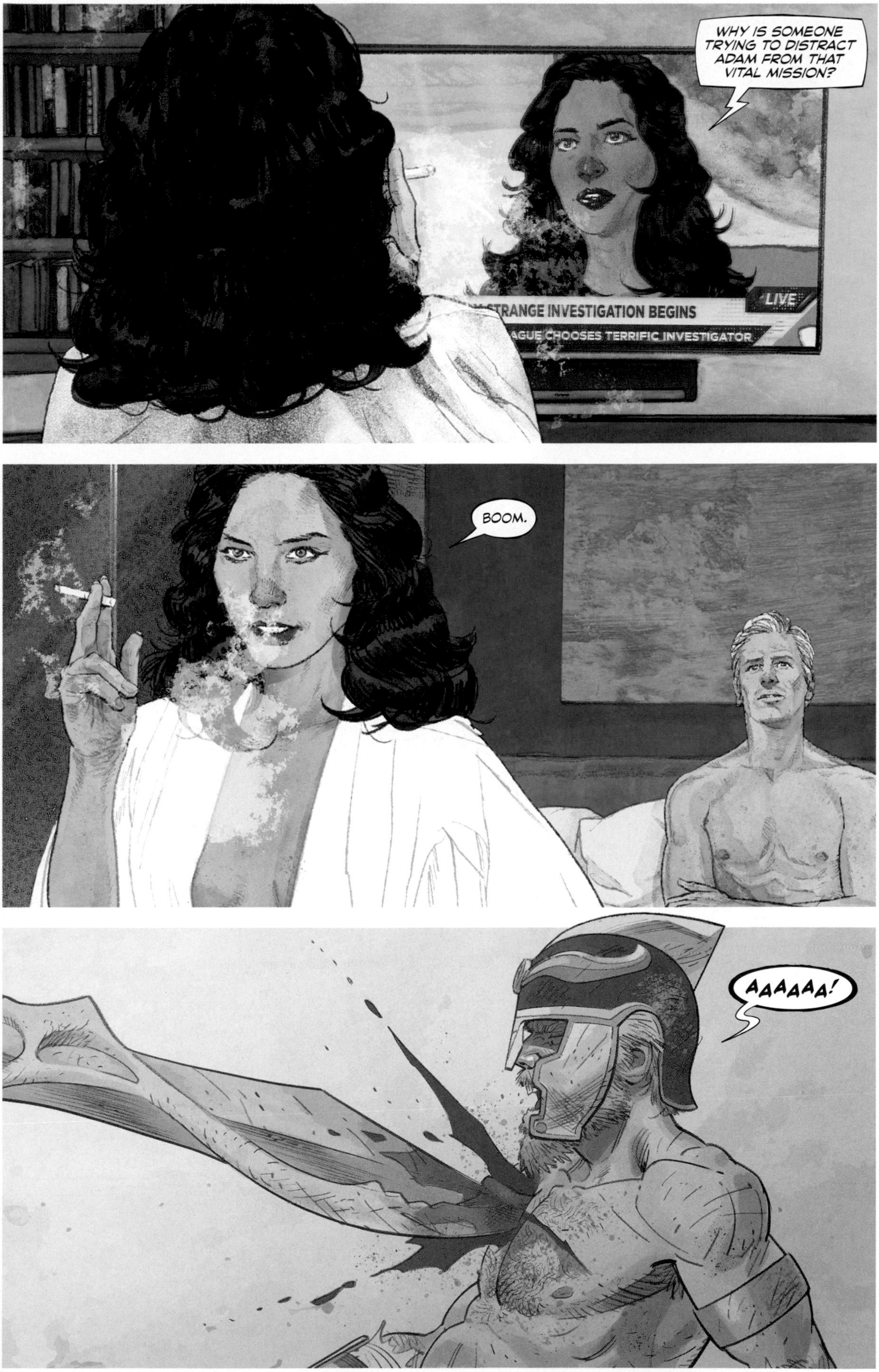
WHY IS SOMEONE TRYING TO DISTRACT ADAM FROM THAT VITAL MISSION?
STRANGE INVESTIGATION BEGINS
LIVE
CHOOSES TERRIFIC INVESTIGATOR
BOOM.
AAAAAA!

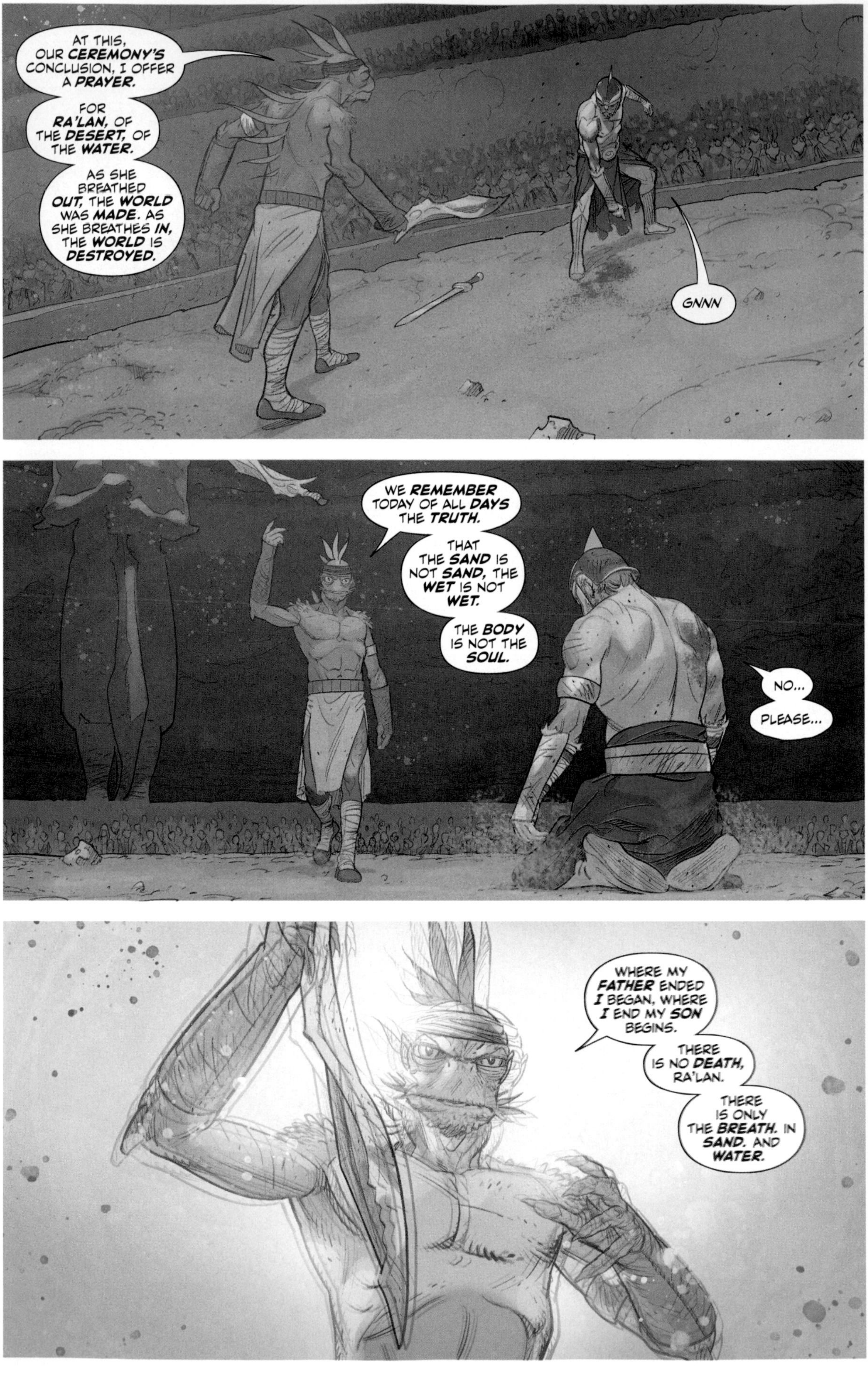
AT THIS, OUR CEREMONY'S CONCLUSION, I OFFER A PRAYER.
FOR RA'LAN, OF THE DESERT, OF THE WATER.
AS SHE BREATHED OUT, THE WORLD WAS MADE. AS SHE BREATHES IN, THE WORLD IS DESTROYED.
GNNN
WE REMEMBER TODAY OF ALL DAYS THE TRUTH.
THAT THE SAND IS NOT SAND, THE WET IS NOT WET.
THE BODY IS NOT THE SOUL.
NO...
PLEASE...
WHERE MY FATHER ENDED I BEGAN, WHERE I END MY SON BEGINS.
THERE IS NO DEATH, RA'LAN.
THERE IS ONLY THE BREATH. IN SAND. AND WATER.

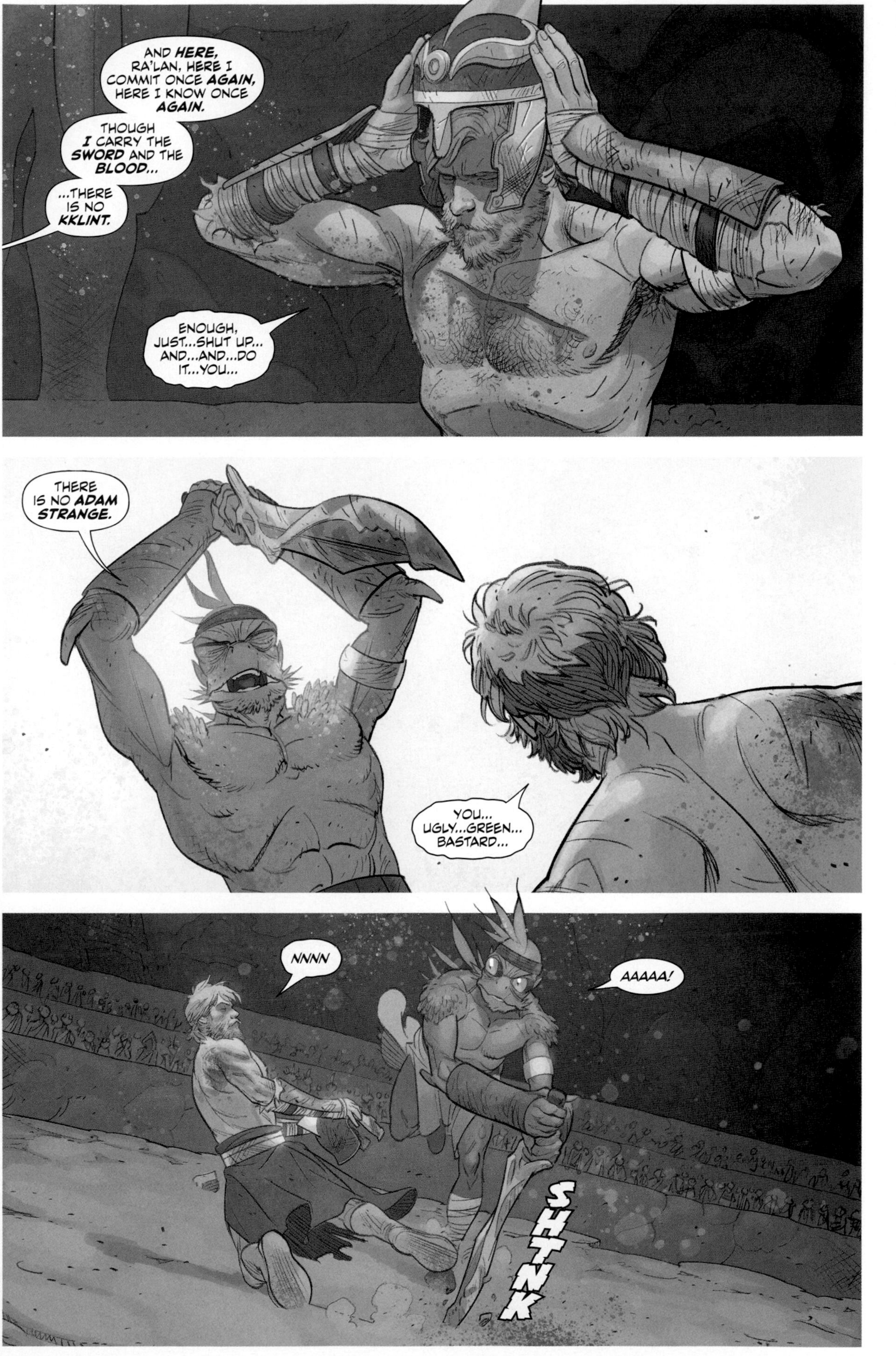
AND HERE, RA'LAN, HERE I COMMIT ONCE AGAIN, HERE I KNOW ONCE AGAIN.
THOUGH I CARRY THE SWORD AND THE BLOOD...
...THERE IS NO KKLINT.
ENOUGH, JUST...SHUT UP... AND...AND...DO IT...YOU...
THERE IS NO ADAM STRANGE.
YOU... UGLY...GREEN... BASTARD...
NNNN
AAAAA!
SHTNK

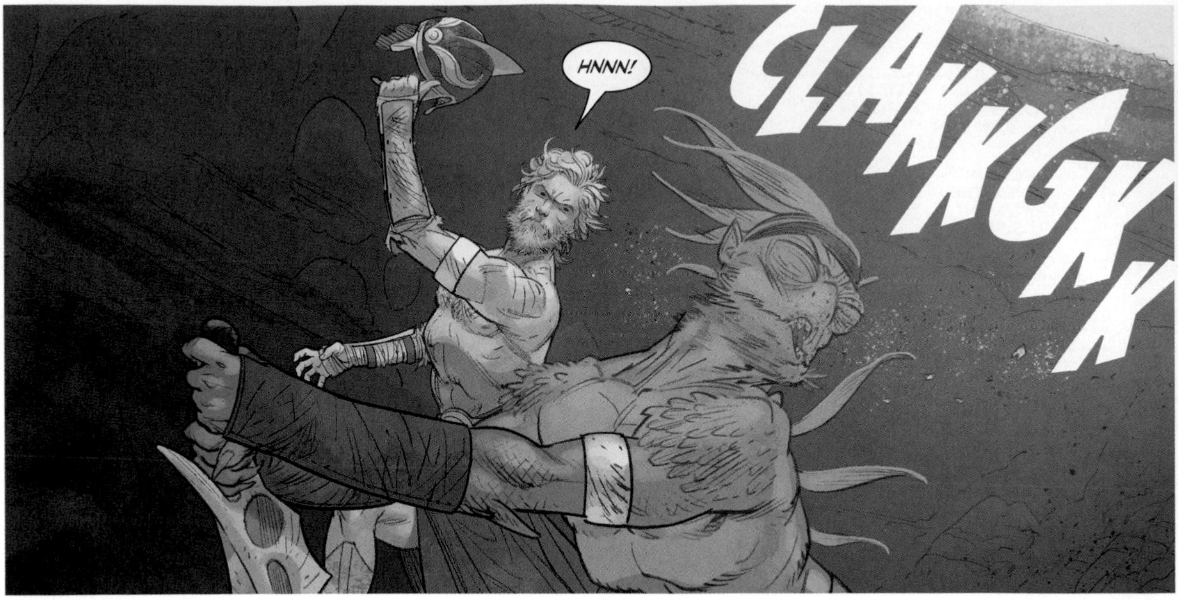
HNNN!
CLAKKGKKK

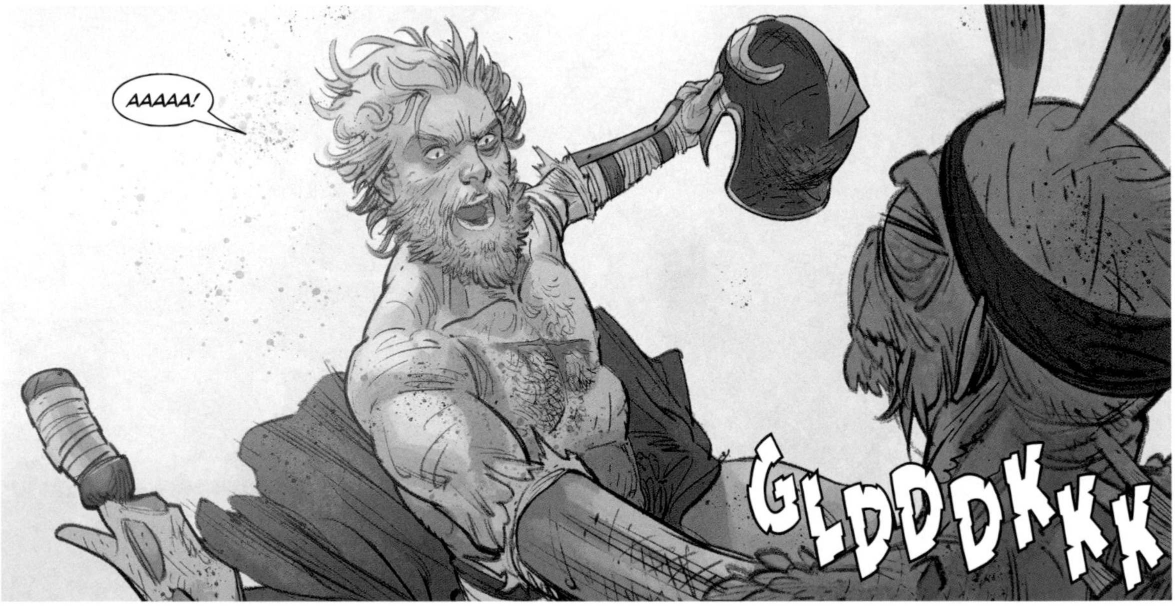
AAAAA!
GLDDDKKK

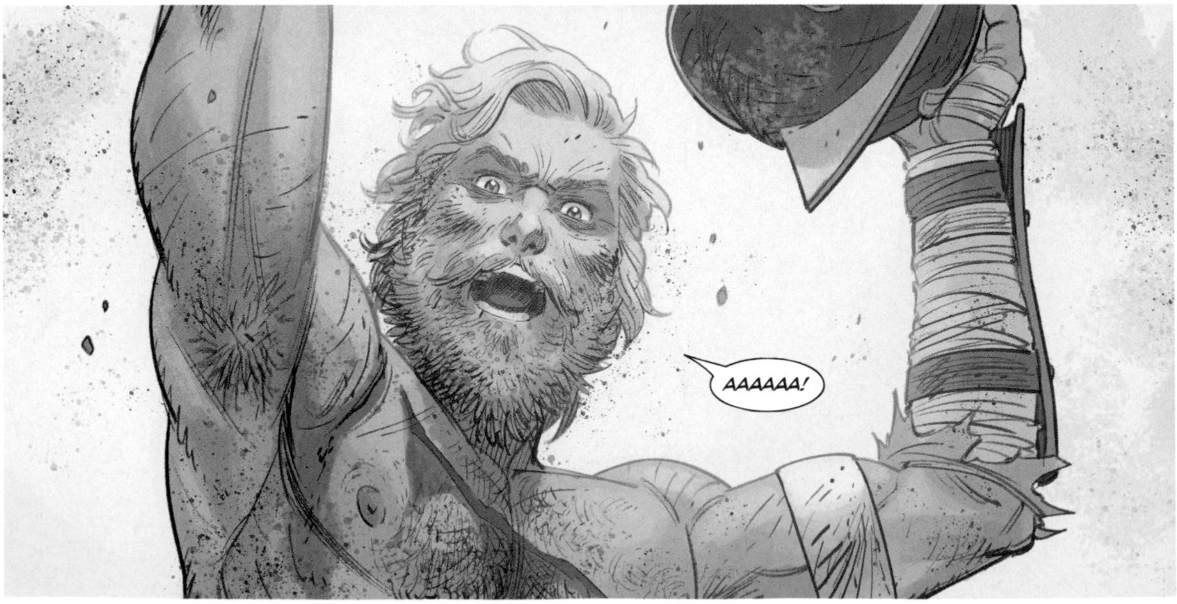
AAAAAA!

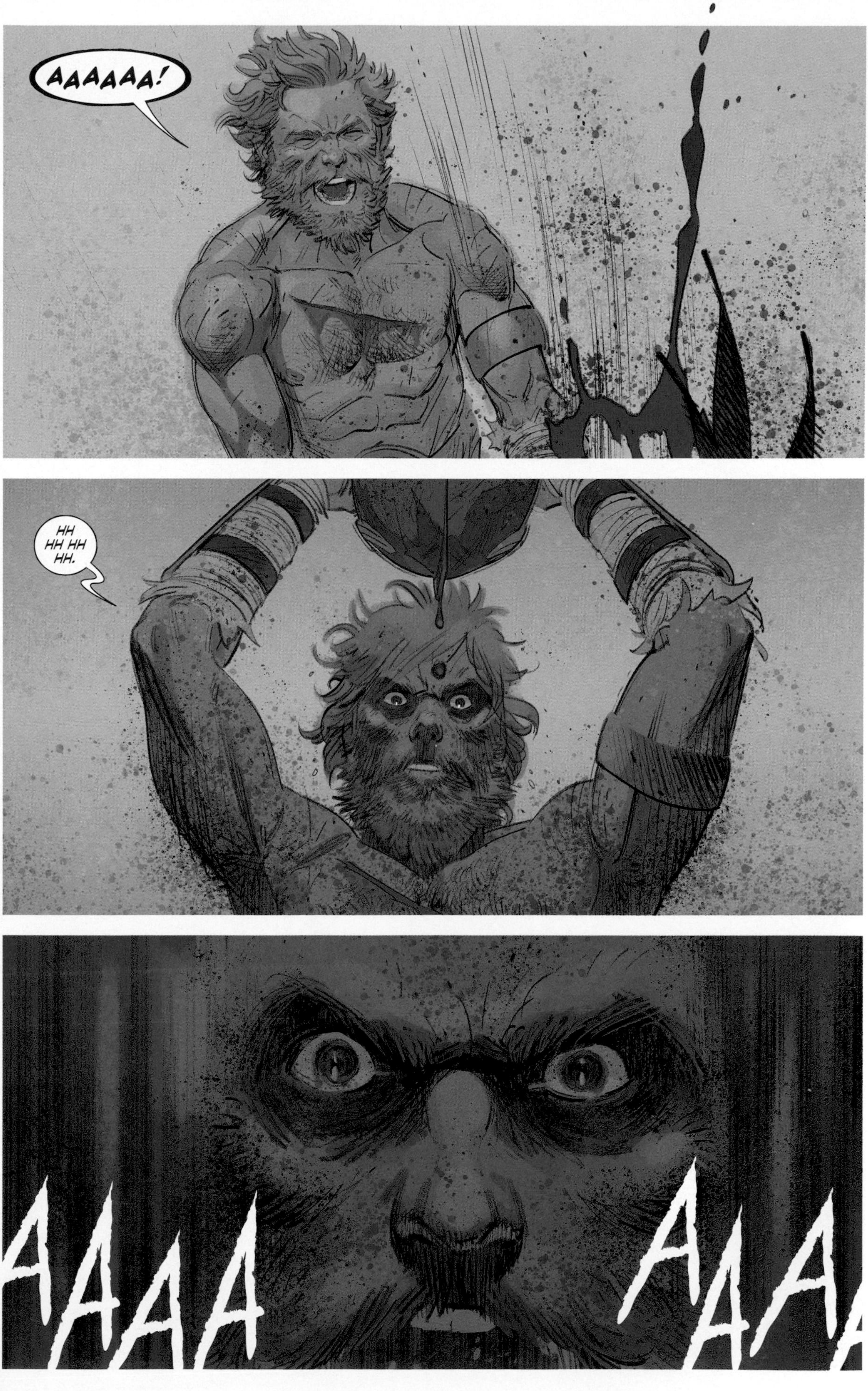
AAAAAA!
HH HH HH HH.
AAAA AAAA

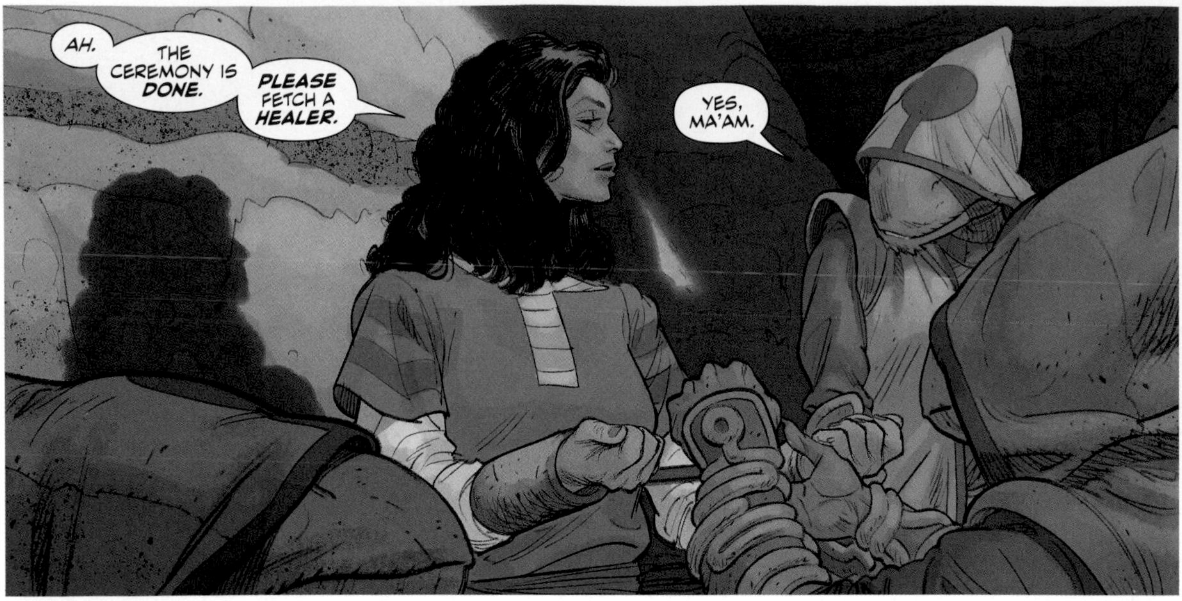
AH.
THE CEREMONY IS DONE.
PLEASE FETCH A HEALER.
YES, MA'AM.

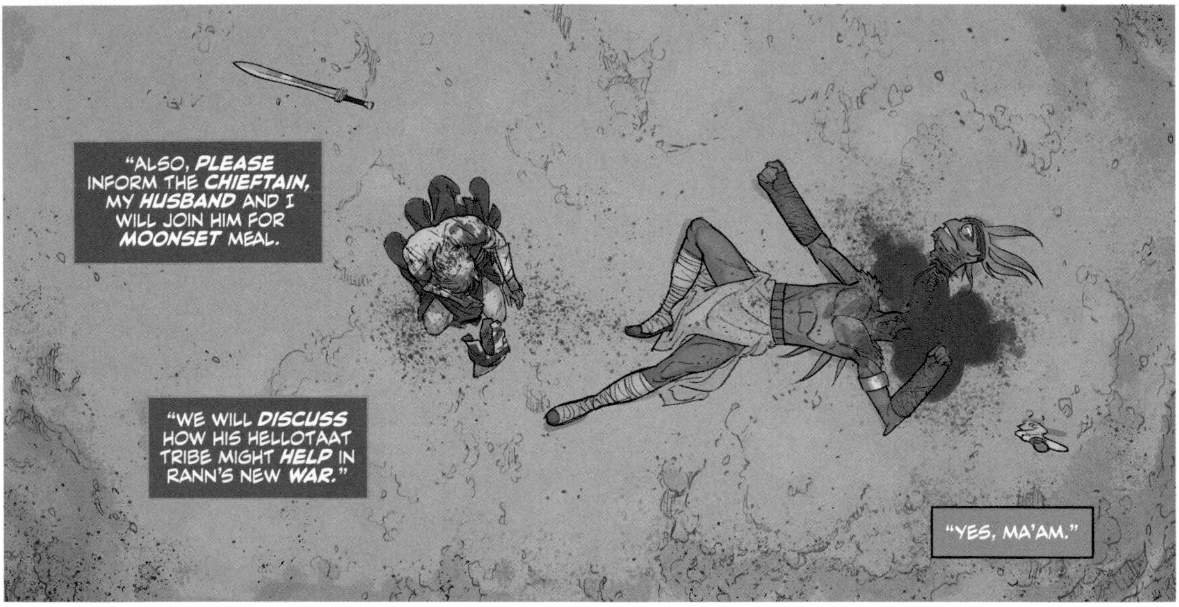
"ALSO, PLEASE INFORM THE CHIEFTAIN, MY HUSBAND AND I WILL JOIN HIM FOR MOONSET MEAL.
"WE WILL DISCUSS HOW HIS HELLOTAAT TRIBE MIGHT HELP IN RANN'S NEW WAR."
"YES, MA'AM."

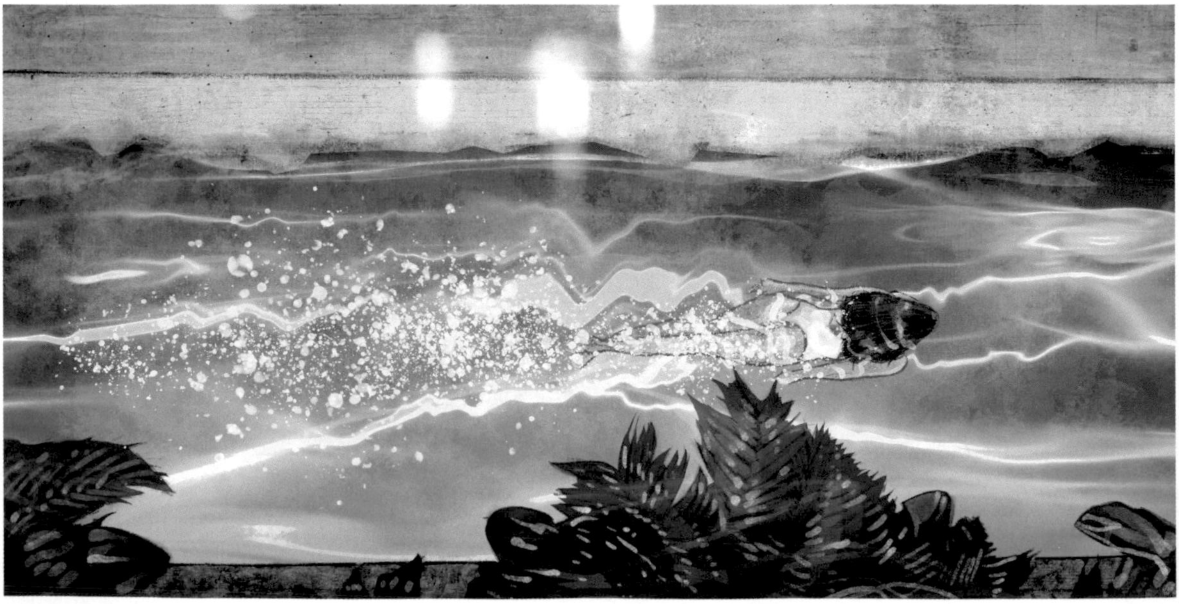

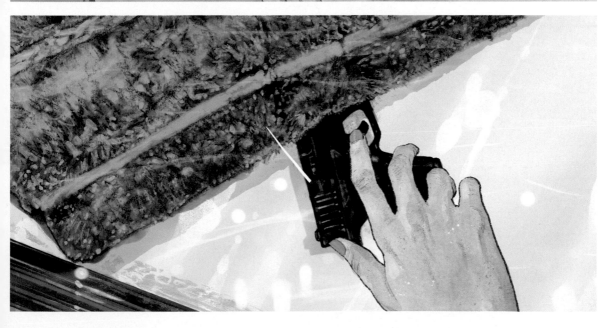

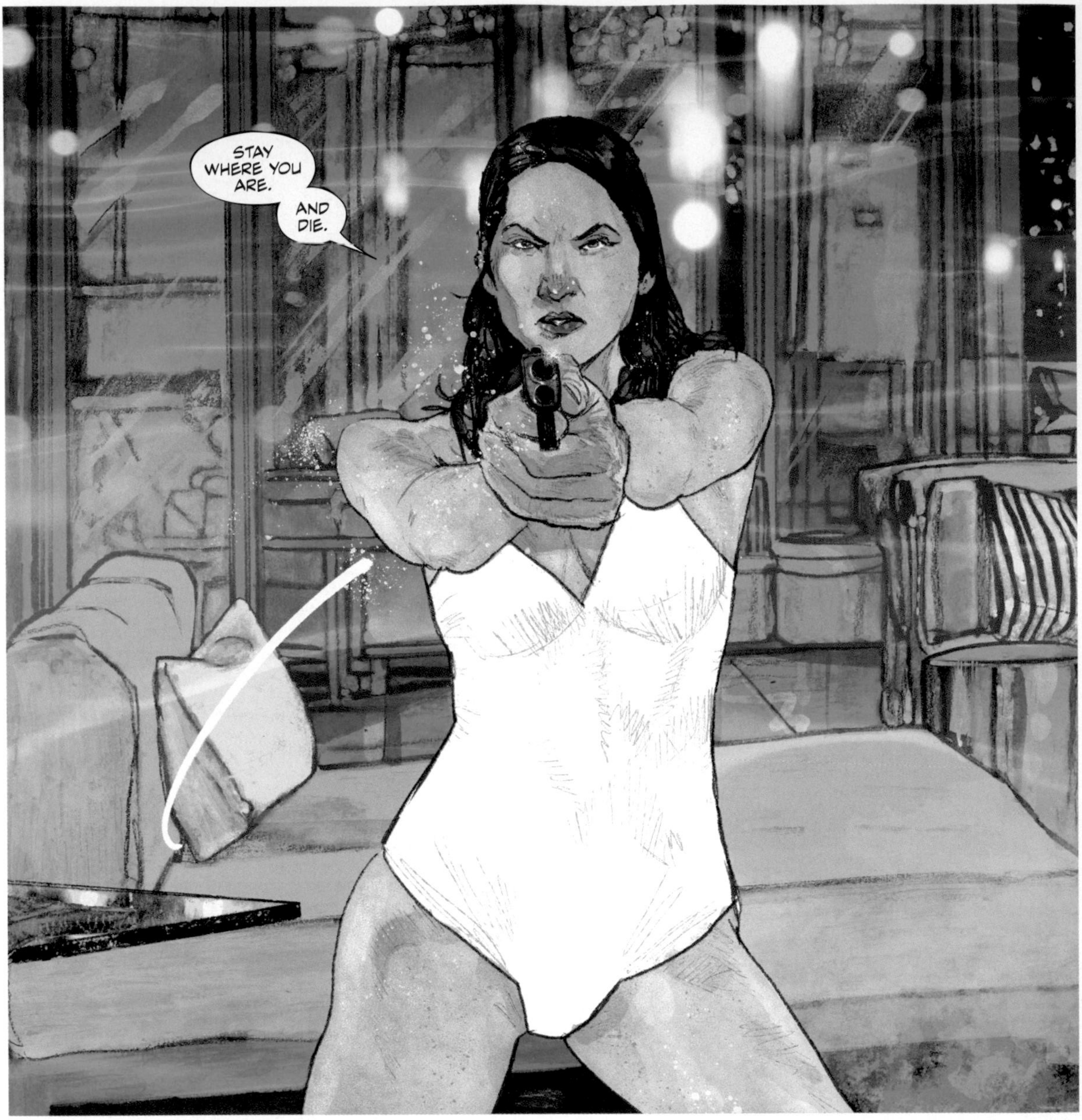
STAY WHERE YOU ARE.
AND DIE.
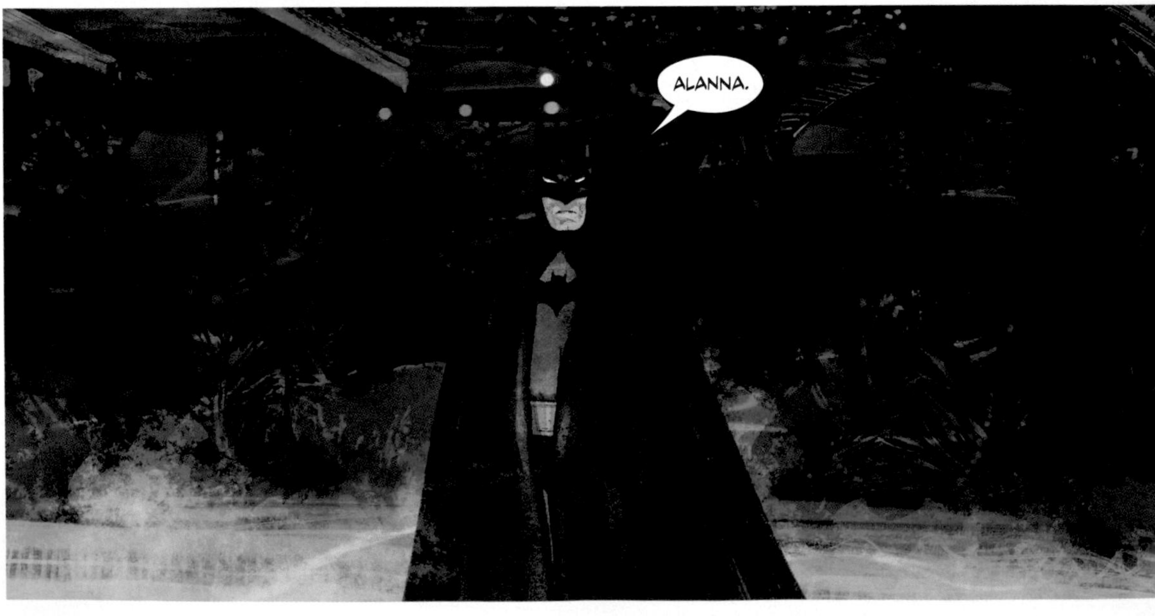
ALANNA.

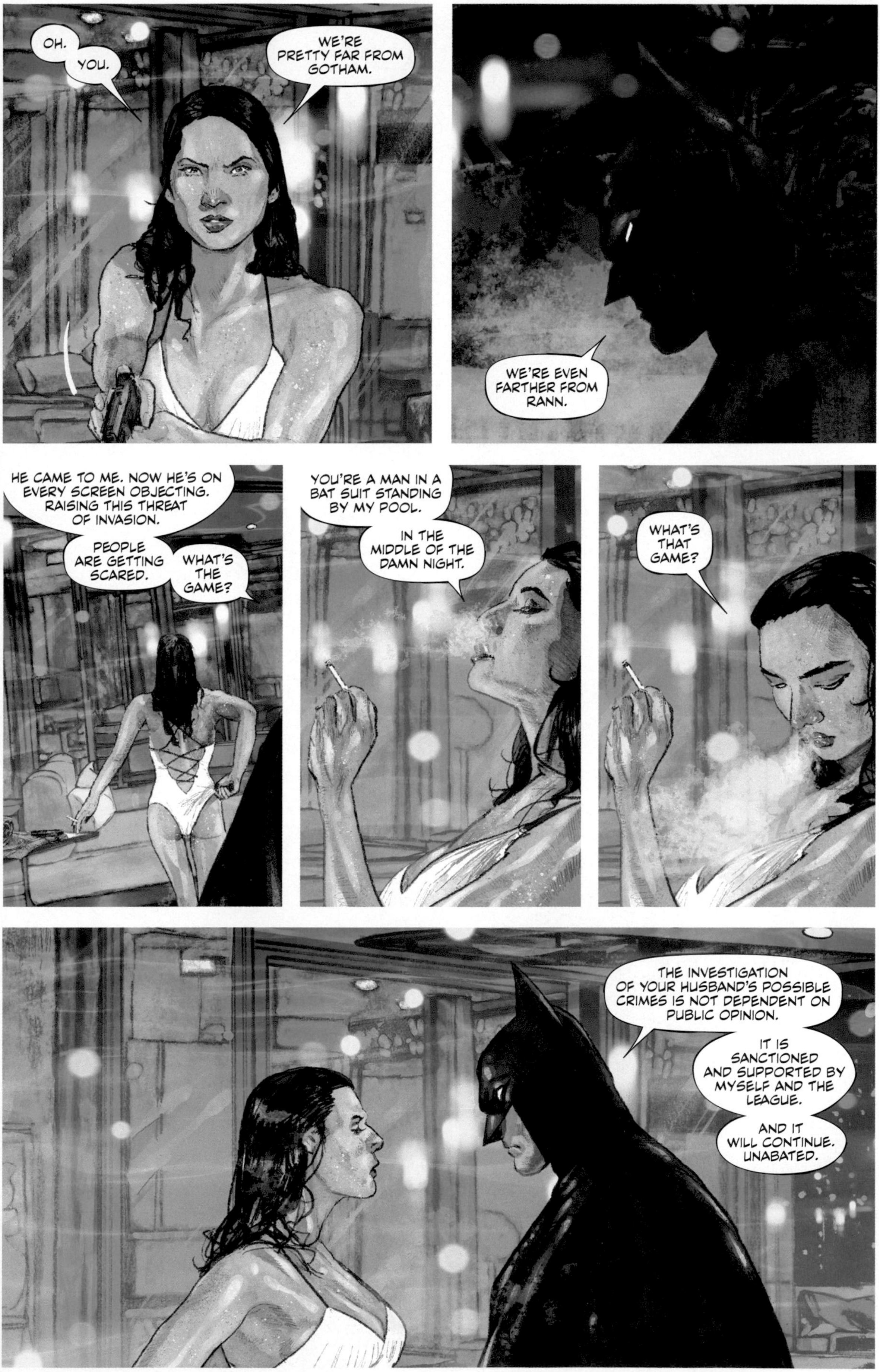
OH.
YOU.
WE'RE PRETTY FAR FROM GOTHAM.
WE'RE EVEN FARTHER FROM RANN.
HE CAME TO ME. NOW HE'S ON EVERY SCREEN OBJECTING. RAISING THIS THREAT OF INVASION.
PEOPLE ARE GETTING SCARED.
WHAT'S THE GAME?
YOU'RE A MAN IN A BAT SUIT STANDING BY MY POOL.
IN THE MIDDLE OF THE DAMN NIGHT.
WHAT'S THAT GAME?
THE INVESTIGATION OF YOUR HUSBAND'S POSSIBLE CRIMES IS NOT DEPENDENT ON PUBLIC OPINION.
IT IS SANCTIONED AND SUPPORTED BY MYSELF AND THE LEAGUE.
AND IT WILL CONTINUE. UNABATED.

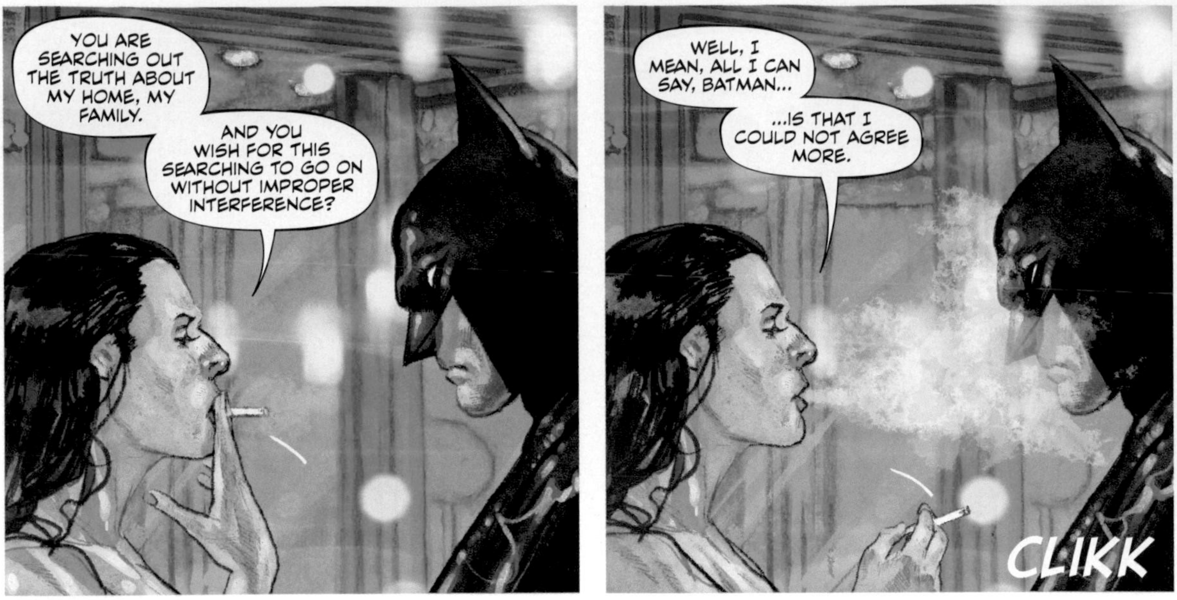
YOU ARE SEARCHING OUT THE TRUTH ABOUT MY HOME, MY FAMILY.
AND YOU WISH FOR THIS SEARCHING TO GO ON WITHOUT IMPROPER INTERFERENCE?
WELL, I MEAN, ALL I CAN SAY, BATMAN...
...IS THAT I COULD NOT AGREE MORE.
CLIKK

There were good guys
and bad guys.
And the job of the
good guys is to kill
the bad guys.

—Wally Wood

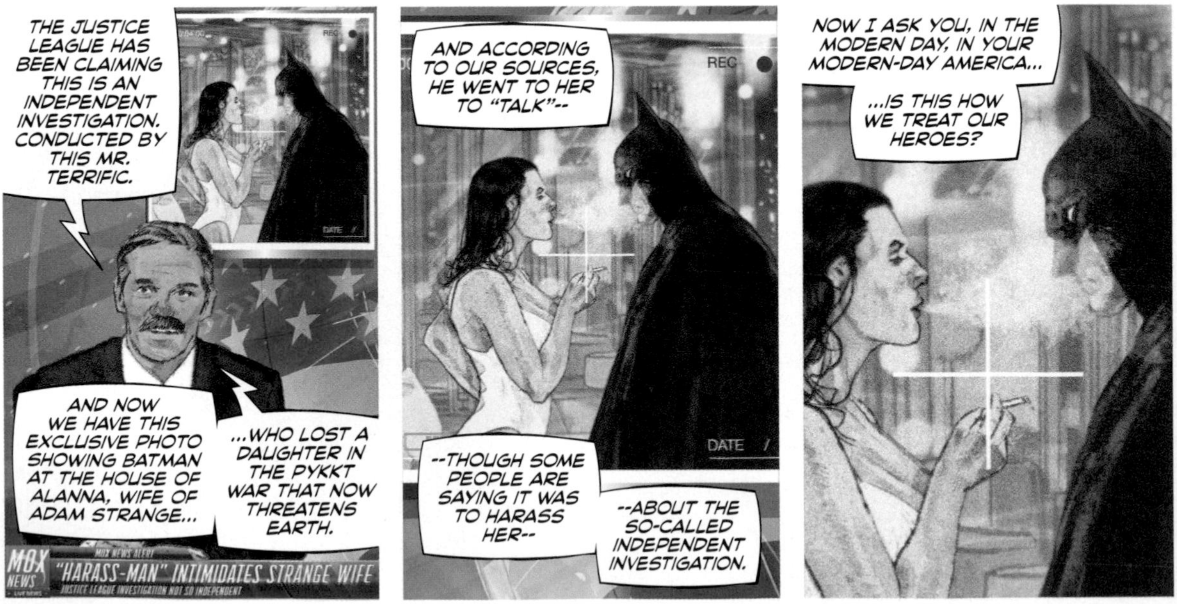
THE JUSTICE LEAGUE HAS BEEN CLAIMING THIS IS AN INDEPENDENT INVESTIGATION. CONDUCTED BY THIS MR. TERRIFIC.
AND NOW WE HAVE THIS EXCLUSIVE PHOTO SHOWING BATMAN AT THE HOUSE OF ALANNA, WIFE OF ADAM STRANGE...
...WHO LOST A DAUGHTER IN THE PYKKT WAR THAT NOW THREATENS EARTH.
MOX NEWS
"HARASS-MAN" INTIMIDATES STRANGE WIFE
JUSTICE LEAGUE INVESTIGATION NOT SO INDEPENDENT
AND ACCORDING TO OUR SOURCES, HE WENT TO HER TO "TALK"--
--THOUGH SOME PEOPLE ARE SAYING IT WAS TO HARASS HER--
--ABOUT THE SO-CALLED INDEPENDENT INVESTIGATION.
NOW I ASK YOU, IN THE MODERN DAY, IN YOUR MODERN-DAY AMERICA...
...IS THIS HOW WE TREAT OUR HEROES?

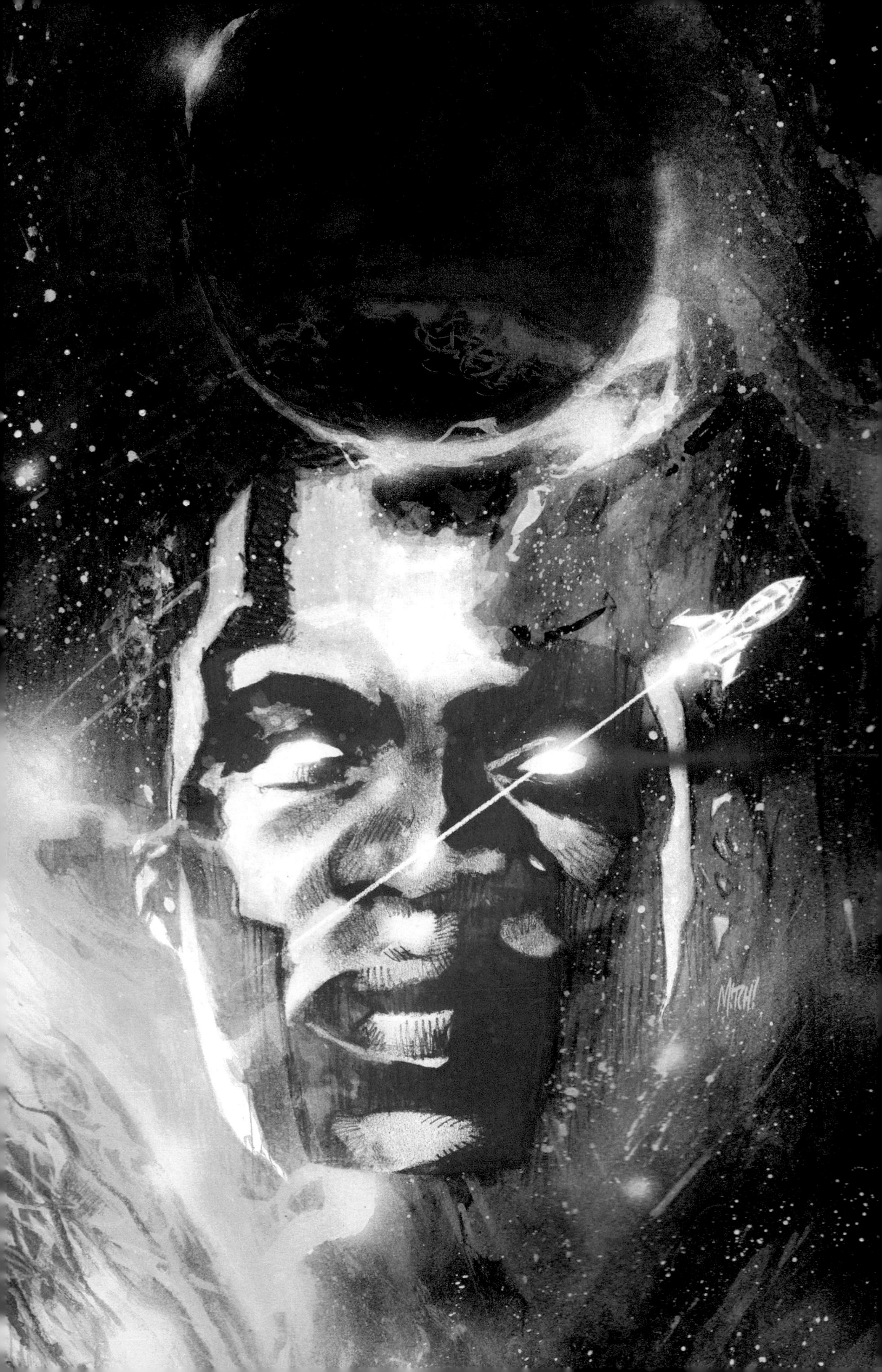

"THERE'S ALWAYS A CRISIS SOMEWHERE."

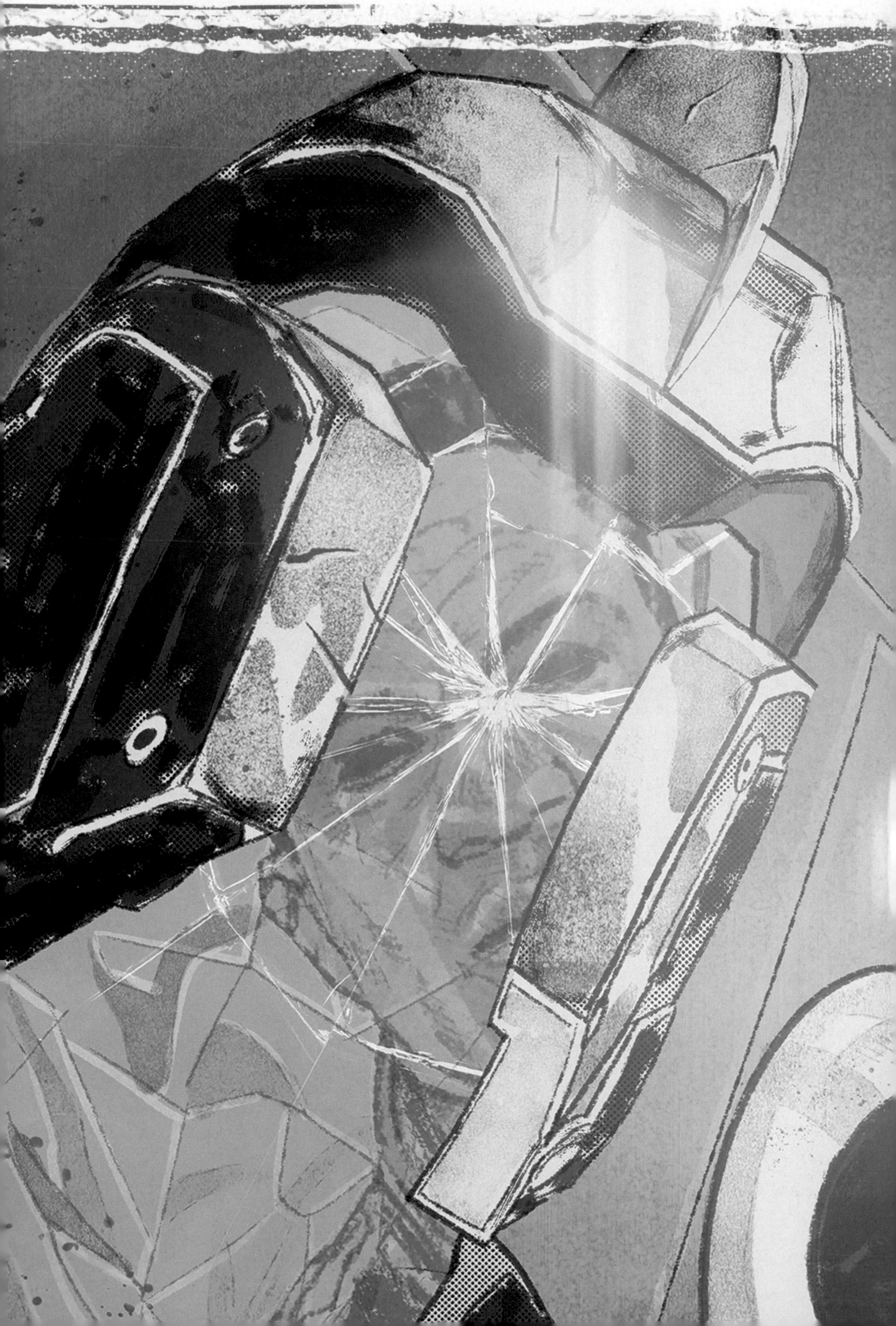

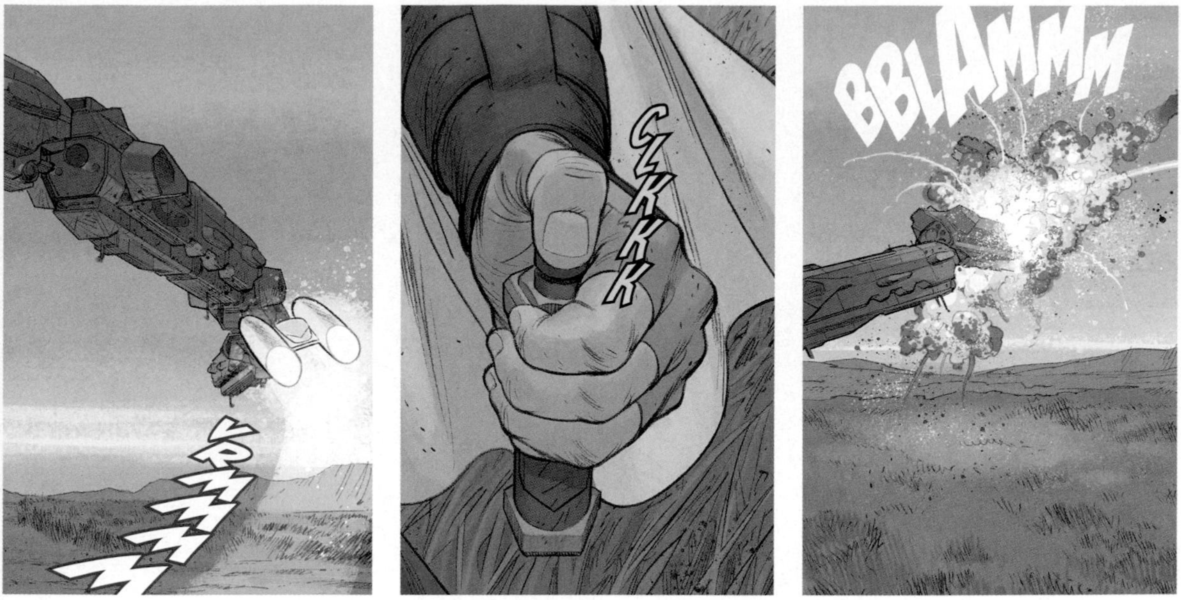
VRMMMM
CLKKK
BBLAMMM

Chapter 4

Out the window

TOM KING	...Writer
MITCH GERADS EVAN "DOC" SHANER	...Interior & Cover Artists
CLAYTON COWLES	...Letterer
BIXIE MATHIEU	...Assistant Editor
BRITTANY HOLZHERR	...Associate Editor
JAMIE S. RICH	...Editor

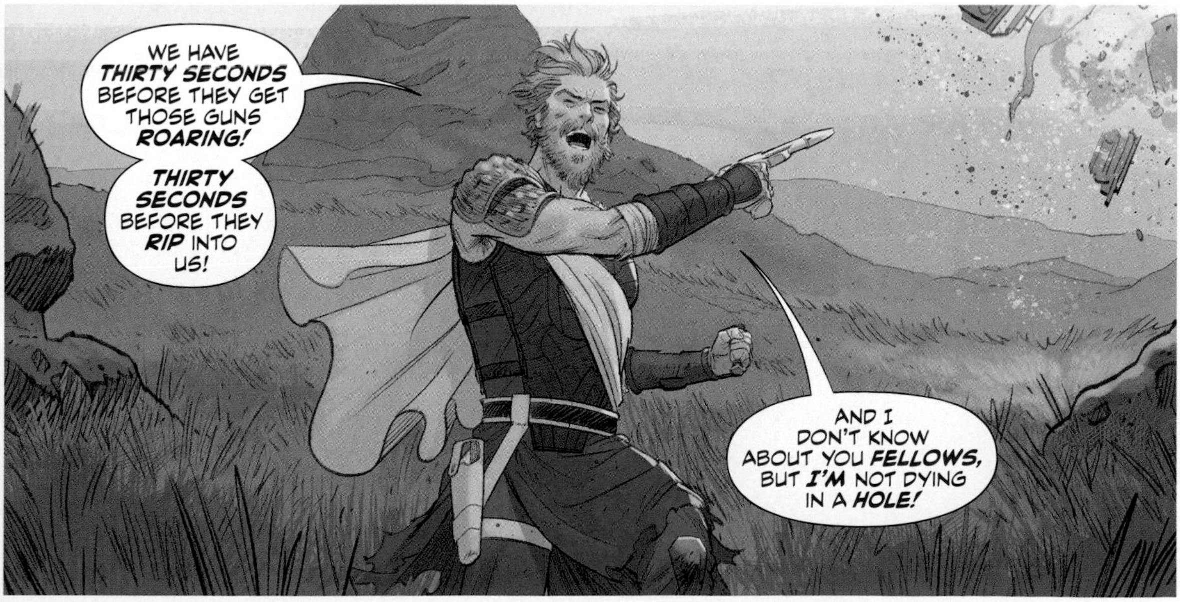
WE HAVE *THIRTY SECONDS* BEFORE THEY GET THOSE GUNS *ROARING!*
THIRTY SECONDS BEFORE THEY *RIP* INTO US!
AND I DON'T KNOW ABOUT YOU *FELLOWS,* BUT *I'M* NOT DYING IN A *HOLE!*

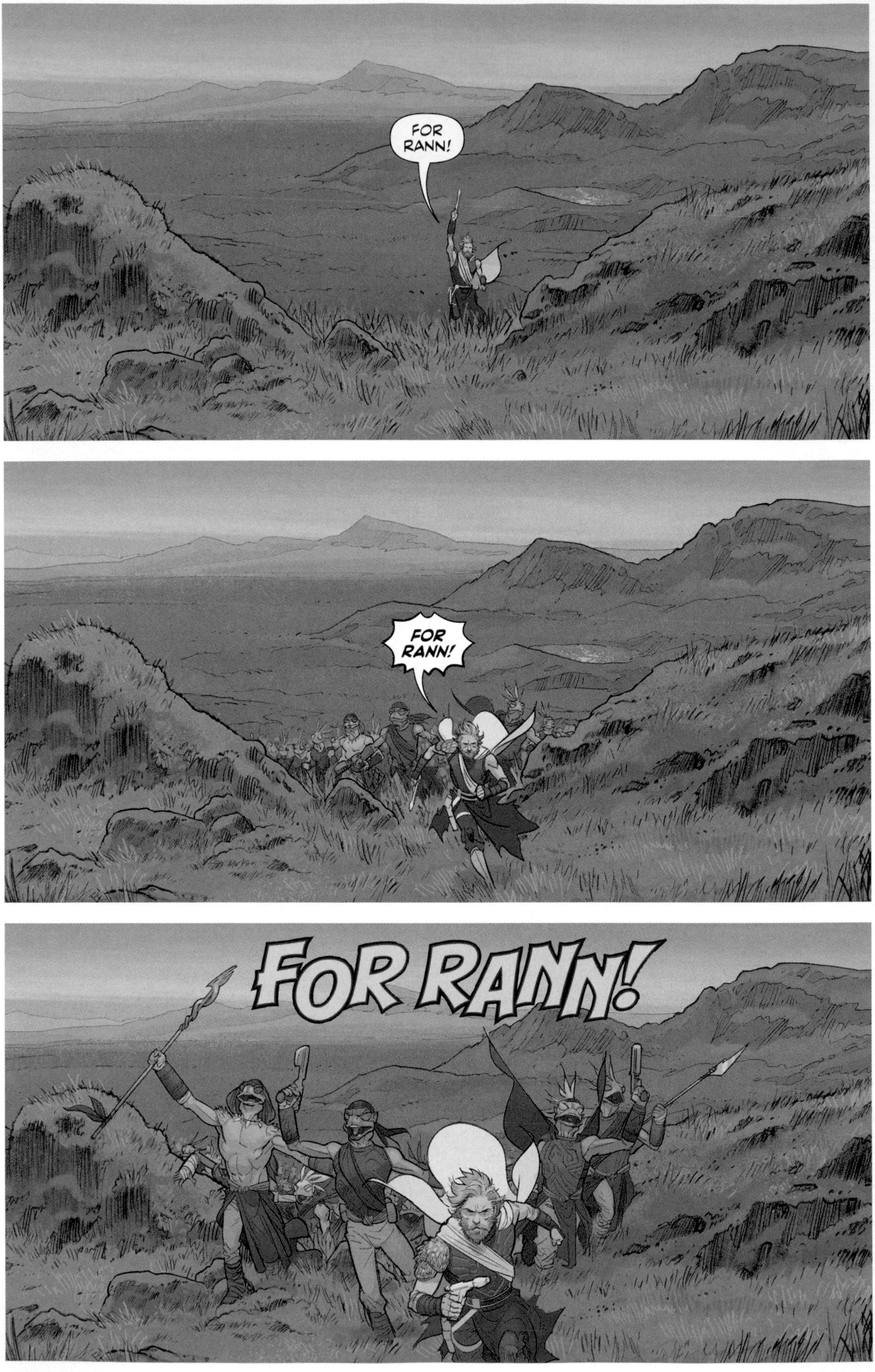
FOR RANN!
FOR RANN!
FOR RANN!

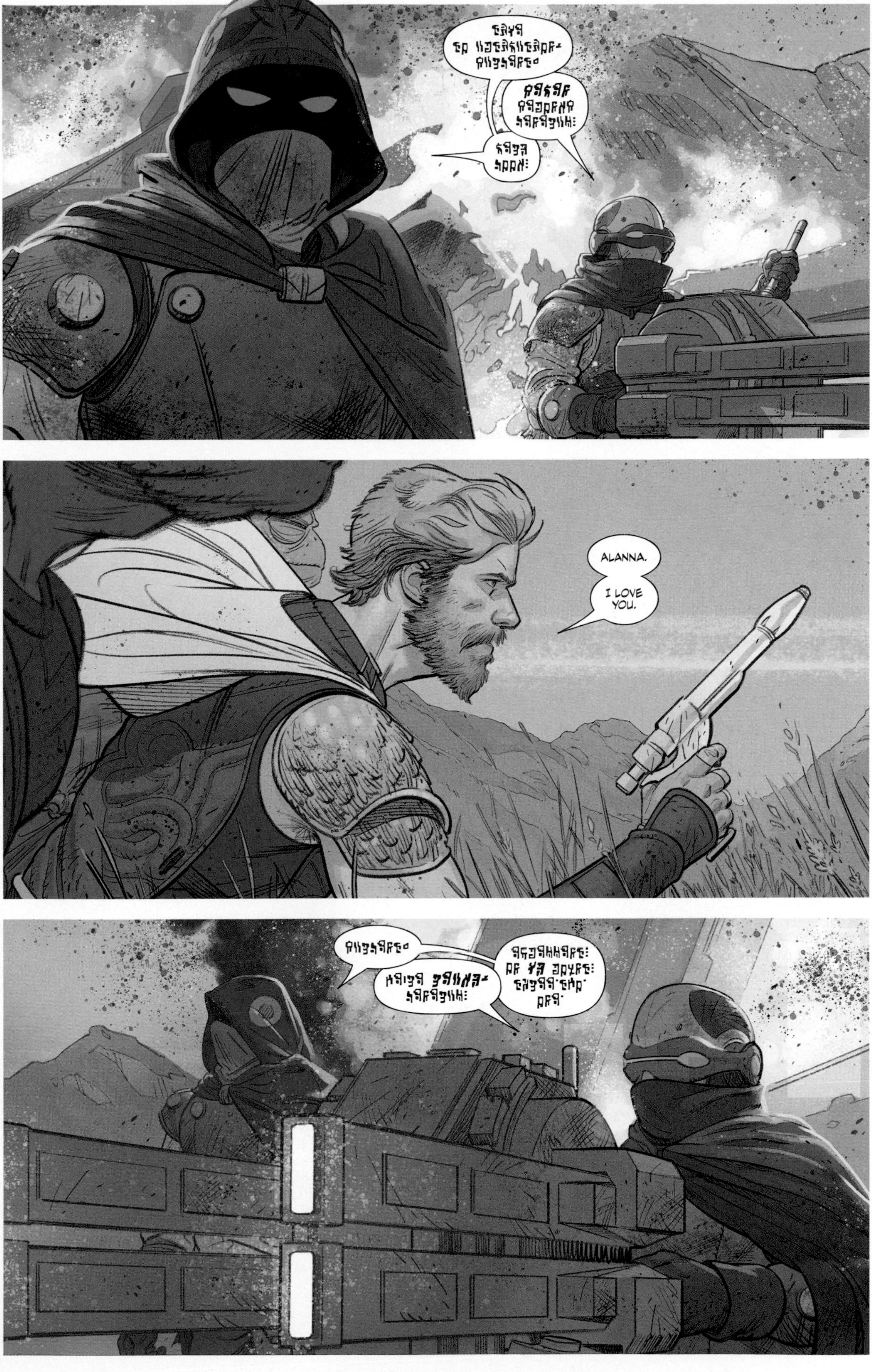
ALANNA.
I LOVE YOU.

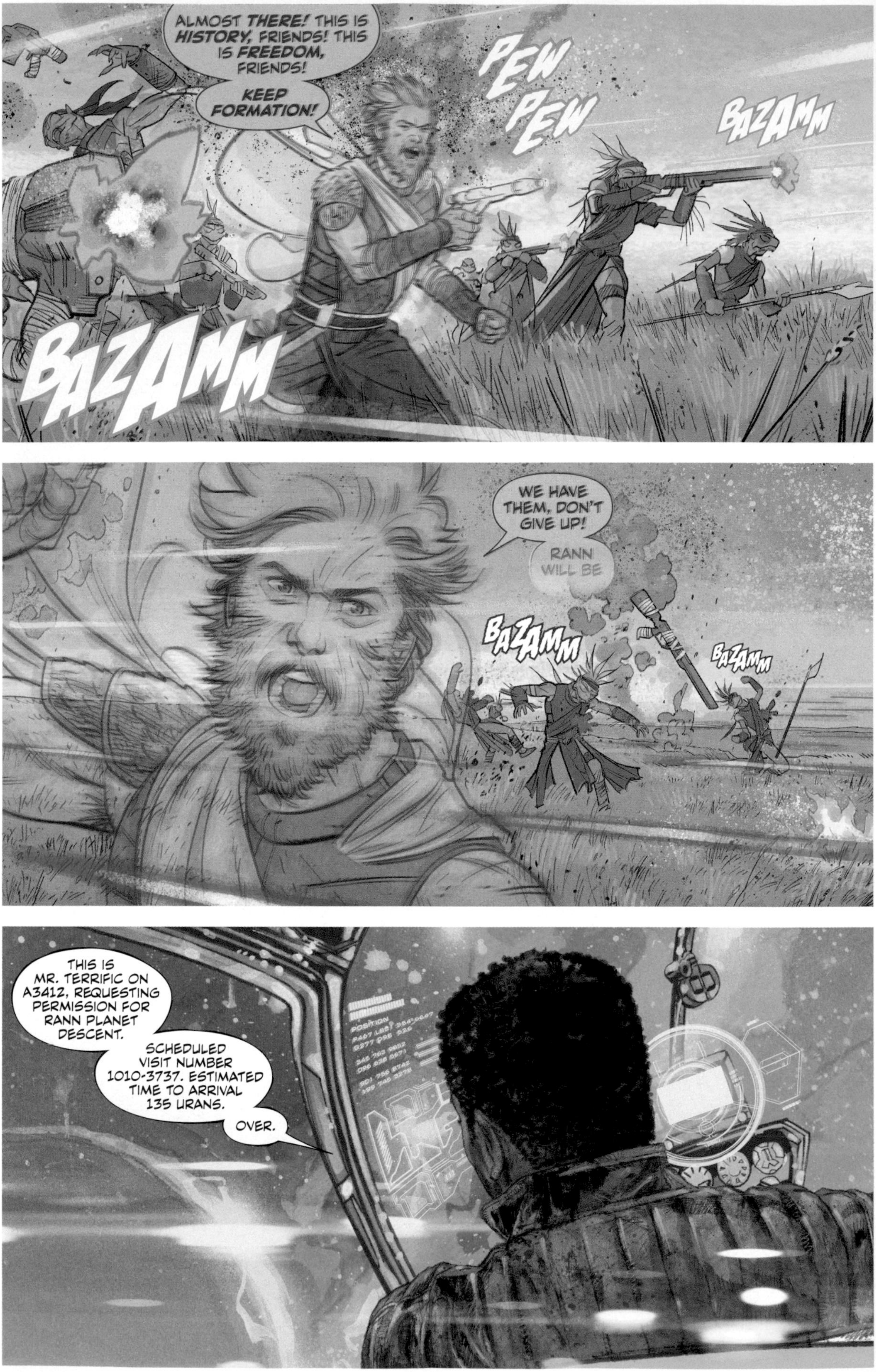
ALMOST THERE! THIS IS HISTORY, FRIENDS! THIS IS FREEDOM, FRIENDS!
KEEP FORMATION!
PEW PEW
PEW PEW
BAZAMM
BAZAMM
WE HAVE THEM, DON'T GIVE UP!
RANN WILL BE
BAZAMM
BAZAMM
THIS IS MR. TERRIFIC ON A3412, REQUESTING PERMISSION FOR RANN PLANET DESCENT.
SCHEDULED VISIT NUMBER 1010-3737. ESTIMATED TIME TO ARRIVAL 135 URANS.
OVER.

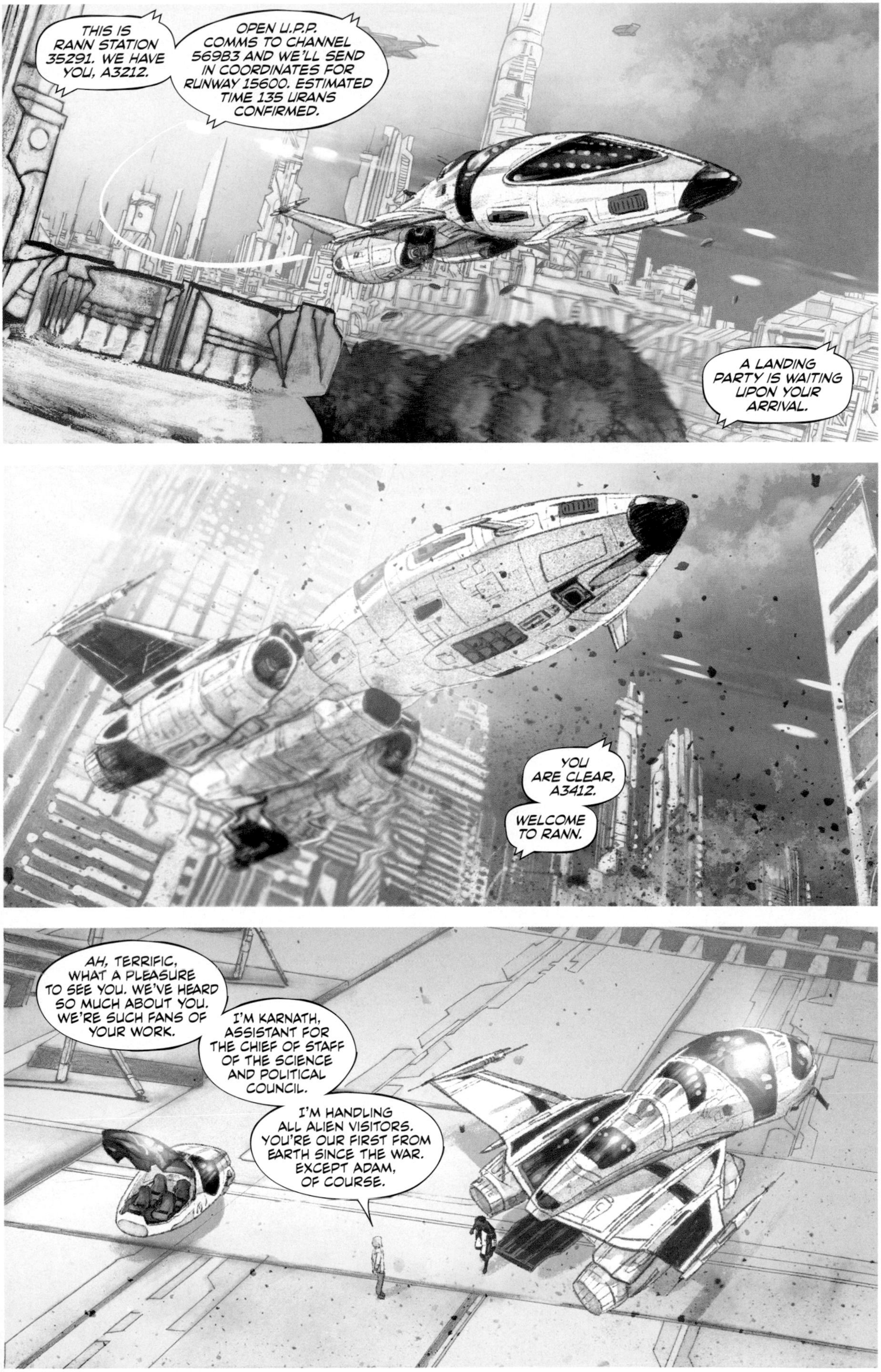
THIS IS RANN STATION 35291. WE HAVE YOU, A3212.
OPEN U.P.P. COMMS TO CHANNEL 569B3 AND WE'LL SEND IN COORDINATES FOR RUNWAY 15600. ESTIMATED TIME 135 URANS CONFIRMED.
A LANDING PARTY IS WAITING UPON YOUR ARRIVAL.
YOU ARE CLEAR, A3412.
WELCOME TO RANN.
AH, TERRIFIC, WHAT A PLEASURE TO SEE YOU. WE'VE HEARD SO MUCH ABOUT YOU. WE'RE SUCH FANS OF YOUR WORK.
I'M KARNATH, ASSISTANT FOR THE CHIEF OF STAFF OF THE SCIENCE AND POLITICAL COUNCIL.
I'M HANDLING ALL ALIEN VISITORS. YOU'RE OUR FIRST FROM EARTH SINCE THE WAR. EXCEPT ADAM, OF COURSE.

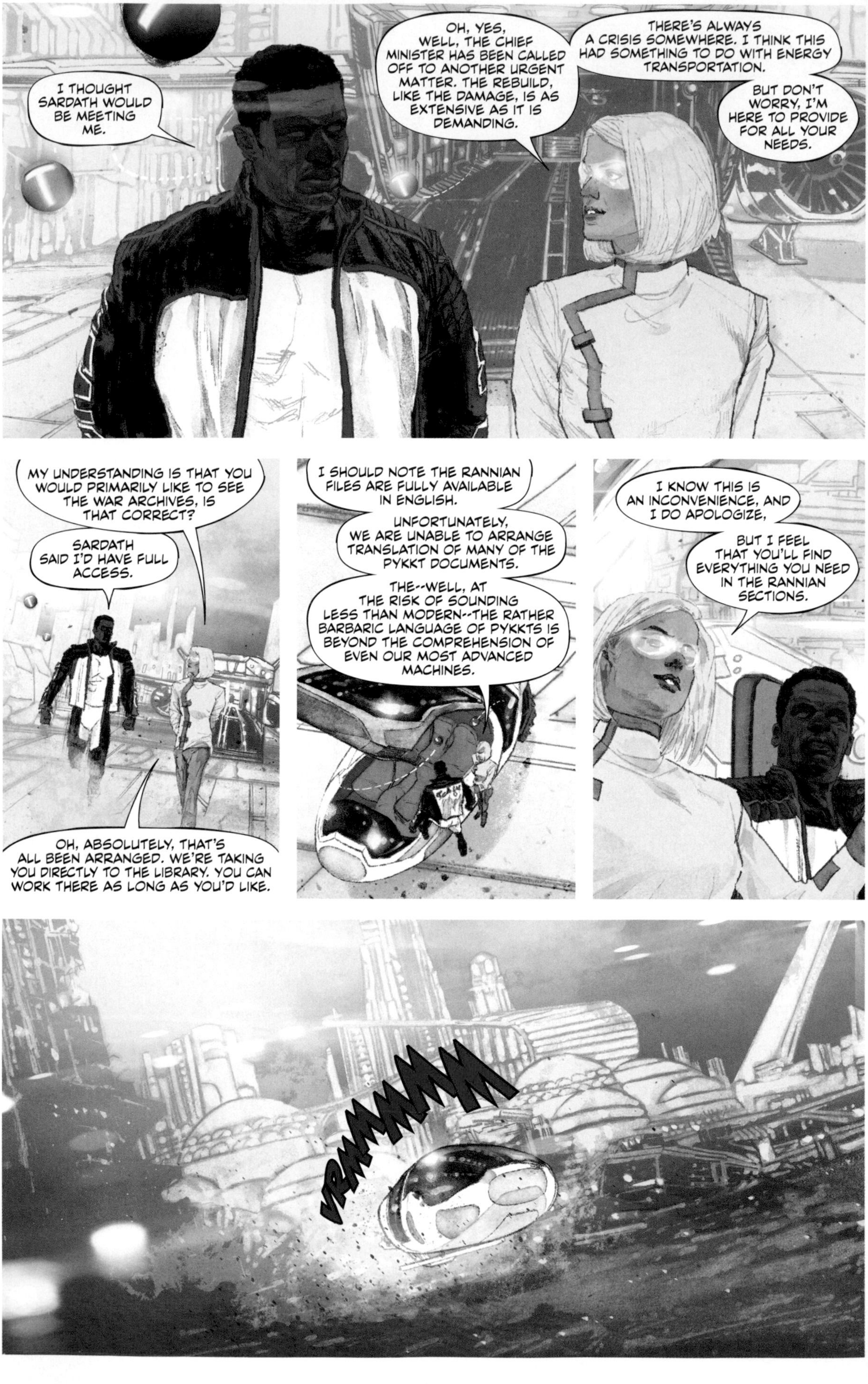
I THOUGHT SARDATH WOULD BE MEETING ME.
OH, YES, WELL, THE CHIEF MINISTER HAS BEEN CALLED OFF TO ANOTHER URGENT MATTER. THE REBUILD, LIKE THE DAMAGE, IS AS EXTENSIVE AS IT IS DEMANDING.
THERE'S ALWAYS A CRISIS SOMEWHERE. I THINK THIS HAD SOMETHING TO DO WITH ENERGY TRANSPORTATION.
BUT DON'T WORRY, I'M HERE TO PROVIDE FOR ALL YOUR NEEDS.
MY UNDERSTANDING IS THAT YOU WOULD PRIMARILY LIKE TO SEE THE WAR ARCHIVES, IS THAT CORRECT?
SARDATH SAID I'D HAVE FULL ACCESS.
OH, ABSOLUTELY, THAT'S ALL BEEN ARRANGED. WE'RE TAKING YOU DIRECTLY TO THE LIBRARY. YOU CAN WORK THERE AS LONG AS YOU'D LIKE.
I SHOULD NOTE THE RANNIAN FILES ARE FULLY AVAILABLE IN ENGLISH.
UNFORTUNATELY, WE ARE UNABLE TO ARRANGE TRANSLATION OF MANY OF THE PYKKT DOCUMENTS.
THE--WELL, AT THE RISK OF SOUNDING LESS THAN MODERN--THE RATHER BARBARIC LANGUAGE OF PYKKTS IS BEYOND THE COMPREHENSION OF EVEN OUR MOST ADVANCED MACHINES.
I KNOW THIS IS AN INCONVENIENCE, AND I DO APOLOGIZE,
BUT I FEEL THAT YOU'LL FIND EVERYTHING YOU NEED IN THE RANNIAN SECTIONS.
VRMMMMM

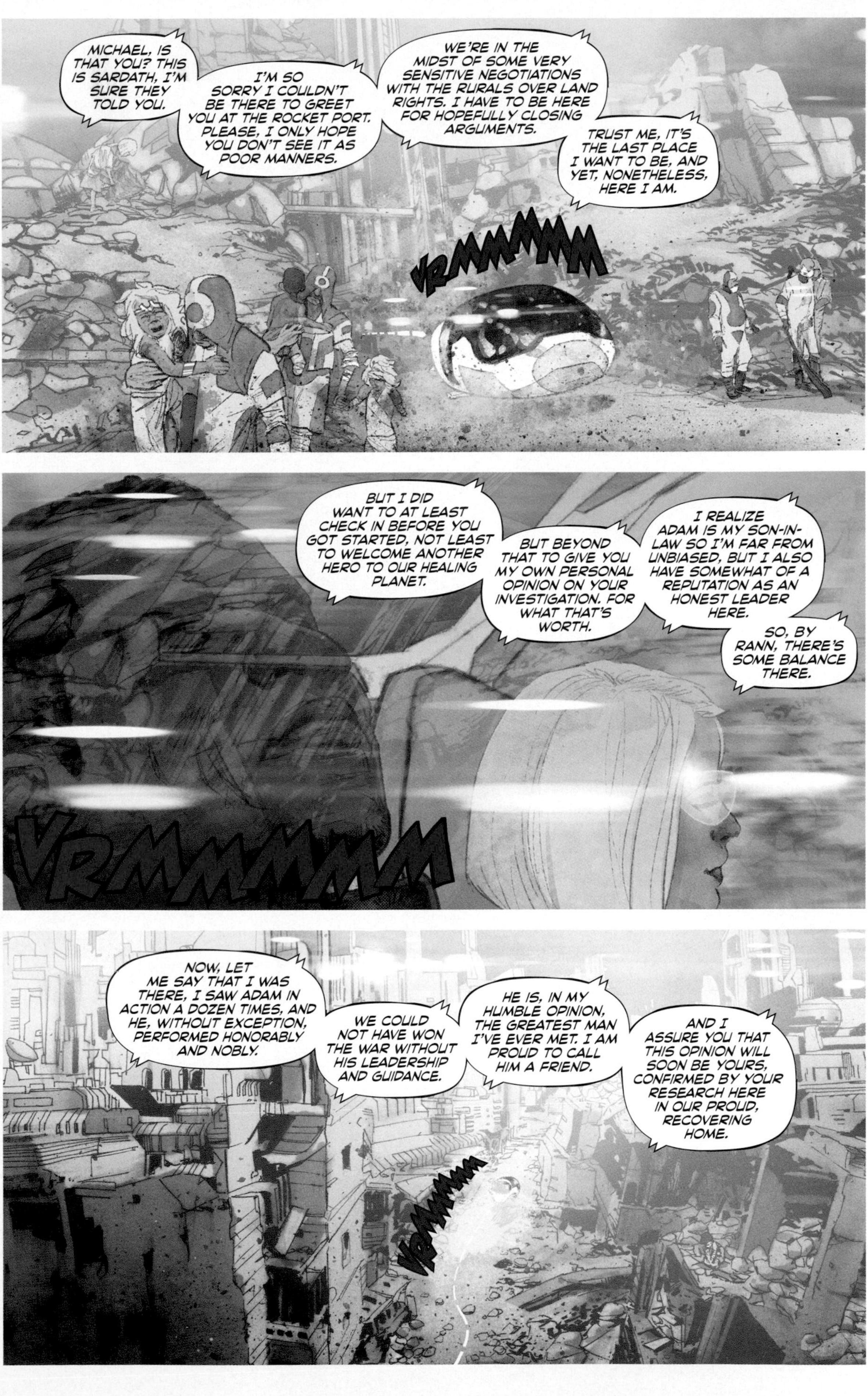
MICHAEL, IS THAT YOU? THIS IS SARDATH, I'M SURE THEY TOLD YOU.
I'M SO SORRY I COULDN'T BE THERE TO GREET YOU AT THE ROCKET PORT. PLEASE, I ONLY HOPE YOU DON'T SEE IT AS POOR MANNERS.
WE'RE IN THE MIDST OF SOME VERY SENSITIVE NEGOTIATIONS WITH THE RURALS OVER LAND RIGHTS. I HAVE TO BE HERE FOR HOPEFULLY CLOSING ARGUMENTS.
TRUST ME, IT'S THE LAST PLACE I WANT TO BE, AND YET, NONETHELESS, HERE I AM.
VRMMMMM
BUT I DID WANT TO AT LEAST CHECK IN BEFORE YOU GOT STARTED, NOT LEAST TO WELCOME ANOTHER HERO TO OUR HEALING PLANET.
BUT BEYOND THAT TO GIVE YOU MY OWN PERSONAL OPINION ON YOUR INVESTIGATION. FOR WHAT THAT'S WORTH.
I REALIZE ADAM IS MY SON-IN-LAW SO I'M FAR FROM UNBIASED, BUT I ALSO HAVE SOMEWHAT OF A REPUTATION AS AN HONEST LEADER HERE.
SO, BY RANN, THERE'S SOME BALANCE THERE.
VRMMMMM
NOW, LET ME SAY THAT I WAS THERE, I SAW ADAM IN ACTION A DOZEN TIMES, AND HE, WITHOUT EXCEPTION, PERFORMED HONORABLY AND NOBLY.
WE COULD NOT HAVE WON THE WAR WITHOUT HIS LEADERSHIP AND GUIDANCE.
HE IS, IN MY HUMBLE OPINION, THE GREATEST MAN I'VE EVER MET. I AM PROUD TO CALL HIM A FRIEND.
AND I ASSURE YOU THAT THIS OPINION WILL SOON BE YOURS, CONFIRMED BY YOUR RESEARCH HERE IN OUR PROUD, RECOVERING HOME.
VRMMMMM

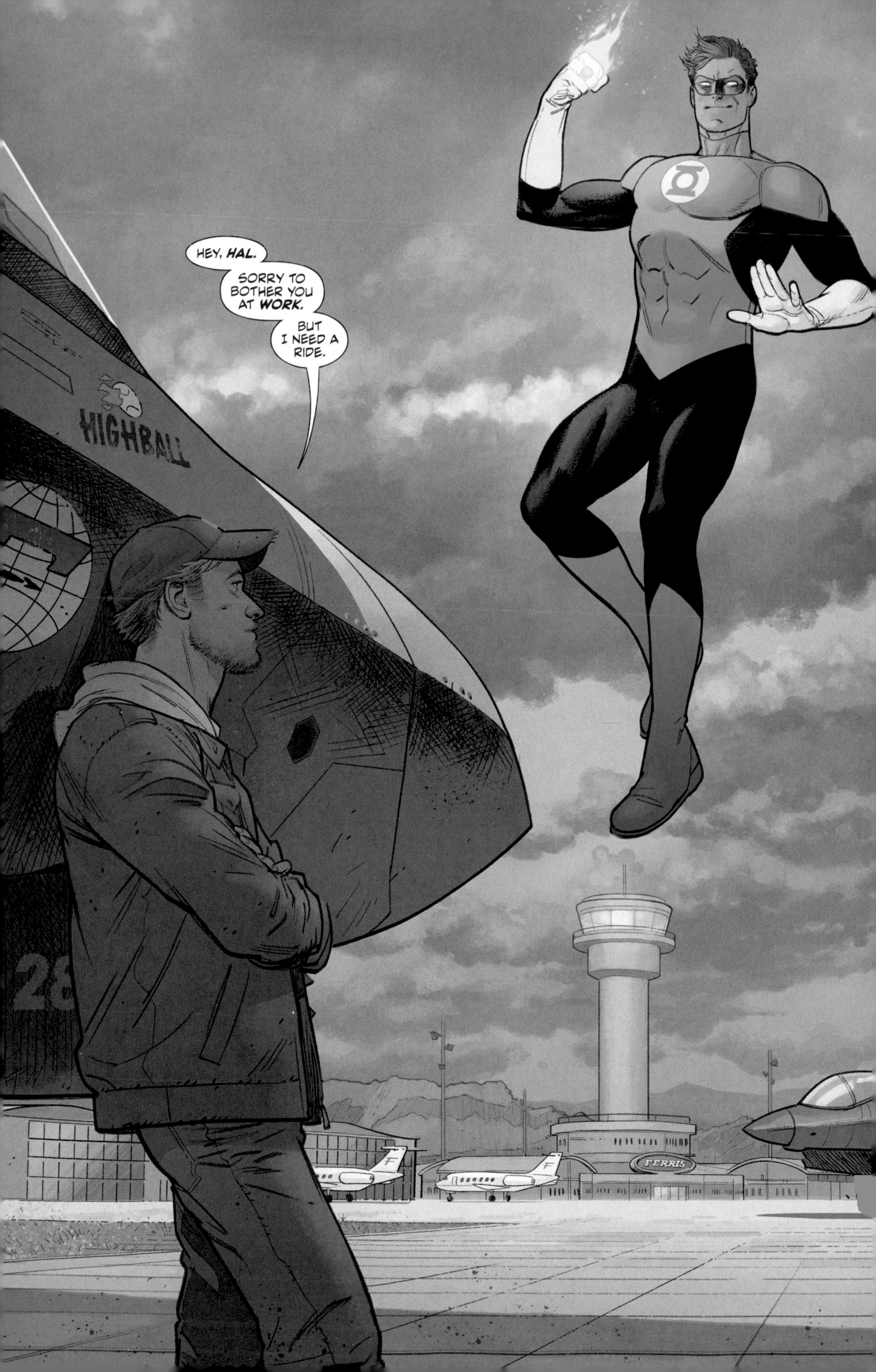
HEY, **HAL.**
SORRY TO BOTHER YOU AT **WORK.**
BUT I NEED A RIDE.
HIGHBALL
FERRIS

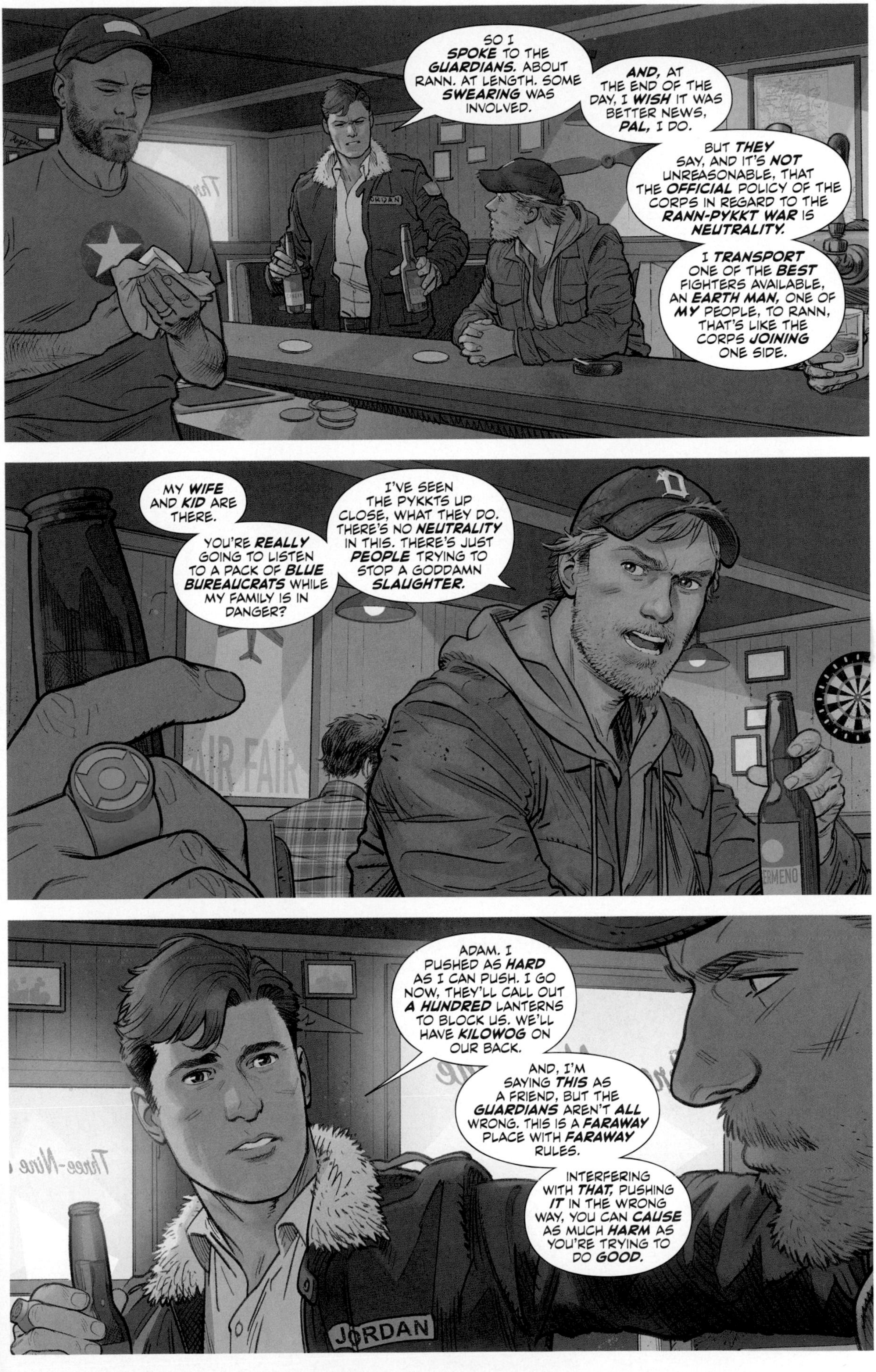

SO I SPOKE TO THE GUARDIANS. ABOUT RANN. AT LENGTH. SOME SWEARING WAS INVOLVED.
AND, AT THE END OF THE DAY, I WISH IT WAS BETTER NEWS, PAL, I DO.
BUT THEY SAY, AND IT'S NOT UNREASONABLE, THAT THE OFFICIAL POLICY OF THE CORPS IN REGARD TO THE RANN-PYKKT WAR IS NEUTRALITY.
I TRANSPORT ONE OF THE BEST FIGHTERS AVAILABLE, AN EARTH MAN, ONE OF MY PEOPLE, TO RANN, THAT'S LIKE THE CORPS JOINING ONE SIDE.
MY WIFE AND KID ARE THERE.
YOU'RE REALLY GOING TO LISTEN TO A PACK OF BLUE BUREAUCRATS WHILE MY FAMILY IS IN DANGER?
I'VE SEEN THE PYKKTS UP CLOSE, WHAT THEY DO. THERE'S NO NEUTRALITY IN THIS. THERE'S JUST PEOPLE TRYING TO STOP A GODDAMN SLAUGHTER.
AIR FAIR
ADAM. I PUSHED AS HARD AS I CAN PUSH. I GO NOW, THEY'LL CALL OUT A HUNDRED LANTERNS TO BLOCK US. WE'LL HAVE KILOWOG ON OUR BACK.
AND, I'M SAYING THIS AS A FRIEND, BUT THE GUARDIANS AREN'T ALL WRONG. THIS IS A FARAWAY PLACE WITH FARAWAY RULES.
INTERFERING WITH THAT, PUSHING IT IN THE WRONG WAY, YOU CAN CAUSE AS MUCH HARM AS YOU'RE TRYING TO DO GOOD.
JORDAN

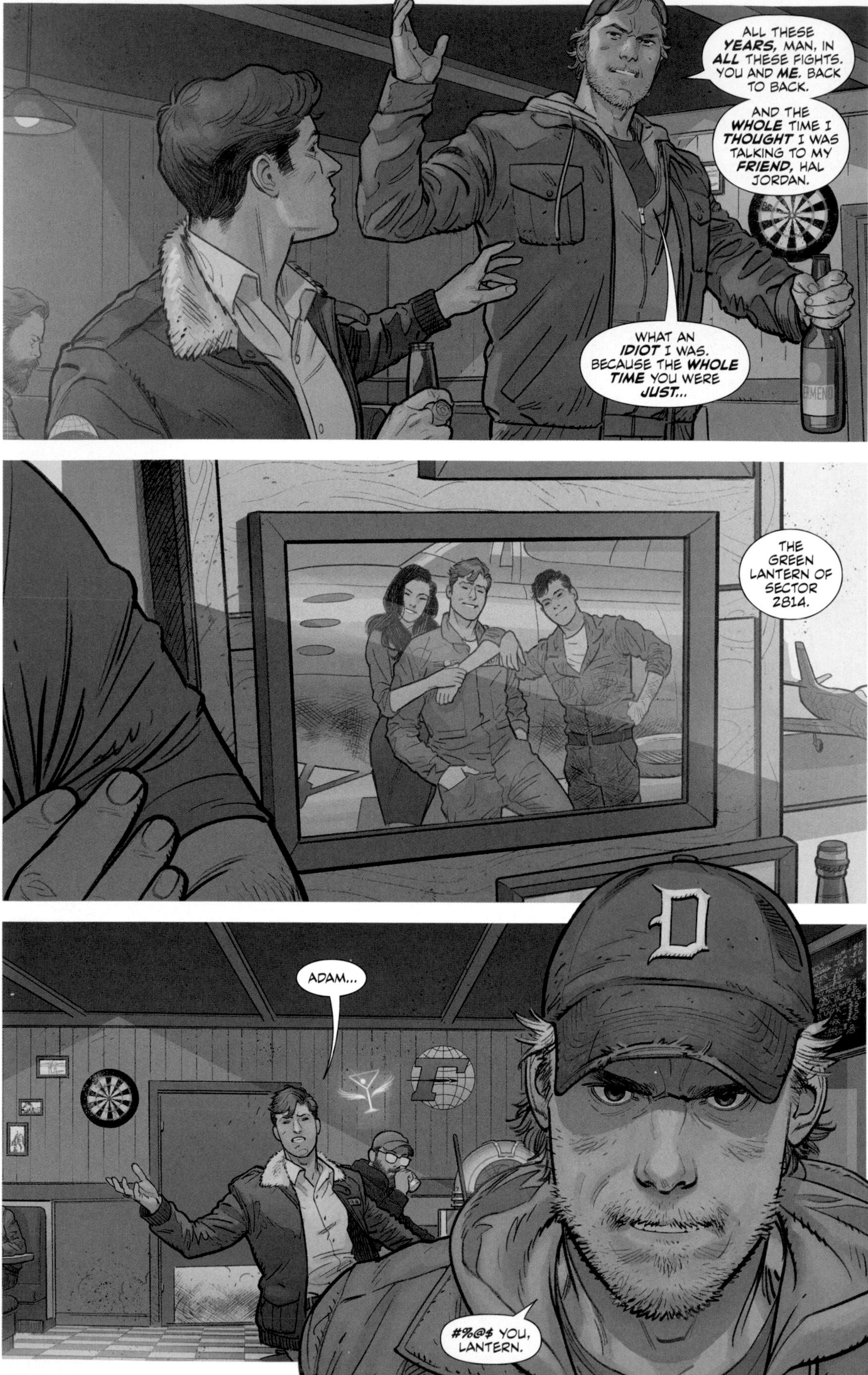

ALL THESE *YEARS*, MAN, IN *ALL* THESE FIGHTS. YOU AND *ME*. BACK TO BACK.
AND THE *WHOLE* TIME I *THOUGHT* I WAS TALKING TO MY *FRIEND*, HAL JORDAN.
WHAT AN *IDIOT* I WAS. BECAUSE THE *WHOLE TIME* YOU WERE *JUST*...
THE GREEN LANTERN OF SECTOR 2814.
ADAM...
#%@$ YOU, LANTERN.

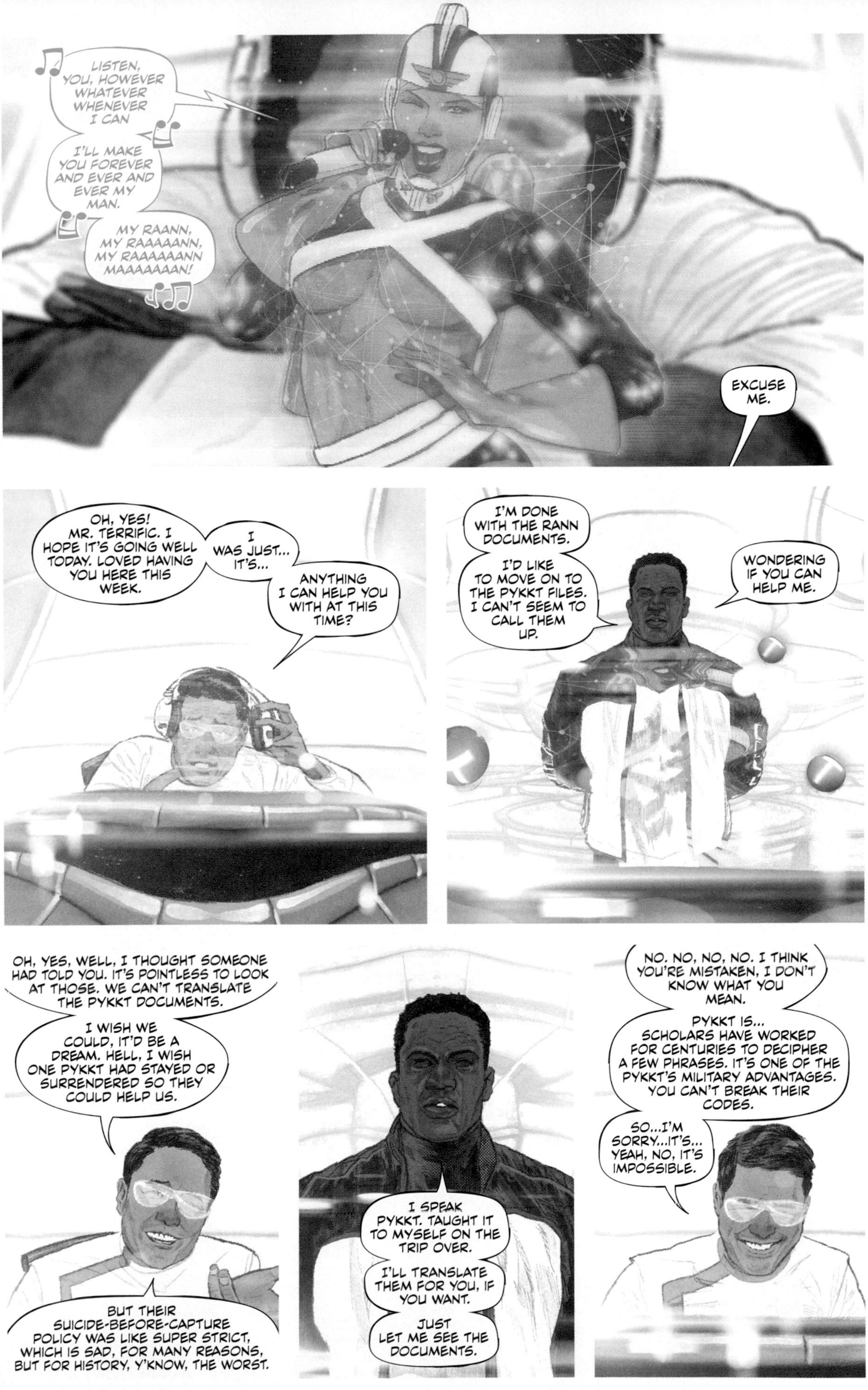
LISTEN, YOU, HOWEVER WHATEVER WHENEVER I CAN
I'LL MAKE YOU FOREVER AND EVER AND EVER MY MAN.
MY RAANN, MY RAAAAANN, MY RAAAAAANN MAAAAAAAN!
EXCUSE ME.
OH, YES! MR. TERRIFIC. I HOPE IT'S GOING WELL TODAY. LOVED HAVING YOU HERE THIS WEEK.
I WAS JUST... IT'S...
ANYTHING I CAN HELP YOU WITH AT THIS TIME?
I'M DONE WITH THE RANN DOCUMENTS.
I'D LIKE TO MOVE ON TO THE PYKKT FILES. I CAN'T SEEM TO CALL THEM UP.
WONDERING IF YOU CAN HELP ME.
OH, YES, WELL, I THOUGHT SOMEONE HAD TOLD YOU. IT'S POINTLESS TO LOOK AT THOSE. WE CAN'T TRANSLATE THE PYKKT DOCUMENTS.
I WISH WE COULD, IT'D BE A DREAM. HELL, I WISH ONE PYKKT HAD STAYED OR SURRENDERED SO THEY COULD HELP US.
BUT THEIR SUICIDE-BEFORE-CAPTURE POLICY WAS LIKE SUPER STRICT, WHICH IS SAD, FOR MANY REASONS, BUT FOR HISTORY, Y'KNOW, THE WORST.
I SPEAK PYKKT. TAUGHT IT TO MYSELF ON THE TRIP OVER.
I'LL TRANSLATE THEM FOR YOU, IF YOU WANT.
JUST LET ME SEE THE DOCUMENTS.
NO. NO, NO, NO. I THINK YOU'RE MISTAKEN, I DON'T KNOW WHAT YOU MEAN.
PYKKT IS... SCHOLARS HAVE WORKED FOR CENTURIES TO DECIPHER A FEW PHRASES. IT'S ONE OF THE PYKKT'S MILITARY ADVANTAGES. YOU CAN'T BREAK THEIR CODES.
SO...I'M SORRY...IT'S... YEAH, NO, IT'S IMPOSSIBLE.

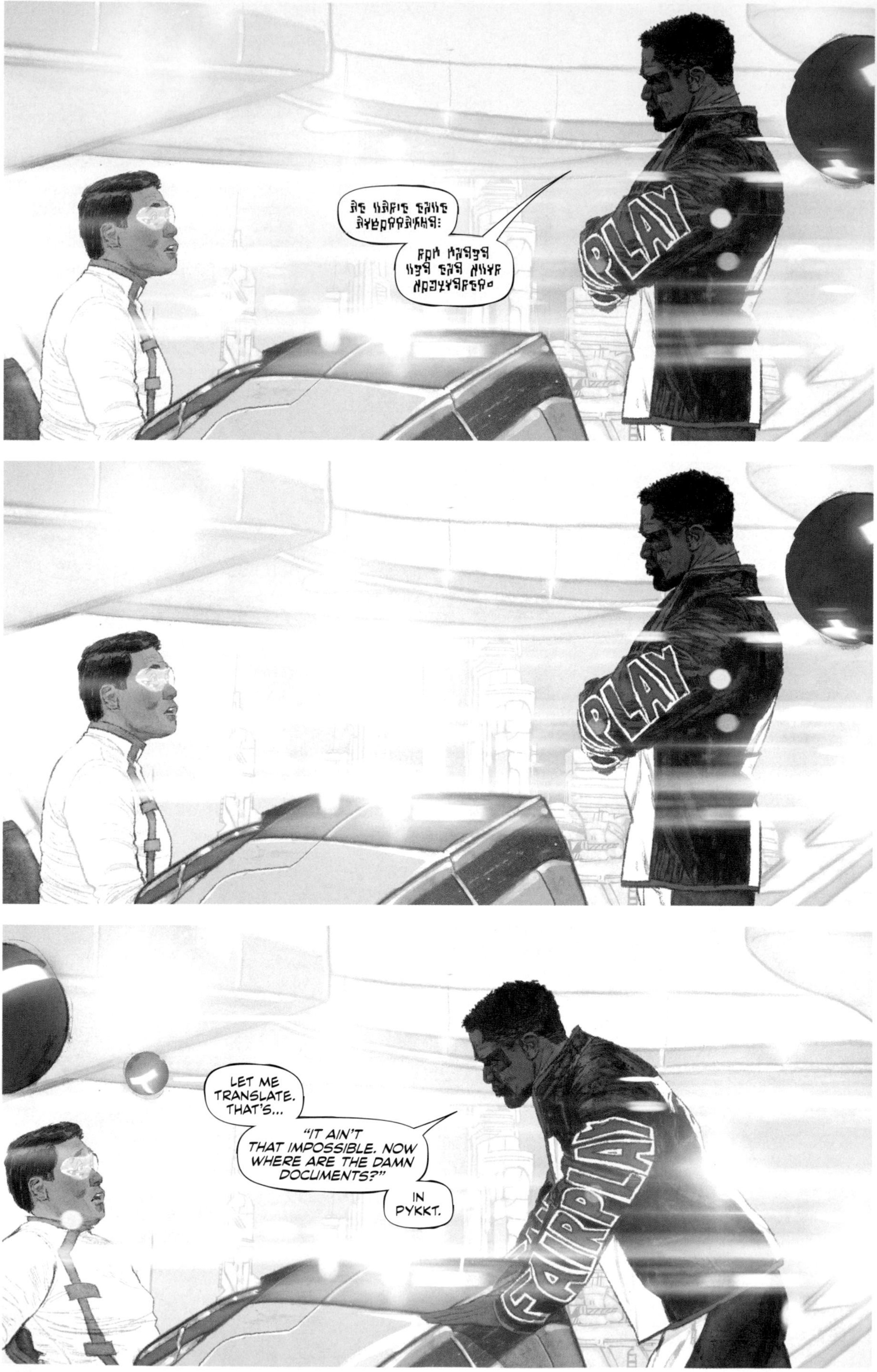
PLAY
PLAY
LET ME TRANSLATE. THAT'S...
"IT AIN'T THAT IMPOSSIBLE. NOW WHERE ARE THE DAMN DOCUMENTS?"
IN PYKKT.
FAIRPLAY

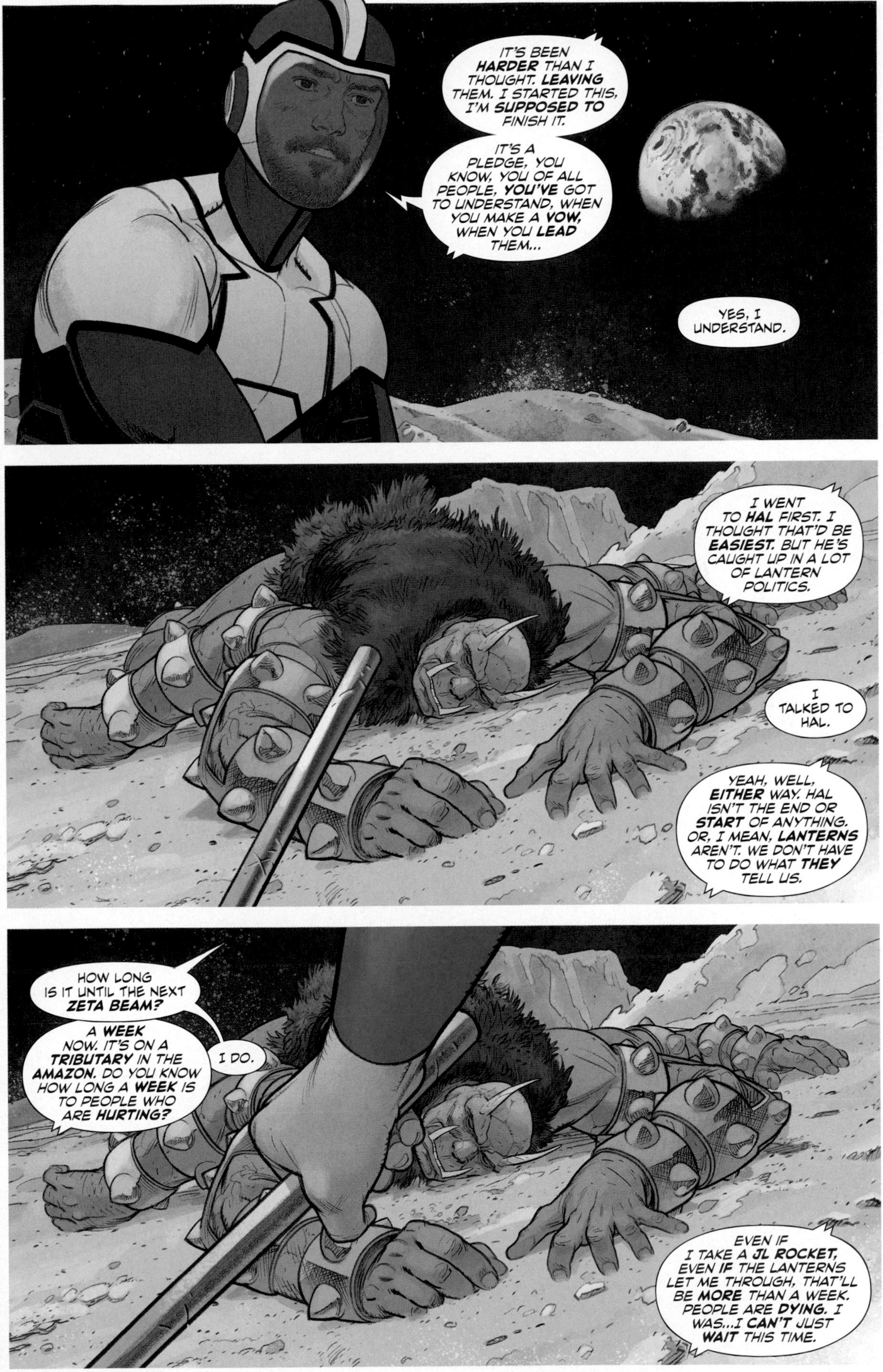
IT'S BEEN HARDER THAN I THOUGHT. LEAVING THEM. I STARTED THIS, I'M SUPPOSED TO FINISH IT.
IT'S A PLEDGE, YOU KNOW, YOU OF ALL PEOPLE, YOU'VE GOT TO UNDERSTAND, WHEN YOU MAKE A VOW, WHEN YOU LEAD THEM...
YES, I UNDERSTAND.
I WENT TO HAL FIRST. I THOUGHT THAT'D BE EASIEST. BUT HE'S CAUGHT UP IN A LOT OF LANTERN POLITICS.
I TALKED TO HAL.
YEAH, WELL, EITHER WAY. HAL ISN'T THE END OR START OF ANYTHING. OR, I MEAN, LANTERNS AREN'T. WE DON'T HAVE TO DO WHAT THEY TELL US.
HOW LONG IS IT UNTIL THE NEXT ZETA BEAM?
A WEEK NOW. IT'S ON A TRIBUTARY IN THE AMAZON. DO YOU KNOW HOW LONG A WEEK IS TO PEOPLE WHO ARE HURTING?
I DO.
EVEN IF I TAKE A JL ROCKET, EVEN IF THE LANTERNS LET ME THROUGH, THAT'LL BE MORE THAN A WEEK. PEOPLE ARE DYING. I WAS...I CAN'T JUST WAIT THIS TIME.

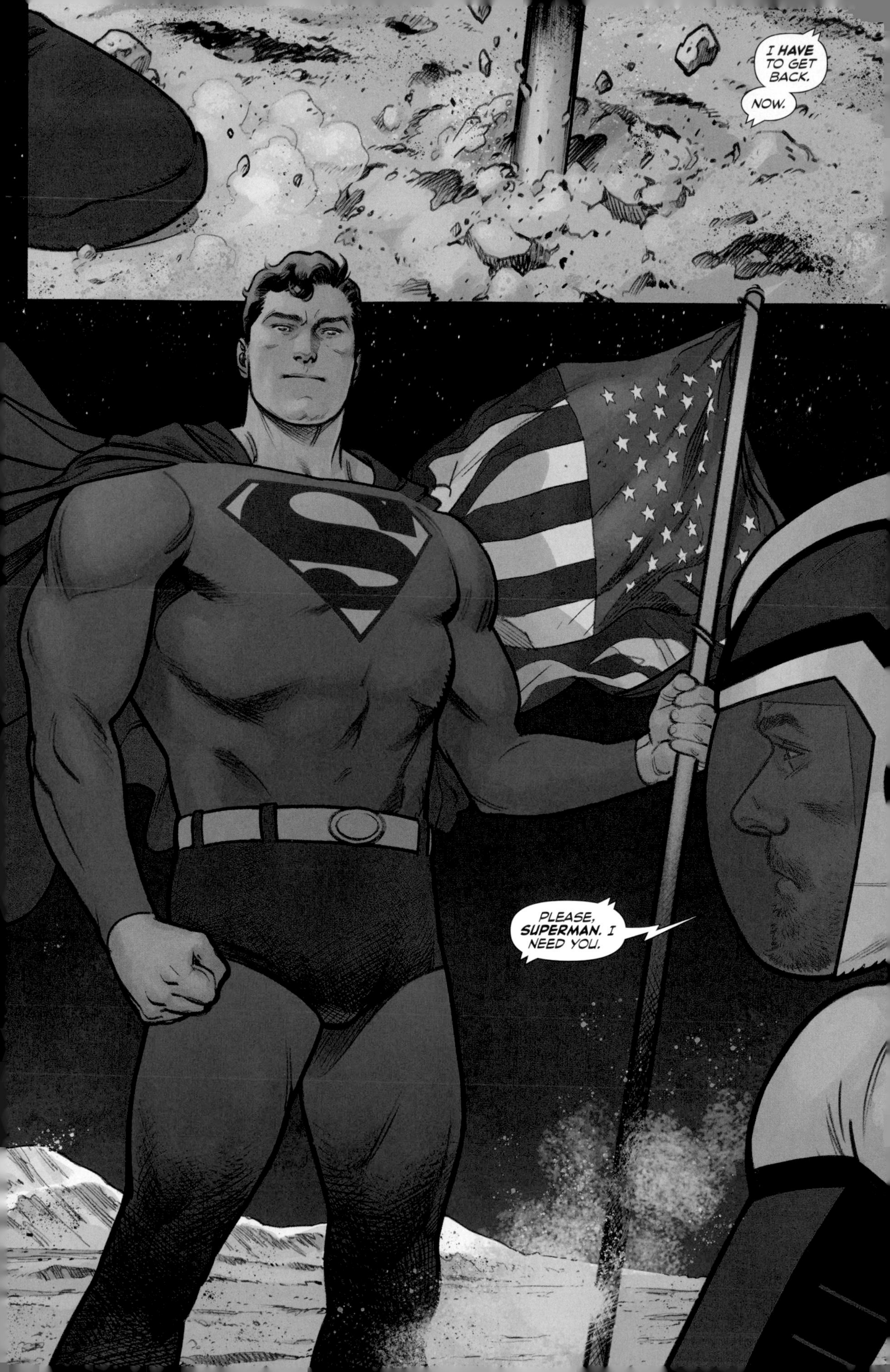

I HAVE TO GET BACK.
NOW.
PLEASE, SUPERMAN. I NEED YOU.

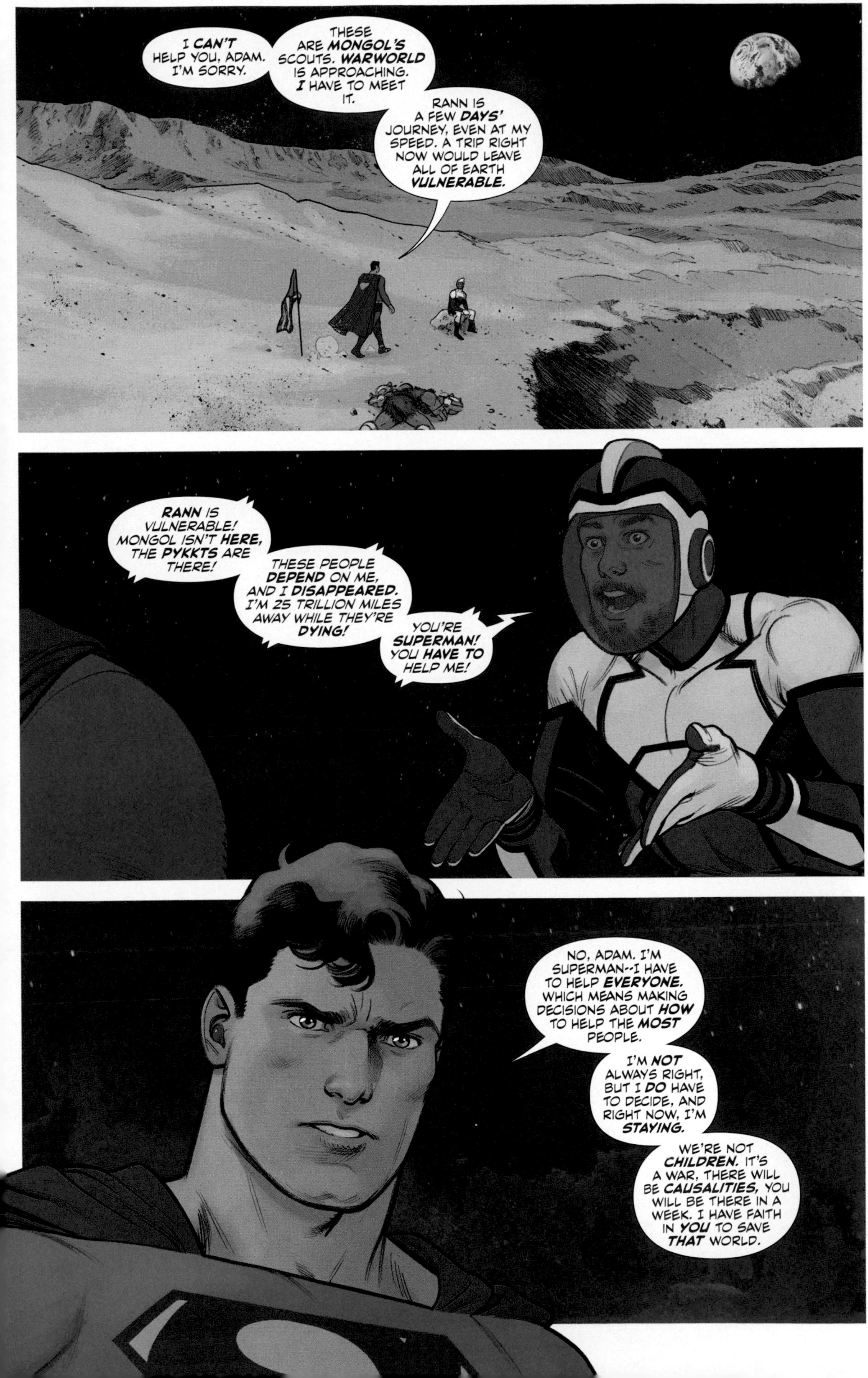
I CAN'T HELP YOU, ADAM. I'M SORRY.
THESE ARE MONGOL'S SCOUTS. WARWORLD IS APPROACHING. I HAVE TO MEET IT.
RANN IS A FEW DAYS' JOURNEY, EVEN AT MY SPEED. A TRIP RIGHT NOW WOULD LEAVE ALL OF EARTH VULNERABLE.
RANN IS VULNERABLE! MONGOL ISN'T HERE, THE PYKKTS ARE THERE!
THESE PEOPLE DEPEND ON ME, AND I DISAPPEARED. I'M 25 TRILLION MILES AWAY WHILE THEY'RE DYING!
YOU'RE SUPERMAN! YOU HAVE TO HELP ME!
NO, ADAM. I'M SUPERMAN--I HAVE TO HELP EVERYONE. WHICH MEANS MAKING DECISIONS ABOUT HOW TO HELP THE MOST PEOPLE.
I'M NOT ALWAYS RIGHT, BUT I DO HAVE TO DECIDE, AND RIGHT NOW, I'M STAYING.
WE'RE NOT CHILDREN. IT'S A WAR, THERE WILL BE CAUSALITIES, YOU WILL BE THERE IN A WEEK. I HAVE FAITH IN YOU TO SAVE THAT WORLD.

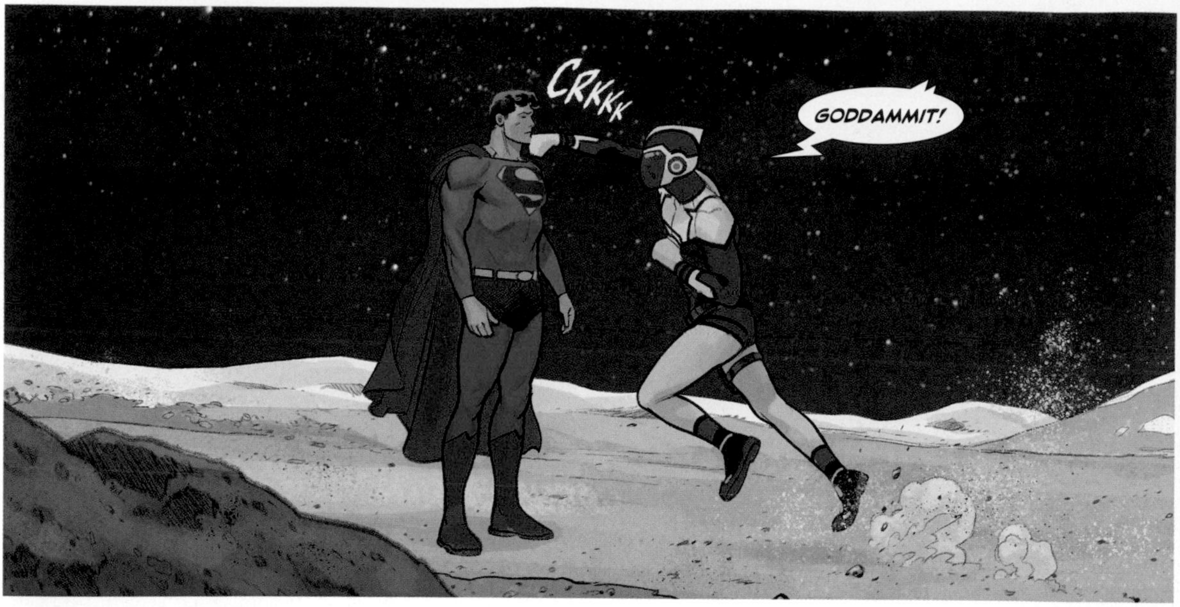
CRKKK
GODDAMMIT!

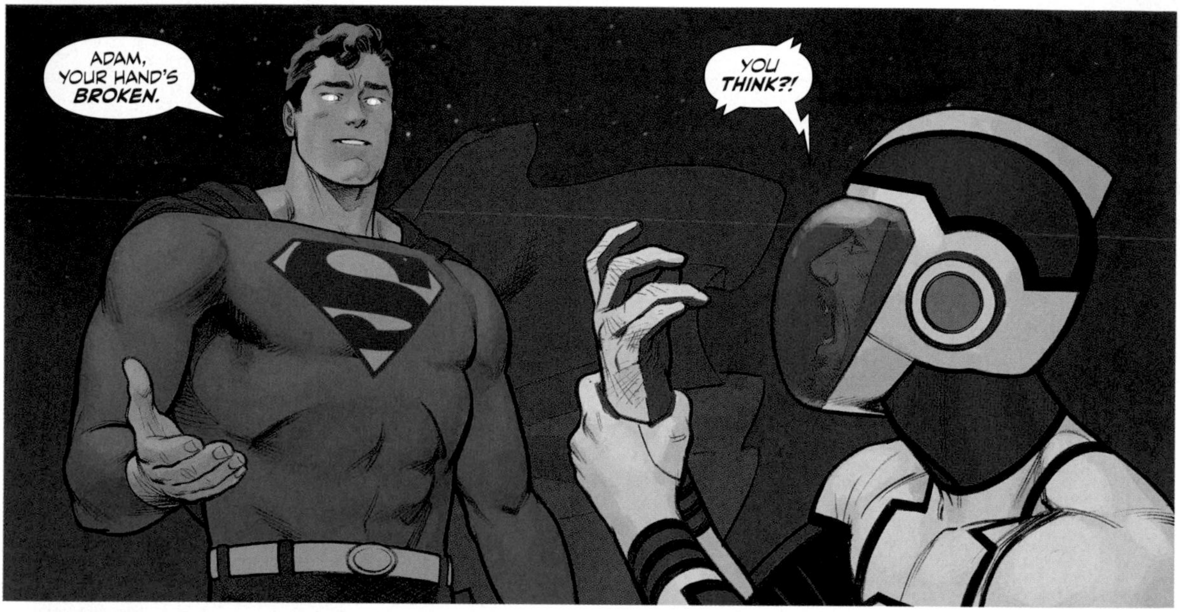
ADAM, YOUR HAND'S BROKEN.
YOU THINK?!

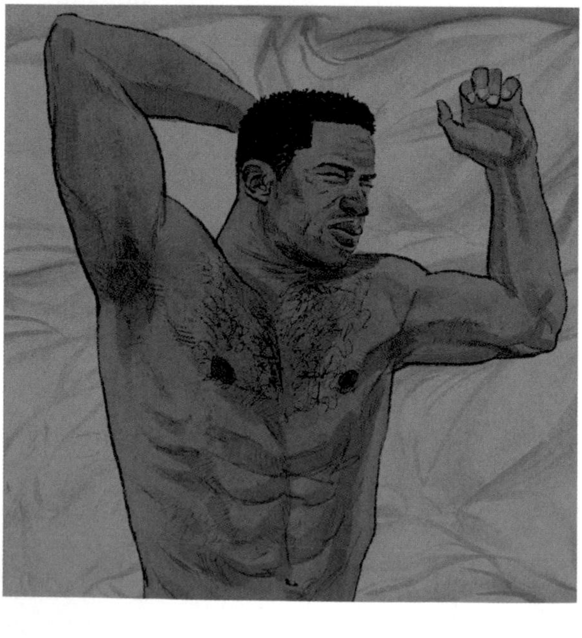

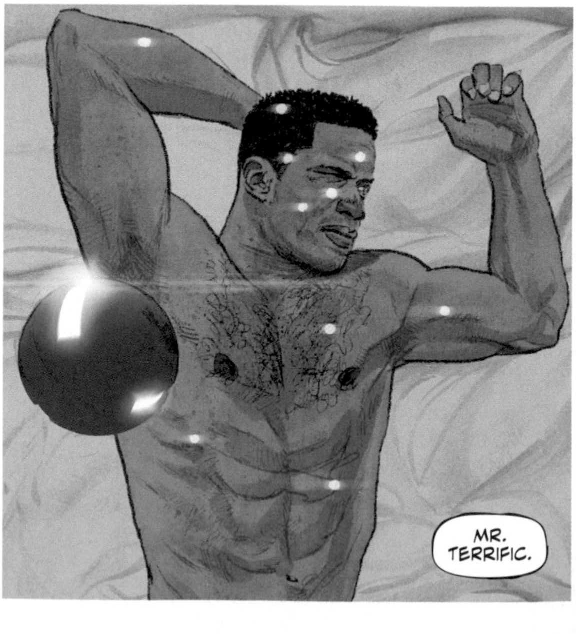
MR. TERRIFIC.

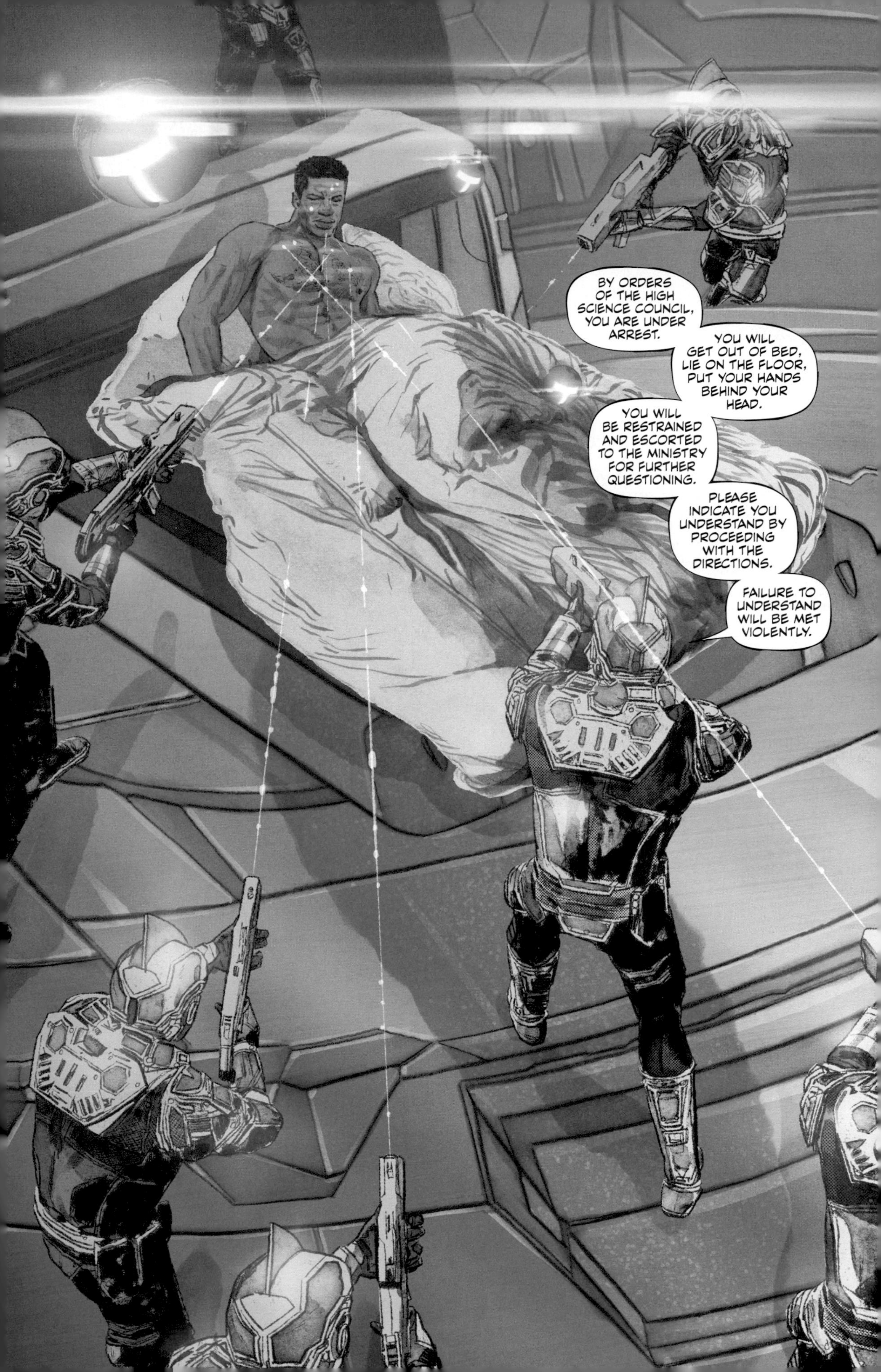
BY ORDERS OF THE HIGH SCIENCE COUNCIL, YOU ARE UNDER ARREST.
YOU WILL GET OUT OF BED, LIE ON THE FLOOR, PUT YOUR HANDS BEHIND YOUR HEAD.
YOU WILL BE RESTRAINED AND ESCORTED TO THE MINISTRY FOR FURTHER QUESTIONING.
PLEASE INDICATE YOU UNDERSTAND BY PROCEEDING WITH THE DIRECTIONS.
FAILURE TO UNDERSTAND WILL BE MET VIOLENTLY.

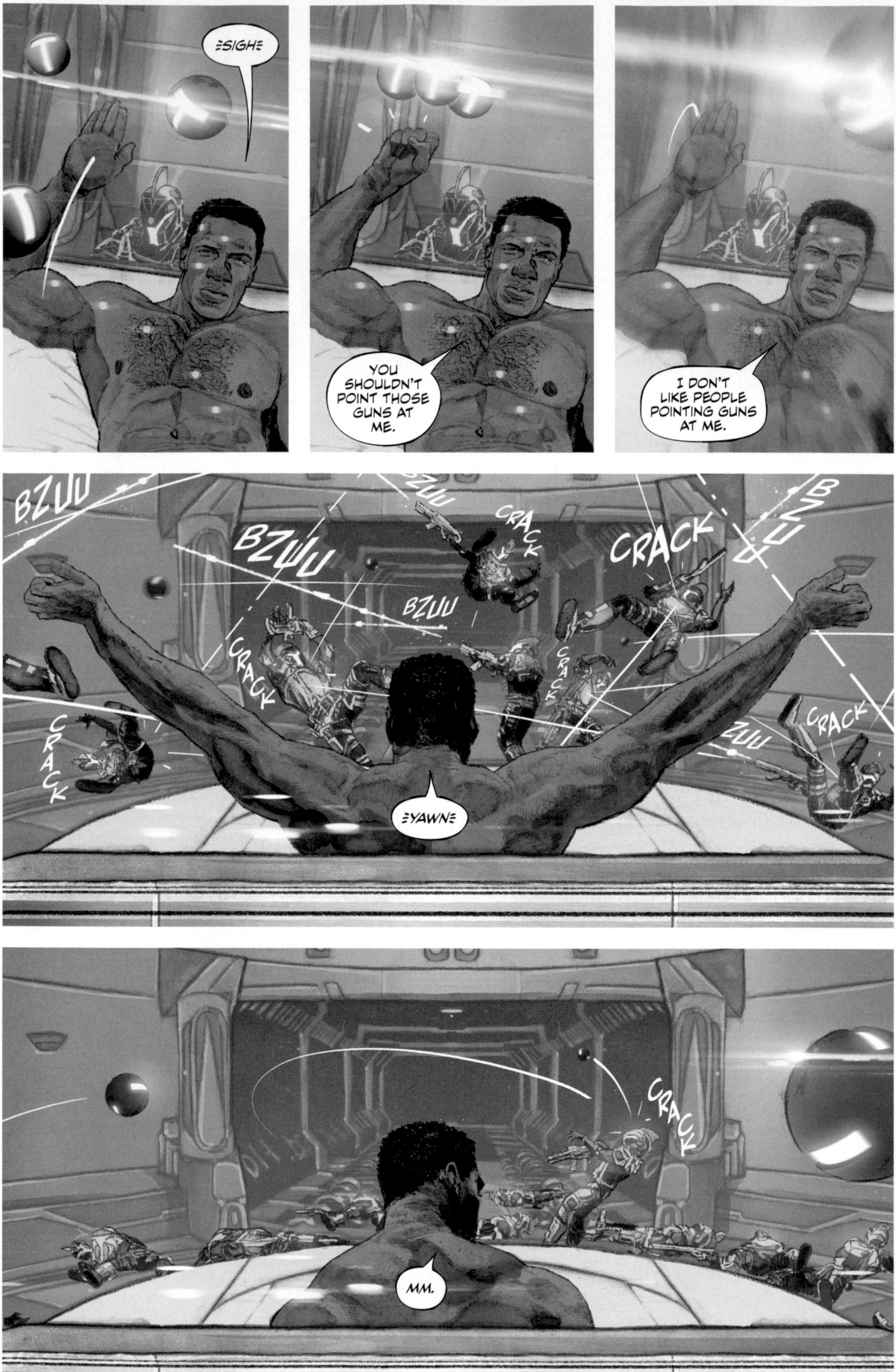
SIGH
YOU SHOULDN'T POINT THOSE GUNS AT ME.
I DON'T LIKE PEOPLE POINTING GUNS AT ME.
BZUU
BZUU
CRACK
BZUU
CRACK
BZUU
CRACK
CRACK
CRACK
BZUU
CRACK
CRACK
ZUU
YAWN
CRACK
MM.

GUH

LISTEN, YOU...

HOWEVER WHATEVER WHENEVER I CAN.

I'LL MAKE YOU FOREVER AND EVER AND EVER MY MAN.

YEAH, FOREVER AND EVER AND EVER MY MAN.

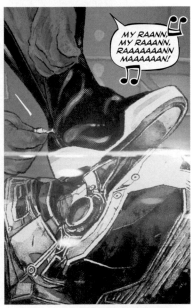

MY RAANN, MY RAANN, RAAAAAAANN MAAAAAAN!

THIS IS A %@%@ED-UP PLANET.

BUT THAT SONG IS FIRE.

FOREVER AND EVER AND EVER MY MAN...

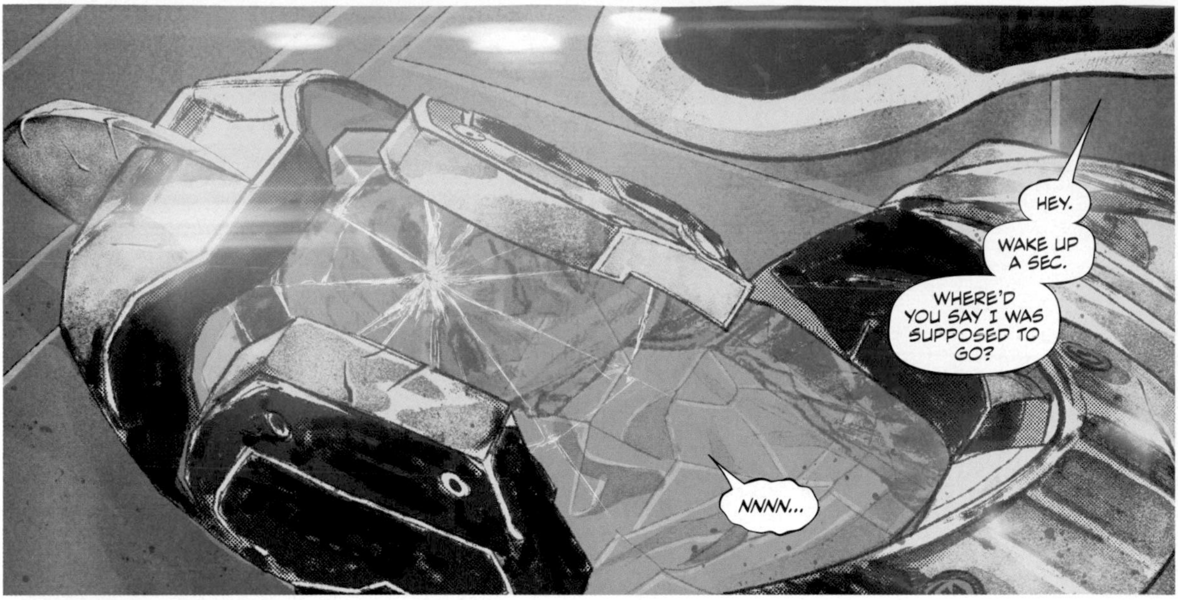
HEY.
WAKE UP A SEC.
WHERE'D YOU SAY I WAS SUPPOSED TO GO?
NNNN...
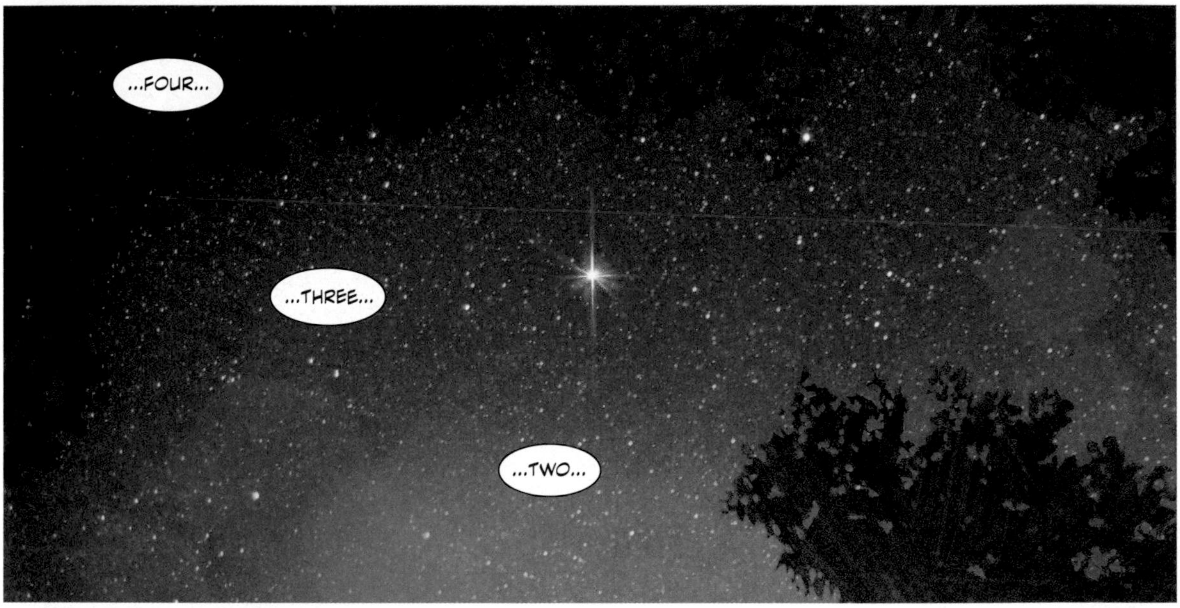
...FOUR...
...THREE...
...TWO...
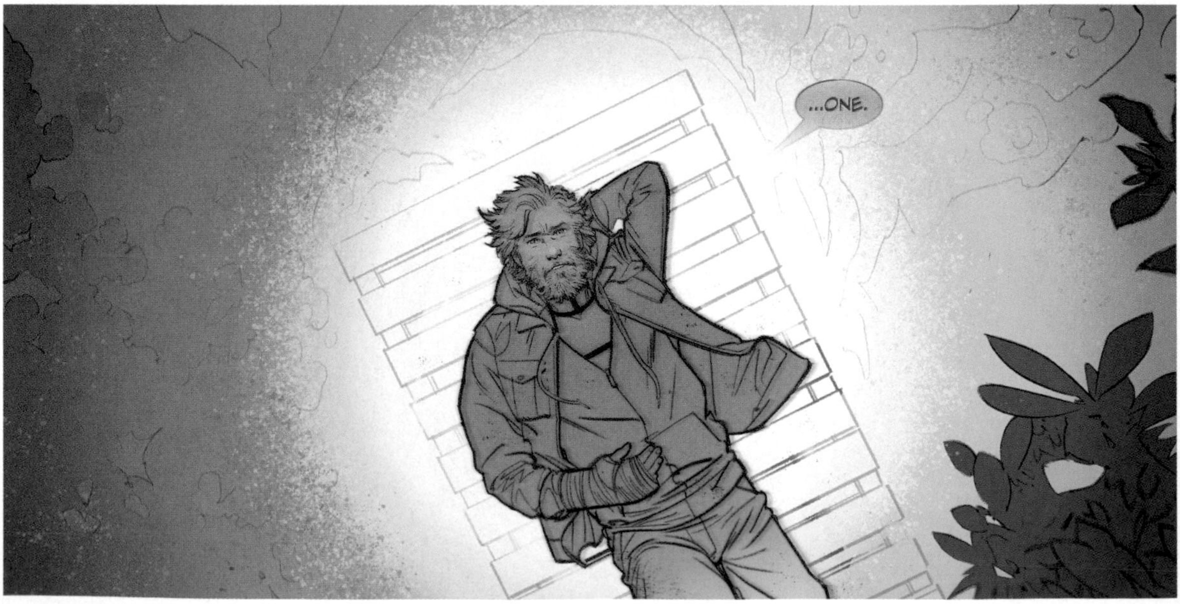
...ONE.

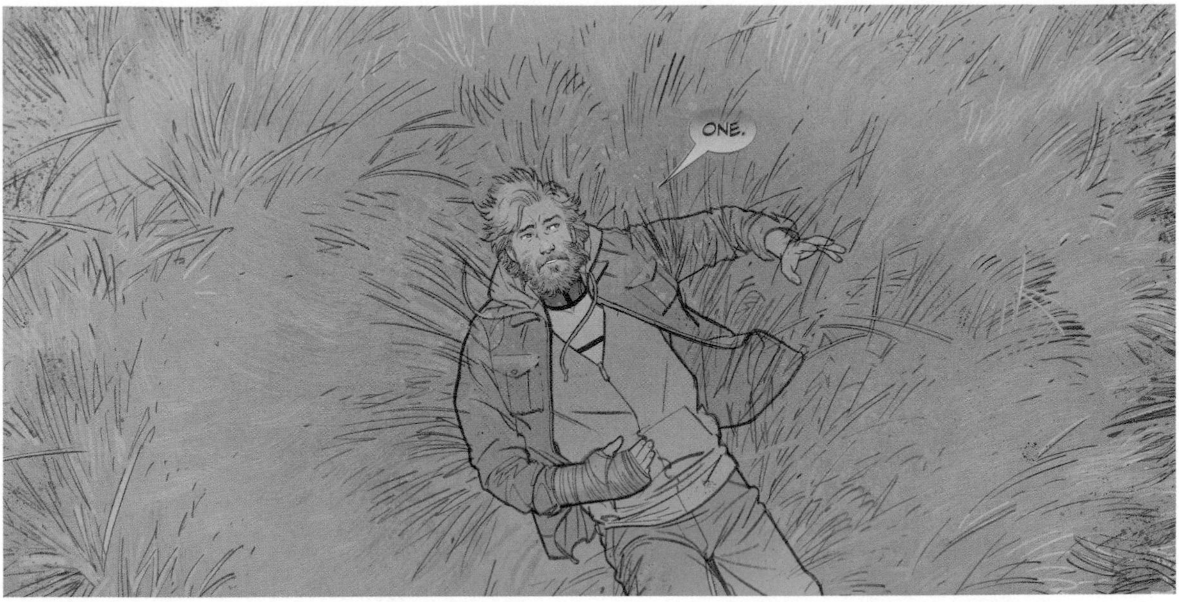
ONE.

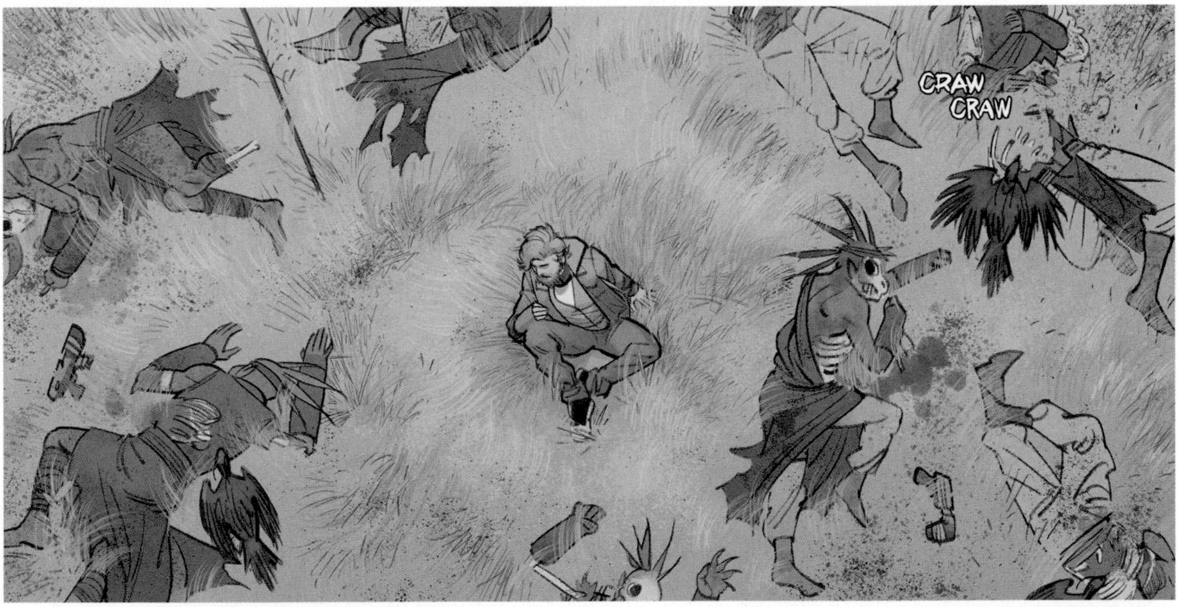
CRAW
CRAW

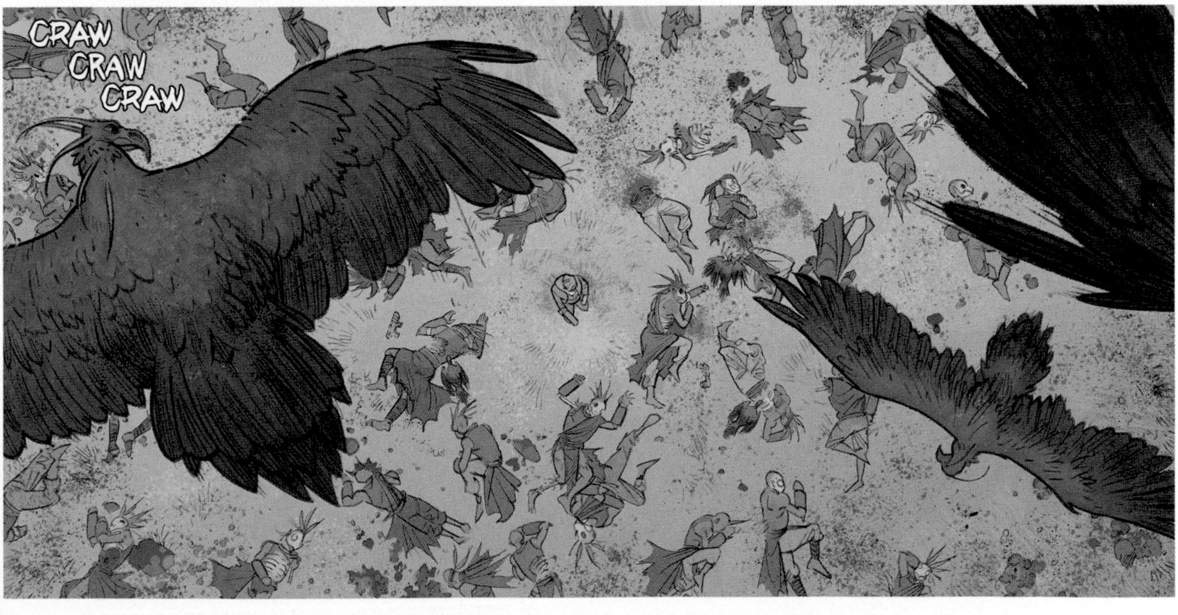
CRAW
CRAW
CRAW

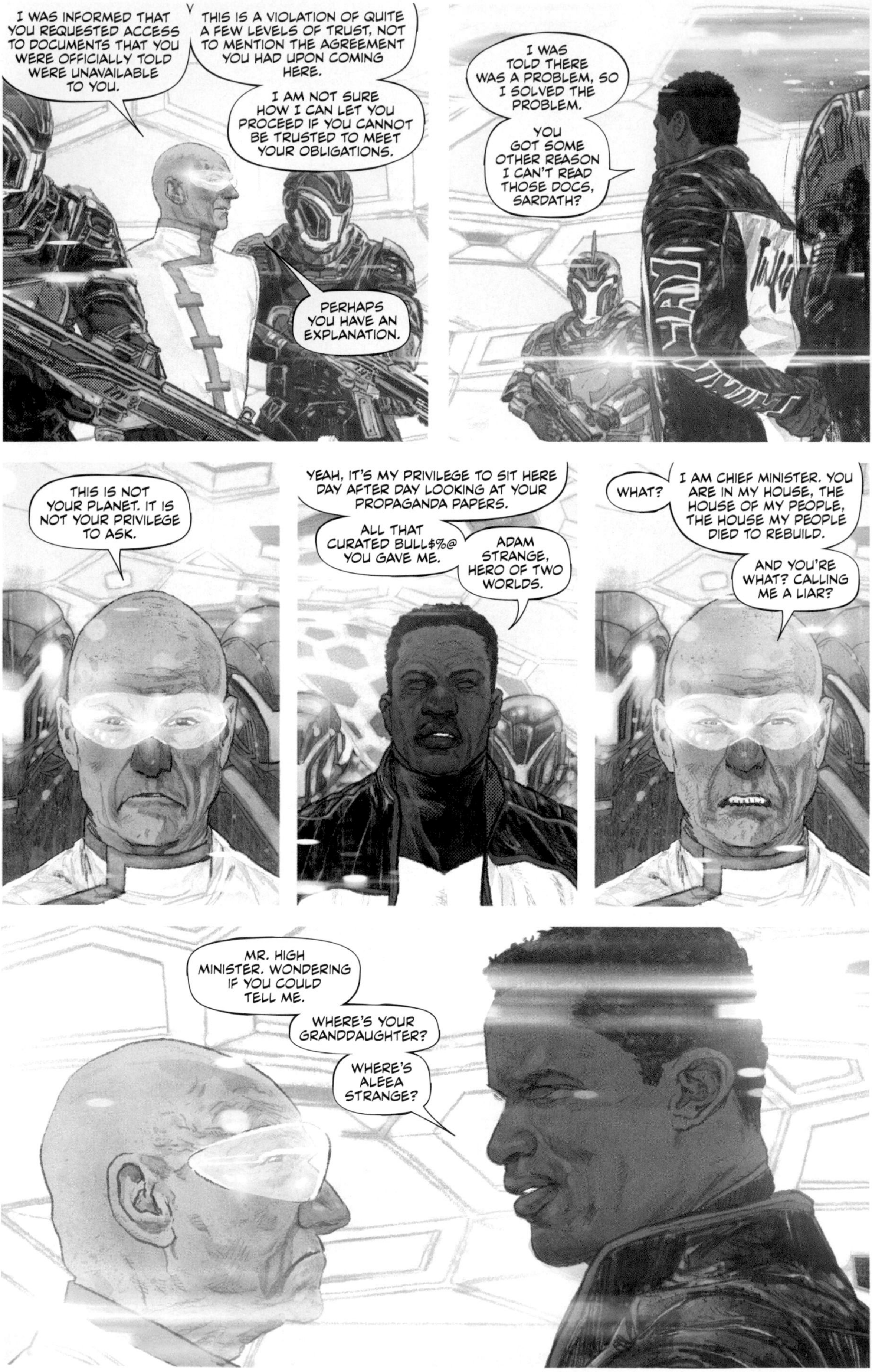

I WAS INFORMED THAT YOU REQUESTED ACCESS TO DOCUMENTS THAT YOU WERE OFFICIALLY TOLD WERE UNAVAILABLE TO YOU.
THIS IS A VIOLATION OF QUITE A FEW LEVELS OF TRUST, NOT TO MENTION THE AGREEMENT YOU HAD UPON COMING HERE.
I AM NOT SURE HOW I CAN LET YOU PROCEED IF YOU CANNOT BE TRUSTED TO MEET YOUR OBLIGATIONS.
PERHAPS YOU HAVE AN EXPLANATION.
I WAS TOLD THERE WAS A PROBLEM, SO I SOLVED THE PROBLEM.
YOU GOT SOME OTHER REASON I CAN'T READ THOSE DOCS, SARDATH?
THIS IS NOT YOUR PLANET. IT IS NOT YOUR PRIVILEGE TO ASK.
YEAH, IT'S MY PRIVILEGE TO SIT HERE DAY AFTER DAY LOOKING AT YOUR PROPAGANDA PAPERS.
ALL THAT CURATED BULL$%@ YOU GAVE ME.
ADAM STRANGE, HERO OF TWO WORLDS.
WHAT?
I AM CHIEF MINISTER. YOU ARE IN MY HOUSE, THE HOUSE OF MY PEOPLE, THE HOUSE MY PEOPLE DIED TO REBUILD.
AND YOU'RE WHAT? CALLING ME A LIAR?
MR. HIGH MINISTER. WONDERING IF YOU COULD TELL ME.
WHERE'S YOUR GRANDDAUGHTER?
WHERE'S ALEEA STRANGE?

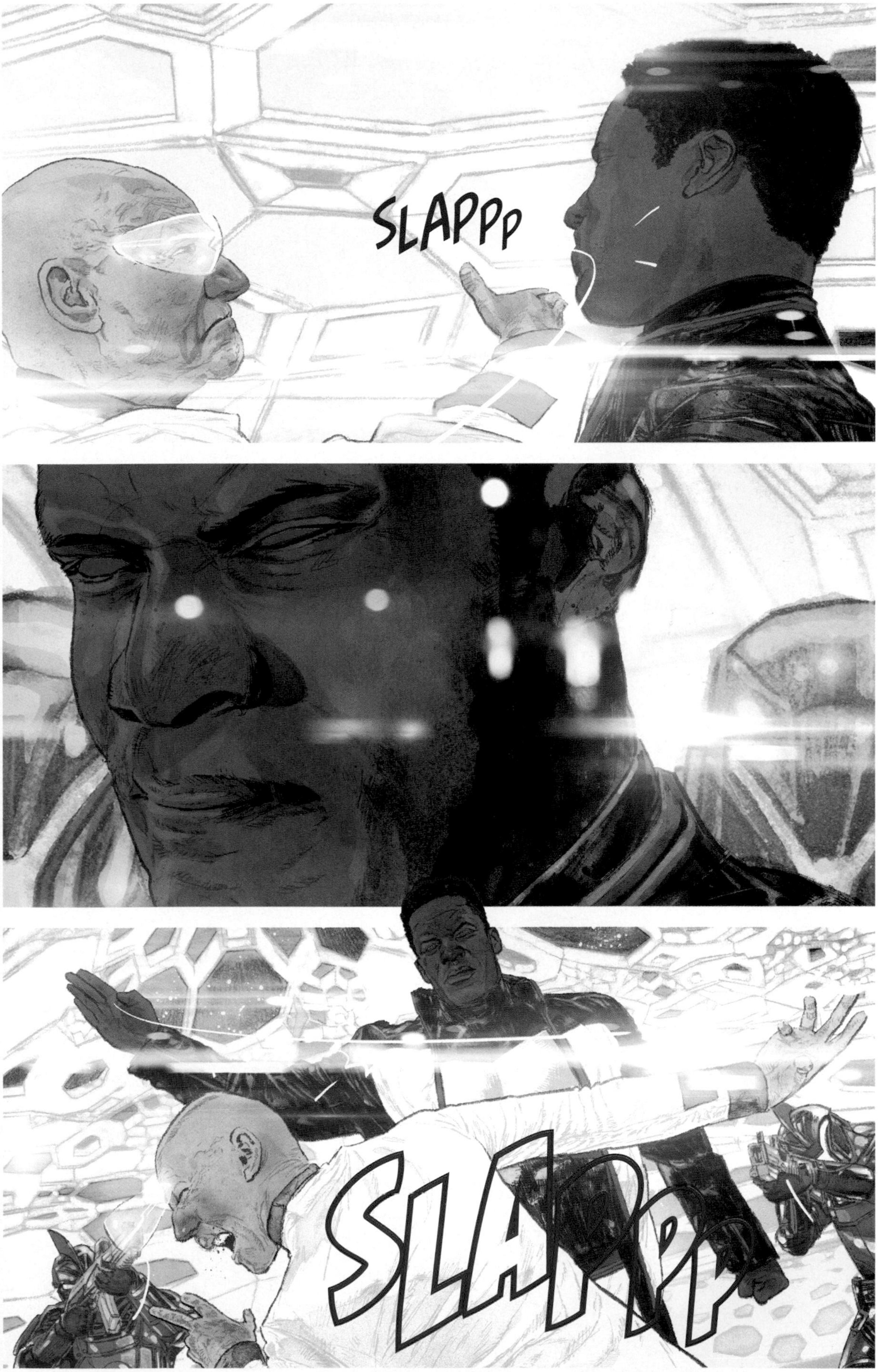
SLAPPP
SLAPPP

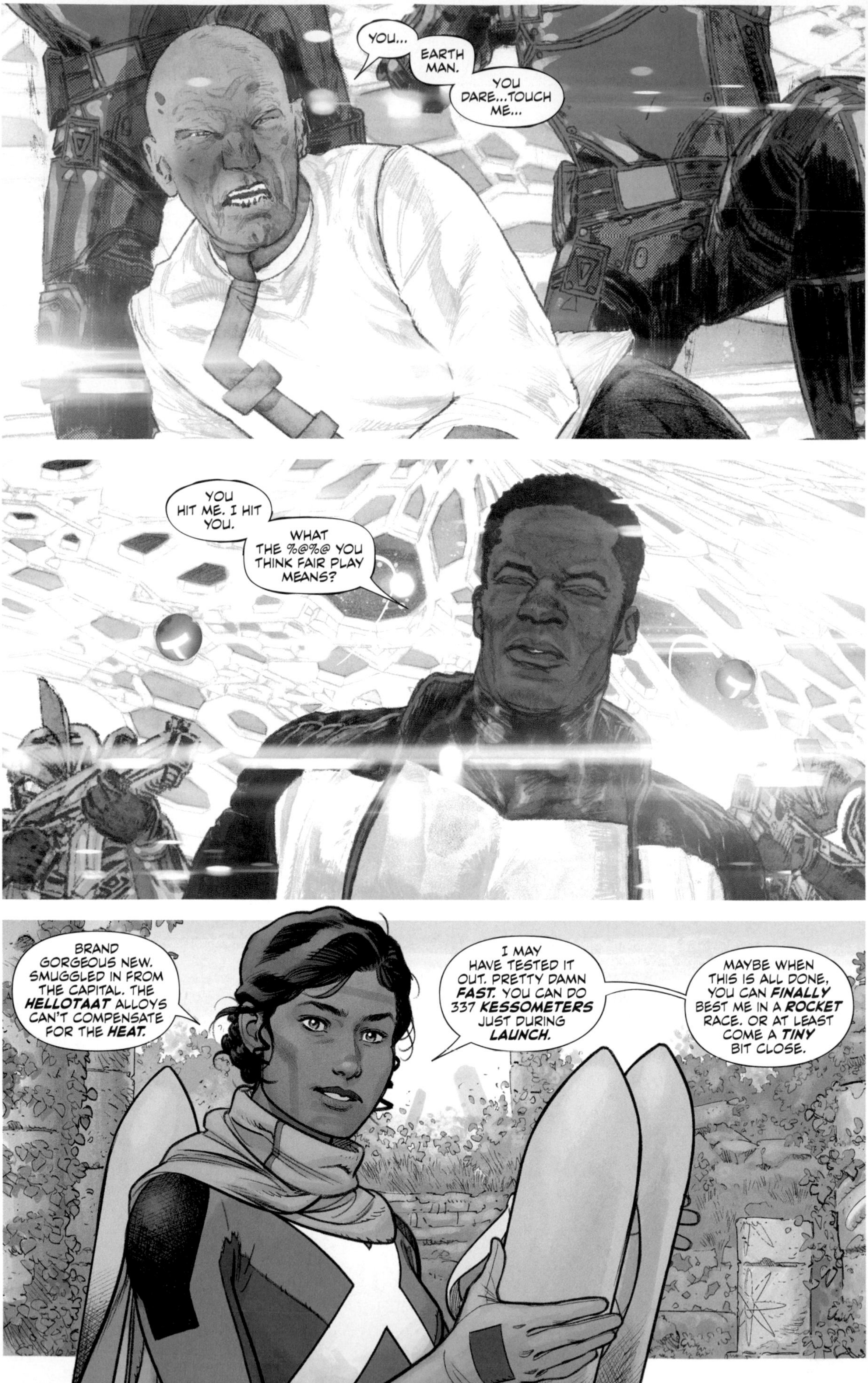
YOU... EARTH MAN.
YOU DARE...TOUCH ME...
YOU HIT ME. I HIT YOU.
WHAT THE %@%@ YOU THINK FAIR PLAY MEANS?
BRAND GORGEOUS NEW. SMUGGLED IN FROM THE CAPITAL. THE HELLOTAAT ALLOYS CAN'T COMPENSATE FOR THE HEAT.
I MAY HAVE TESTED IT OUT. PRETTY DAMN FAST. YOU CAN DO 337 KESSOMETERS JUST DURING LAUNCH.
MAYBE WHEN THIS IS ALL DONE, YOU CAN FINALLY BEST ME IN A ROCKET RACE. OR AT LEAST COME A TINY BIT CLOSE.

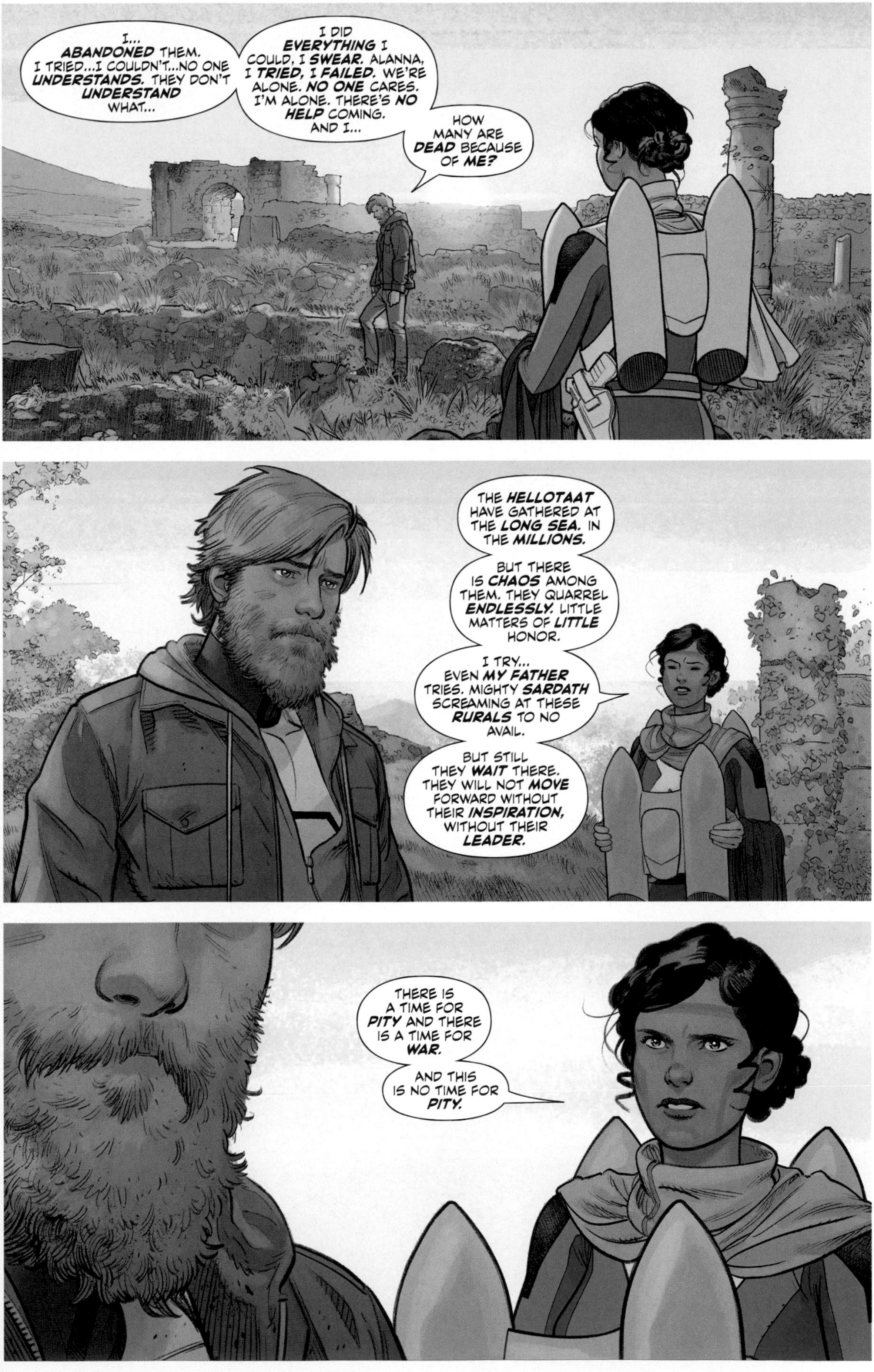
I... ABANDONED THEM. I TRIED...I COULDN'T...NO ONE UNDERSTANDS. THEY DON'T UNDERSTAND WHAT...
I DID EVERYTHING I COULD, I SWEAR. ALANNA, I TRIED, I FAILED. WE'RE ALONE. NO ONE CARES. I'M ALONE. THERE'S NO HELP COMING. AND I...
HOW MANY ARE DEAD BECAUSE OF ME?
THE HELLOTAAT HAVE GATHERED AT THE LONG SEA. IN THE MILLIONS.
BUT THERE IS CHAOS AMONG THEM. THEY QUARREL ENDLESSLY. LITTLE MATTERS OF LITTLE HONOR.
I TRY... EVEN MY FATHER TRIES. MIGHTY SARDATH SCREAMING AT THESE RURALS TO NO AVAIL.
BUT STILL THEY WAIT THERE. THEY WILL NOT MOVE FORWARD WITHOUT THEIR INSPIRATION, WITHOUT THEIR LEADER.
THERE IS A TIME FOR PITY AND THERE IS A TIME FOR WAR.
AND THIS IS NO TIME FOR PITY.

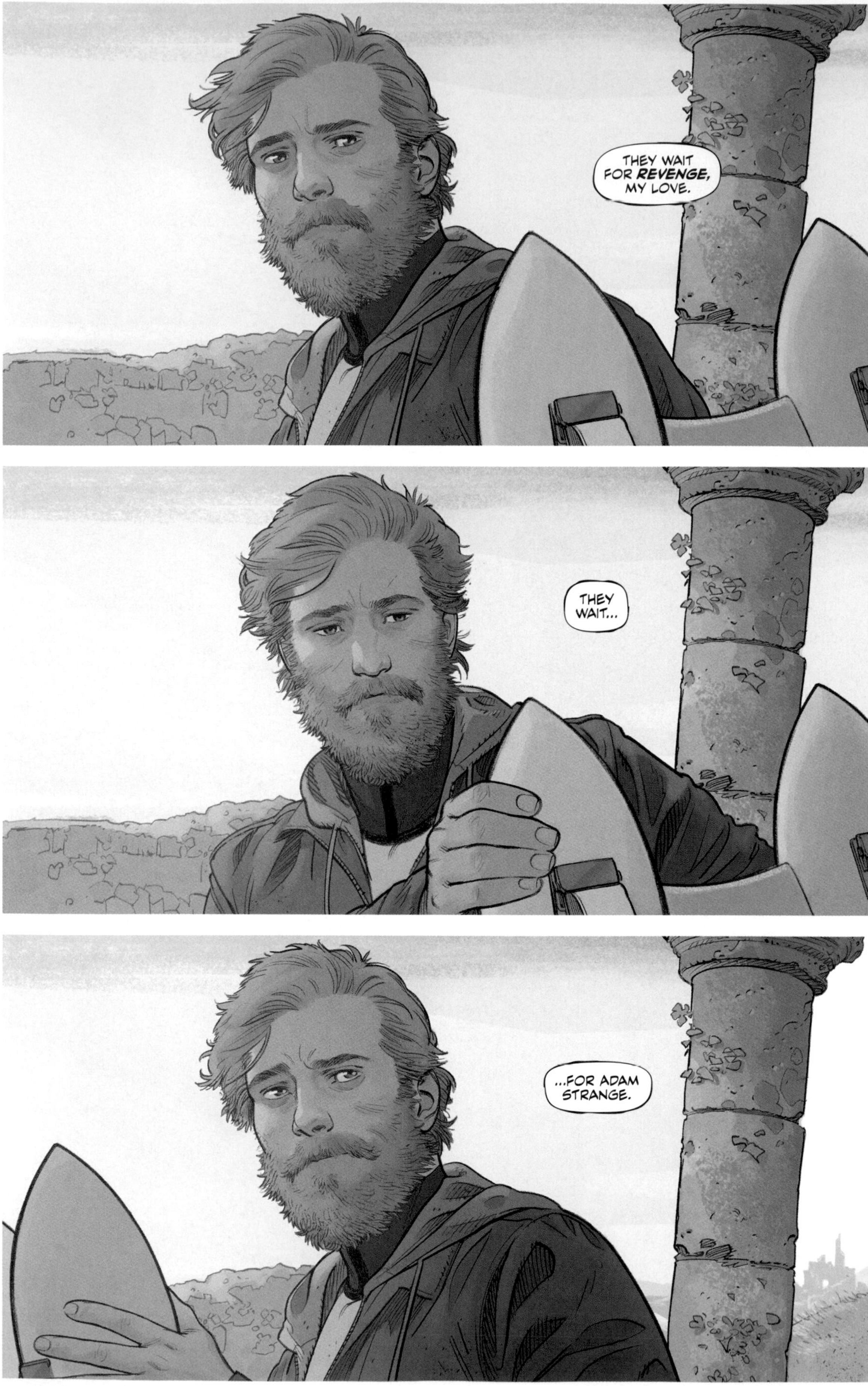
THEY WAIT FOR *REVENGE*, MY LOVE.
THEY WAIT...
...FOR ADAM STRANGE.

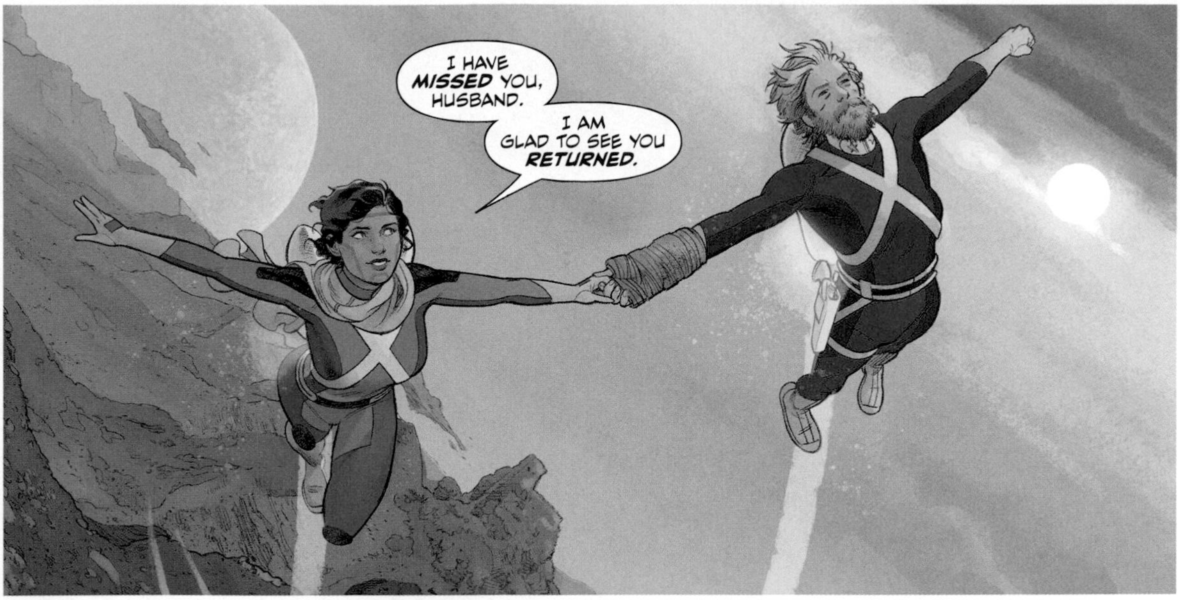
I HAVE MISSED YOU, HUSBAND.
I AM GLAD TO SEE YOU RETURNED.

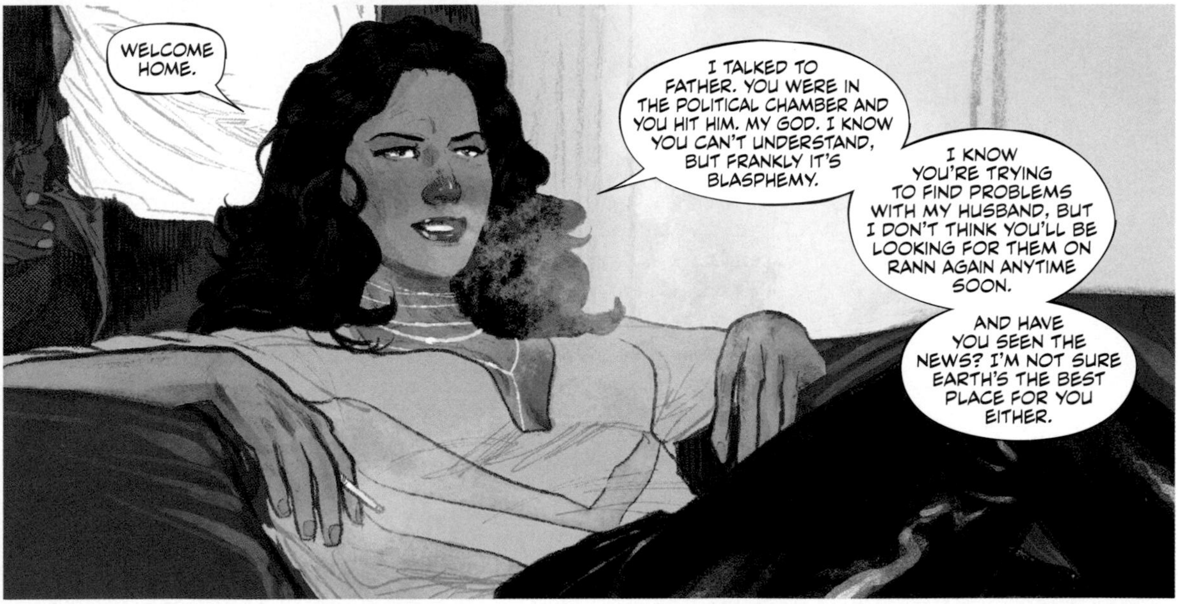
WELCOME HOME.
I TALKED TO FATHER. YOU WERE IN THE POLITICAL CHAMBER AND YOU HIT HIM. MY GOD. I KNOW YOU CAN'T UNDERSTAND, BUT FRANKLY IT'S BLASPHEMY.
I KNOW YOU'RE TRYING TO FIND PROBLEMS WITH MY HUSBAND, BUT I DON'T THINK YOU'LL BE LOOKING FOR THEM ON RANN AGAIN ANYTIME SOON.
AND HAVE YOU SEEN THE NEWS? I'M NOT SURE EARTH'S THE BEST PLACE FOR YOU EITHER.

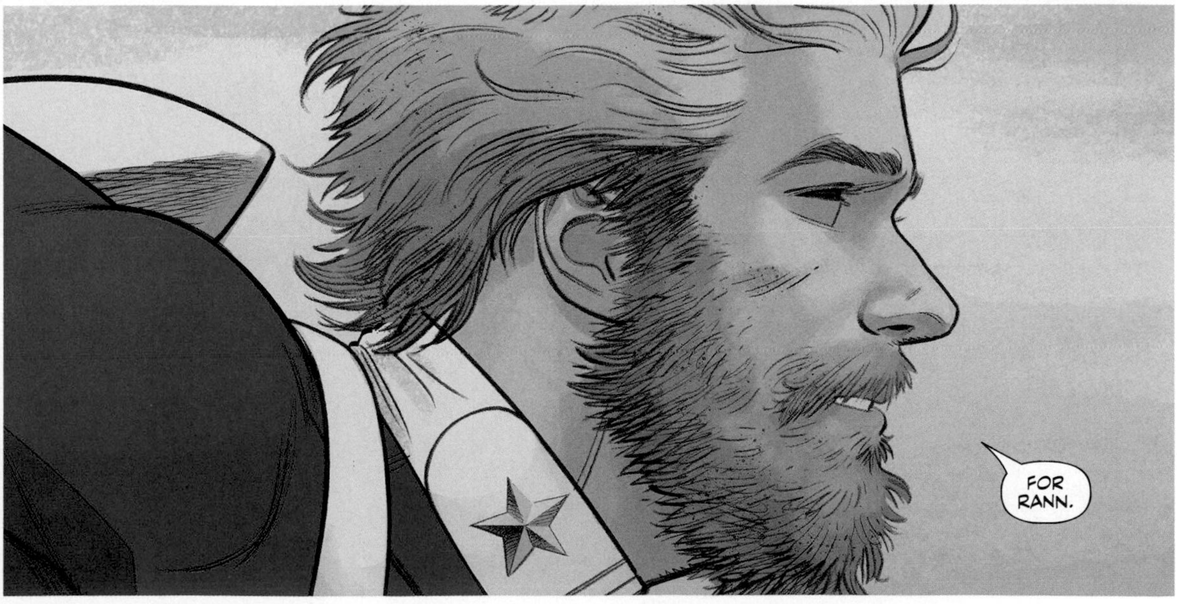
FOR RANN.

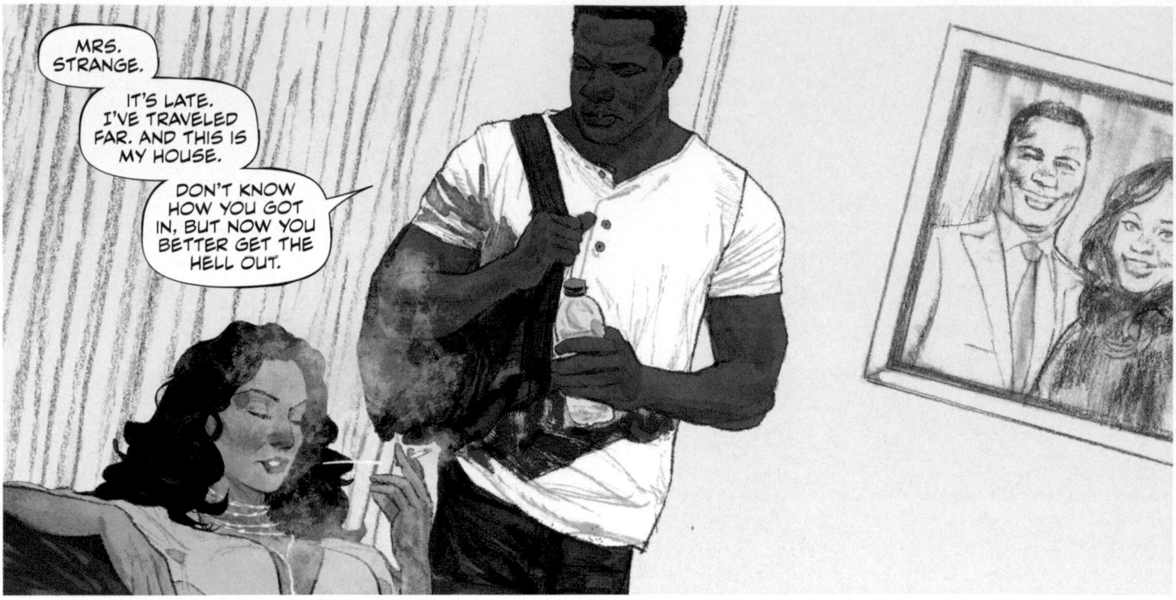
MRS. STRANGE.
IT'S LATE. I'VE TRAVELED FAR. AND THIS IS MY HOUSE.
DON'T KNOW HOW YOU GOT IN, BUT NOW YOU BETTER GET THE HELL OUT.

We had a sense of purpose
and superiority only when
things were going well.
When things were going
badly, of course, it all
went out the window.

—Harvey Kurtzman

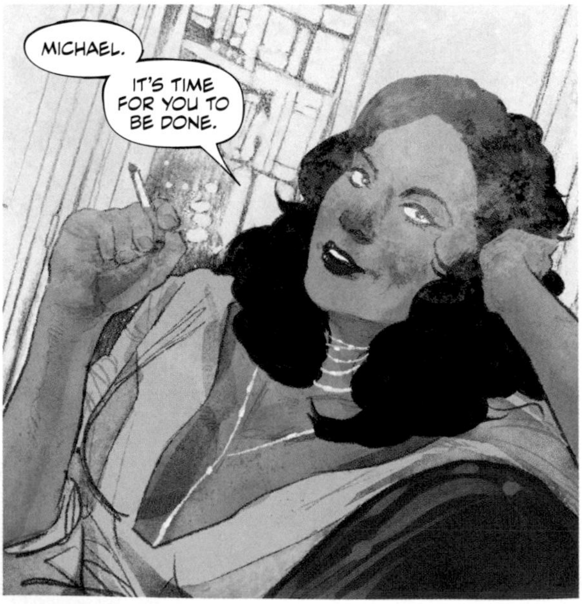
MICHAEL.
IT'S TIME FOR YOU TO BE DONE.

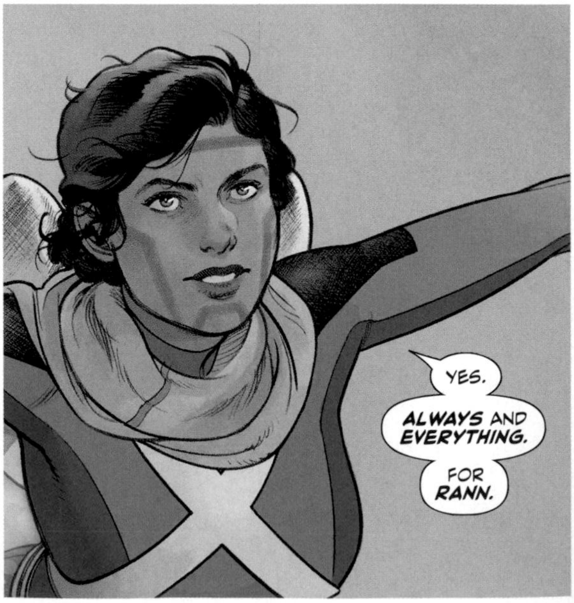
YES.
ALWAYS AND *EVERYTHING.*
FOR *RANN.*

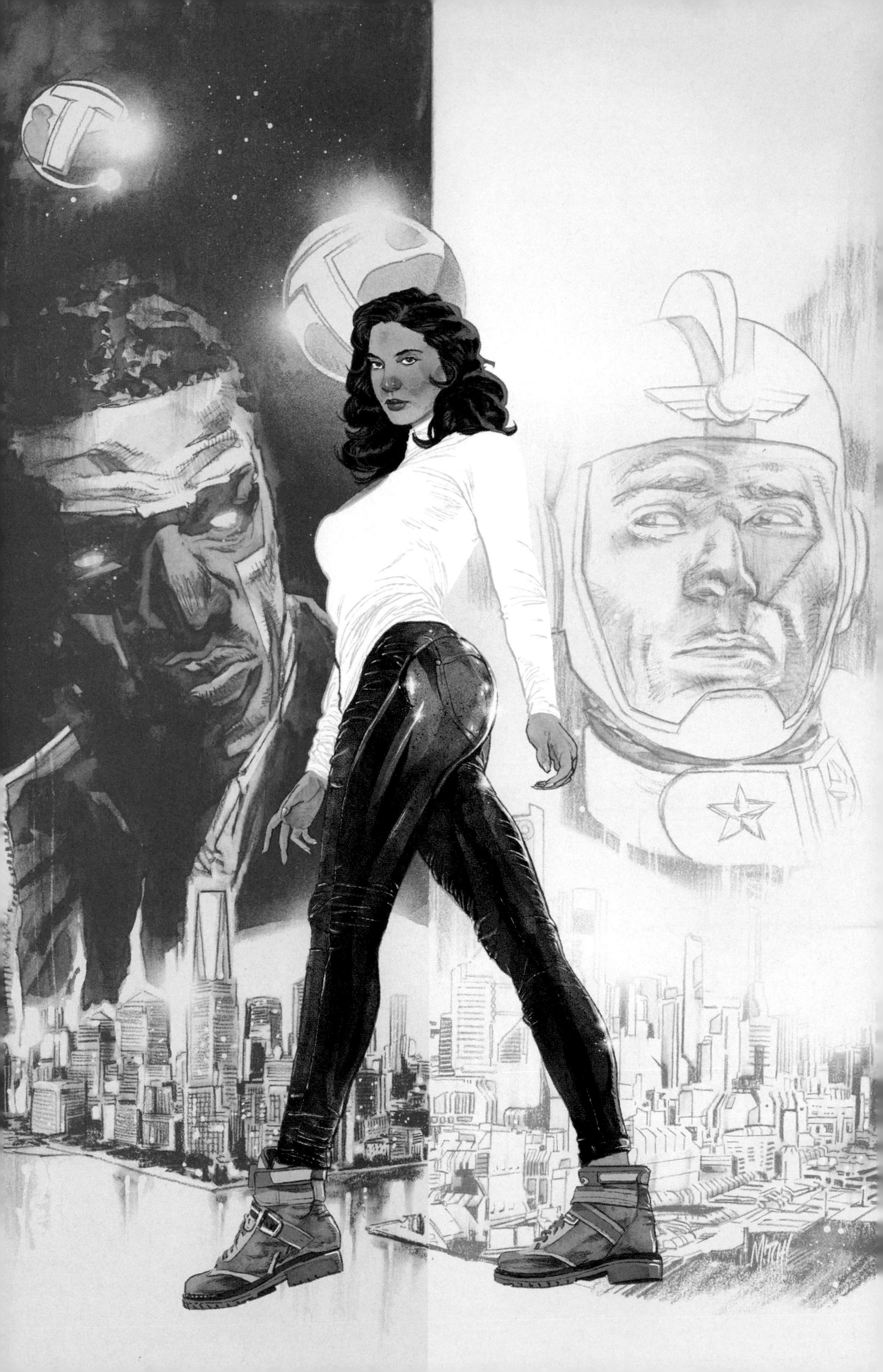

"SUPERHEROES ARE JUST NEEDY CELEBRITIES IN CAPES."

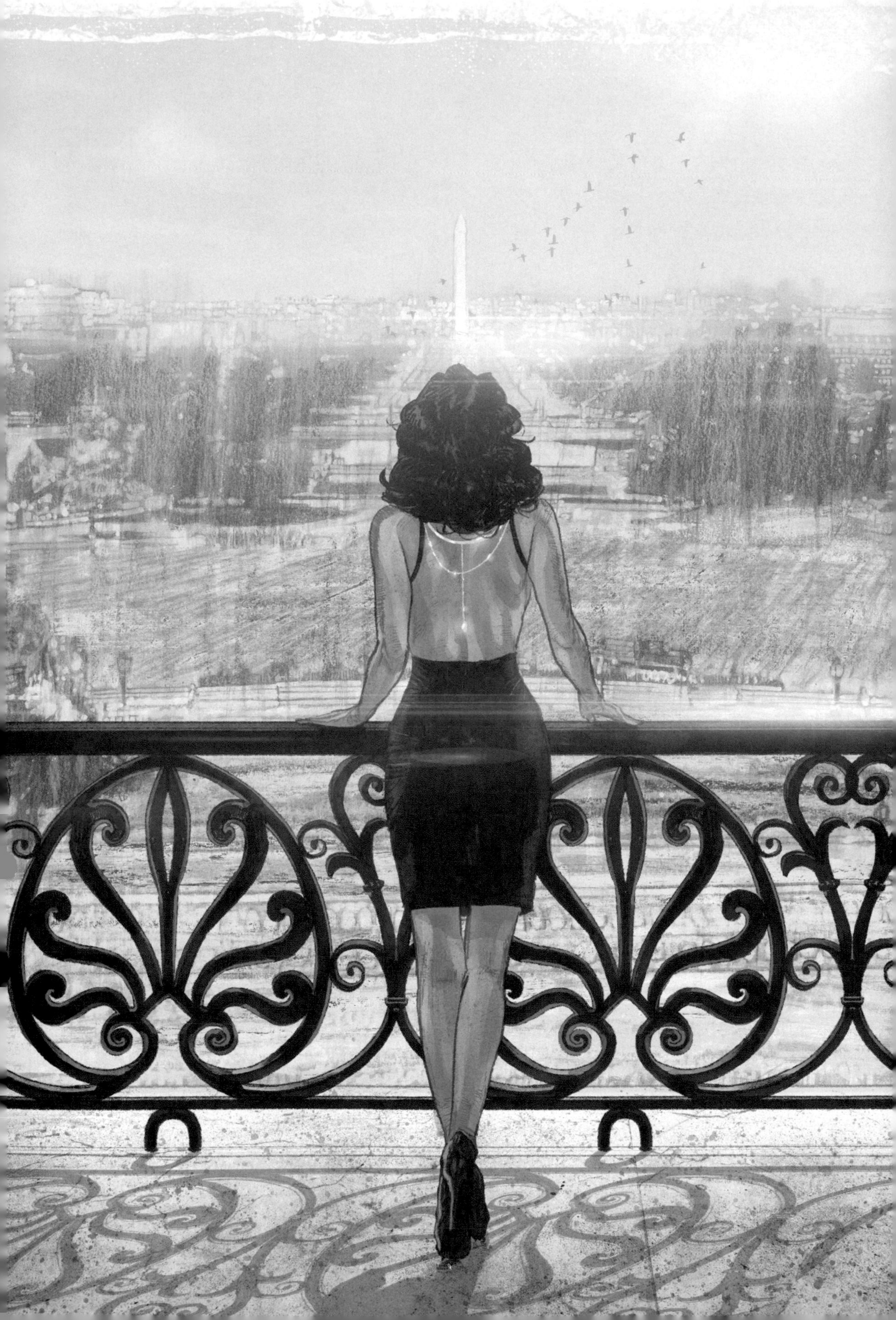

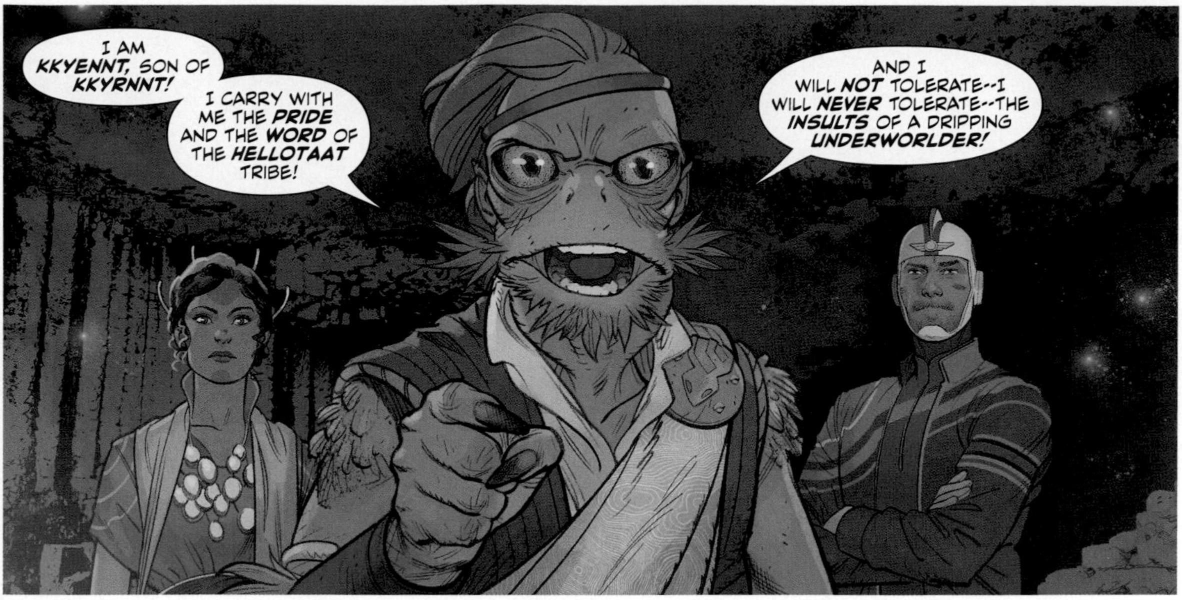
I AM KKYENNT, SON OF KKYRNNT!
I CARRY WITH ME THE PRIDE AND THE WORD OF THE HELLOTAAT TRIBE!
AND I WILL NOT TOLERATE--I WILL NEVER TOLERATE--THE INSULTS OF A DRIPPING UNDERWORLDER!

Chapter 5

On the other hand

TOM KING	...Writer
MITCH GERADS EVAN "DOC" SHANER	...Interior & Cover Artists
CLAYTON COWLES	...Letterer
BIXIE MATHIEU	...Assistant Editor
BRITTANY HOLZHERR	...Associate Editor
JAMIE S. RICH	...Editor

Superman created by Jerry Siegel and Joe Shuster.
By special arrangement with the Jerry Siegel family.

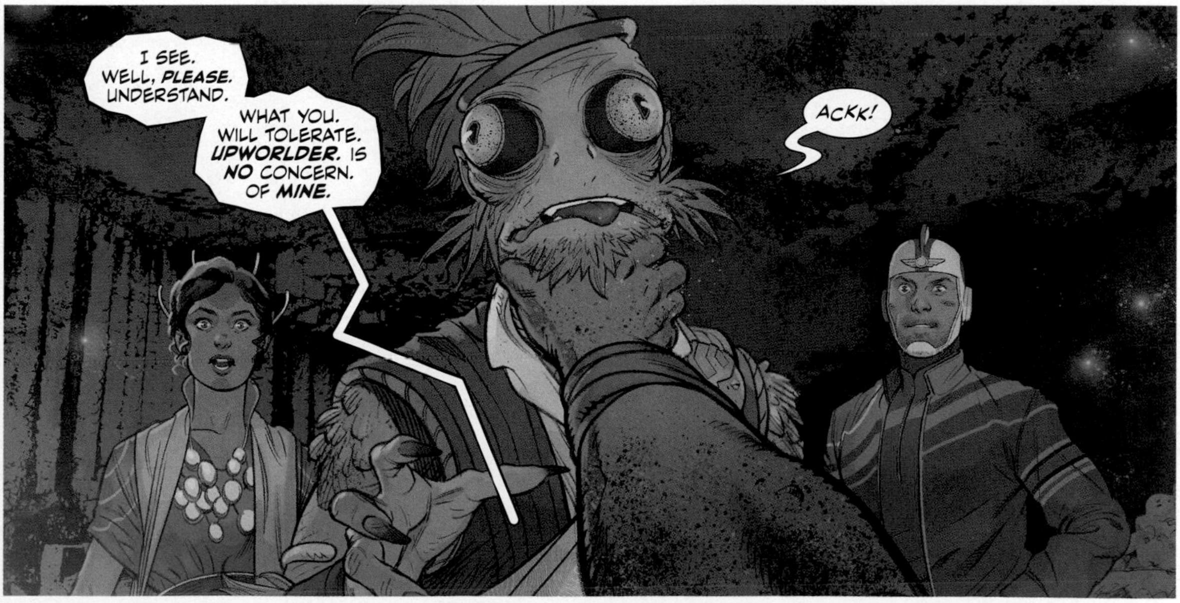
I SEE. WELL, PLEASE. UNDERSTAND.
WHAT YOU. WILL TOLERATE. UPWORLDER. IS NO CONCERN. OF MINE.
ACKK!

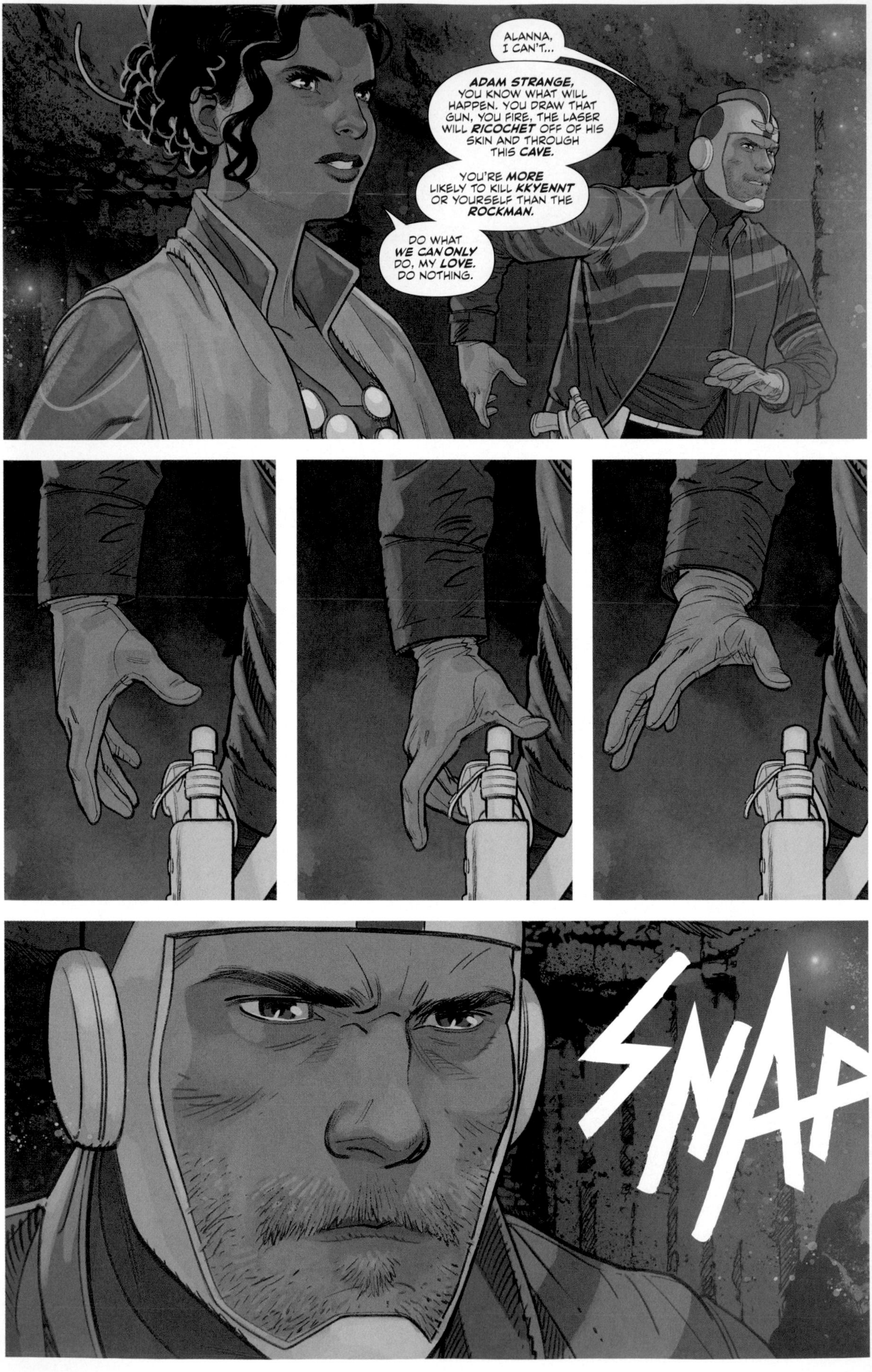
ALANNA, I CAN'T...
ADAM STRANGE, YOU KNOW WHAT WILL HAPPEN. YOU DRAW THAT GUN, YOU FIRE, THE LASER WILL RICOCHET OFF OF HIS SKIN AND THROUGH THIS CAVE.
YOU'RE MORE LIKELY TO KILL KKYENNT OR YOURSELF THAN THE ROCKMAN.
DO WHAT WE CAN ONLY DO, MY LOVE. DO NOTHING.
SNAP

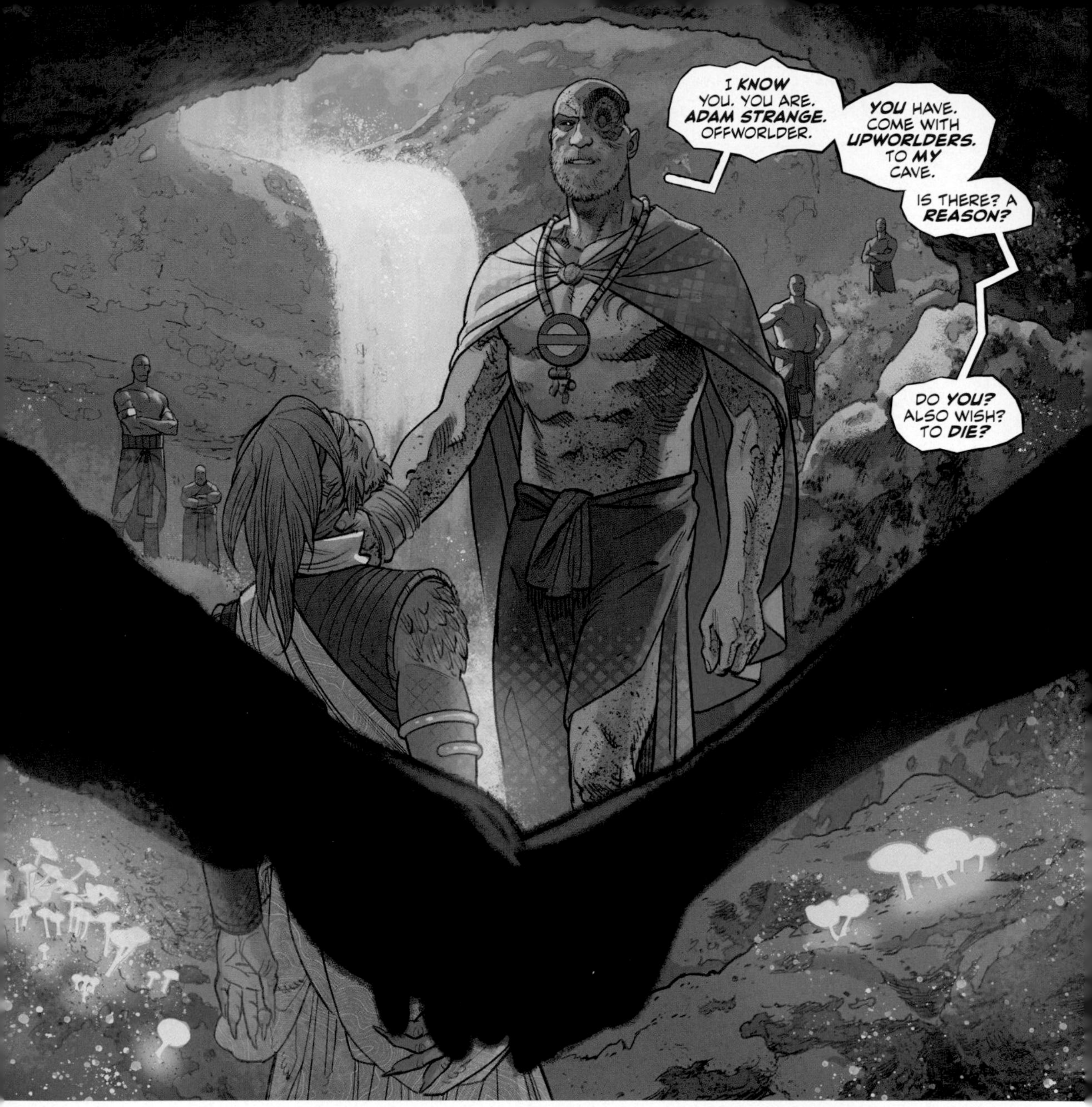
I KNOW YOU. YOU ARE. ADAM STRANGE. OFFWORLDER.
YOU HAVE. COME WITH UPWORLDERS. TO MY CAVE.
IS THERE? A REASON?
DO YOU? ALSO WISH? TO DIE?

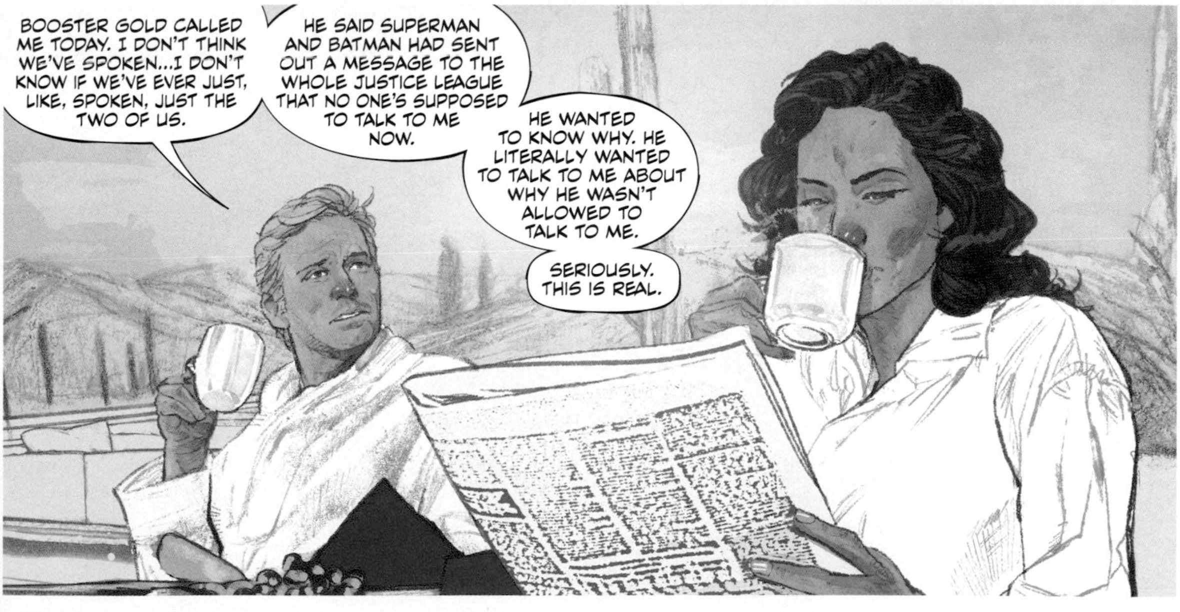
BOOSTER GOLD CALLED ME TODAY. I DON'T THINK WE'VE SPOKEN...I DON'T KNOW IF WE'VE EVER JUST, LIKE, SPOKEN, JUST THE TWO OF US.
HE SAID SUPERMAN AND BATMAN HAD SENT OUT A MESSAGE TO THE WHOLE JUSTICE LEAGUE THAT NO ONE'S SUPPOSED TO TALK TO ME NOW.
HE WANTED TO KNOW WHY. HE LITERALLY WANTED TO TALK TO ME ABOUT WHY HE WASN'T ALLOWED TO TALK TO ME.
SERIOUSLY. THIS IS REAL.

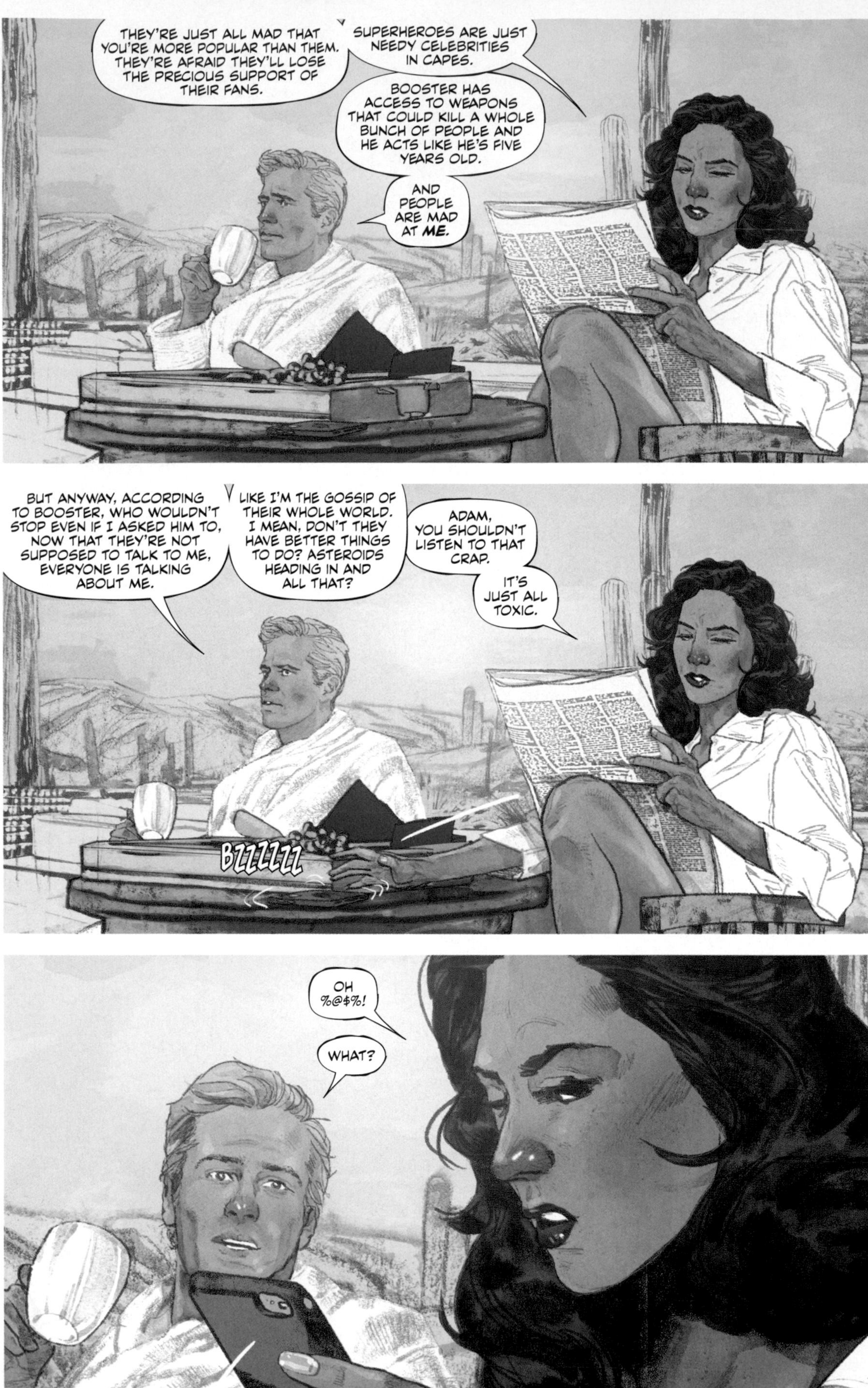
THEY'RE JUST ALL MAD THAT YOU'RE MORE POPULAR THAN THEM. THEY'RE AFRAID THEY'LL LOSE THE PRECIOUS SUPPORT OF THEIR FANS.
SUPERHEROES ARE JUST NEEDY CELEBRITIES IN CAPES.
BOOSTER HAS ACCESS TO WEAPONS THAT COULD KILL A WHOLE BUNCH OF PEOPLE AND HE ACTS LIKE HE'S FIVE YEARS OLD.
AND PEOPLE ARE MAD AT *ME.*
BUT ANYWAY, ACCORDING TO BOOSTER, WHO WOULDN'T STOP EVEN IF I ASKED HIM TO, NOW THAT THEY'RE NOT SUPPOSED TO TALK TO ME, EVERYONE IS TALKING ABOUT ME.
LIKE I'M THE GOSSIP OF THEIR WHOLE WORLD. I MEAN, DON'T THEY HAVE BETTER THINGS TO DO? ASTEROIDS HEADING IN AND ALL THAT?
ADAM, YOU SHOULDN'T LISTEN TO THAT CRAP.
IT'S JUST ALL TOXIC.
BZZZZZZ
OH %@$%!
WHAT?

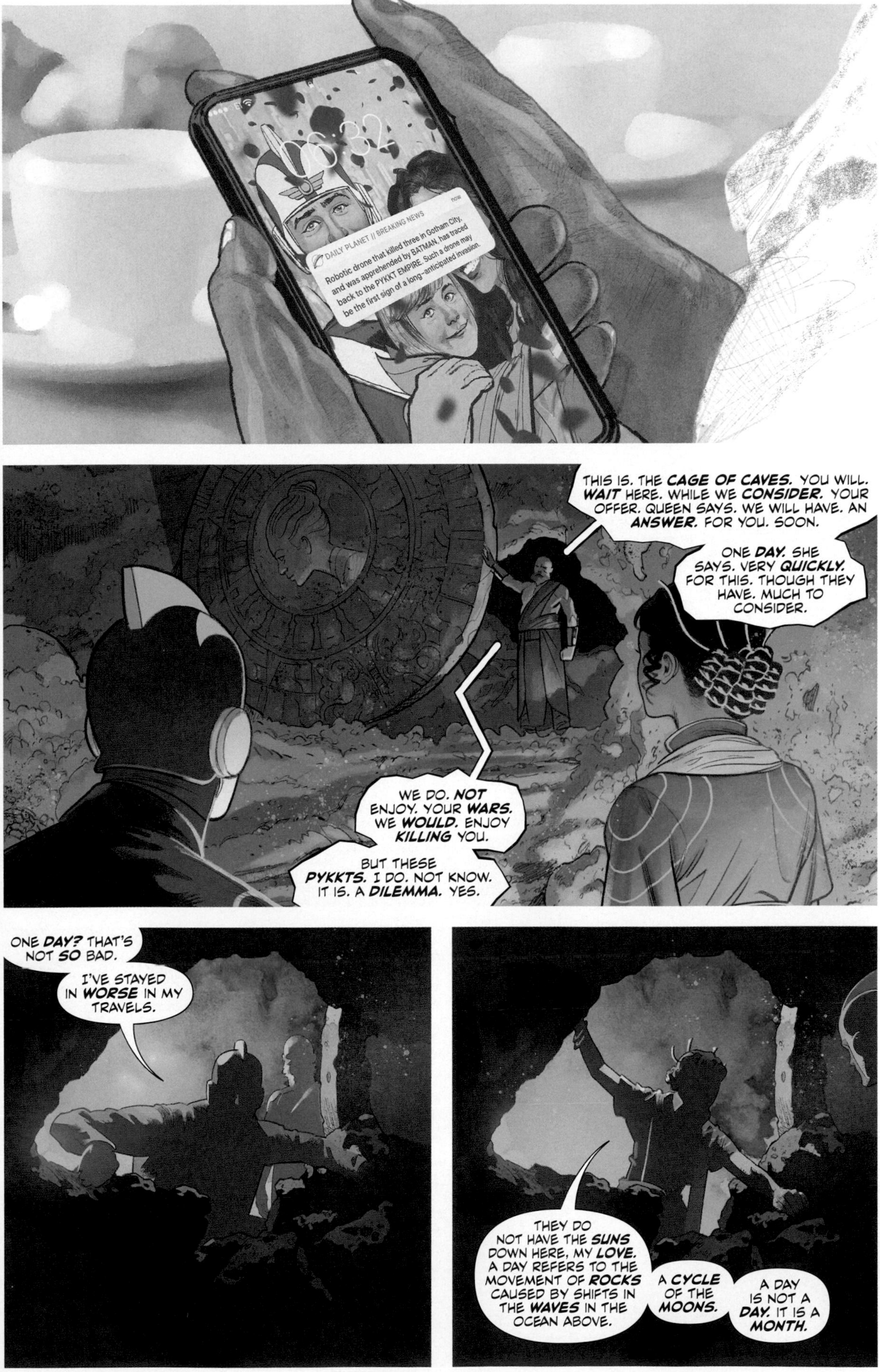
now
DAILY PLANET // BREAKING NEWS
Robotic drone that killed three in Gotham City, and was apprehended by BATMAN, has traced back to the PYKKT EMPIRE. Such a drone may be the first sign of a long-anticipated invasion.
THIS IS. THE CAGE OF CAVES. YOU WILL. WAIT HERE. WHILE WE CONSIDER. YOUR OFFER. QUEEN SAYS. WE WILL HAVE. AN ANSWER. FOR YOU. SOON.
ONE DAY. SHE SAYS. VERY QUICKLY. FOR THIS. THOUGH THEY HAVE. MUCH TO CONSIDER.
WE DO. NOT ENJOY. YOUR WARS. WE WOULD. ENJOY KILLING YOU.
BUT THESE PYKKTS. I DO. NOT KNOW. IT IS. A DILEMMA. YES.
ONE DAY? THAT'S NOT SO BAD.
I'VE STAYED IN WORSE IN MY TRAVELS.
THEY DO NOT HAVE THE SUNS DOWN HERE, MY LOVE. A DAY REFERS TO THE MOVEMENT OF ROCKS CAUSED BY SHIFTS IN THE WAVES IN THE OCEAN ABOVE.
A CYCLE OF THE MOONS.
A DAY IS NOT A DAY. IT IS A MONTH.

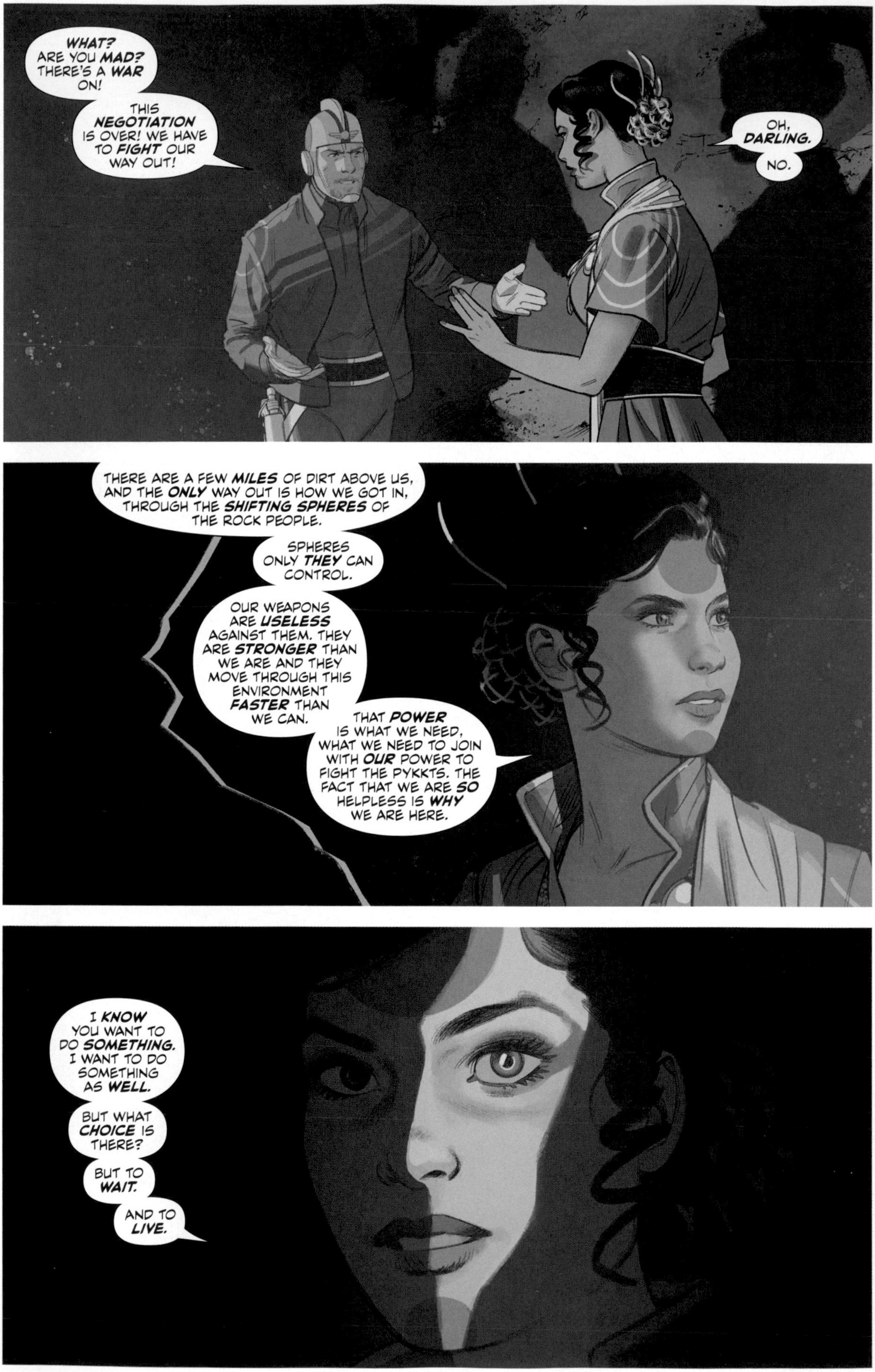
WHAT? ARE YOU MAD? THERE'S A WAR ON!
THIS NEGOTIATION IS OVER! WE HAVE TO FIGHT OUR WAY OUT!
OH, DARLING.
NO.
THERE ARE A FEW MILES OF DIRT ABOVE US, AND THE ONLY WAY OUT IS HOW WE GOT IN, THROUGH THE SHIFTING SPHERES OF THE ROCK PEOPLE.
SPHERES ONLY THEY CAN CONTROL.
OUR WEAPONS ARE USELESS AGAINST THEM. THEY ARE STRONGER THAN WE ARE AND THEY MOVE THROUGH THIS ENVIRONMENT FASTER THAN WE CAN.
THAT POWER IS WHAT WE NEED, WHAT WE NEED TO JOIN WITH OUR POWER TO FIGHT THE PYKKTS. THE FACT THAT WE ARE SO HELPLESS IS WHY WE ARE HERE.
I KNOW YOU WANT TO DO SOMETHING. I WANT TO DO SOMETHING AS WELL.
BUT WHAT CHOICE IS THERE?
BUT TO WAIT.
AND TO LIVE.

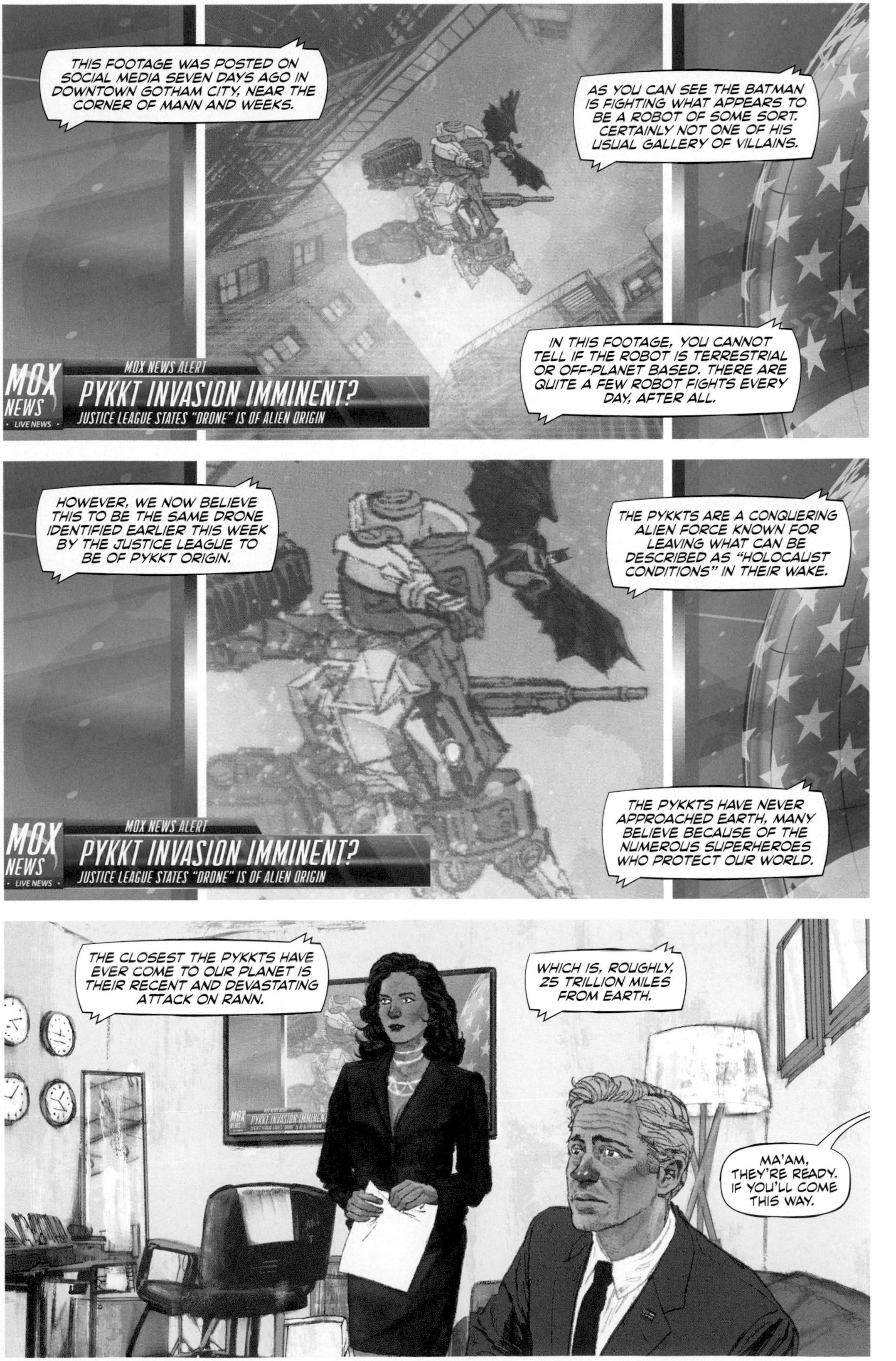
THIS FOOTAGE WAS POSTED ON SOCIAL MEDIA SEVEN DAYS AGO IN DOWNTOWN GOTHAM CITY, NEAR THE CORNER OF MANN AND WEEKS.
AS YOU CAN SEE THE BATMAN IS FIGHTING WHAT APPEARS TO BE A ROBOT OF SOME SORT. CERTAINLY NOT ONE OF HIS USUAL GALLERY OF VILLAINS.
MOX NEWS LIVE NEWS
MOX NEWS ALERT
PYKKT INVASION IMMINENT?
JUSTICE LEAGUE STATES "DRONE" IS OF ALIEN ORIGIN
IN THIS FOOTAGE, YOU CANNOT TELL IF THE ROBOT IS TERRESTRIAL OR OFF-PLANET BASED. THERE ARE QUITE A FEW ROBOT FIGHTS EVERY DAY, AFTER ALL.
HOWEVER, WE NOW BELIEVE THIS TO BE THE SAME DRONE IDENTIFIED EARLIER THIS WEEK BY THE JUSTICE LEAGUE TO BE OF PYKKT ORIGIN.
THE PYKKTS ARE A CONQUERING ALIEN FORCE KNOWN FOR LEAVING WHAT CAN BE DESCRIBED AS "HOLOCAUST CONDITIONS" IN THEIR WAKE.
MOX NEWS LIVE NEWS
MOX NEWS ALERT
PYKKT INVASION IMMINENT?
JUSTICE LEAGUE STATES "DRONE" IS OF ALIEN ORIGIN
THE PYKKTS HAVE NEVER APPROACHED EARTH, MANY BELIEVE BECAUSE OF THE NUMEROUS SUPERHEROES WHO PROTECT OUR WORLD.
THE CLOSEST THE PYKKTS HAVE EVER COME TO OUR PLANET IS THEIR RECENT AND DEVASTATING ATTACK ON RANN.
WHICH IS, ROUGHLY, 25 TRILLION MILES FROM EARTH.
MA'AM, THEY'RE READY. IF YOU'LL COME THIS WAY.

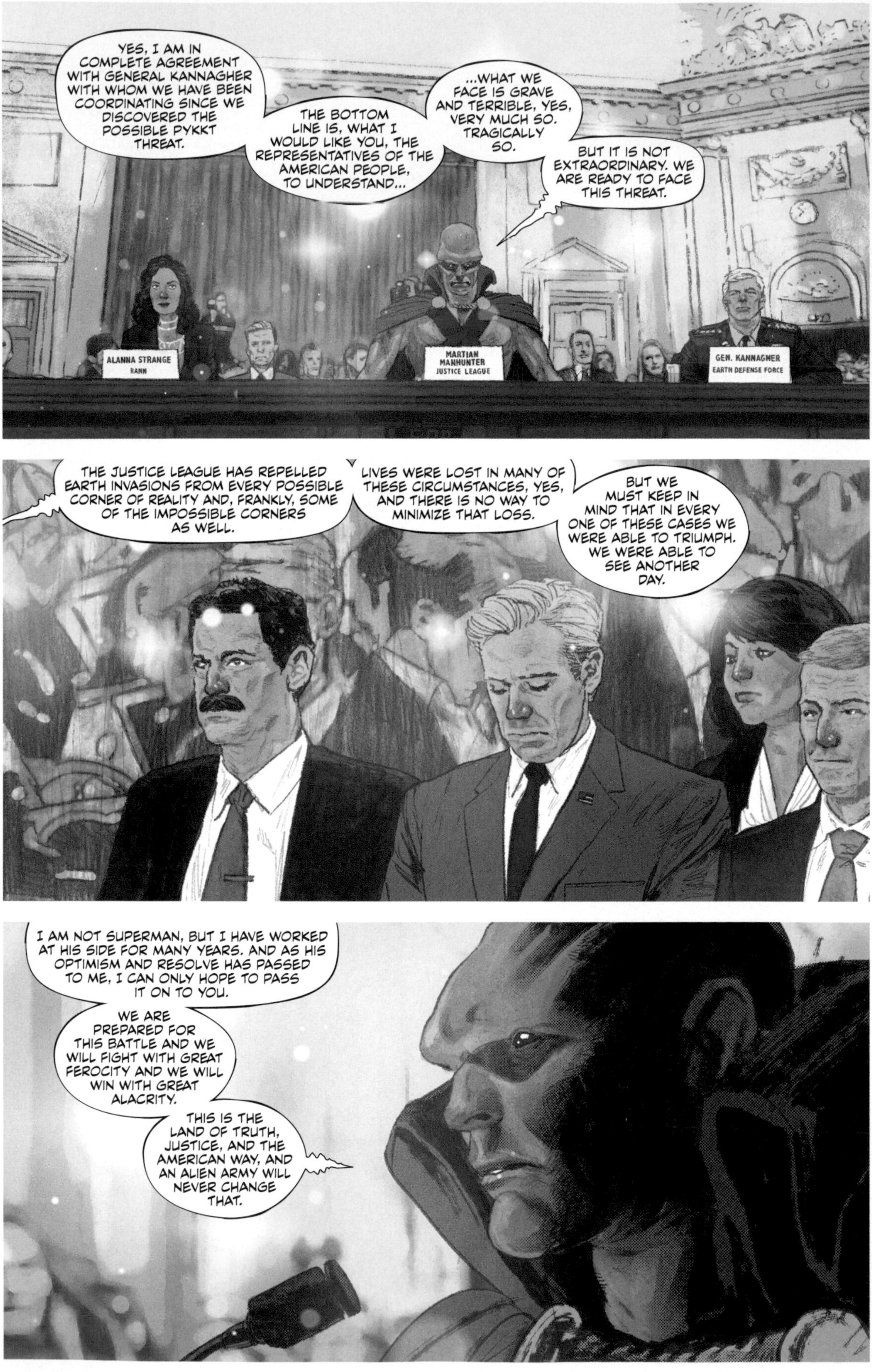
YES, I AM IN COMPLETE AGREEMENT WITH GENERAL KANNAGHER WITH WHOM WE HAVE BEEN COORDINATING SINCE WE DISCOVERED THE POSSIBLE PYKKT THREAT.
THE BOTTOM LINE IS, WHAT I WOULD LIKE YOU, THE REPRESENTATIVES OF THE AMERICAN PEOPLE, TO UNDERSTAND...
...WHAT WE FACE IS GRAVE AND TERRIBLE, YES, VERY MUCH SO. TRAGICALLY SO.
BUT IT IS NOT EXTRAORDINARY. WE ARE READY TO FACE THIS THREAT.
ALANNA STRANGE
RANN
MARTIAN MANHUNTER
JUSTICE LEAGUE
GEN. KANNAGHER
EARTH DEFENSE FORCE
THE JUSTICE LEAGUE HAS REPELLED EARTH INVASIONS FROM EVERY POSSIBLE CORNER OF REALITY AND, FRANKLY, SOME OF THE IMPOSSIBLE CORNERS AS WELL.
LIVES WERE LOST IN MANY OF THESE CIRCUMSTANCES, YES, AND THERE IS NO WAY TO MINIMIZE THAT LOSS.
BUT WE MUST KEEP IN MIND THAT IN EVERY ONE OF THESE CASES WE WERE ABLE TO TRIUMPH. WE WERE ABLE TO SEE ANOTHER DAY.
I AM NOT SUPERMAN, BUT I HAVE WORKED AT HIS SIDE FOR MANY YEARS. AND AS HIS OPTIMISM AND RESOLVE HAS PASSED TO ME, I CAN ONLY HOPE TO PASS IT ON TO YOU.
WE ARE PREPARED FOR THIS BATTLE AND WE WILL FIGHT WITH GREAT FEROCITY AND WE WILL WIN WITH GREAT ALACRITY.
THIS IS THE LAND OF TRUTH, JUSTICE, AND THE AMERICAN WAY, AND AN ALIEN ARMY WILL NEVER CHANGE THAT.

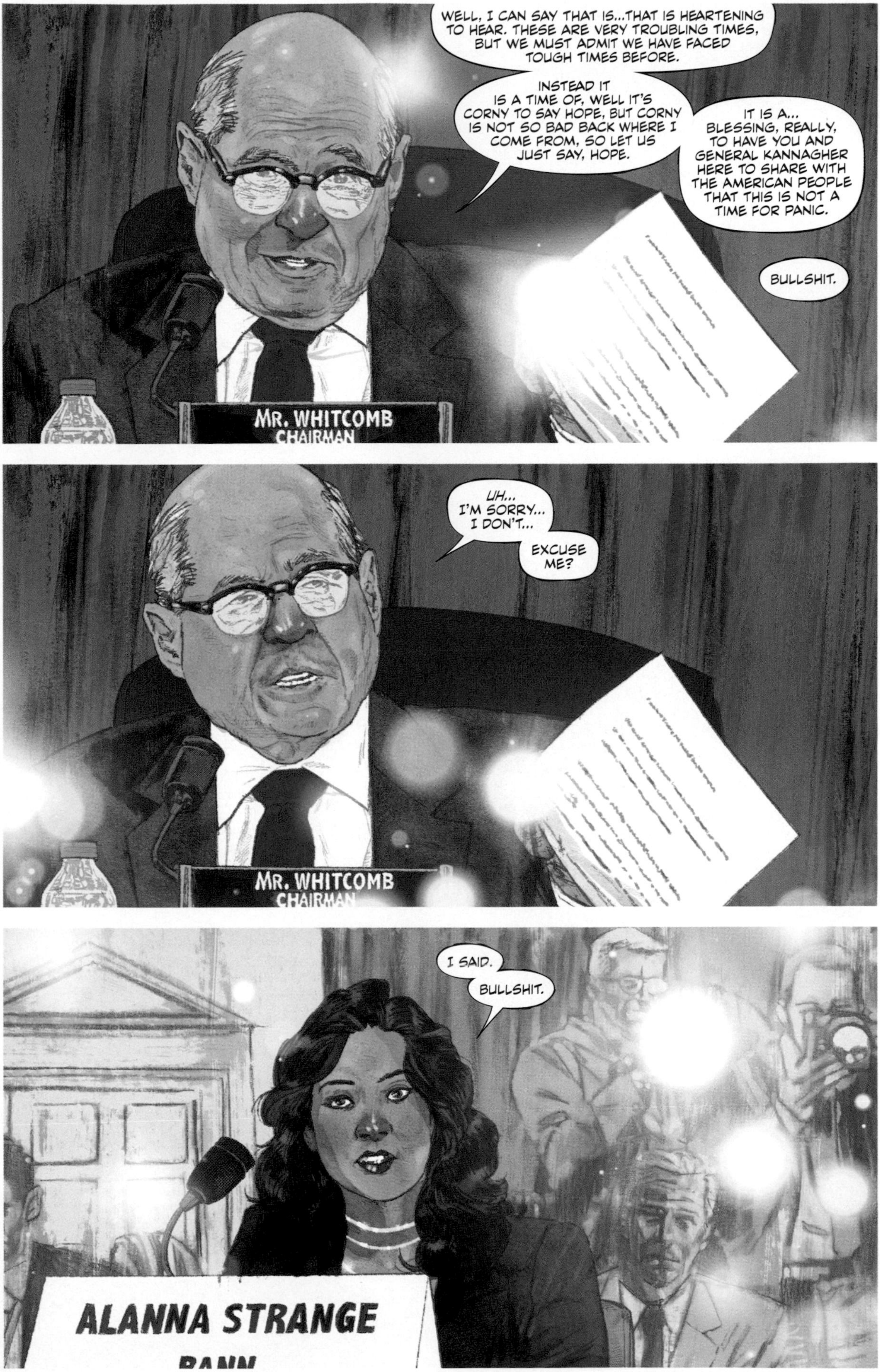
WELL, I CAN SAY THAT IS...THAT IS HEARTENING TO HEAR. THESE ARE VERY TROUBLING TIMES, BUT WE MUST ADMIT WE HAVE FACED TOUGH TIMES BEFORE.
INSTEAD IT IS A TIME OF, WELL IT'S CORNY TO SAY HOPE, BUT CORNY IS NOT SO BAD BACK WHERE I COME FROM, SO LET US JUST SAY, HOPE.
IT IS A... BLESSING, REALLY, TO HAVE YOU AND GENERAL KANNAGHER HERE TO SHARE WITH THE AMERICAN PEOPLE THAT THIS IS NOT A TIME FOR PANIC.
BULLSHIT.
MR. WHITCOMB
CHAIRMAN
UH... I'M SORRY... I DON'T...
EXCUSE ME?
MR. WHITCOMB
CHAIRMAN
I SAID.
BULLSHIT.
ALANNA STRANGE

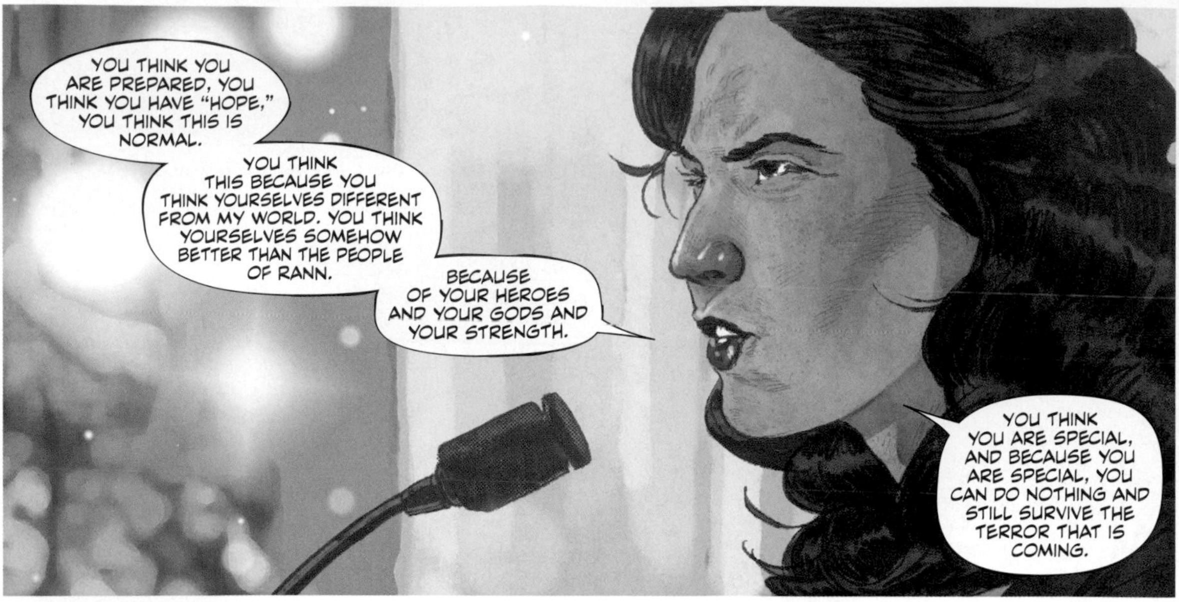
YOU THINK YOU ARE PREPARED, YOU THINK YOU HAVE "HOPE," YOU THINK THIS IS NORMAL.
YOU THINK THIS BECAUSE YOU THINK YOURSELVES DIFFERENT FROM MY WORLD. YOU THINK YOURSELVES SOMEHOW BETTER THAN THE PEOPLE OF RANN.
BECAUSE OF YOUR HEROES AND YOUR GODS AND YOUR STRENGTH.
YOU THINK YOU ARE SPECIAL, AND BECAUSE YOU ARE SPECIAL, YOU CAN DO NOTHING AND STILL SURVIVE THE TERROR THAT IS COMING.

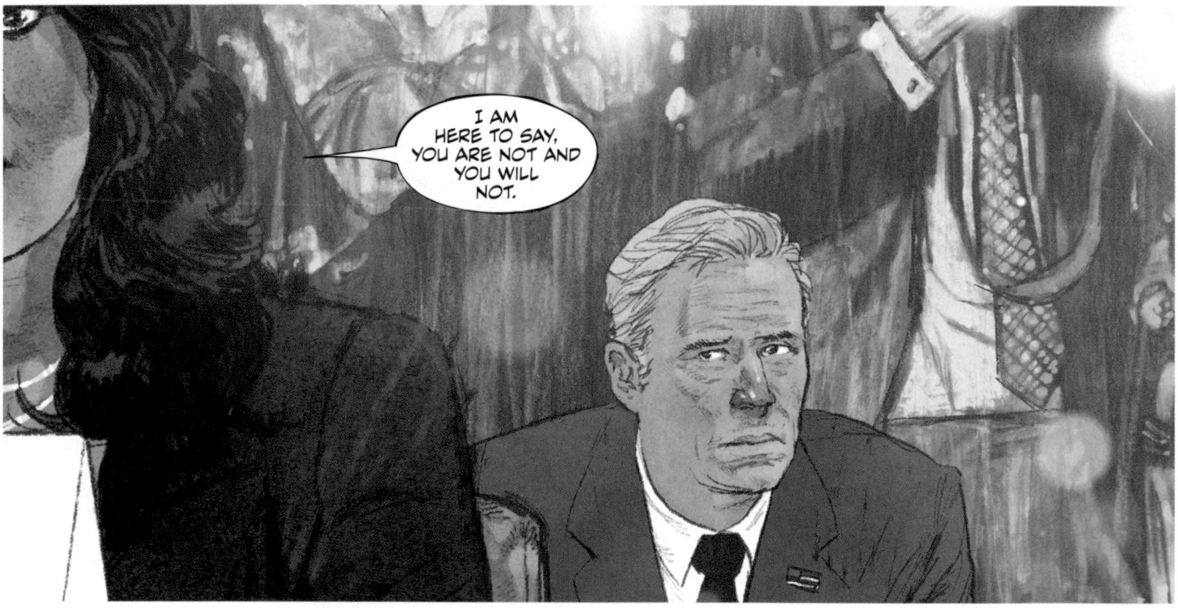
I AM HERE TO SAY, YOU ARE NOT AND YOU WILL NOT.

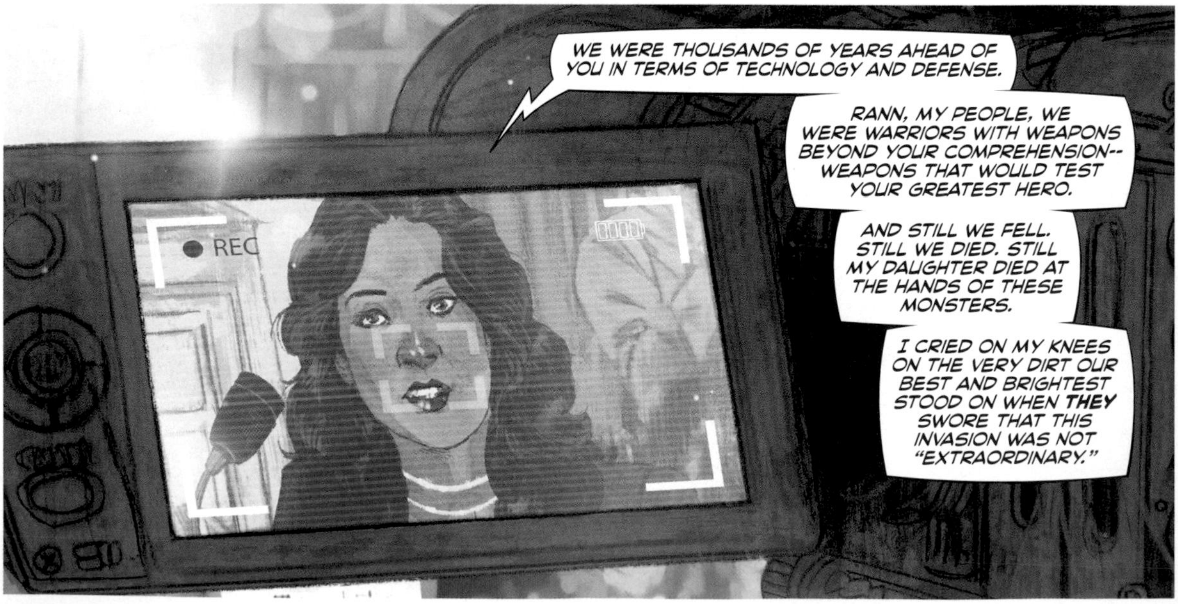
WE WERE THOUSANDS OF YEARS AHEAD OF YOU IN TERMS OF TECHNOLOGY AND DEFENSE.
RANN, MY PEOPLE, WE WERE WARRIORS WITH WEAPONS BEYOND YOUR COMPREHENSION-- WEAPONS THAT WOULD TEST YOUR GREATEST HERO.
AND STILL WE FELL. STILL WE DIED. STILL MY DAUGHTER DIED AT THE HANDS OF THESE MONSTERS.
I CRIED ON MY KNEES ON THE VERY DIRT OUR BEST AND BRIGHTEST STOOD ON WHEN THEY SWORE THAT THIS INVASION WAS NOT "EXTRAORDINARY."
REC

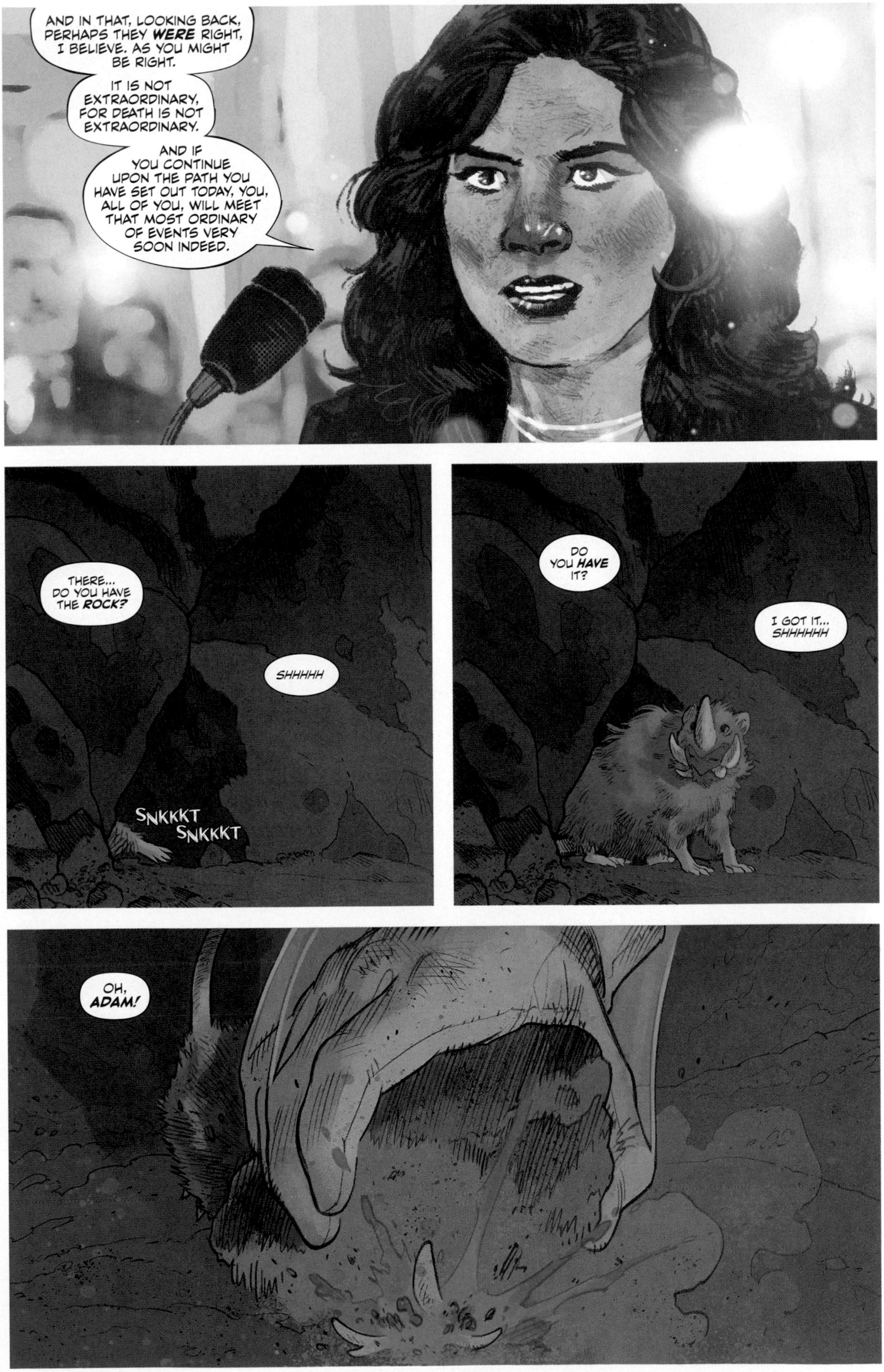
AND IN THAT, LOOKING BACK, PERHAPS THEY **WERE** RIGHT, I BELIEVE. AS YOU MIGHT BE RIGHT.
IT IS NOT EXTRAORDINARY, FOR DEATH IS NOT EXTRAORDINARY.
AND IF YOU CONTINUE UPON THE PATH YOU HAVE SET OUT TODAY, YOU, ALL OF YOU, WILL MEET THAT MOST ORDINARY OF EVENTS VERY SOON INDEED.
THERE... DO YOU HAVE THE **ROCK?**
SHHHHH
SNKKKT SNKKKT
DO YOU **HAVE** IT?
I GOT IT... *SHHHHHH*
OH, **ADAM!**

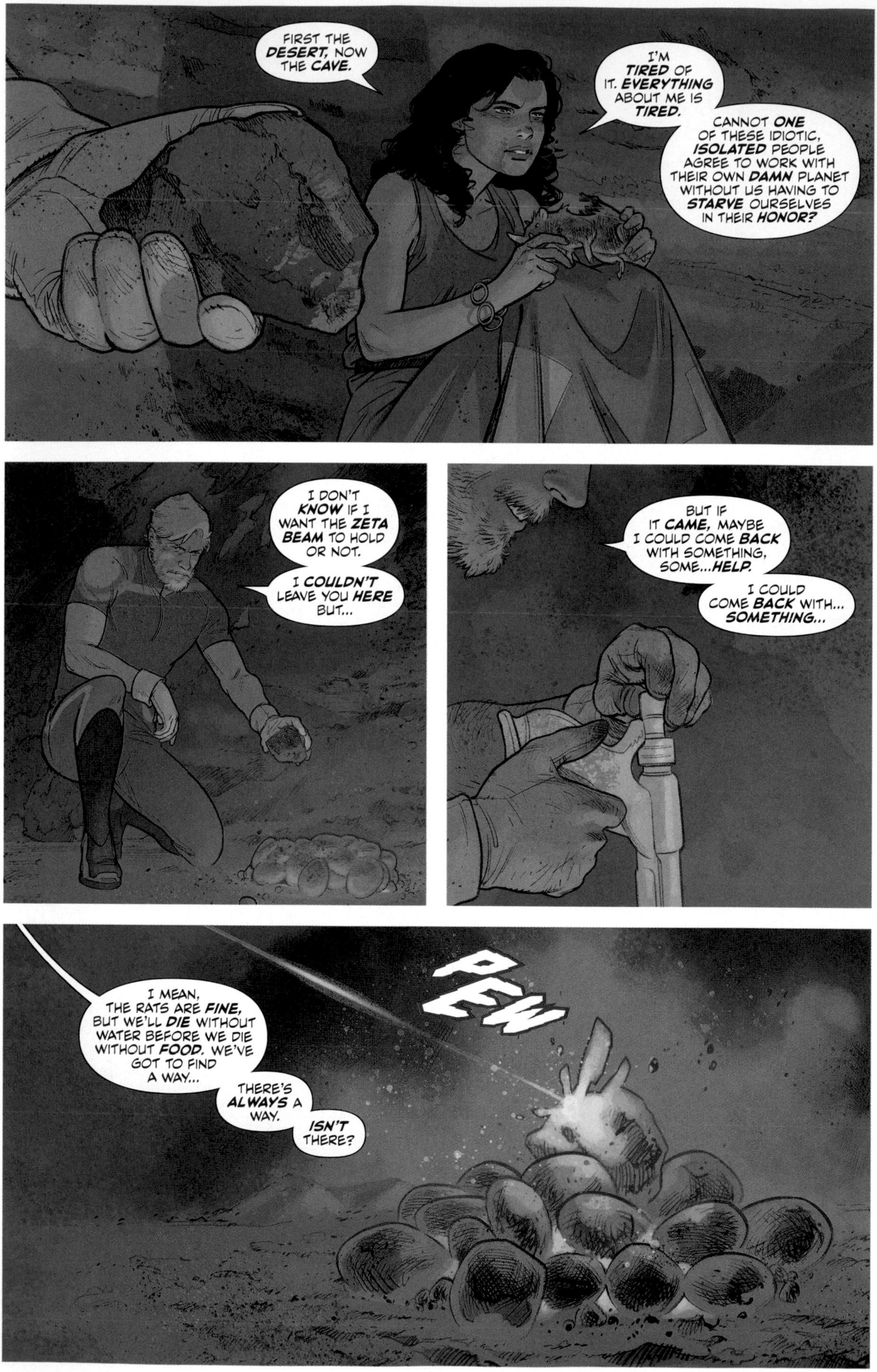

FIRST THE DESERT, NOW THE CAVE.
I'M TIRED OF IT. EVERYTHING ABOUT ME IS TIRED.
CANNOT ONE OF THESE IDIOTIC, ISOLATED PEOPLE AGREE TO WORK WITH THEIR OWN DAMN PLANET WITHOUT US HAVING TO STARVE OURSELVES IN THEIR HONOR?
I DON'T KNOW IF I WANT THE ZETA BEAM TO HOLD OR NOT.
I COULDN'T LEAVE YOU HERE BUT...
BUT IF IT CAME, MAYBE I COULD COME BACK WITH SOMETHING, SOME...HELP.
I COULD COME BACK WITH... SOMETHING...
PEW
I MEAN, THE RATS ARE FINE, BUT WE'LL DIE WITHOUT WATER BEFORE WE DIE WITHOUT FOOD. WE'VE GOT TO FIND A WAY...
THERE'S ALWAYS A WAY.
ISN'T THERE?

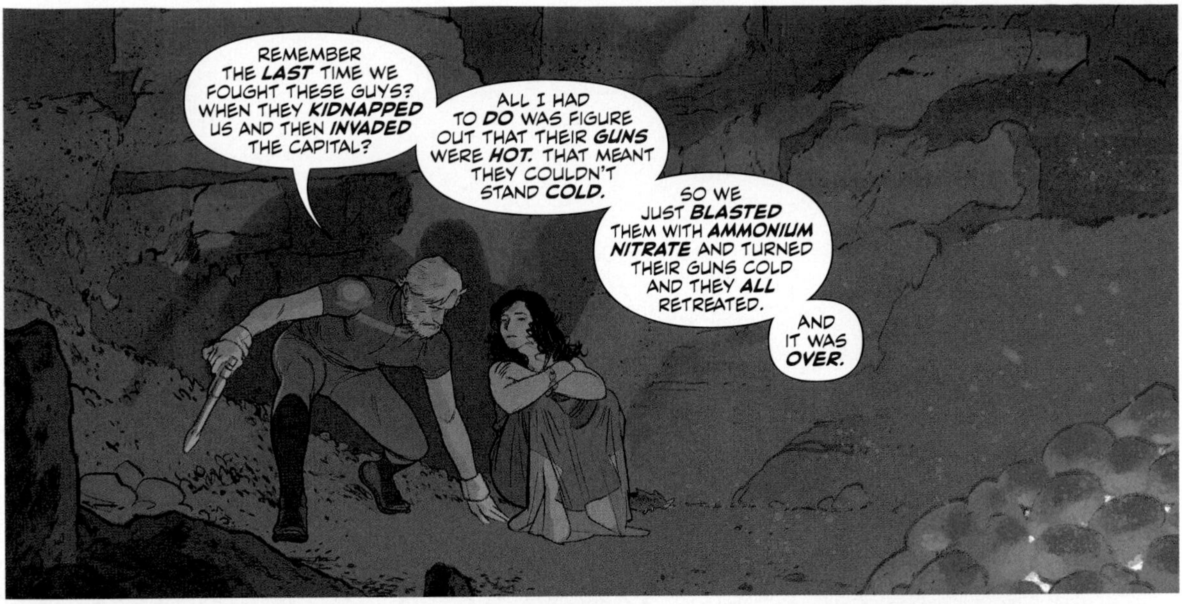
REMEMBER THE LAST TIME WE FOUGHT THESE GUYS? WHEN THEY KIDNAPPED US AND THEN INVADED THE CAPITAL?
ALL I HAD TO DO WAS FIGURE OUT THAT THEIR GUNS WERE HOT. THAT MEANT THEY COULDN'T STAND COLD.
SO WE JUST BLASTED THEM WITH AMMONIUM NITRATE AND TURNED THEIR GUNS COLD AND THEY ALL RETREATED.
AND IT WAS OVER.

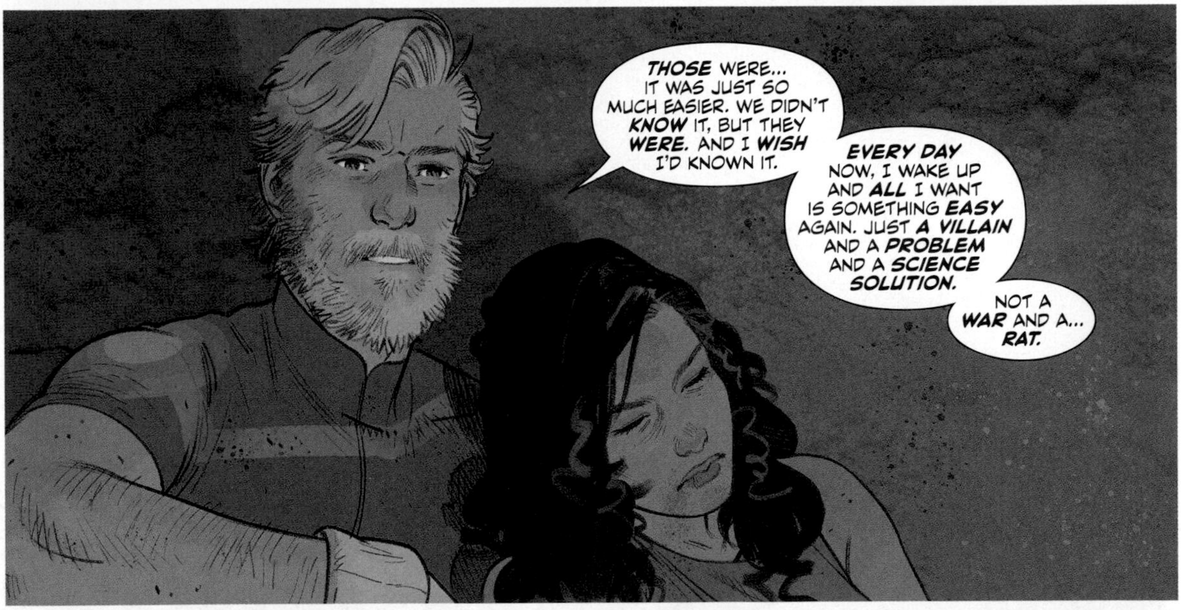
THOSE WERE... IT WAS JUST SO MUCH EASIER. WE DIDN'T KNOW IT, BUT THEY WERE. AND I WISH I'D KNOWN IT.
EVERY DAY NOW, I WAKE UP AND ALL I WANT IS SOMETHING EASY AGAIN. JUST A VILLAIN AND A PROBLEM AND A SCIENCE SOLUTION.
NOT A WAR AND A... RAT.

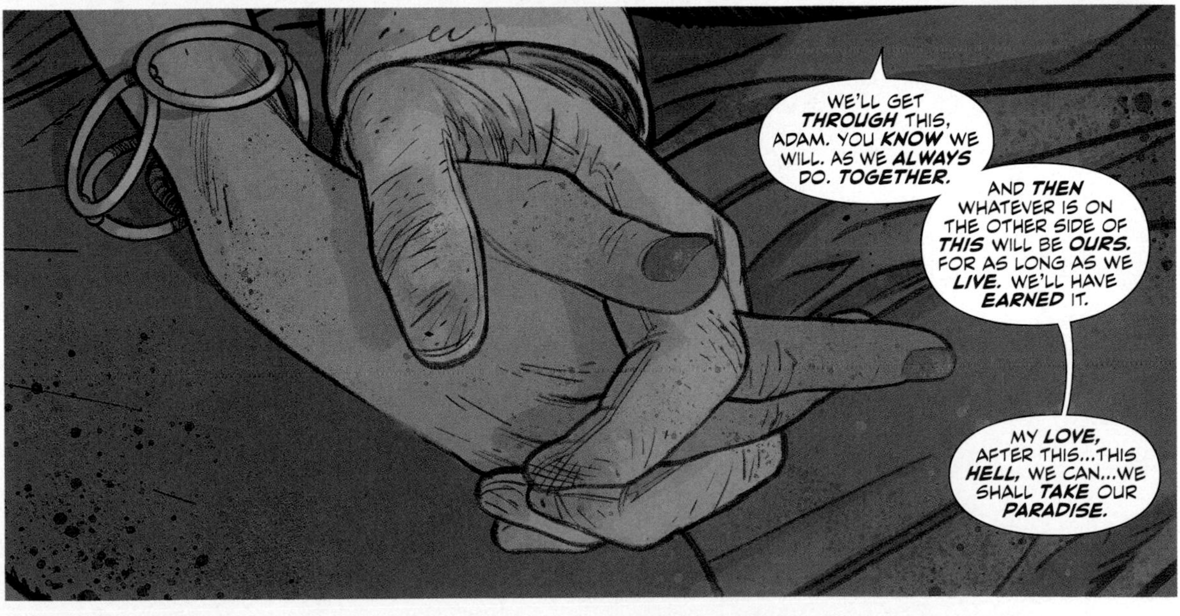
WE'LL GET THROUGH THIS, ADAM. YOU KNOW WE WILL. AS WE ALWAYS DO. TOGETHER.
AND THEN WHATEVER IS ON THE OTHER SIDE OF THIS WILL BE OURS. FOR AS LONG AS WE LIVE. WE'LL HAVE EARNED IT.
MY LOVE, AFTER THIS...THIS HELL, WE CAN...WE SHALL TAKE OUR PARADISE.

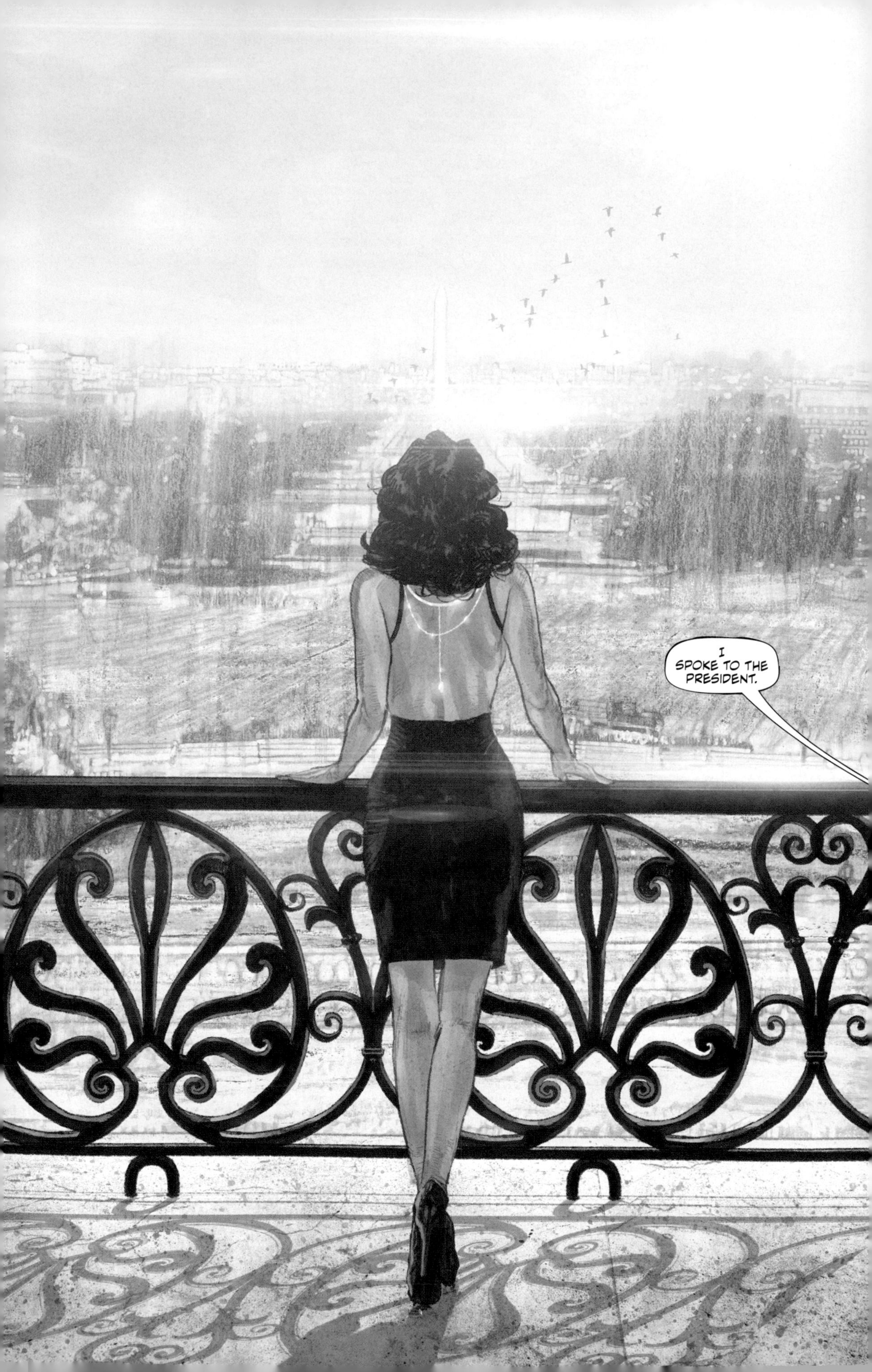
I SPOKE TO THE PRESIDENT.

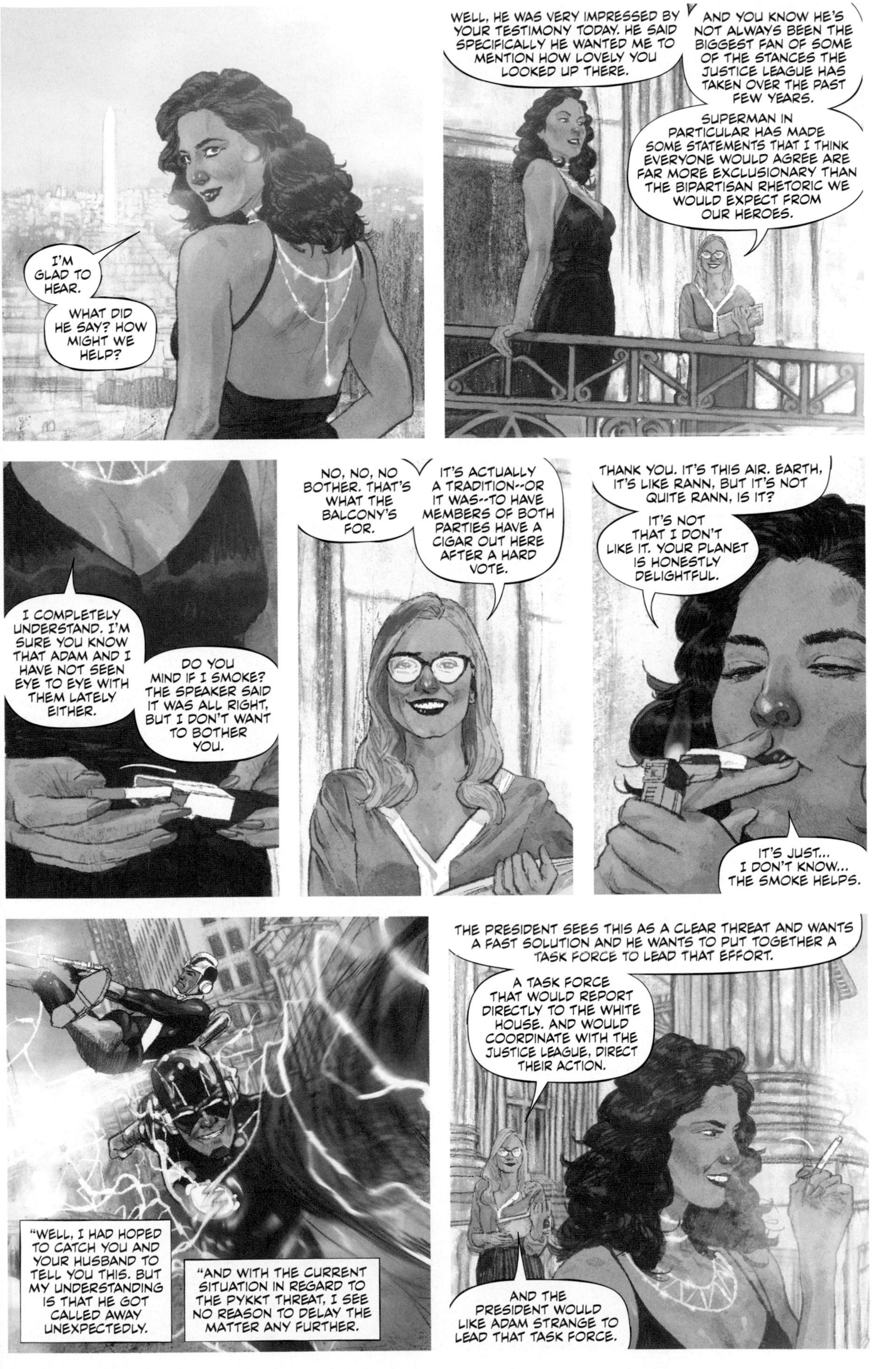
I'M GLAD TO HEAR.
WHAT DID HE SAY? HOW MIGHT WE HELP?
WELL, HE WAS VERY IMPRESSED BY YOUR TESTIMONY TODAY. HE SAID SPECIFICALLY HE WANTED ME TO MENTION HOW LOVELY YOU LOOKED UP THERE.
AND YOU KNOW HE'S NOT ALWAYS BEEN THE BIGGEST FAN OF SOME OF THE STANCES THE JUSTICE LEAGUE HAS TAKEN OVER THE PAST FEW YEARS.
SUPERMAN IN PARTICULAR HAS MADE SOME STATEMENTS THAT I THINK EVERYONE WOULD AGREE ARE FAR MORE EXCLUSIONARY THAN THE BIPARTISAN RHETORIC WE WOULD EXPECT FROM OUR HEROES.
I COMPLETELY UNDERSTAND. I'M SURE YOU KNOW THAT ADAM AND I HAVE NOT SEEN EYE TO EYE WITH THEM LATELY EITHER.
DO YOU MIND IF I SMOKE? THE SPEAKER SAID IT WAS ALL RIGHT, BUT I DON'T WANT TO BOTHER YOU.
NO, NO, NO BOTHER. THAT'S WHAT THE BALCONY'S FOR.
IT'S ACTUALLY A TRADITION--OR IT WAS--TO HAVE MEMBERS OF BOTH PARTIES HAVE A CIGAR OUT HERE AFTER A HARD VOTE.
THANK YOU. IT'S THIS AIR. EARTH, IT'S LIKE RANN, BUT IT'S NOT QUITE RANN, IS IT?
IT'S NOT THAT I DON'T LIKE IT. YOUR PLANET IS HONESTLY DELIGHTFUL.
IT'S JUST... I DON'T KNOW... THE SMOKE HELPS.
"WELL, I HAD HOPED TO CATCH YOU AND YOUR HUSBAND TO TELL YOU THIS. BUT MY UNDERSTANDING IS THAT HE GOT CALLED AWAY UNEXPECTEDLY.
"AND WITH THE CURRENT SITUATION IN REGARD TO THE PYKKT THREAT, I SEE NO REASON TO DELAY THE MATTER ANY FURTHER.
THE PRESIDENT SEES THIS AS A CLEAR THREAT AND WANTS A FAST SOLUTION AND HE WANTS TO PUT TOGETHER A TASK FORCE TO LEAD THAT EFFORT.
A TASK FORCE THAT WOULD REPORT DIRECTLY TO THE WHITE HOUSE. AND WOULD COORDINATE WITH THE JUSTICE LEAGUE, DIRECT THEIR ACTION.
AND THE PRESIDENT WOULD LIKE ADAM STRANGE TO LEAD THAT TASK FORCE.

"WITH YOU AT HIS SIDE, OBVIOUSLY."

BANG

IT'S *THERE*. YOU... I *SEE* IT.

HURRY...

BANG

THERE *MUST* HAVE BEEN A *STORM* OR...

MAYBE *IT'S*...THERE'S... DO YOU...I SEE IT...DO YOU *SEE* IT?

IT'S... *WET*...YES, YES, I SEE IT...

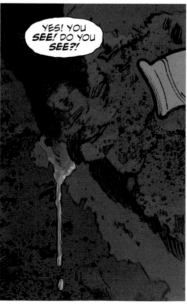

YES! YOU *SEE!* DO YOU *SEE?!*

OH, ADAM...

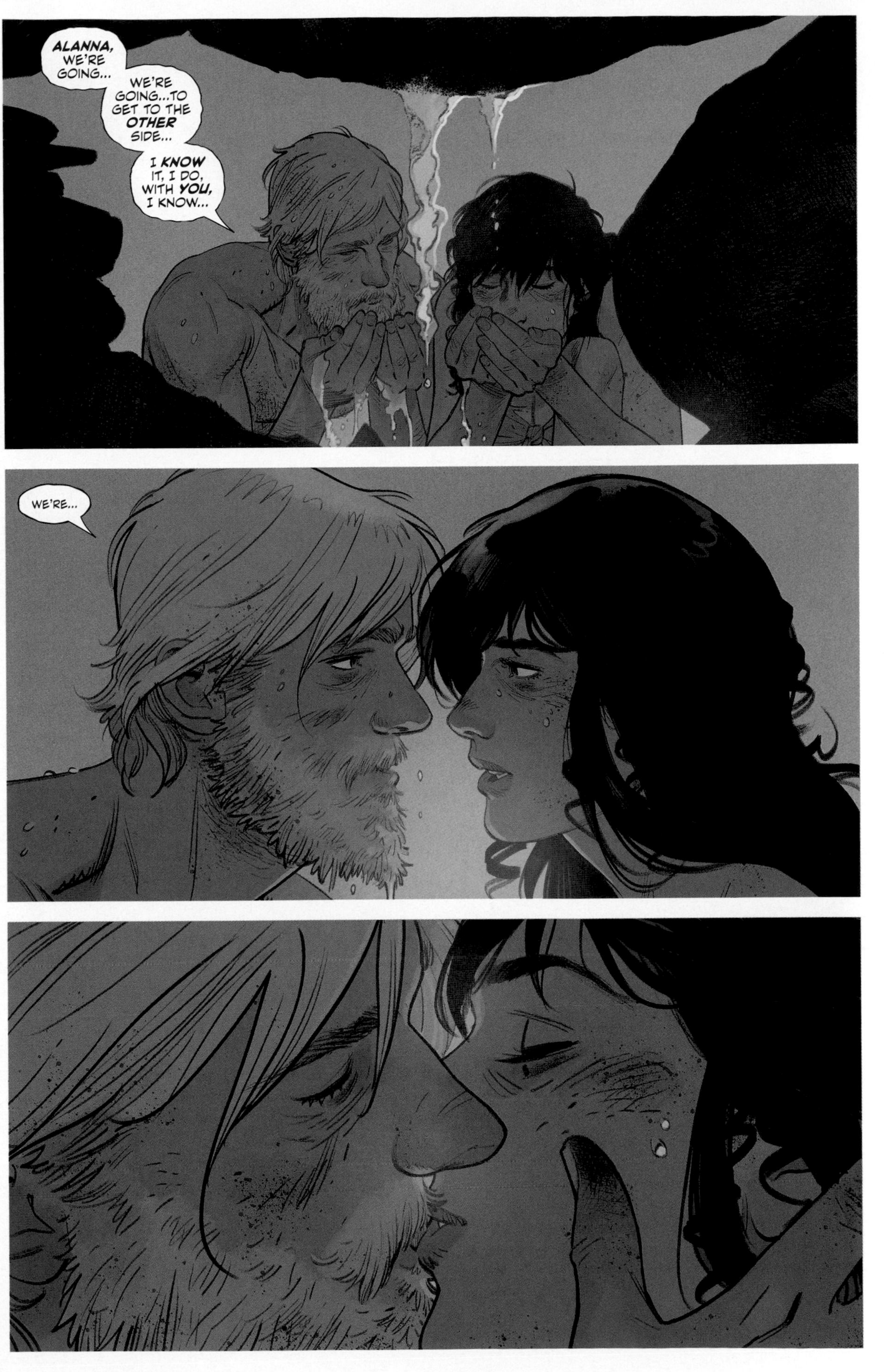
ALANNA, WE'RE GOING...
WE'RE GOING...TO GET TO THE OTHER SIDE...
I KNOW IT, I DO, WITH YOU, I KNOW...
WE'RE...

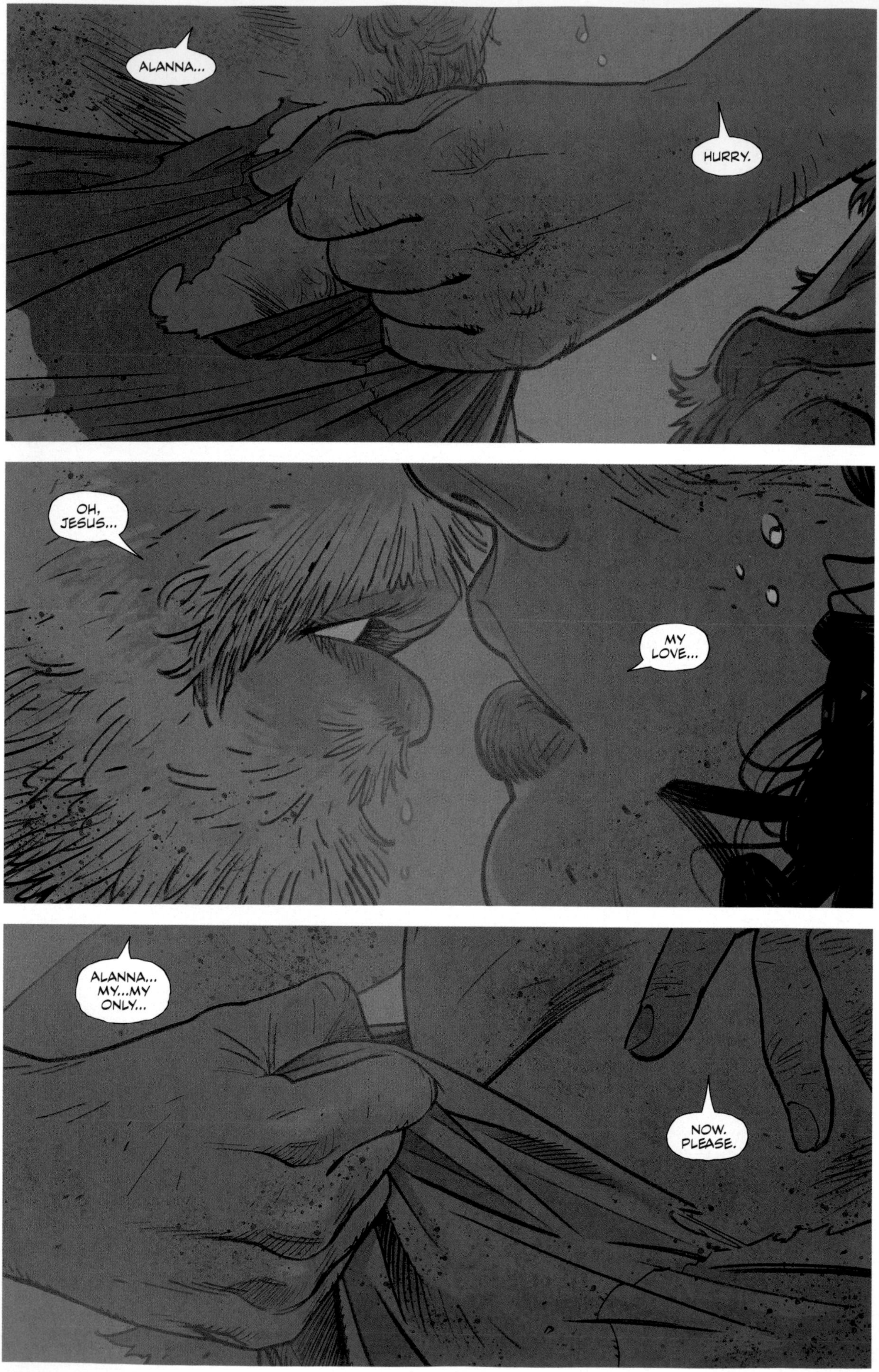
ALANNA...
HURRY.
OH, JESUS...
MY LOVE...
ALANNA... MY...MY ONLY...
NOW. PLEASE.

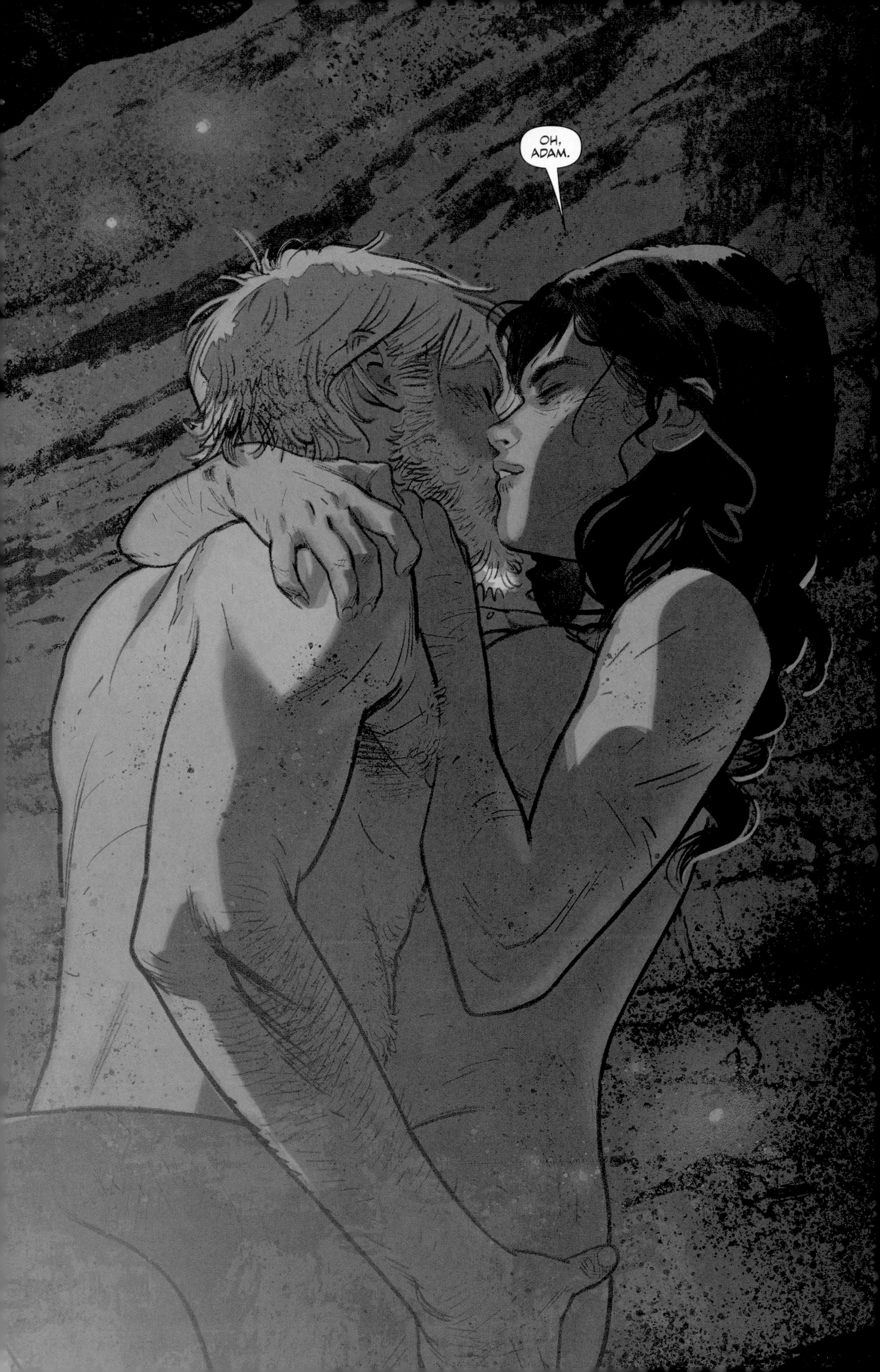
OH, ADAM.

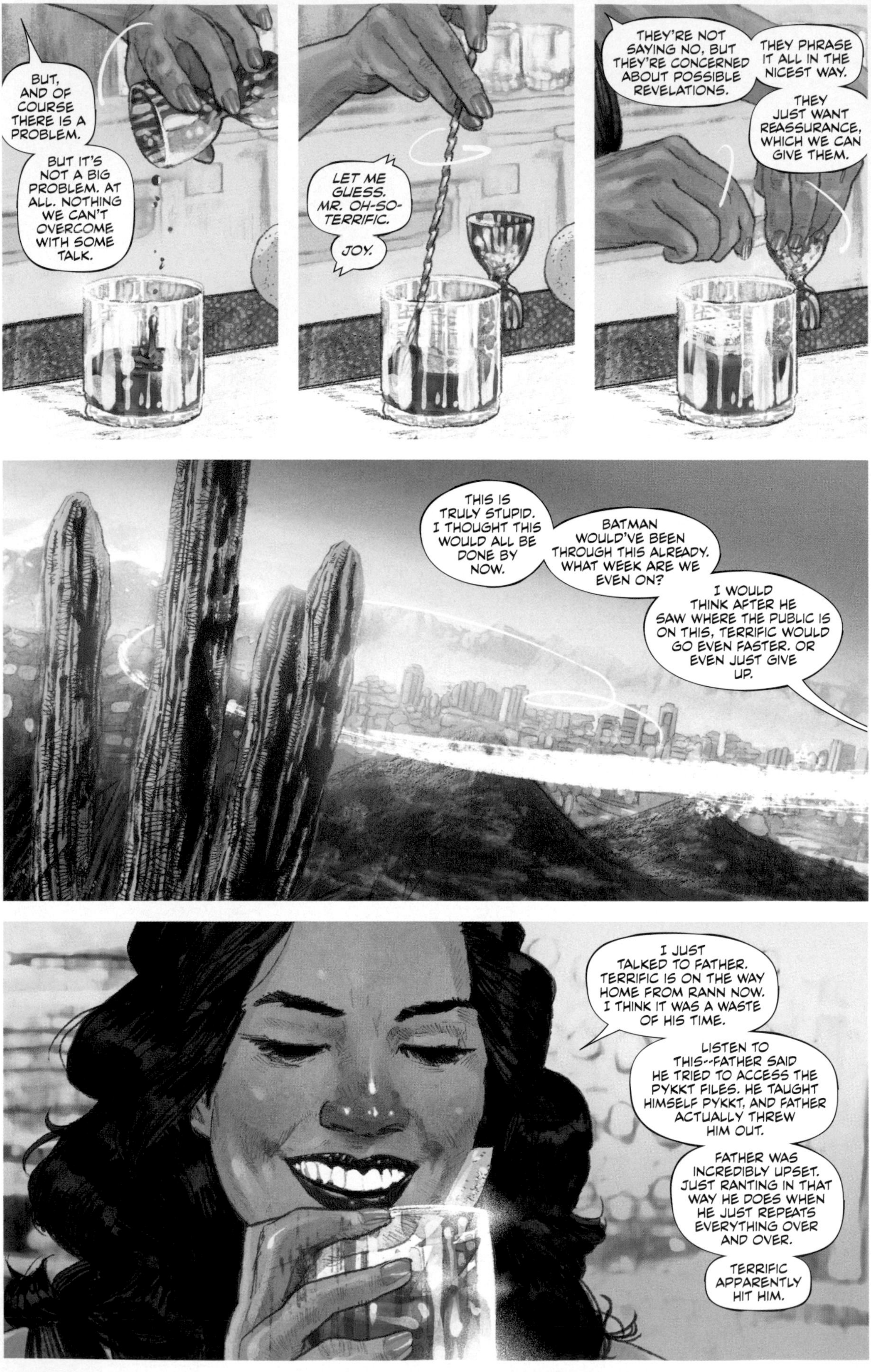
BUT, AND OF COURSE THERE IS A PROBLEM.
BUT IT'S NOT A BIG PROBLEM. AT ALL. NOTHING WE CAN'T OVERCOME WITH SOME TALK.
LET ME GUESS. MR. OH-SO-TERRIFIC.
JOY.
THEY'RE NOT SAYING NO, BUT THEY'RE CONCERNED ABOUT POSSIBLE REVELATIONS.
THEY PHRASE IT ALL IN THE NICEST WAY.
THEY JUST WANT REASSURANCE, WHICH WE CAN GIVE THEM.
THIS IS TRULY STUPID. I THOUGHT THIS WOULD ALL BE DONE BY NOW.
BATMAN WOULD'VE BEEN THROUGH THIS ALREADY. WHAT WEEK ARE WE EVEN ON?
I WOULD THINK AFTER HE SAW WHERE THE PUBLIC IS ON THIS, TERRIFIC WOULD GO EVEN FASTER. OR EVEN JUST GIVE UP.
I JUST TALKED TO FATHER. TERRIFIC IS ON THE WAY HOME FROM RANN NOW. I THINK IT WAS A WASTE OF HIS TIME.
LISTEN TO THIS--FATHER SAID HE TRIED TO ACCESS THE PYKKT FILES. HE TAUGHT HIMSELF PYKKT, AND FATHER ACTUALLY THREW HIM OUT.
FATHER WAS INCREDIBLY UPSET. JUST RANTING IN THAT WAY HE DOES WHEN HE JUST REPEATS EVERYTHING OVER AND OVER.
TERRIFIC APPARENTLY HIT HIM.

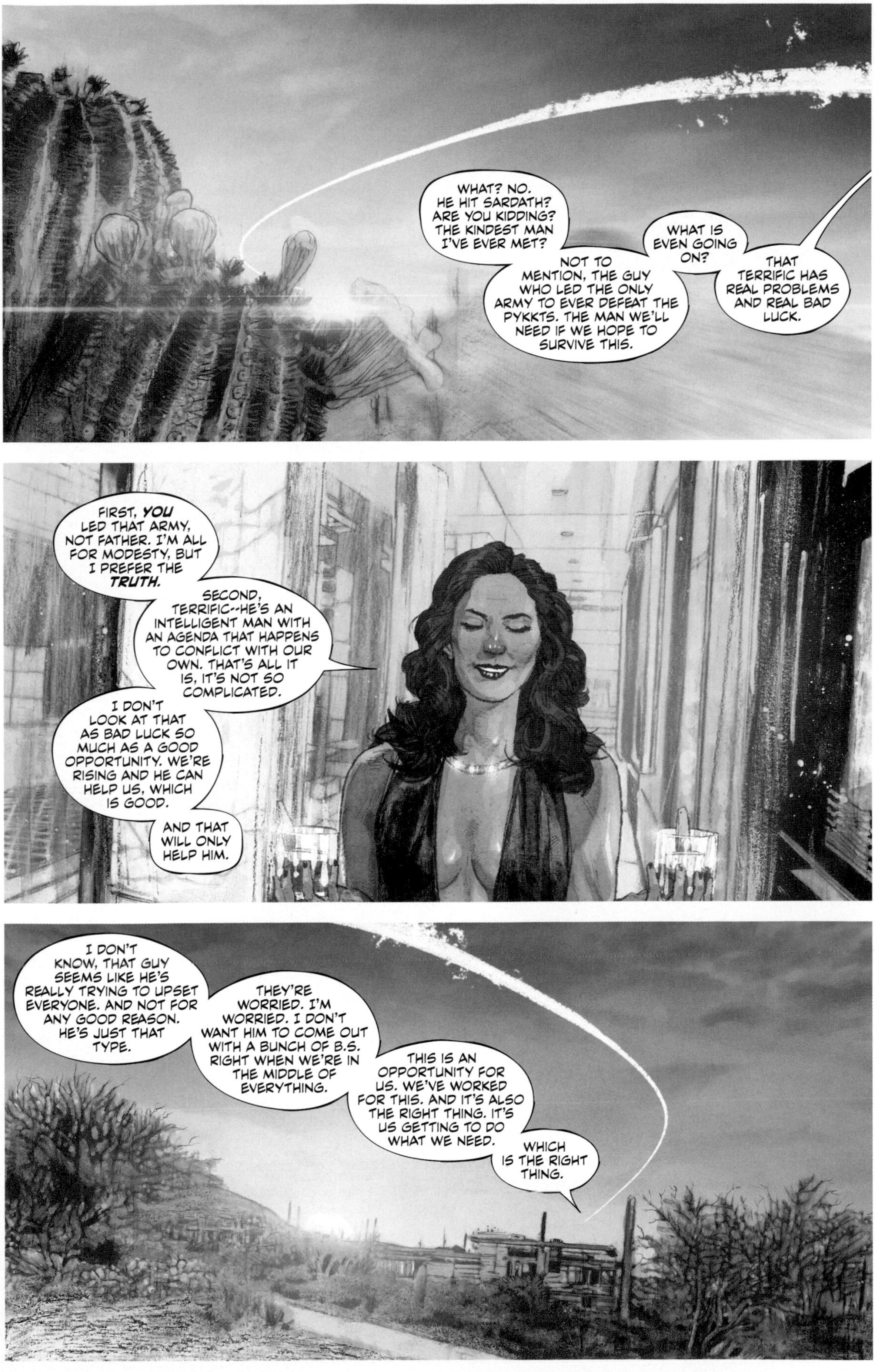
WHAT? NO. HE HIT SARDATH? ARE YOU KIDDING? THE KINDEST MAN I'VE EVER MET?
NOT TO MENTION, THE GUY WHO LED THE ONLY ARMY TO EVER DEFEAT THE PYKKTS. THE MAN WE'LL NEED IF WE HOPE TO SURVIVE THIS.
WHAT IS EVEN GOING ON?
THAT TERRIFIC HAS REAL PROBLEMS AND REAL BAD LUCK.
FIRST, ***YOU*** LED THAT ARMY, NOT FATHER. I'M ALL FOR MODESTY, BUT I PREFER THE ***TRUTH.***
SECOND, TERRIFIC--HE'S AN INTELLIGENT MAN WITH AN AGENDA THAT HAPPENS TO CONFLICT WITH OUR OWN. THAT'S ALL IT IS, IT'S NOT SO COMPLICATED.
I DON'T LOOK AT THAT AS BAD LUCK SO MUCH AS A GOOD OPPORTUNITY. WE'RE RISING AND HE CAN HELP US, WHICH IS GOOD.
AND THAT WILL ONLY HELP HIM.
I DON'T KNOW, THAT GUY SEEMS LIKE HE'S REALLY TRYING TO UPSET EVERYONE. AND NOT FOR ANY GOOD REASON. HE'S JUST THAT TYPE.
THEY'RE WORRIED. I'M WORRIED. I DON'T WANT HIM TO COME OUT WITH A BUNCH OF B.S. RIGHT WHEN WE'RE IN THE MIDDLE OF EVERYTHING.
THIS IS AN OPPORTUNITY FOR US. WE'VE WORKED FOR THIS. AND IT'S ALSO THE RIGHT THING. IT'S US GETTING TO DO WHAT WE NEED.
WHICH IS THE RIGHT THING.

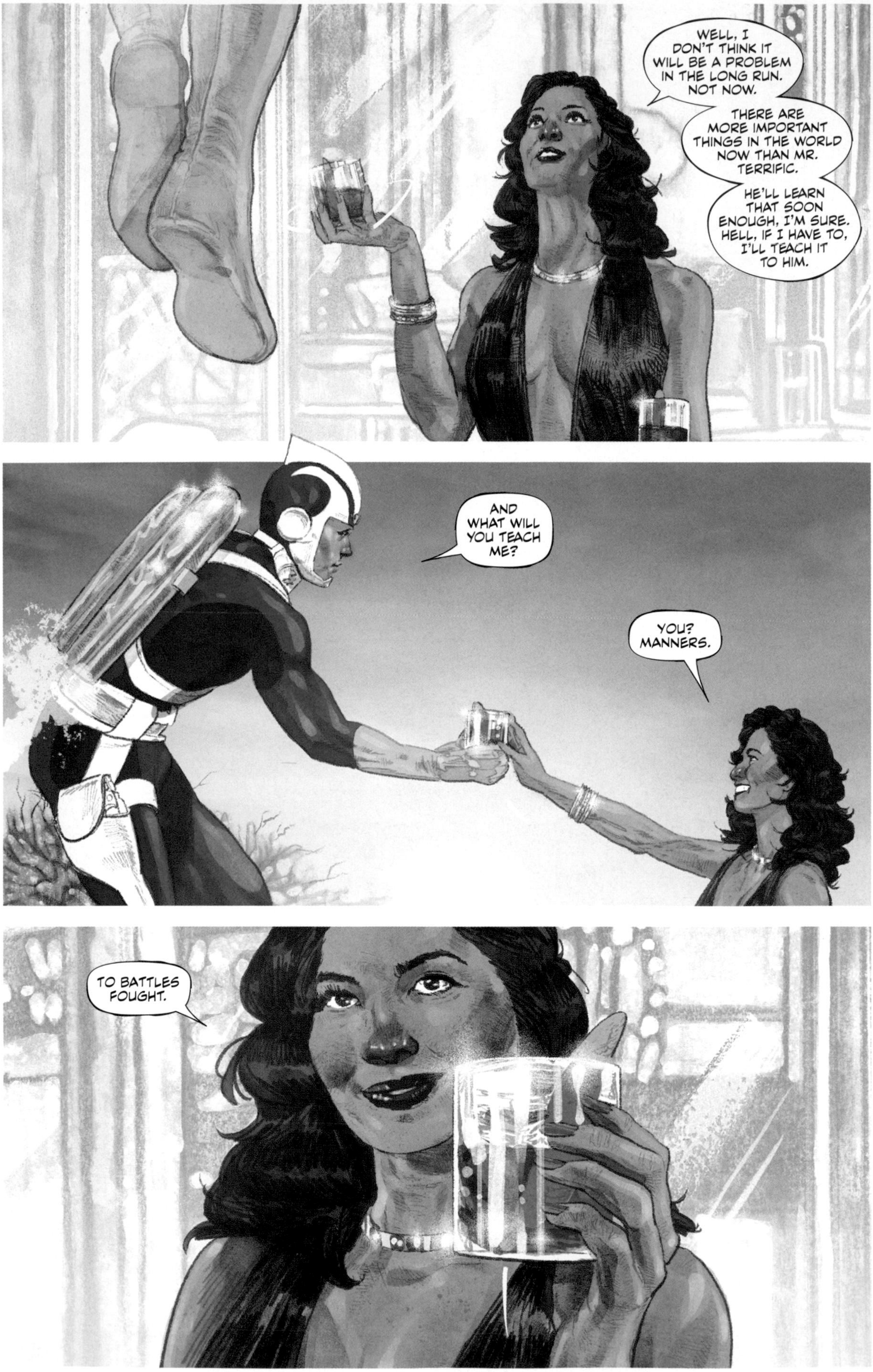
WELL, I DON'T THINK IT WILL BE A PROBLEM IN THE LONG RUN. NOT NOW.
THERE ARE MORE IMPORTANT THINGS IN THE WORLD NOW THAN MR. TERRIFIC.
HE'LL LEARN THAT SOON ENOUGH, I'M SURE. HELL, IF I HAVE TO, I'LL TEACH IT TO HIM.
AND WHAT WILL YOU TEACH ME?
YOU? MANNERS.
TO BATTLES FOUGHT.

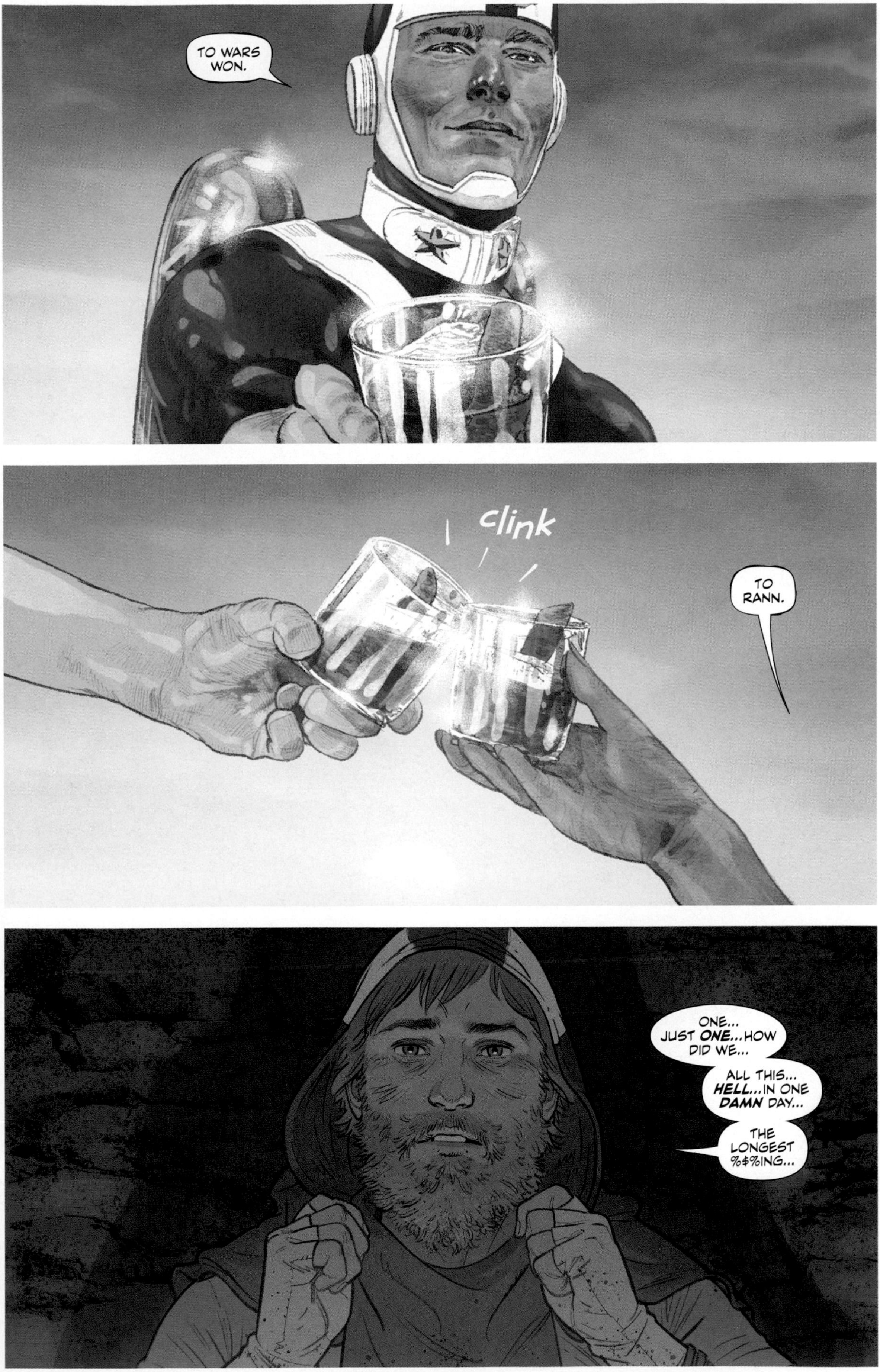
TO WARS WON.
clink
TO RANN.
ONE... JUST ONE...HOW DID WE...
ALL THIS... HELL...IN ONE DAMN DAY...
THE LONGEST %$%ING...

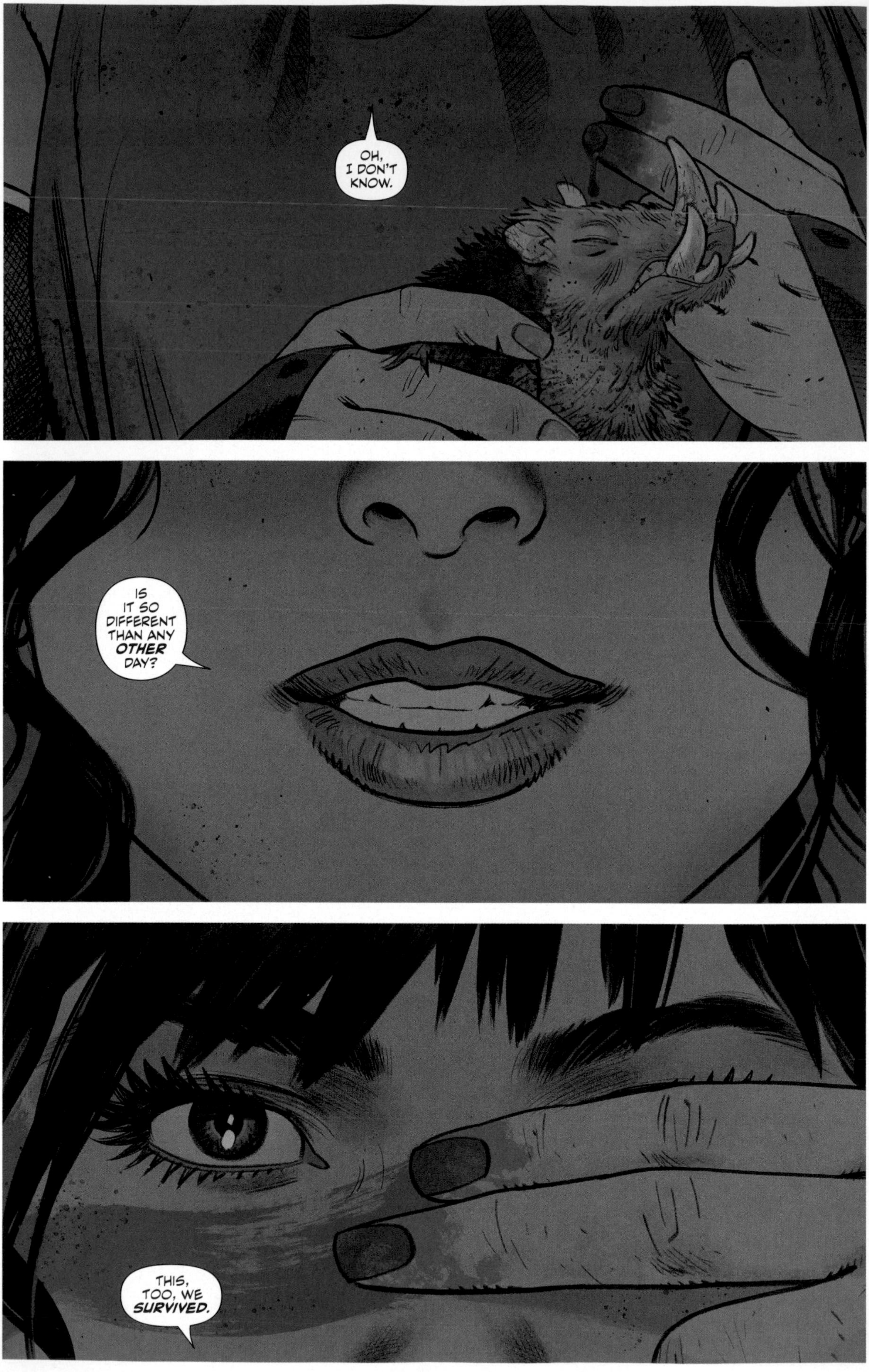
OH, I DON'T KNOW.
IS IT SO DIFFERENT THAN ANY **OTHER** DAY?
THIS, TOO, WE **SURVIVED.**

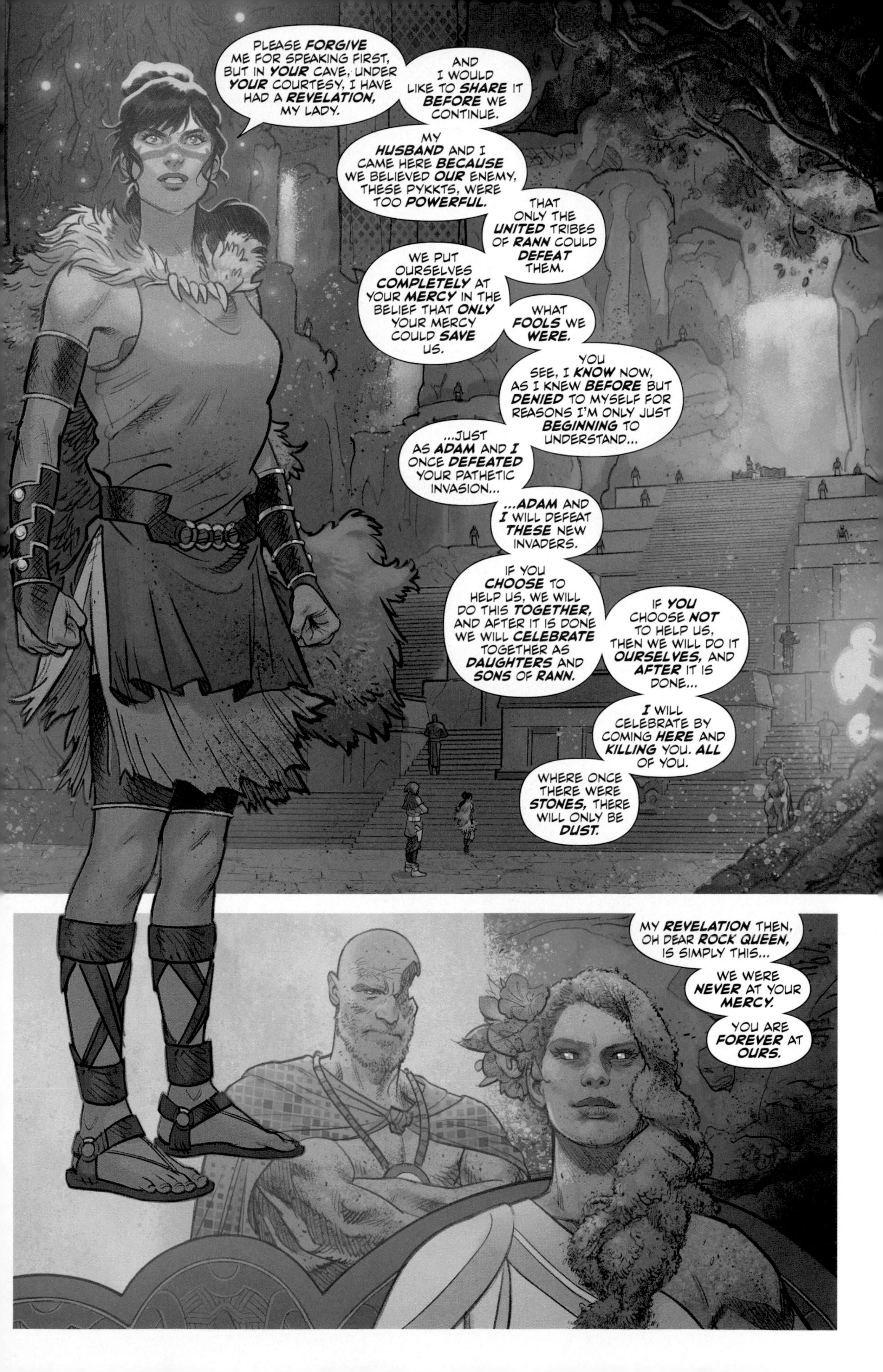
PLEASE FORGIVE ME FOR SPEAKING FIRST, BUT IN YOUR CAVE, UNDER YOUR COURTESY, I HAVE HAD A REVELATION, MY LADY.
AND I WOULD LIKE TO SHARE IT BEFORE WE CONTINUE.
MY HUSBAND AND I CAME HERE BECAUSE WE BELIEVED OUR ENEMY, THESE PYKKTS, WERE TOO POWERFUL.
THAT ONLY THE UNITED TRIBES OF RANN COULD DEFEAT THEM.
WE PUT OURSELVES COMPLETELY AT YOUR MERCY IN THE BELIEF THAT ONLY YOUR MERCY COULD SAVE US.
WHAT FOOLS WE WERE.
YOU SEE, I KNOW NOW, AS I KNEW BEFORE BUT DENIED TO MYSELF FOR REASONS I'M ONLY JUST BEGINNING TO UNDERSTAND...
...JUST AS ADAM AND I ONCE DEFEATED YOUR PATHETIC INVASION...
...ADAM AND I WILL DEFEAT THESE NEW INVADERS.
IF YOU CHOOSE TO HELP US, WE WILL DO THIS TOGETHER, AND AFTER IT IS DONE WE WILL CELEBRATE TOGETHER AS DAUGHTERS AND SONS OF RANN.
IF YOU CHOOSE NOT TO HELP US, THEN WE WILL DO IT OURSELVES, AND AFTER IT IS DONE...
I WILL CELEBRATE BY COMING HERE AND KILLING YOU. ALL OF YOU.
WHERE ONCE THERE WERE STONES, THERE WILL ONLY BE DUST.
MY REVELATION THEN, OH DEAR ROCK QUEEN, IS SIMPLY THIS...
WE WERE NEVER AT YOUR MERCY.
YOU ARE FOREVER AT OURS.

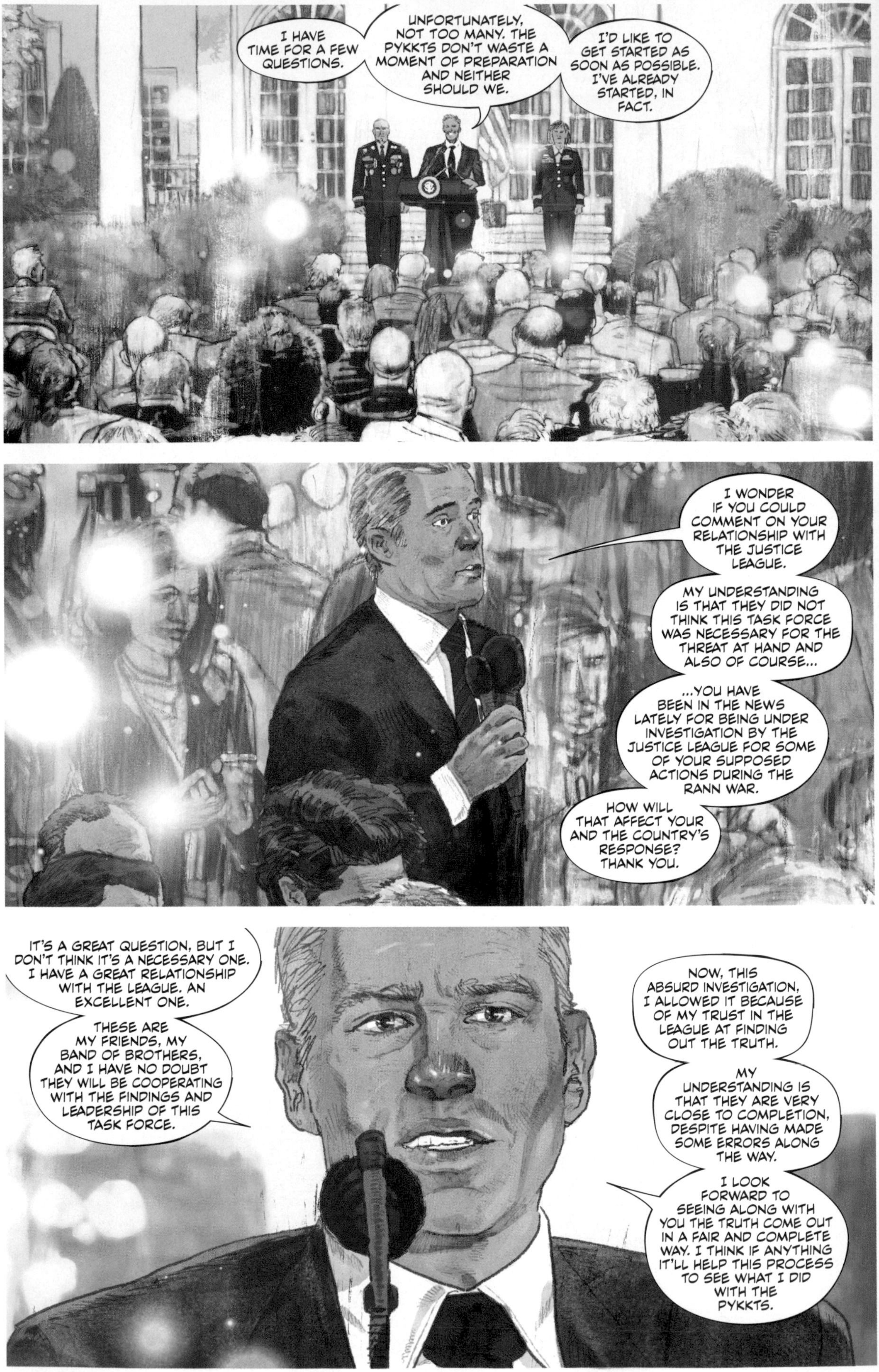
I HAVE TIME FOR A FEW QUESTIONS.
UNFORTUNATELY, NOT TOO MANY. THE PYKKTS DON'T WASTE A MOMENT OF PREPARATION AND NEITHER SHOULD WE.
I'D LIKE TO GET STARTED AS SOON AS POSSIBLE. I'VE ALREADY STARTED, IN FACT.
I WONDER IF YOU COULD COMMENT ON YOUR RELATIONSHIP WITH THE JUSTICE LEAGUE.
MY UNDERSTANDING IS THAT THEY DID NOT THINK THIS TASK FORCE WAS NECESSARY FOR THE THREAT AT HAND AND ALSO OF COURSE...
...YOU HAVE BEEN IN THE NEWS LATELY FOR BEING UNDER INVESTIGATION BY THE JUSTICE LEAGUE FOR SOME OF YOUR SUPPOSED ACTIONS DURING THE RANN WAR.
HOW WILL THAT AFFECT YOUR AND THE COUNTRY'S RESPONSE? THANK YOU.
IT'S A GREAT QUESTION, BUT I DON'T THINK IT'S A NECESSARY ONE. I HAVE A GREAT RELATIONSHIP WITH THE LEAGUE. AN EXCELLENT ONE.
THESE ARE MY FRIENDS, MY BAND OF BROTHERS, AND I HAVE NO DOUBT THEY WILL BE COOPERATING WITH THE FINDINGS AND LEADERSHIP OF THIS TASK FORCE.
NOW, THIS ABSURD INVESTIGATION, I ALLOWED IT BECAUSE OF MY TRUST IN THE LEAGUE AT FINDING OUT THE TRUTH.
MY UNDERSTANDING IS THAT THEY ARE VERY CLOSE TO COMPLETION, DESPITE HAVING MADE SOME ERRORS ALONG THE WAY.
I LOOK FORWARD TO SEEING ALONG WITH YOU THE TRUTH COME OUT IN A FAIR AND COMPLETE WAY. I THINK IF ANYTHING IT'LL HELP THIS PROCESS TO SEE WHAT I DID WITH THE PYKKTS.

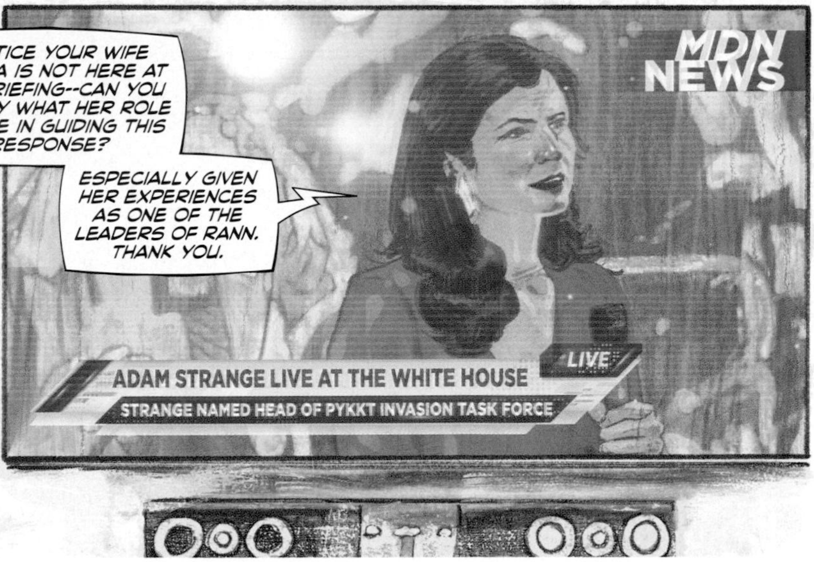
I NOTICE YOUR WIFE ALANNA IS NOT HERE AT THE BRIEFING--CAN YOU SPECIFY WHAT HER ROLE WILL BE IN GUIDING THIS RESPONSE?
ESPECIALLY GIVEN HER EXPERIENCES AS ONE OF THE LEADERS OF RANN. THANK YOU.
MDN NEWS
LIVE
ADAM STRANGE LIVE AT THE WHITE HOUSE
STRANGE NAMED HEAD OF PYKKT INVASION TASK FORCE

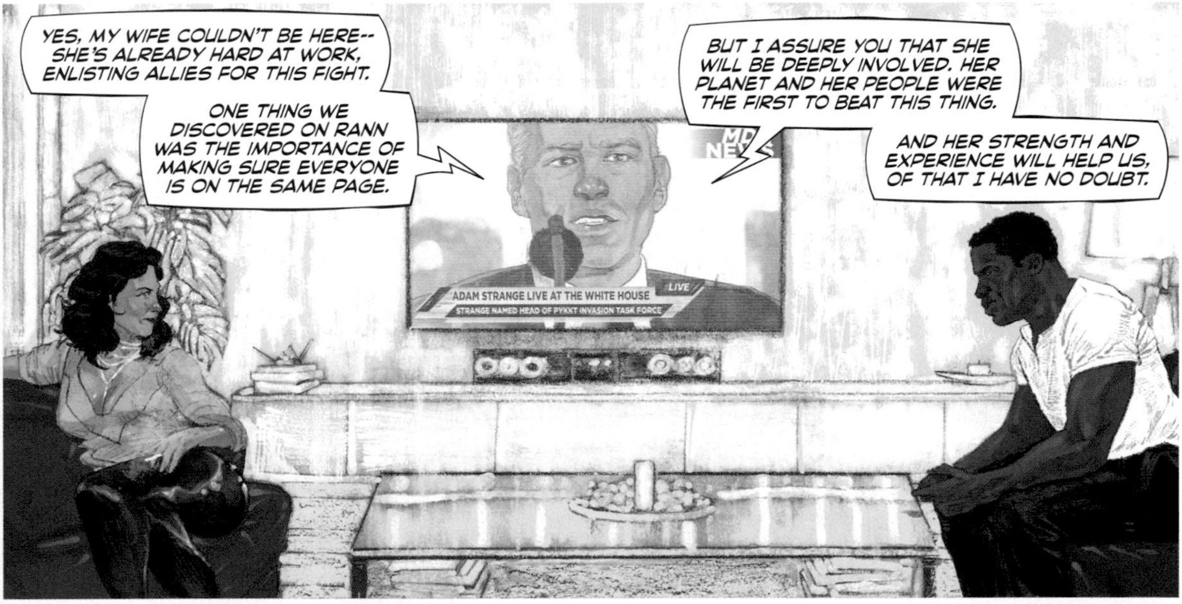
YES, MY WIFE COULDN'T BE HERE--SHE'S ALREADY HARD AT WORK, ENLISTING ALLIES FOR THIS FIGHT.
ONE THING WE DISCOVERED ON RANN WAS THE IMPORTANCE OF MAKING SURE EVERYONE IS ON THE SAME PAGE.
BUT I ASSURE YOU THAT SHE WILL BE DEEPLY INVOLVED. HER PLANET AND HER PEOPLE WERE THE FIRST TO BEAT THIS THING.
AND HER STRENGTH AND EXPERIENCE WILL HELP US, OF THAT I HAVE NO DOUBT.
ADAM STRANGE LIVE AT THE WHITE HOUSE
STRANGE NAMED HEAD OF PYKKT INVASION TASK FORCE
LIVE

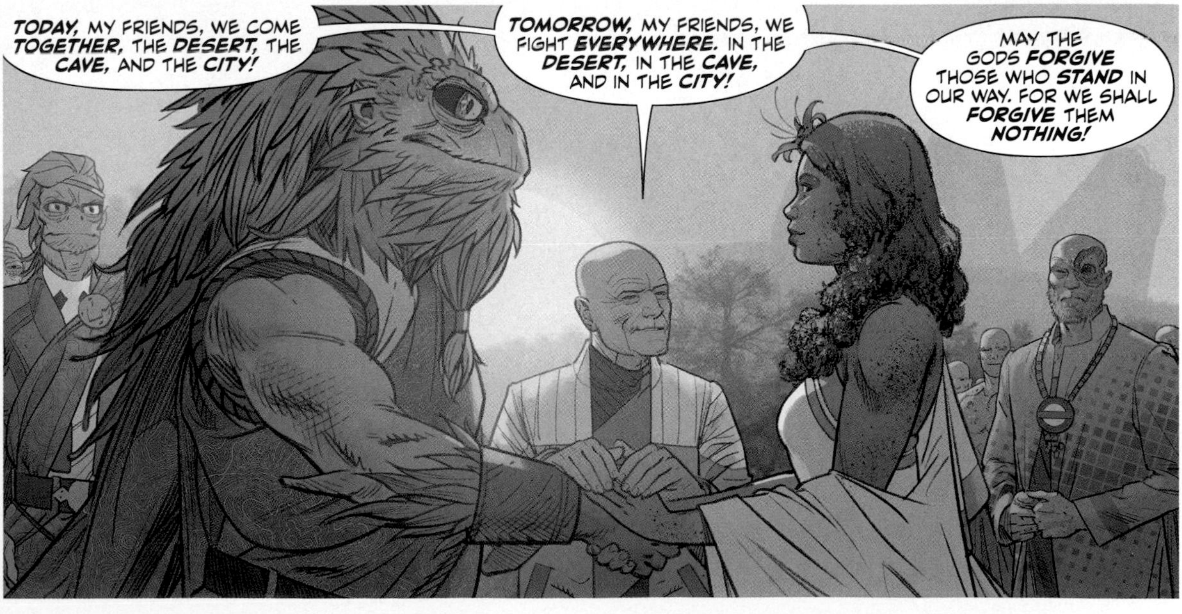
TODAY, MY FRIENDS, WE COME TOGETHER, THE DESERT, THE CAVE, AND THE CITY!
TOMORROW, MY FRIENDS, WE FIGHT EVERYWHERE. IN THE DESERT, IN THE CAVE, AND IN THE CITY!
MAY THE GODS FORGIVE THOSE WHO STAND IN OUR WAY. FOR WE SHALL FORGIVE THEM NOTHING!

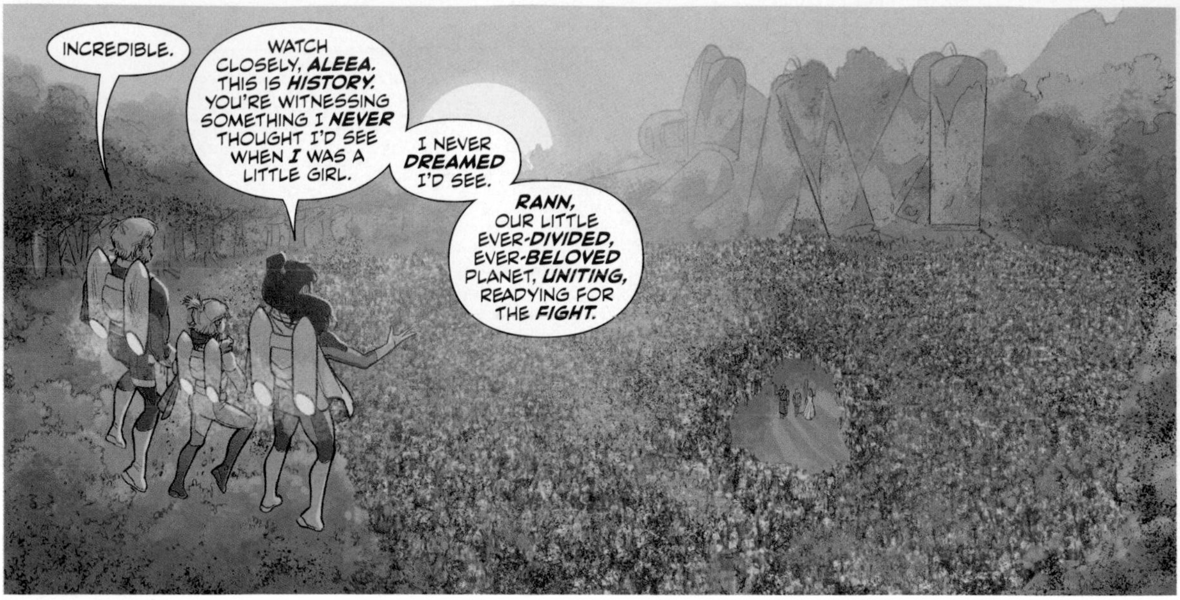
INCREDIBLE.
WATCH CLOSELY, ALEEA. THIS IS HISTORY. YOU'RE WITNESSING SOMETHING I NEVER THOUGHT I'D SEE WHEN I WAS A LITTLE GIRL.
I NEVER DREAMED I'D SEE.
RANN, OUR LITTLE EVER-DIVIDED, EVER-BELOVED PLANET, UNITING, READYING FOR THE FIGHT.

And you like to know that somebody out there appreciated what you were doing. You know, you have a mixed feeling about these things as you work on them. And you have other things, obligations, on the other hand.

—Murphy Anderson

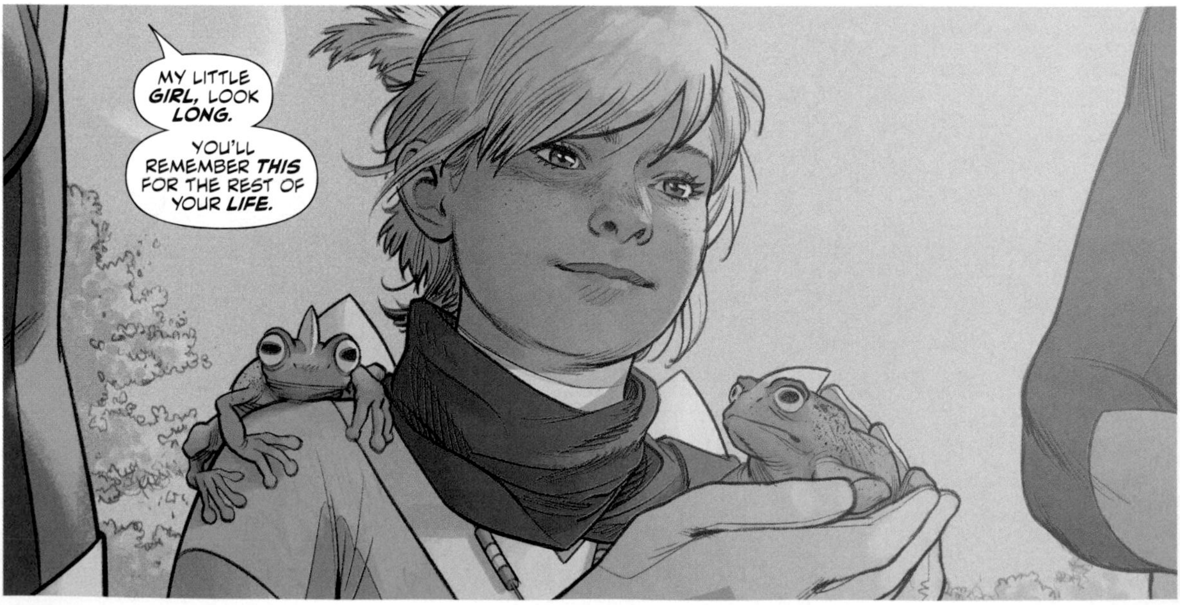
MY LITTLE GIRL, LOOK LONG.
YOU'LL REMEMBER THIS FOR THE REST OF YOUR LIFE.

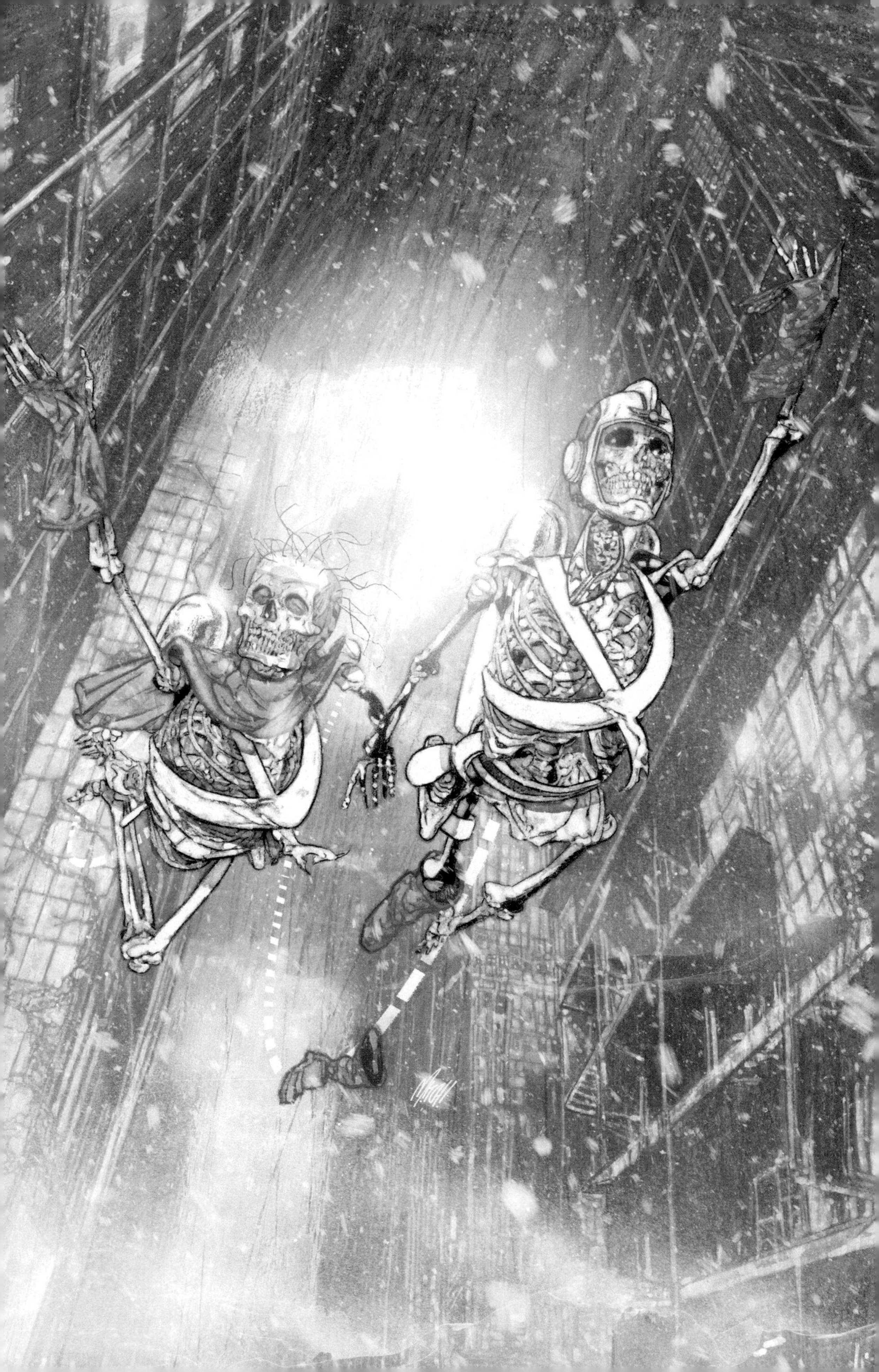

"I'M ASHAMED OF OUR ACTIONS, BUT I'M NOT AFRAID OF THEM."

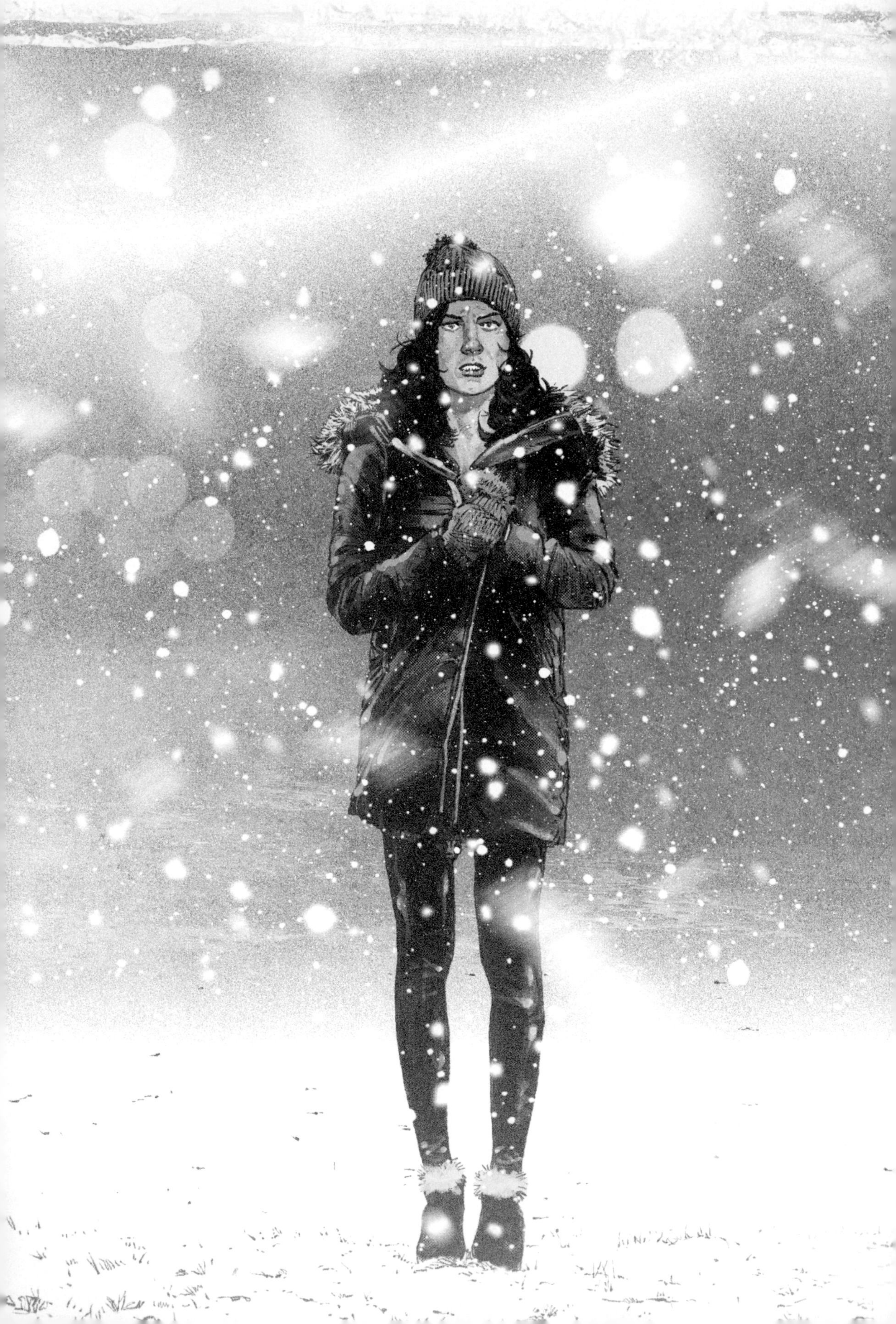

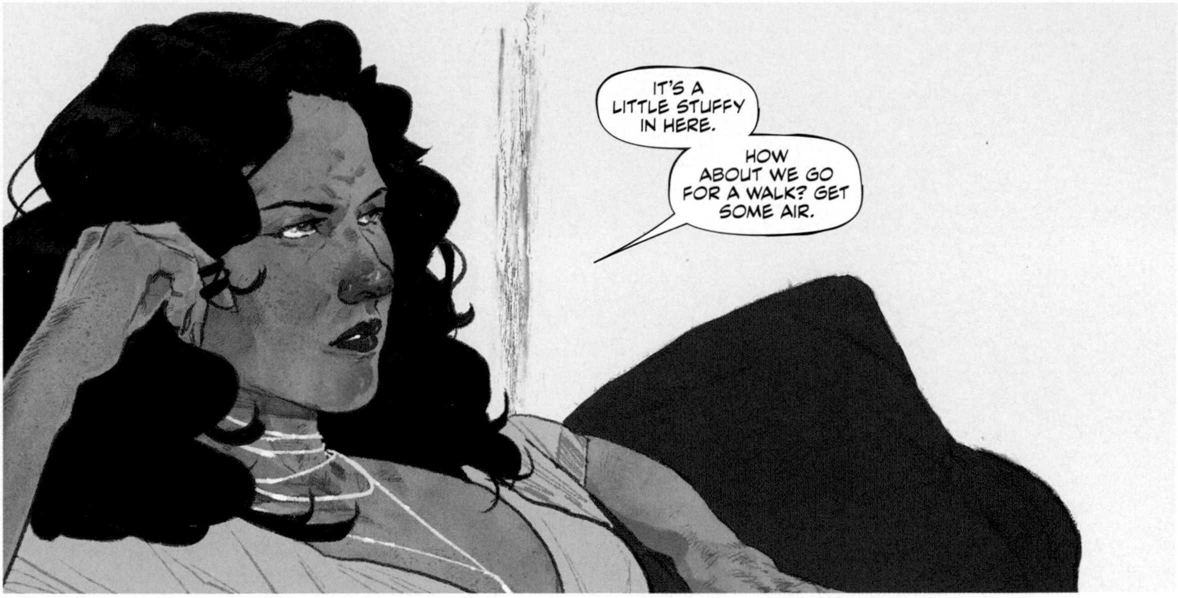
IT'S A LITTLE STUFFY IN HERE.
HOW ABOUT WE GO FOR A WALK? GET SOME AIR.

Chapter 6

Another thing

TOM KING ...Writer

MITCH GERADS
EVAN "DOC" SHANER ...Interior & Cover Artists

CLAYTON COWLES ...Letterer
BIXIE MATHIEU ...Assistant Editor
BRITTANY HOLZHERR ...Associate Editor
JAMIE S. RICH ...Editor

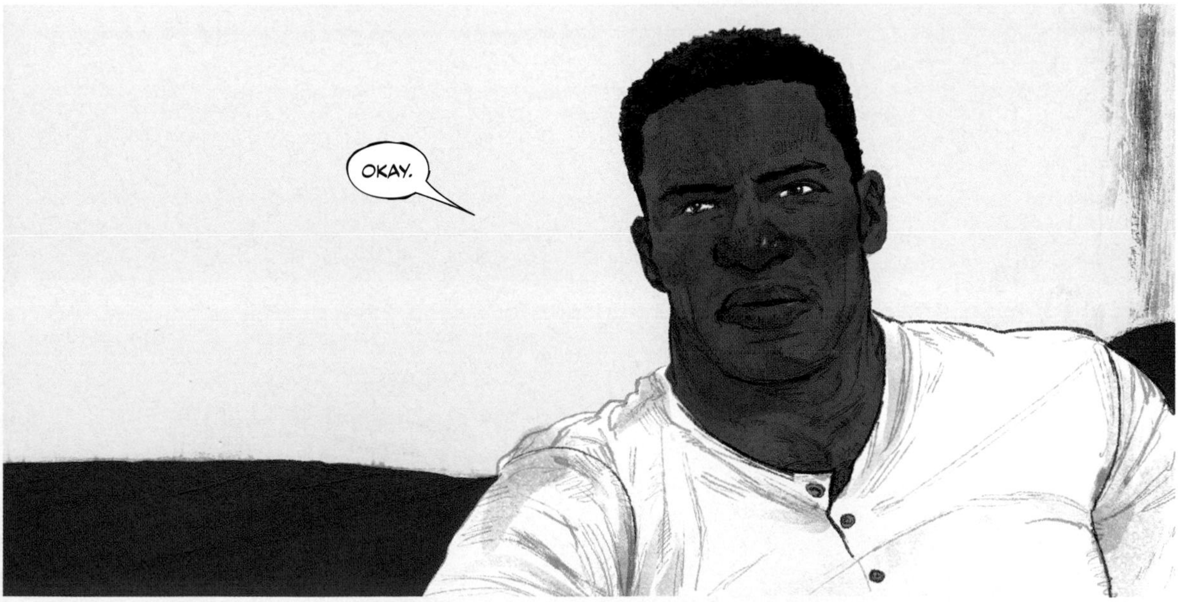
OKAY.

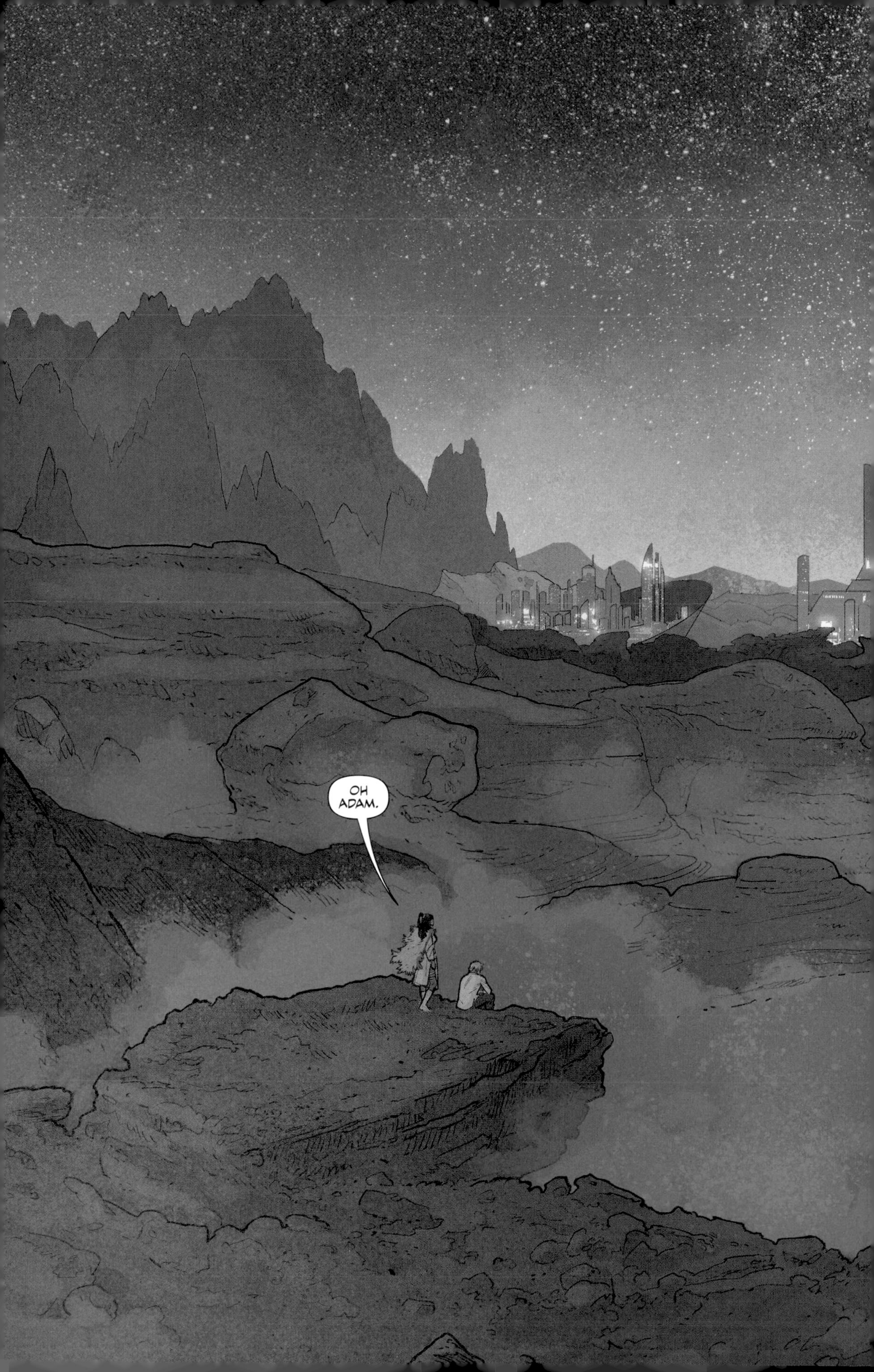
OH ADAM.

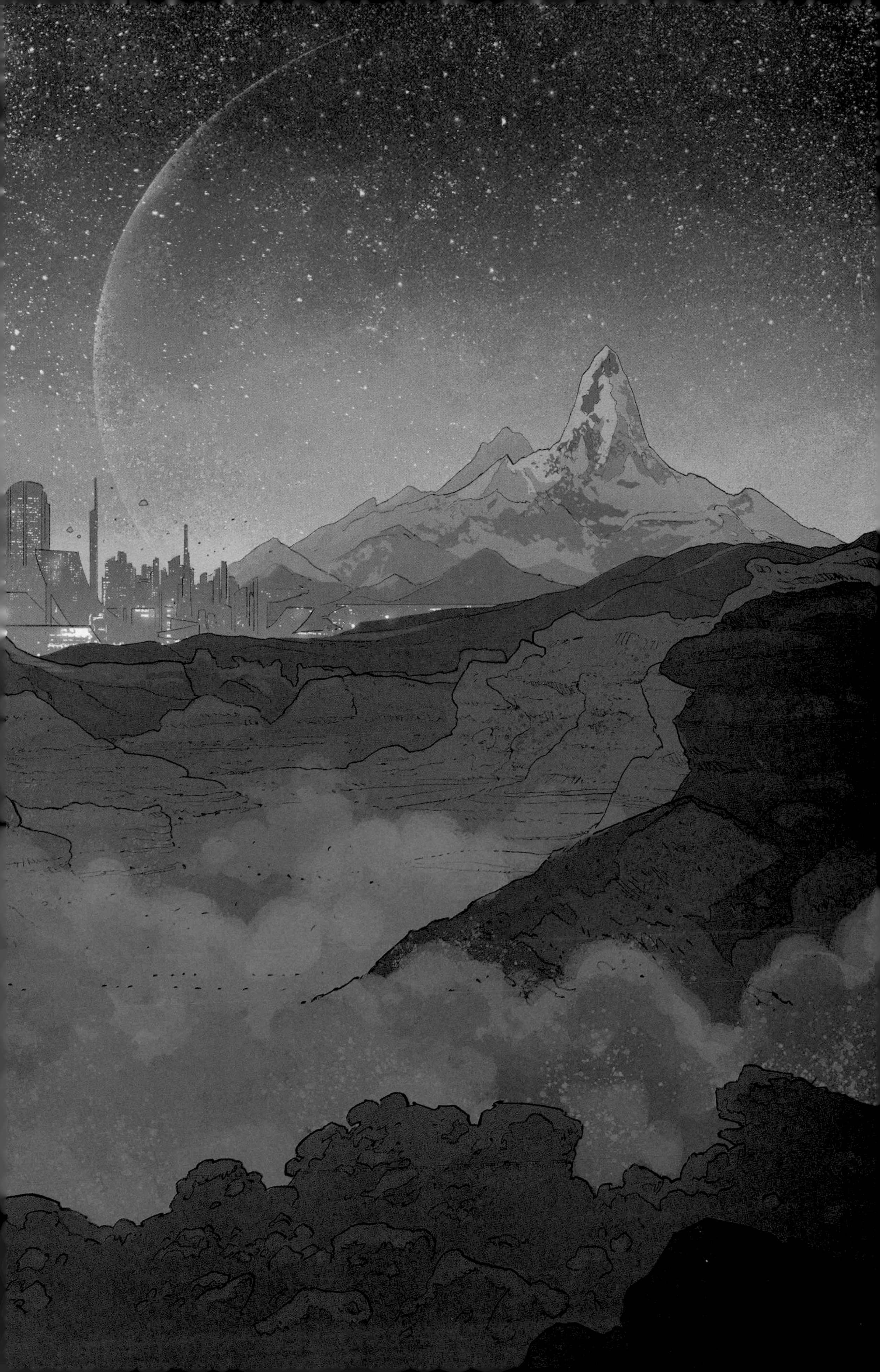

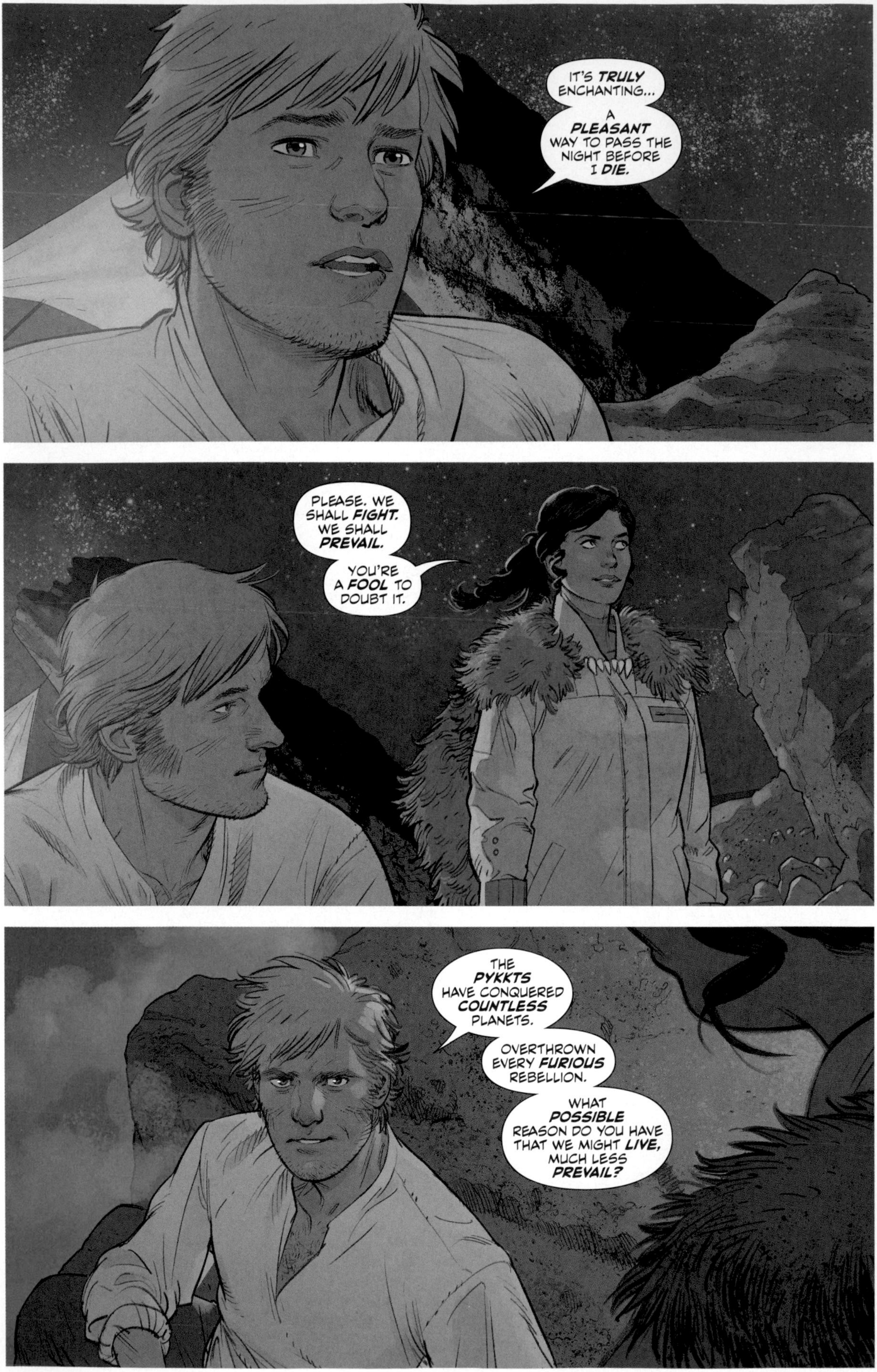
IT'S TRULY ENCHANTING...
A PLEASANT WAY TO PASS THE NIGHT BEFORE I DIE.
PLEASE. WE SHALL FIGHT. WE SHALL PREVAIL.
YOU'RE A FOOL TO DOUBT IT.
THE PYKKTS HAVE CONQUERED COUNTLESS PLANETS.
OVERTHROWN EVERY FURIOUS REBELLION.
WHAT POSSIBLE REASON DO YOU HAVE THAT WE MIGHT LIVE, MUCH LESS PREVAIL?

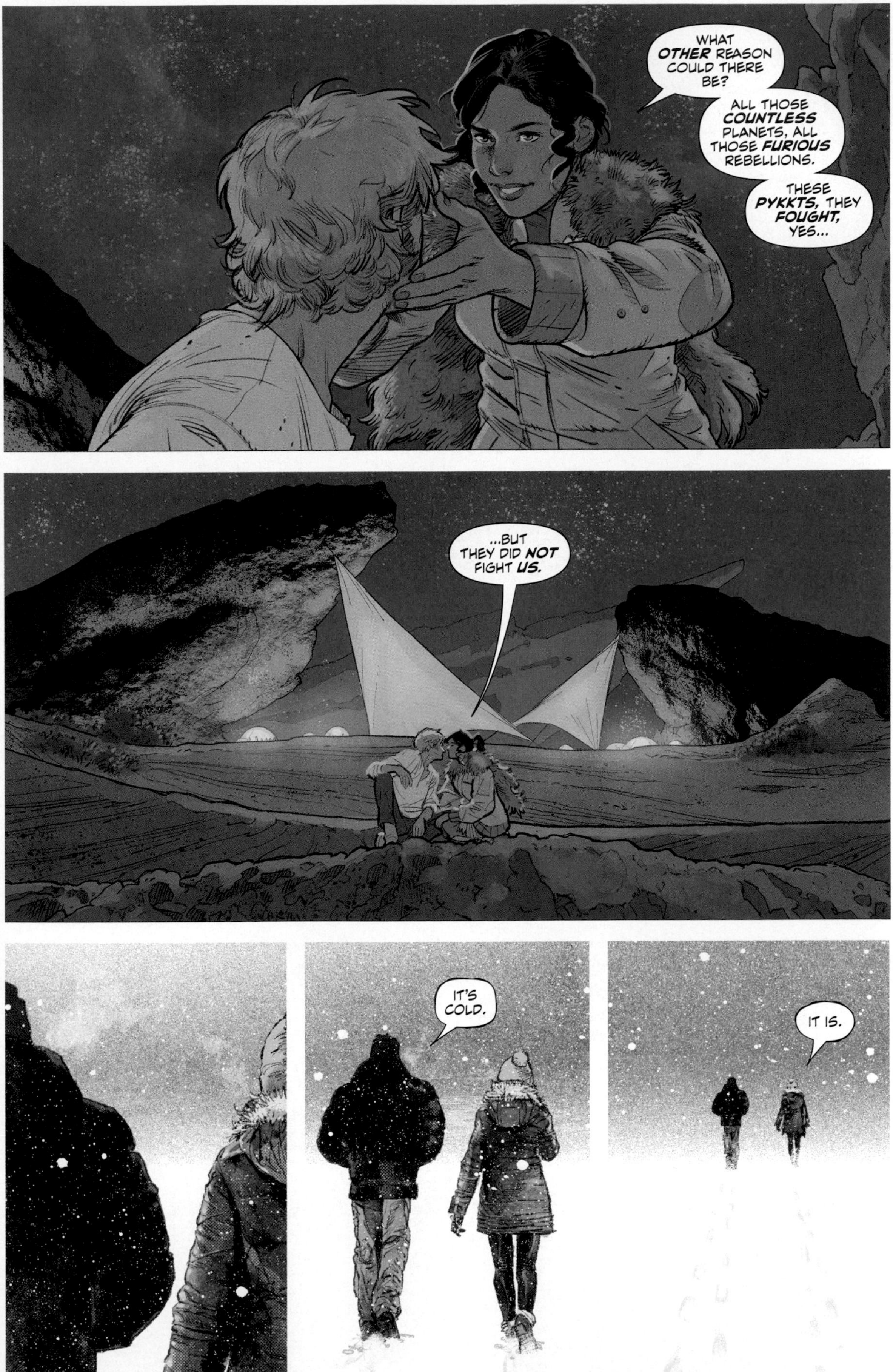
WHAT OTHER REASON COULD THERE BE?
ALL THOSE COUNTLESS PLANETS, ALL THOSE FURIOUS REBELLIONS.
THESE PYKKTS, THEY FOUGHT, YES...
...BUT THEY DID NOT FIGHT US.
IT'S COLD.
IT IS.

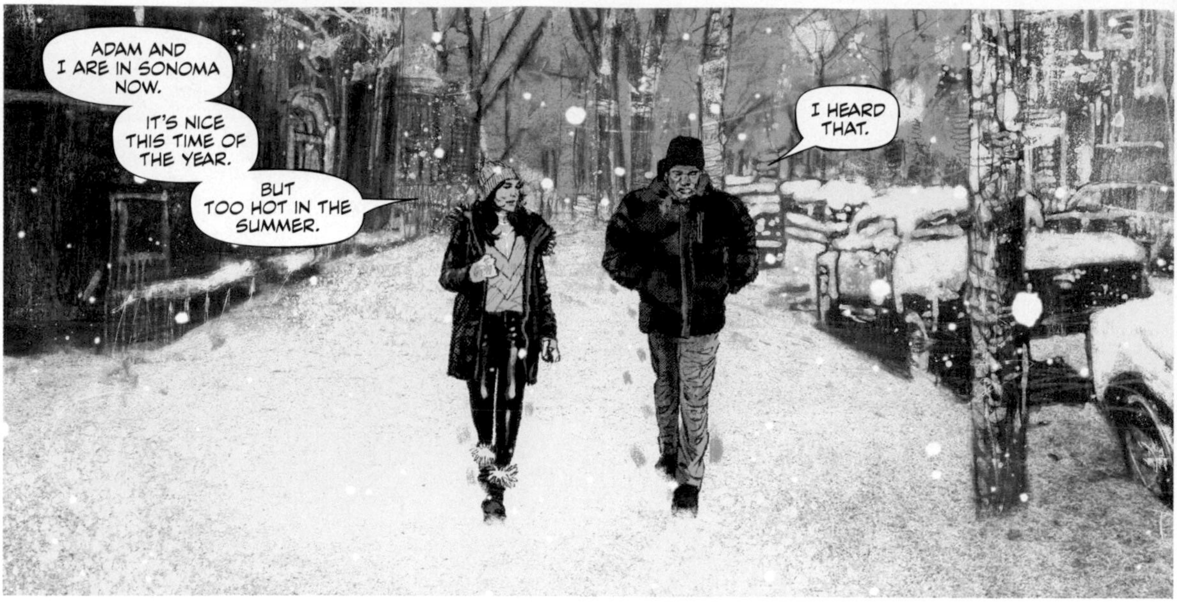
ADAM AND I ARE IN SONOMA NOW.
IT'S NICE THIS TIME OF THE YEAR.
BUT TOO HOT IN THE SUMMER.
I HEARD THAT.

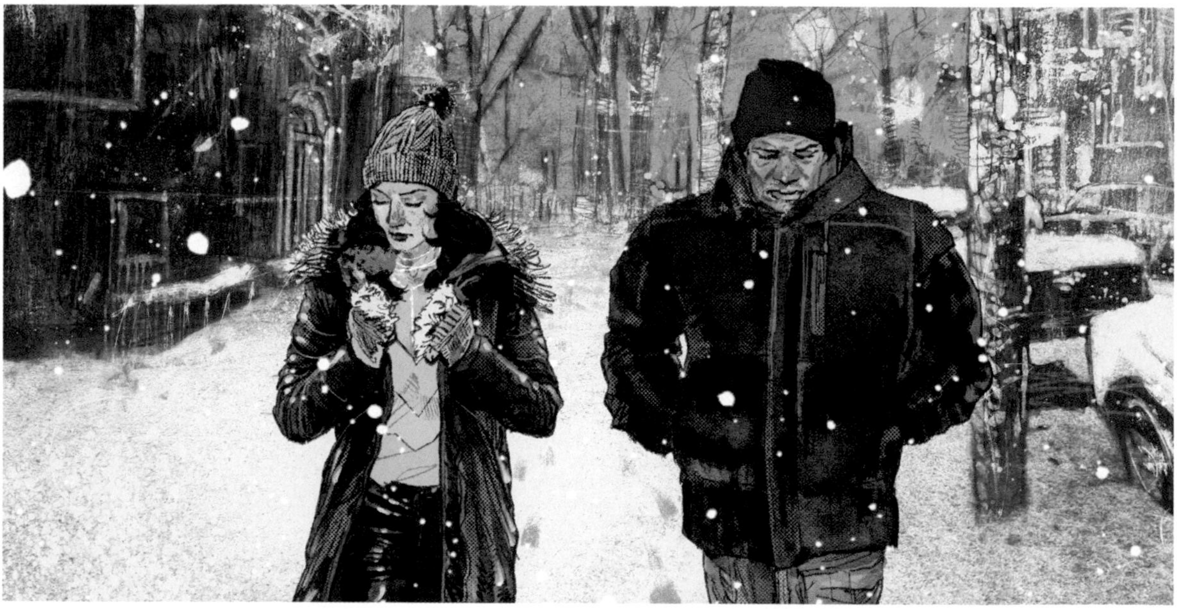

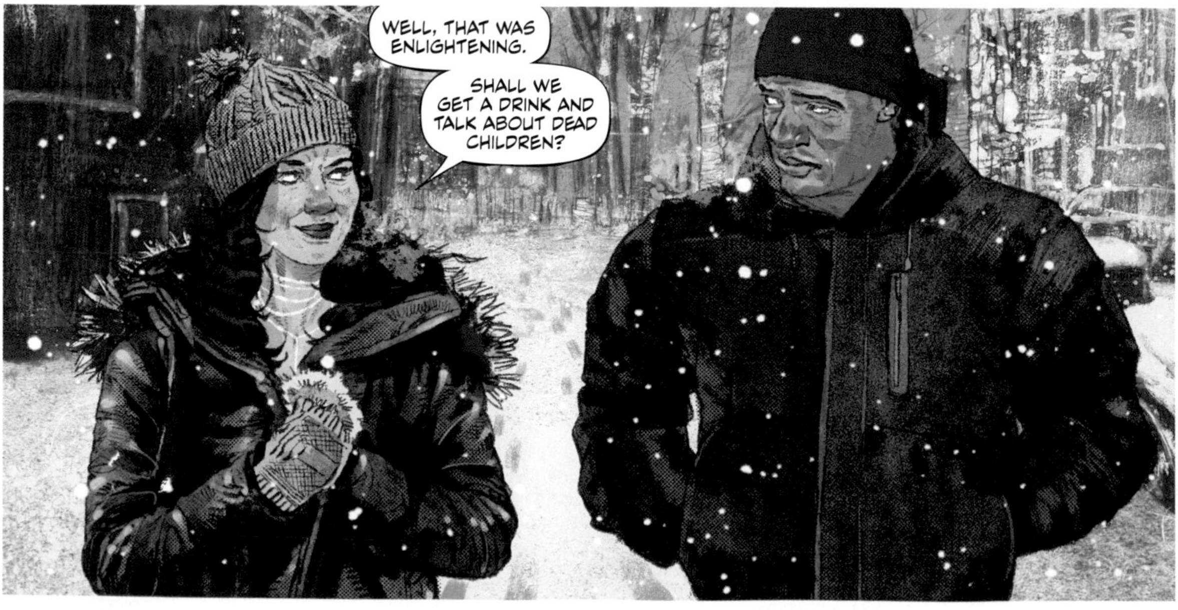
WELL, THAT WAS ENLIGHTENING.
SHALL WE GET A DRINK AND TALK ABOUT DEAD CHILDREN?

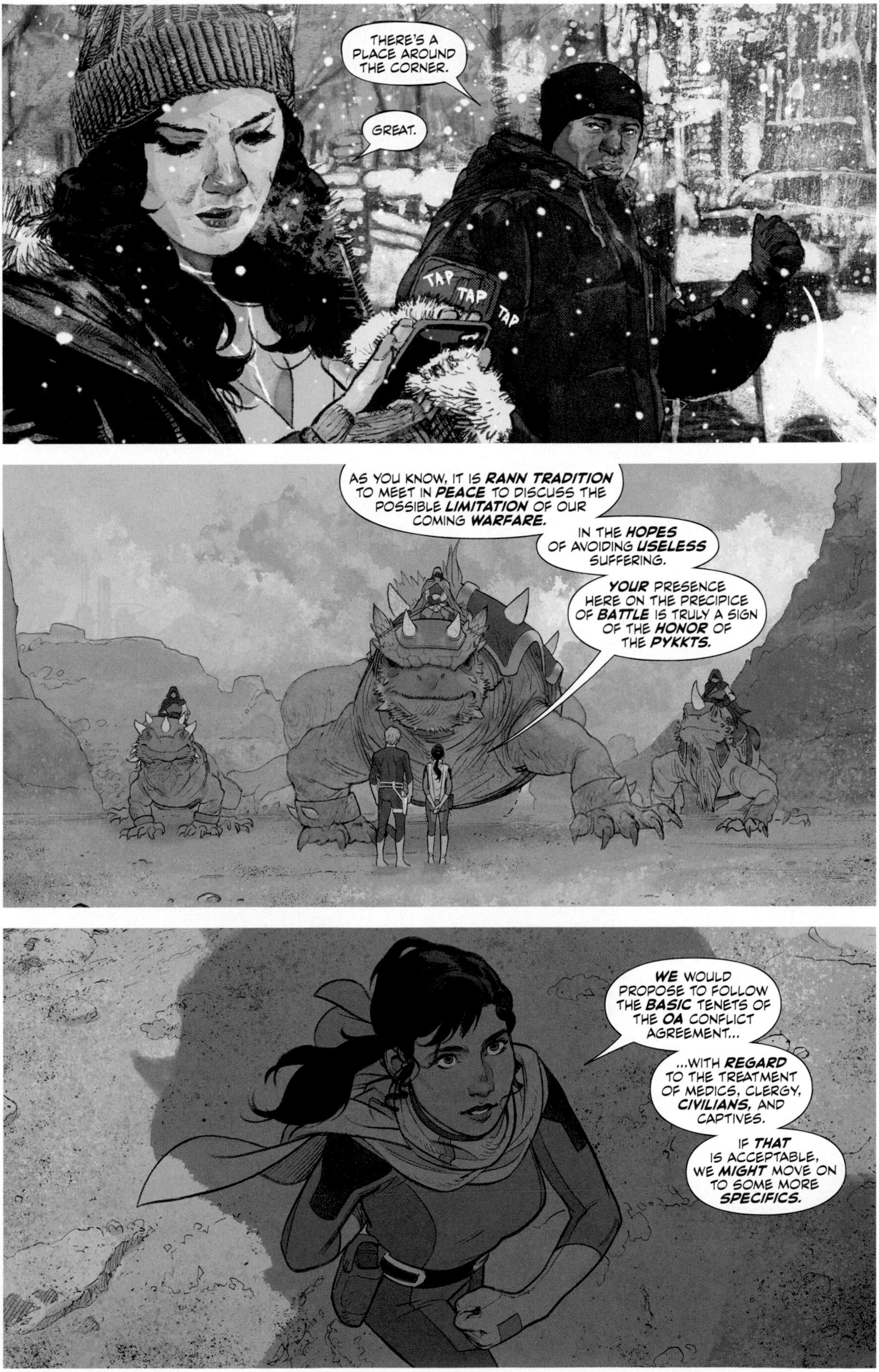

THERE'S A PLACE AROUND THE CORNER.
GREAT.
TAP TAP TAP
AS YOU KNOW, IT IS **RANN TRADITION** TO MEET IN **PEACE** TO DISCUSS THE POSSIBLE **LIMITATION** OF OUR COMING **WARFARE.**
IN THE **HOPES** OF AVOIDING **USELESS** SUFFERING.
YOUR PRESENCE HERE ON THE PRECIPICE OF **BATTLE** IS TRULY A SIGN OF THE **HONOR** OF THE **PYKKTS.**
WE WOULD PROPOSE TO FOLLOW THE **BASIC** TENETS OF THE **OA** CONFLICT AGREEMENT...
...WITH **REGARD** TO THE TREATMENT OF MEDICS, CLERGY, **CIVILIANS,** AND CAPTIVES.
IF **THAT** IS ACCEPTABLE, WE **MIGHT** MOVE ON TO SOME MORE **SPECIFICS.**

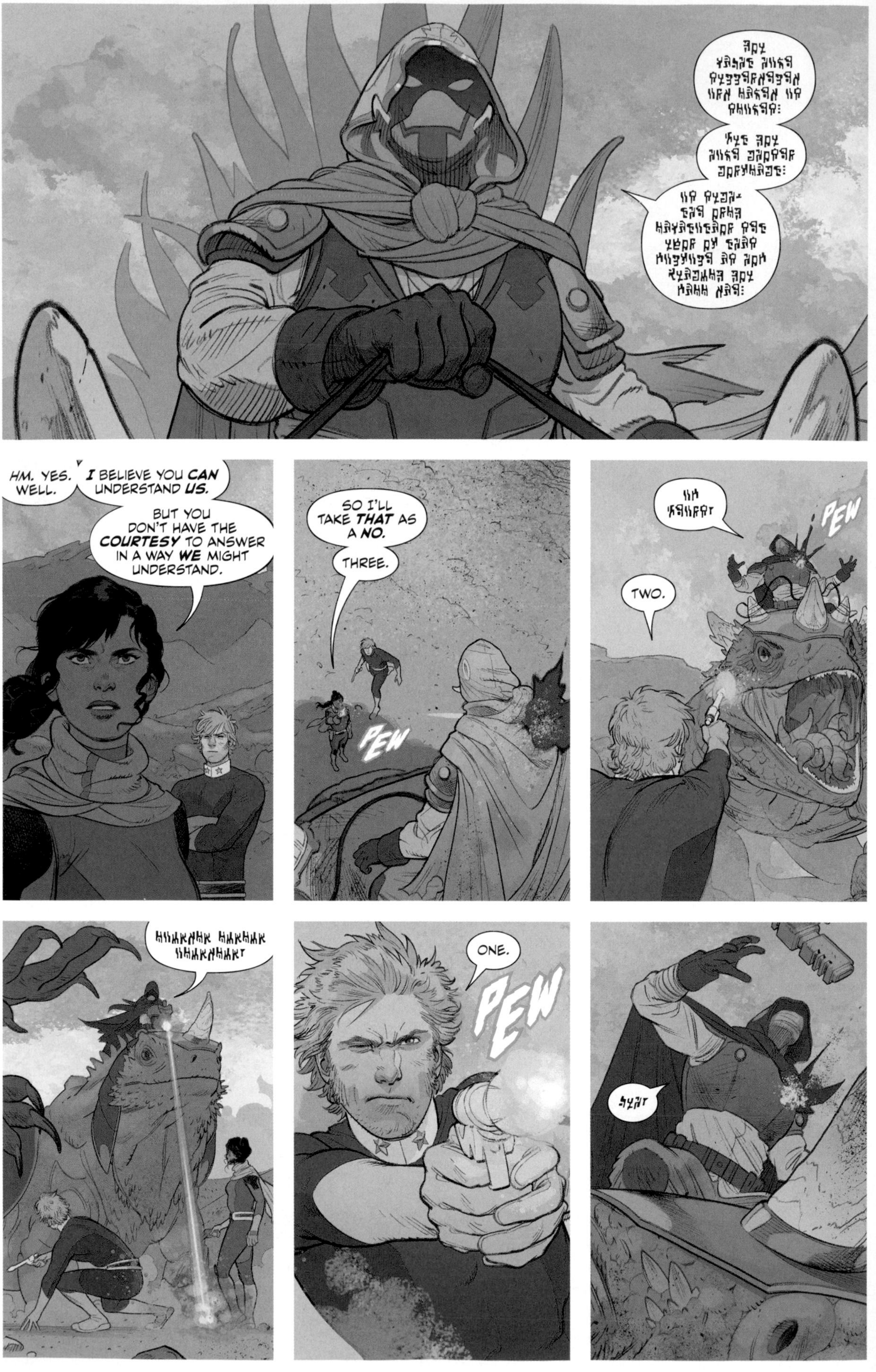
HM. YES. WELL.
I BELIEVE YOU CAN UNDERSTAND US.
BUT YOU DON'T HAVE THE COURTESY TO ANSWER IN A WAY WE MIGHT UNDERSTAND.
SO I'LL TAKE THAT AS A NO.
THREE.
PEW
TWO.
PEW
ONE.
PEW

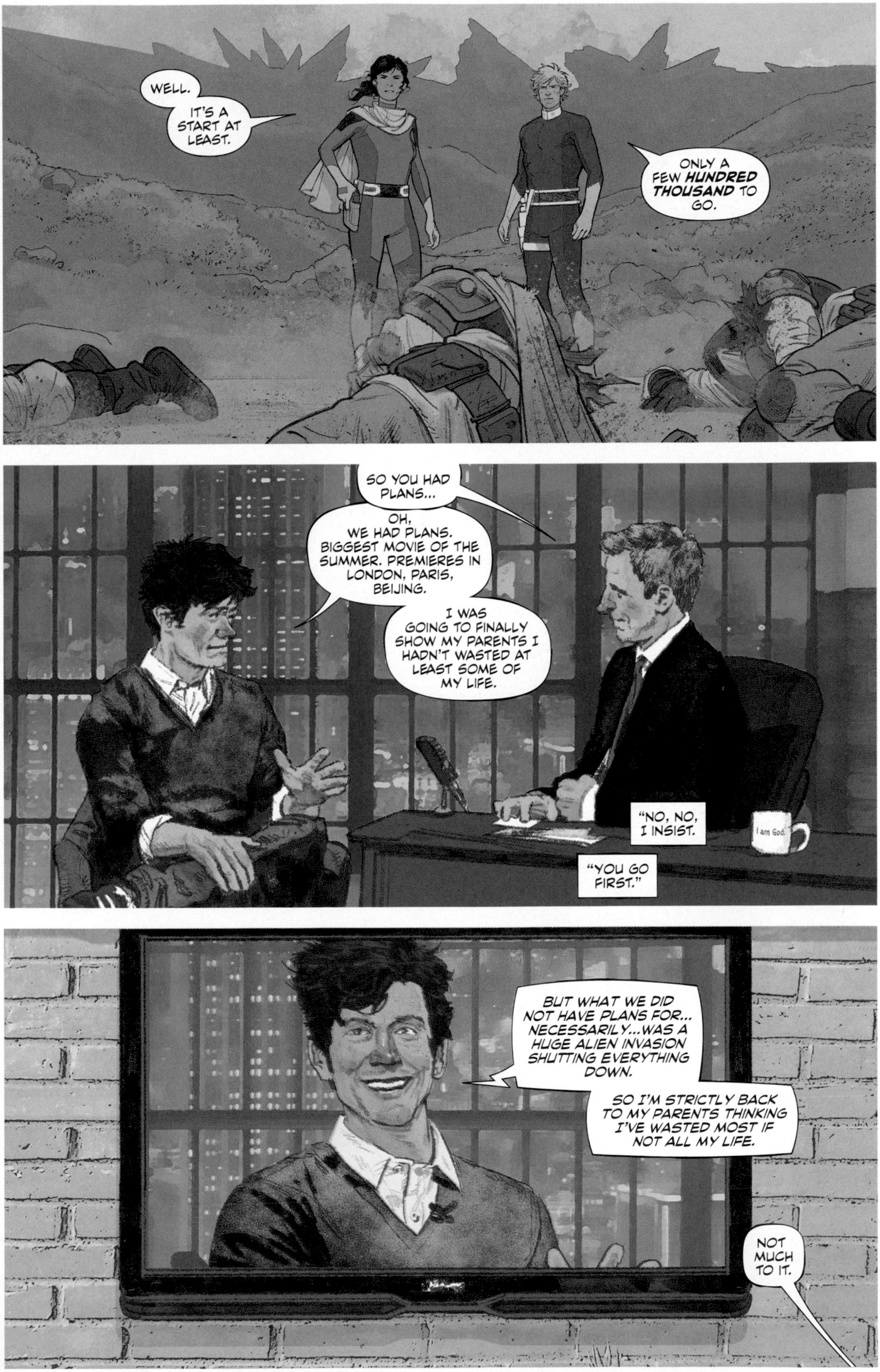
WELL.
IT'S A START AT LEAST.
ONLY A FEW **HUNDRED THOUSAND** TO GO.
SO YOU HAD PLANS...
OH, WE HAD PLANS. BIGGEST MOVIE OF THE SUMMER. PREMIERES IN LONDON, PARIS, BEIJING.
I WAS GOING TO FINALLY SHOW MY PARENTS I HADN'T WASTED AT LEAST SOME OF MY LIFE.
"NO, NO, I INSIST.
I am God.
"YOU GO FIRST."
BUT WHAT WE DID NOT HAVE PLANS FOR... NECESSARILY...WAS A HUGE ALIEN INVASION SHUTTING EVERYTHING DOWN.
SO I'M STRICTLY BACK TO MY PARENTS THINKING I'VE WASTED MOST IF NOT ALL MY LIFE.
NOT MUCH TO IT.

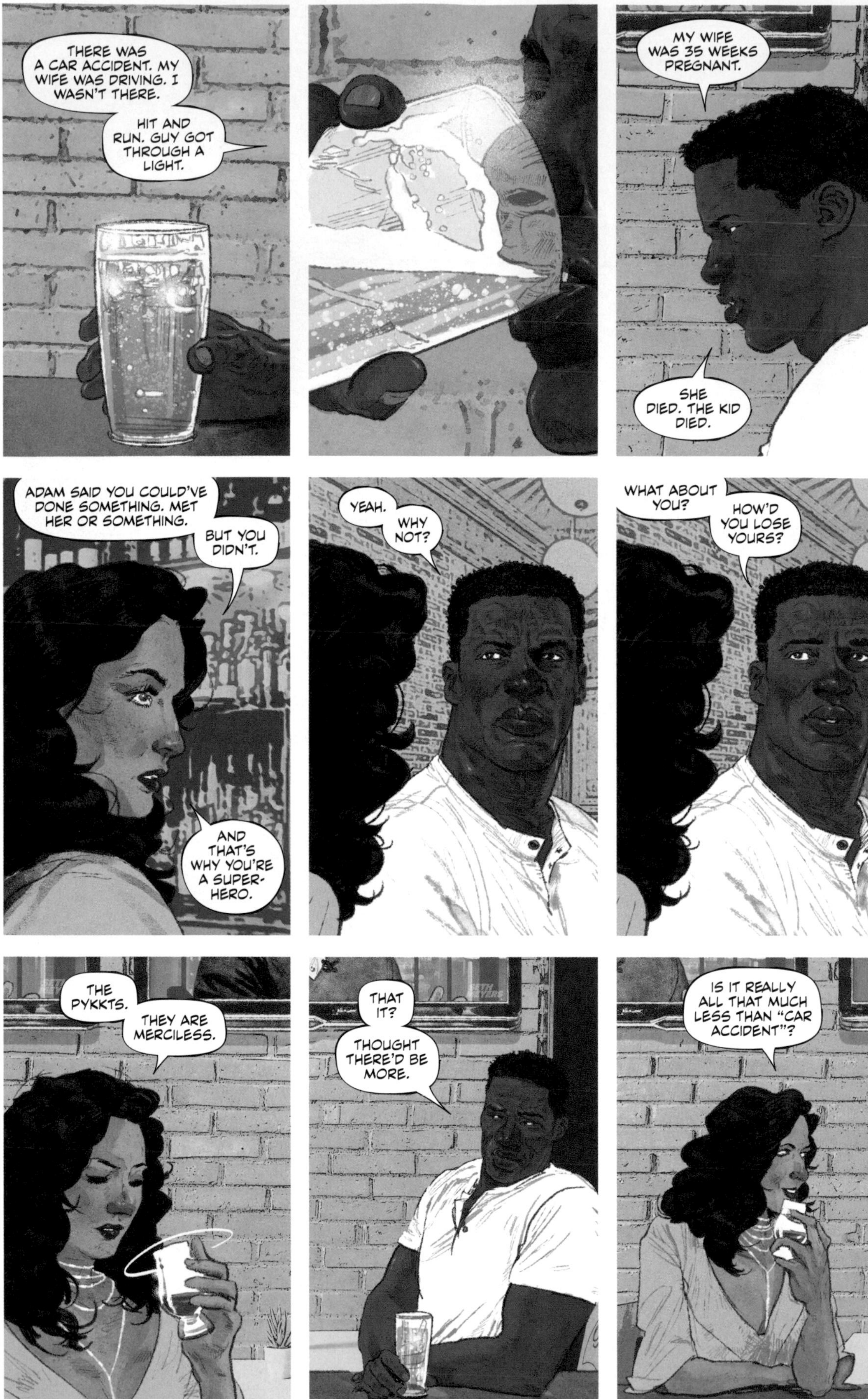
THERE WAS A CAR ACCIDENT. MY WIFE WAS DRIVING. I WASN'T THERE.
HIT AND RUN. GUY GOT THROUGH A LIGHT.
MY WIFE WAS 35 WEEKS PREGNANT.
SHE DIED. THE KID DIED.
ADAM SAID YOU COULD'VE DONE SOMETHING. MET HER OR SOMETHING.
BUT YOU DIDN'T.
AND THAT'S WHY YOU'RE A SUPER-HERO.
YEAH.
WHY NOT?
WHAT ABOUT YOU?
HOW'D YOU LOSE YOURS?
THE PYKKTS.
THEY ARE MERCILESS.
THAT IT?
THOUGHT THERE'D BE MORE.
IS IT REALLY ALL THAT MUCH LESS THAN "CAR ACCIDENT"?

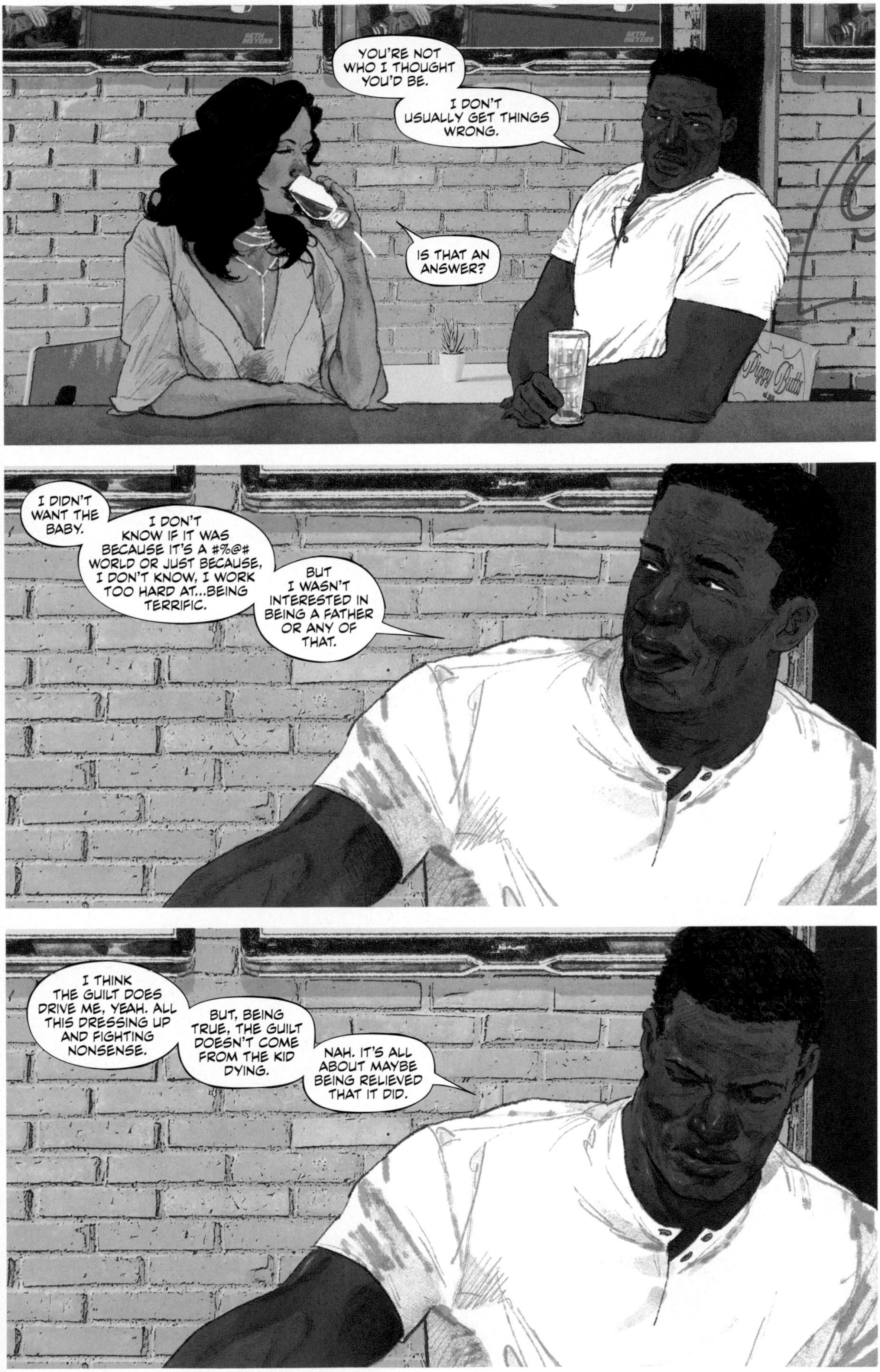
YOU'RE NOT WHO I THOUGHT YOU'D BE.
I DON'T USUALLY GET THINGS WRONG.
IS THAT AN ANSWER?
I DIDN'T WANT THE BABY.
I DON'T KNOW IF IT WAS BECAUSE IT'S A #%@# WORLD OR JUST BECAUSE, I DON'T KNOW, I WORK TOO HARD AT...BEING TERRIFIC.
BUT I WASN'T INTERESTED IN BEING A FATHER OR ANY OF THAT.
I THINK THE GUILT DOES DRIVE ME, YEAH. ALL THIS DRESSING UP AND FIGHTING NONSENSE.
BUT, BEING TRUE, THE GUILT DOESN'T COME FROM THE KID DYING.
NAH. IT'S ALL ABOUT MAYBE BEING RELIEVED THAT IT DID.

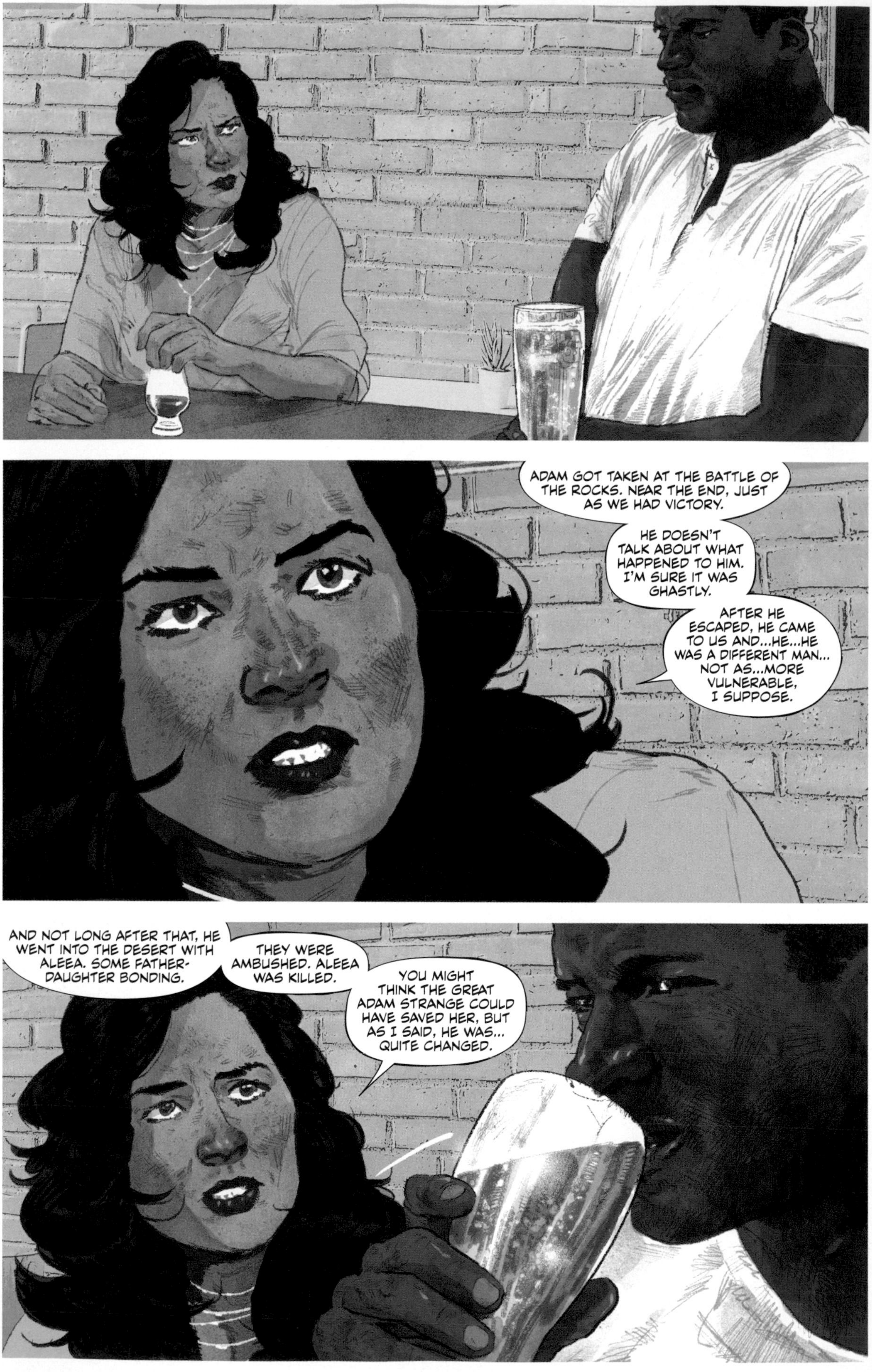
ADAM GOT TAKEN AT THE BATTLE OF THE ROCKS. NEAR THE END, JUST AS WE HAD VICTORY.
HE DOESN'T TALK ABOUT WHAT HAPPENED TO HIM. I'M SURE IT WAS GHASTLY.
AFTER HE ESCAPED, HE CAME TO US AND...HE...HE WAS A DIFFERENT MAN... NOT AS...MORE VULNERABLE, I SUPPOSE.
AND NOT LONG AFTER THAT, HE WENT INTO THE DESERT WITH ALEEA. SOME FATHER-DAUGHTER BONDING.
THEY WERE AMBUSHED. ALEEA WAS KILLED.
YOU MIGHT THINK THE GREAT ADAM STRANGE COULD HAVE SAVED HER, BUT AS I SAID, HE WAS... QUITE CHANGED.

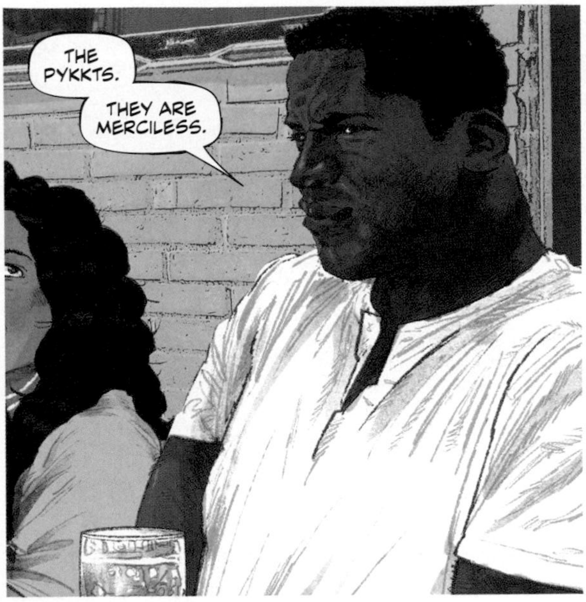
THE PYKKTS.
THEY ARE MERCILESS.

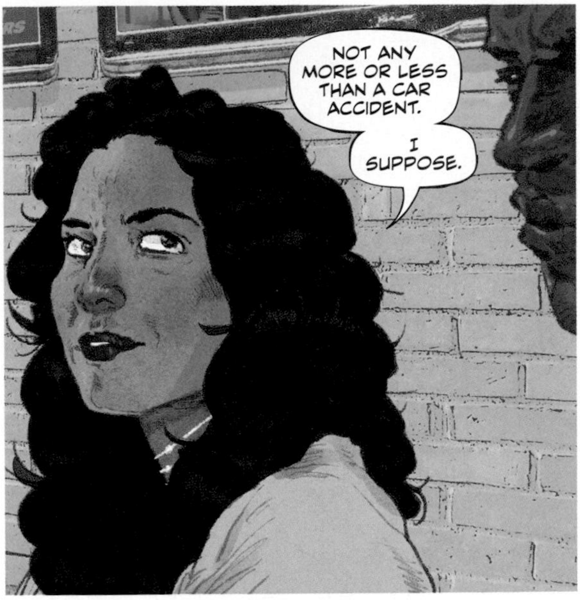
NOT ANY MORE OR LESS THAN A CAR ACCIDENT.
I SUPPOSE.

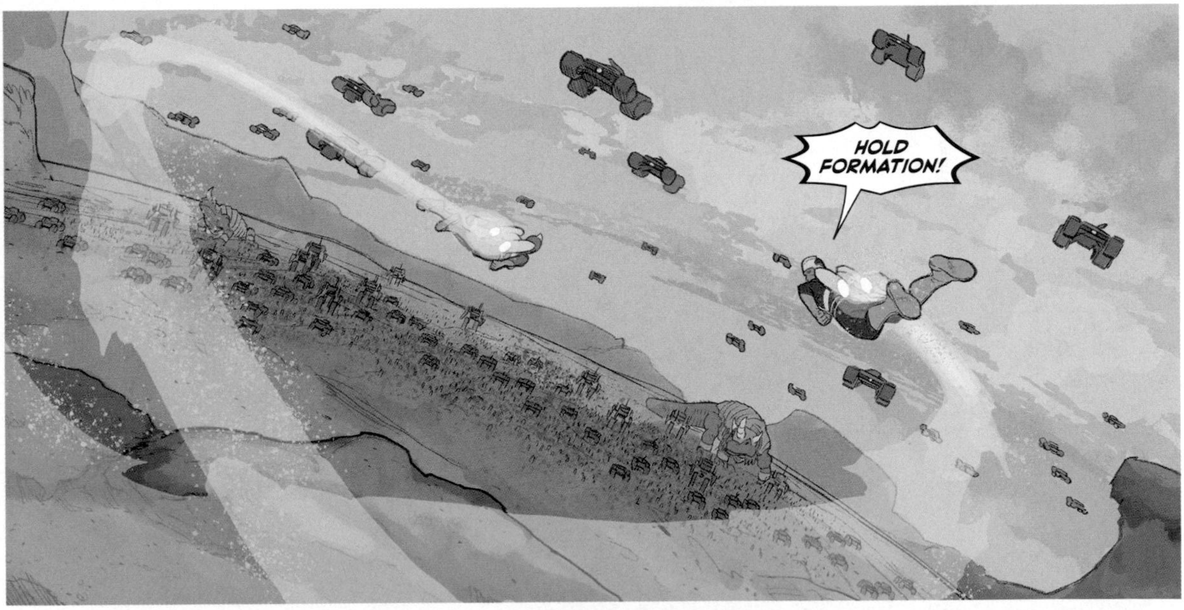
HOLD FORMATION!

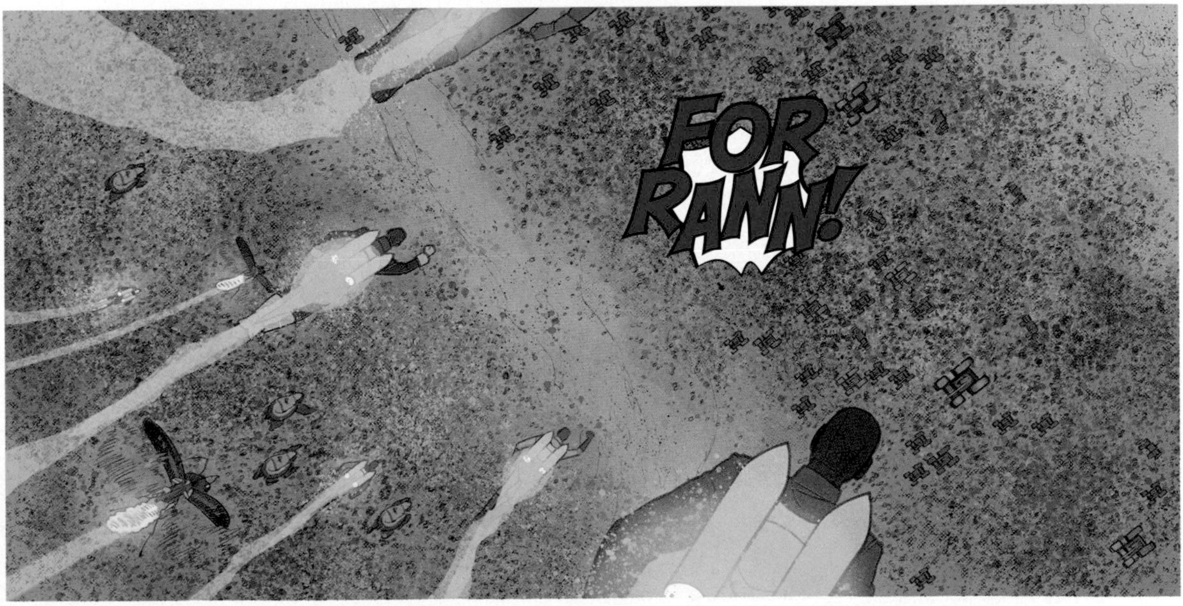
FOR RANN!

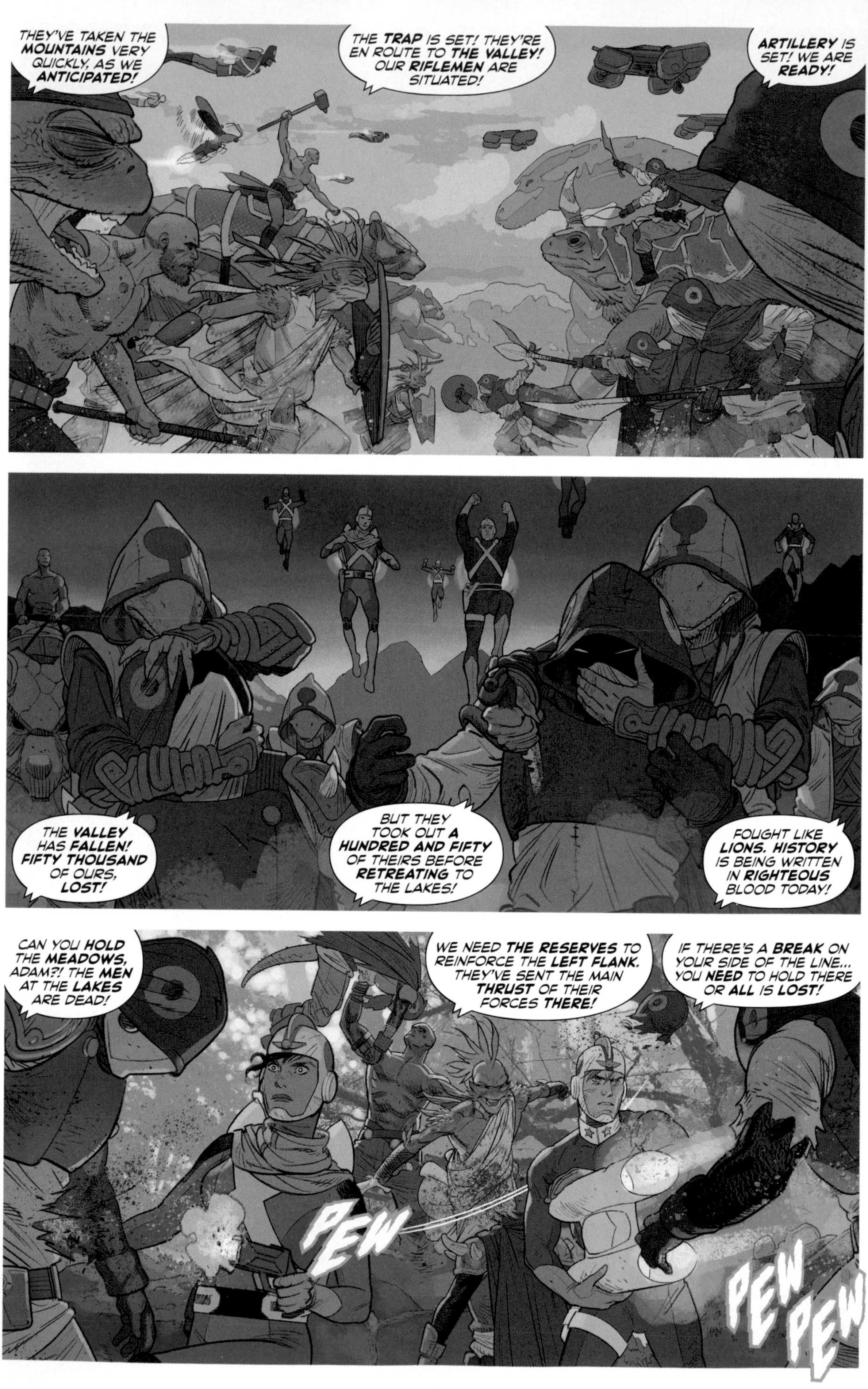
THEY'VE TAKEN THE MOUNTAINS VERY QUICKLY, AS WE ANTICIPATED!
THE TRAP IS SET! THEY'RE EN ROUTE TO THE VALLEY! OUR RIFLEMEN ARE SITUATED!
ARTILLERY IS SET! WE ARE READY!
THE VALLEY HAS FALLEN! FIFTY THOUSAND OF OURS, LOST!
BUT THEY TOOK OUT A HUNDRED AND FIFTY OF THEIRS BEFORE RETREATING TO THE LAKES!
FOUGHT LIKE LIONS. HISTORY IS BEING WRITTEN IN RIGHTEOUS BLOOD TODAY!
CAN YOU HOLD THE MEADOWS, ADAM?! THE MEN AT THE LAKES ARE DEAD!
WE NEED THE RESERVES TO REINFORCE THE LEFT FLANK. THEY'VE SENT THE MAIN THRUST OF THEIR FORCES THERE!
IF THERE'S A BREAK ON YOUR SIDE OF THE LINE... YOU NEED TO HOLD THERE OR ALL IS LOST!
PEW
PEW PEW

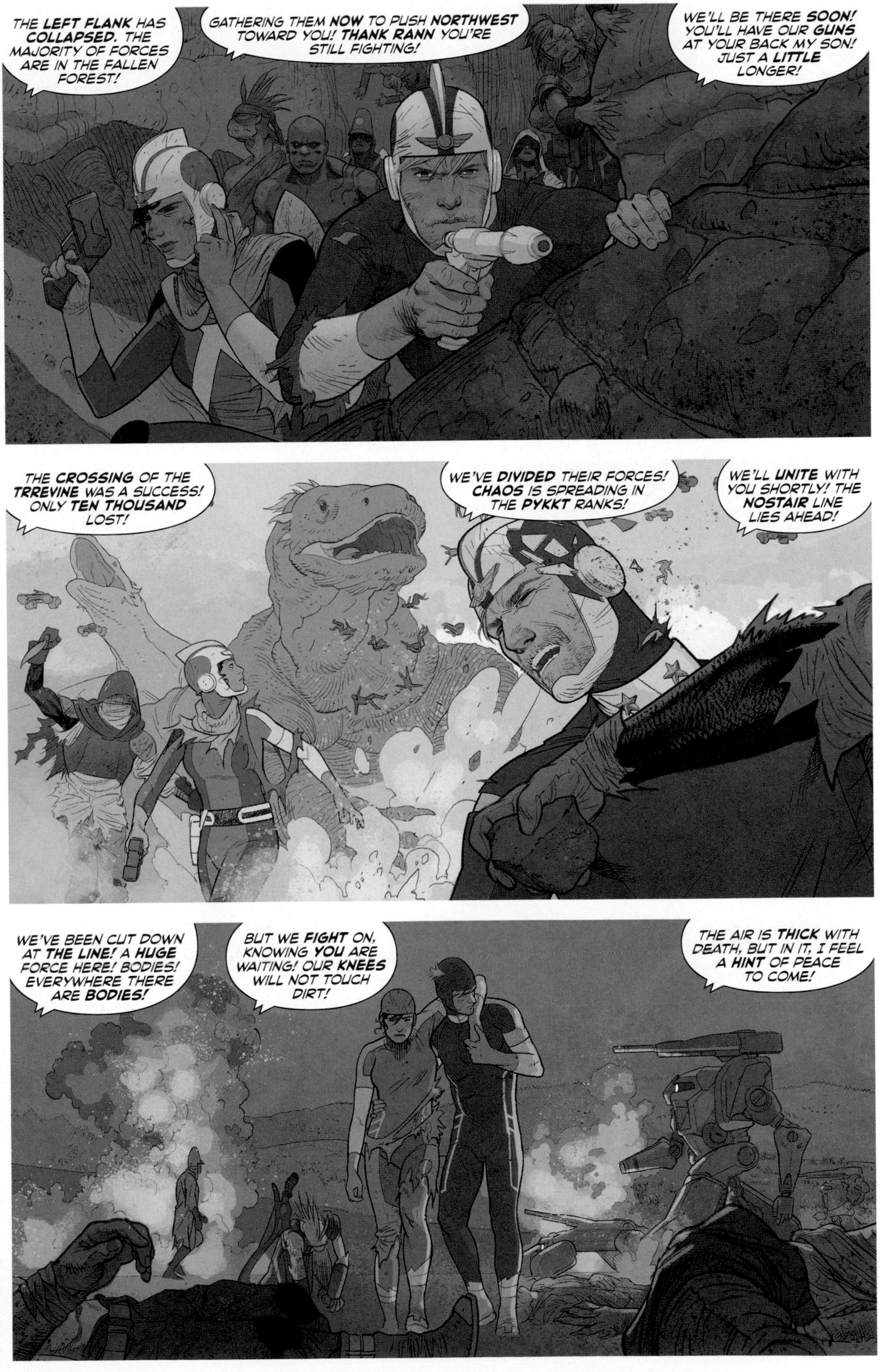
THE LEFT FLANK HAS COLLAPSED. THE MAJORITY OF FORCES ARE IN THE FALLEN FOREST!
GATHERING THEM NOW TO PUSH NORTHWEST TOWARD YOU! THANK RANN YOU'RE STILL FIGHTING!
WE'LL BE THERE SOON! YOU'LL HAVE OUR GUNS AT YOUR BACK MY SON! JUST A LITTLE LONGER!
THE CROSSING OF THE TREVINE WAS A SUCCESS! ONLY TEN THOUSAND LOST!
WE'VE DIVIDED THEIR FORCES! CHAOS IS SPREADING IN THE PYKKT RANKS!
WE'LL UNITE WITH YOU SHORTLY! THE NOSTAIR LINE LIES AHEAD!
WE'VE BEEN CUT DOWN AT THE LINE! A HUGE FORCE HERE! BODIES! EVERYWHERE THERE ARE BODIES!
BUT WE FIGHT ON, KNOWING YOU ARE WAITING! OUR KNEES WILL NOT TOUCH DIRT!
THE AIR IS THICK WITH DEATH, BUT IN IT, I FEEL A HINT OF PEACE TO COME!

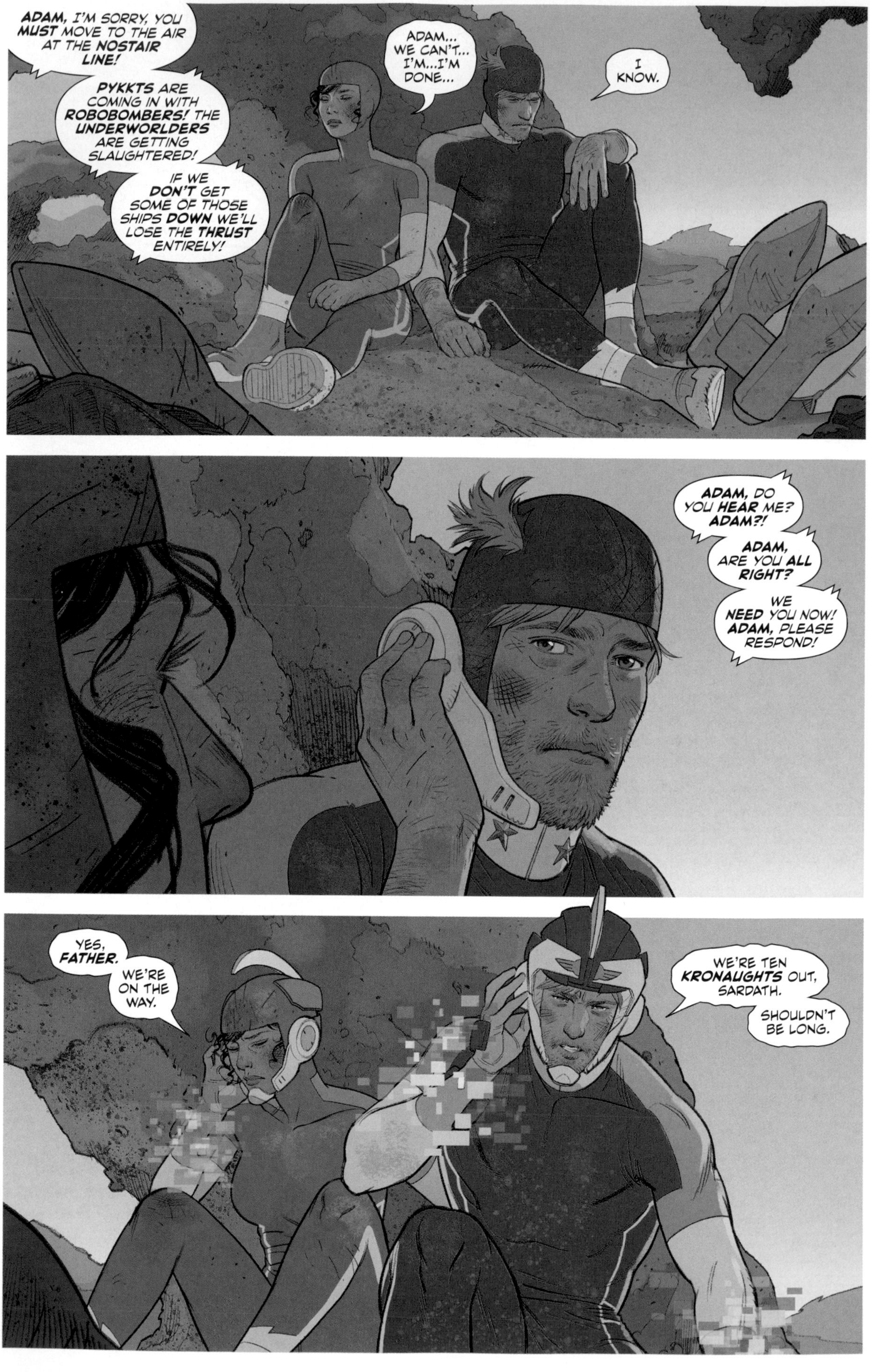
ADAM, I'M SORRY, YOU MUST MOVE TO THE AIR AT THE NOSTAIR LINE!
PYKKTS ARE COMING IN WITH ROBOBOMBERS! THE UNDERWORLDERS ARE GETTING SLAUGHTERED!
IF WE DON'T GET SOME OF THOSE SHIPS DOWN WE'LL LOSE THE THRUST ENTIRELY!
ADAM... WE CAN'T... I'M...I'M DONE...
I KNOW.
ADAM, DO YOU HEAR ME? ADAM?!
ADAM, ARE YOU ALL RIGHT?
WE NEED YOU NOW! ADAM, PLEASE RESPOND!
YES, FATHER.
WE'RE ON THE WAY.
WE'RE TEN KRONAUGHTS OUT, SARDATH.
SHOULDN'T BE LONG.

THANKS TO YOU, THE **HELLOTAAT** CAVALRY HAS PASSED **ERGOS** RIVER!

REPORTING **TWENTY THOUSAND** CASUALTIES!

BUT STILL **BULLING** FORWARD! IT'S **MAGNIFICENT!**

RESERVES ARE NOW **COMPLETELY** WIPED OUT. **NO** ONE IS COMING!

IT'S **US** AND THE **PYKKTS.** WE **STAND** OR WE **RETREAT!**

WE **DIE** ON THIS **GROUND** OR WE ARE **SHAMED** ON IT!

PEW PEW

RANN **BLESS** US, WE'VE TAKEN **TWO** FOR EVERY **ONE** OF THEIRS!

THE **TROOPS** WON'T RETREAT! THEY **CHARGE** AND **CHARGE** AND **CHARGE!**

ADAM STRANGE! THEY **SHOUT** YOUR NAME AS THEY DIE!

PEW

PEW

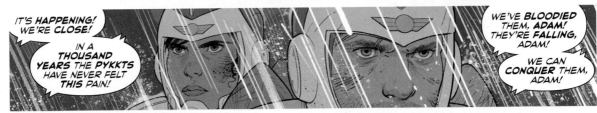

IT'S **HAPPENING!** WE'RE **CLOSE!**

IN A **THOUSAND YEARS** THE PYKKTS HAVE NEVER FELT **THIS** PAIN!

WE'VE **BLOODIED** THEM, **ADAM!** THEY'RE **FALLING,** ADAM!

WE CAN **CONQUER** THEM, ADAM!

YOU'RE RIGHT.

IT IS A VERY LARGE SPOON.

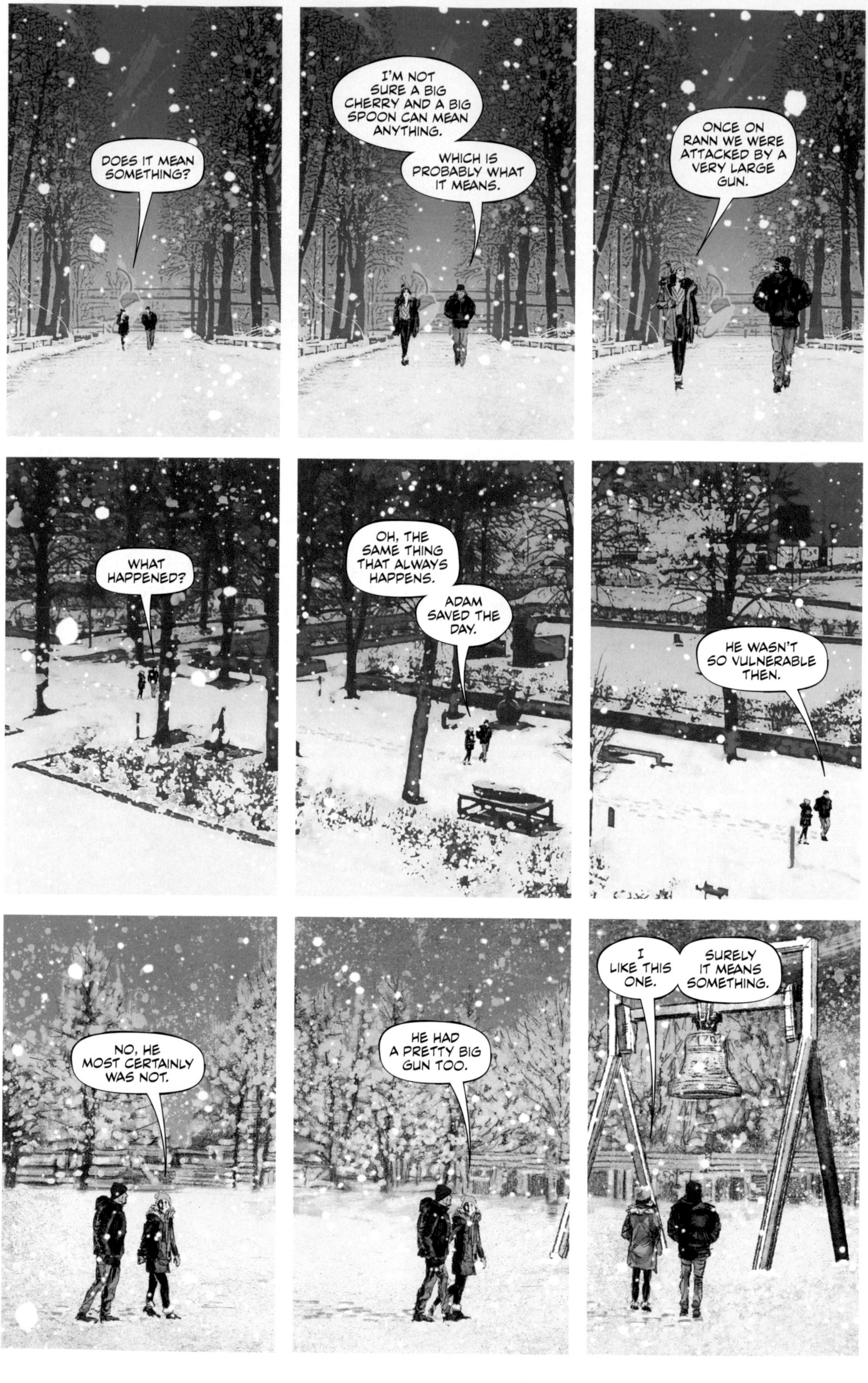
DOES IT MEAN SOMETHING?
I'M NOT SURE A BIG CHERRY AND A BIG SPOON CAN MEAN ANYTHING.
WHICH IS PROBABLY WHAT IT MEANS.
ONCE ON RANN WE WERE ATTACKED BY A VERY LARGE GUN.
WHAT HAPPENED?
OH, THE SAME THING THAT ALWAYS HAPPENS.
ADAM SAVED THE DAY.
HE WASN'T SO VULNERABLE THEN.
NO, HE MOST CERTAINLY WAS NOT.
HE HAD A PRETTY BIG GUN TOO.
I LIKE THIS ONE.
SURELY IT MEANS SOMETHING.

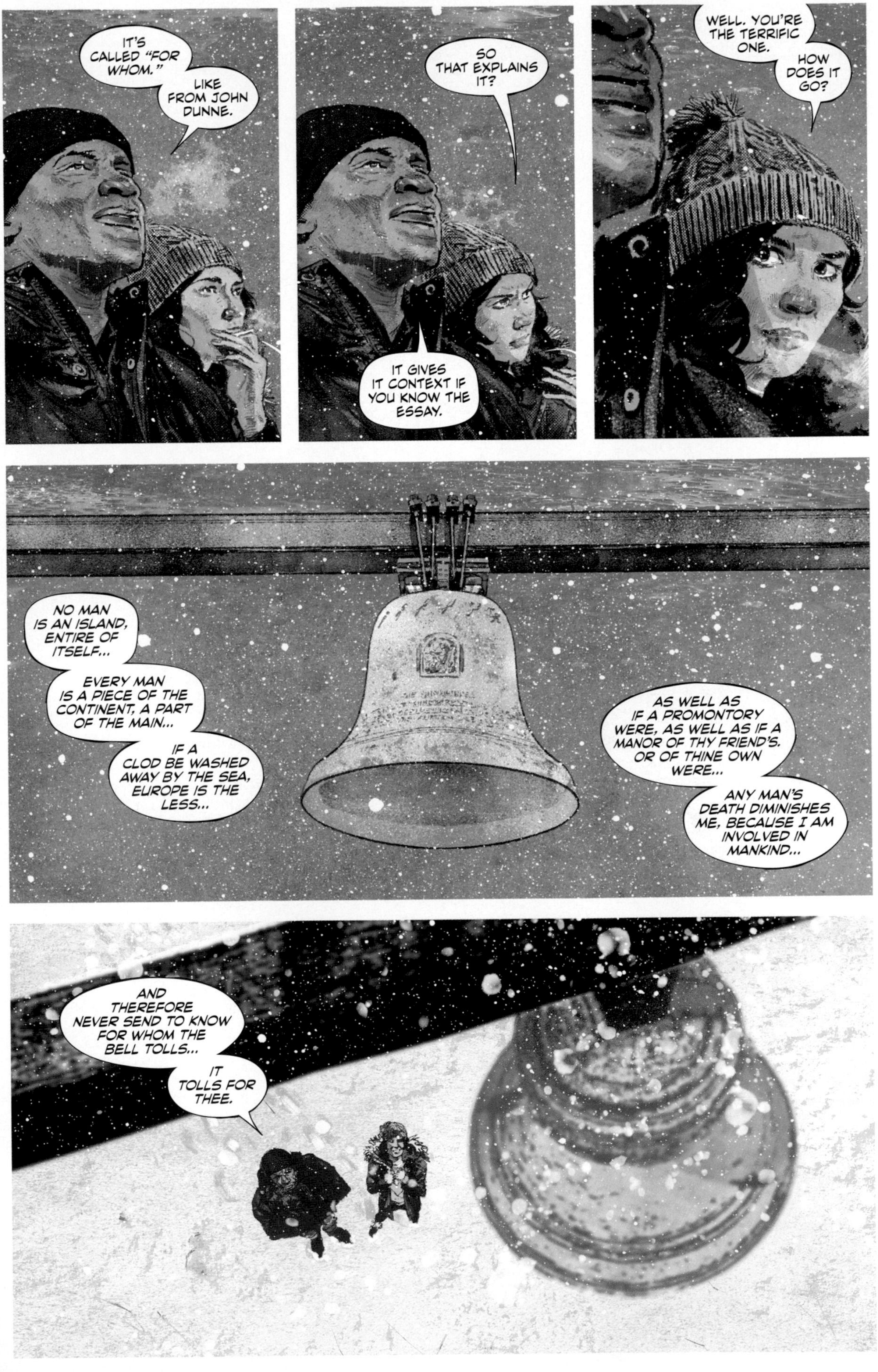

IT'S CALLED "FOR WHOM."
LIKE FROM JOHN DUNNE.
SO THAT EXPLAINS IT?
IT GIVES IT CONTEXT IF YOU KNOW THE ESSAY.
WELL. YOU'RE THE TERRIFIC ONE.
HOW DOES IT GO?
NO MAN IS AN ISLAND, ENTIRE OF ITSELF...
EVERY MAN IS A PIECE OF THE CONTINENT, A PART OF THE MAIN...
IF A CLOD BE WASHED AWAY BY THE SEA, EUROPE IS THE LESS...
AS WELL AS IF A PROMONTORY WERE, AS WELL AS IF A MANOR OF THY FRIEND'S. OR OF THINE OWN WERE...
ANY MAN'S DEATH DIMINISHES ME, BECAUSE I AM INVOLVED IN MANKIND...
AND THEREFORE NEVER SEND TO KNOW FOR WHOM THE BELL TOLLS...
IT TOLLS FOR THEE.

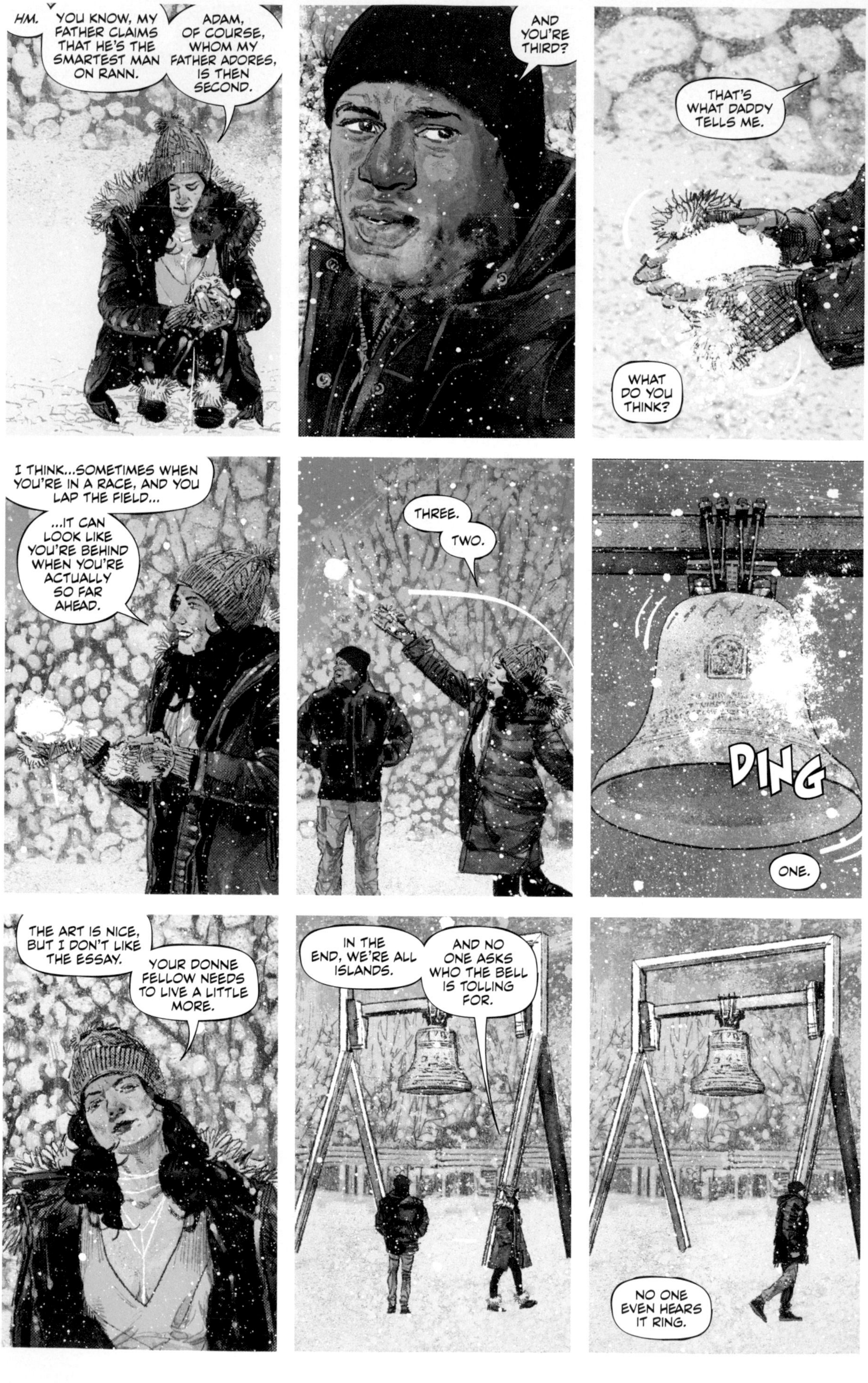
HM.
YOU KNOW, MY FATHER CLAIMS THAT HE'S THE SMARTEST MAN ON RANN.
ADAM, OF COURSE, WHOM MY FATHER ADORES, IS THEN SECOND.
AND YOU'RE THIRD?
THAT'S WHAT DADDY TELLS ME.
WHAT DO YOU THINK?
I THINK...SOMETIMES WHEN YOU'RE IN A RACE, AND YOU LAP THE FIELD...
...IT CAN LOOK LIKE YOU'RE BEHIND WHEN YOU'RE ACTUALLY SO FAR AHEAD.
THREE.
TWO.
DING
ONE.
THE ART IS NICE, BUT I DON'T LIKE THE ESSAY.
YOUR DONNE FELLOW NEEDS TO LIVE A LITTLE MORE.
IN THE END, WE'RE ALL ISLANDS.
AND NO ONE ASKS WHO THE BELL IS TOLLING FOR.
NO ONE EVEN HEARS IT RING.

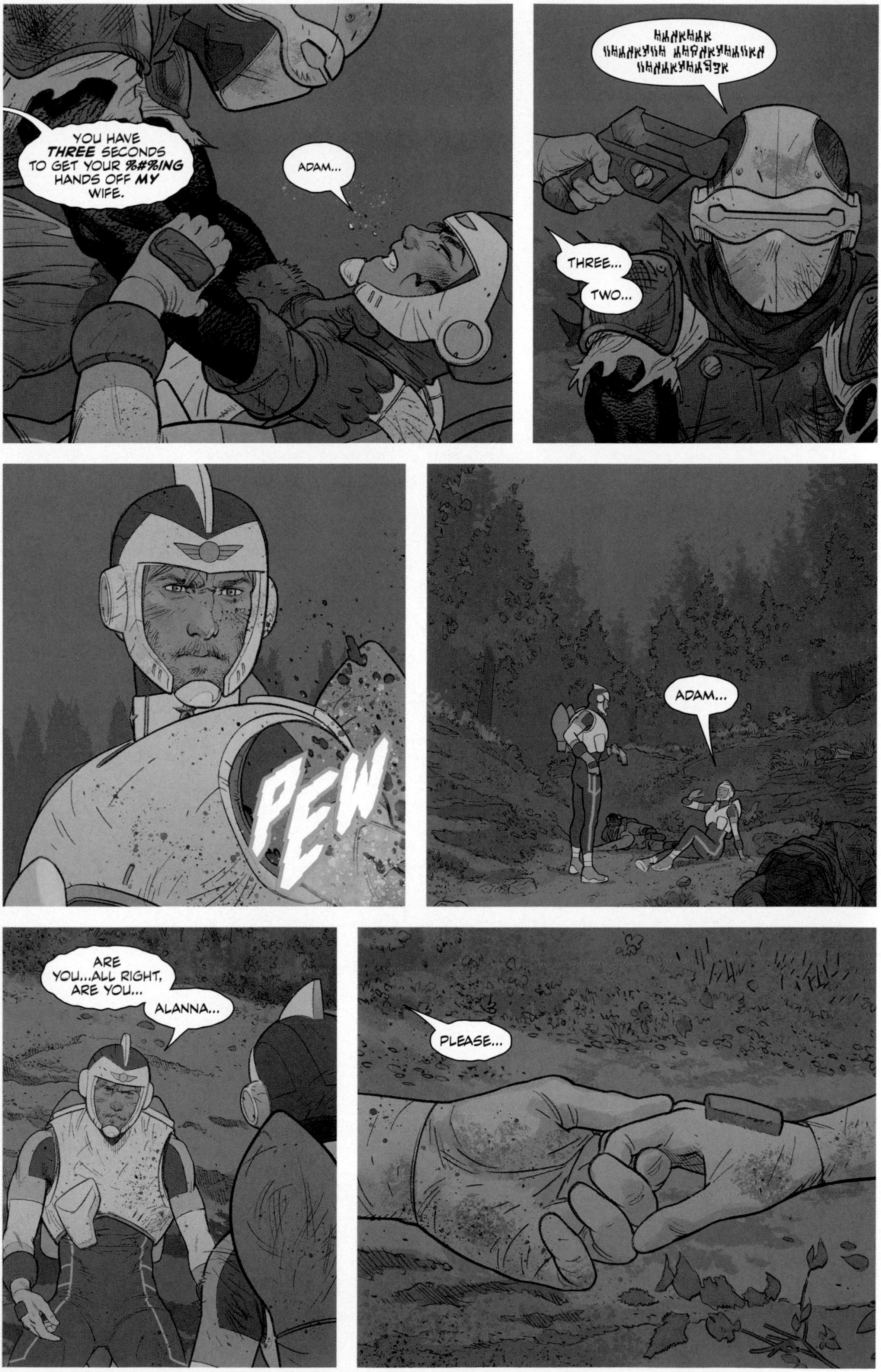

YOU HAVE THREE SECONDS TO GET YOUR %#%ING HANDS OFF MY WIFE.
ADAM...
THREE...
TWO...
PEW
ADAM...
ARE YOU...ALL RIGHT, ARE YOU...
ALANNA...
PLEASE...

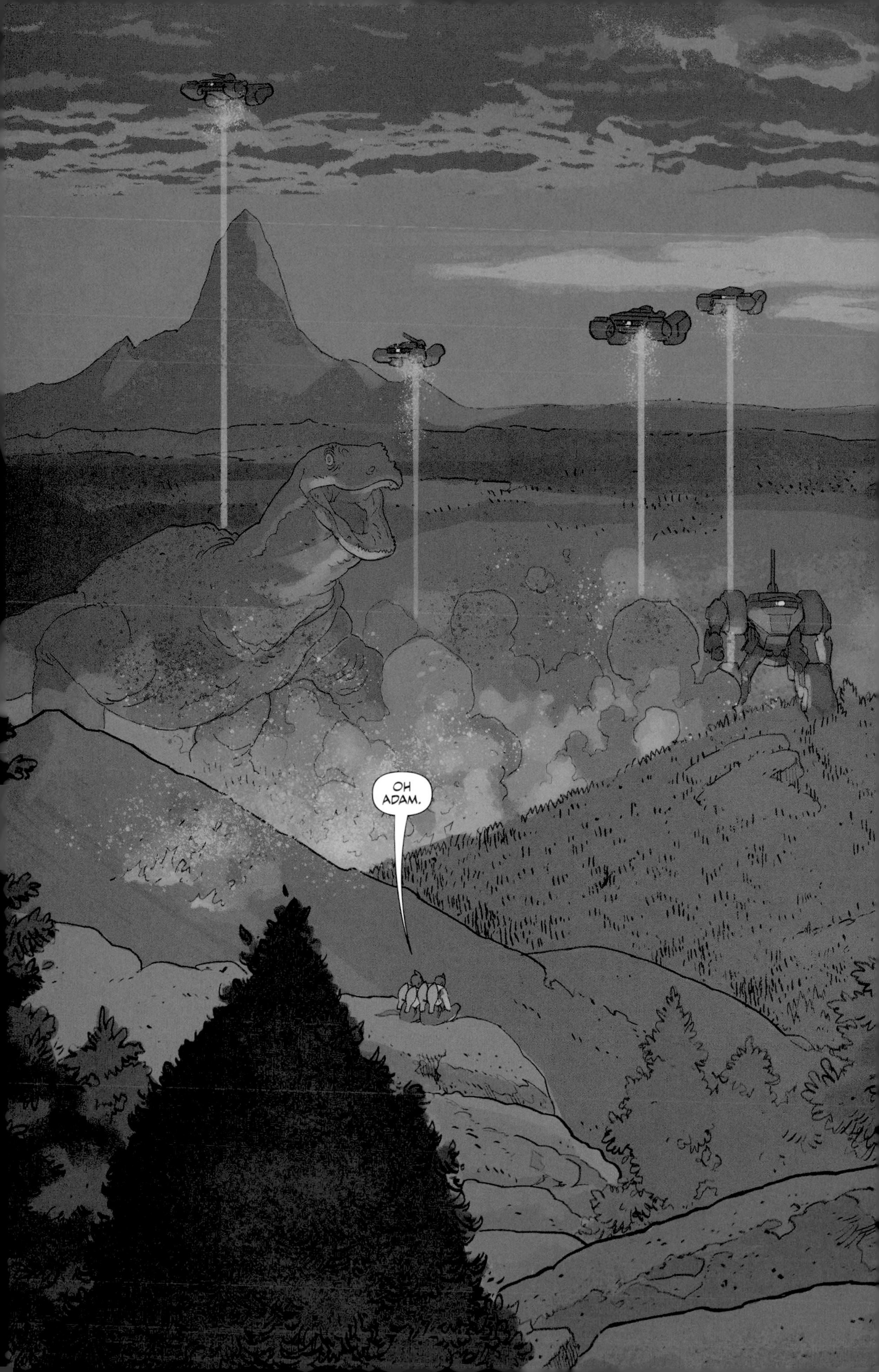
OH ADAM.

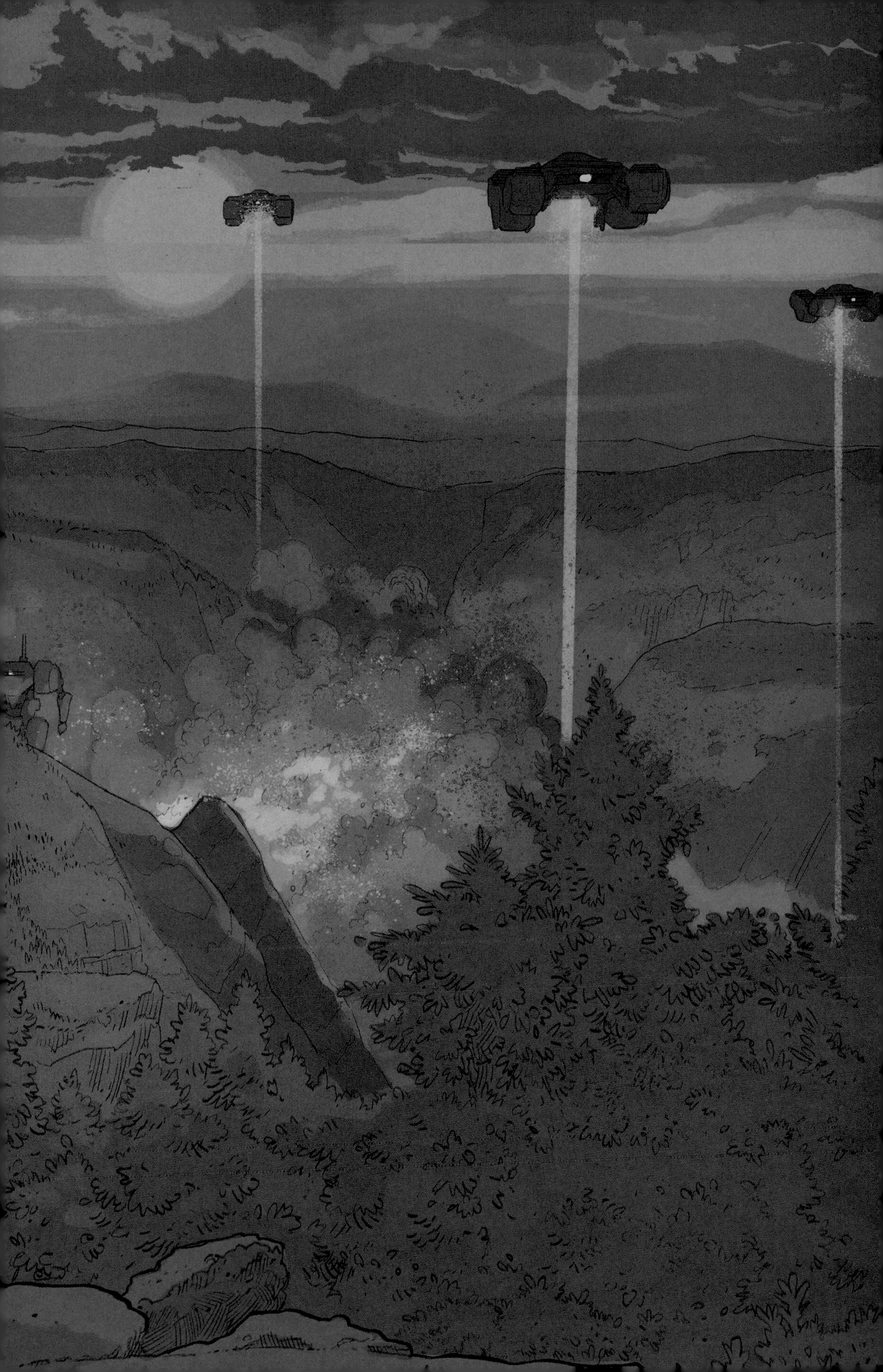

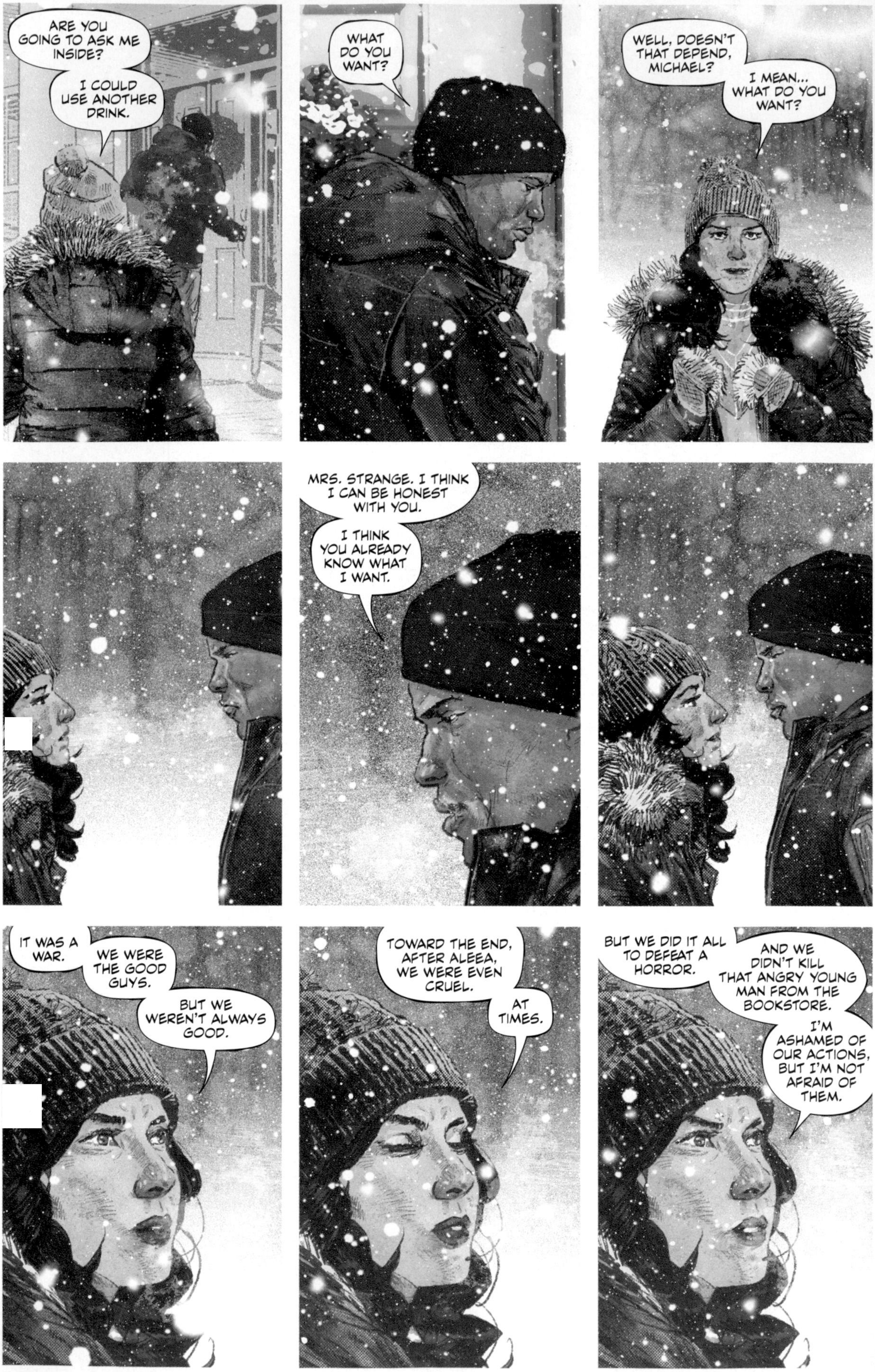

ARE YOU GOING TO ASK ME INSIDE?
I COULD USE ANOTHER DRINK.
WHAT DO YOU WANT?
WELL, DOESN'T THAT DEPEND, MICHAEL?
I MEAN... WHAT DO YOU WANT?
MRS. STRANGE. I THINK I CAN BE HONEST WITH YOU.
I THINK YOU ALREADY KNOW WHAT I WANT.
IT WAS A WAR.
WE WERE THE GOOD GUYS.
BUT WE WEREN'T ALWAYS GOOD.
TOWARD THE END, AFTER ALEEA, WE WERE EVEN CRUEL.
AT TIMES.
BUT WE DID IT ALL TO DEFEAT A HORROR.
AND WE DIDN'T KILL THAT ANGRY YOUNG MAN FROM THE BOOKSTORE.
I'M ASHAMED OF OUR ACTIONS, BUT I'M NOT AFRAID OF THEM.

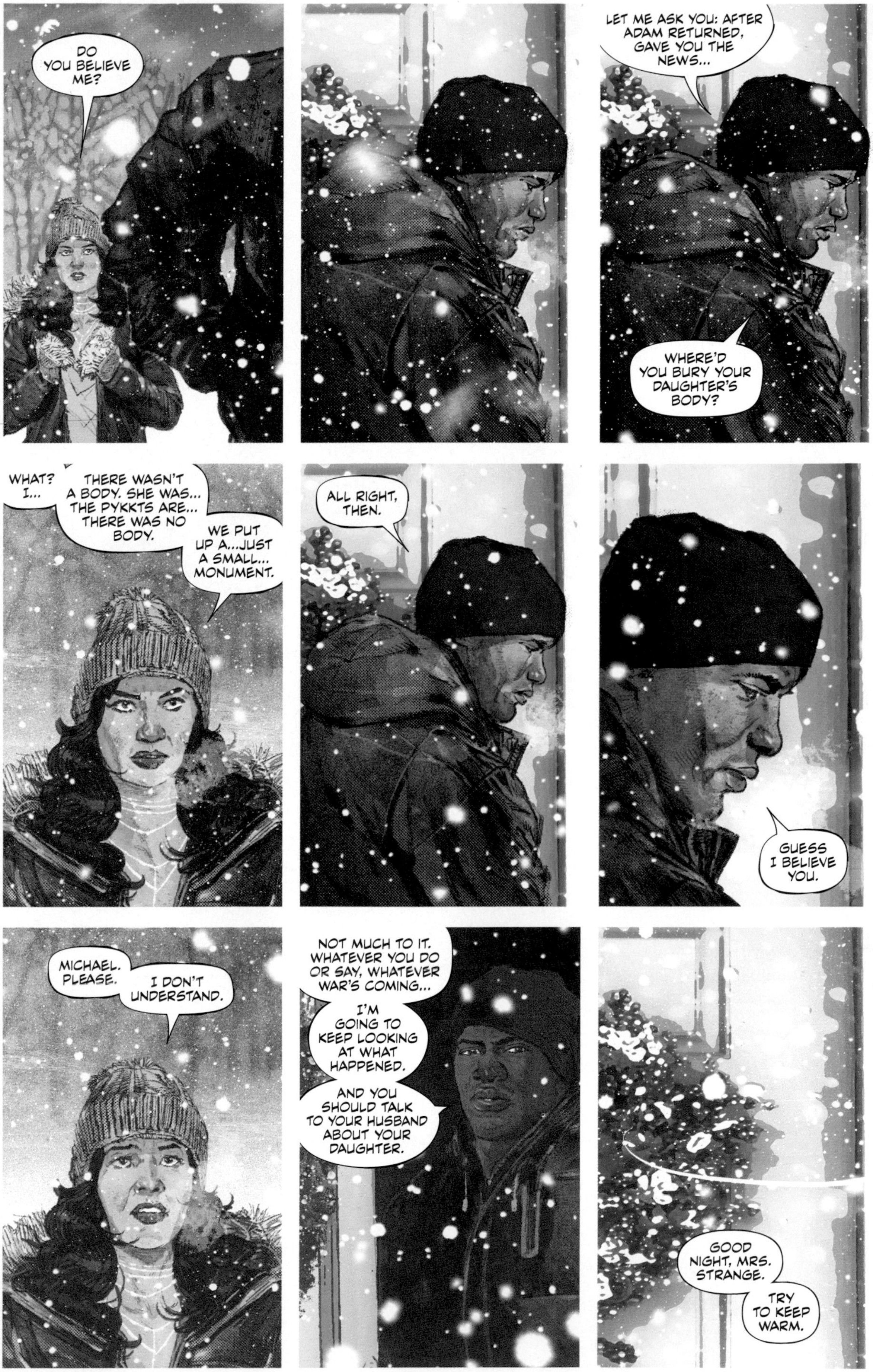
DO YOU BELIEVE ME?
LET ME ASK YOU: AFTER ADAM RETURNED, GAVE YOU THE NEWS...
WHERE'D YOU BURY YOUR DAUGHTER'S BODY?
WHAT? I...
THERE WASN'T A BODY. SHE WAS... THE PYKKTS ARE... THERE WAS NO BODY.
WE PUT UP A...JUST A SMALL... MONUMENT.
ALL RIGHT, THEN.
GUESS I BELIEVE YOU.
MICHAEL. PLEASE.
I DON'T UNDERSTAND.
NOT MUCH TO IT. WHATEVER YOU DO OR SAY, WHATEVER WAR'S COMING...
I'M GOING TO KEEP LOOKING AT WHAT HAPPENED.
AND YOU SHOULD TALK TO YOUR HUSBAND ABOUT YOUR DAUGHTER.
GOOD NIGHT, MRS. STRANGE.
TRY TO KEEP WARM.

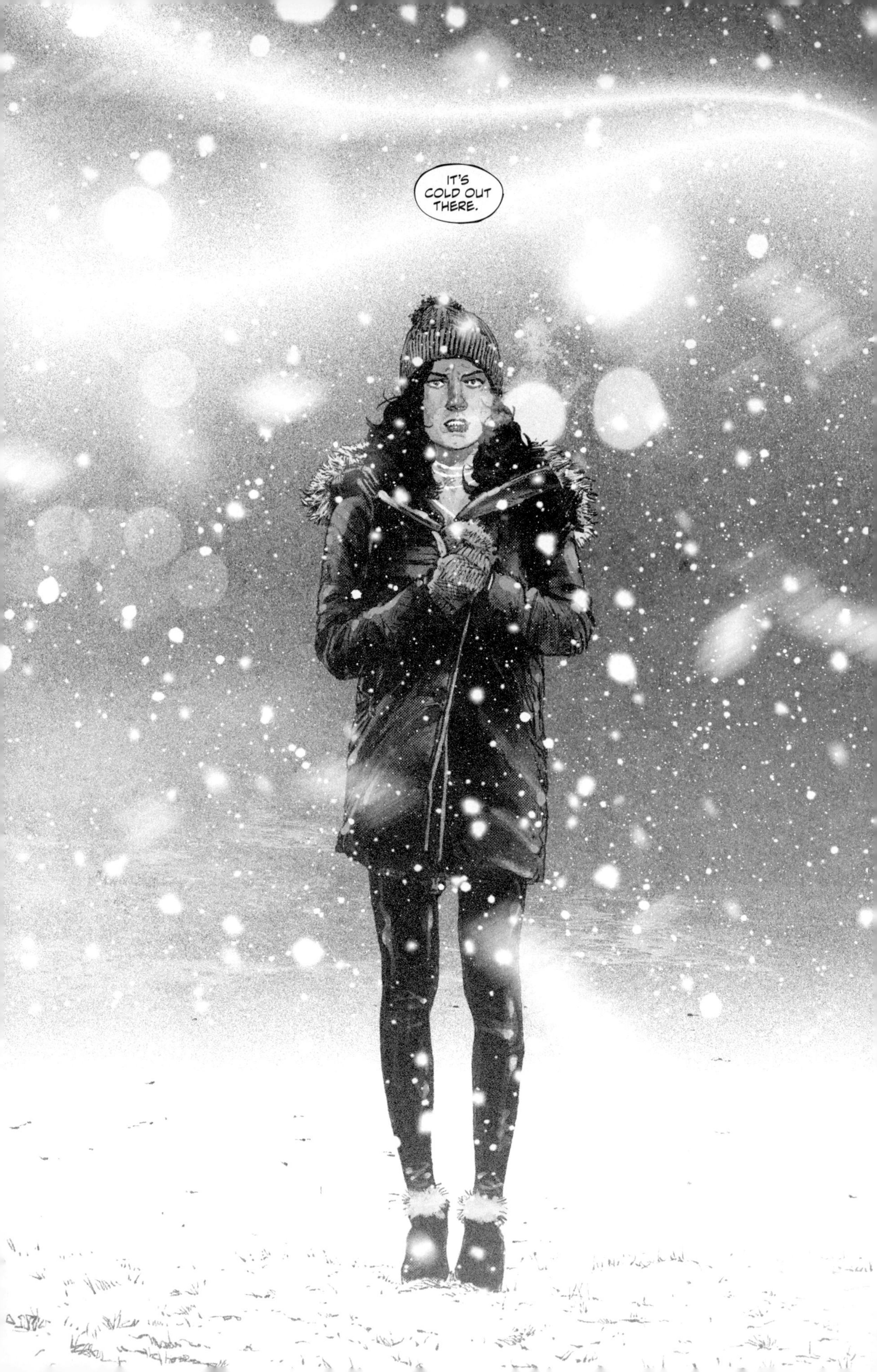
IT'S COLD OUT THERE.

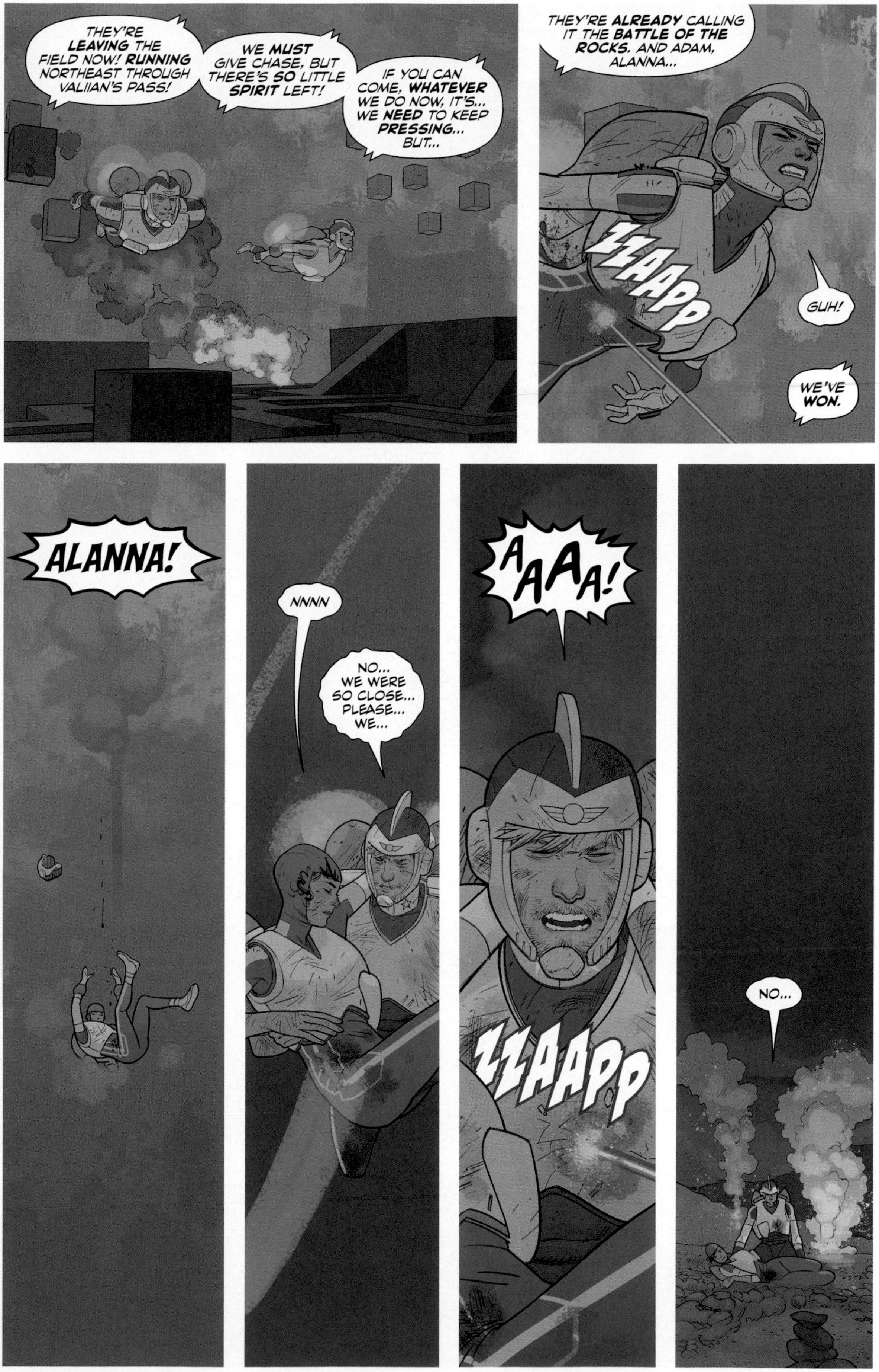

THEY'RE LEAVING THE FIELD NOW! RUNNING NORTHEAST THROUGH VALIIAN'S PASS!
WE MUST GIVE CHASE, BUT THERE'S SO LITTLE SPIRIT LEFT!
IF YOU CAN COME, WHATEVER WE DO NOW, IT'S... WE NEED TO KEEP PRESSING... BUT...
THEY'RE ALREADY CALLING IT THE BATTLE OF THE ROCKS. AND ADAM, ALANNA...
ZZAAPP
GUH!
WE'VE WON.
ALANNA!
NNNN
NO... WE WERE SO CLOSE... PLEASE... WE...
AAAA!
ZZAAPP
NO...

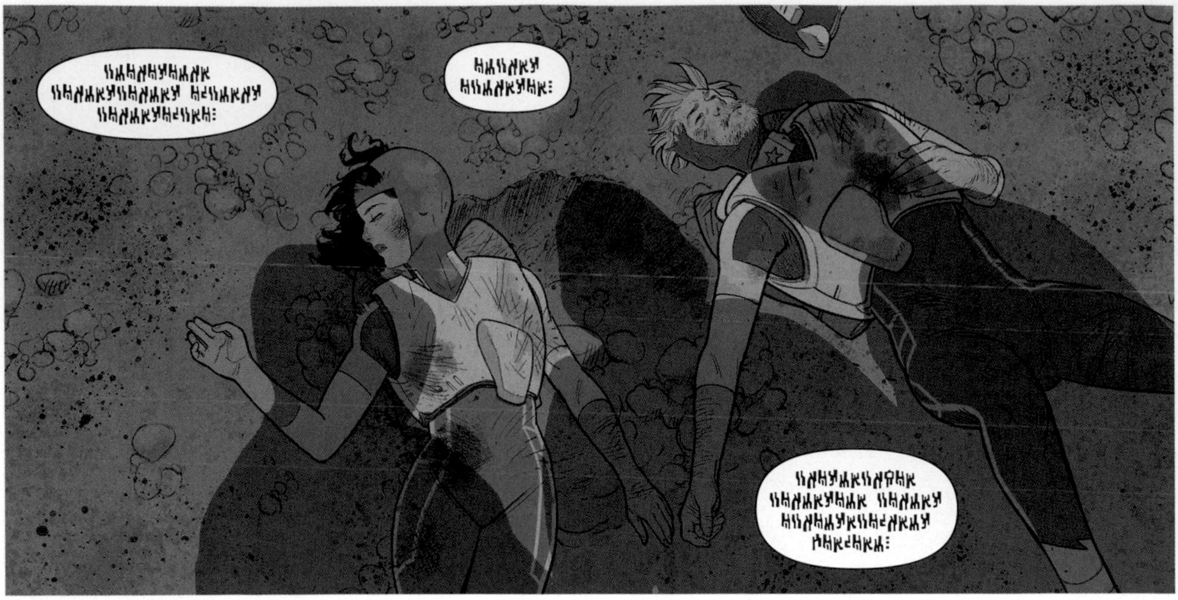

Yeah. It's one thing to tell a joke about it, but it's another thing to spend your whole day doing a mass-murder and dismembering scene and, you know, it's not exactly uplifting.

—Marie Severin

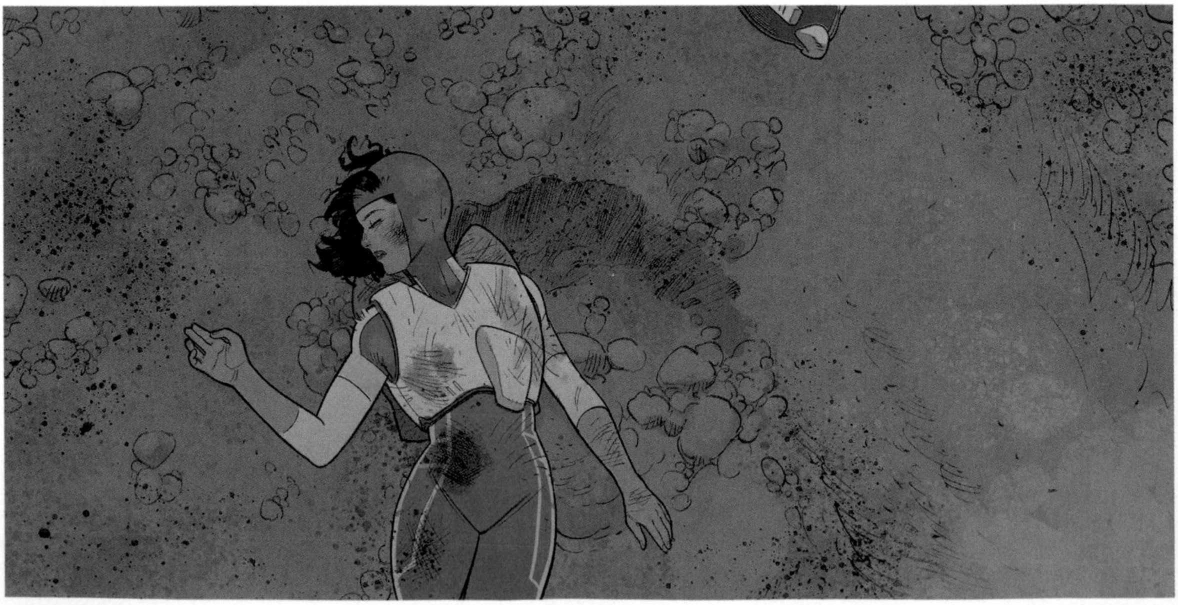

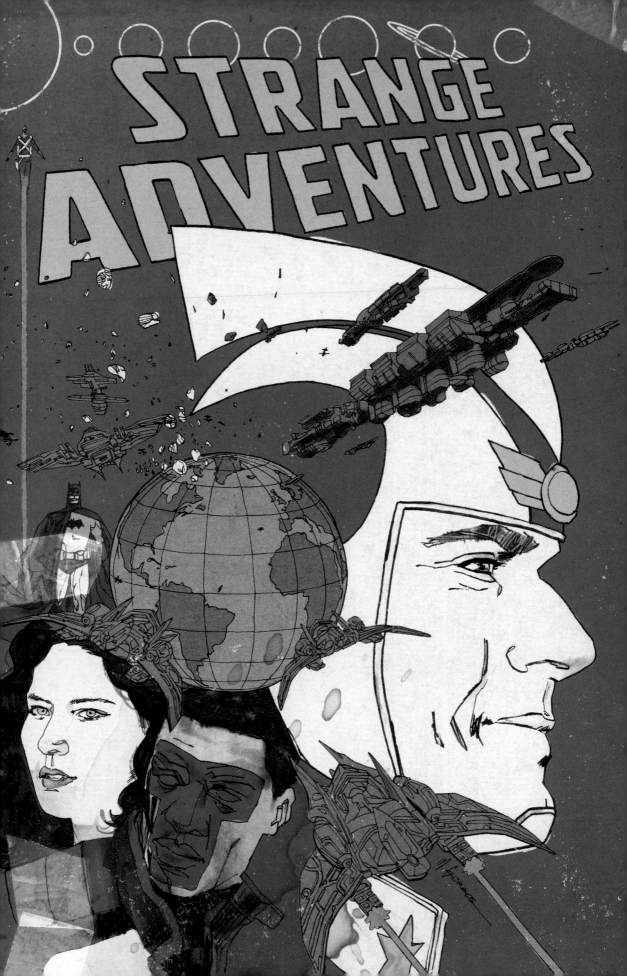

STRANGE
ADVENTURES

"...YOU'RE A SUPERHERO. I'M SOMETHING ELSE."

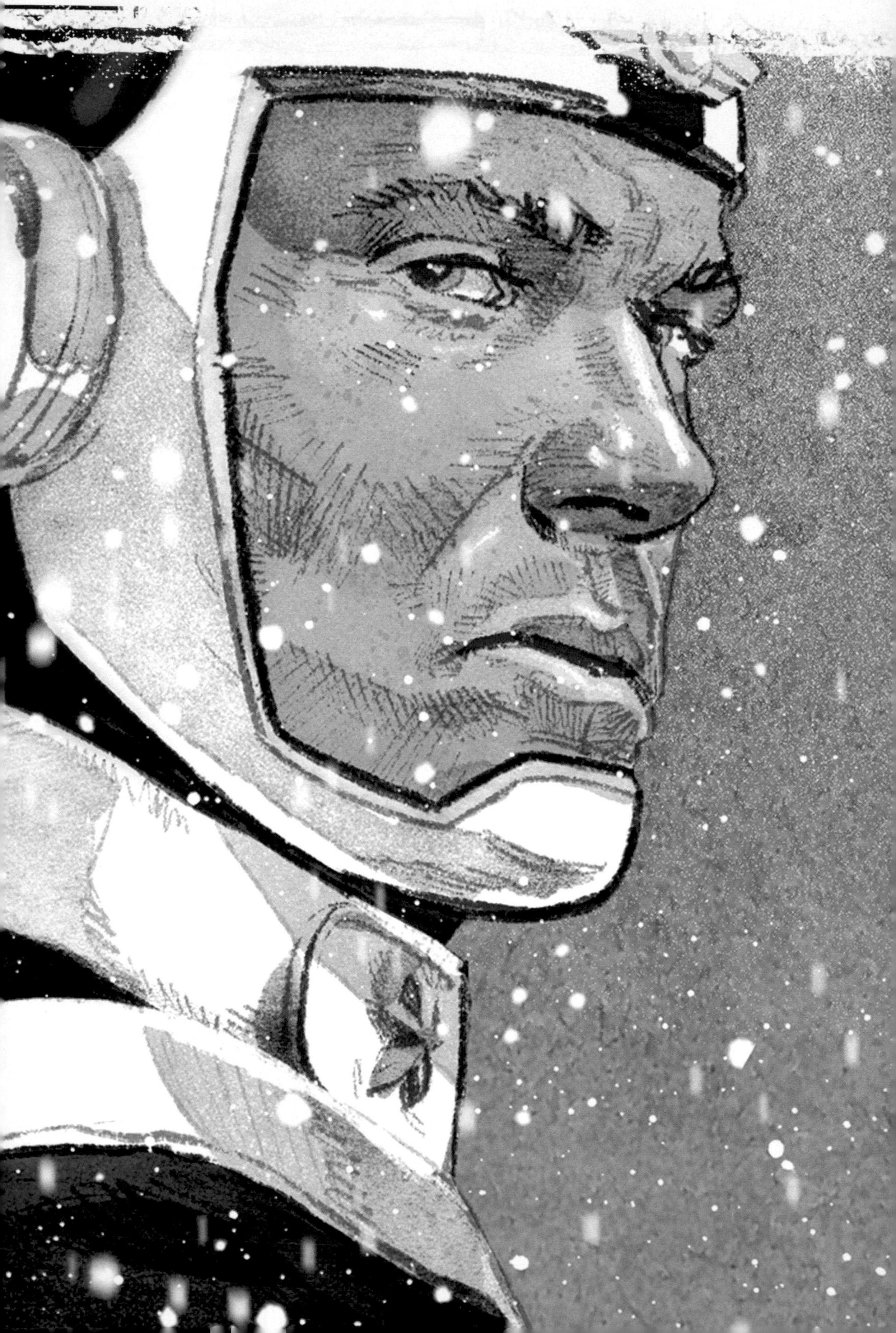

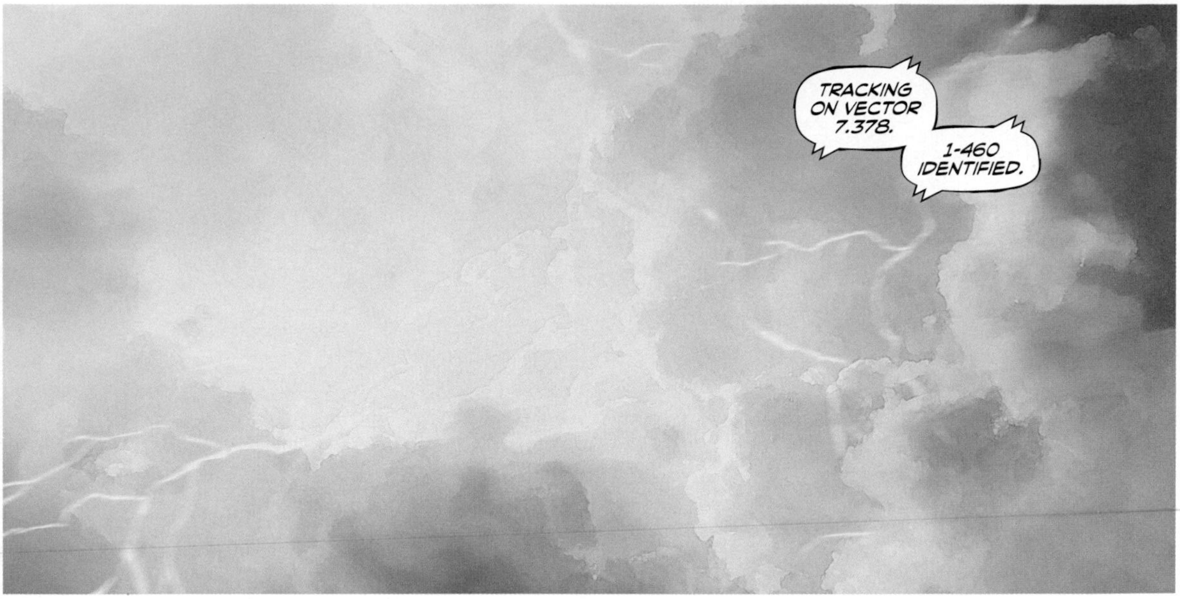
TRACKING ON VECTOR 7.378.
1-460 IDENTIFIED.

Chapter 7

It should happen to everybody

TOM KING ...Writer

MITCH GERADS
EVAN "DOC" SHANER ...Interior & Cover Artists

CLAYTON COWLES ...Letterer
BIXIE MATHIEU ...Assistant Editor
BRITTANY HOLZHERR ...Associate Editor
JAMIE S. RICH ...Editor

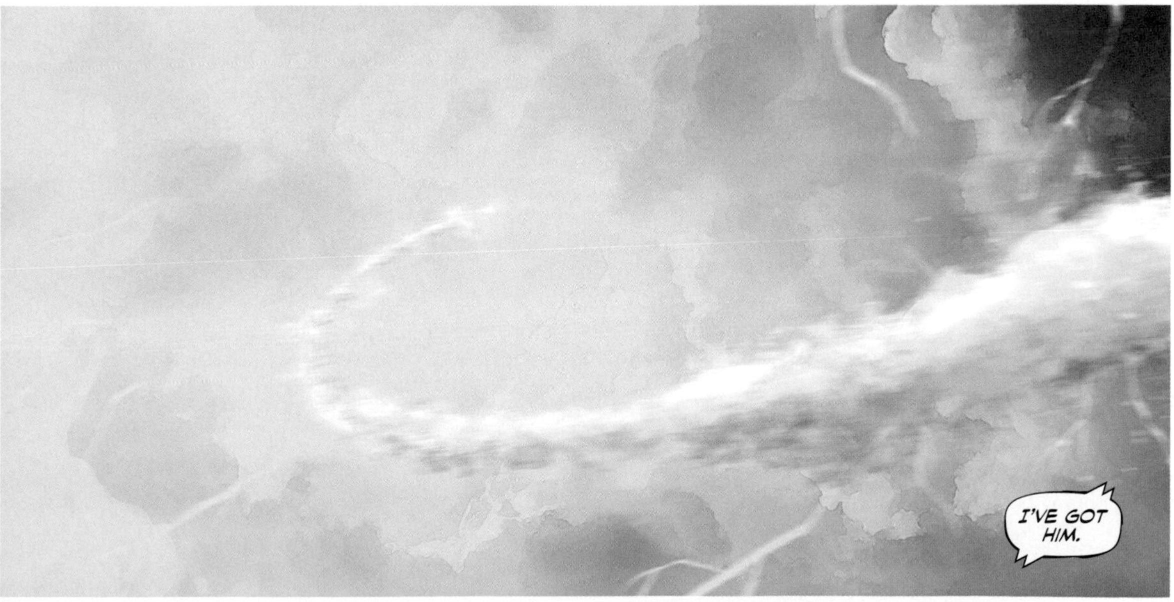
I'VE GOT HIM.

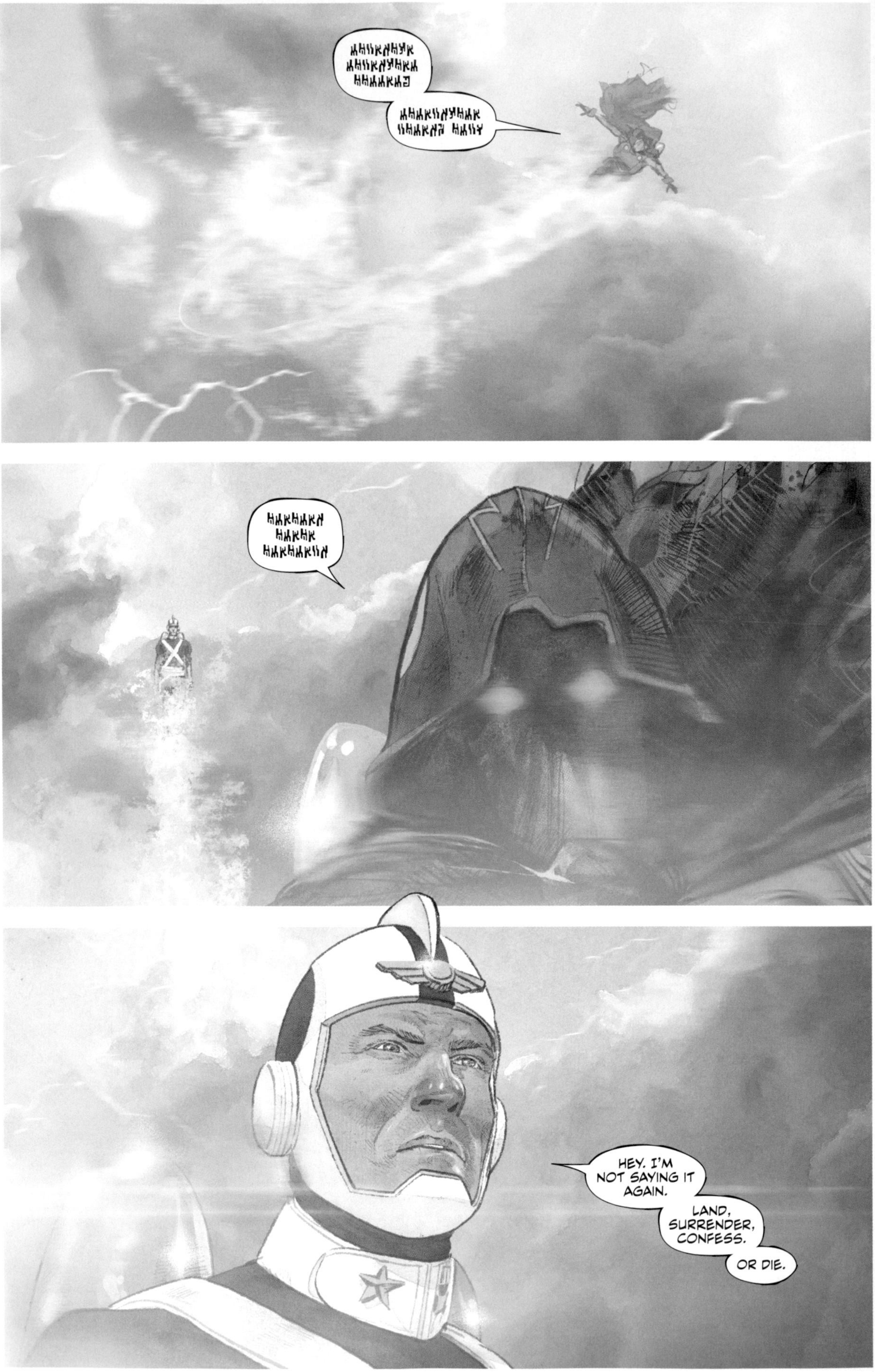
HEY. I'M NOT SAYING IT AGAIN.
LAND, SURRENDER, CONFESS.
OR DIE.

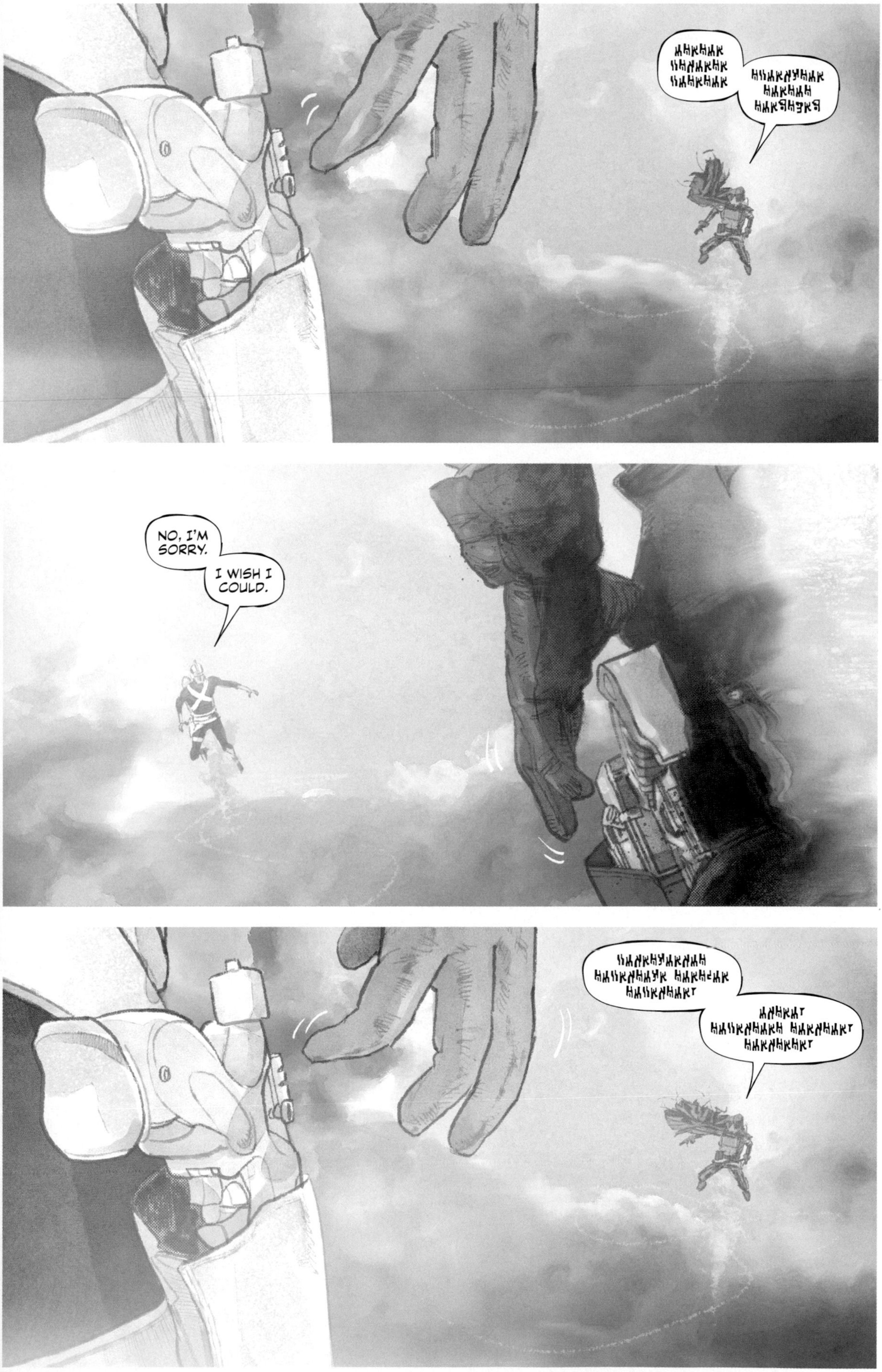
NO, I'M SORRY.
I WISH I COULD.

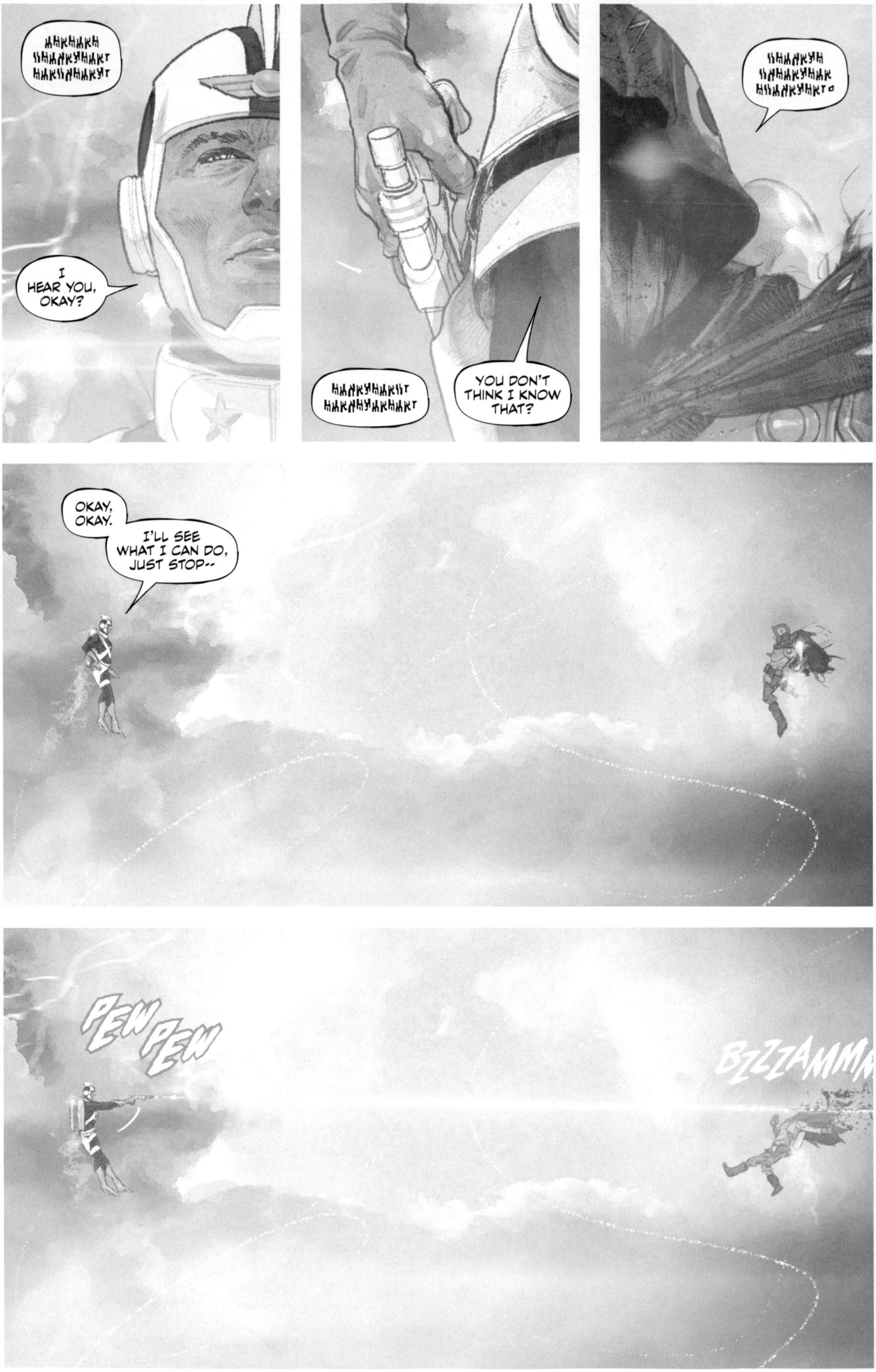
I HEAR YOU, OKAY?
YOU DON'T THINK I KNOW THAT?
OKAY, OKAY.
I'LL SEE WHAT I CAN DO, JUST STOP--
PEW PEW
BZZZAMM

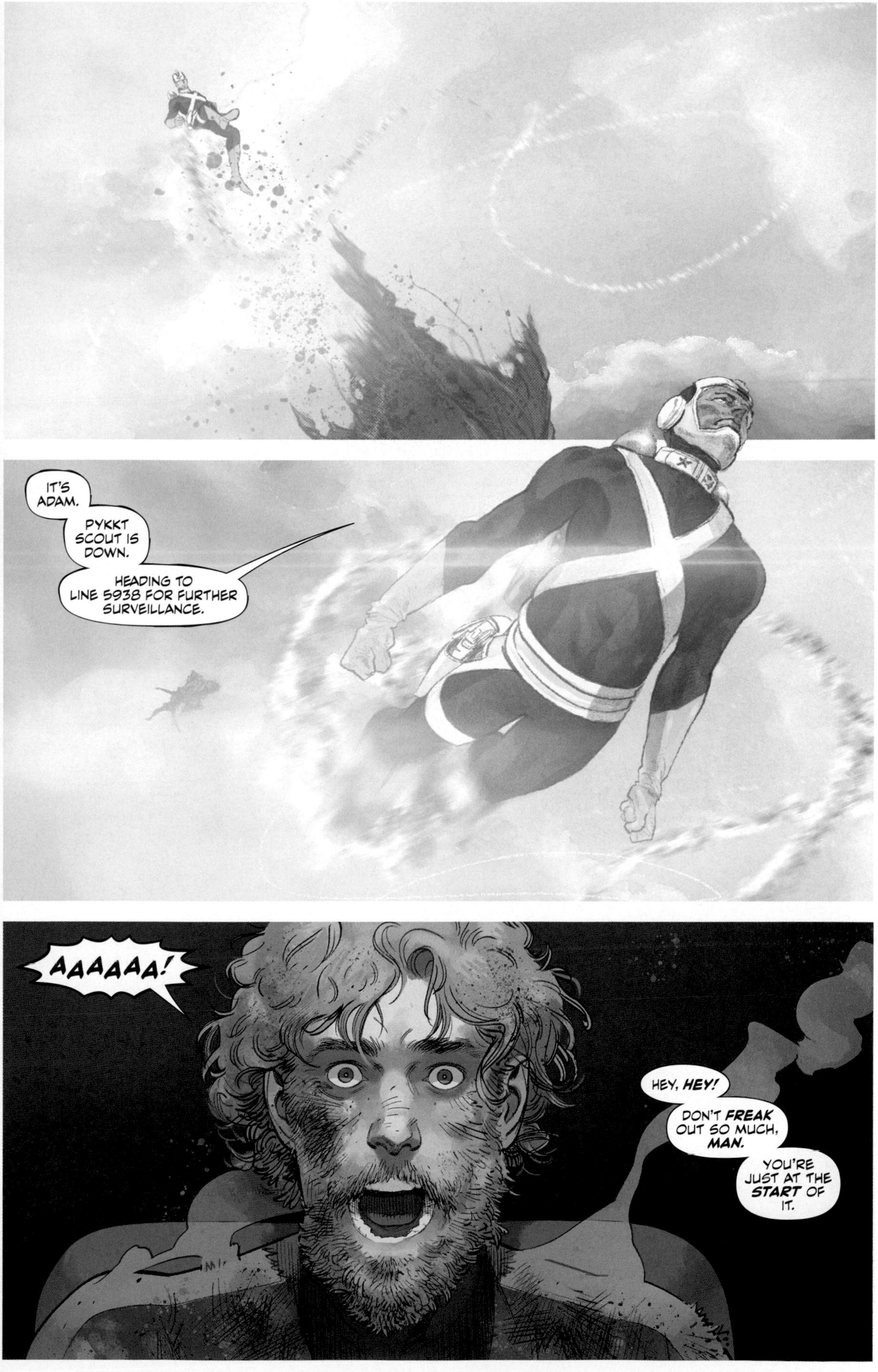
IT'S ADAM.
PYKKT SCOUT IS DOWN.
HEADING TO LINE 5938 FOR FURTHER SURVEILLANCE.
AAAAAA!
HEY, HEY!
DON'T FREAK OUT SO MUCH, MAN.
YOU'RE JUST AT THE START OF IT.

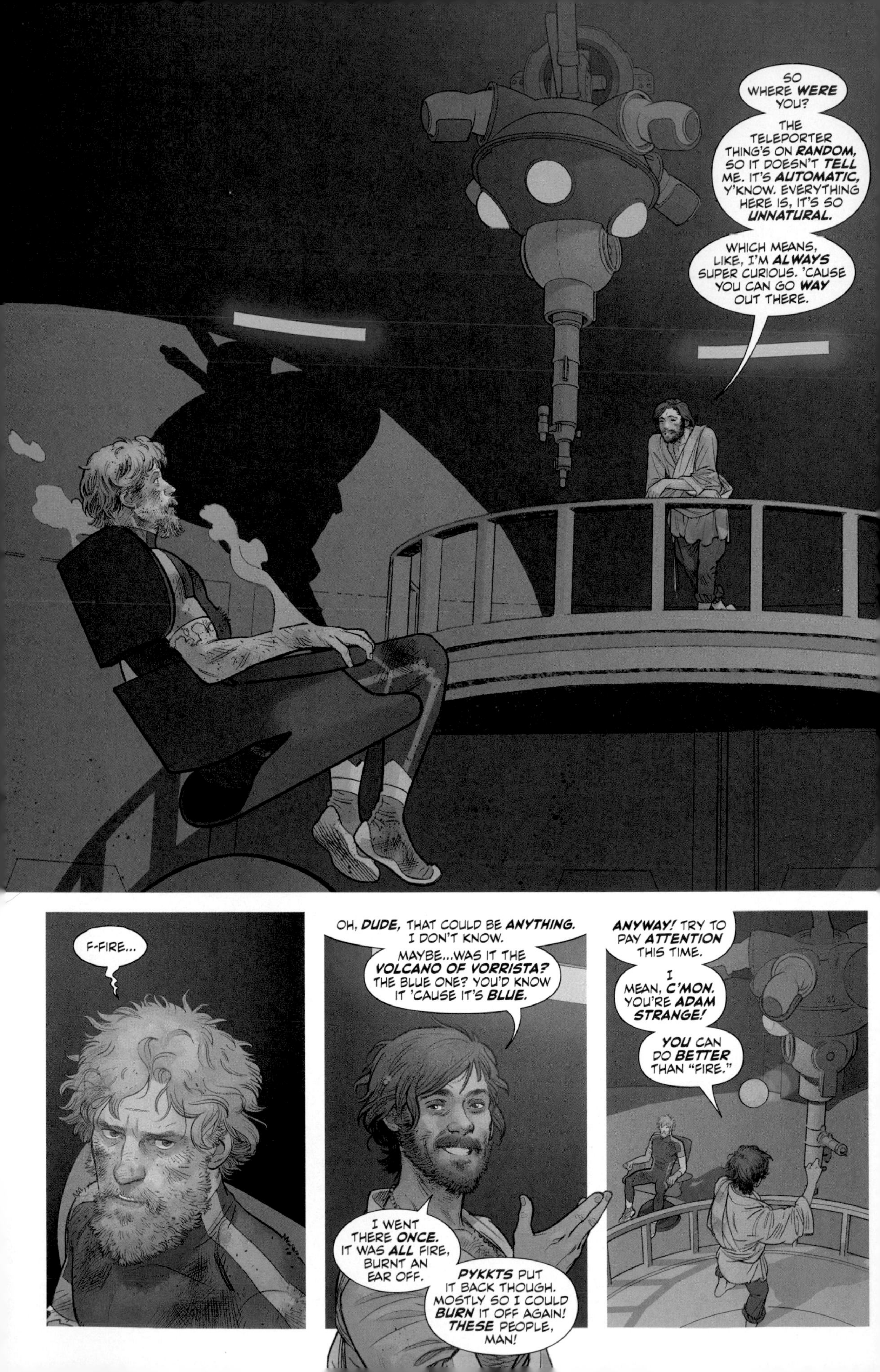
SO WHERE WERE YOU?
THE TELEPORTER THING'S ON RANDOM, SO IT DOESN'T TELL ME. IT'S AUTOMATIC, Y'KNOW. EVERYTHING HERE IS, IT'S SO UNNATURAL.
WHICH MEANS, LIKE, I'M ALWAYS SUPER CURIOUS. 'CAUSE YOU CAN GO WAY OUT THERE.
F-FIRE...
OH, DUDE, THAT COULD BE ANYTHING. I DON'T KNOW.
MAYBE...WAS IT THE VOLCANO OF VORRISTA? THE BLUE ONE? YOU'D KNOW IT 'CAUSE IT'S BLUE.
I WENT THERE ONCE. IT WAS ALL FIRE, BURNT AN EAR OFF.
PYKKTS PUT IT BACK THOUGH. MOSTLY SO I COULD BURN IT OFF AGAIN! THESE PEOPLE, MAN!
ANYWAY! TRY TO PAY ATTENTION THIS TIME.
I MEAN, C'MON. YOU'RE ADAM STRANGE!
YOU CAN DO BETTER THAN "FIRE."

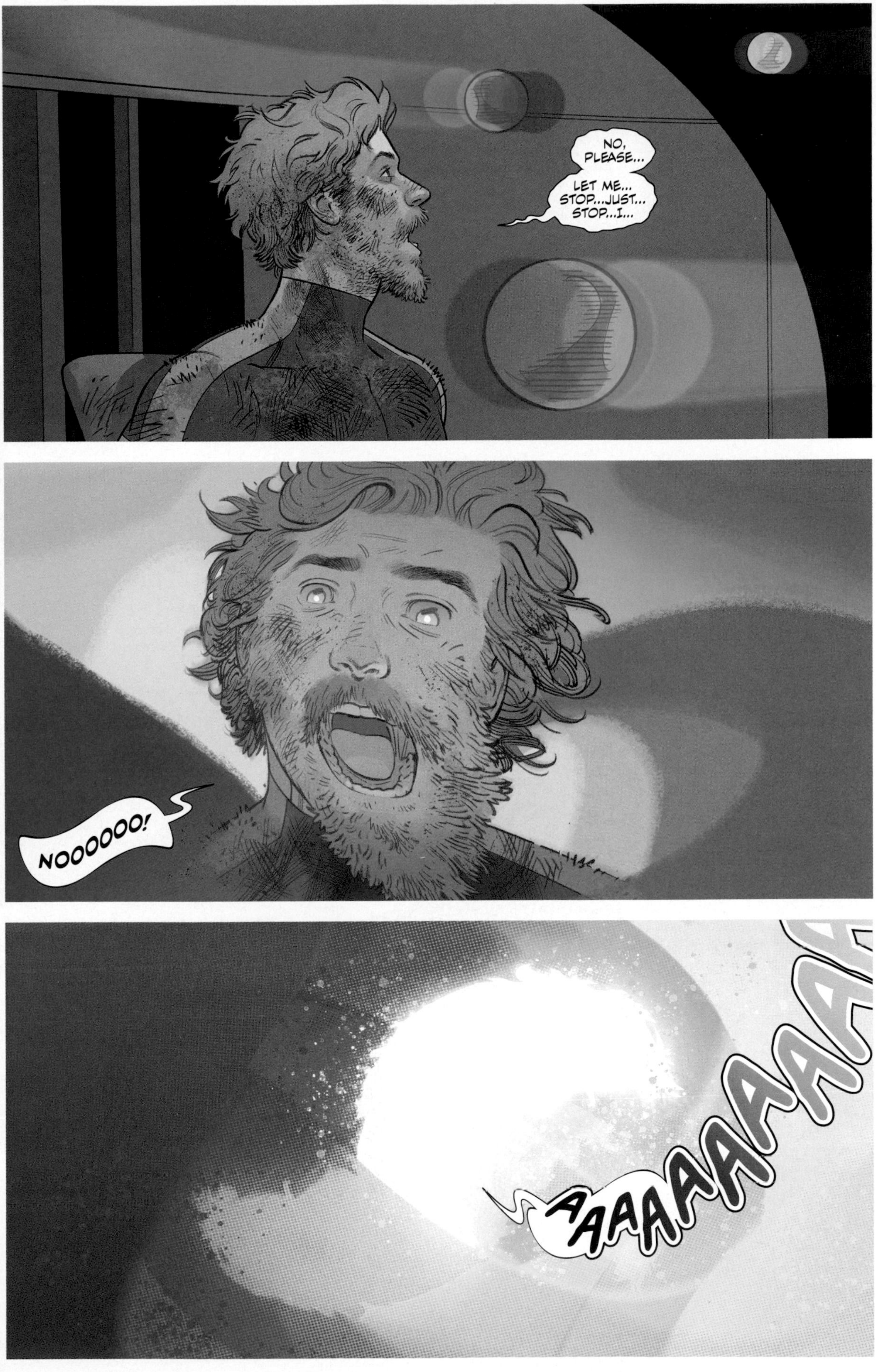
NO, PLEASE...
LET ME... STOP...JUST... STOP...I...
NOOOOOO!
AAAAAAAAAAA

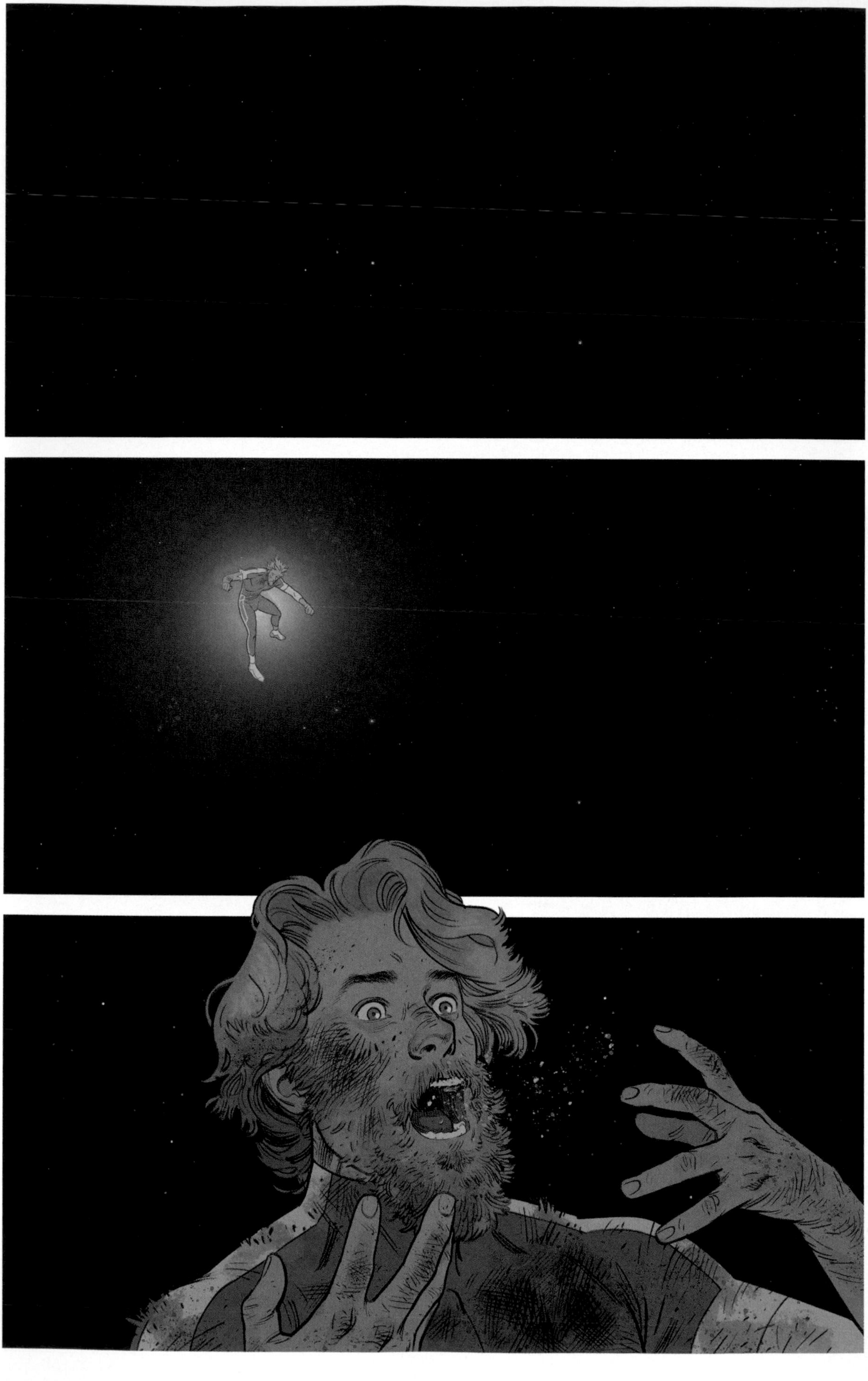

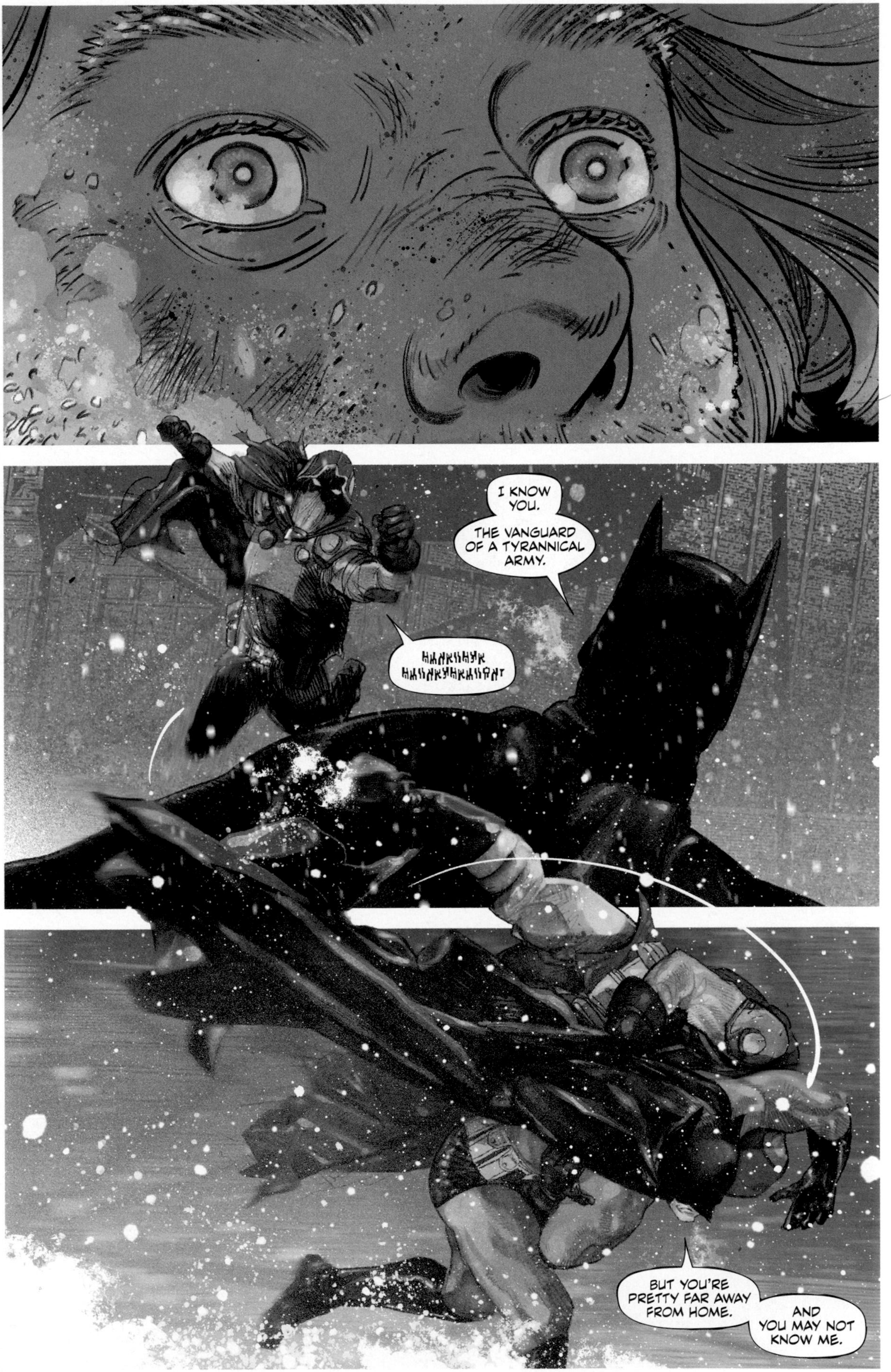
I KNOW YOU.
THE VANGUARD OF A TYRANNICAL ARMY.
BUT YOU'RE PRETTY FAR AWAY FROM HOME.
AND YOU MAY NOT KNOW ME.

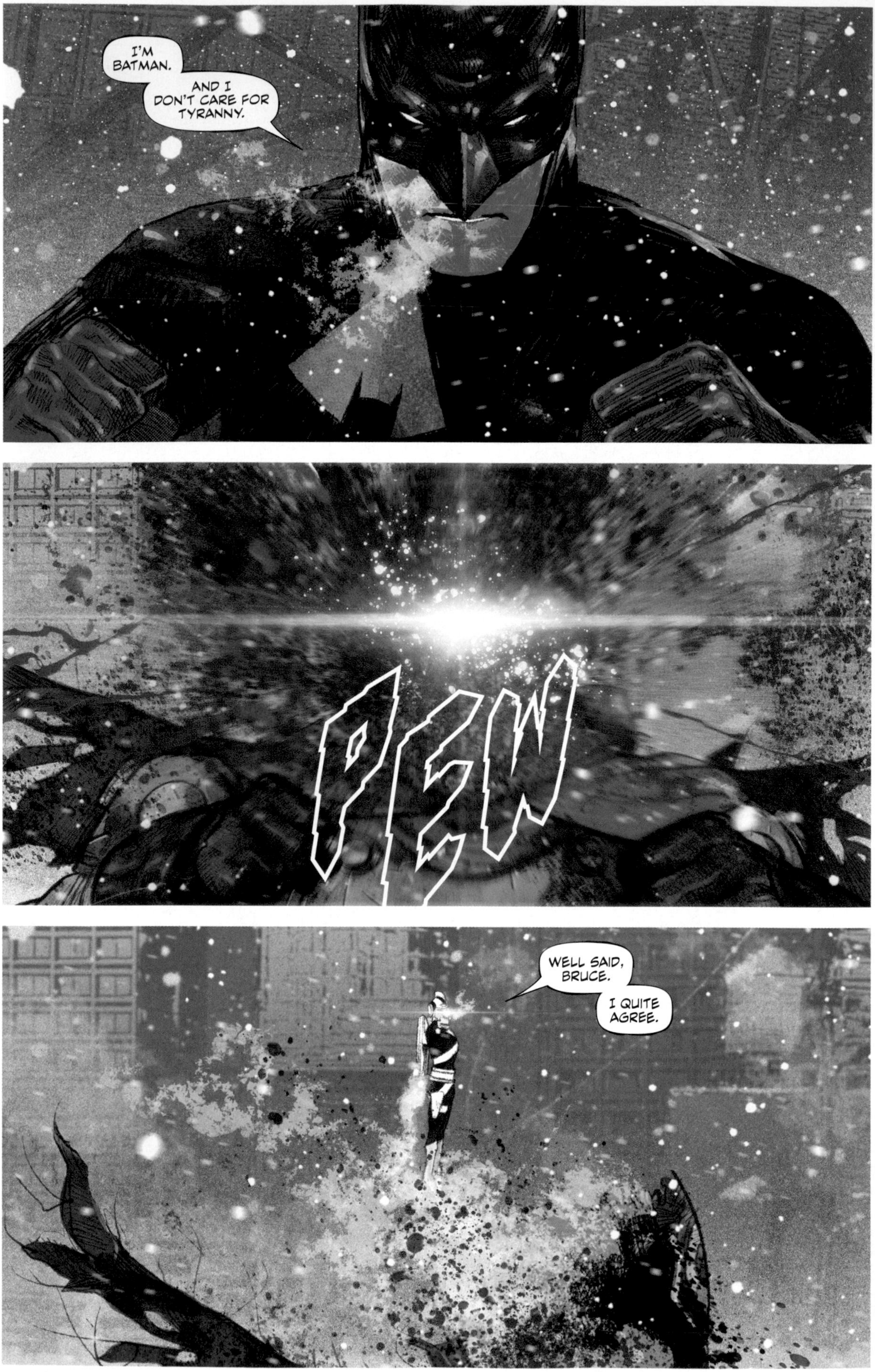
I'M BATMAN.
AND I DON'T CARE FOR TYRANNY.
PEW
WELL SAID, BRUCE.
I QUITE AGREE.

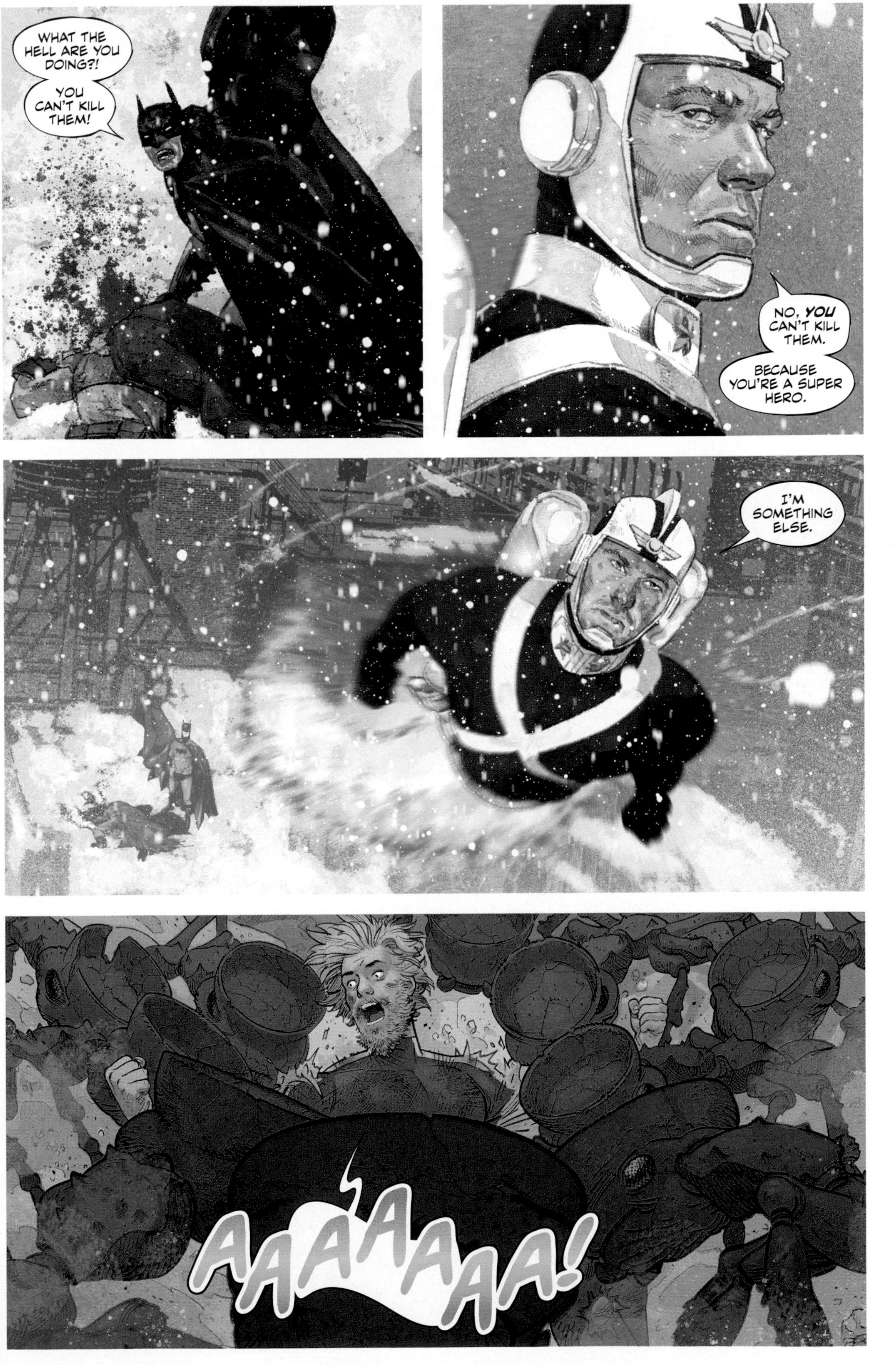
WHAT THE HELL ARE YOU DOING?!
YOU CAN'T KILL THEM!
NO, YOU CAN'T KILL THEM.
BECAUSE YOU'RE A SUPER HERO.
I'M SOMETHING ELSE.
AAAAAAAA!

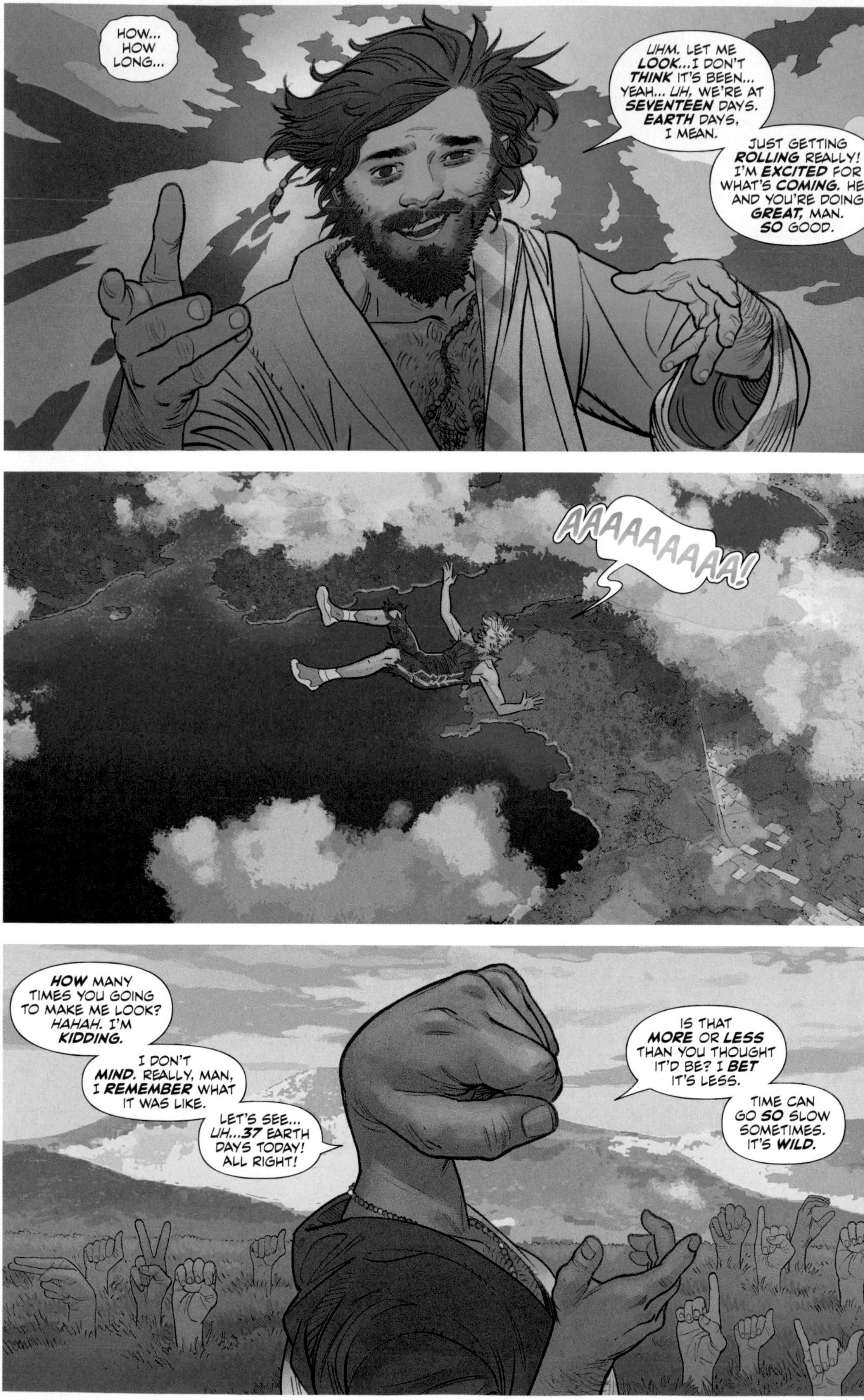
HOW... HOW LONG...
UHM. LET ME LOOK...I DON'T THINK IT'S BEEN... YEAH... UH, WE'RE AT SEVENTEEN DAYS. EARTH DAYS, I MEAN.
JUST GETTING ROLLING REALLY! I'M EXCITED FOR WHAT'S COMING. HEY, AND YOU'RE DOING GREAT, MAN. SO GOOD.
AAAAAAAAA!
HOW MANY TIMES YOU GOING TO MAKE ME LOOK? HAHAH. I'M KIDDING.
I DON'T MIND. REALLY, MAN, I REMEMBER WHAT IT WAS LIKE.
LET'S SEE... UH...37 EARTH DAYS TODAY! ALL RIGHT!
IS THAT MORE OR LESS THAN YOU THOUGHT IT'D BE? I BET IT'S LESS.
TIME CAN GO SO SLOW SOMETIMES. IT'S WILD.

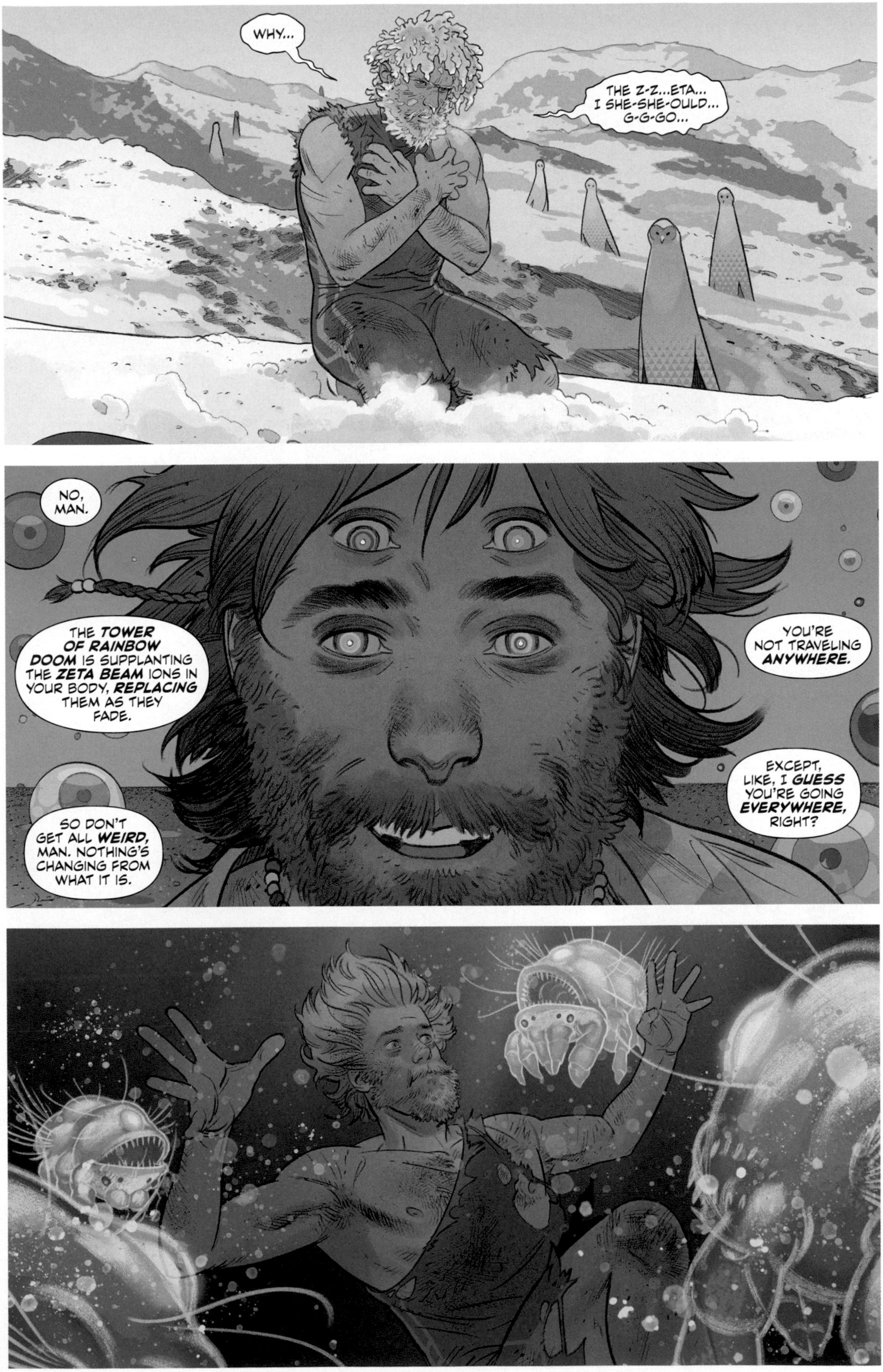
WHY...
THE Z-Z...ETA... I SHE-SHE-OULD... G-G-GO...
NO, MAN.
THE TOWER OF RAINBOW DOOM IS SUPPLANTING THE ZETA BEAM IONS IN YOUR BODY, REPLACING THEM AS THEY FADE.
YOU'RE NOT TRAVELING ANYWHERE.
SO DON'T GET ALL WEIRD, MAN. NOTHING'S CHANGING FROM WHAT IT IS.
EXCEPT, LIKE, I GUESS YOU'RE GOING EVERYWHERE, RIGHT?

DO...YOU... YOU...KNOW... I DON'T... WHY... WHY...

DUDE, I ASKED THE **SAME THING** WHEN THE **PYKKTS** CAME TO MY PLANET, **ANTHORANN.** WHERE WE'RE AT **NOW.**

AFTER WE **PLEADED** FOR RANN TO HELP, Y'KNOW. WHEN RANN DID **NOTHING** AND THEN PYKKTS CAME AND THEY JUST **KILLED** EVERYONE.

AND **I** WAS LIKE, "WHY **US?**" AND THEN WHEN THEY CAPTURED **ME...**

I WAS ALL, "WHY **ME?**"

IT WASN'T UNTIL **THE END,** AFTER A **TON** OF PAIN, THAT THEY TOLD ME, LIKE, **WHY** AND WHAT **I** COULD DO, Y'KNOW, TO STOP IT.

IT WAS A **RELIEF!** BY **THAT** POINT, MAN, I WOULD'VE DONE **ANYTHING.**

I MEAN, I JUST **WANTED** TO DIE. **YOU** WANT TO DIE, RIGHT? **YOU** GET IT.

I WAS JUST LIKE, "JUST **LET** ME DO IT AND **KILL** ME."

AND **THEN** THEY TOLD ME, AND **I** WAS LIKE, "GREAT, **WHATEVER.** LET'S **DO** IT!"

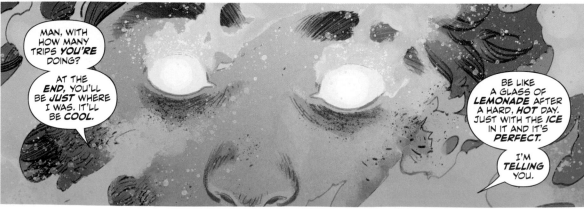

MAN, WITH HOW MANY TRIPS **YOU'RE** DOING?

AT THE **END,** YOU'LL BE **JUST** WHERE I WAS. IT'LL BE **COOL.**

BE LIKE A GLASS OF **LEMONADE** AFTER A HARD, **HOT** DAY. JUST WITH THE **ICE** IN IT AND IT'S **PERFECT.**

I'M **TELLING** YOU.

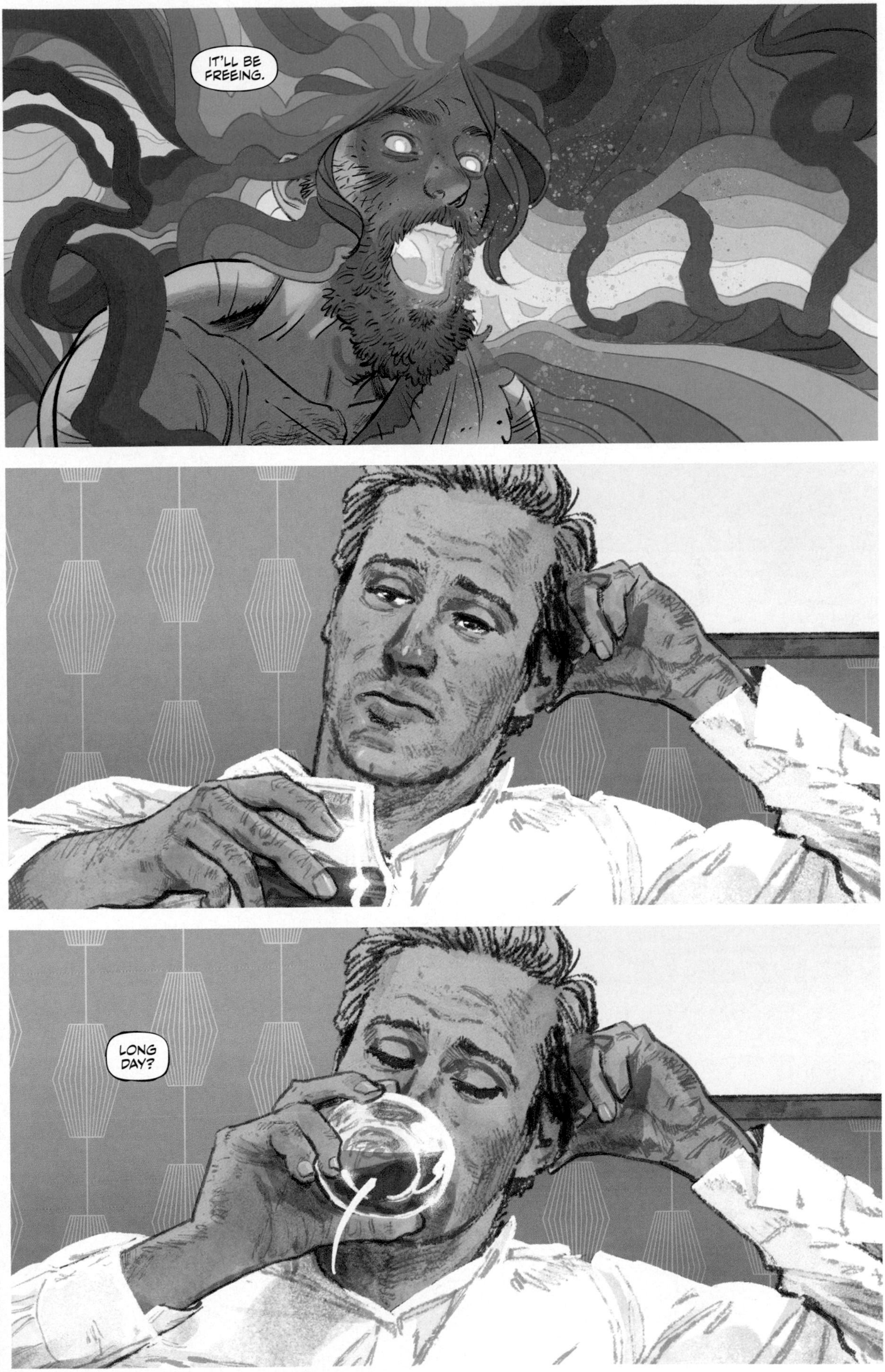
IT'LL BE FREEING.
LONG DAY?

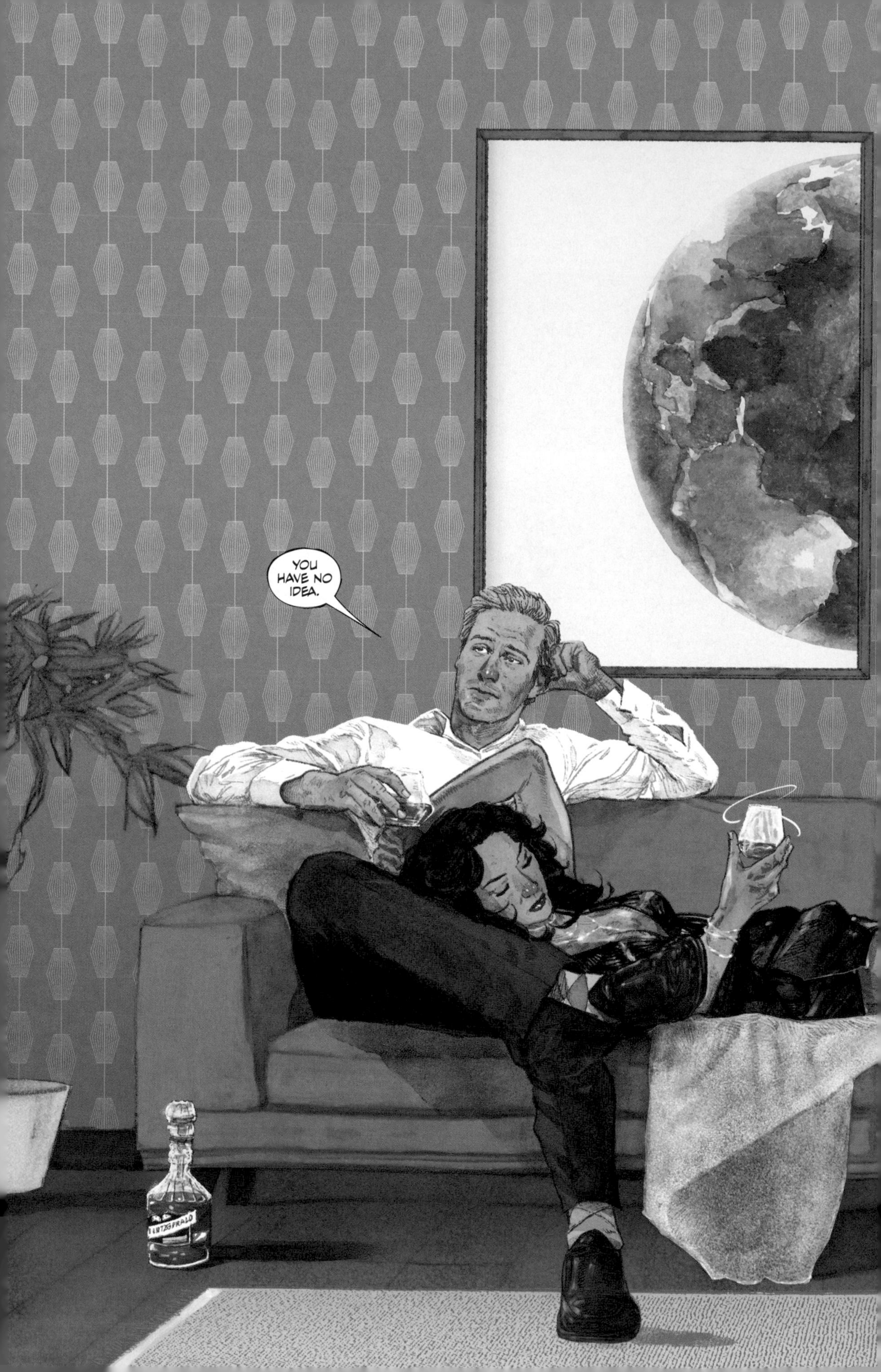
YOU HAVE NO IDEA.

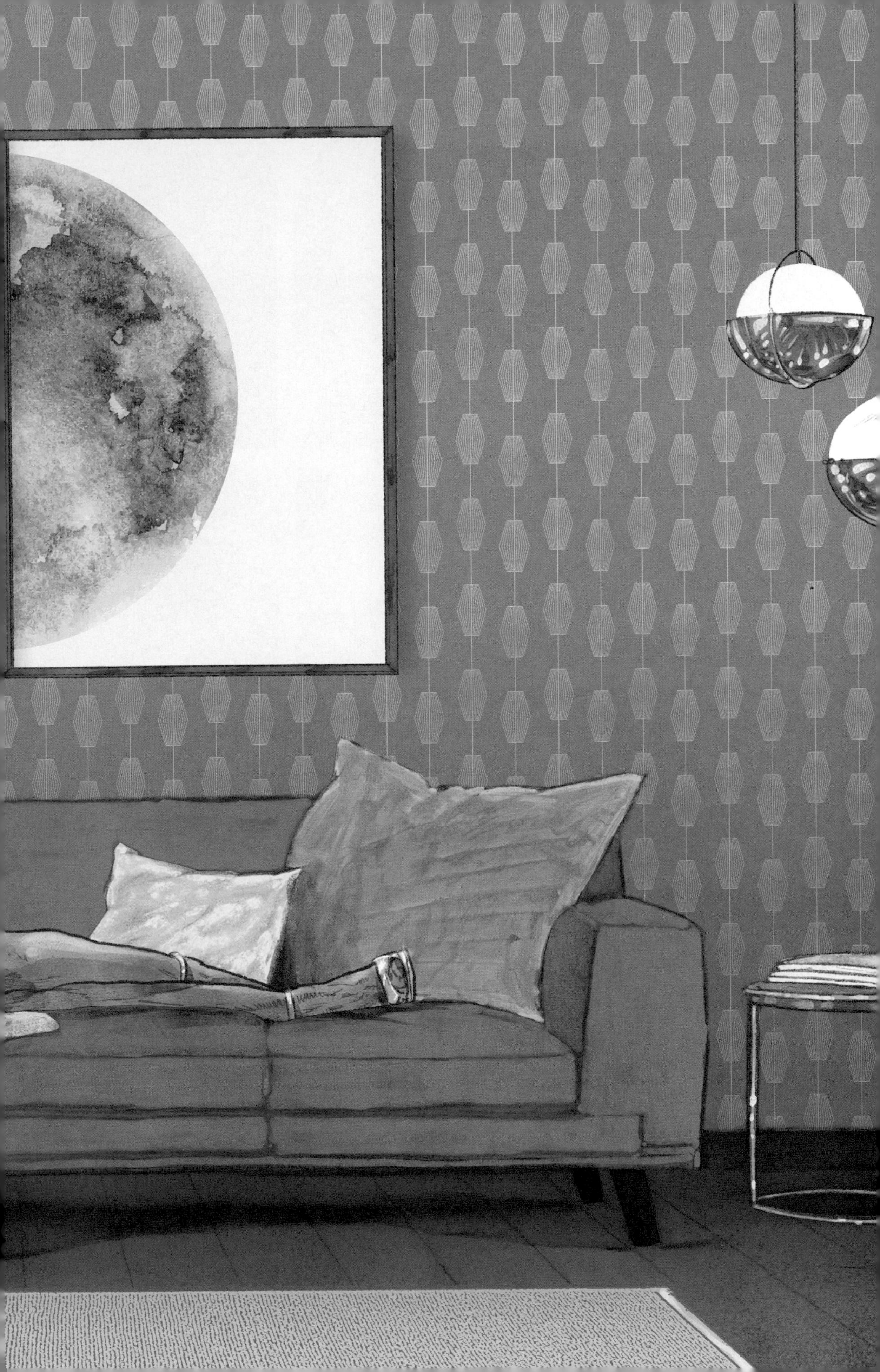

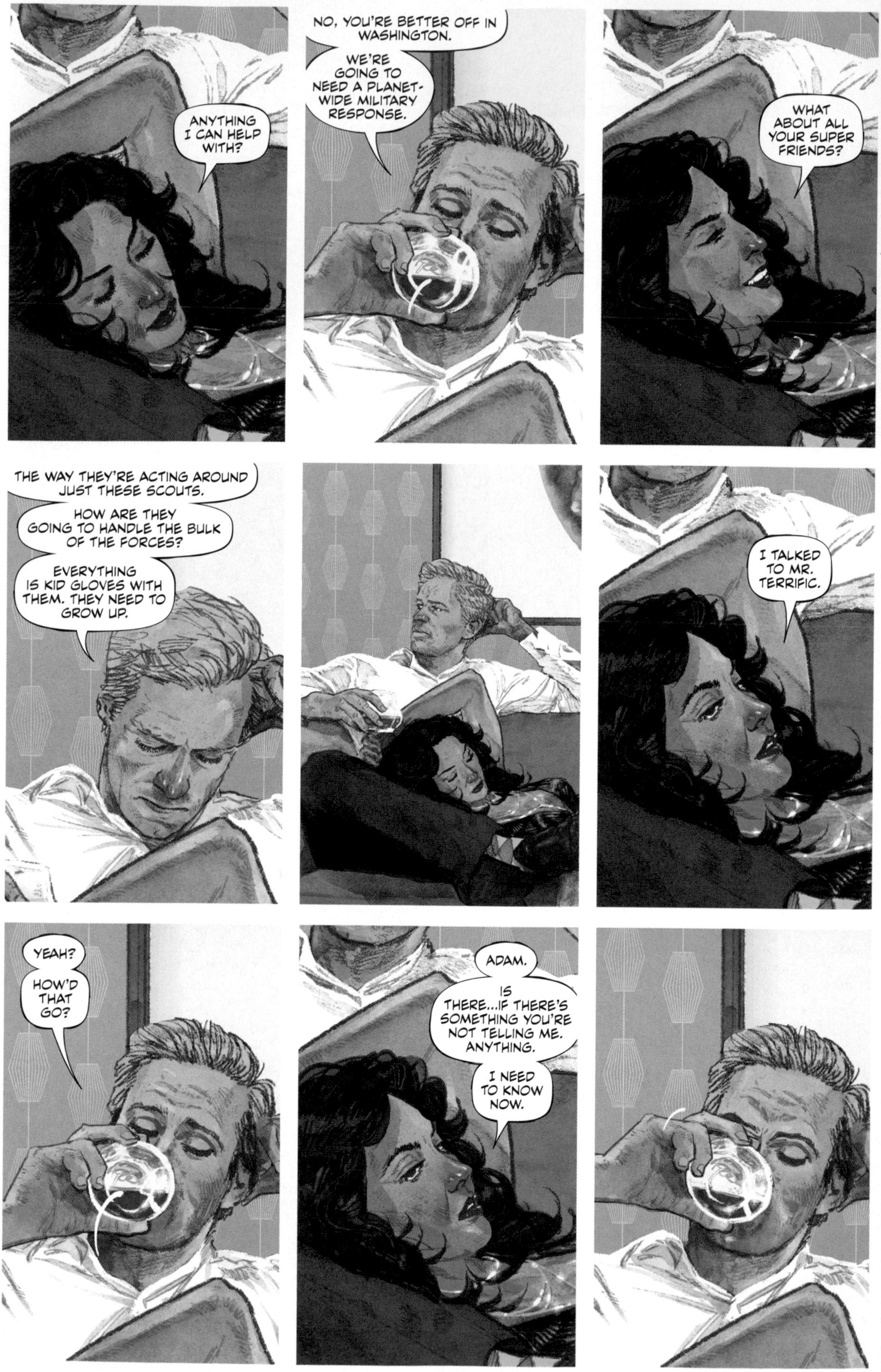
ANYTHING I CAN HELP WITH?
NO, YOU'RE BETTER OFF IN WASHINGTON.
WE'RE GOING TO NEED A PLANET-WIDE MILITARY RESPONSE.
WHAT ABOUT ALL YOUR SUPER FRIENDS?
THE WAY THEY'RE ACTING AROUND JUST THESE SCOUTS.
HOW ARE THEY GOING TO HANDLE THE BULK OF THE FORCES?
EVERYTHING IS KID GLOVES WITH THEM. THEY NEED TO GROW UP.
I TALKED TO MR. TERRIFIC.
YEAH?
HOW'D THAT GO?
ADAM.
IS THERE...IF THERE'S SOMETHING YOU'RE NOT TELLING ME. ANYTHING.
I NEED TO KNOW NOW.

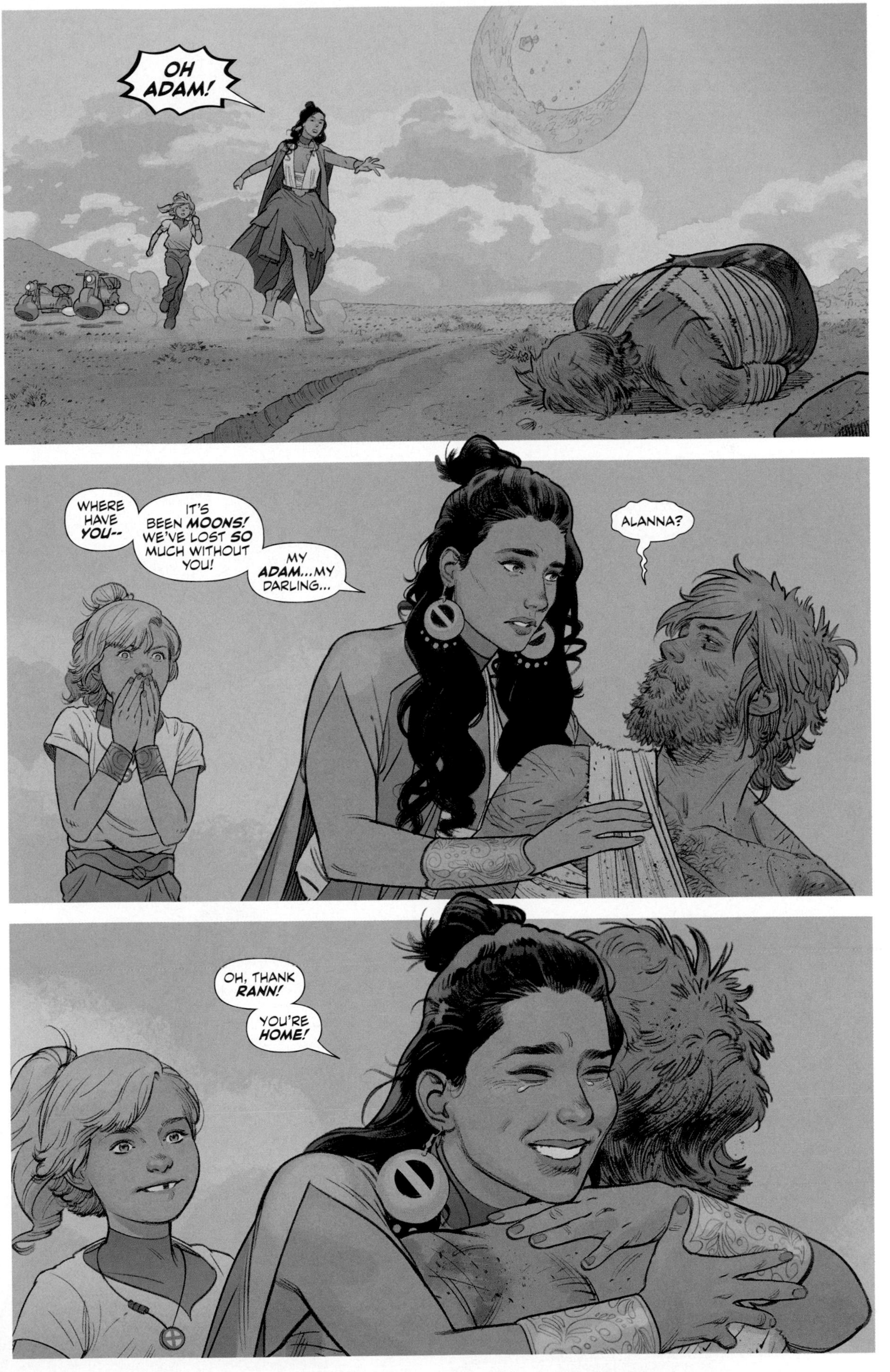
OH ADAM!
WHERE HAVE YOU--
IT'S BEEN MOONS! WE'VE LOST SO MUCH WITHOUT YOU!
MY ADAM...MY DARLING...
ALANNA?
OH, THANK RANN!
YOU'RE HOME!

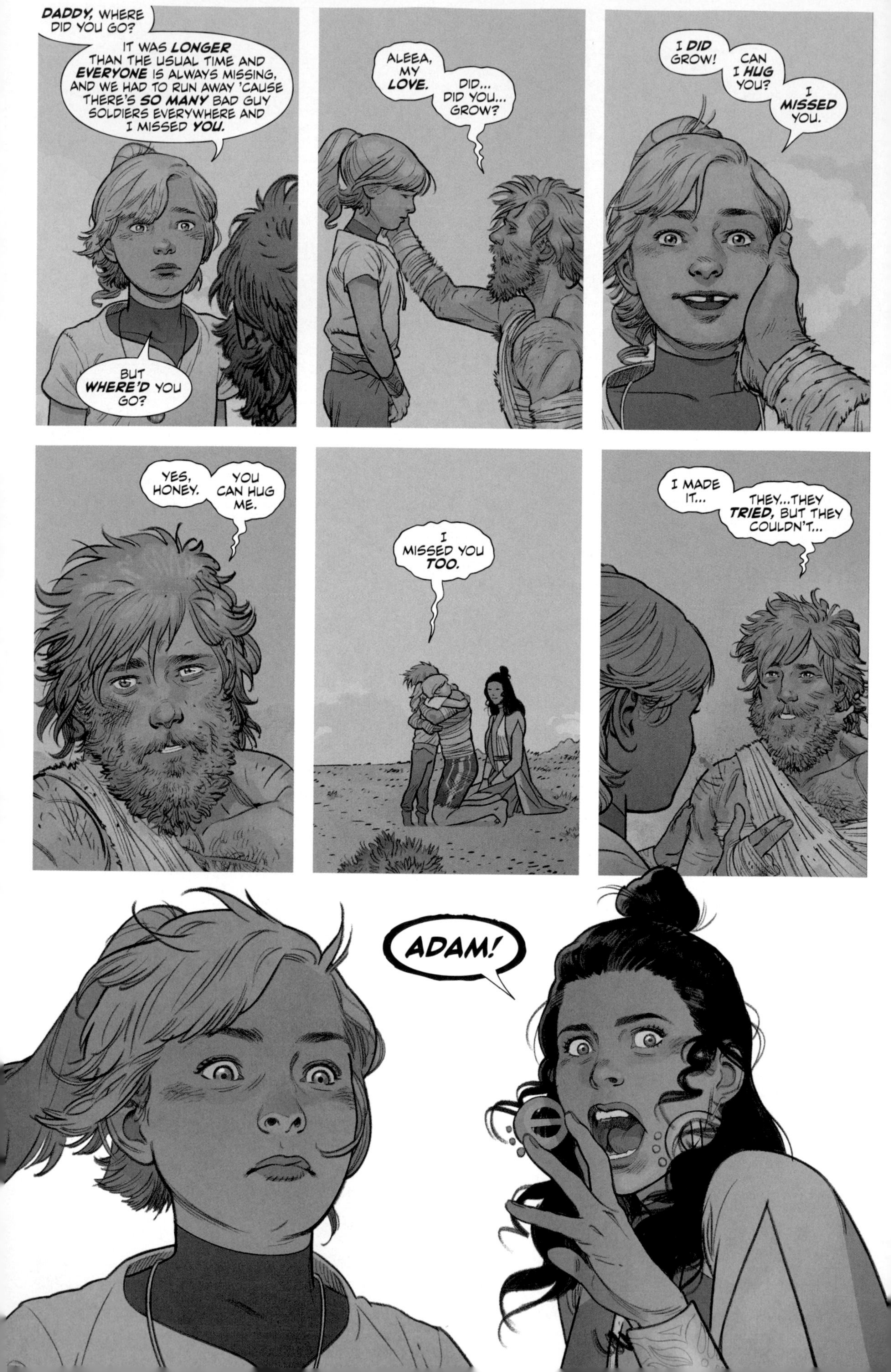
DADDY, WHERE DID YOU GO?
IT WAS LONGER THAN THE USUAL TIME AND EVERYONE IS ALWAYS MISSING, AND WE HAD TO RUN AWAY 'CAUSE THERE'S SO MANY BAD GUY SOLDIERS EVERYWHERE AND I MISSED YOU.
BUT WHERE'D YOU GO?
ALEEA, MY LOVE.
DID... DID YOU... GROW?
I DID GROW!
CAN I HUG YOU?
I MISSED YOU.
YES, HONEY.
YOU CAN HUG ME.
I MISSED YOU TOO.
I MADE IT...
THEY...THEY TRIED, BUT THEY COULDN'T...
ADAM!

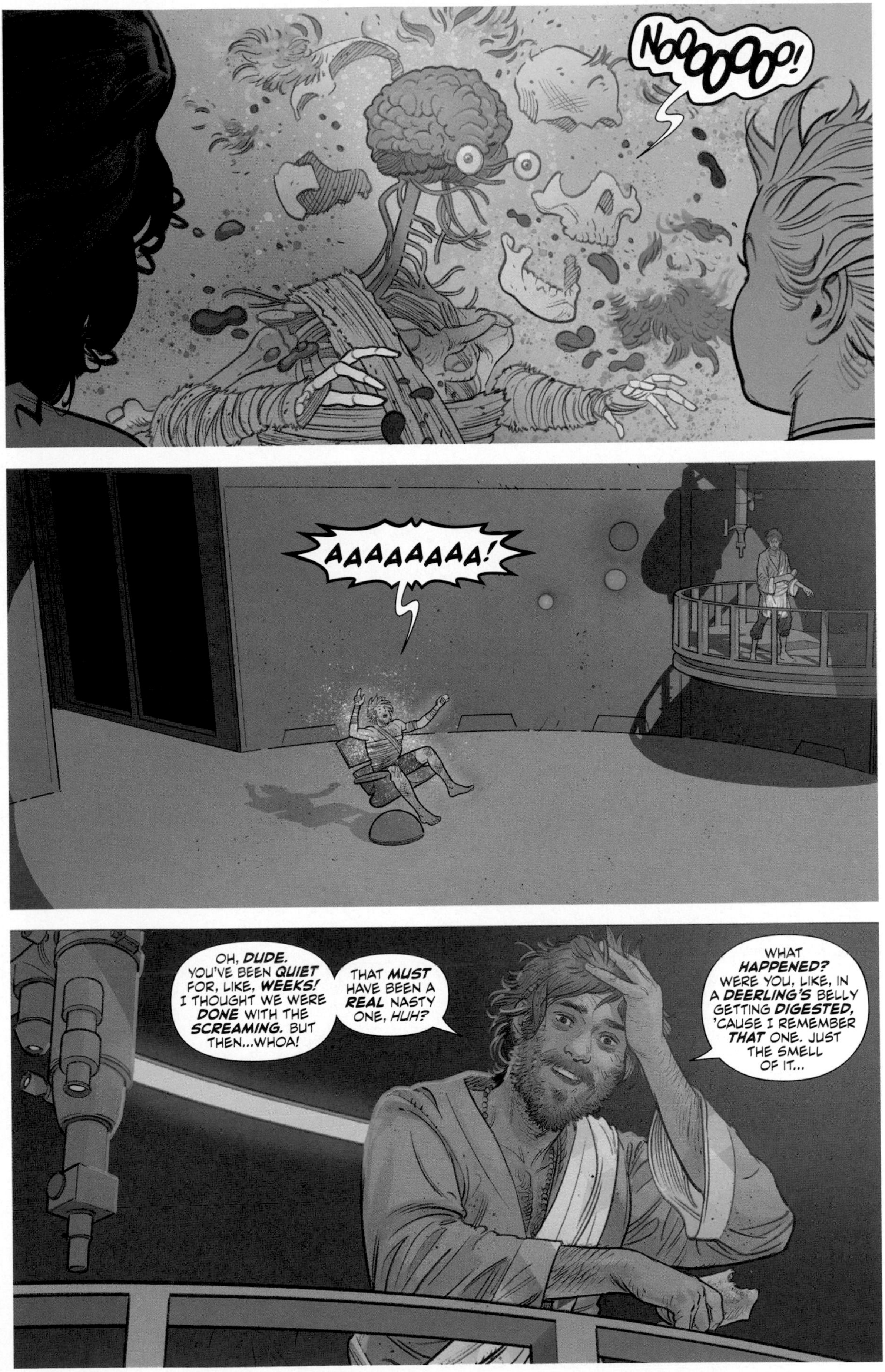
NOOOOOOO!
AAAAAAAA!
OH, DUDE. YOU'VE BEEN QUIET FOR, LIKE, WEEKS! I THOUGHT WE WERE DONE WITH THE SCREAMING. BUT THEN...WHOA!
THAT MUST HAVE BEEN A REAL NASTY ONE, HUH?
WHAT HAPPENED? WERE YOU, LIKE, IN A DEERLING'S BELLY GETTING DIGESTED, 'CAUSE I REMEMBER THAT ONE. JUST THE SMELL OF IT...

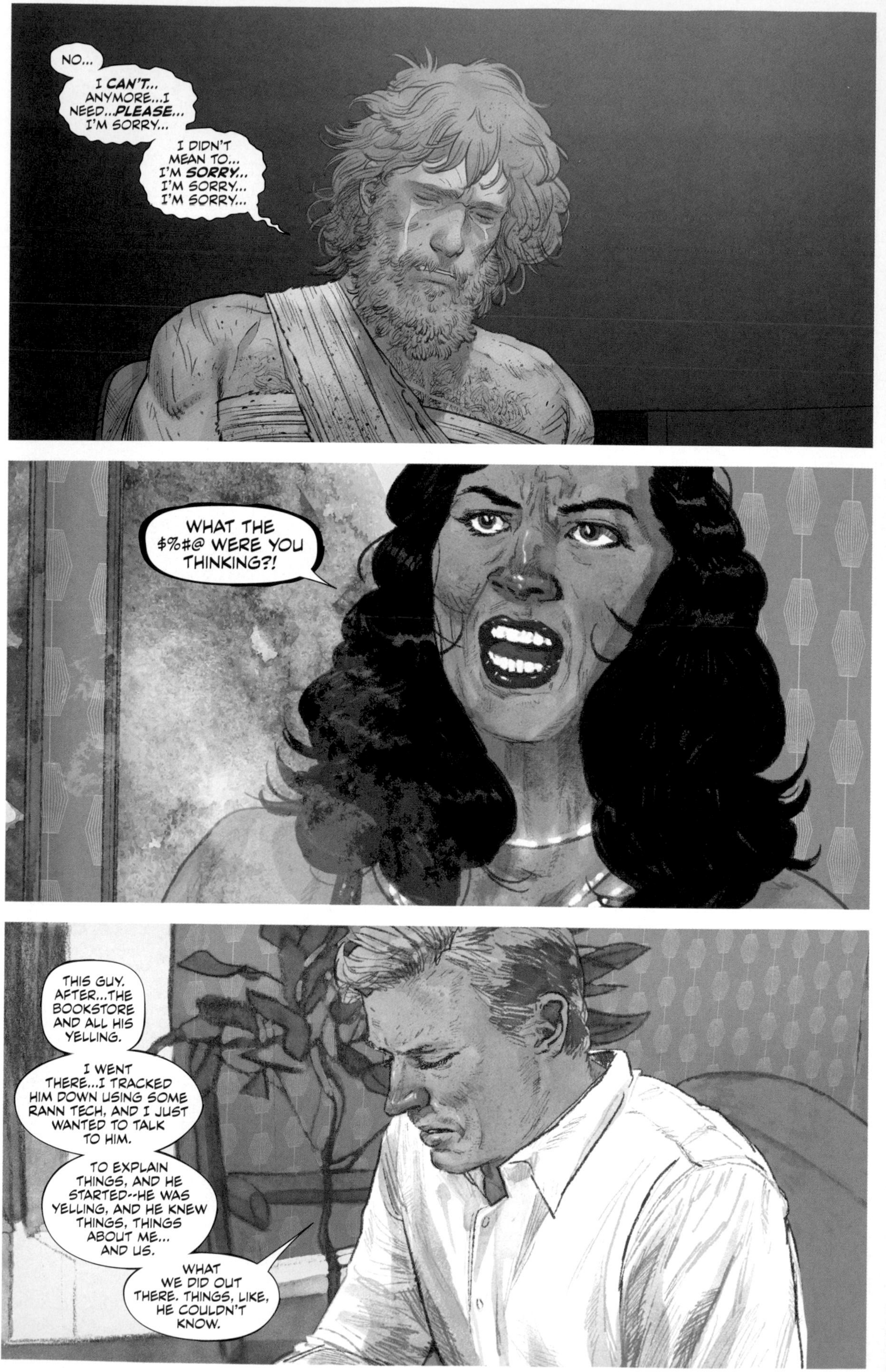
NO...
I CAN'T... ANYMORE...I NEED...PLEASE... I'M SORRY...
I DIDN'T MEAN TO... I'M SORRY... I'M SORRY... I'M SORRY...
WHAT THE $%#@ WERE YOU THINKING?!
THIS GUY. AFTER...THE BOOKSTORE AND ALL HIS YELLING.
I WENT THERE...I TRACKED HIM DOWN USING SOME RANN TECH, AND I JUST WANTED TO TALK TO HIM.
TO EXPLAIN THINGS, AND HE STARTED--HE WAS YELLING, AND HE KNEW THINGS, THINGS ABOUT ME... AND US.
WHAT WE DID OUT THERE. THINGS, LIKE, HE COULDN'T KNOW.

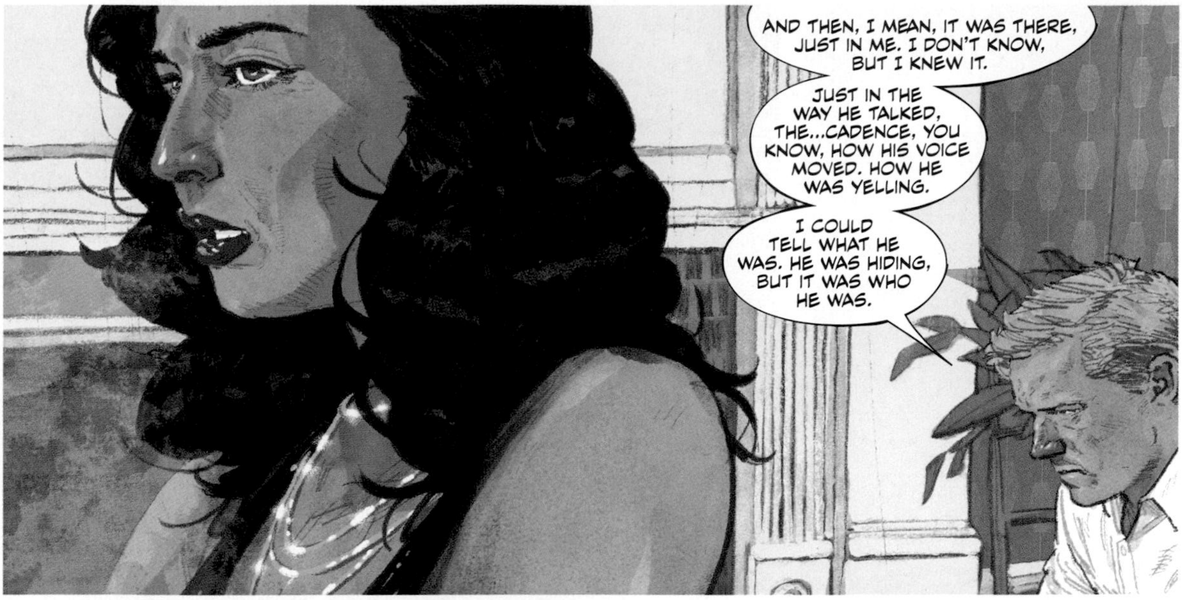
AND THEN, I MEAN, IT WAS THERE, JUST IN ME. I DON'T KNOW, BUT I KNEW IT.
JUST IN THE WAY HE TALKED, THE...CADENCE, YOU KNOW, HOW HIS VOICE MOVED. HOW HE WAS YELLING.
I COULD TELL WHAT HE WAS. HE WAS HIDING, BUT IT WAS WHO HE WAS.

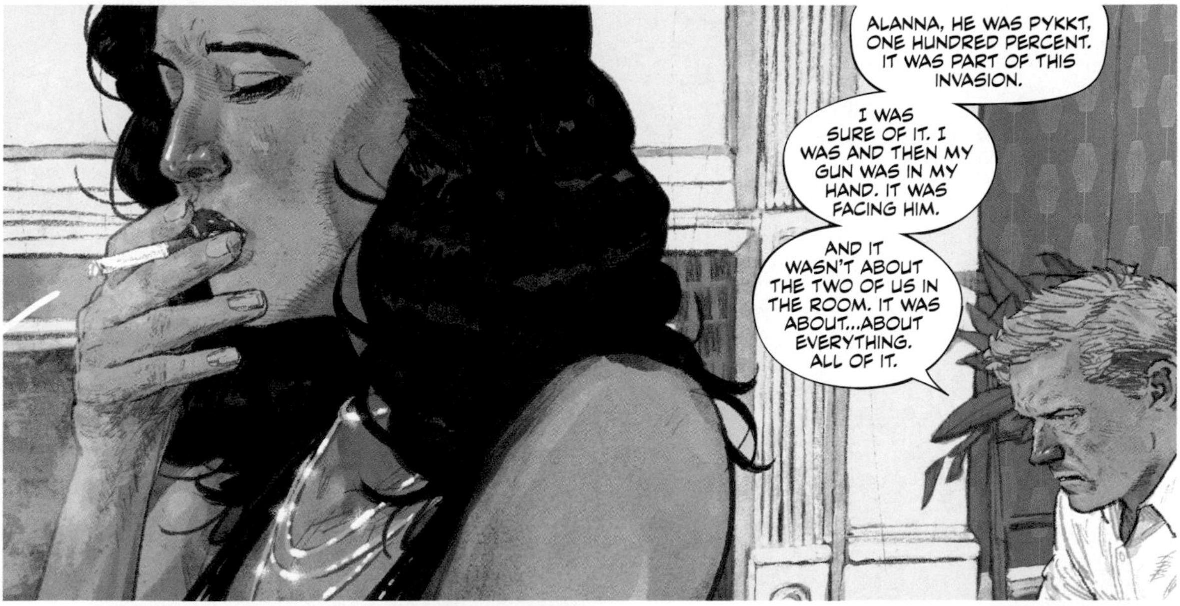
ALANNA, HE WAS PYKKT, ONE HUNDRED PERCENT. IT WAS PART OF THIS INVASION.
I WAS SURE OF IT. I WAS AND THEN MY GUN WAS IN MY HAND. IT WAS FACING HIM.
AND IT WASN'T ABOUT THE TWO OF US IN THE ROOM. IT WAS ABOUT...ABOUT EVERYTHING. ALL OF IT.

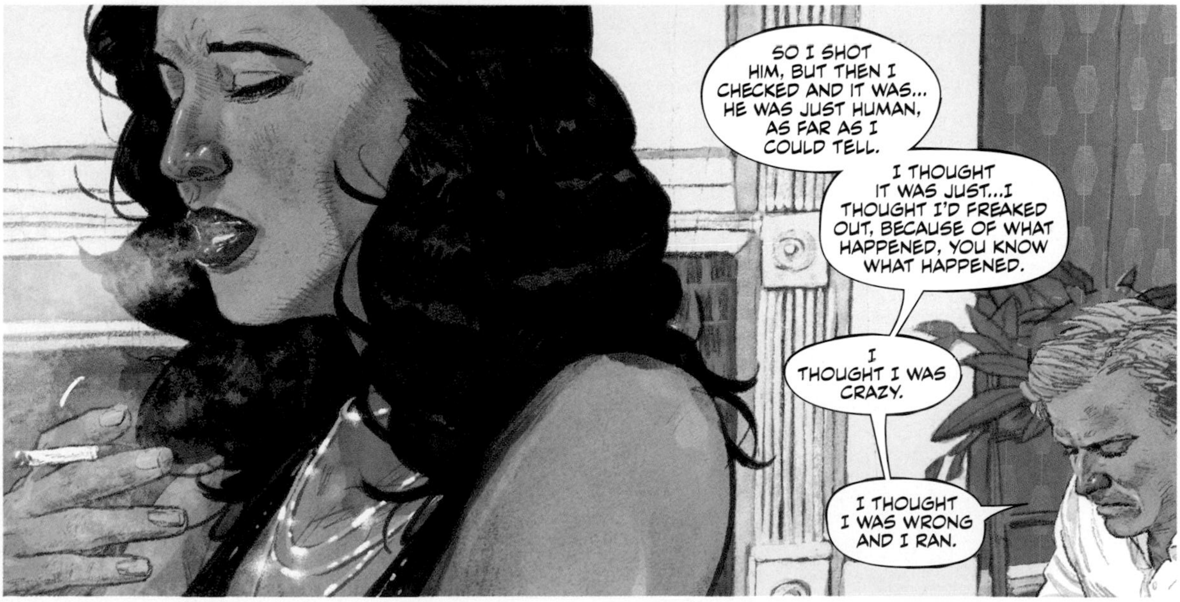
SO I SHOT HIM, BUT THEN I CHECKED AND IT WAS... HE WAS JUST HUMAN, AS FAR AS I COULD TELL.
I THOUGHT IT WAS JUST...I THOUGHT I'D FREAKED OUT, BECAUSE OF WHAT HAPPENED, YOU KNOW WHAT HAPPENED.
I THOUGHT I WAS CRAZY.
I THOUGHT I WAS WRONG AND I RAN.

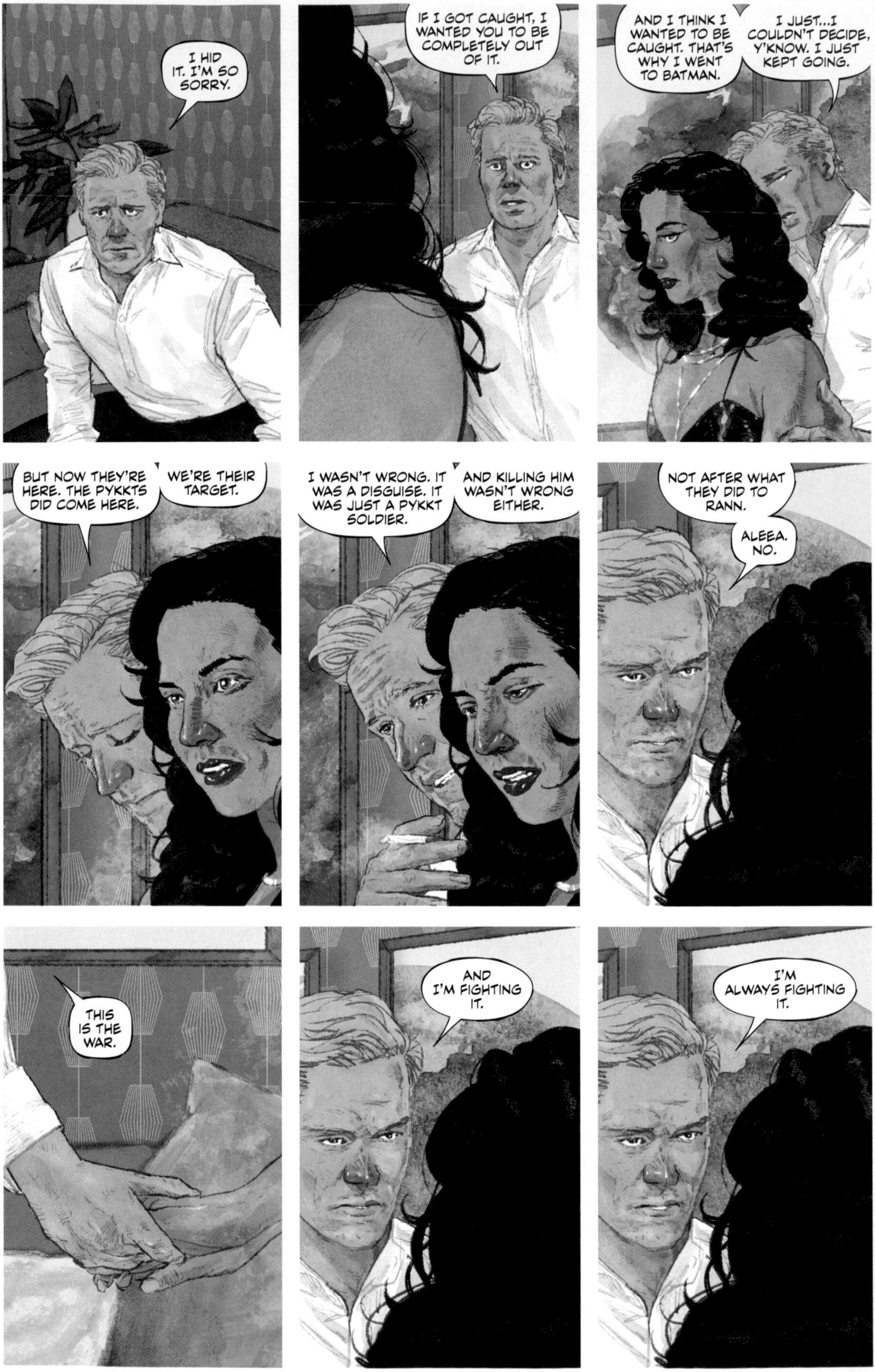
I HID IT. I'M SO SORRY.
IF I GOT CAUGHT, I WANTED YOU TO BE COMPLETELY OUT OF IT.
AND I THINK I WANTED TO BE CAUGHT. THAT'S WHY I WENT TO BATMAN.
I JUST...I COULDN'T DECIDE, Y'KNOW. I JUST KEPT GOING.
BUT NOW THEY'RE HERE. THE PYKKTS DID COME HERE.
WE'RE THEIR TARGET.
I WASN'T WRONG. IT WAS A DISGUISE. IT WAS JUST A PYKKT SOLDIER.
AND KILLING HIM WASN'T WRONG EITHER.
NOT AFTER WHAT THEY DID TO RANN.
ALEEA. NO.
THIS IS THE WAR.
AND I'M FIGHTING IT.
I'M ALWAYS FIGHTING IT.

AND THAT'S IT? EVERYTHING?

THERE'S NO... THERE'S NOT SOMETHING ABOUT ALEEA OR SOMETHING.

WHAT? NO, THERE'S NOTHING, THAT'S IT. WHAT ABOUT ALEEA? I DON'T UNDERSTAND.

YOU SWEAR, ON OUR DAUGHTER, ON YOUR LOVE FOR YOUR DAUGHTER, YOUR LOVE FOR ME, ON EARTH AND RANN, YOU SWEAR, ADAM.

THERE'S NOTHING ELSE.

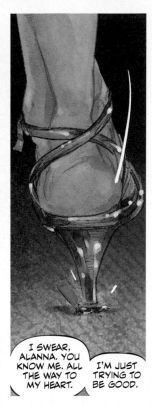

I SWEAR, ALANNA. YOU KNOW ME. ALL THE WAY TO MY HEART.

I'M JUST TRYING TO BE GOOD.

OH ADAM...

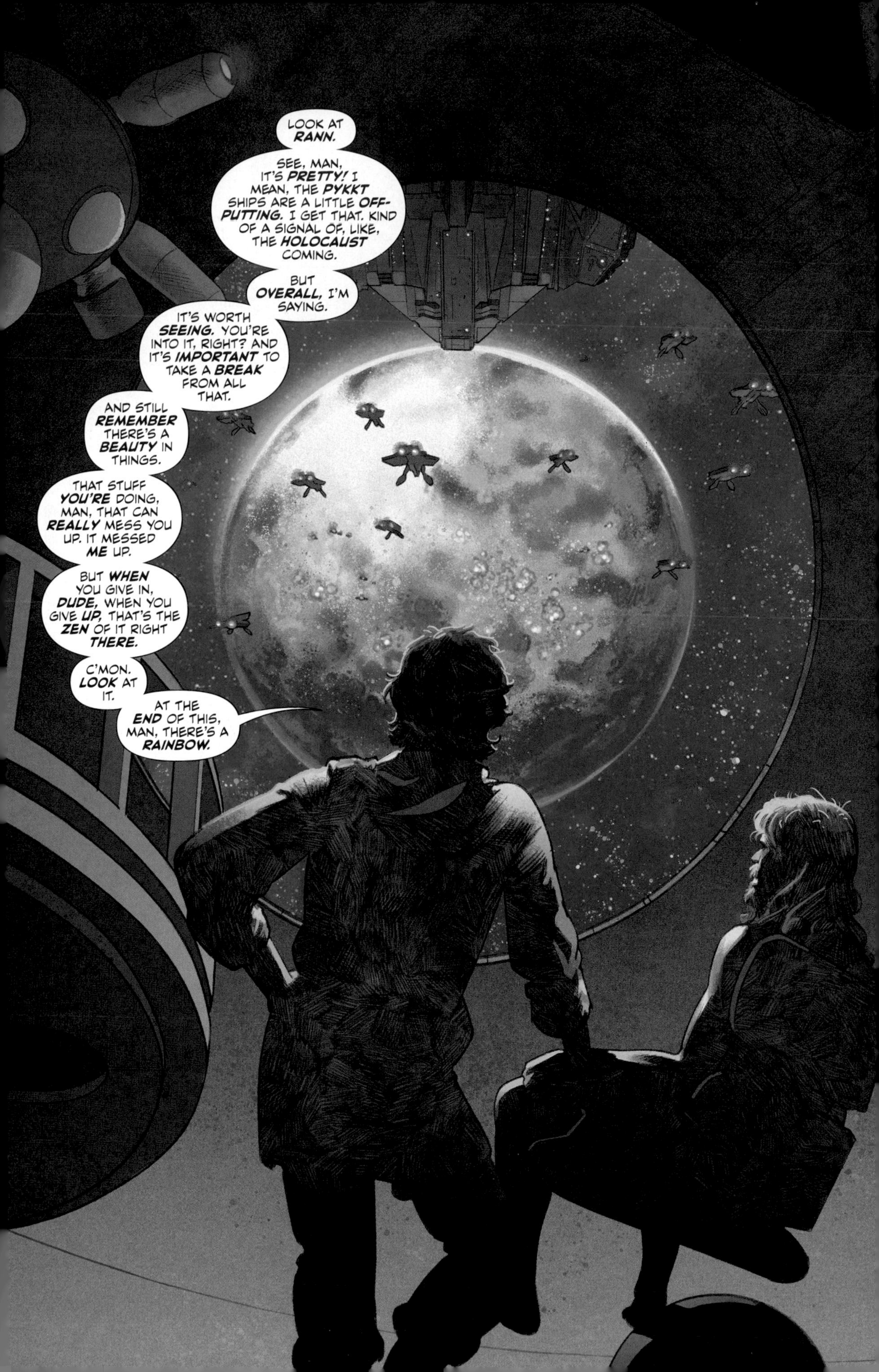
LOOK AT **RANN.**
SEE, MAN, IT'S **PRETTY!** I MEAN, THE **PYKKT** SHIPS ARE A LITTLE **OFF-PUTTING.** I GET THAT. KIND OF A SIGNAL OF, LIKE, THE **HOLOCAUST** COMING.
BUT **OVERALL,** I'M SAYING.
IT'S WORTH **SEEING.** YOU'RE INTO IT, RIGHT? AND IT'S **IMPORTANT** TO TAKE A **BREAK** FROM ALL THAT.
AND STILL **REMEMBER** THERE'S A **BEAUTY** IN THINGS.
THAT STUFF **YOU'RE** DOING, MAN, THAT CAN **REALLY** MESS YOU UP. IT MESSED **ME** UP.
BUT **WHEN** YOU GIVE IN, **DUDE,** WHEN YOU GIVE **UP,** THAT'S THE **ZEN** OF IT RIGHT **THERE.**
C'MON. **LOOK** AT IT.
AT THE **END** OF THIS, MAN, THERE'S A **RAINBOW.**

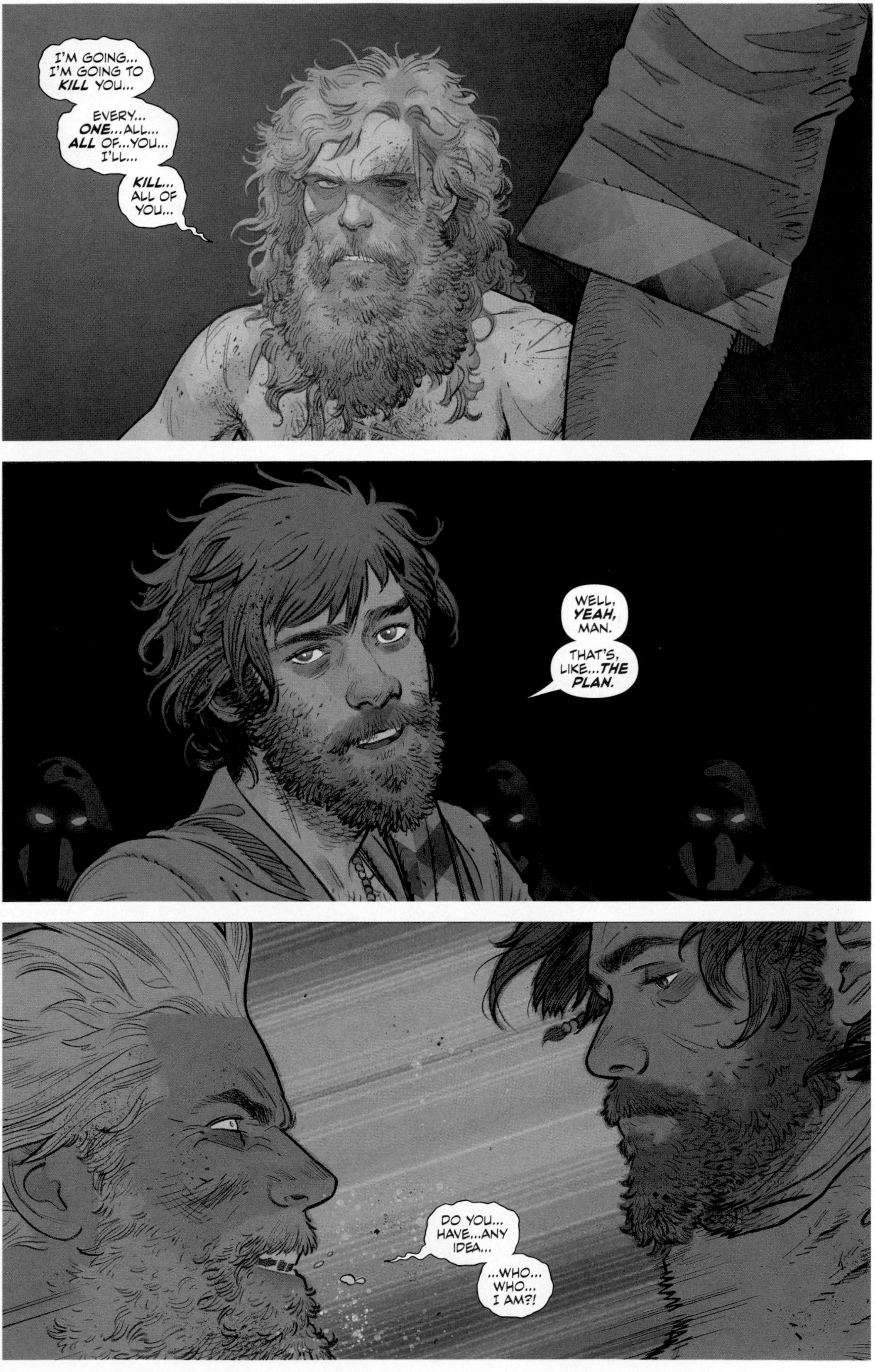
I'M GOING... I'M GOING TO **KILL** YOU...
EVERY... **ONE**...ALL... **ALL** OF...YOU... I'LL...
KILL... ALL OF YOU...
WELL, **YEAH,** MAN.
THAT'S, LIKE...**THE PLAN.**
DO YOU... HAVE...ANY IDEA...
...WHO... WHO... I AM?!

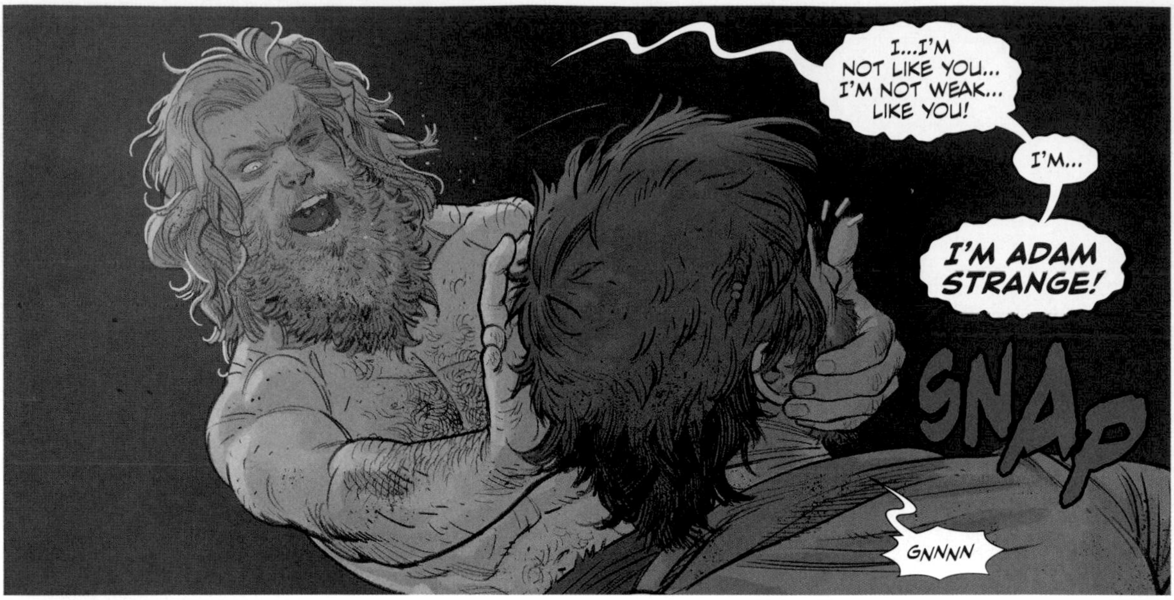
I...I'M NOT LIKE YOU... I'M NOT WEAK... LIKE YOU!
I'M...
I'M ADAM STRANGE!
SNAP
GNNNN

I mean in one of my stories, the guy gets killed, he goes to another world, the bad guy gets it, and then he goes back to this beautiful world with this beautiful girl. I think that's lovely. That's a lovely story. It should happen to everybody.

—Al Williamson

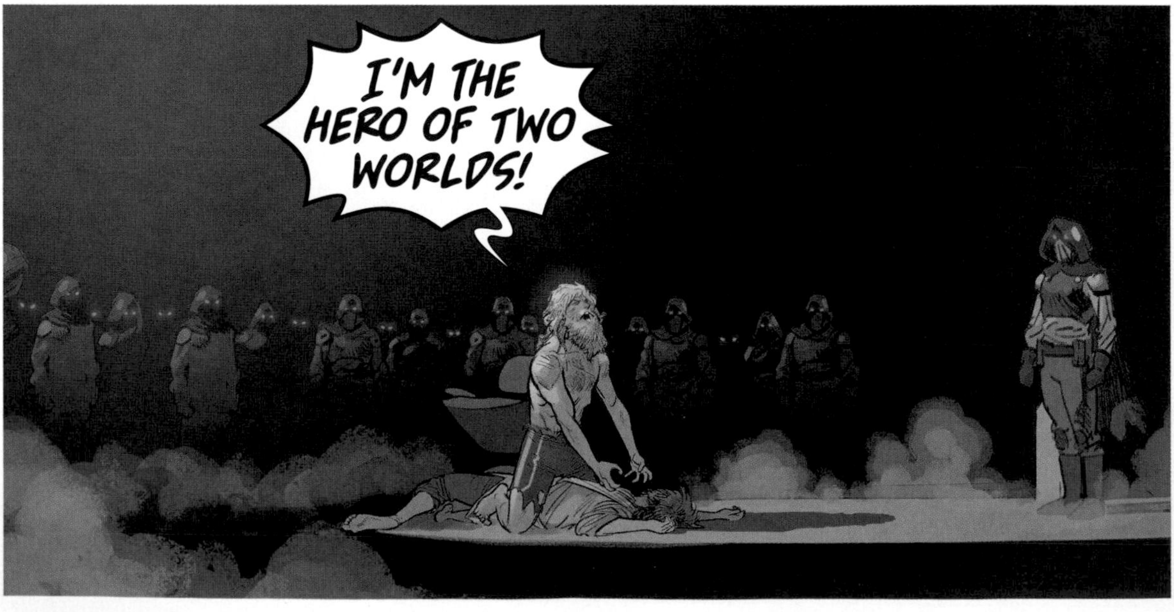
I'M THE HERO OF TWO WORLDS!

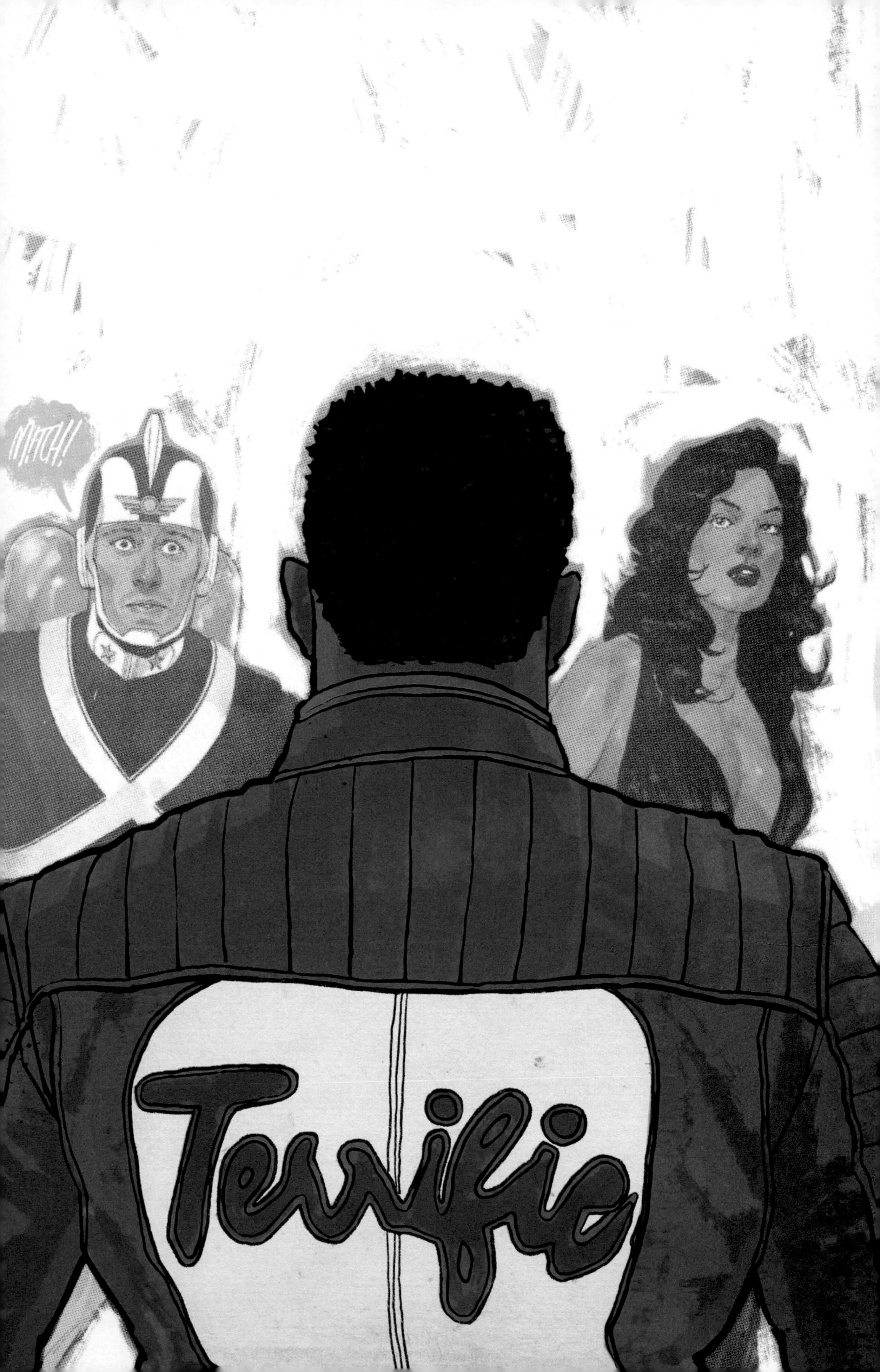
MITCH!
Terrific

"I'M TRYING TO FIGHT A WAR, A WAR THAT WAS LOST WHILE I WAS AWAY."

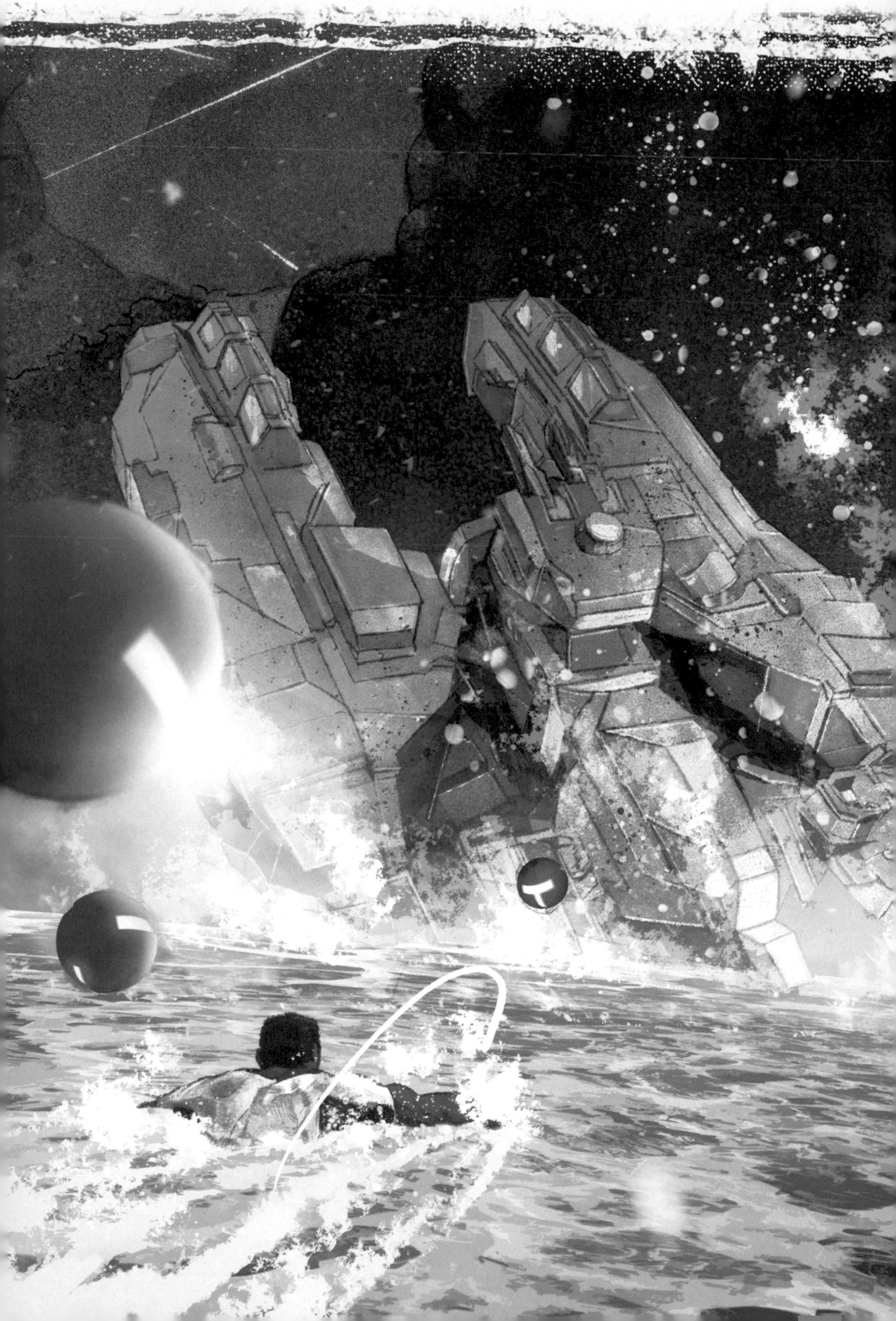

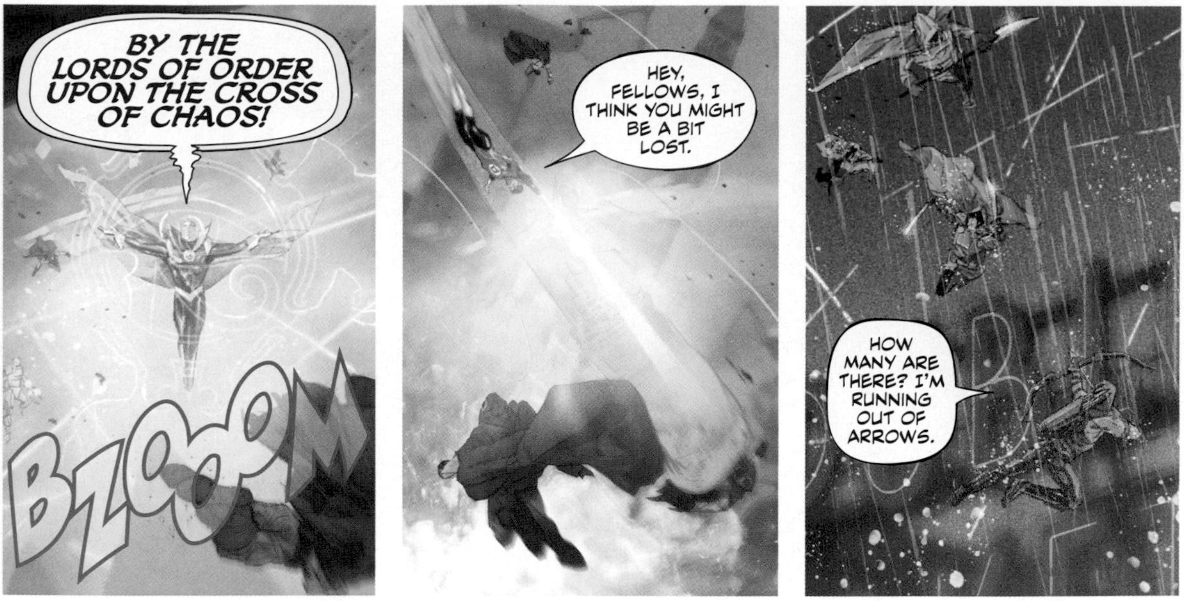
BY THE LORDS OF ORDER UPON THE CROSS OF CHAOS!
BZOOOM
HEY, FELLOWS, I THINK YOU MIGHT BE A BIT LOST.
HOW MANY ARE THERE? I'M RUNNING OUT OF ARROWS.

Chapter 8

It could've been worse

TOM KING	...Writer
MITCH GERADS EVAN "DOC" SHANER	...Interior & Cover Artists
CLAYTON COWLES	...Letterer
BIXIE MATHIEU	...Assistant Editor
BRITTANY HOLZHERR	...Associate Editor
JAMIE S. RICH	...Editor

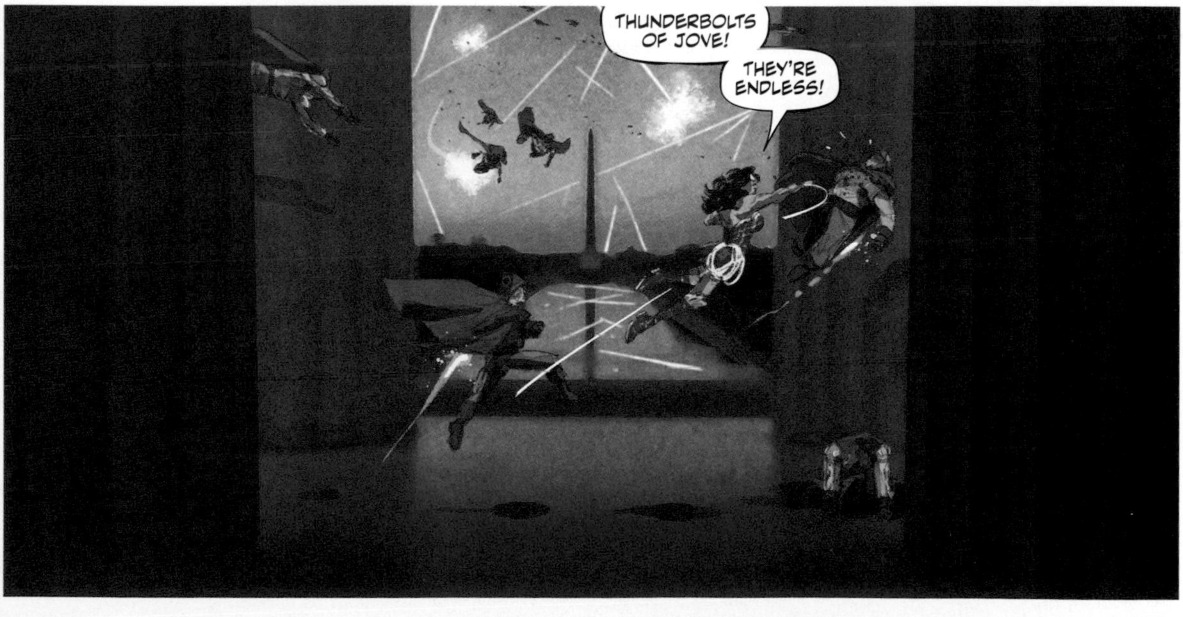
THUNDERBOLTS OF JOVE!
THEY'RE ENDLESS!

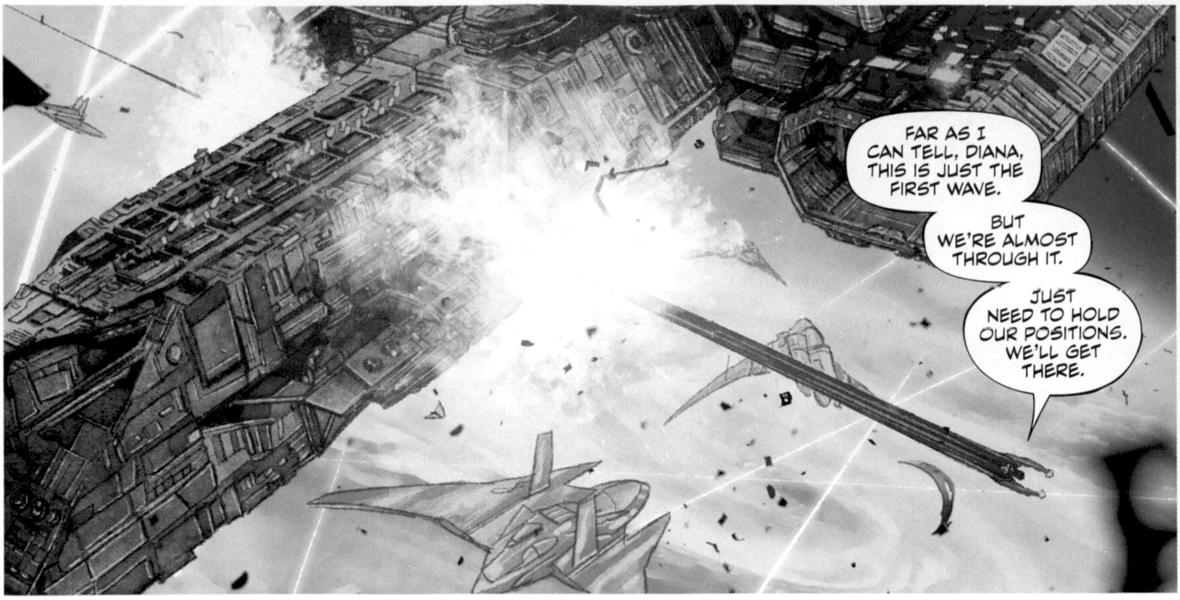
FAR AS I CAN TELL, DIANA, THIS IS JUST THE FIRST WAVE.
BUT WE'RE ALMOST THROUGH IT.
JUST NEED TO HOLD OUR POSITIONS. WE'LL GET THERE.

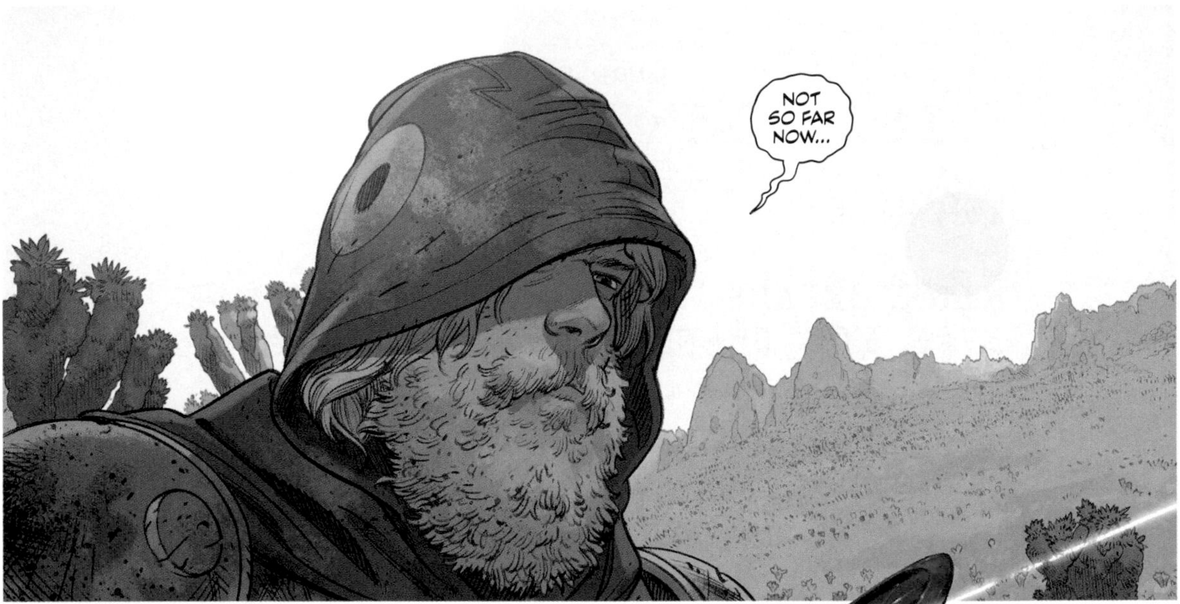
NOT SO FAR NOW...

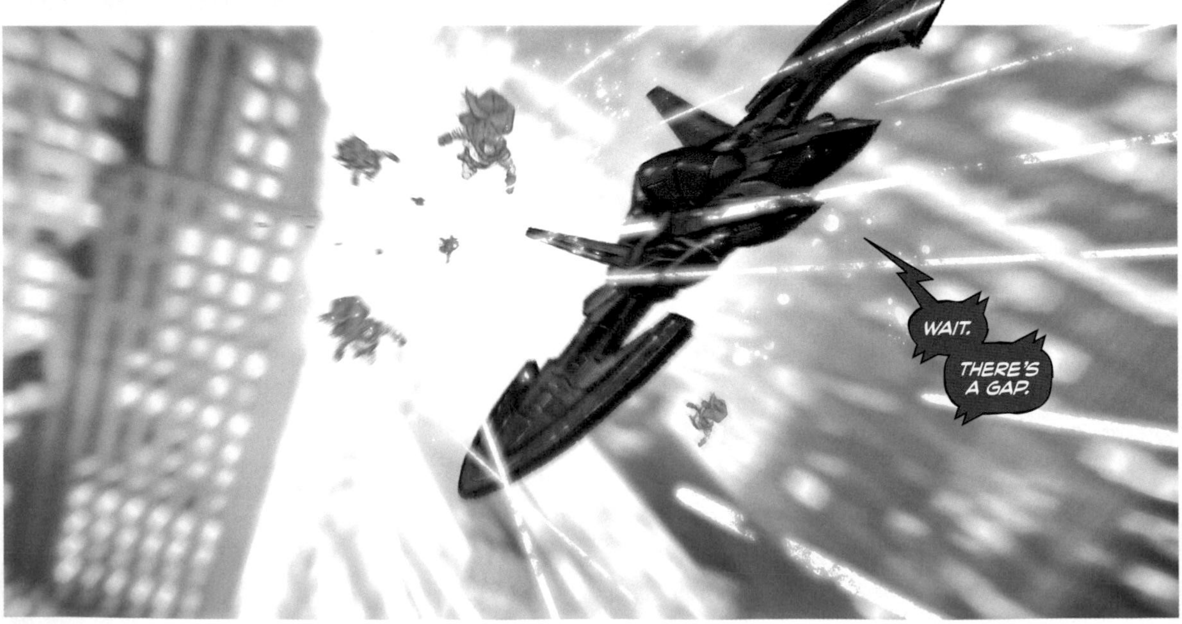
WAIT.
THERE'S A GAP.

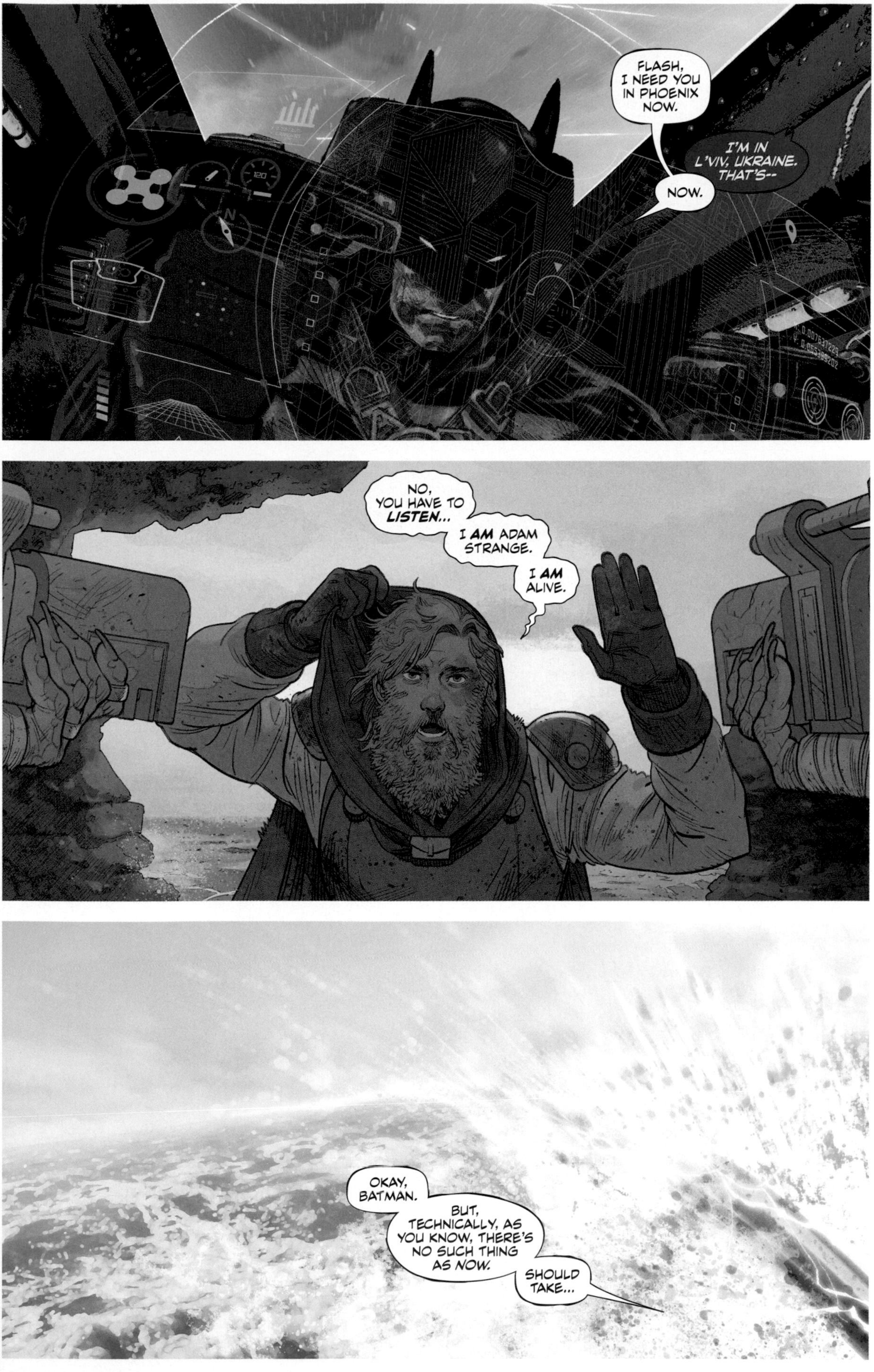
FLASH, I NEED YOU IN PHOENIX NOW.
I'M IN L'VIV, UKRAINE. THAT'S--
NOW.
NO, YOU HAVE TO **LISTEN...**
I **AM** ADAM STRANGE.
I **AM** ALIVE.
OKAY, BATMAN.
BUT, TECHNICALLY, AS YOU KNOW, THERE'S NO SUCH THING AS *NOW.*
SHOULD TAKE...

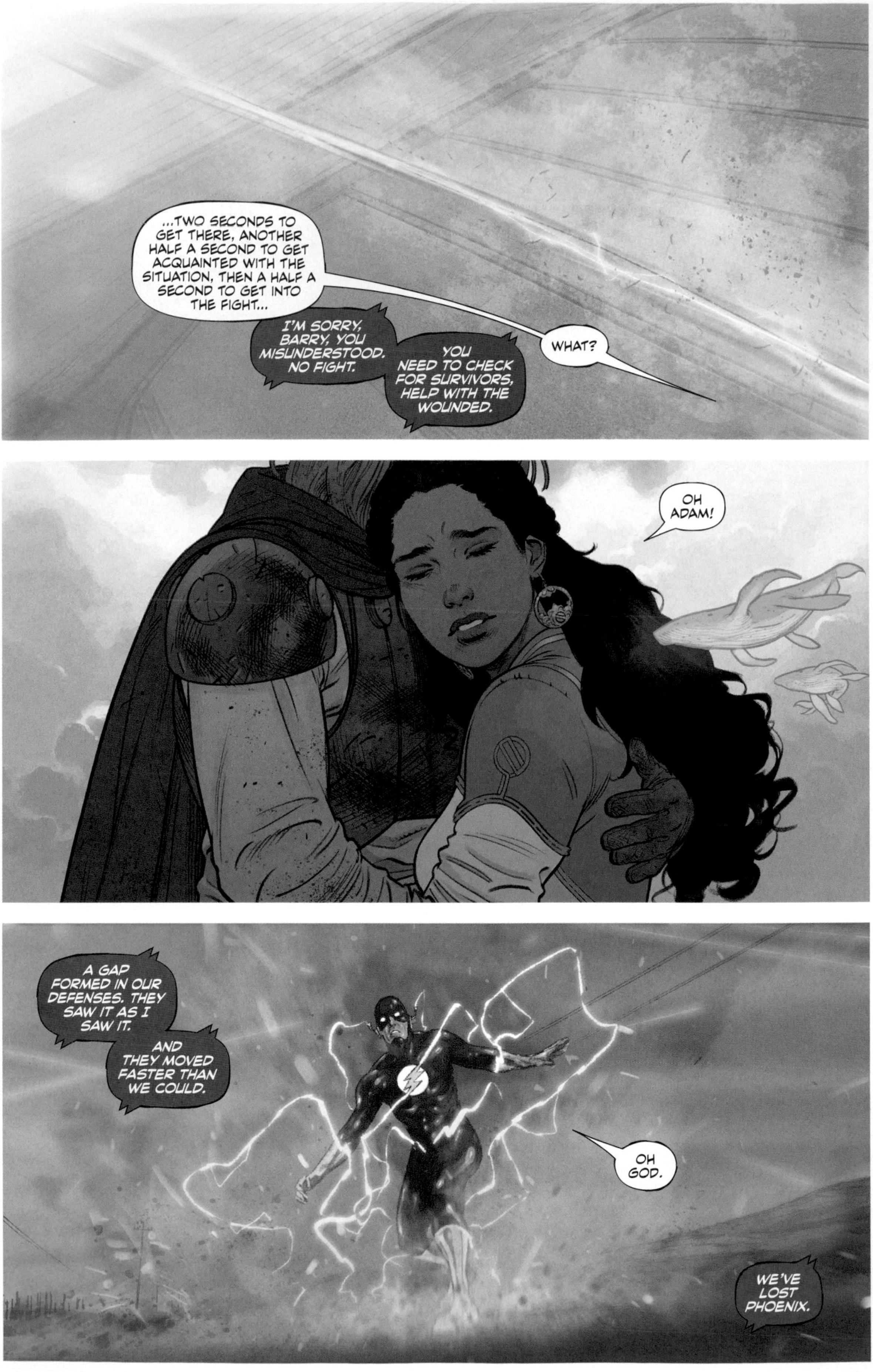
...TWO SECONDS TO GET THERE, ANOTHER HALF A SECOND TO GET ACQUAINTED WITH THE SITUATION, THEN A HALF A SECOND TO GET INTO THE FIGHT...
I'M SORRY, BARRY, YOU MISUNDERSTOOD. NO FIGHT.
YOU NEED TO CHECK FOR SURVIVORS, HELP WITH THE WOUNDED.
WHAT?
OH ADAM!
A GAP FORMED IN OUR DEFENSES. THEY SAW IT AS I SAW IT.
AND THEY MOVED FASTER THAN WE COULD.
OH GOD.
WE'VE LOST PHOENIX.

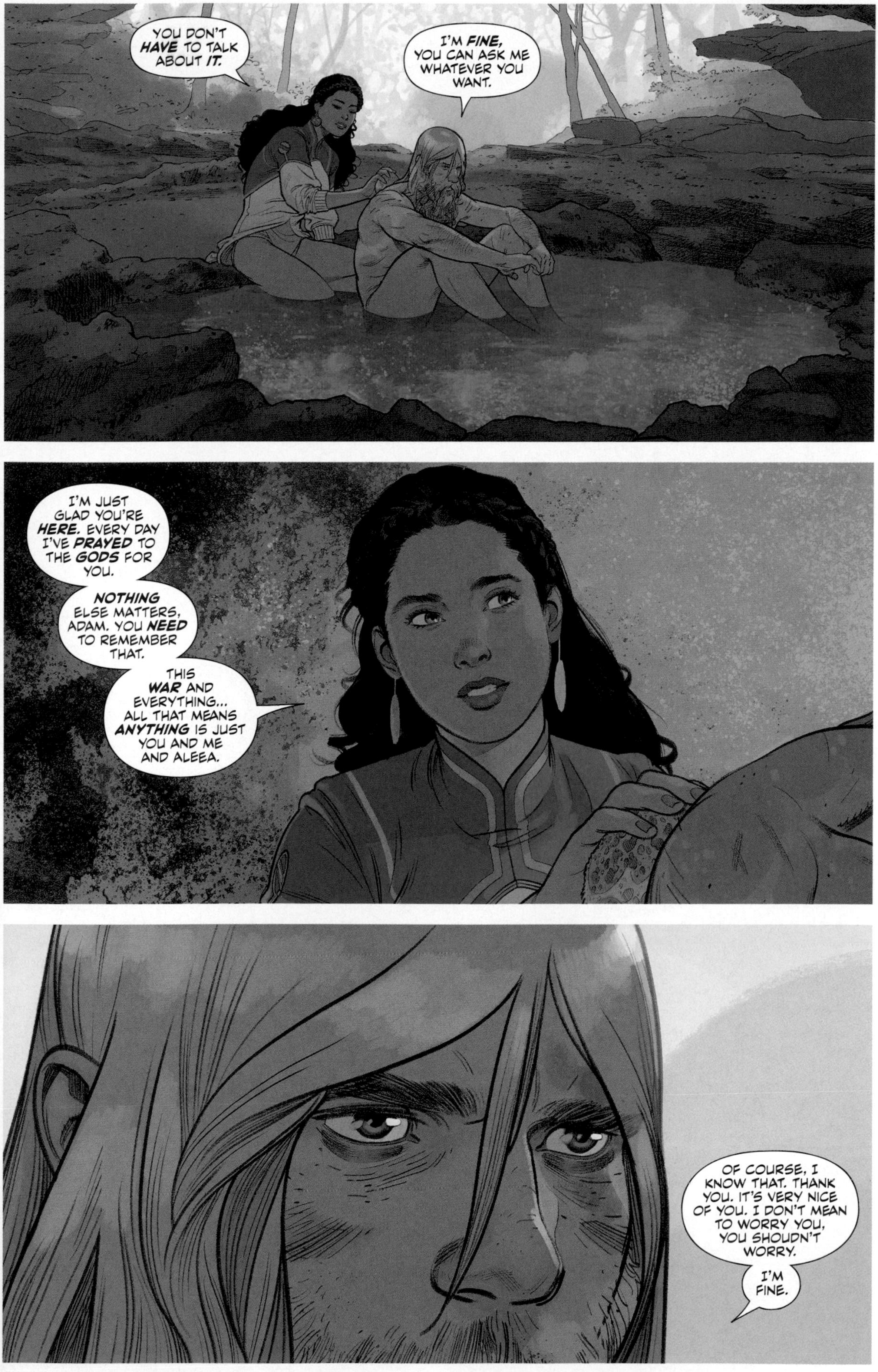
YOU DON'T HAVE TO TALK ABOUT IT.
I'M FINE, YOU CAN ASK ME WHATEVER YOU WANT.
I'M JUST GLAD YOU'RE HERE. EVERY DAY I'VE PRAYED TO THE GODS FOR YOU.
NOTHING ELSE MATTERS, ADAM. YOU NEED TO REMEMBER THAT.
THIS WAR AND EVERYTHING... ALL THAT MEANS ANYTHING IS JUST YOU AND ME AND ALEEA.
OF COURSE, I KNOW THAT. THANK YOU. IT'S VERY NICE OF YOU. I DON'T MEAN TO WORRY YOU, YOU SHOUDN'T WORRY.
I'M FINE.

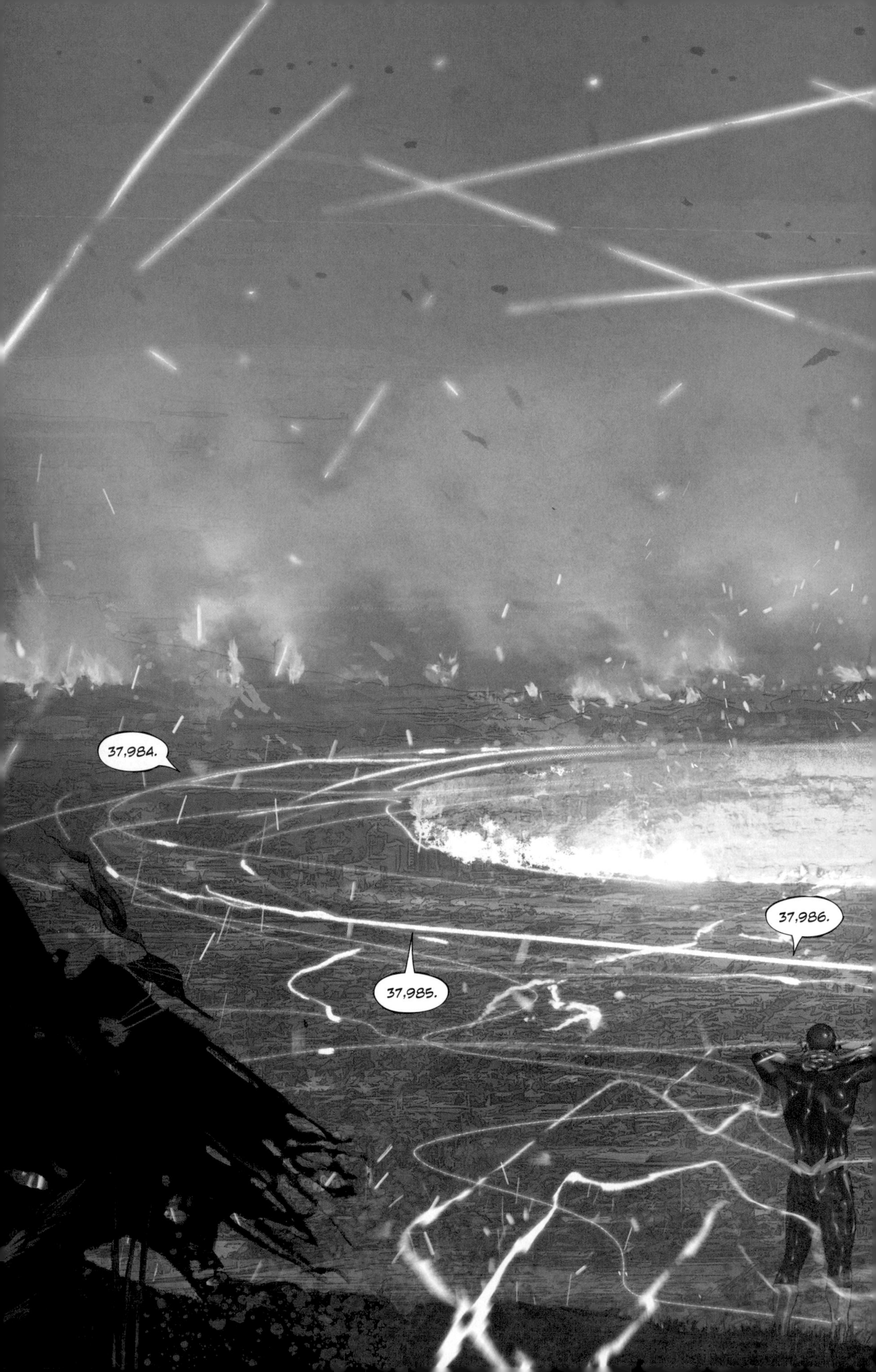
37,984.
37,985.
37,986.

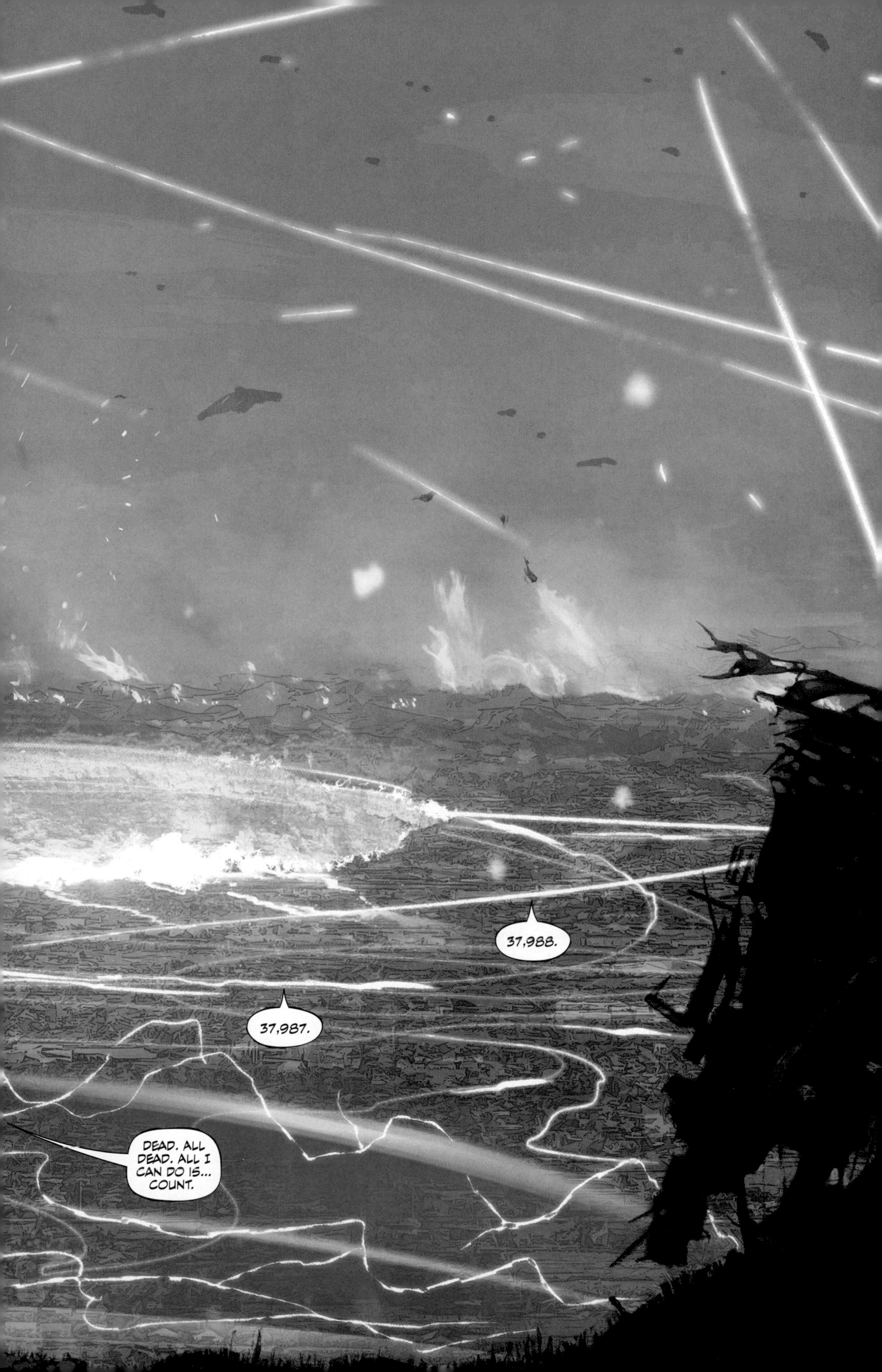
37,988.
37,987.
DEAD. ALL DEAD. ALL I CAN DO IS... COUNT.

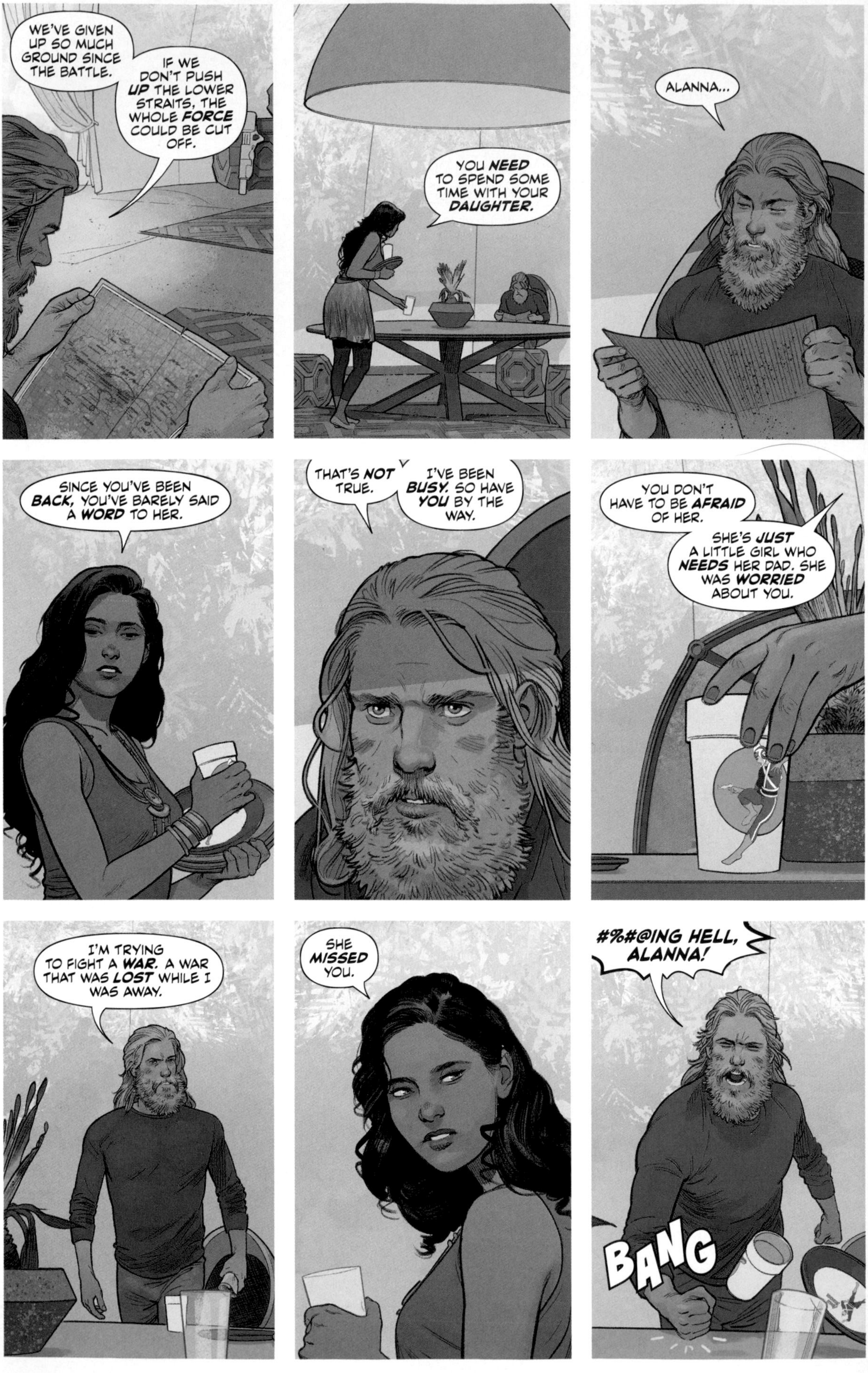
WE'VE GIVEN UP SO MUCH GROUND SINCE THE BATTLE.
IF WE DON'T PUSH UP THE LOWER STRAITS, THE WHOLE FORCE COULD BE CUT OFF.
YOU NEED TO SPEND SOME TIME WITH YOUR DAUGHTER.
ALANNA...
SINCE YOU'VE BEEN BACK, YOU'VE BARELY SAID A WORD TO HER.
THAT'S NOT TRUE.
I'VE BEEN BUSY. SO HAVE YOU BY THE WAY.
YOU DON'T HAVE TO BE AFRAID OF HER.
SHE'S JUST A LITTLE GIRL WHO NEEDS HER DAD. SHE WAS WORRIED ABOUT YOU.
I'M TRYING TO FIGHT A WAR. A WAR THAT WAS LOST WHILE I WAS AWAY.
SHE MISSED YOU.
#%#@ING HELL, ALANNA!
BANG

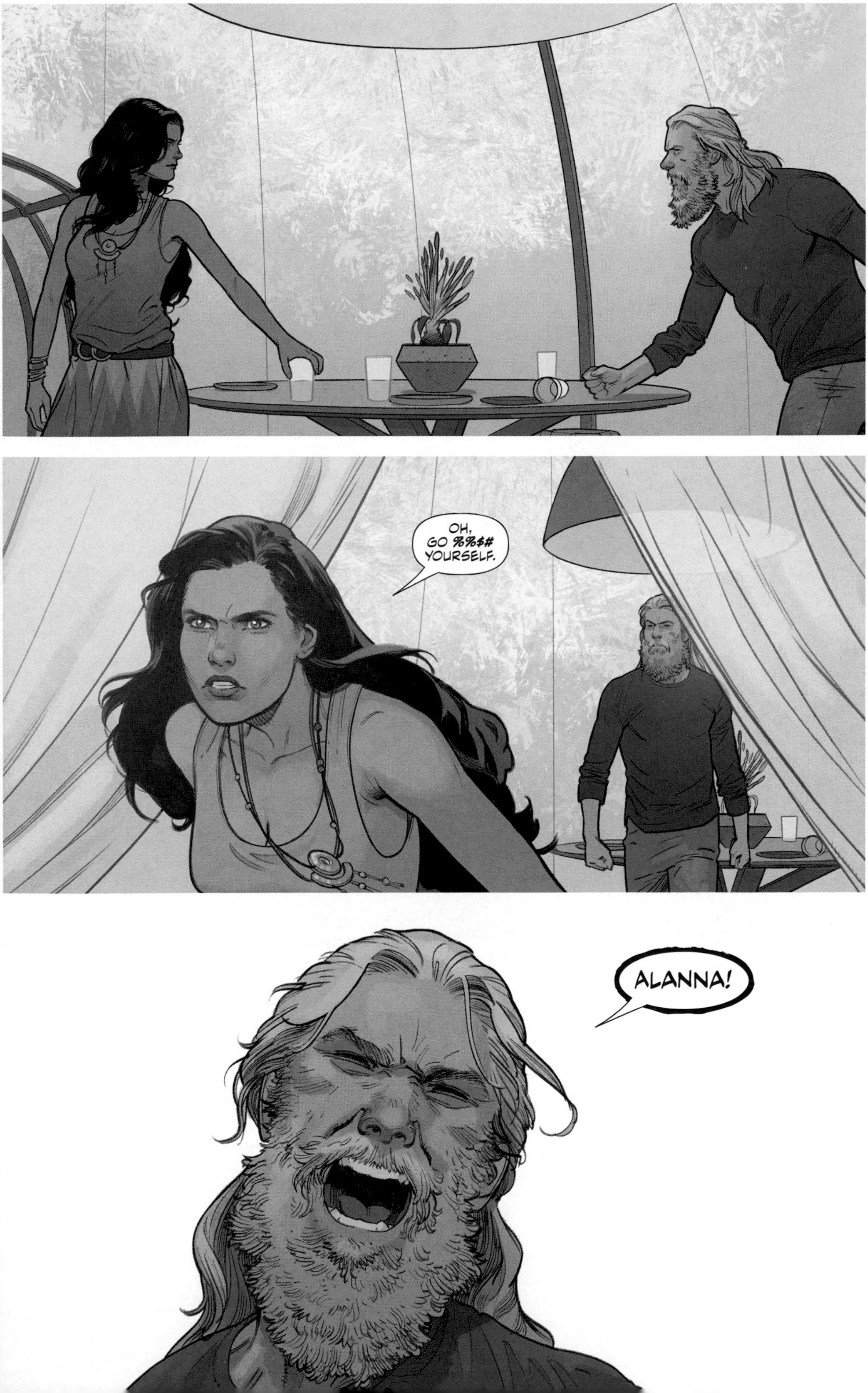

OH, GO %%$# YOURSELF.
ALANNA!

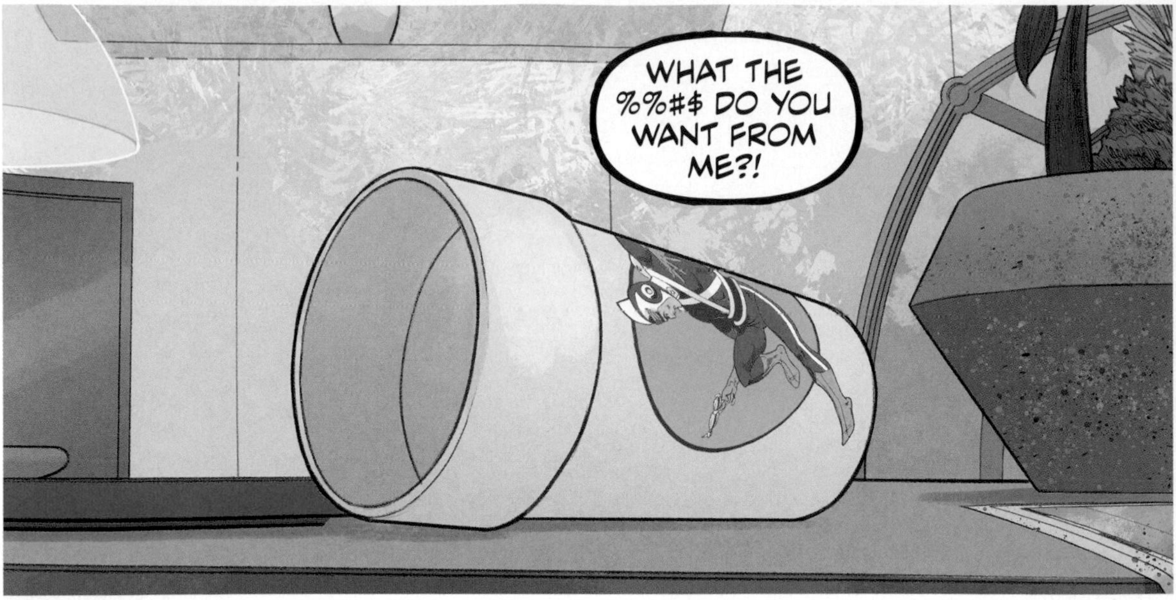
WHAT THE %%#$ DO YOU WANT FROM ME?!

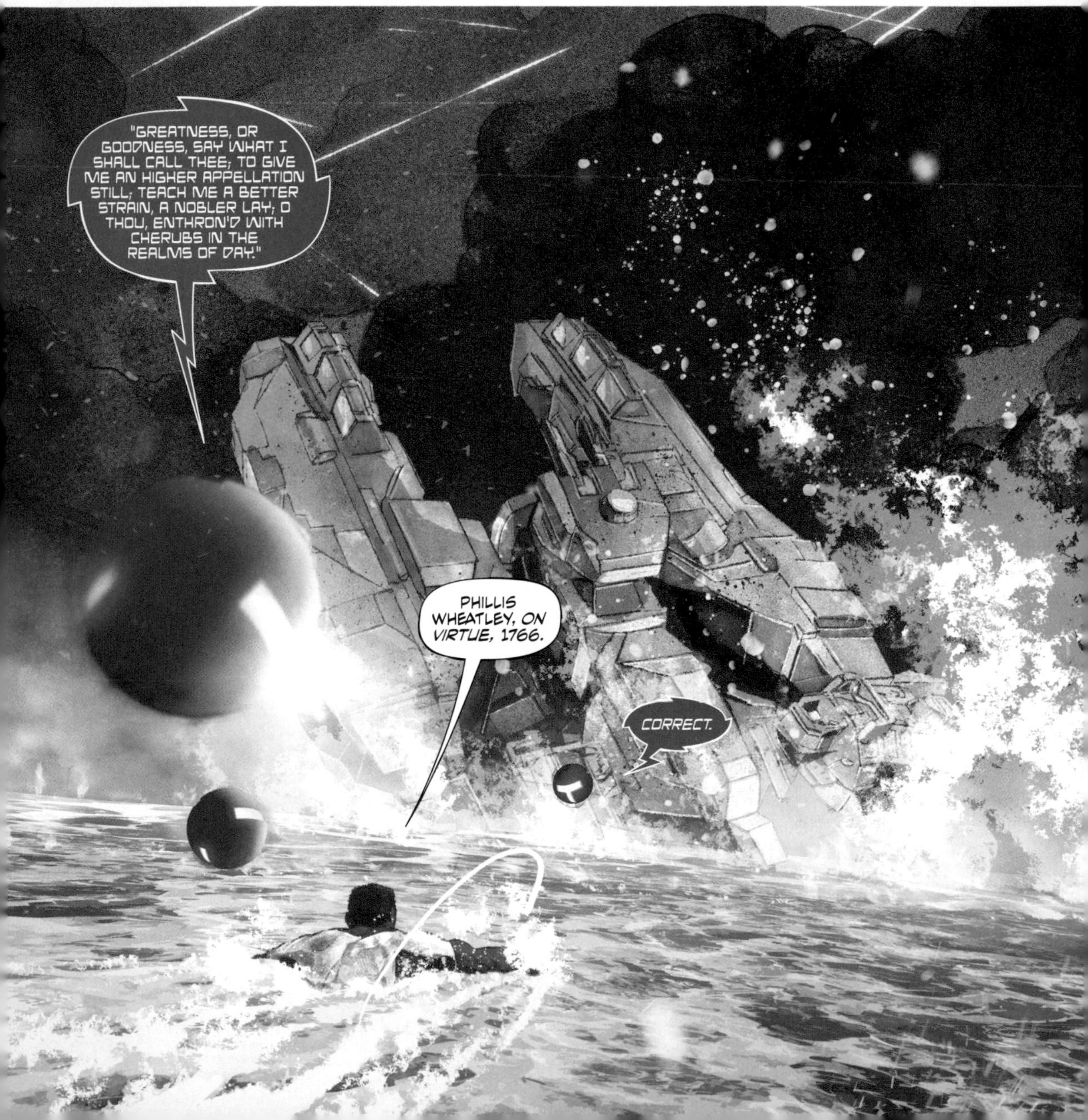
"GREATNESS, OR GOODNESS, SAY WHAT I SHALL CALL THEE; TO GIVE ME AN HIGHER APPELLATION STILL; TEACH ME A BETTER STRAIN, A NOBLER LAY; O THOU, ENTHRON'D WITH CHERUBS IN THE REALMS OF DAY."
PHILLIS WHEATLEY, ON *VIRTUE*, 1766.
CORRECT.

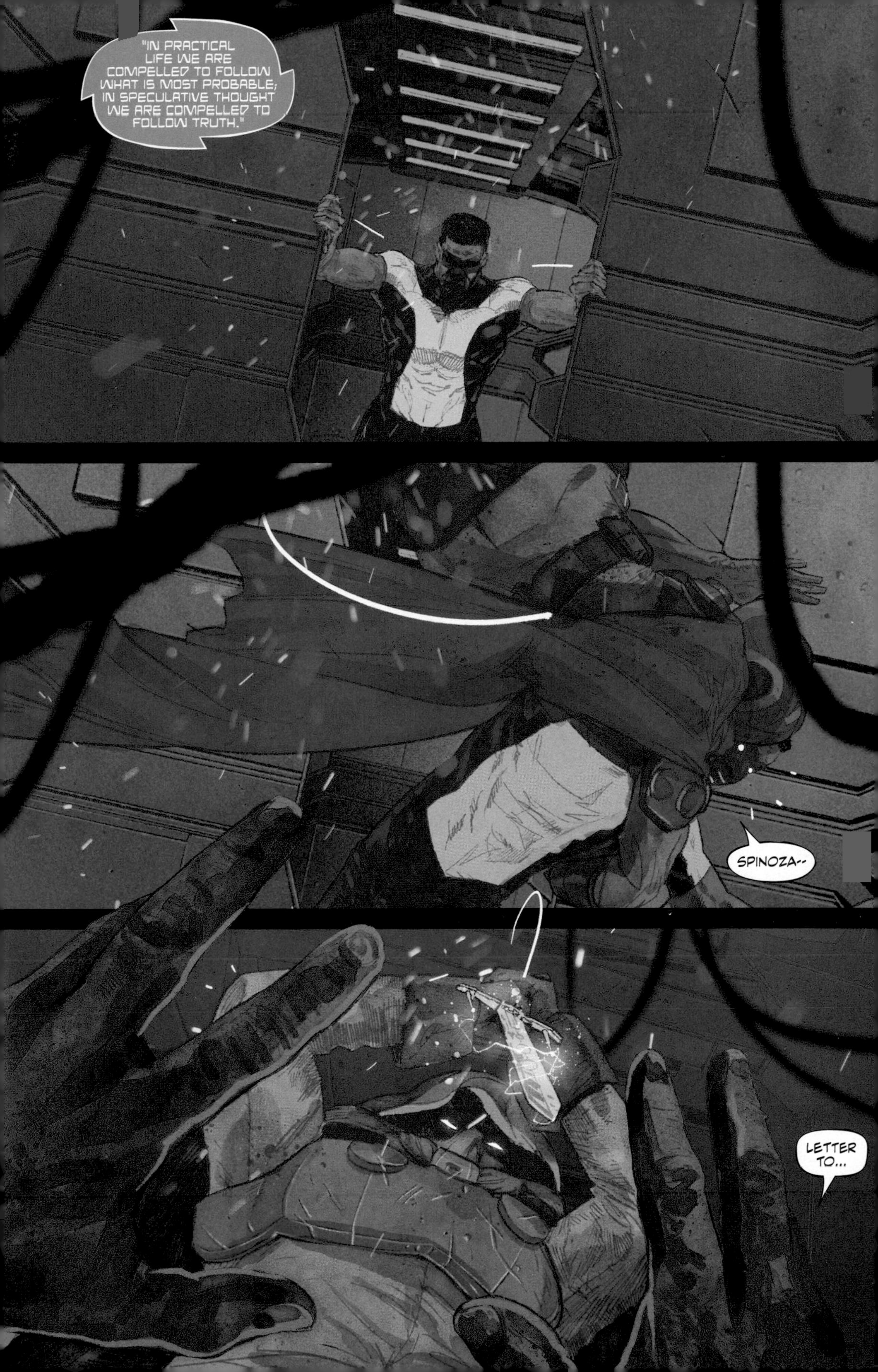
"IN PRACTICAL LIFE WE ARE COMPELLED TO FOLLOW WHAT IS MOST PROBABLE; IN SPECULATIVE THOUGHT WE ARE COMPELLED TO FOLLOW TRUTH."
SPINOZA--
LETTER TO...

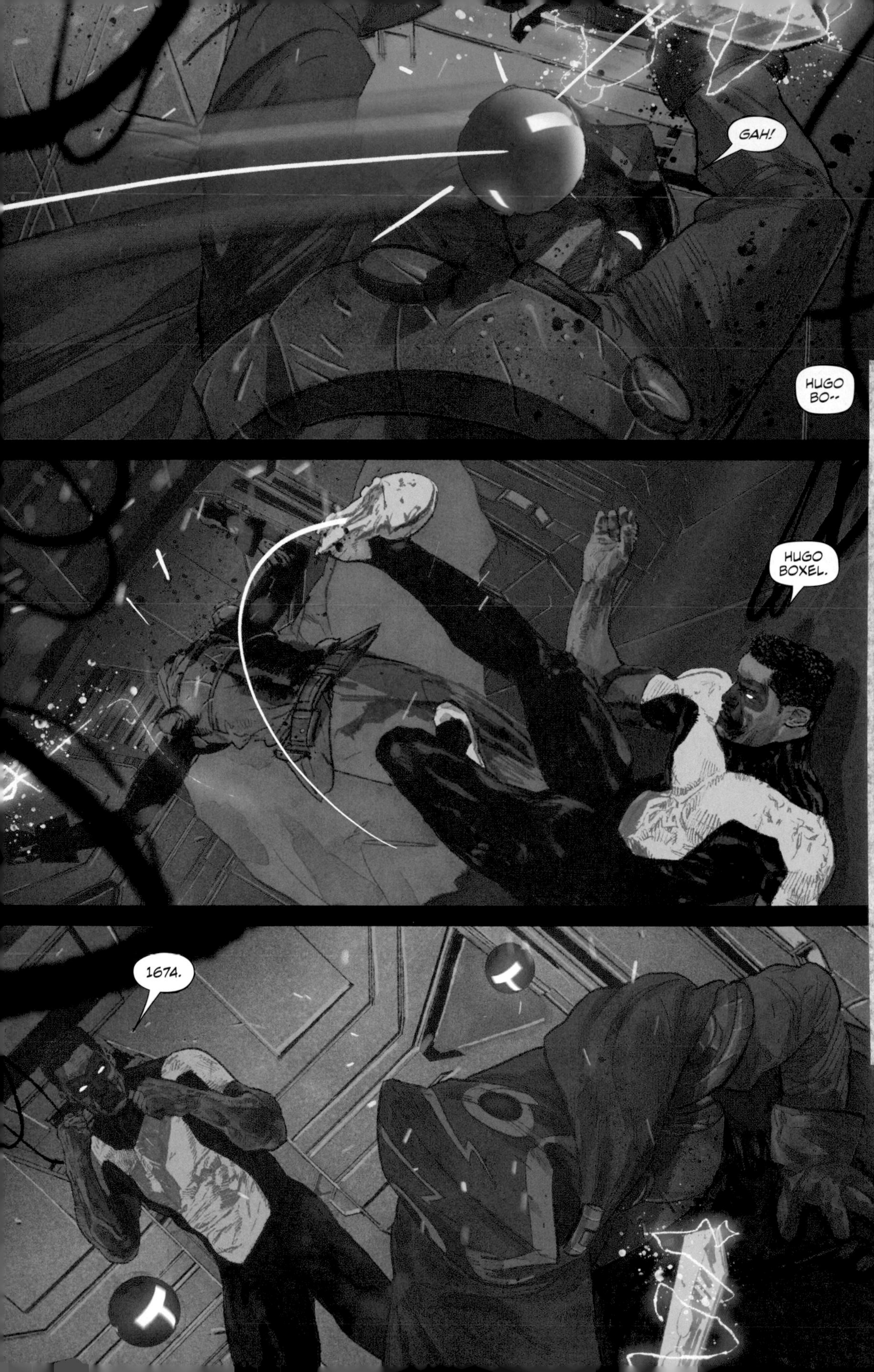
GAH!
HUGO BO--
HUGO BOXEL.
1674.

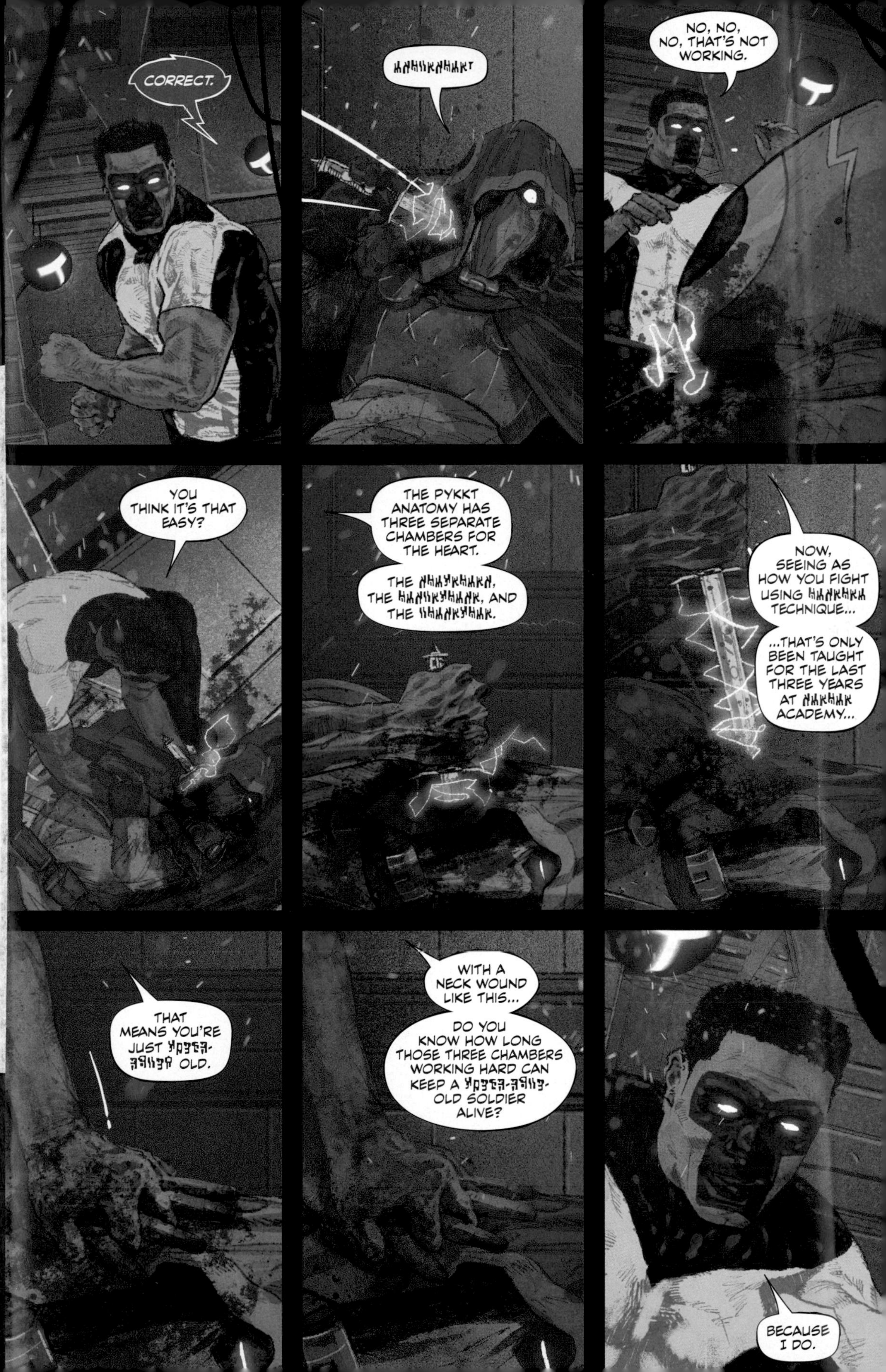
CORRECT.
NO, NO, NO, THAT'S NOT WORKING.
YOU THINK IT'S THAT EASY?
THE PYKKT ANATOMY HAS THREE SEPARATE CHAMBERS FOR THE HEART.
THE , THE , AND THE .
NOW, SEEING AS HOW YOU FIGHT USING TECHNIQUE...
...THAT'S ONLY BEEN TAUGHT FOR THE LAST THREE YEARS AT ACADEMY...
THAT MEANS YOU'RE JUST OLD.
WITH A NECK WOUND LIKE THIS...
DO YOU KNOW HOW LONG THOSE THREE CHAMBERS WORKING HARD CAN KEEP A OLD SOLDIER ALIVE?
BECAUSE I DO.

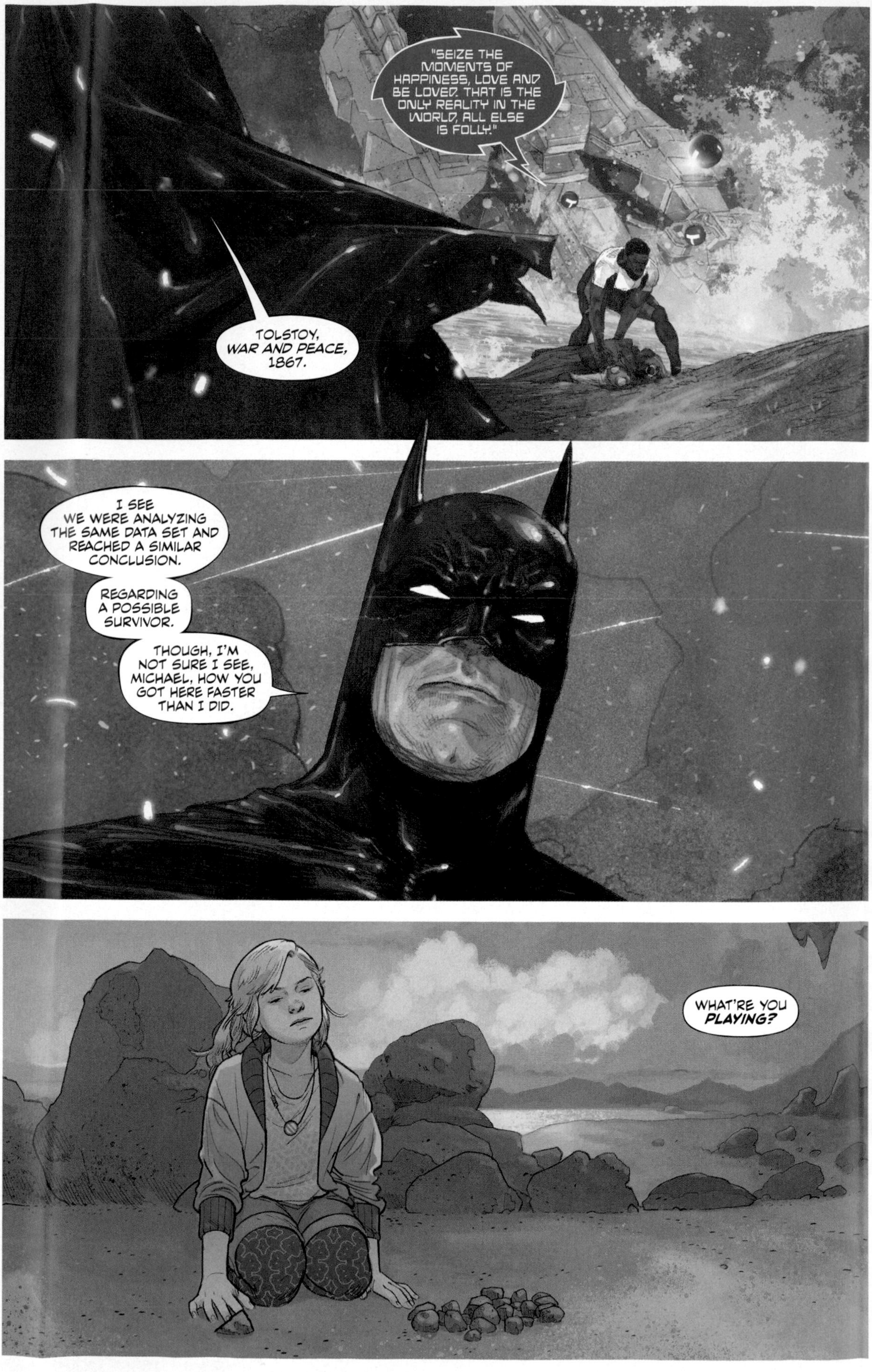
"SEIZE THE MOMENTS OF HAPPINESS, LOVE AND BE LOVED. THAT IS THE ONLY REALITY IN THE WORLD, ALL ELSE IS FOLLY."
TOLSTOY, *WAR AND PEACE,* 1867.
I SEE WE WERE ANALYZING THE SAME DATA SET AND REACHED A SIMILAR CONCLUSION.
REGARDING A POSSIBLE SURVIVOR.
THOUGH, I'M NOT SURE I SEE, MICHAEL, HOW YOU GOT HERE FASTER THAN I DID.
WHAT'RE YOU *PLAYING?*

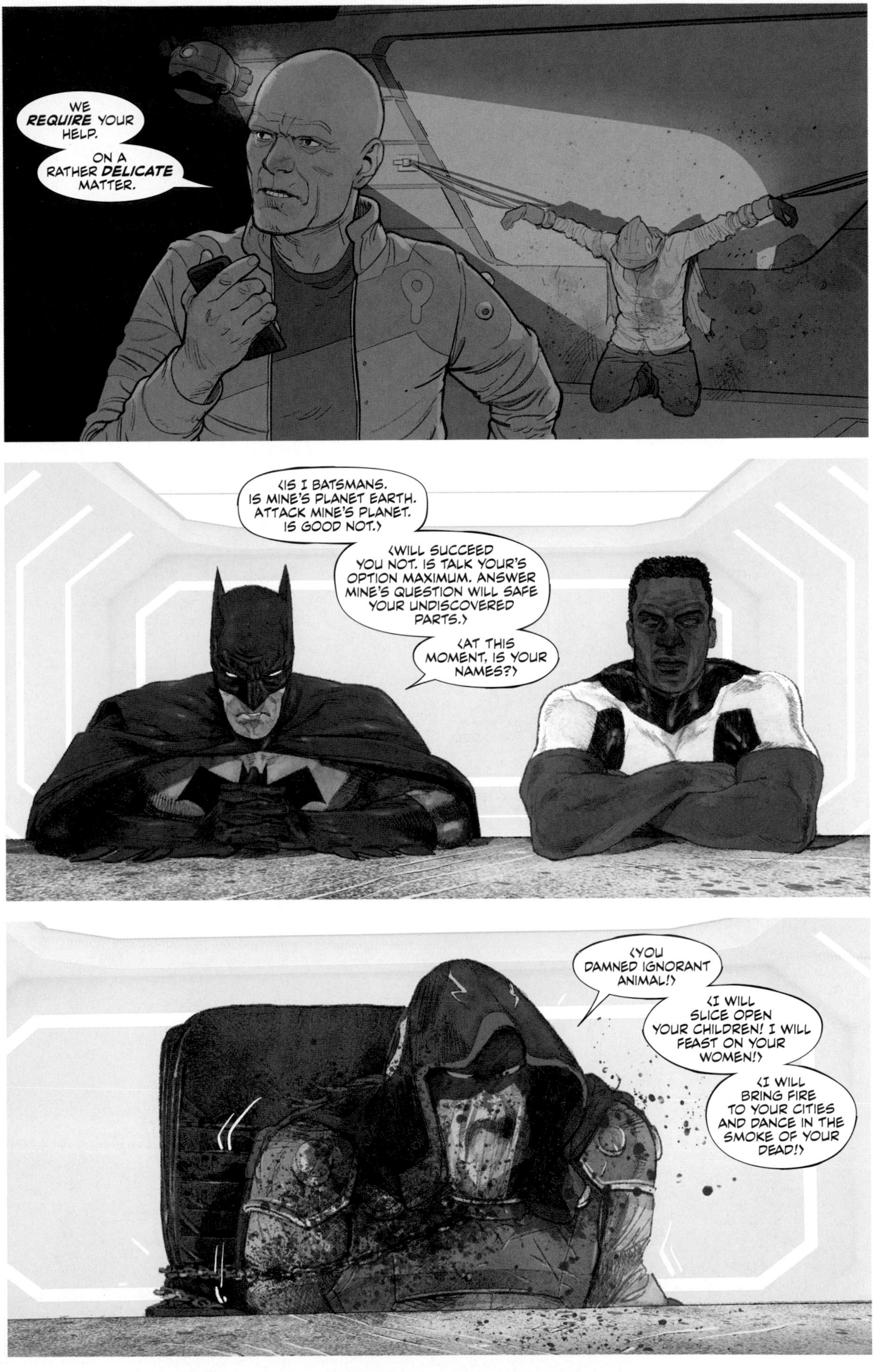
WE REQUIRE YOUR HELP.
ON A RATHER DELICATE MATTER.
‹IS I BATSMANS. IS MINE'S PLANET EARTH. ATTACK MINE'S PLANET. IS GOOD NOT.›
‹WILL SUCCEED YOU NOT. IS TALK YOUR'S OPTION MAXIMUM. ANSWER MINE'S QUESTION WILL SAFE YOUR UNDISCOVERED PARTS.›
‹AT THIS MOMENT, IS YOUR NAMES?›
‹YOU DAMNED IGNORANT ANIMAL!›
‹I WILL SLICE OPEN YOUR CHILDREN! I WILL FEAST ON YOUR WOMEN!›
‹I WILL BRING FIRE TO YOUR CITIES AND DANCE IN THE SMOKE OF YOUR DEAD!›

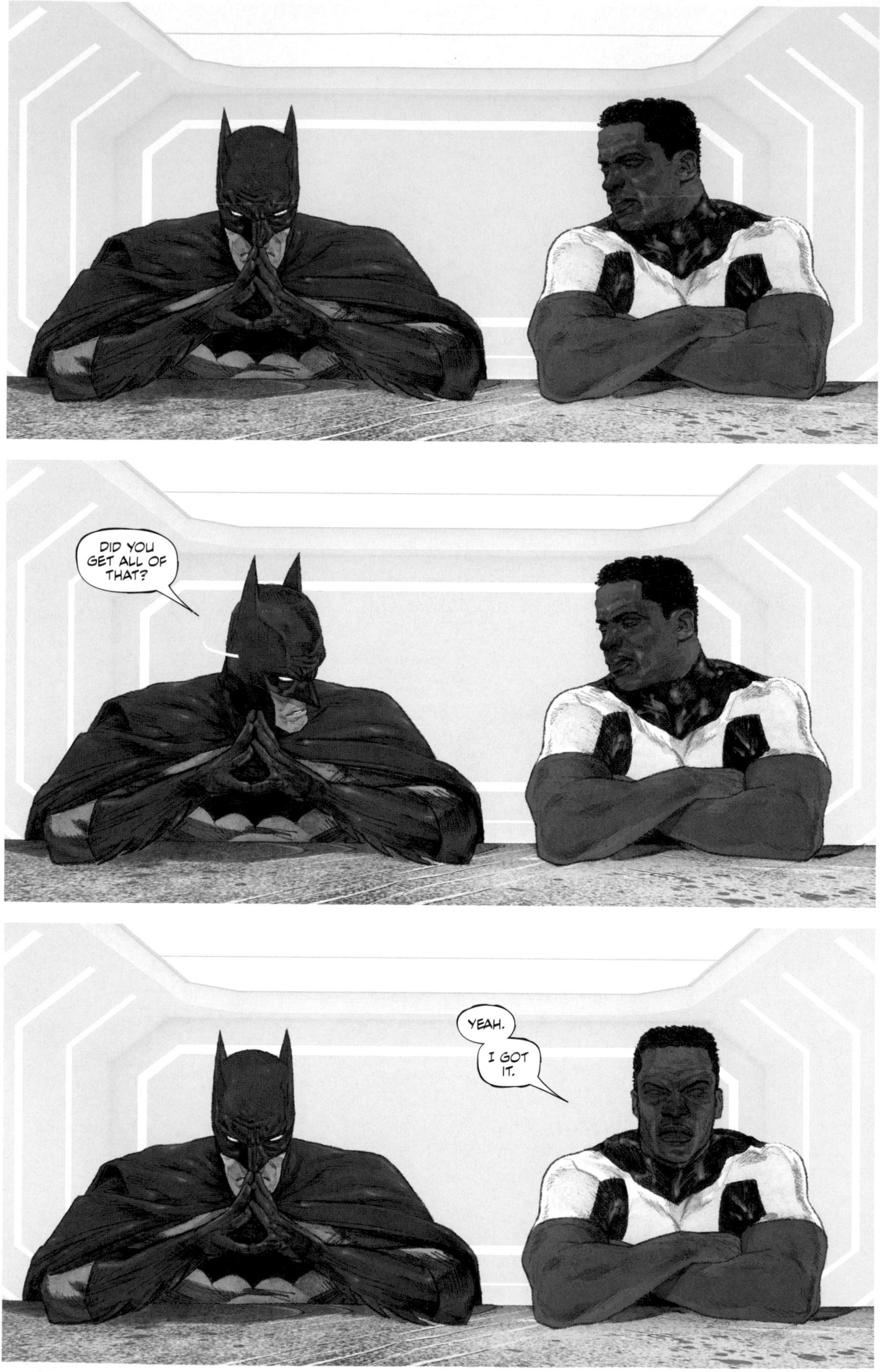
DID YOU GET ALL OF THAT?
YEAH.
I GOT IT.

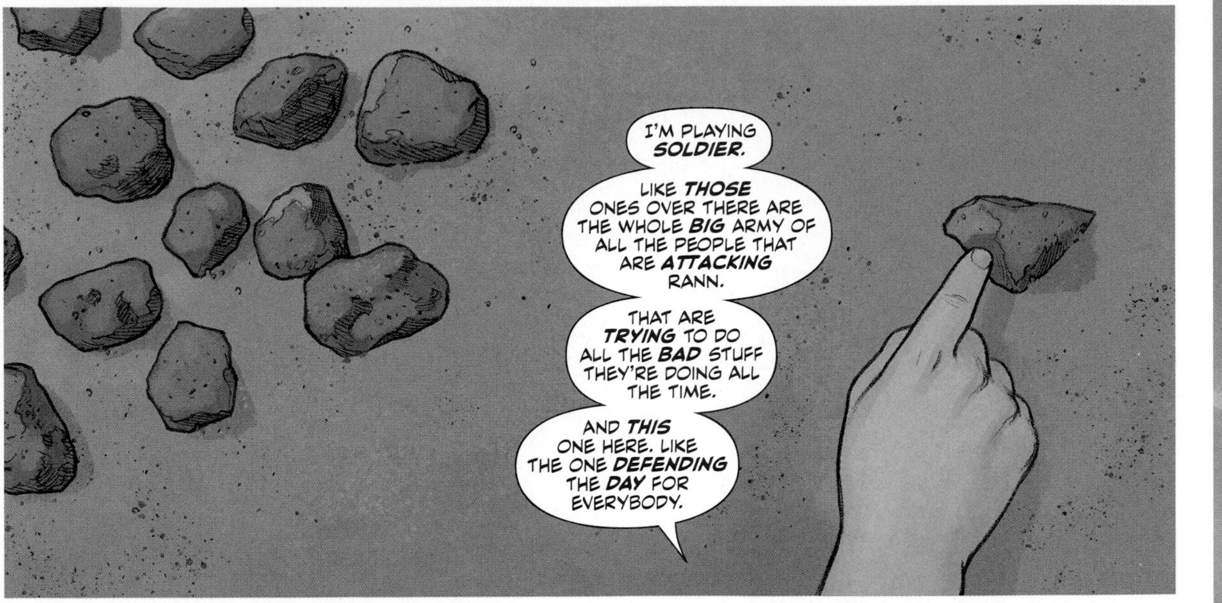
I'M PLAYING SOLDIER.
LIKE THOSE ONES OVER THERE ARE THE WHOLE BIG ARMY OF ALL THE PEOPLE THAT ARE ATTACKING RANN.
THAT ARE TRYING TO DO ALL THE BAD STUFF THEY'RE DOING ALL THE TIME.
AND THIS ONE HERE. LIKE THE ONE DEFENDING THE DAY FOR EVERYBODY.

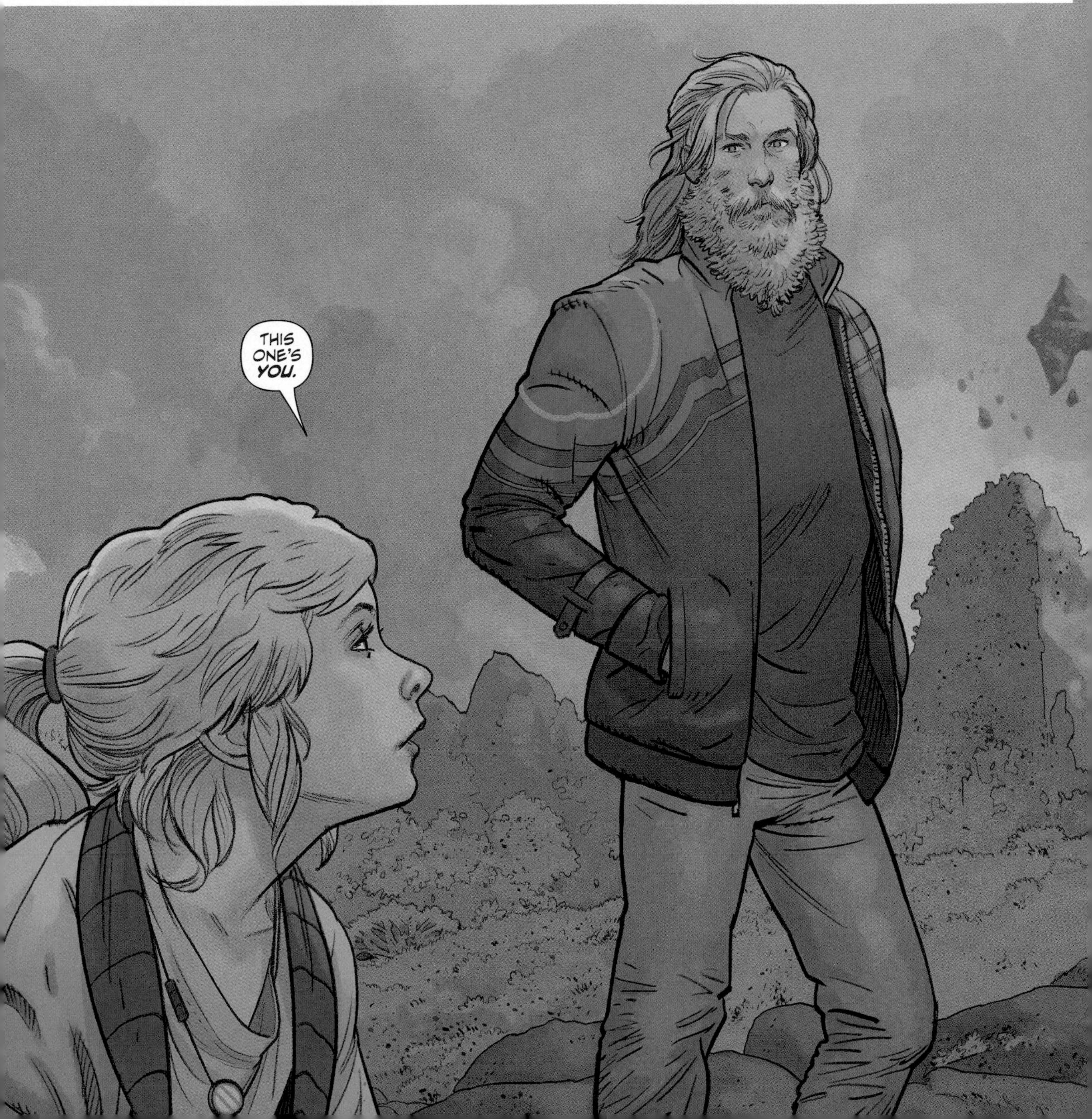
THIS ONE'S YOU.

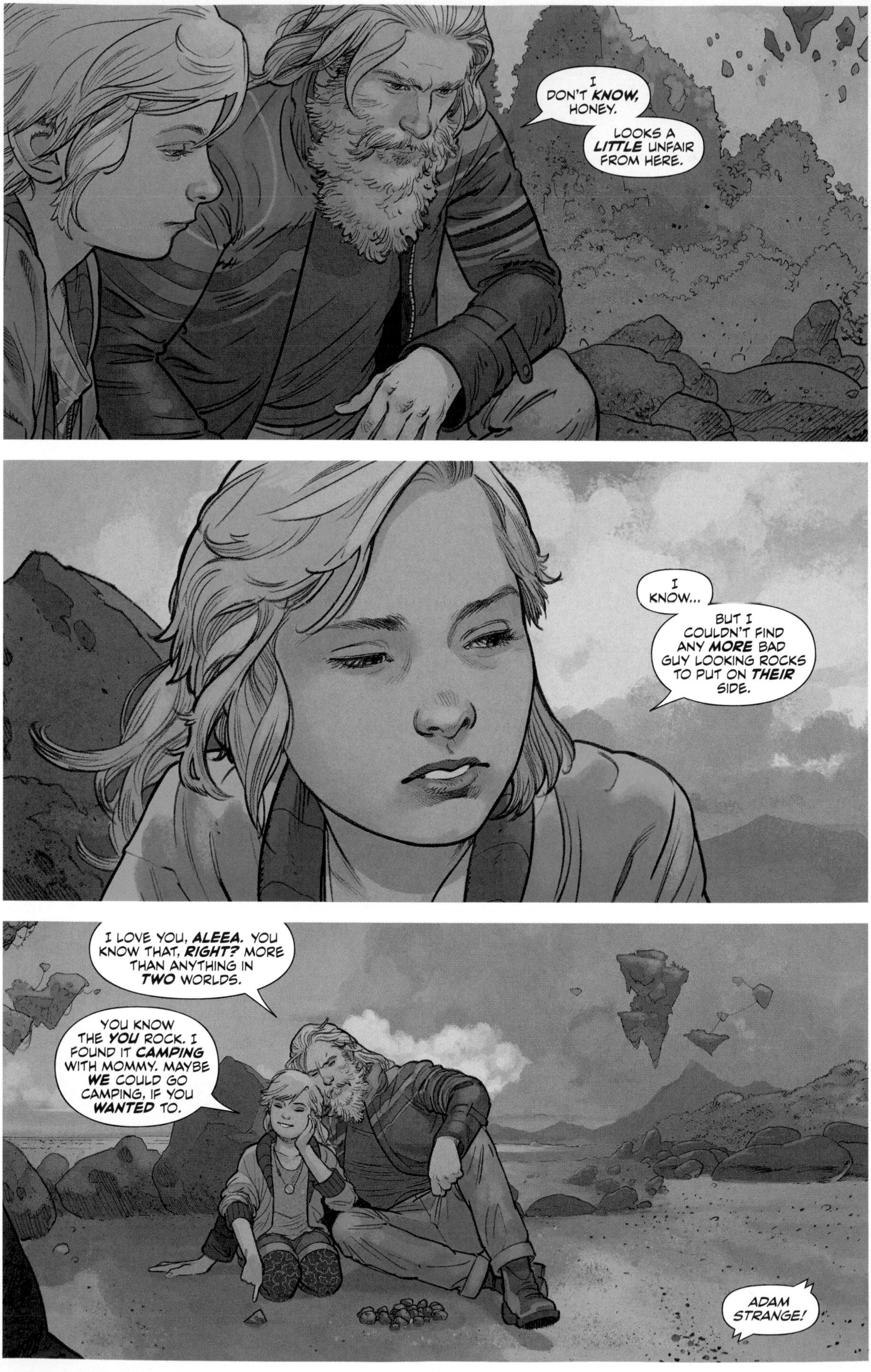
I DON'T KNOW, HONEY.
LOOKS A LITTLE UNFAIR FROM HERE.
I KNOW...
BUT I COULDN'T FIND ANY MORE BAD GUY LOOKING ROCKS TO PUT ON THEIR SIDE.
I LOVE YOU, ALEEA. YOU KNOW THAT, RIGHT? MORE THAN ANYTHING IN TWO WORLDS.
YOU KNOW THE YOU ROCK. I FOUND IT CAMPING WITH MOMMY. MAYBE WE COULD GO CAMPING, IF YOU WANTED TO.
ADAM STRANGE!

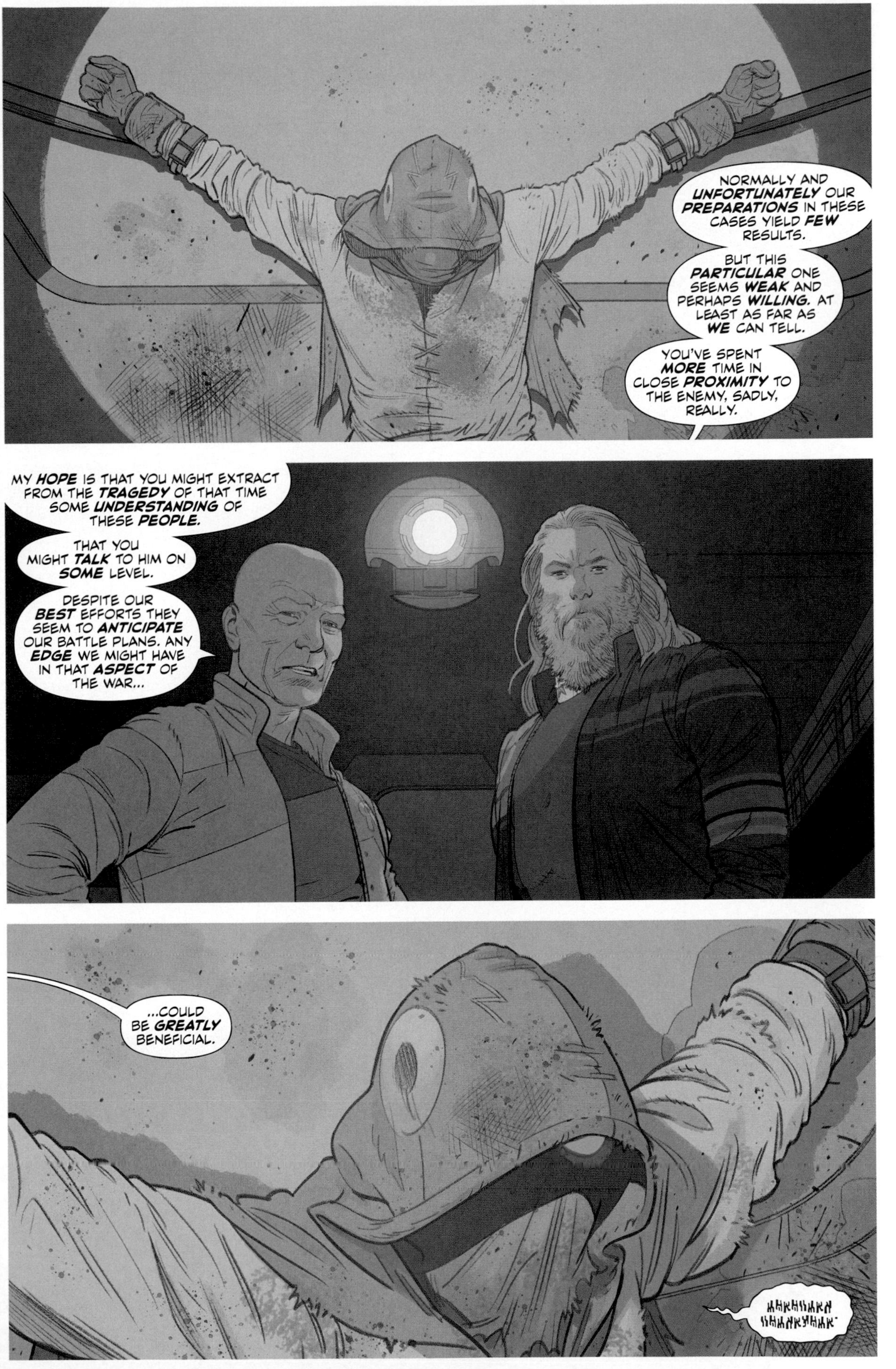
NORMALLY AND UNFORTUNATELY OUR PREPARATIONS IN THESE CASES YIELD FEW RESULTS.
BUT THIS PARTICULAR ONE SEEMS WEAK AND PERHAPS WILLING. AT LEAST AS FAR AS WE CAN TELL.
YOU'VE SPENT MORE TIME IN CLOSE PROXIMITY TO THE ENEMY, SADLY, REALLY.
MY HOPE IS THAT YOU MIGHT EXTRACT FROM THE TRAGEDY OF THAT TIME SOME UNDERSTANDING OF THESE PEOPLE.
THAT YOU MIGHT TALK TO HIM ON SOME LEVEL.
DESPITE OUR BEST EFFORTS THEY SEEM TO ANTICIPATE OUR BATTLE PLANS. ANY EDGE WE MIGHT HAVE IN THAT ASPECT OF THE WAR...
...COULD BE GREATLY BENEFICIAL.

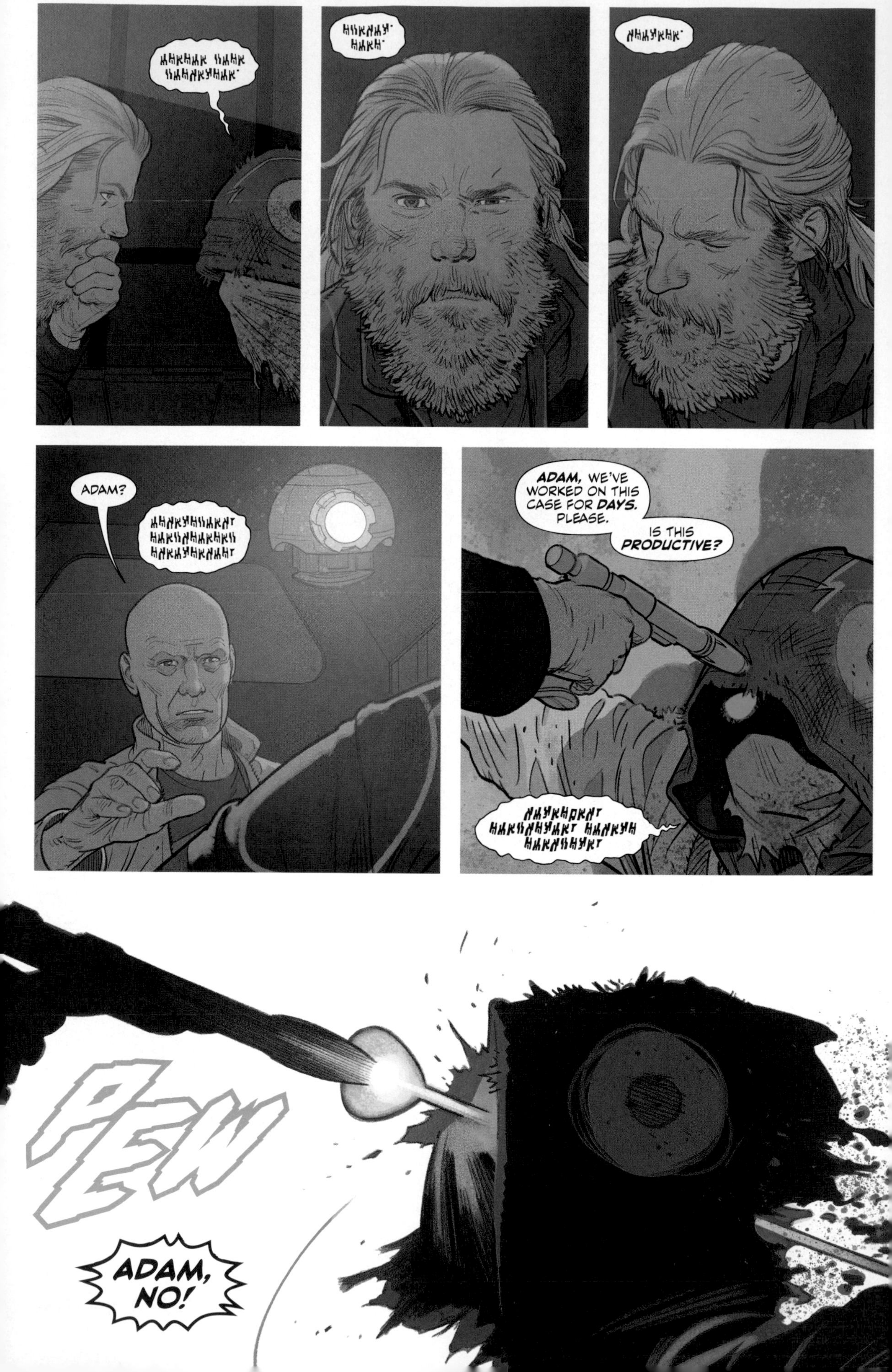
ADAM?
ADAM, WE'VE WORKED ON THIS CASE FOR DAYS. PLEASE.
IS THIS PRODUCTIVE?
PEW
ADAM, NO!

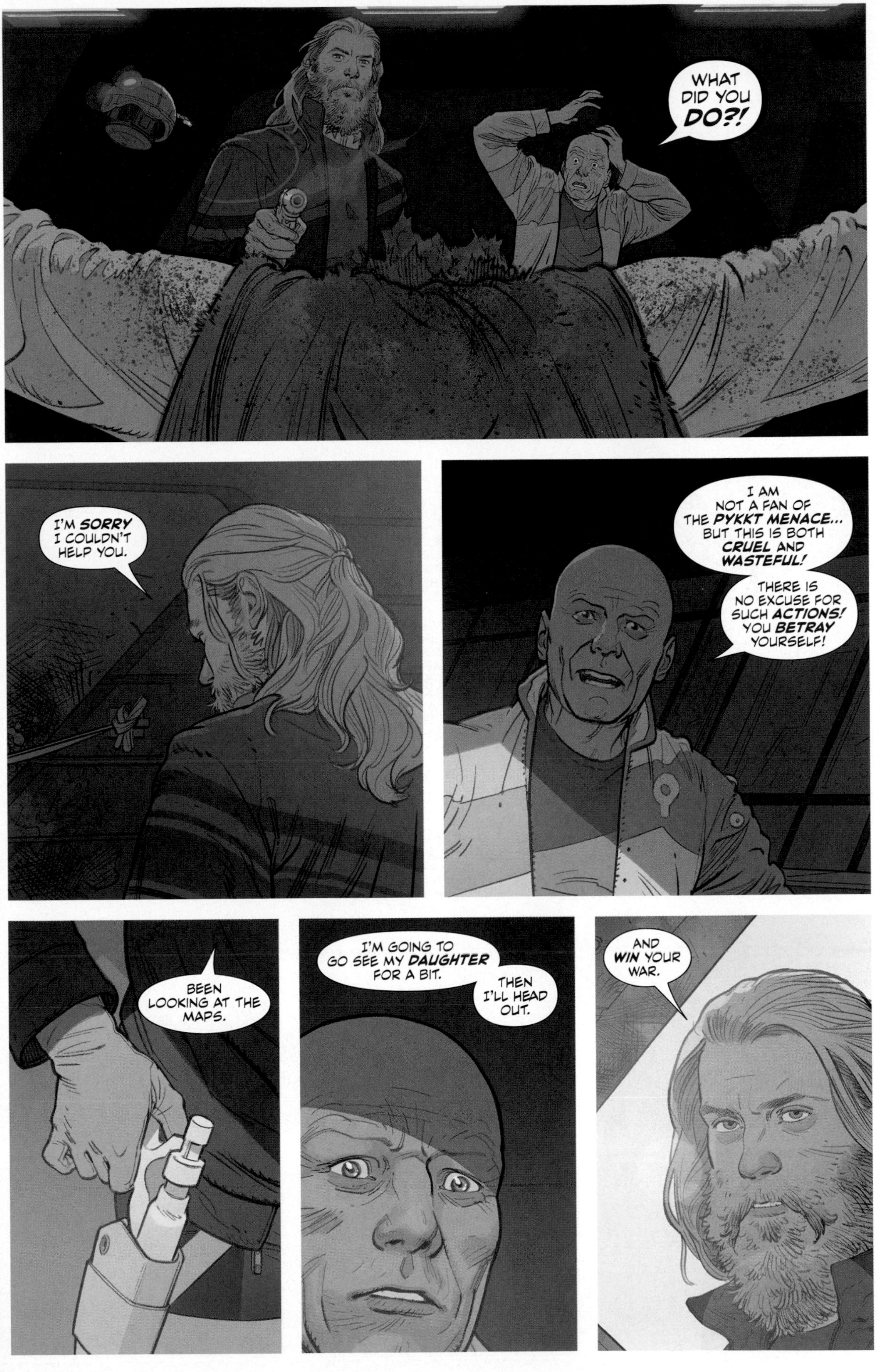
WHAT DID YOU DO?!
I'M SORRY I COULDN'T HELP YOU.
I AM NOT A FAN OF THE PYKKT MENACE... BUT THIS IS BOTH CRUEL AND WASTEFUL!
THERE IS NO EXCUSE FOR SUCH ACTIONS! YOU BETRAY YOURSELF!
BEEN LOOKING AT THE MAPS.
I'M GOING TO GO SEE MY DAUGHTER FOR A BIT.
THEN I'LL HEAD OUT.
AND WIN YOUR WAR.

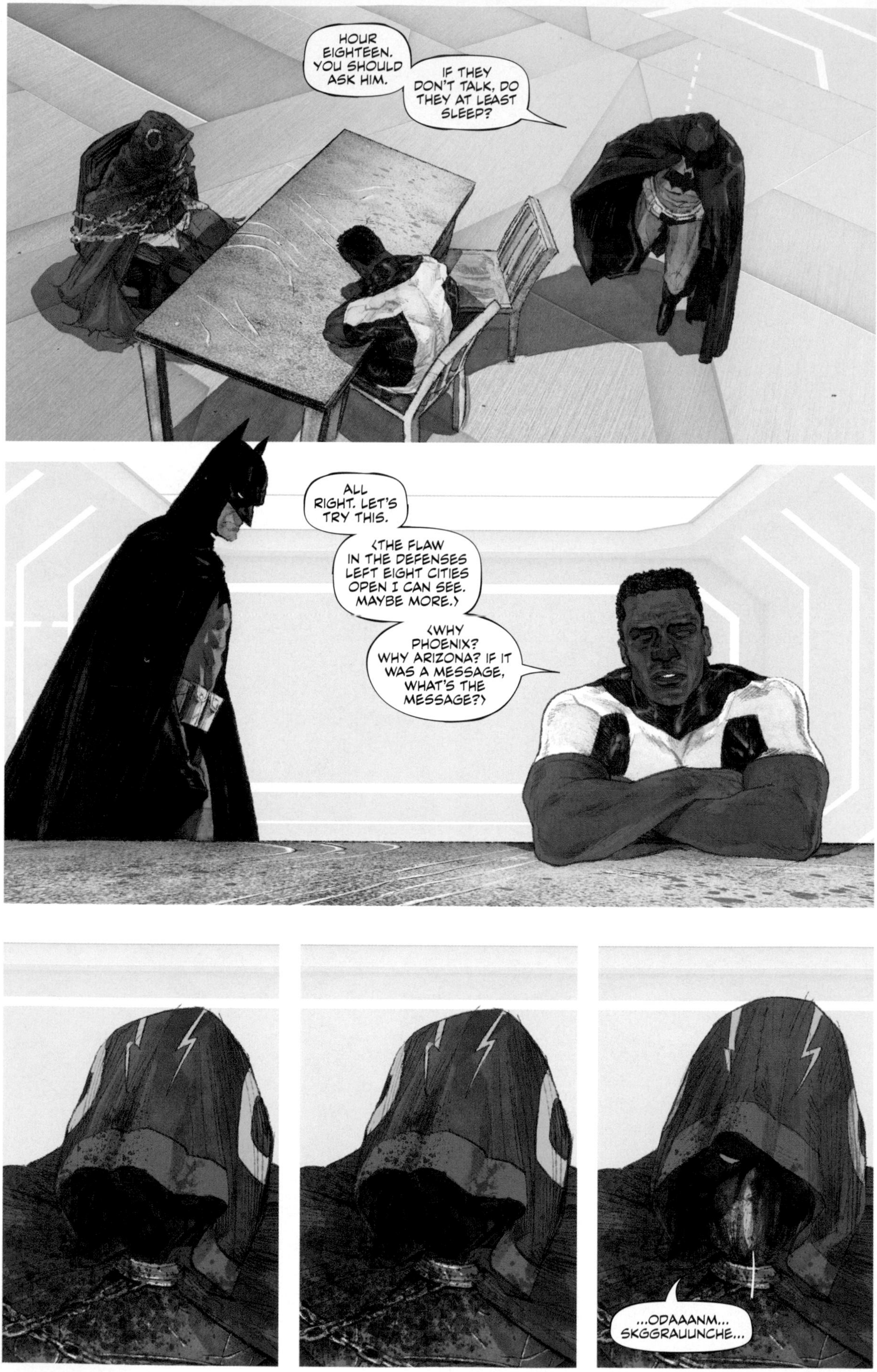
HOUR EIGHTEEN. YOU SHOULD ASK HIM.
IF THEY DON'T TALK, DO THEY AT LEAST SLEEP?
ALL RIGHT. LET'S TRY THIS.
‹THE FLAW IN THE DEFENSES LEFT EIGHT CITIES OPEN I CAN SEE. MAYBE MORE.›
‹WHY PHOENIX? WHY ARIZONA? IF IT WAS A MESSAGE, WHAT'S THE MESSAGE?›
...ODAAANM... SKGGRAUUNCHE...

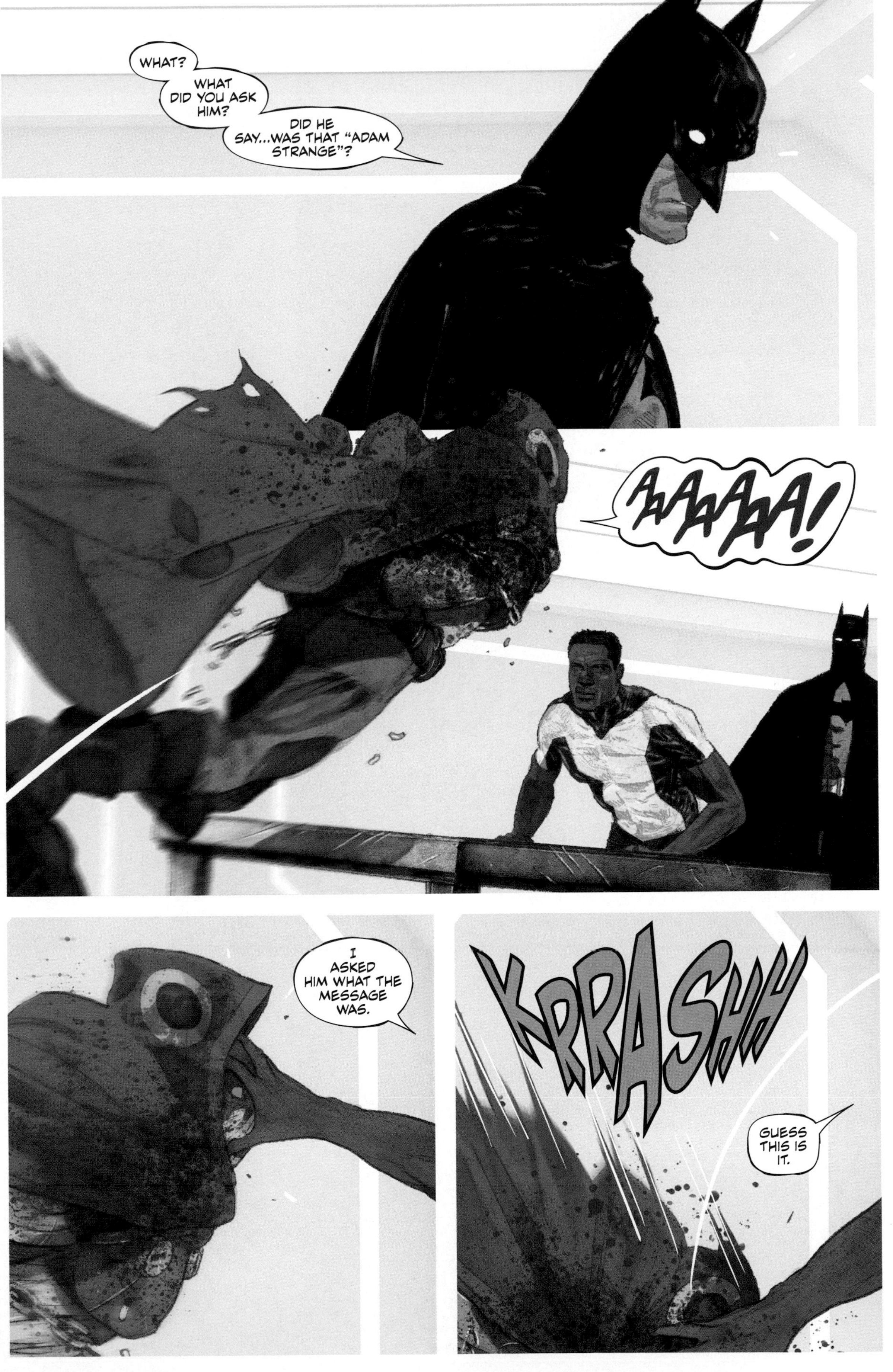
WHAT?
WHAT DID YOU ASK HIM?
DID HE SAY...WAS THAT "ADAM STRANGE"?
AAAAAA!
I ASKED HIM WHAT THE MESSAGE WAS.
KRRASHH
GUESS THIS IS IT.

‹YOU KNOW, MR. PYKKT, I WENT TO RANN. GOT TO SEE THE WHOLE HISTORY OF THEIR WAR WITH YOU. IT WAS SOMETHING.›

‹HOW THE RANNIANS FOUGHT WITH HONOR AND GRACE...›

‹...THE WAY I'D ALWAYS HEARD THE PYKKTS FIGHT, BUT I GUESS DON'T ANYMORE.›

‹THEY SAID THE WHOLE TIME THEY WERE JUST FOLLOWING ADAM'S LEAD.›

‹THEY KEPT SAYING...›

‹...ADAM STRANGE WAS A GOOD MAN LEADING A GOOD WAR.›

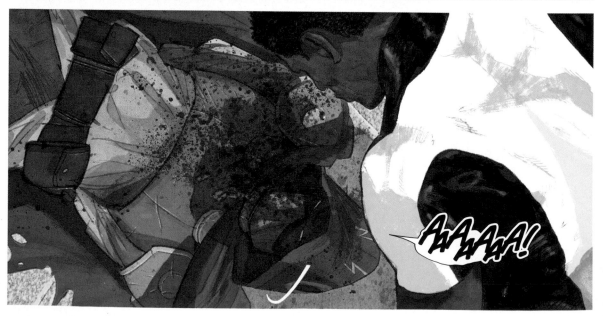

AAAAAA!

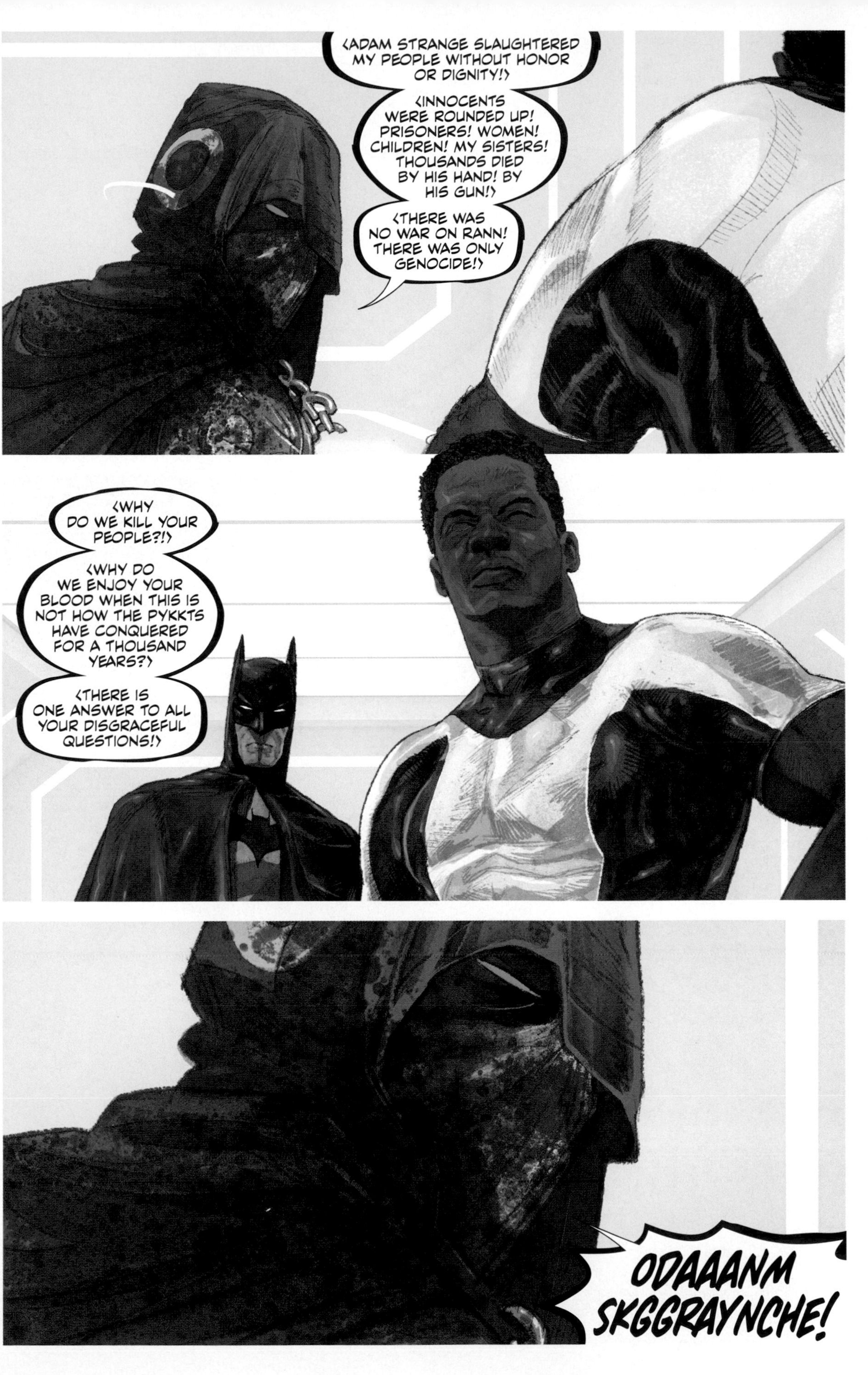

<ADAM STRANGE SLAUGHTERED MY PEOPLE WITHOUT HONOR OR DIGNITY!>
<INNOCENTS WERE ROUNDED UP! PRISONERS! WOMEN! CHILDREN! MY SISTERS! THOUSANDS DIED BY HIS HAND! BY HIS GUN!>
<THERE WAS NO WAR ON RANN! THERE WAS ONLY GENOCIDE!>
<WHY DO WE KILL YOUR PEOPLE?!>
<WHY DO WE ENJOY YOUR BLOOD WHEN THIS IS NOT HOW THE PYKKTS HAVE CONQUERED FOR A THOUSAND YEARS?>
<THERE IS ONE ANSWER TO ALL YOUR DISGRACEFUL QUESTIONS!>
ODAAANM SKGGRAYNCHE!

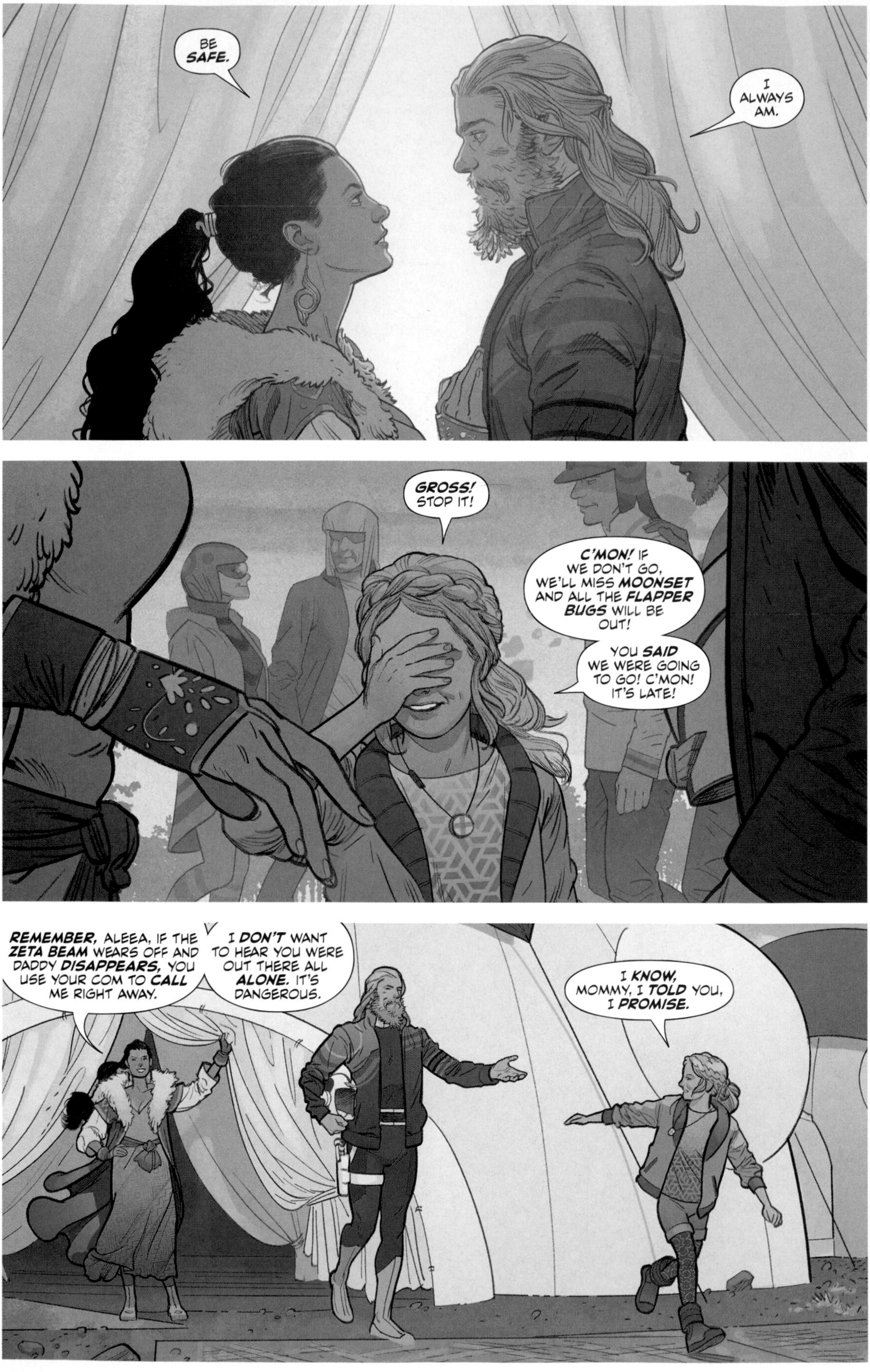
BE SAFE.
I ALWAYS AM.
GROSS! STOP IT!
C'MON! IF WE DON'T GO, WE'LL MISS MOONSET AND ALL THE FLAPPER BUGS WILL BE OUT!
YOU SAID WE WERE GOING TO GO! C'MON! IT'S LATE!
REMEMBER, ALEEA, IF THE ZETA BEAM WEARS OFF AND DADDY DISAPPEARS, YOU USE YOUR COM TO CALL ME RIGHT AWAY.
I DON'T WANT TO HEAR YOU WERE OUT THERE ALL ALONE. IT'S DANGEROUS.
I KNOW, MOMMY, I TOLD YOU, I PROMISE.

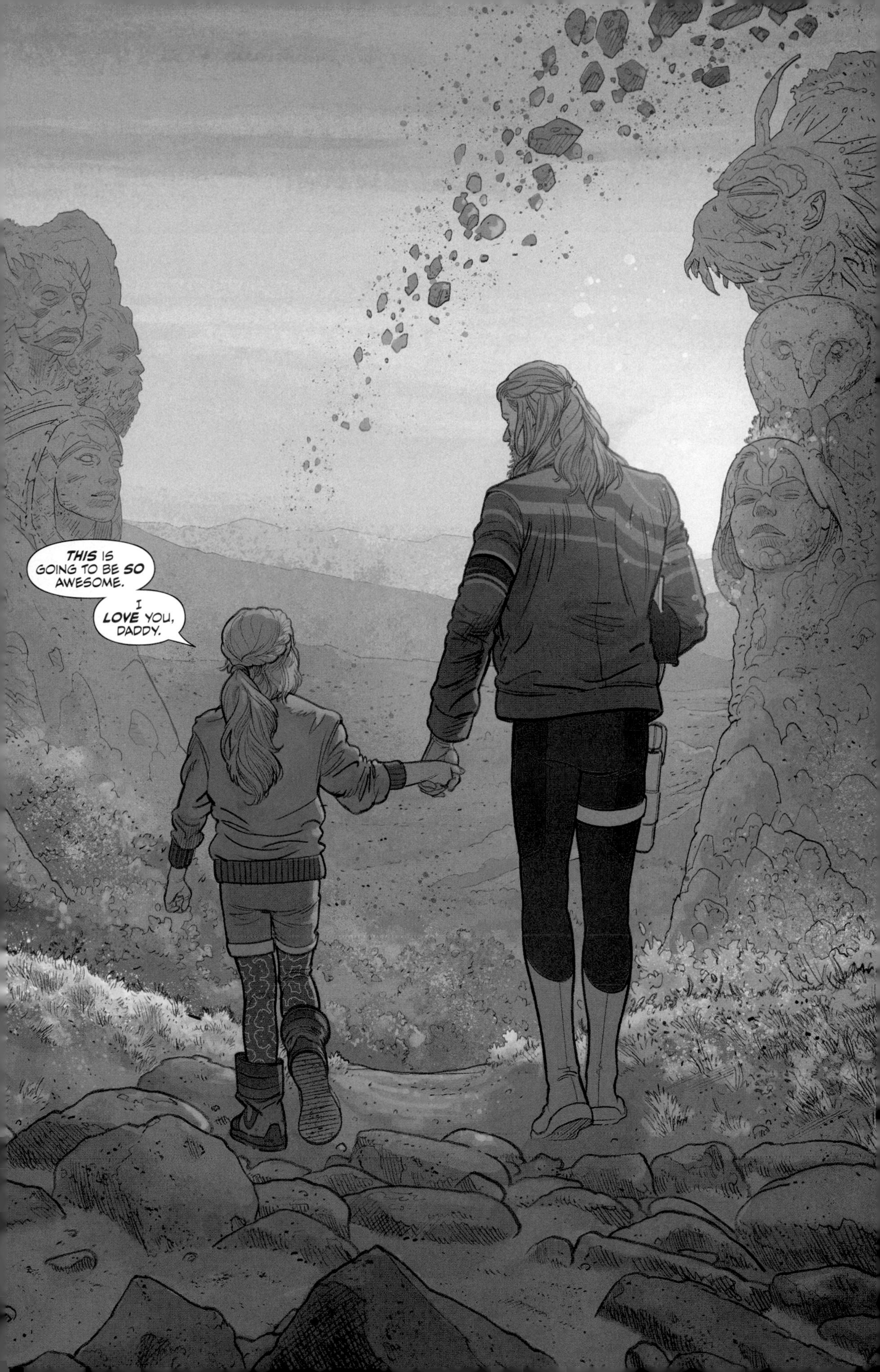
THIS IS GOING TO BE SO AWESOME.
I LOVE YOU, DADDY.

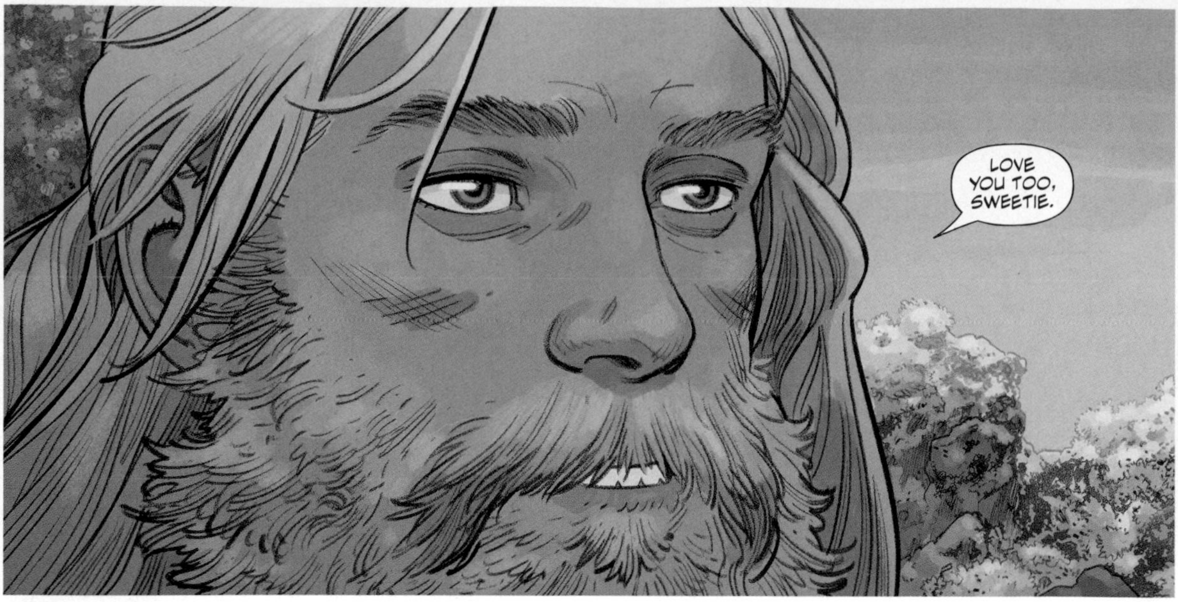
LOVE YOU TOO, SWEETIE.

But no, the whole thing was just great.
Life is not easy, but this was pleasant.
It was good. It could've been worse.

—Jack Davis

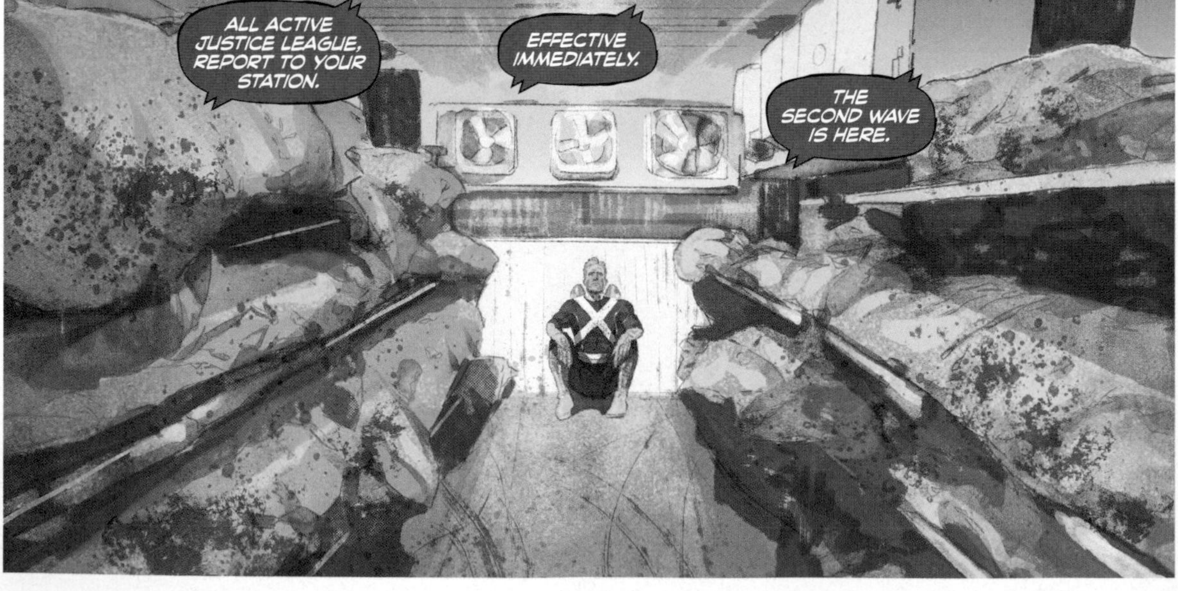
ALL ACTIVE JUSTICE LEAGUE, REPORT TO YOUR STATION.
EFFECTIVE IMMEDIATELY.
THE SECOND WAVE IS HERE.

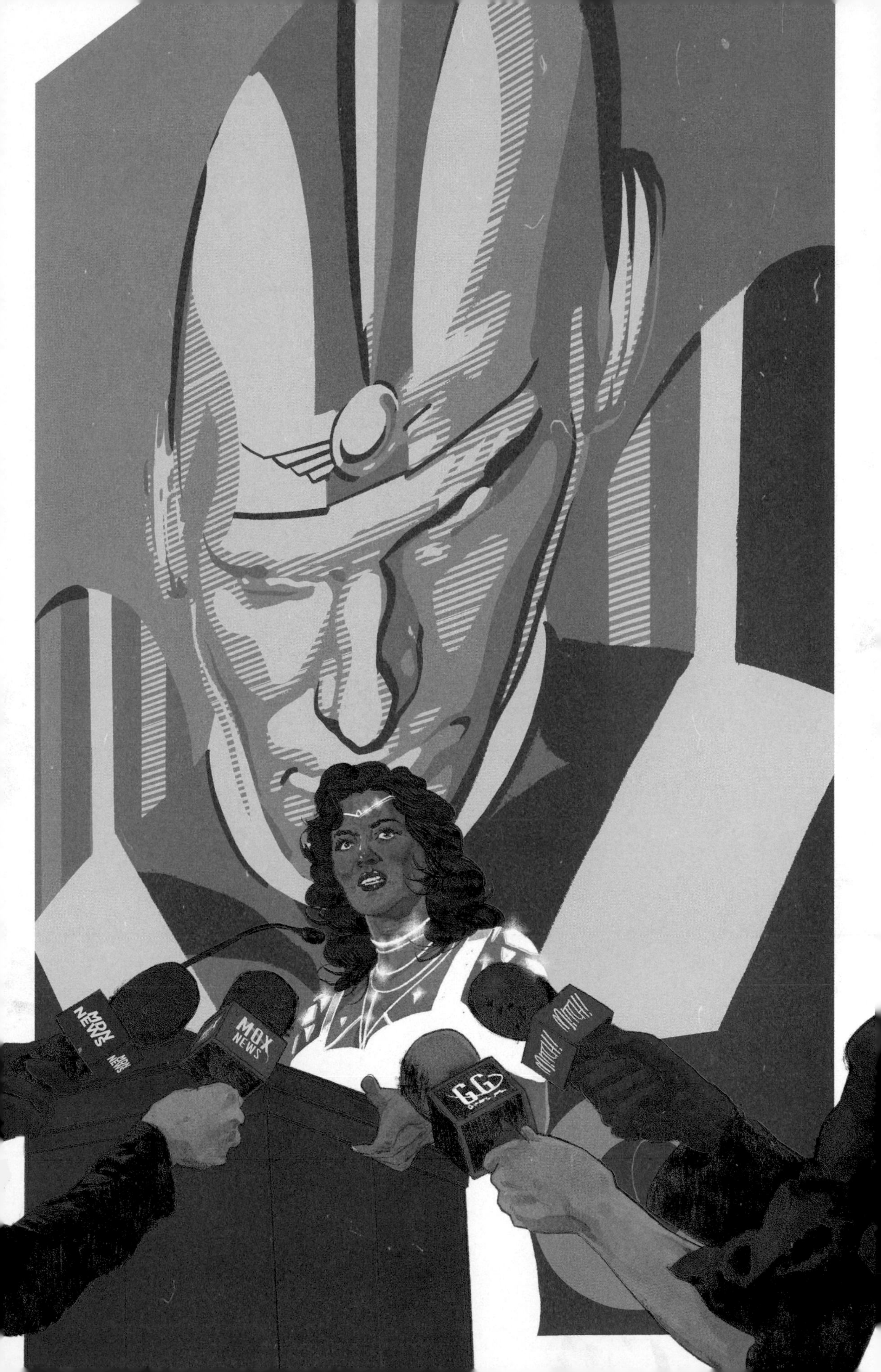
MRN NEWS
MOX NEWS
GG

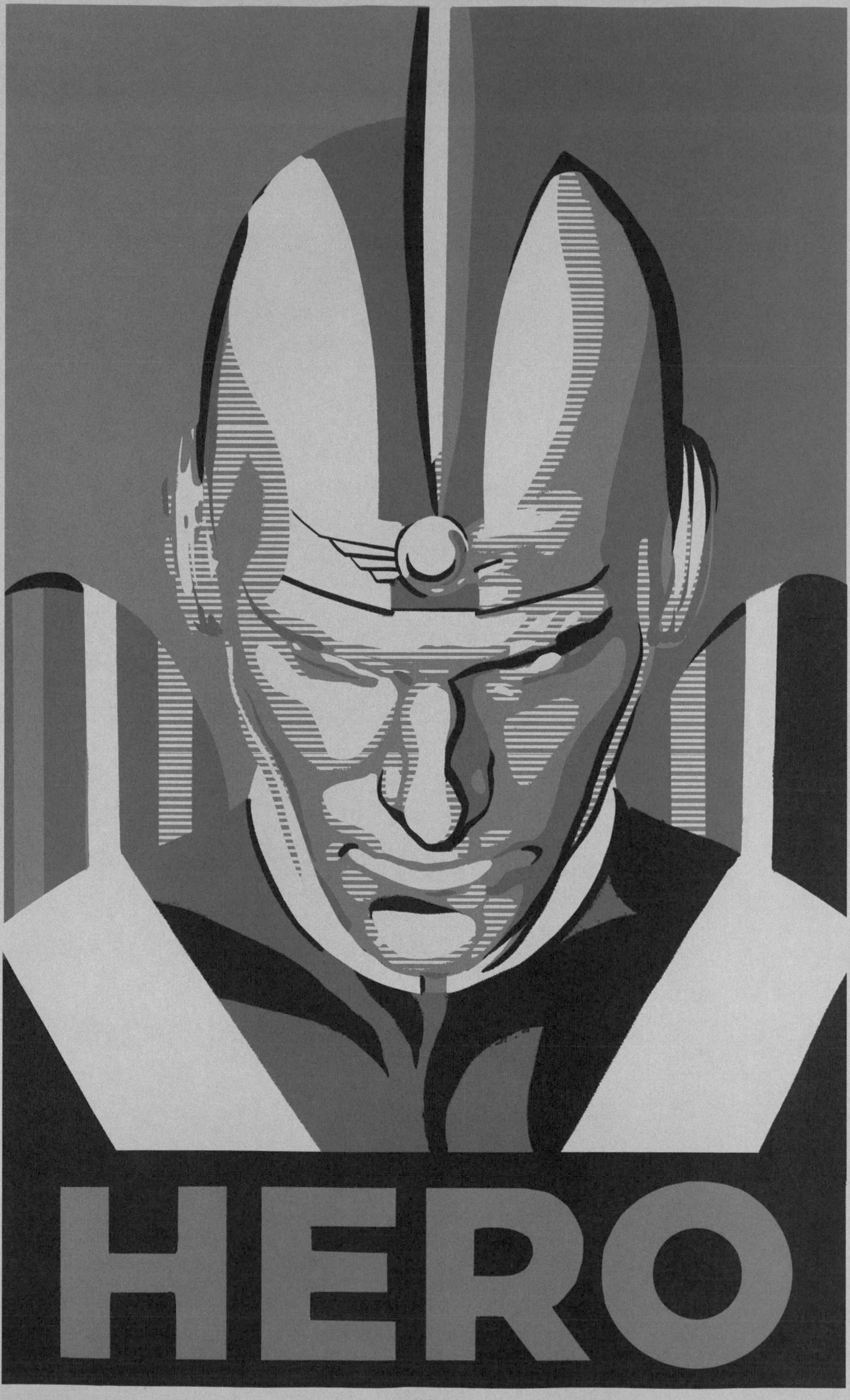
HERO

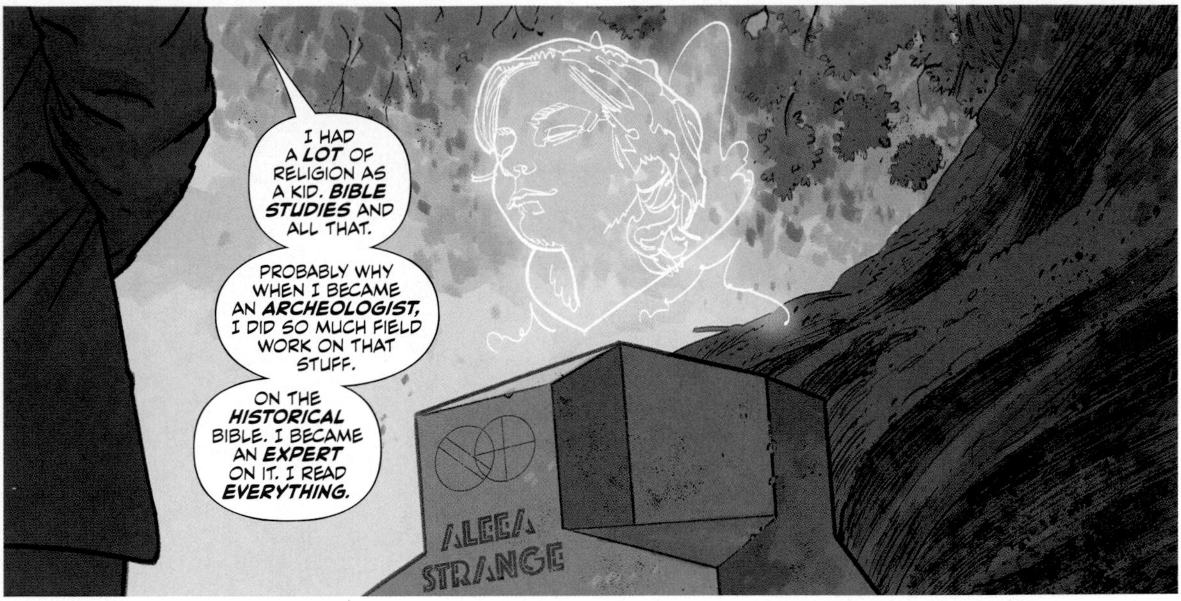
I HAD A LOT OF RELIGION AS A KID. BIBLE STUDIES AND ALL THAT.
PROBABLY WHY WHEN I BECAME AN ARCHEOLOGIST, I DID SO MUCH FIELD WORK ON THAT STUFF.
ON THE HISTORICAL BIBLE. I BECAME AN EXPERT ON IT. I READ EVERYTHING.
ALEEA STRANGE

Chapter 9

The whole world's looking

TOM KING ...Writer

MITCH GERADS
EVAN "DOC" SHANER ...Interior & Cover Artists

CLAYTON COWLES ...Letterer
BIXIE MATHIEU ...Assistant Editor
BRITTANY HOLZHERR ...Associate Editor
JAMIE S. RICH ...Editor

SUPERMAN created by JERRY SIEGEL & JOE SHUSTER.
By special arrangement with the JERRY SIEGEL FAMILY.

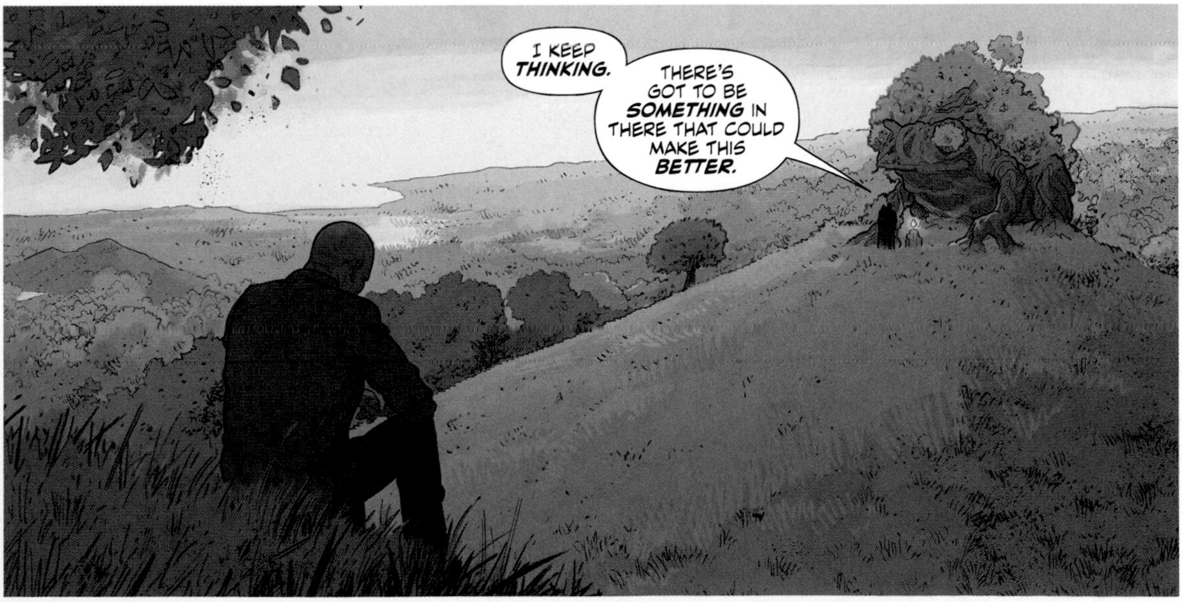
I KEEP THINKING.
THERE'S GOT TO BE SOMETHING IN THERE THAT COULD MAKE THIS BETTER.

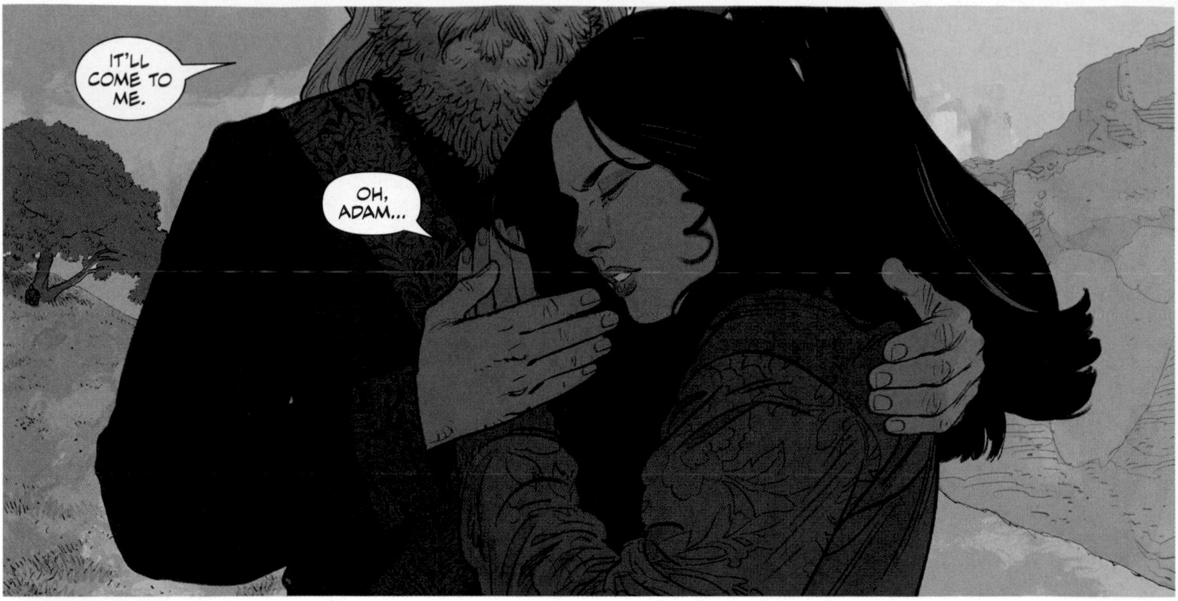
IT'LL COME TO ME.
OH, ADAM...

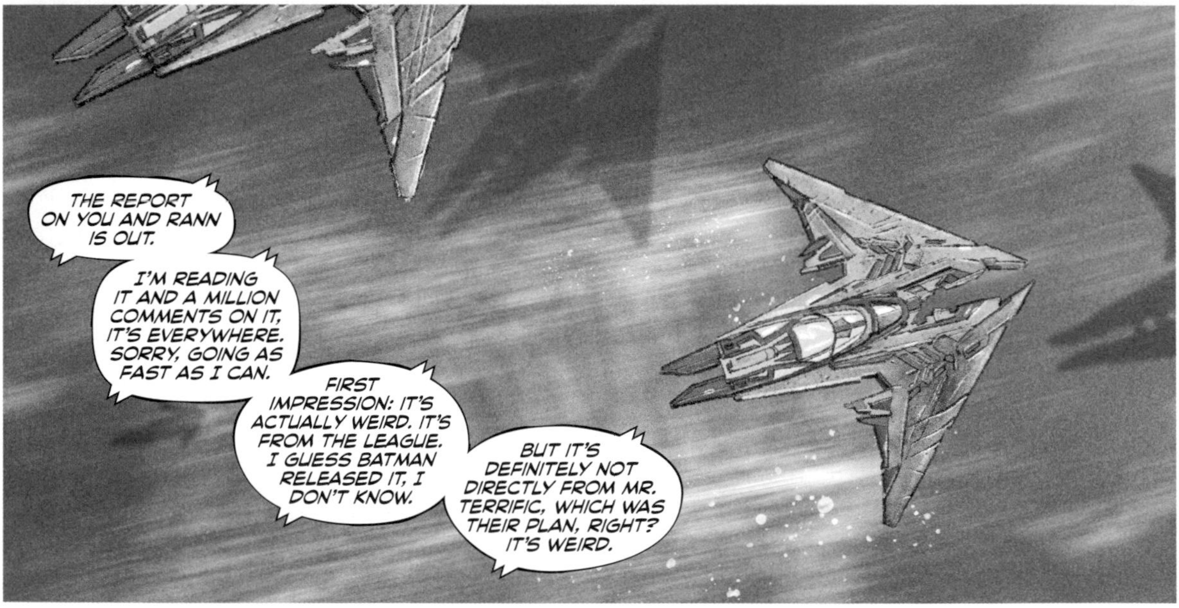
THE REPORT ON YOU AND RANN IS OUT.
I'M READING IT AND A MILLION COMMENTS ON IT, IT'S EVERYWHERE. SORRY, GOING AS FAST AS I CAN.
FIRST IMPRESSION: IT'S ACTUALLY WEIRD. IT'S FROM THE LEAGUE. I GUESS BATMAN RELEASED IT, I DON'T KNOW.
BUT IT'S DEFINITELY NOT DIRECTLY FROM MR. TERRIFIC, WHICH WAS THEIR PLAN, RIGHT? IT'S WEIRD.

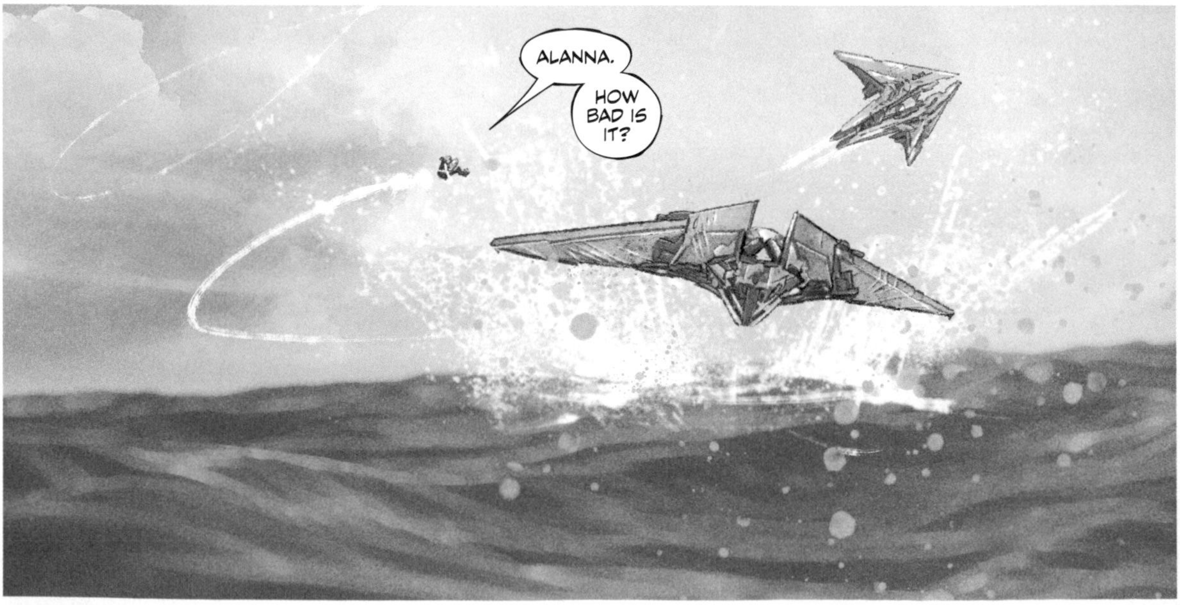
ALANNA.
HOW BAD IS IT?

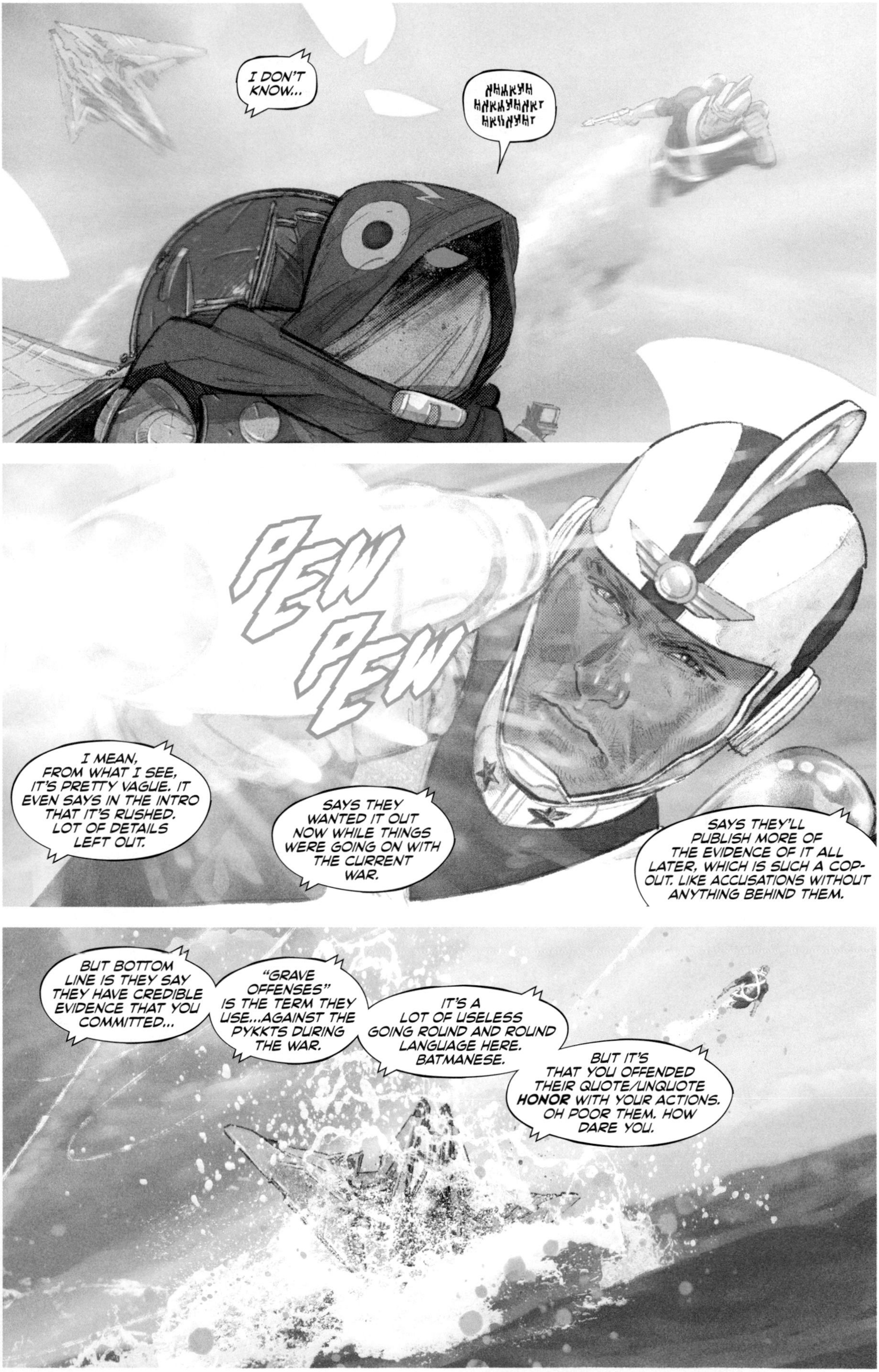
I DON'T KNOW...
PEW PEW
I MEAN, FROM WHAT I SEE, IT'S PRETTY VAGUE. IT EVEN SAYS IN THE INTRO THAT IT'S RUSHED. LOT OF DETAILS LEFT OUT.
SAYS THEY WANTED IT OUT NOW WHILE THINGS WERE GOING ON WITH THE CURRENT WAR.
SAYS THEY'LL PUBLISH MORE OF THE EVIDENCE OF IT ALL LATER, WHICH IS SUCH A COP-OUT. LIKE ACCUSATIONS WITHOUT ANYTHING BEHIND THEM.
BUT BOTTOM LINE IS THEY SAY THEY HAVE CREDIBLE EVIDENCE THAT YOU COMMITTED...
"GRAVE OFFENSES" IS THE TERM THEY USE...AGAINST THE PYKKTS DURING THE WAR.
IT'S A LOT OF USELESS GOING ROUND AND ROUND LANGUAGE HERE. BATMANESE.
BUT IT'S THAT YOU OFFENDED THEIR QUOTE/UNQUOTE **HONOR** WITH YOUR ACTIONS. OH POOR THEM. HOW DARE YOU.

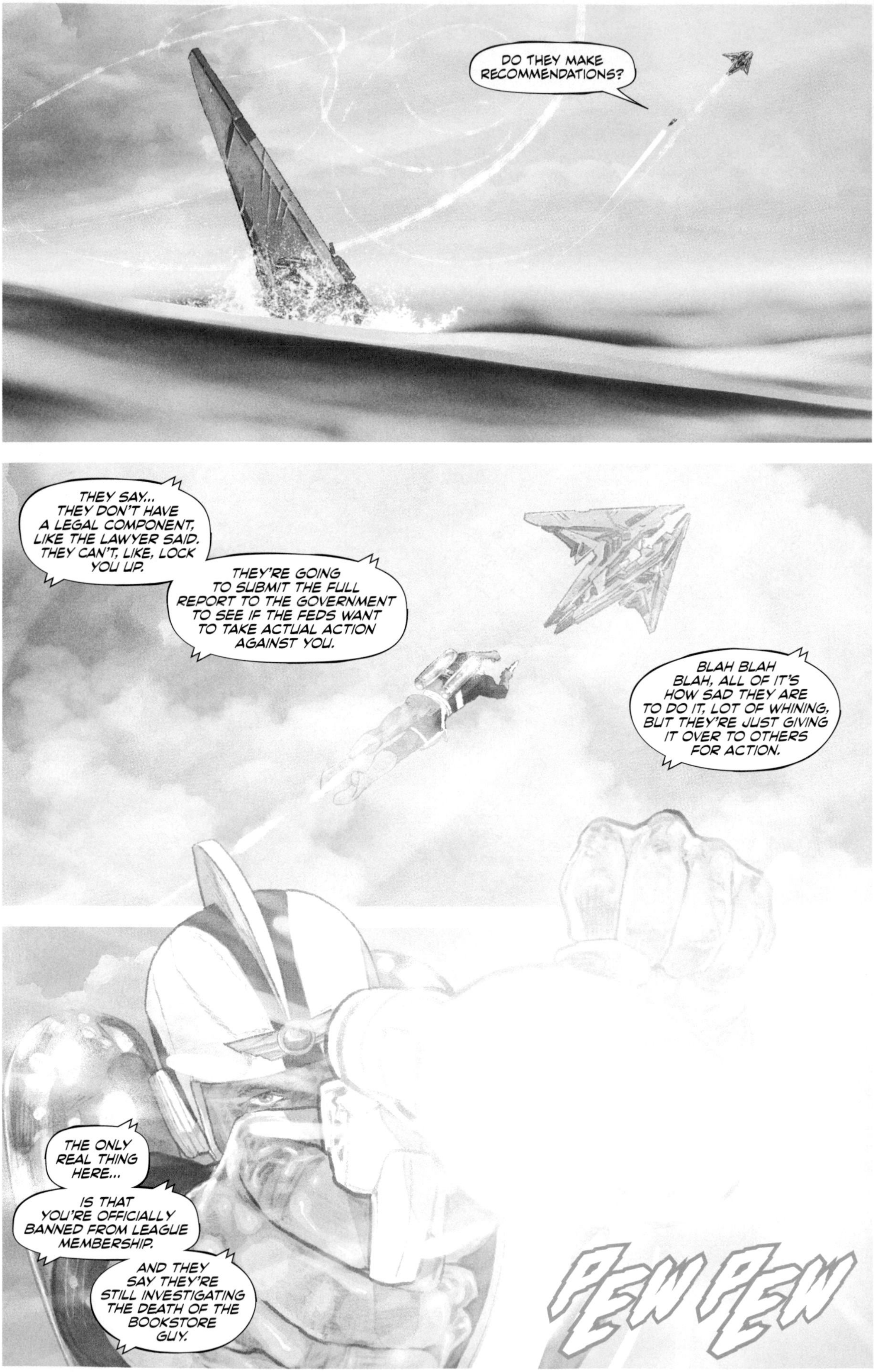
DO THEY MAKE RECOMMENDATIONS?
THEY SAY... THEY DON'T HAVE A LEGAL COMPONENT, LIKE THE LAWYER SAID. THEY CAN'T, LIKE, LOCK YOU UP.
THEY'RE GOING TO SUBMIT THE FULL REPORT TO THE GOVERNMENT TO SEE IF THE FEDS WANT TO TAKE ACTUAL ACTION AGAINST YOU.
BLAH BLAH BLAH, ALL OF IT'S HOW SAD THEY ARE TO DO IT, LOT OF WHINING, BUT THEY'RE JUST GIVING IT OVER TO OTHERS FOR ACTION.
THE ONLY REAL THING HERE...
IS THAT YOU'RE OFFICIALLY BANNED FROM LEAGUE MEMBERSHIP.
AND THEY SAY THEY'RE STILL INVESTIGATING THE DEATH OF THE BOOKSTORE GUY.
PEW PEW

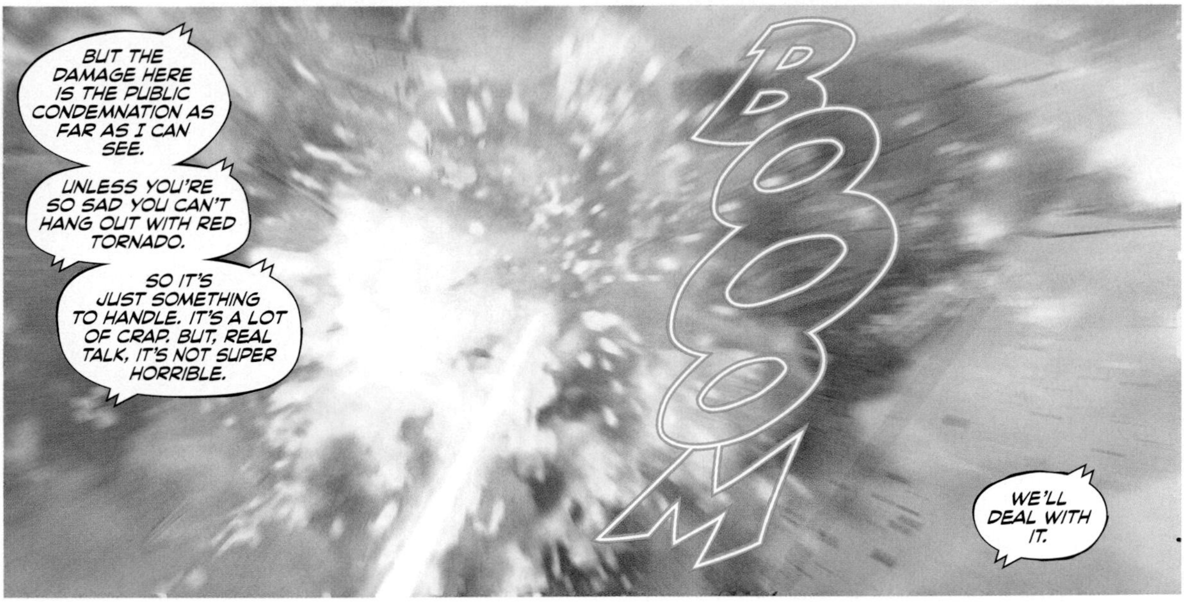
BUT THE DAMAGE HERE IS THE PUBLIC CONDEMNATION AS FAR AS I CAN SEE.
UNLESS YOU'RE SO SAD YOU CAN'T HANG OUT WITH RED TORNADO.
SO IT'S JUST SOMETHING TO HANDLE. IT'S A LOT OF CRAP. BUT, REAL TALK, IT'S NOT SUPER HORRIBLE.
BOOOOM
WE'LL DEAL WITH IT.

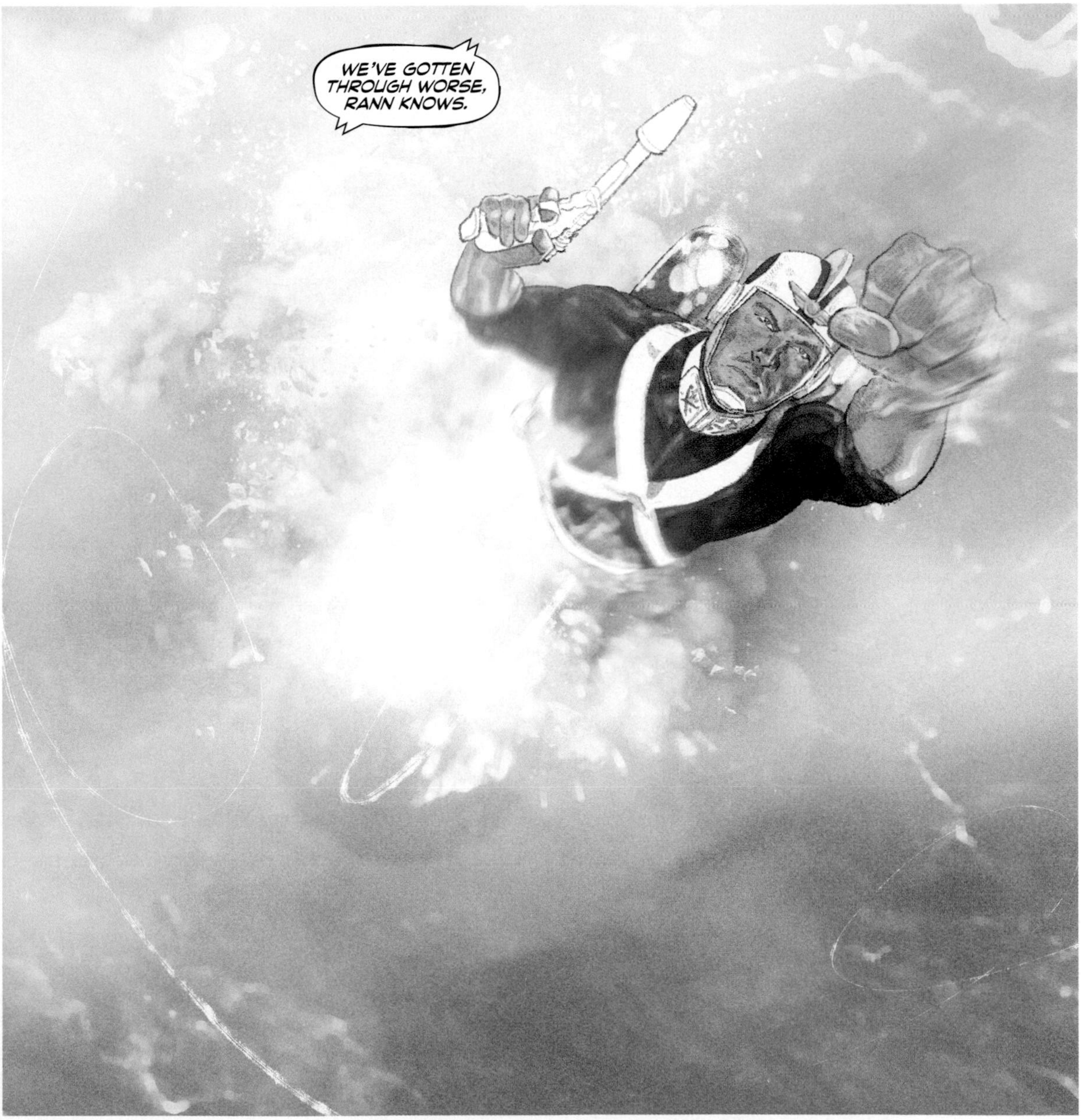
WE'VE GOTTEN THROUGH WORSE, RANN KNOWS.

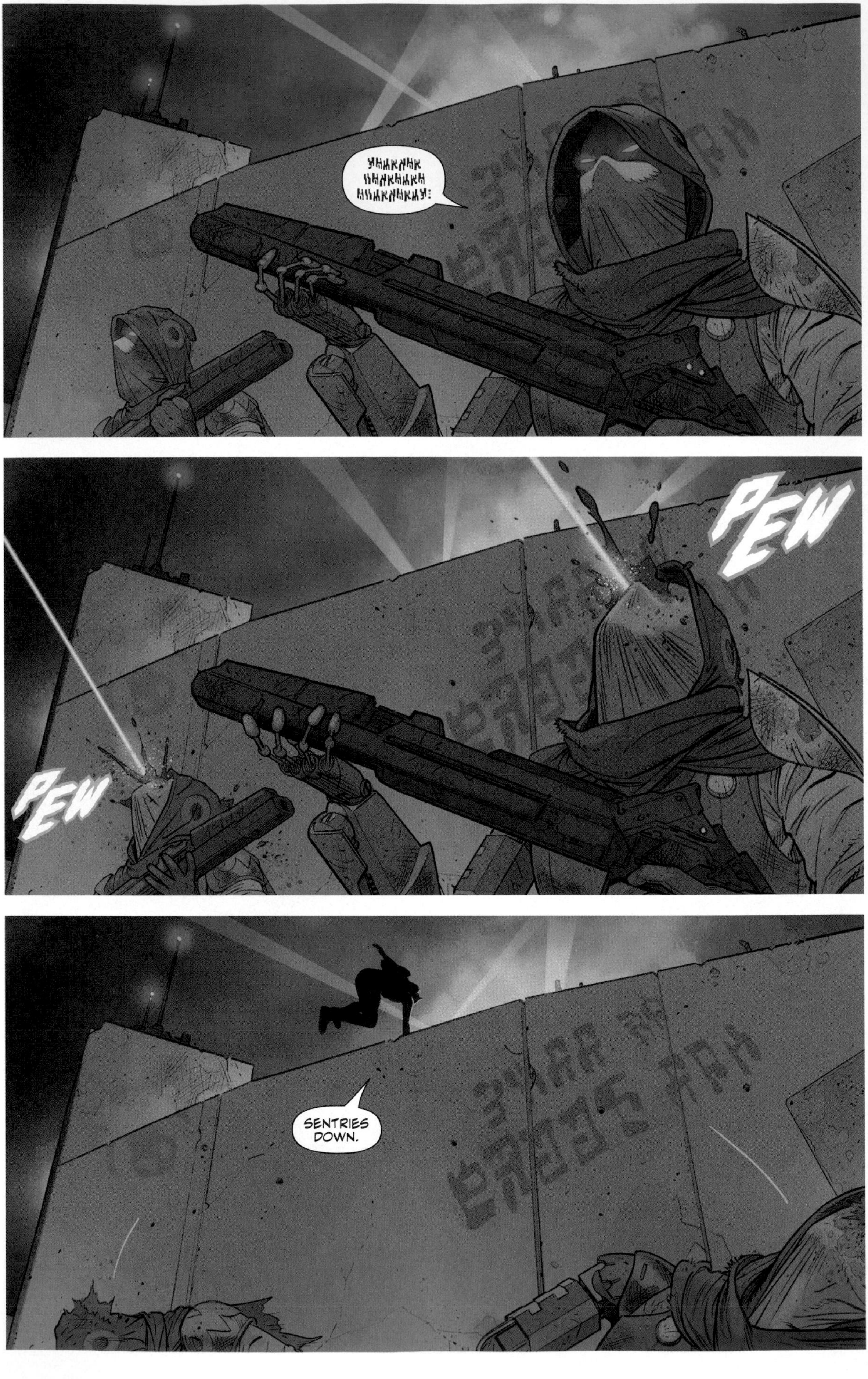
PEW
PEW
SENTRIES DOWN.

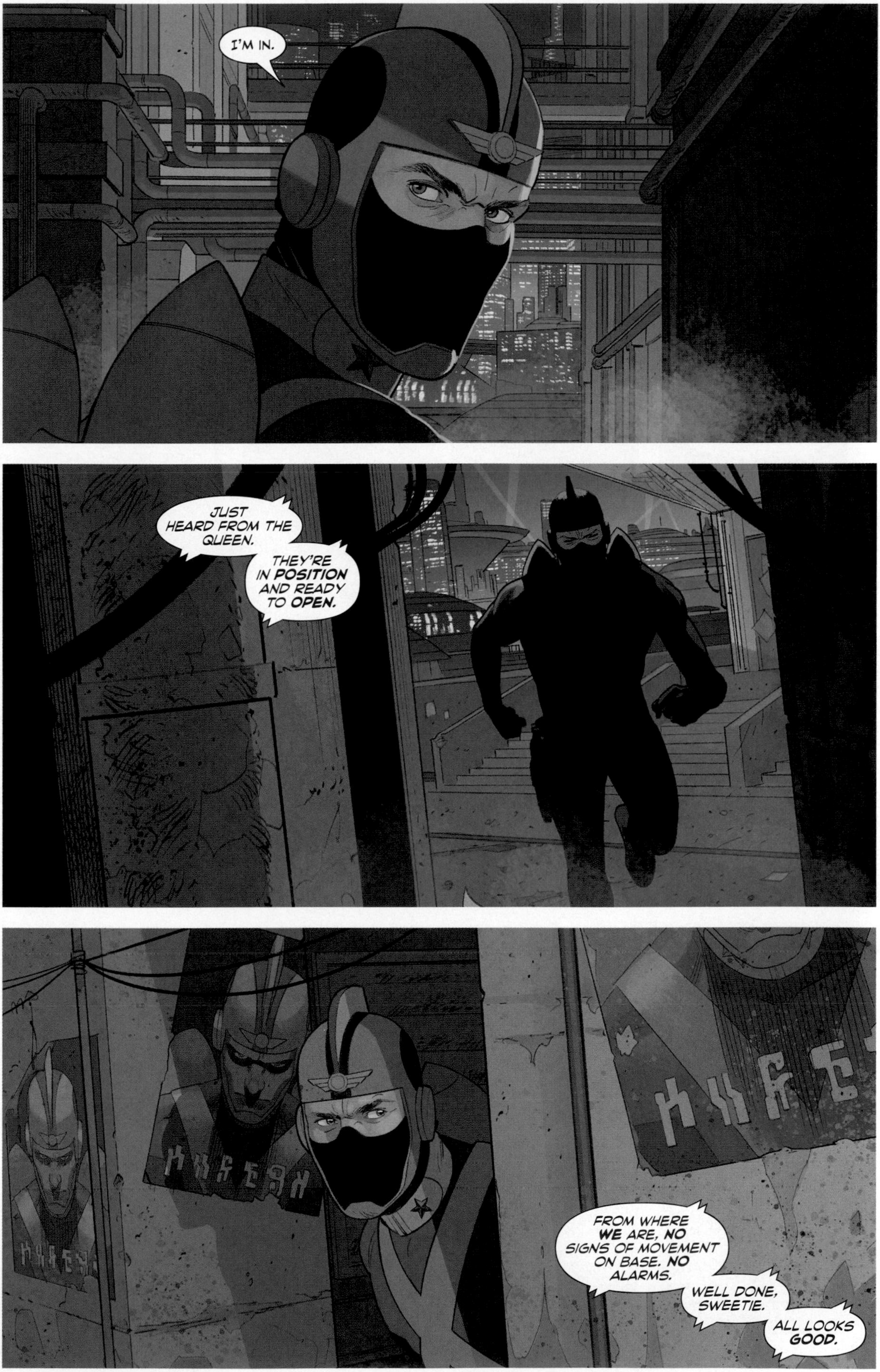
I'M IN.
JUST HEARD FROM THE QUEEN.
THEY'RE IN **POSITION** AND READY TO **OPEN.**
FROM WHERE **WE** ARE, **NO** SIGNS OF MOVEMENT ON BASE. **NO** ALARMS.
WELL DONE, SWEETIE.
ALL LOOKS **GOOD.**

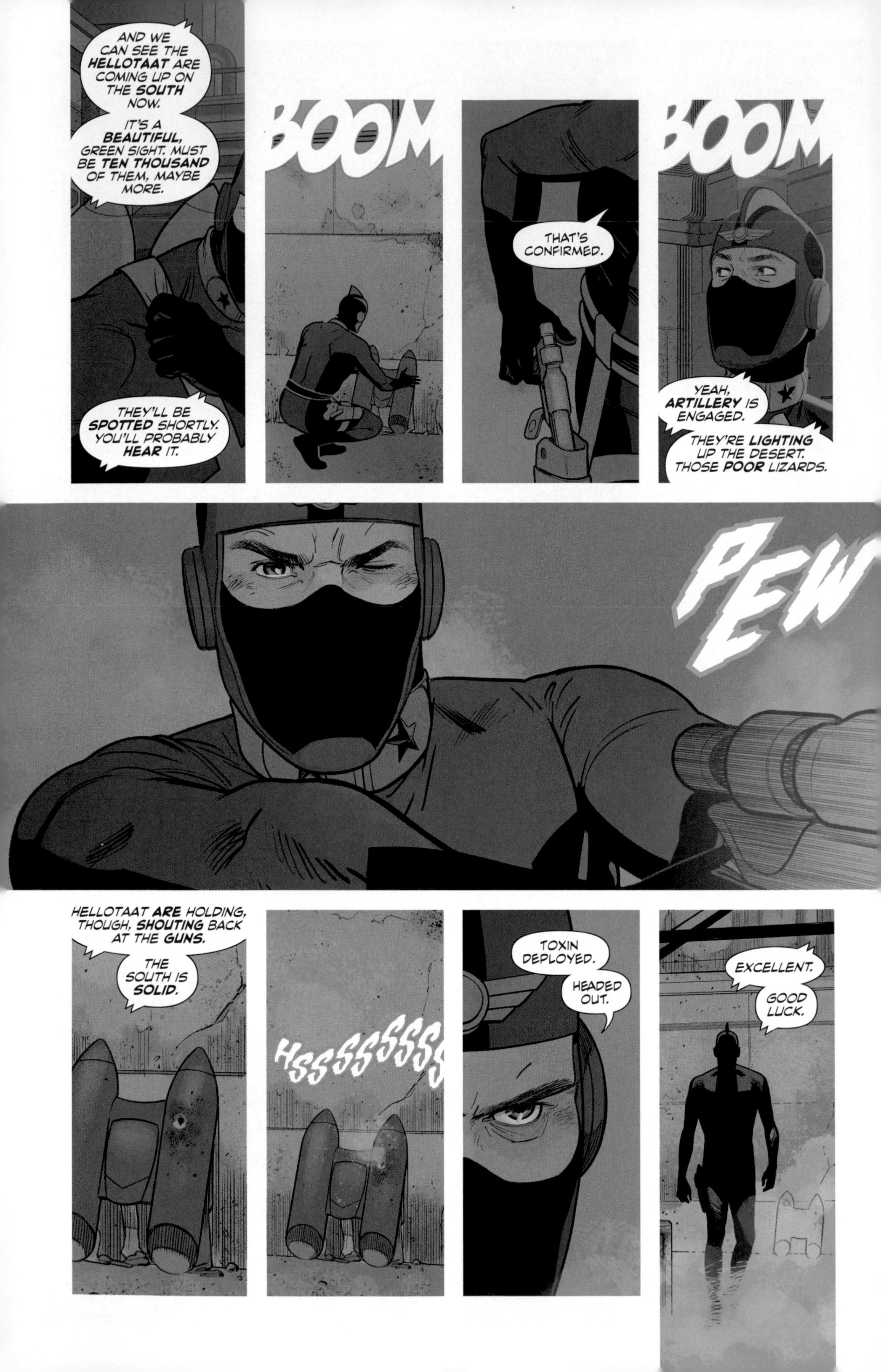
AND WE CAN SEE THE HELLOTAAT ARE COMING UP ON THE SOUTH NOW.
IT'S A BEAUTIFUL, GREEN SIGHT. MUST BE TEN THOUSAND OF THEM, MAYBE MORE.
THEY'LL BE SPOTTED SHORTLY. YOU'LL PROBABLY HEAR IT.
BOOM
THAT'S CONFIRMED.
BOOM
YEAH, ARTILLERY IS ENGAGED.
THEY'RE LIGHTING UP THE DESERT. THOSE POOR LIZARDS.
PEW
HELLOTAAT ARE HOLDING, THOUGH, SHOUTING BACK AT THE GUNS.
THE SOUTH IS SOLID.
HSSSSSSSS
TOXIN DEPLOYED.
HEADED OUT.
EXCELLENT.
GOOD LUCK.

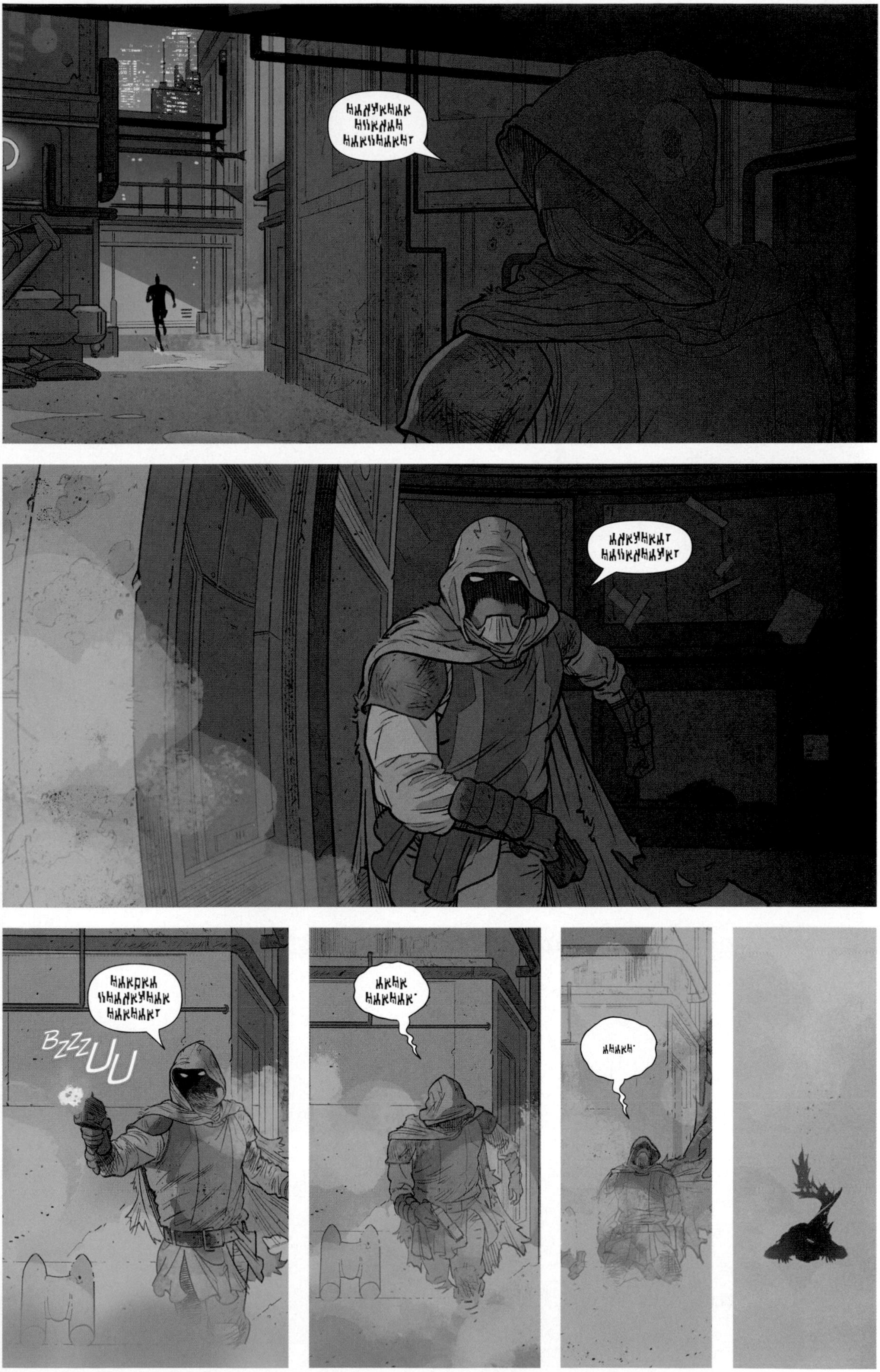
BZZZUU

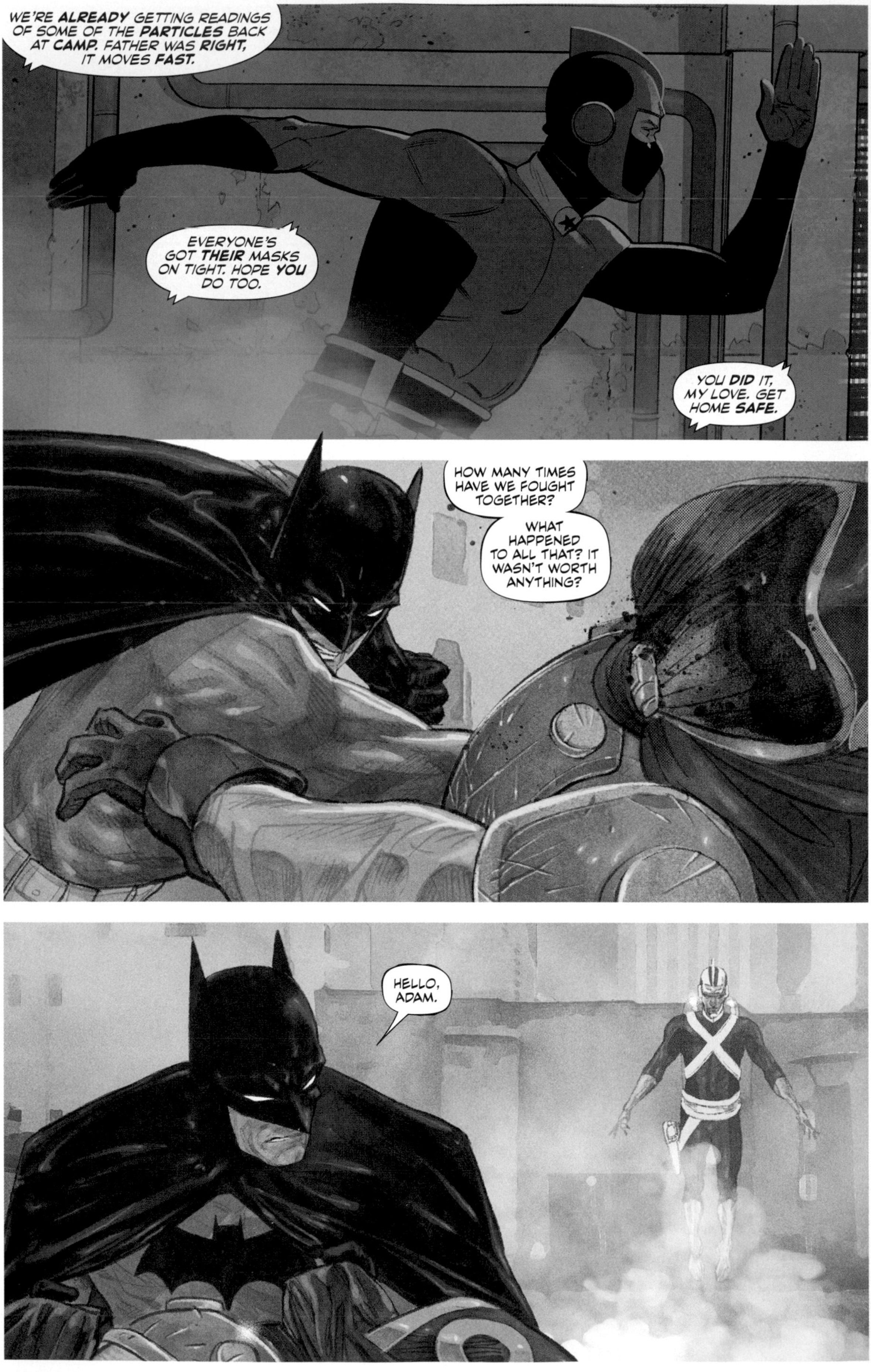
WE'RE **ALREADY** GETTING READINGS OF SOME OF THE **PARTICLES** BACK AT **CAMP.** FATHER WAS **RIGHT,** IT MOVES **FAST.**
EVERYONE'S GOT **THEIR** MASKS ON TIGHT. HOPE **YOU** DO TOO.
YOU **DID** IT, MY LOVE. GET HOME **SAFE.**
HOW MANY TIMES HAVE WE FOUGHT TOGETHER?
WHAT HAPPENED TO ALL THAT? IT WASN'T WORTH ANYTHING?
HELLO, ADAM.

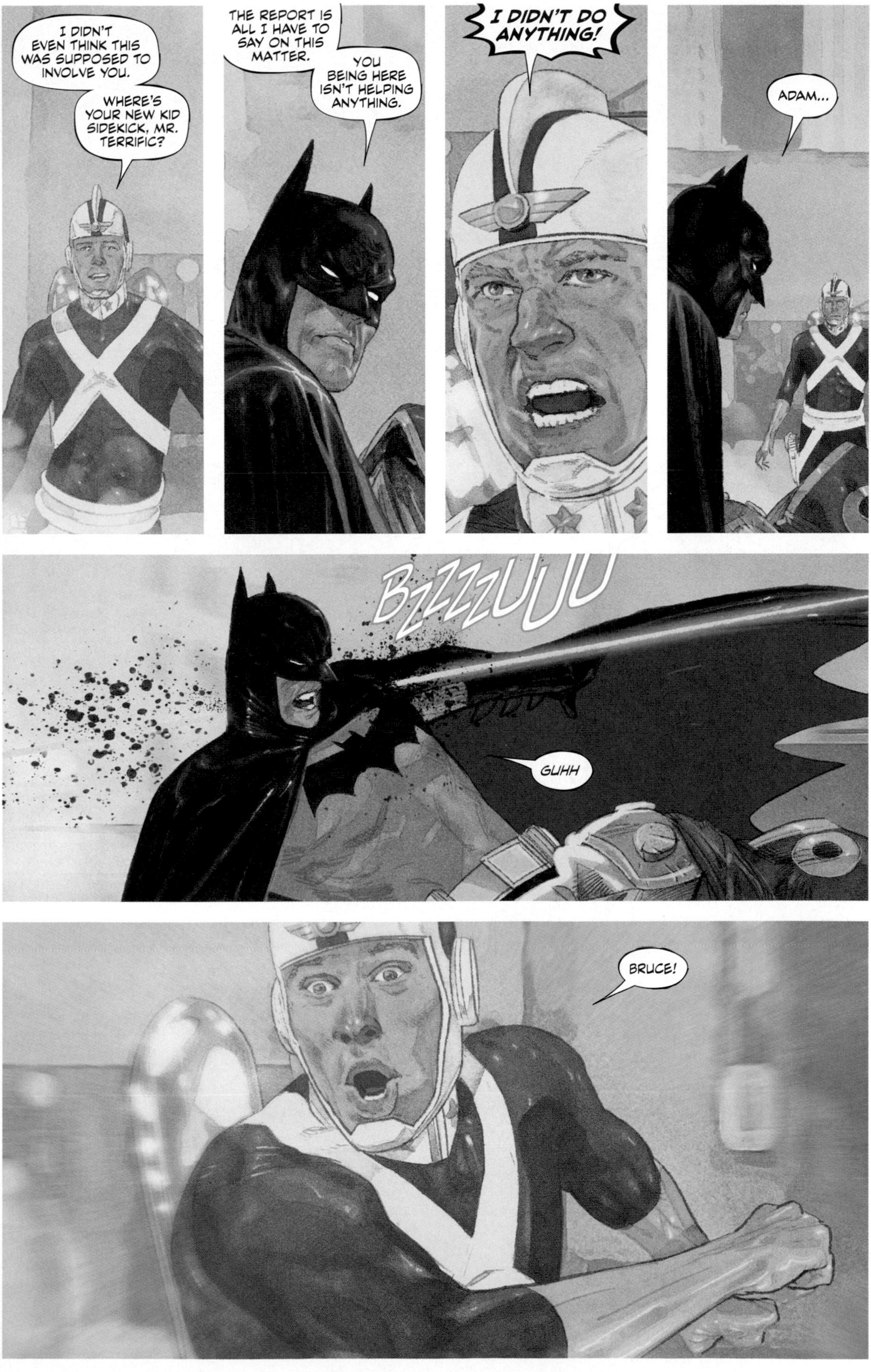
I DIDN'T EVEN THINK THIS WAS SUPPOSED TO INVOLVE YOU.
WHERE'S YOUR NEW KID SIDEKICK, MR. TERRIFIC?
THE REPORT IS ALL I HAVE TO SAY ON THIS MATTER.
YOU BEING HERE ISN'T HELPING ANYTHING.
I DIDN'T DO ANYTHING!
ADAM...
BZZZZUUU
GUHH
BRUCE!

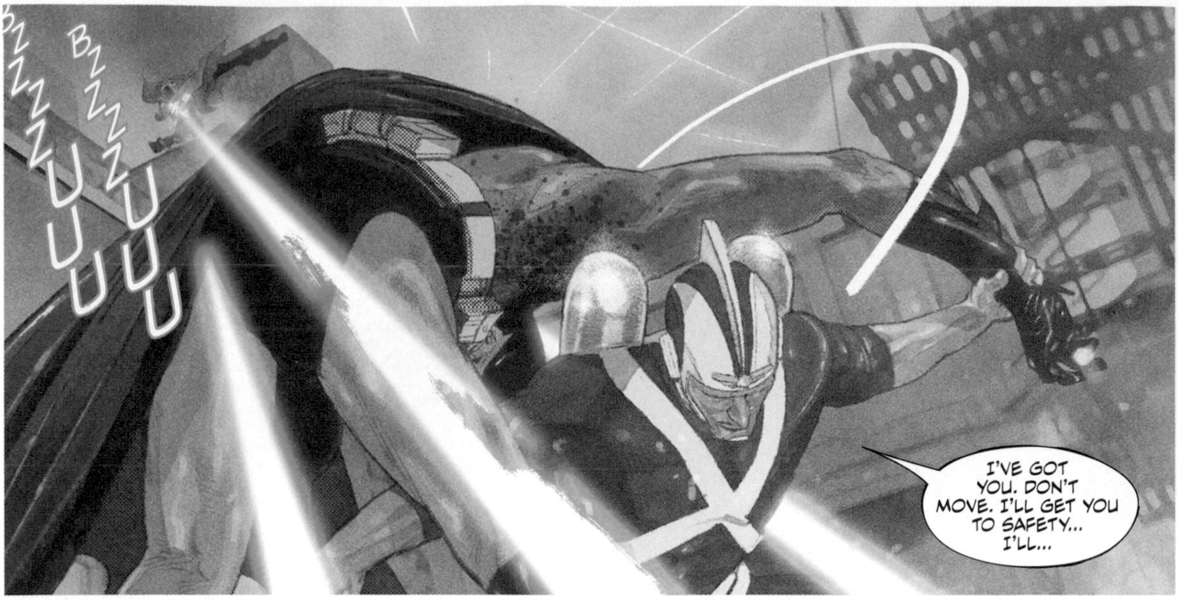
BZZZZUUUU
BZZZZUUUU
I'VE GOT YOU. DON'T MOVE. I'LL GET YOU TO SAFETY... I'LL...

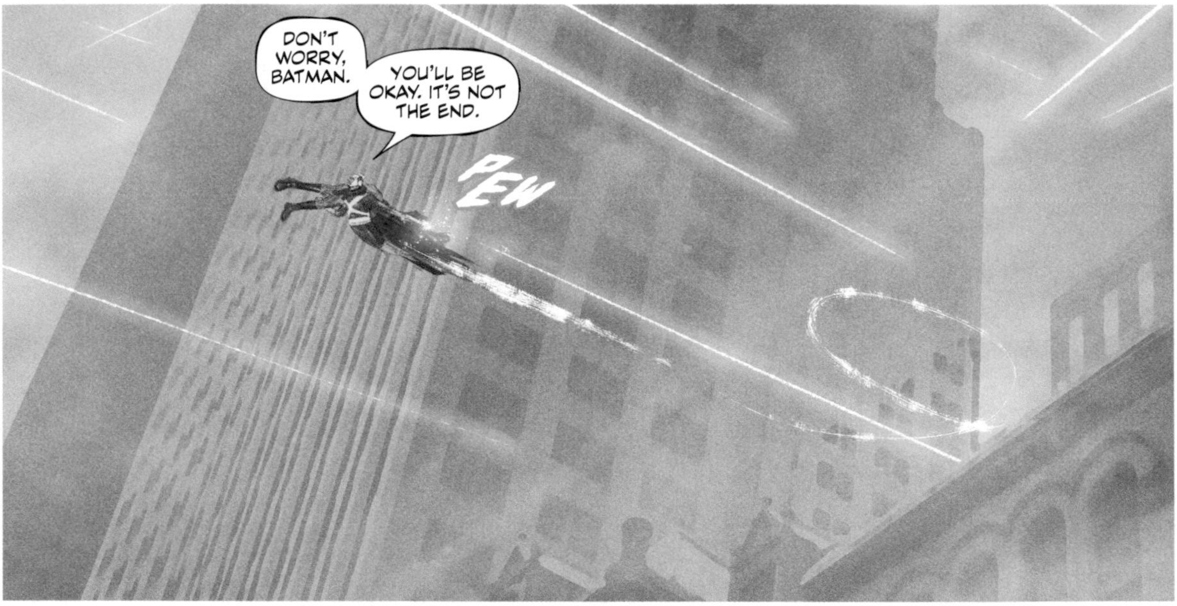
DON'T WORRY, BATMAN.
YOU'LL BE OKAY. IT'S NOT THE END.
PEW

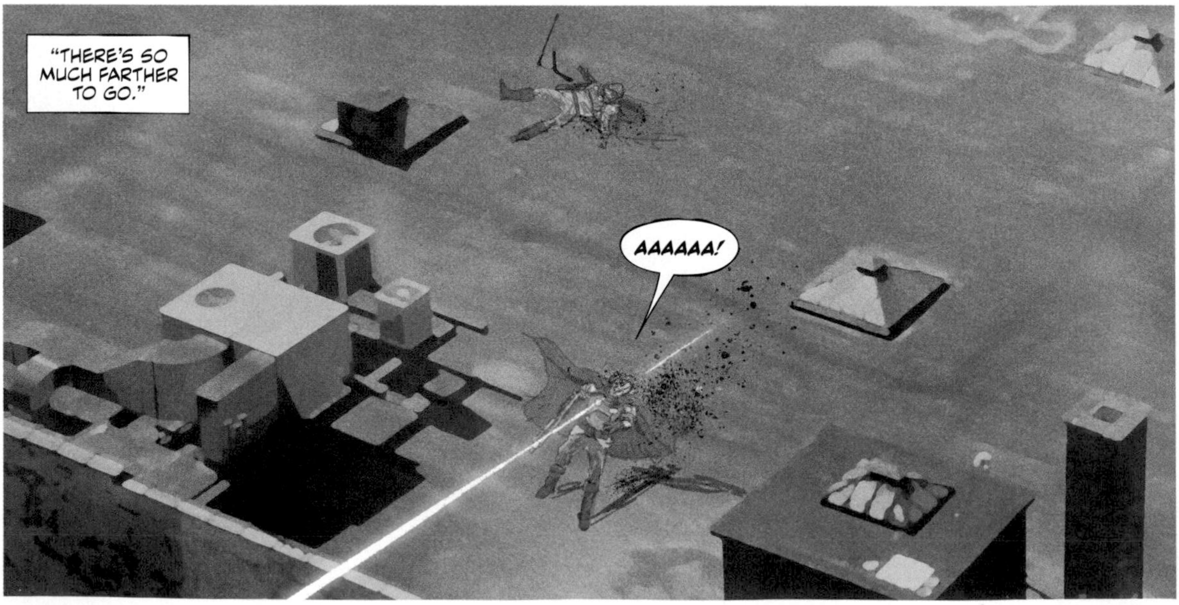
"THERE'S SO MUCH FARTHER TO GO."
AAAAAA!

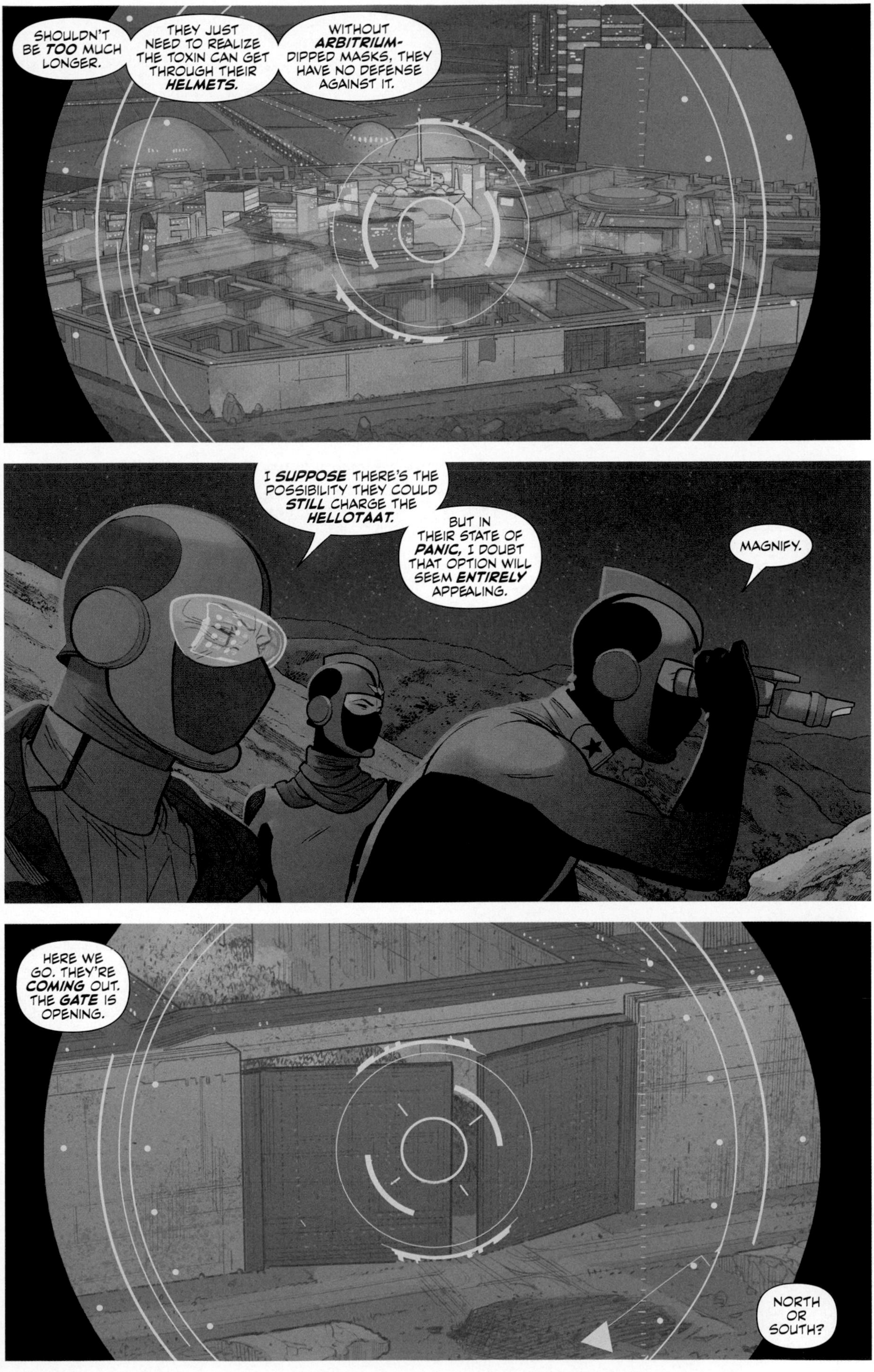
SHOULDN'T BE TOO MUCH LONGER.
THEY JUST NEED TO REALIZE THE TOXIN CAN GET THROUGH THEIR HELMETS.
WITHOUT ARBITRIUM-DIPPED MASKS, THEY HAVE NO DEFENSE AGAINST IT.
I SUPPOSE THERE'S THE POSSIBILITY THEY COULD STILL CHARGE THE HELLOTAAT.
BUT IN THEIR STATE OF PANIC, I DOUBT THAT OPTION WILL SEEM ENTIRELY APPEALING.
MAGNIFY.
HERE WE GO. THEY'RE COMING OUT. THE GATE IS OPENING.
NORTH OR SOUTH?

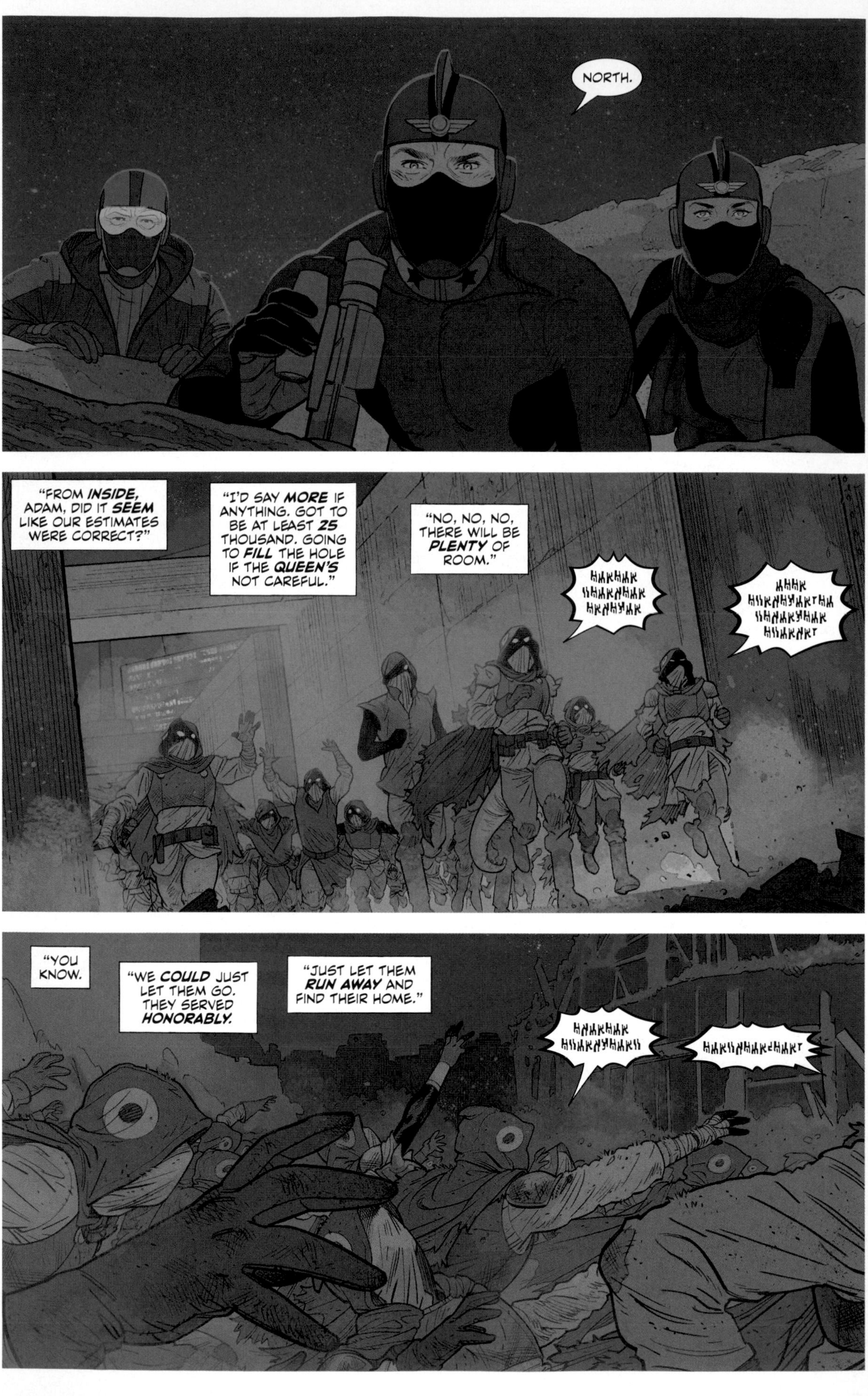
NORTH.
"FROM INSIDE, ADAM, DID IT SEEM LIKE OUR ESTIMATES WERE CORRECT?"
"I'D SAY MORE IF ANYTHING. GOT TO BE AT LEAST 25 THOUSAND. GOING TO FILL THE HOLE IF THE QUEEN'S NOT CAREFUL."
"NO, NO, NO, THERE WILL BE PLENTY OF ROOM."
"YOU KNOW.
"WE COULD JUST LET THEM GO. THEY SERVED HONORABLY.
"JUST LET THEM RUN AWAY AND FIND THEIR HOME."

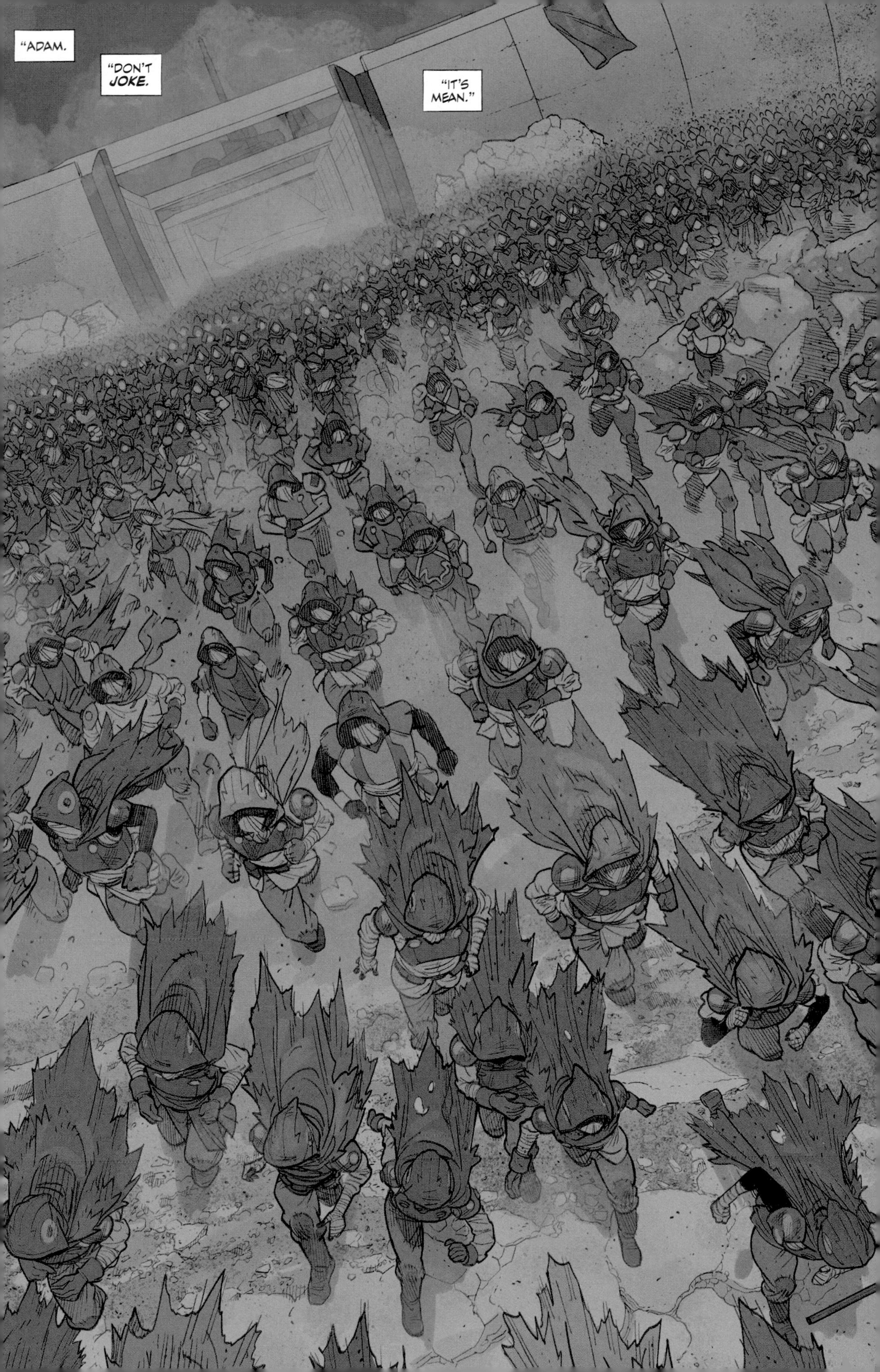
"ADAM.
"DON'T JOKE.
"IT'S MEAN."

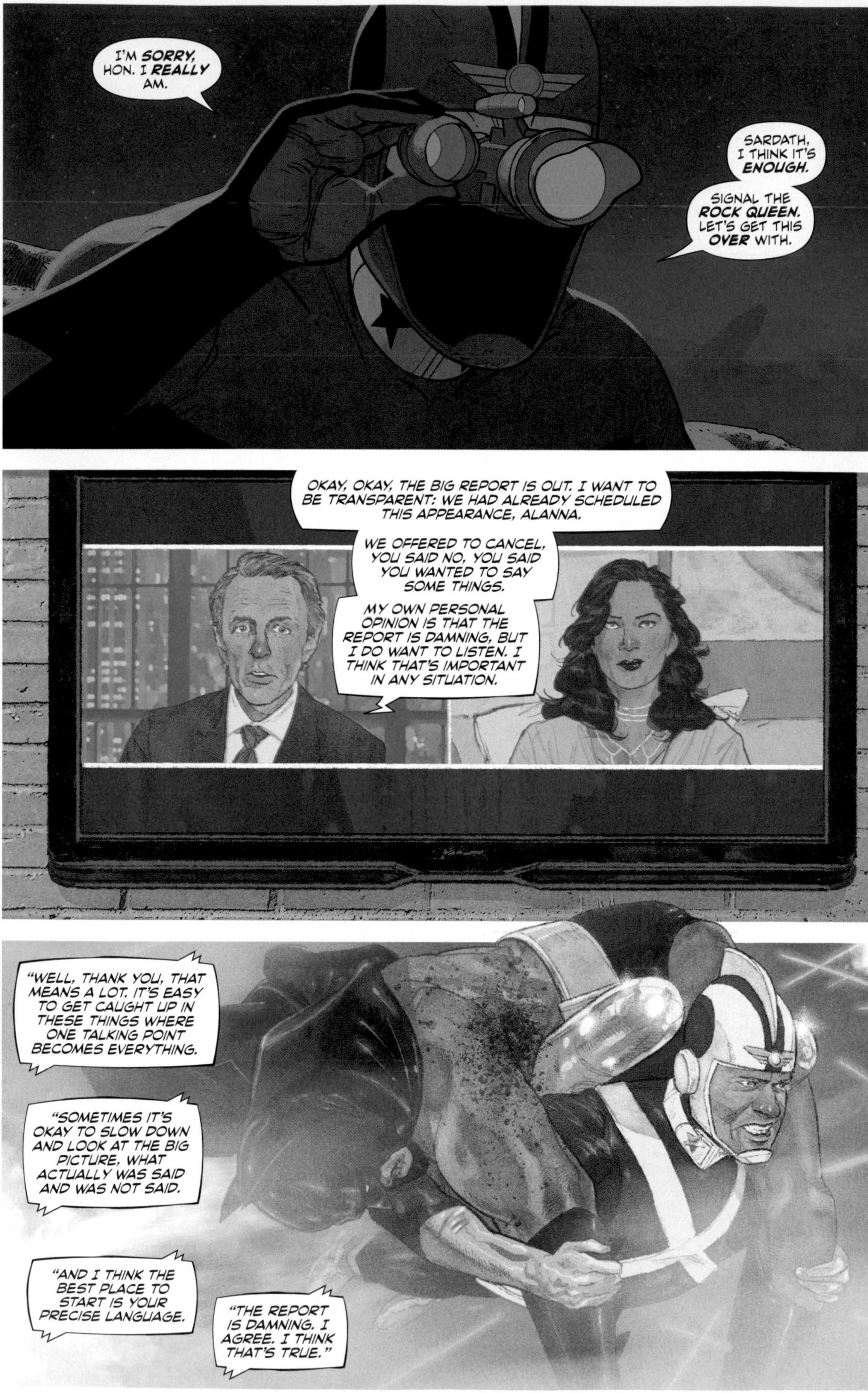
I'M SORRY, HON. I REALLY AM.
SARDATH, I THINK IT'S ENOUGH.
SIGNAL THE ROCK QUEEN. LET'S GET THIS OVER WITH.
OKAY, OKAY, THE BIG REPORT IS OUT. I WANT TO BE TRANSPARENT: WE HAD ALREADY SCHEDULED THIS APPEARANCE, ALANNA.
WE OFFERED TO CANCEL, YOU SAID NO, YOU SAID YOU WANTED TO SAY SOME THINGS.
MY OWN PERSONAL OPINION IS THAT THE REPORT IS DAMNING, BUT I DO WANT TO LISTEN. I THINK THAT'S IMPORTANT IN ANY SITUATION.
"WELL, THANK YOU, THAT MEANS A LOT. IT'S EASY TO GET CAUGHT UP IN THESE THINGS WHERE ONE TALKING POINT BECOMES EVERYTHING.
"SOMETIMES IT'S OKAY TO SLOW DOWN AND LOOK AT THE BIG PICTURE, WHAT ACTUALLY WAS SAID AND WAS NOT SAID.
"AND I THINK THE BEST PLACE TO START IS YOUR PRECISE LANGUAGE.
"THE REPORT IS DAMNING. I AGREE. I THINK THAT'S TRUE."

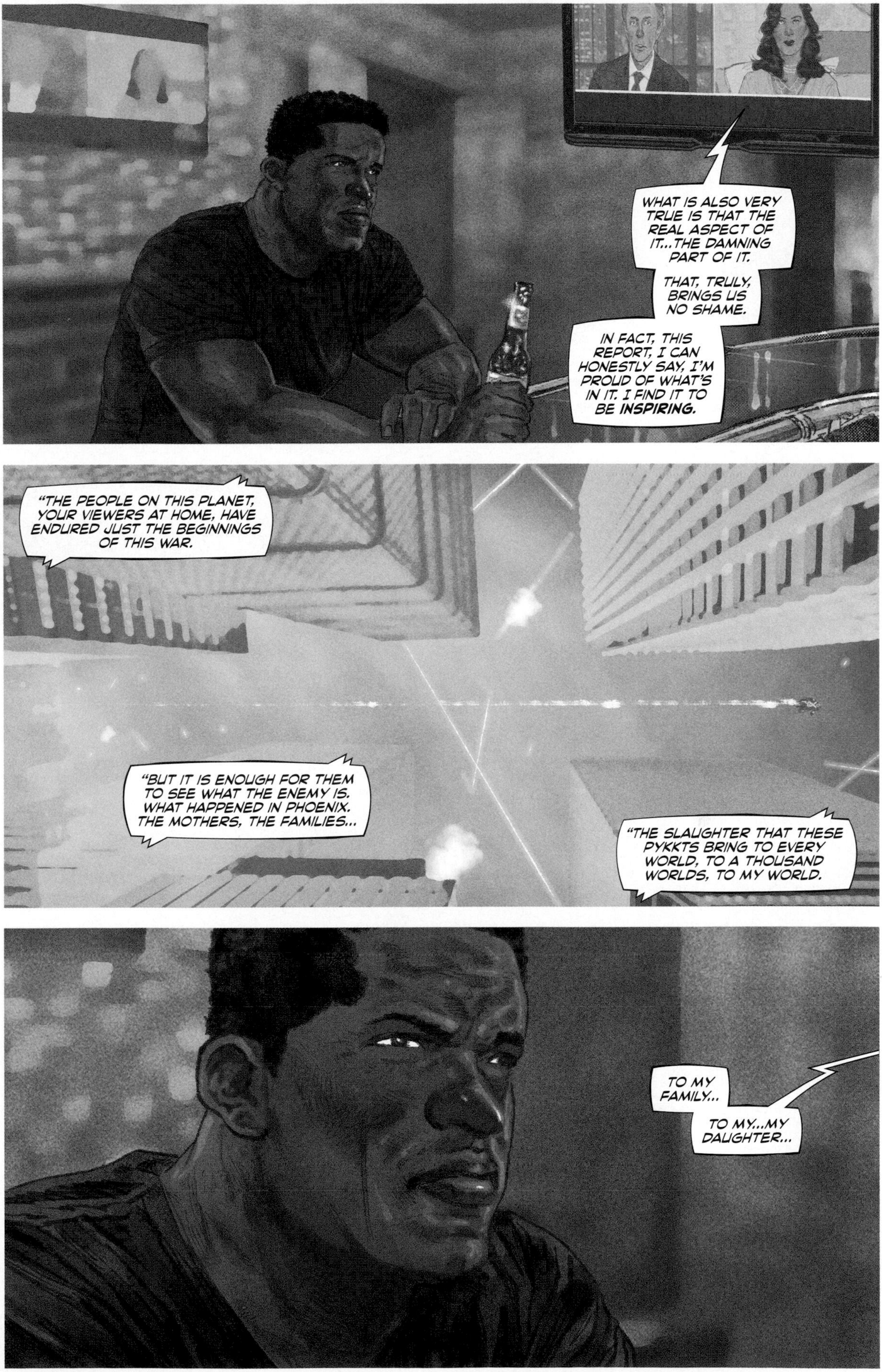
WHAT IS ALSO VERY TRUE IS THAT THE REAL ASPECT OF IT...THE DAMNING PART OF IT.
THAT, TRULY, BRINGS US NO SHAME.
IN FACT, THIS REPORT, I CAN HONESTLY SAY, I'M PROUD OF WHAT'S IN IT. I FIND IT TO BE INSPIRING.
"THE PEOPLE ON THIS PLANET, YOUR VIEWERS AT HOME, HAVE ENDURED JUST THE BEGINNINGS OF THIS WAR.
"BUT IT IS ENOUGH FOR THEM TO SEE WHAT THE ENEMY IS. WHAT HAPPENED IN PHOENIX. THE MOTHERS, THE FAMILIES...
"THE SLAUGHTER THAT THESE PYKKTS BRING TO EVERY WORLD, TO A THOUSAND WORLDS, TO MY WORLD.
TO MY FAMILY...
TO MY...MY DAUGHTER...

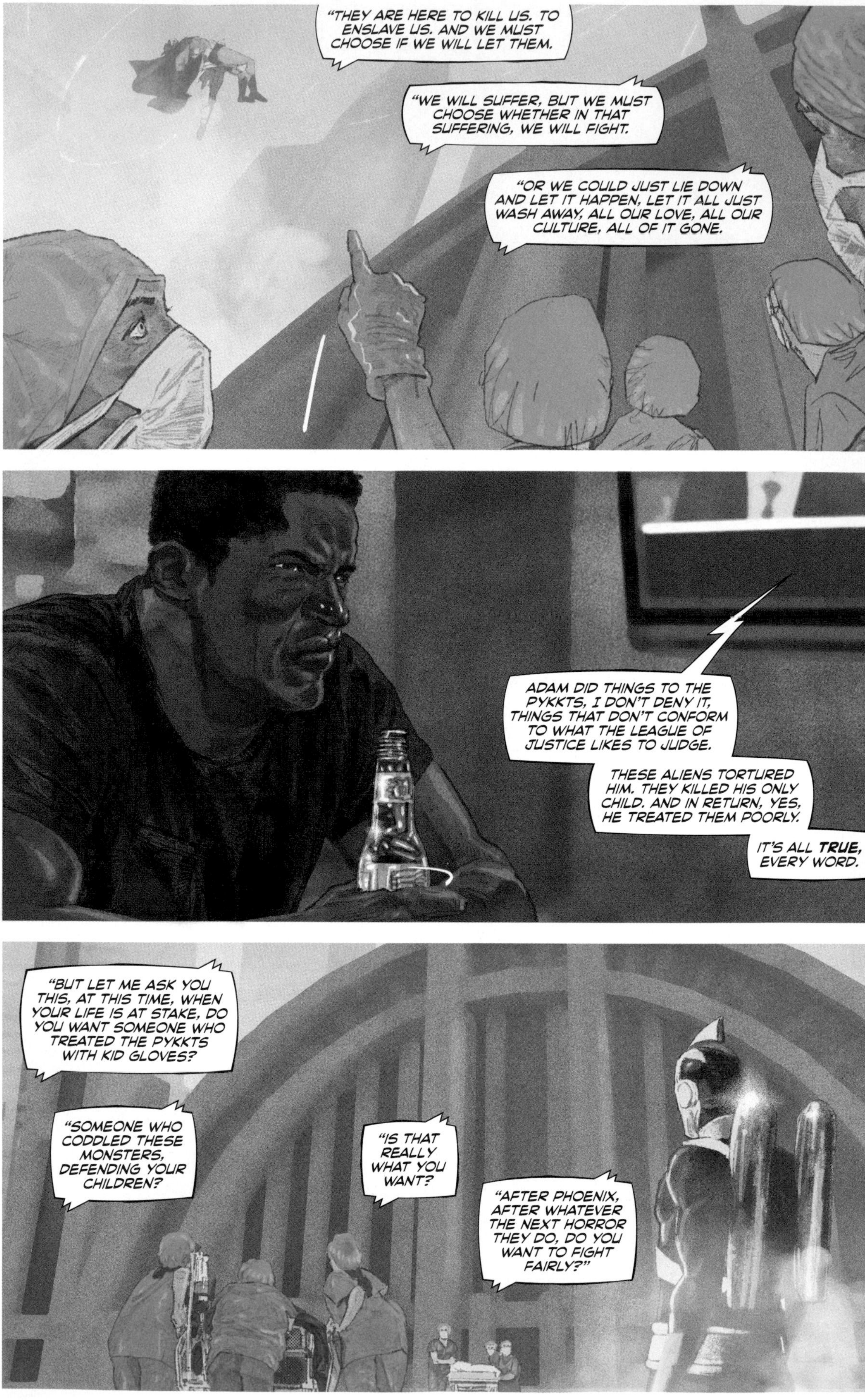
"THEY ARE HERE TO KILL US. TO ENSLAVE US. AND WE MUST CHOOSE IF WE WILL LET THEM.
"WE WILL SUFFER, BUT WE MUST CHOOSE WHETHER IN THAT SUFFERING, WE WILL FIGHT.
"OR WE COULD JUST LIE DOWN AND LET IT HAPPEN, LET IT ALL JUST WASH AWAY, ALL OUR LOVE, ALL OUR CULTURE, ALL OF IT GONE.
ADAM DID THINGS TO THE PYKKTS, I DON'T DENY IT, THINGS THAT DON'T CONFORM TO WHAT THE LEAGUE OF JUSTICE LIKES TO JUDGE.
THESE ALIENS TORTURED HIM. THEY KILLED HIS ONLY CHILD. AND IN RETURN, YES, HE TREATED THEM POORLY.
IT'S ALL **TRUE,** EVERY WORD.
"BUT LET ME ASK YOU THIS, AT THIS TIME, WHEN YOUR LIFE IS AT STAKE, DO YOU WANT SOMEONE WHO TREATED THE PYKKTS WITH KID GLOVES?
"SOMEONE WHO CODDLED THESE MONSTERS, DEFENDING YOUR CHILDREN?
"IS THAT REALLY WHAT YOU WANT?
"AFTER PHOENIX, AFTER WHATEVER THE NEXT HORROR THEY DO, DO YOU WANT TO FIGHT FAIRLY?"

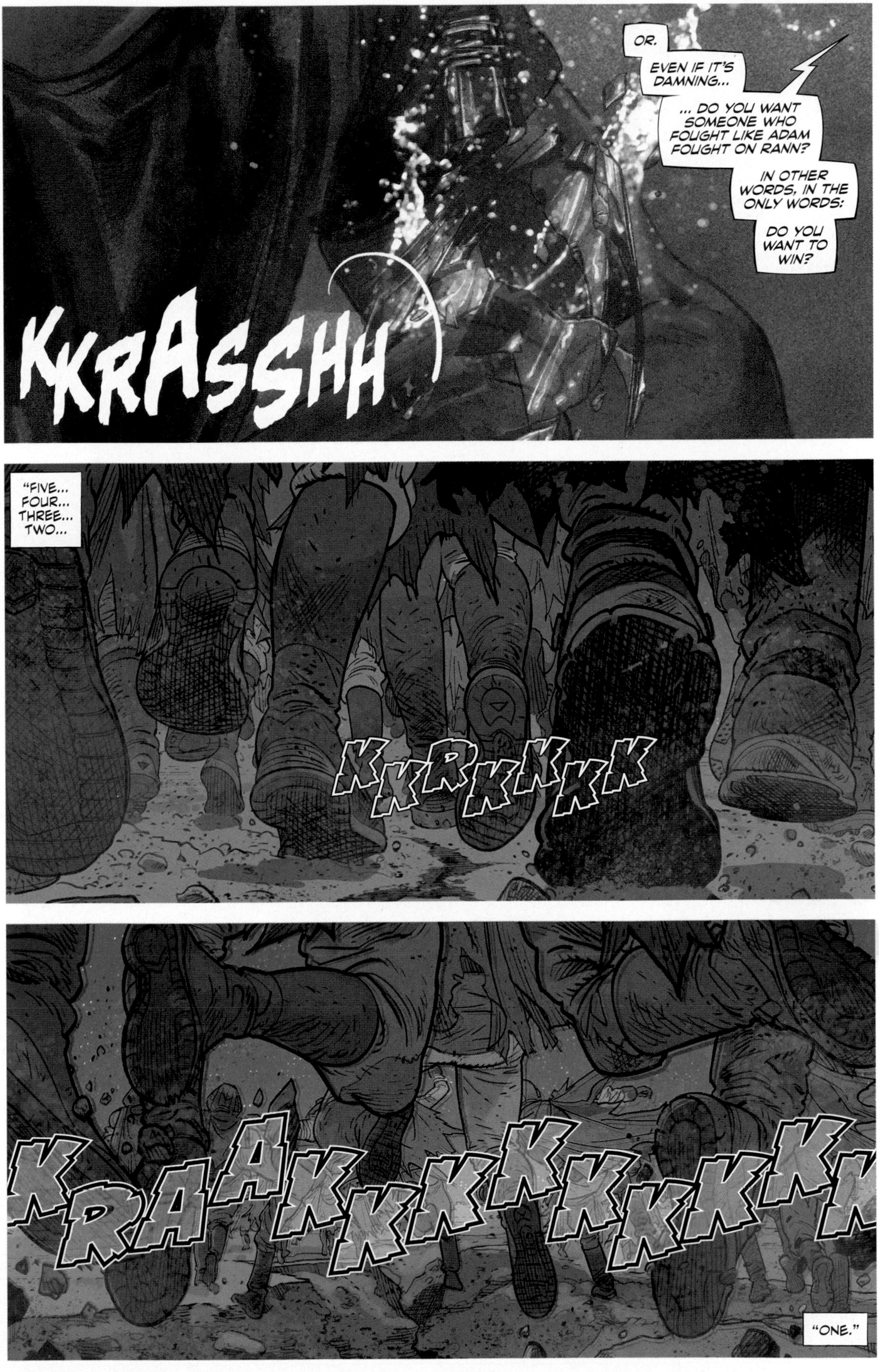
OR.
EVEN IF IT'S DAMNING...
... DO YOU WANT SOMEONE WHO FOUGHT LIKE ADAM FOUGHT ON RANN?
IN OTHER WORDS, IN THE ONLY WORDS:
DO YOU WANT TO WIN?
KKRASSHH
"FIVE... FOUR... THREE... TWO...
KKRKKKK
KRAAKKKKKKKKK
"ONE."

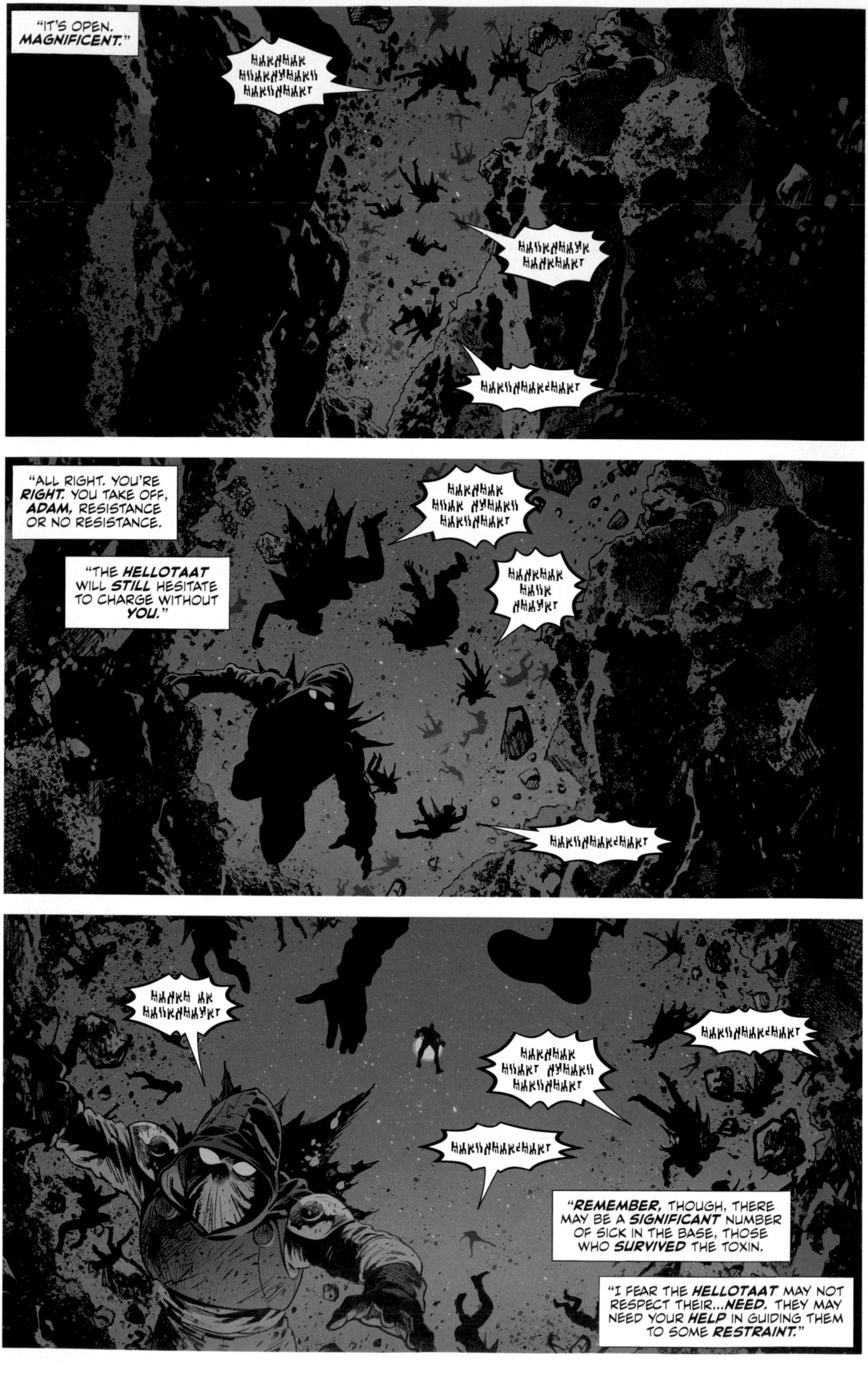
"IT'S OPEN. MAGNIFICENT."
"ALL RIGHT. YOU'RE RIGHT. YOU TAKE OFF, ADAM, RESISTANCE OR NO RESISTANCE.
"THE HELLOTAAT WILL STILL HESITATE TO CHARGE WITHOUT YOU."
"REMEMBER, THOUGH, THERE MAY BE A SIGNIFICANT NUMBER OF SICK IN THE BASE, THOSE WHO SURVIVED THE TOXIN.
"I FEAR THE HELLOTAAT MAY NOT RESPECT THEIR...NEED. THEY MAY NEED YOUR HELP IN GUIDING THEM TO SOME RESTRAINT."

"DON'T WORRY, SARDATH."

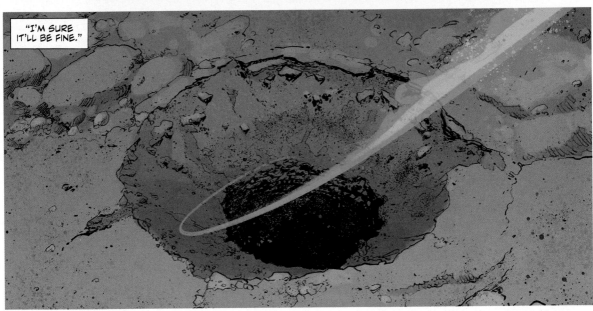

"I'M SURE IT'LL BE FINE."

LOOK, HE MADE MISTAKES. THAT SEEMS CLEAR. THEY WERE BAD MISTAKES.

NO ONE IS DENYING THAT.

THEY WERE.

THEY'VE SAID THE TRUTH, THEY STUCK BY THE TRUTH.

EXACTLY.

LIVE ELLIE & BRYAN

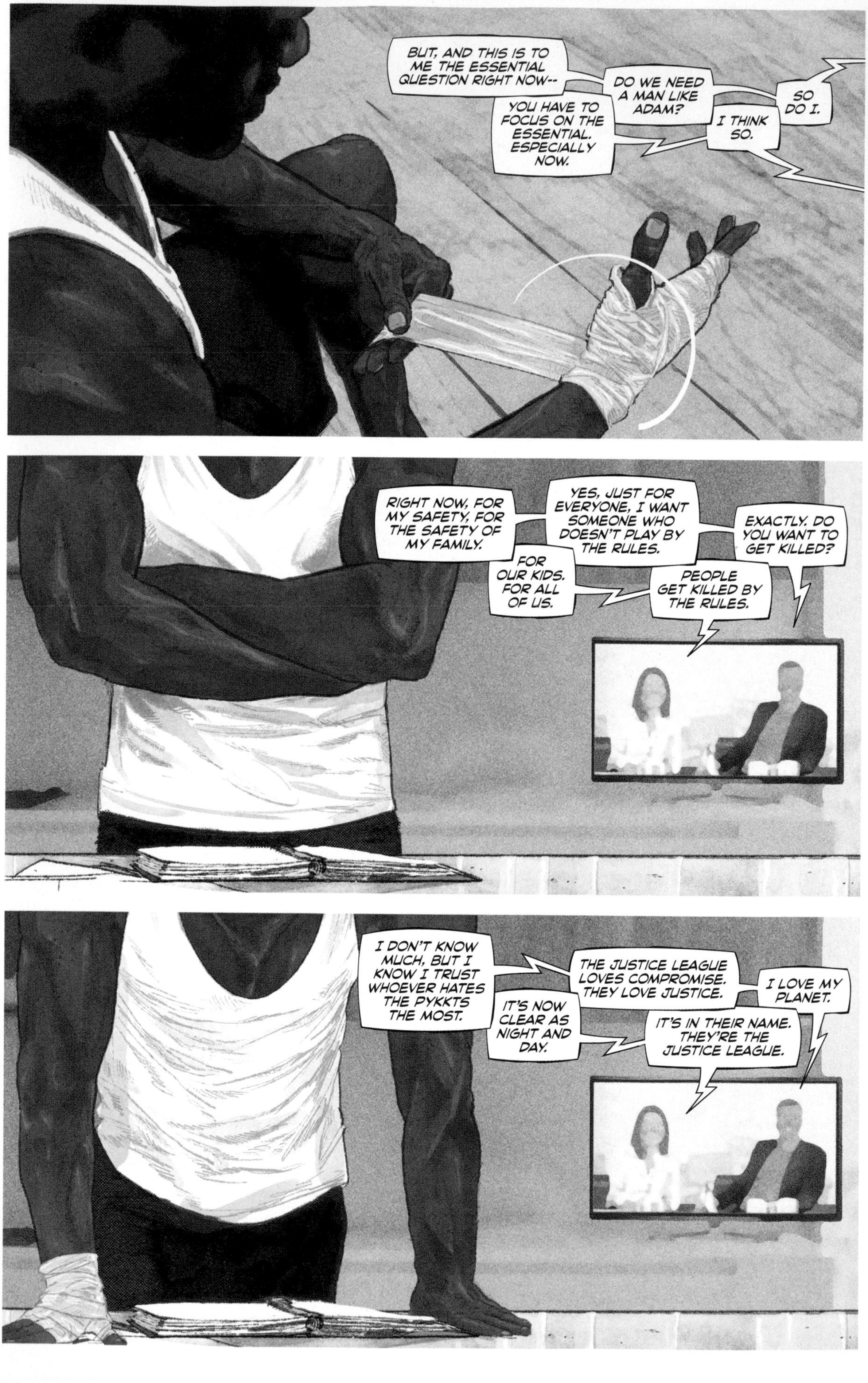
BUT, AND THIS IS TO ME THE ESSENTIAL QUESTION RIGHT NOW--
DO WE NEED A MAN LIKE ADAM?
SO DO I.
YOU HAVE TO FOCUS ON THE ESSENTIAL. ESPECIALLY NOW.
I THINK SO.
RIGHT NOW, FOR MY SAFETY, FOR THE SAFETY OF MY FAMILY.
YES, JUST FOR EVERYONE, I WANT SOMEONE WHO DOESN'T PLAY BY THE RULES.
EXACTLY. DO YOU WANT TO GET KILLED?
FOR OUR KIDS. FOR ALL OF US.
PEOPLE GET KILLED BY THE RULES.
I DON'T KNOW MUCH, BUT I KNOW I TRUST WHOEVER HATES THE PYKKTS THE MOST.
THE JUSTICE LEAGUE LOVES COMPROMISE. THEY LOVE JUSTICE.
I LOVE MY PLANET.
IT'S NOW CLEAR AS NIGHT AND DAY.
IT'S IN THEIR NAME. THEY'RE THE JUSTICE LEAGUE.

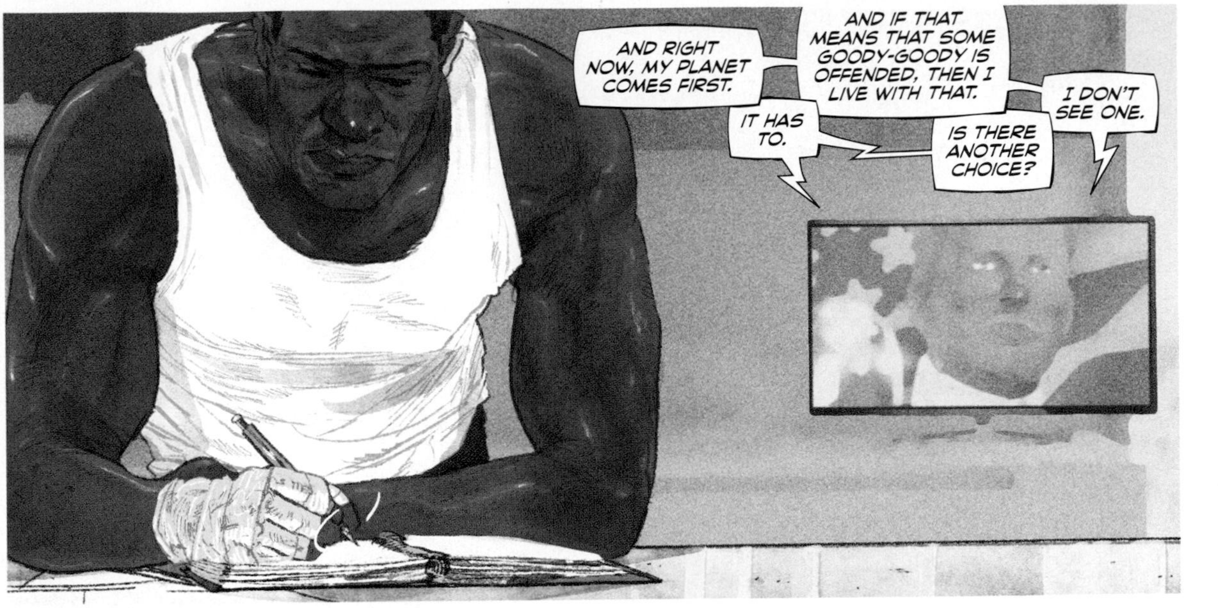
AND RIGHT NOW, MY PLANET COMES FIRST.
IT HAS TO.
AND IF THAT MEANS THAT SOME GOODY-GOODY IS OFFENDED, THEN I LIVE WITH THAT.
IS THERE ANOTHER CHOICE?
I DON'T SEE ONE.

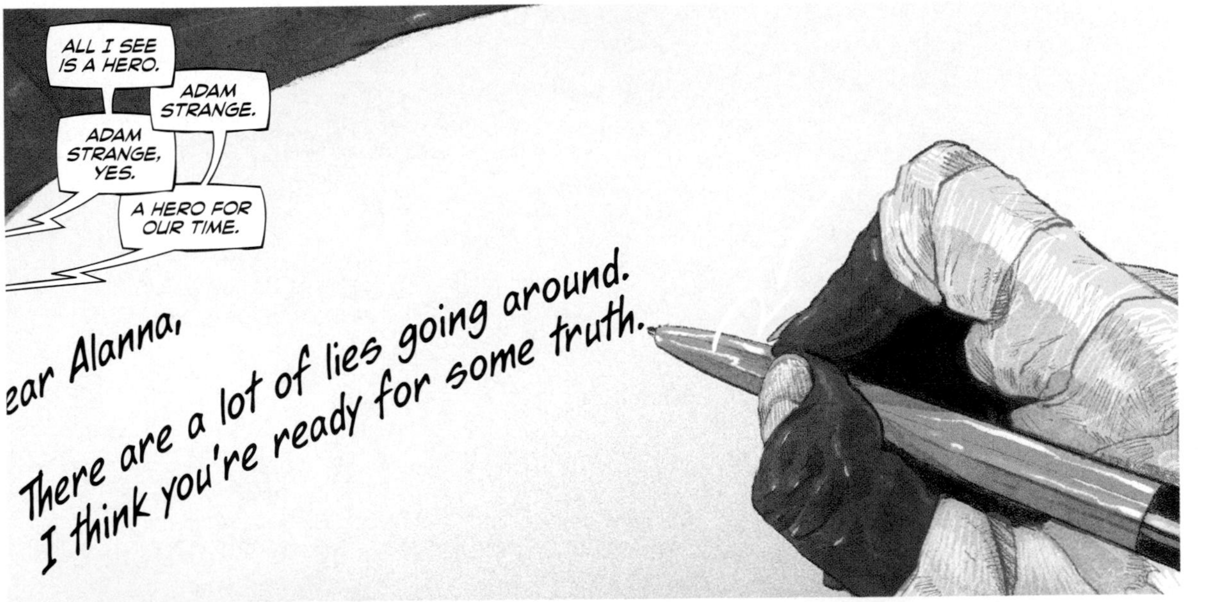
ALL I SEE IS A HERO.
ADAM STRANGE.
ADAM STRANGE, YES.
A HERO FOR OUR TIME.
ear Alanna,
There are a lot of lies going around.
I think you're ready for some truth.

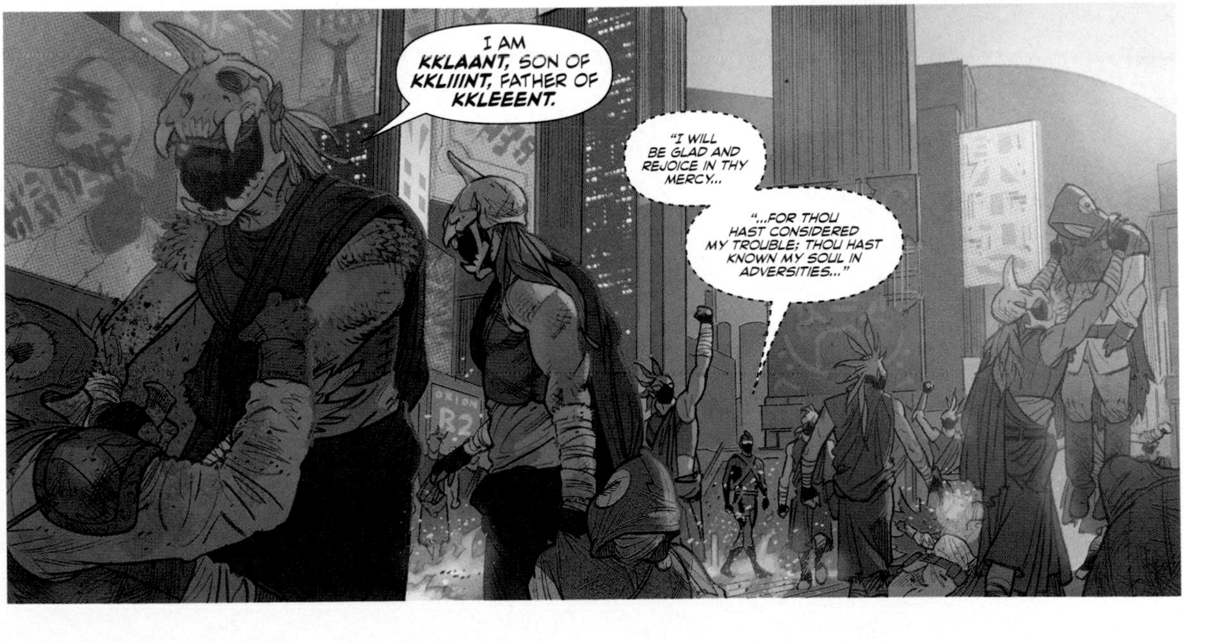
I AM KKLAANT, SON OF KKLIIINT, FATHER OF KKLEEENT.
"I WILL BE GLAD AND REJOICE IN THY MERCY...
"...FOR THOU HAST CONSIDERED MY TROUBLE; THOU HAST KNOWN MY SOUL IN ADVERSITIES..."

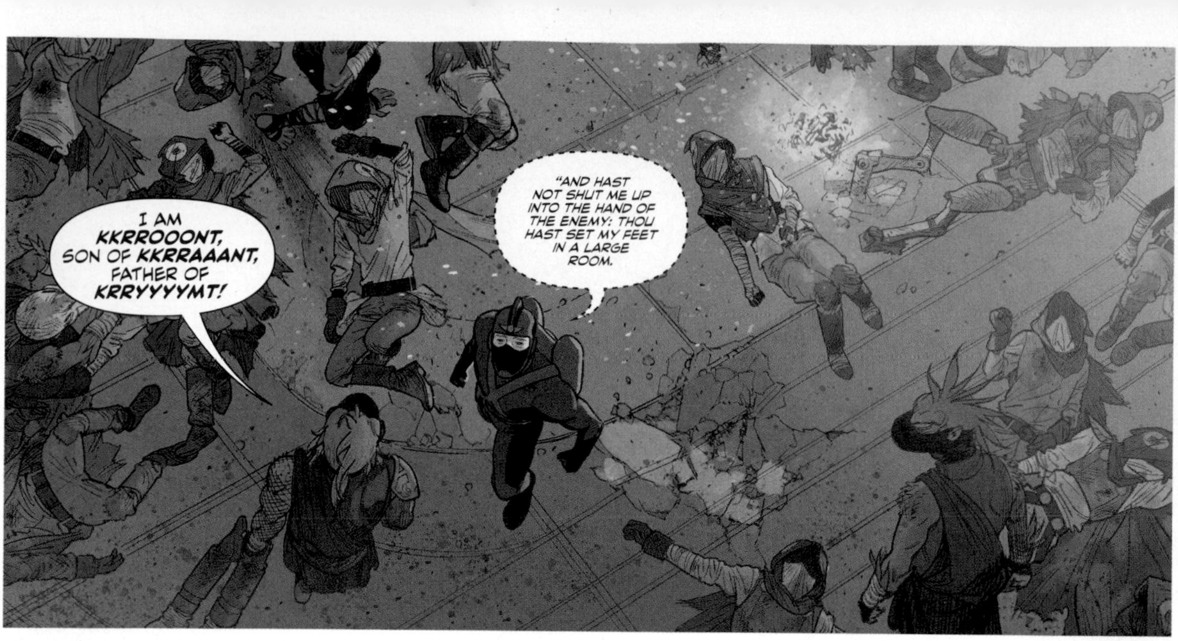
I AM KKRROOONT, SON OF KKRRAAANT, FATHER OF KRRYYYYMT!
"AND HAST NOT SHUT ME UP INTO THE HAND OF THE ENEMY: THOU HAST SET MY FEET IN A LARGE ROOM.

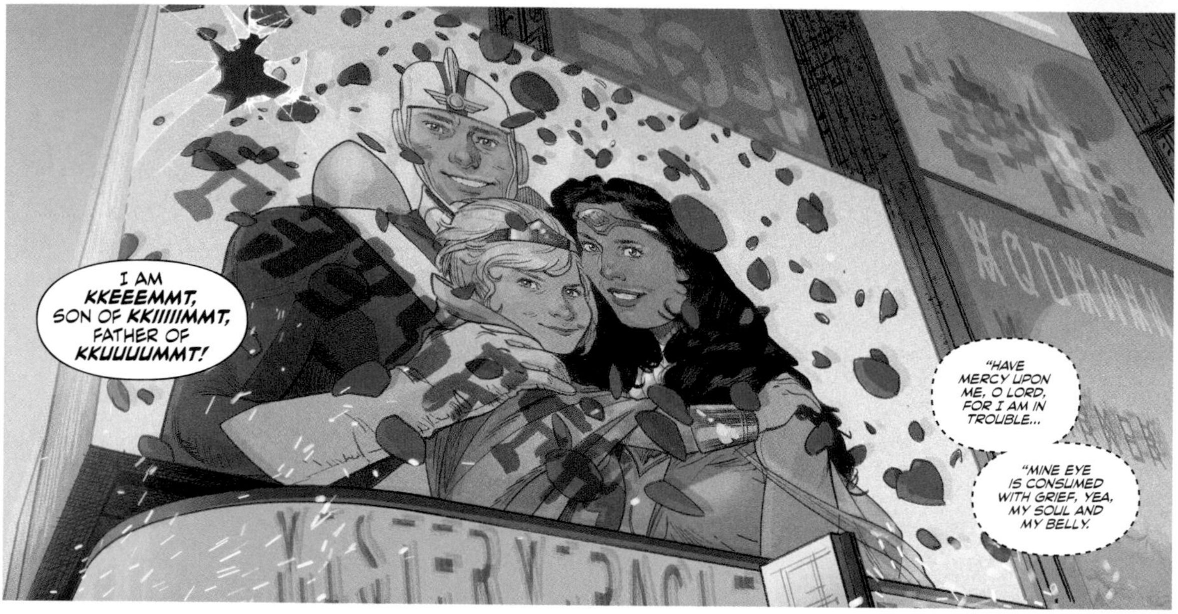
I AM KKEEEMMT, SON OF KKIIIIIMMT, FATHER OF KKUUUUUMMT!
"HAVE MERCY UPON ME, O LORD, FOR I AM IN TROUBLE...
"MINE EYE IS CONSUMED WITH GRIEF, YEA, MY SOUL AND MY BELLY.

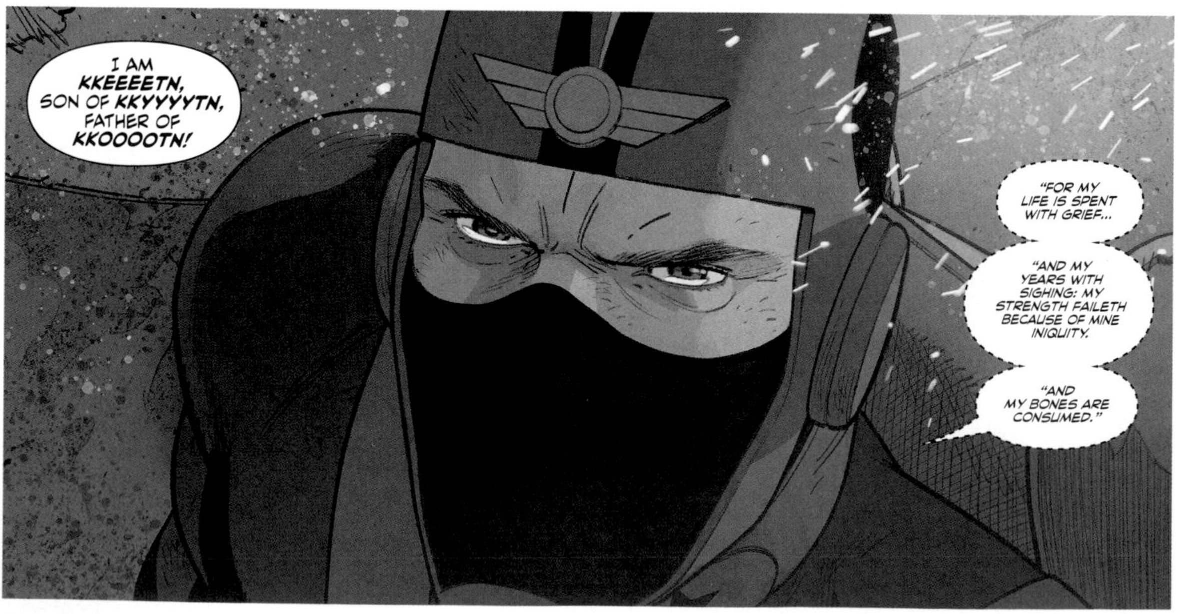
I AM KKEEEETN, SON OF KKYYYYTN, FATHER OF KKOOOOTN!
"FOR MY LIFE IS SPENT WITH GRIEF...
"AND MY YEARS WITH SIGHING: MY STRENGTH FAILETH BECAUSE OF MINE INIQUITY.
"AND MY BONES ARE CONSUMED."

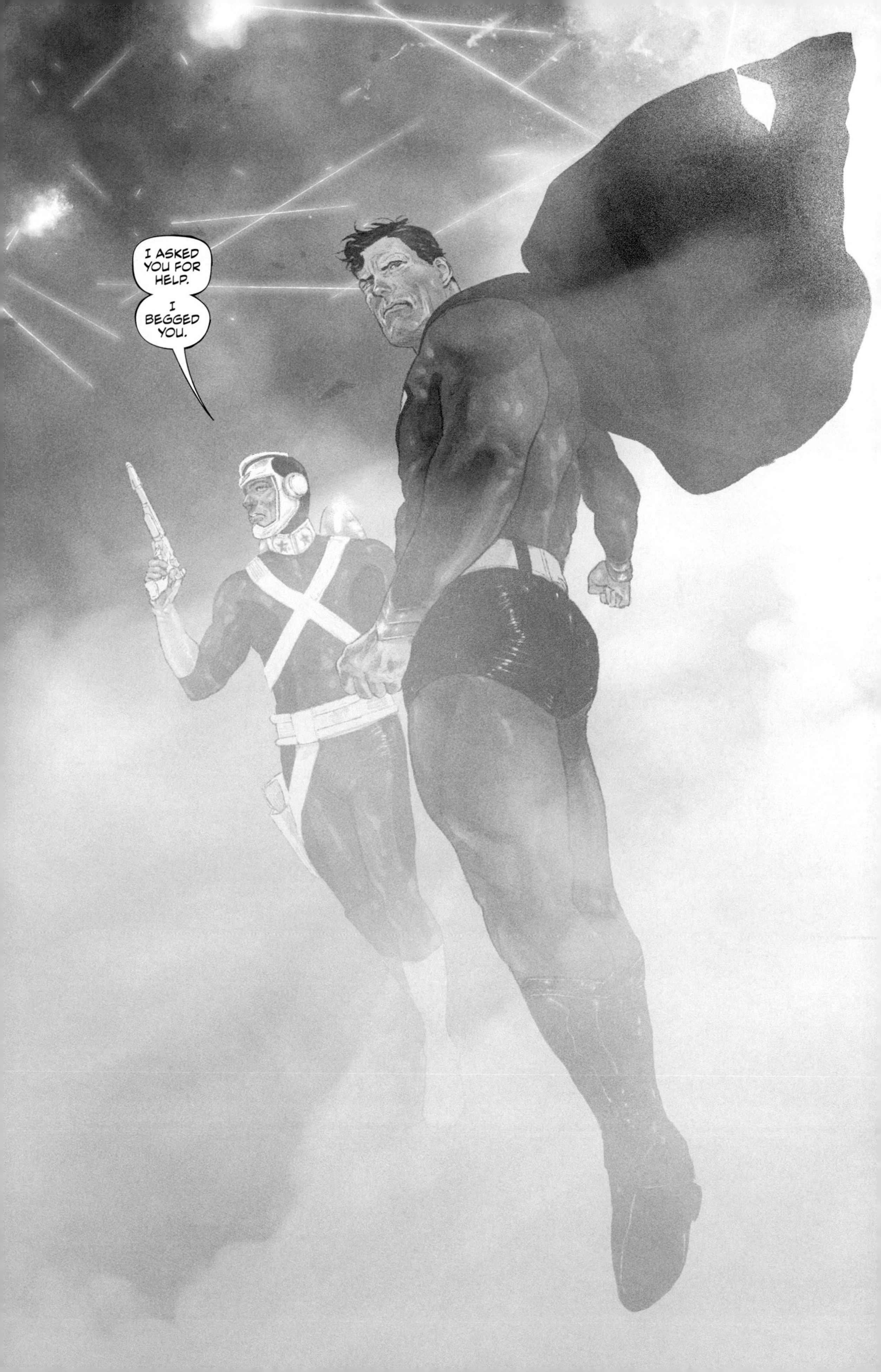
I ASKED YOU FOR HELP.
I BEGGED YOU.

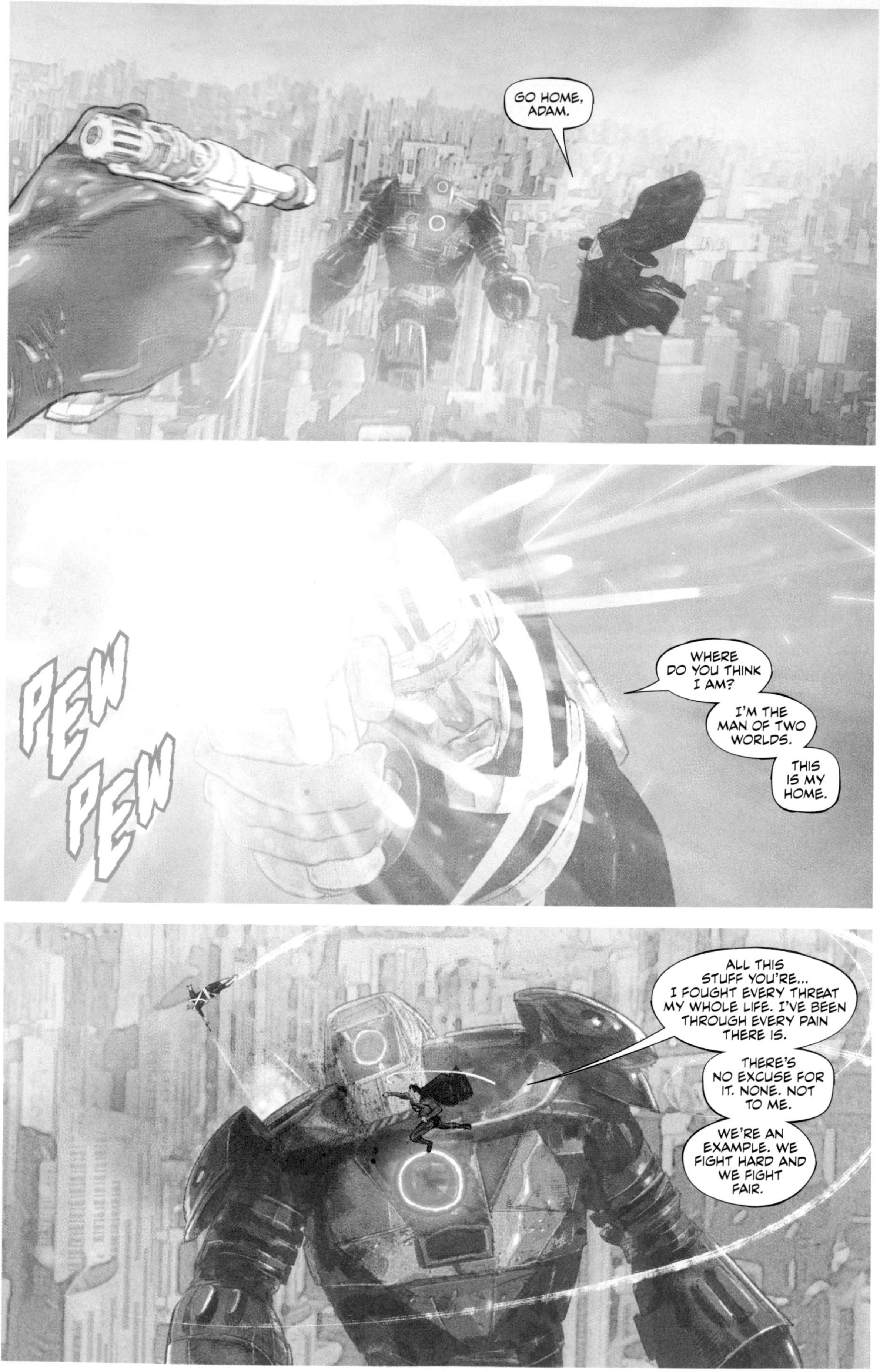

GO HOME, ADAM.
PEW PEW
WHERE DO YOU THINK I AM?
I'M THE MAN OF TWO WORLDS.
THIS IS MY HOME.
ALL THIS STUFF YOU'RE... I FOUGHT EVERY THREAT MY WHOLE LIFE. I'VE BEEN THROUGH EVERY PAIN THERE IS.
THERE'S NO EXCUSE FOR IT. NONE. NOT TO ME.
WE'RE AN EXAMPLE. WE FIGHT HARD AND WE FIGHT FAIR.

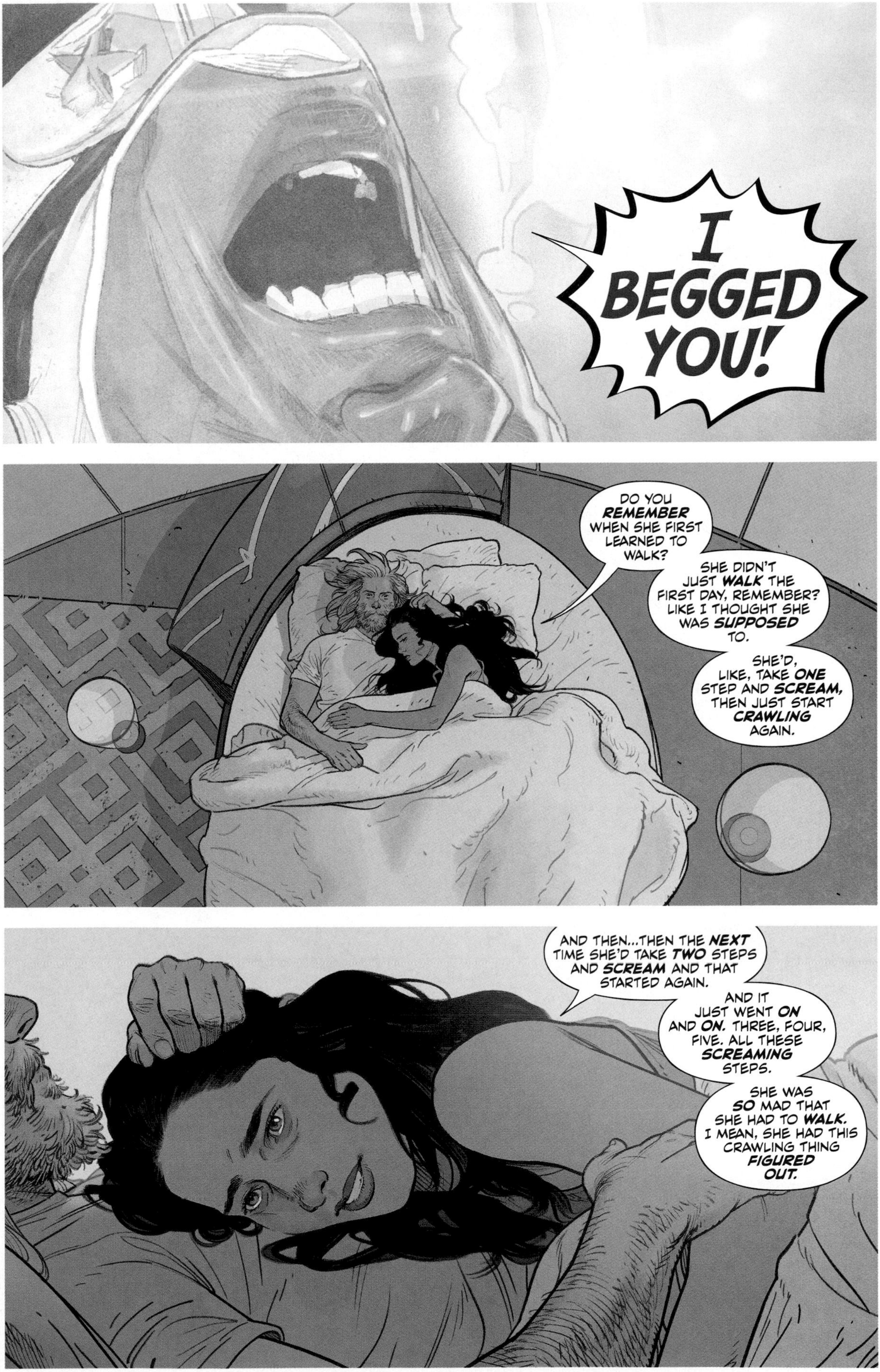
I BEGGED YOU!
DO YOU REMEMBER WHEN SHE FIRST LEARNED TO WALK?
SHE DIDN'T JUST WALK THE FIRST DAY, REMEMBER? LIKE I THOUGHT SHE WAS SUPPOSED TO.
SHE'D, LIKE, TAKE ONE STEP AND SCREAM, THEN JUST START CRAWLING AGAIN.
AND THEN...THEN THE NEXT TIME SHE'D TAKE TWO STEPS AND SCREAM AND THAT STARTED AGAIN.
AND IT JUST WENT ON AND ON. THREE, FOUR, FIVE. ALL THESE SCREAMING STEPS.
SHE WAS SO MAD THAT SHE HAD TO WALK. I MEAN, SHE HAD THIS CRAWLING THING FIGURED OUT.

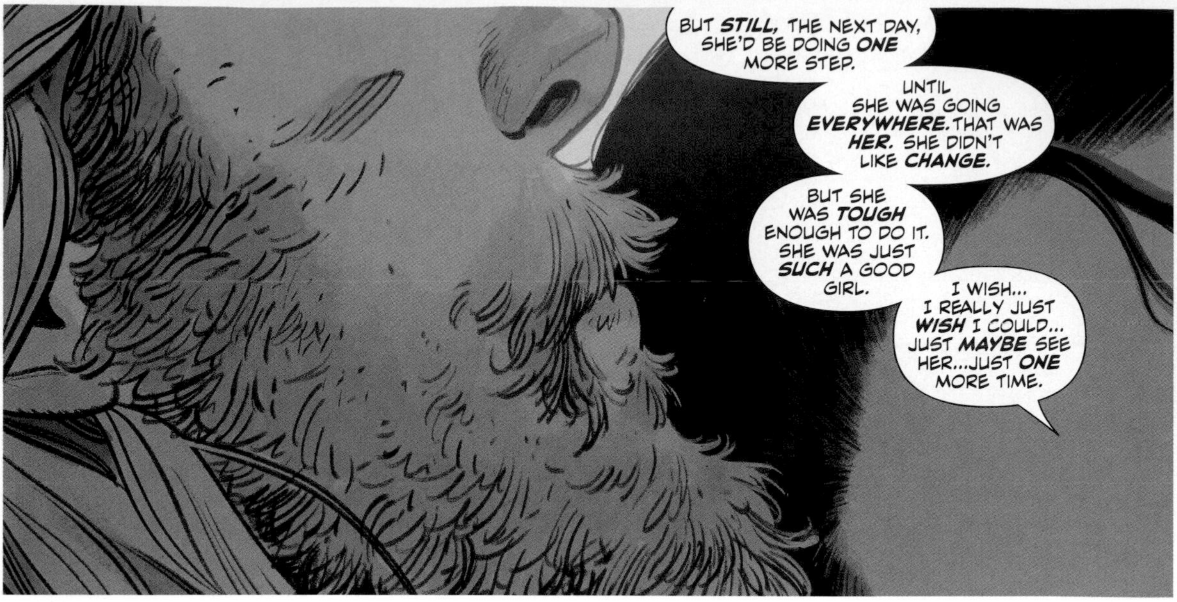
BUT STILL, THE NEXT DAY, SHE'D BE DOING ONE MORE STEP.
UNTIL SHE WAS GOING EVERYWHERE. THAT WAS HER. SHE DIDN'T LIKE CHANGE.
BUT SHE WAS TOUGH ENOUGH TO DO IT. SHE WAS JUST SUCH A GOOD GIRL.
I WISH... I REALLY JUST WISH I COULD... JUST MAYBE SEE HER...JUST ONE MORE TIME.

We were all so anonymous, we never had our name on anything, it was just total anonymity. I happen to think it made for some of the richness of comics in those days because when you're sitting by yourself in a room, you're going to think of things that you're not going to think of if you think the whole world's looking.

—Ramona Fradon,
Comic Book Artist #10
(TwoMorrows, October 2000)

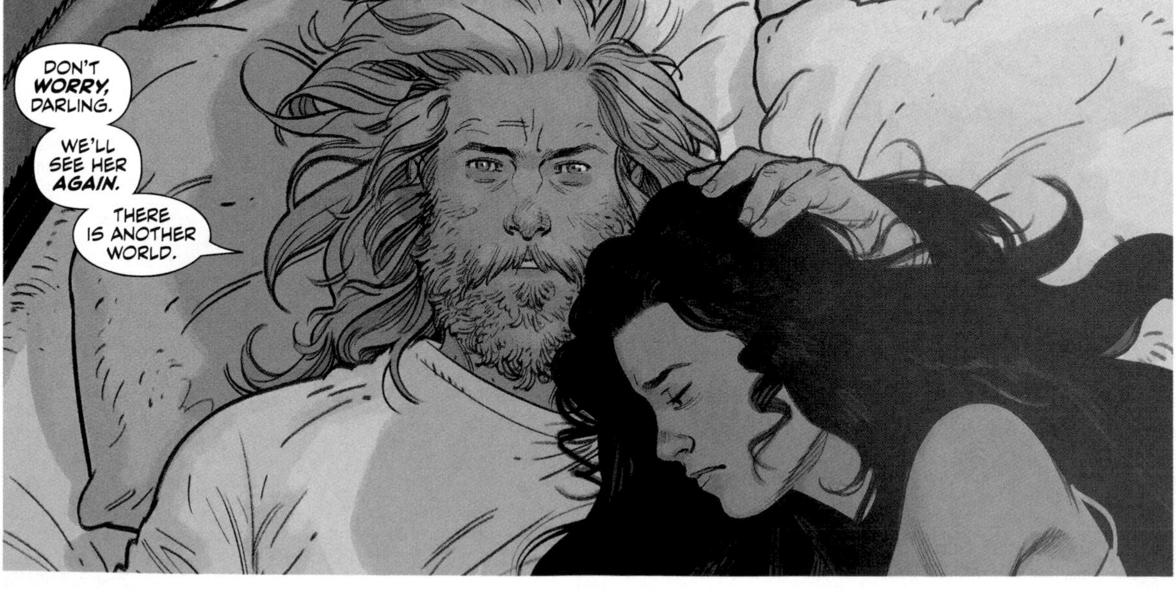
DON'T WORRY, DARLING.
WE'LL SEE HER AGAIN.
THERE IS ANOTHER WORLD.

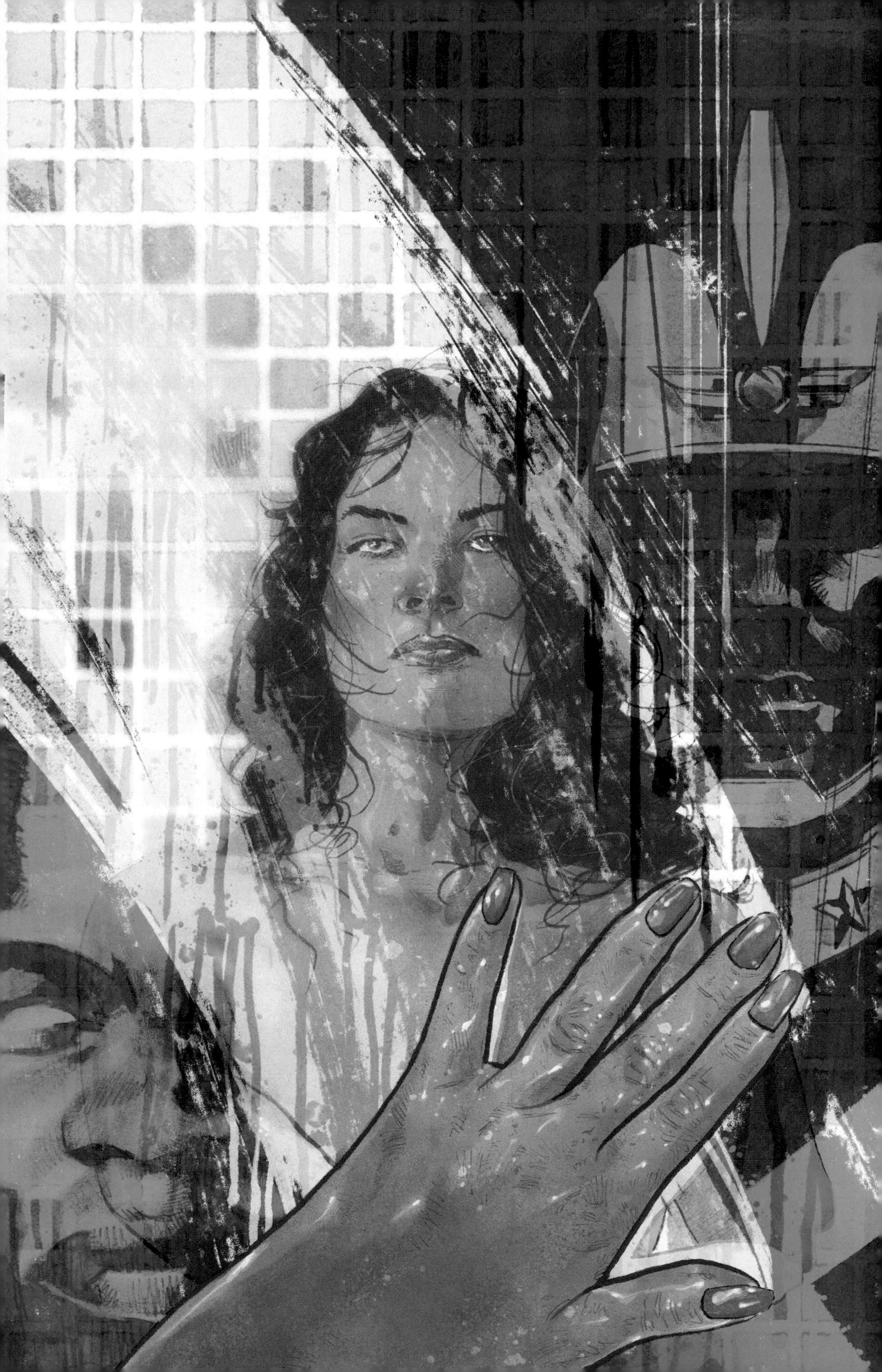

"LET'S START WITH YOUR WAR."

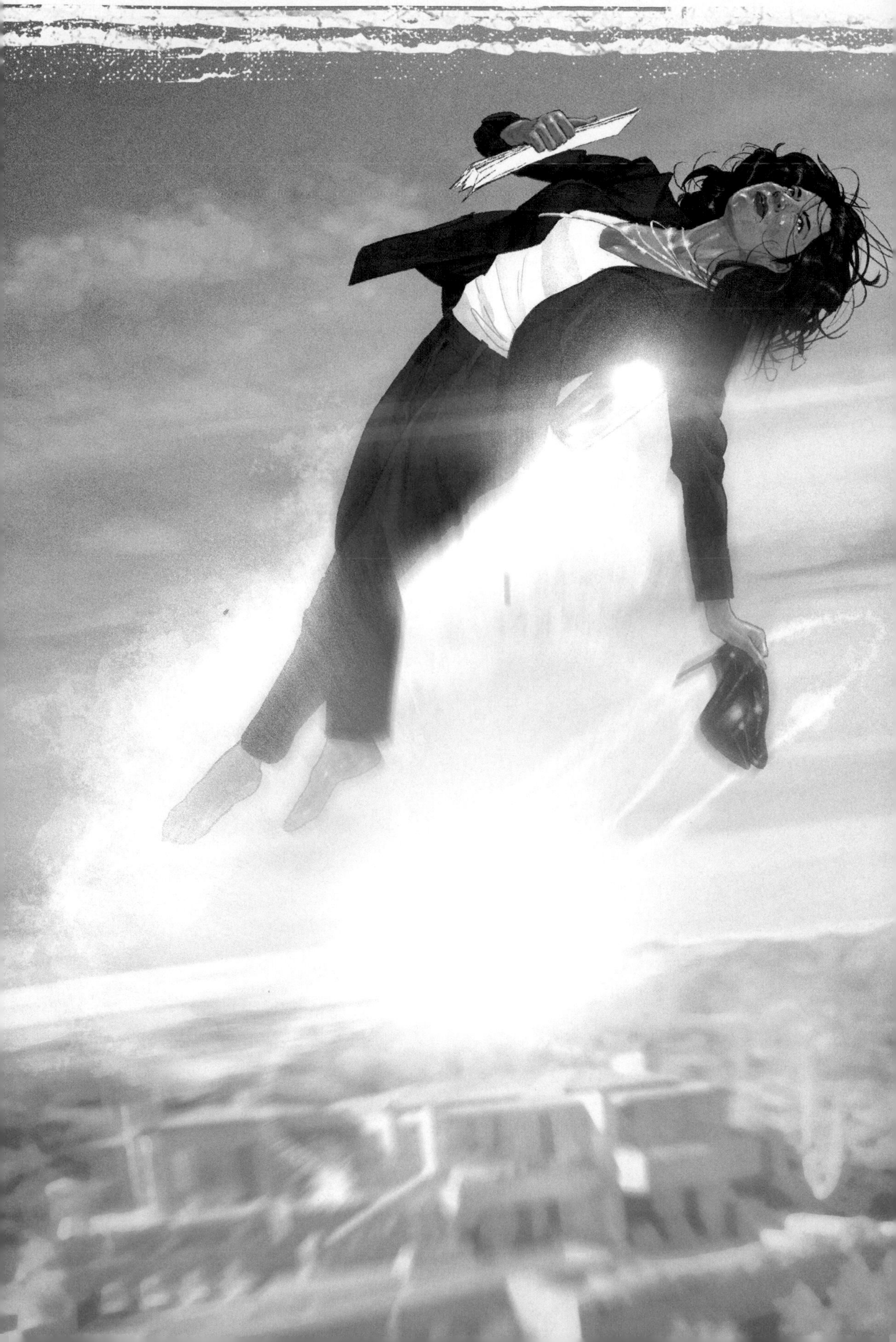

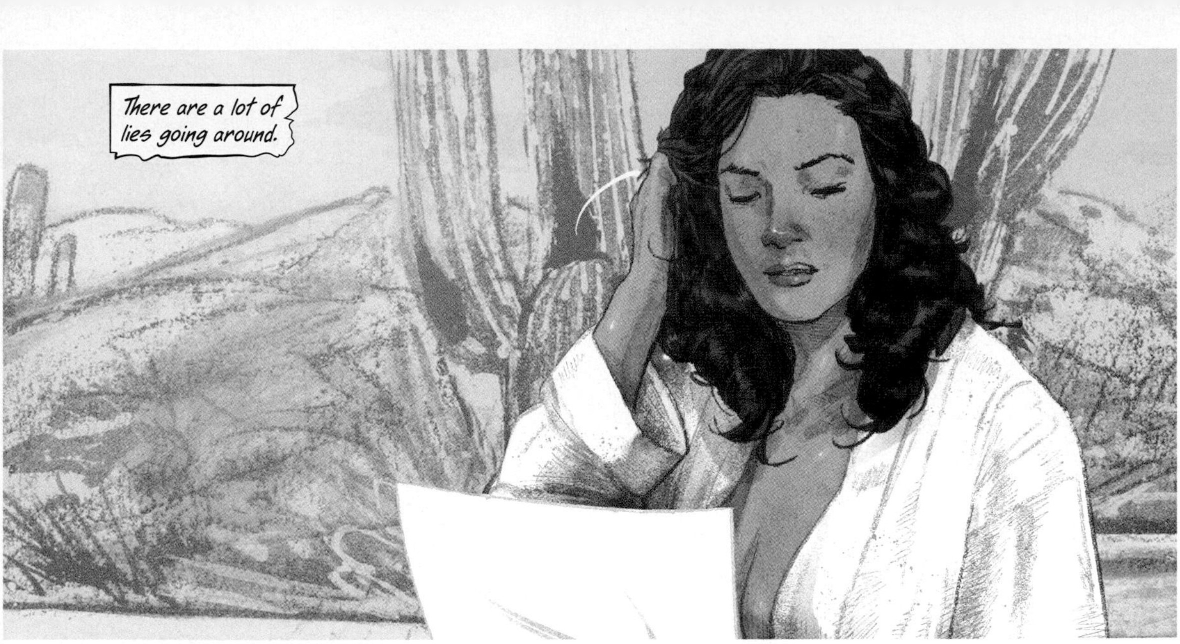
There are a lot of lies going around.

Chapter 10

You rule supreme

TOM KING	...Writer
MITCH GERADS EVAN "DOC" SHANER	...Interior & Cover Artists
CLAYTON COWLES	...Letterer
BIXIE MATHIEU	...Assistant Editor
BRITTANY HOLZHERR	...Associate Editor
JAMIE S. RICH	...Editor

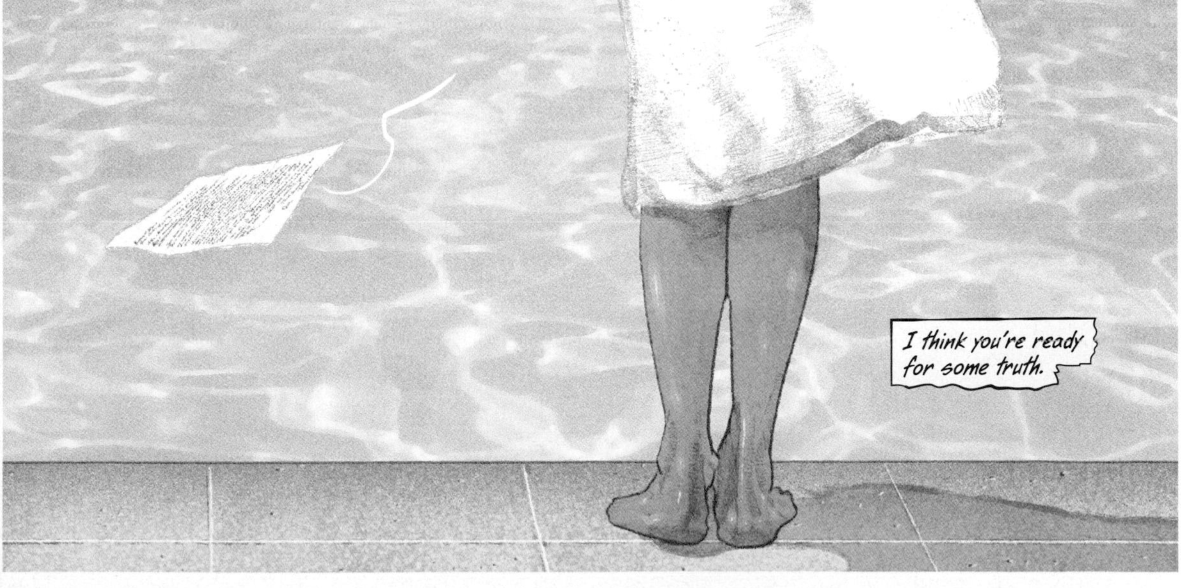
I think you're ready for some truth.

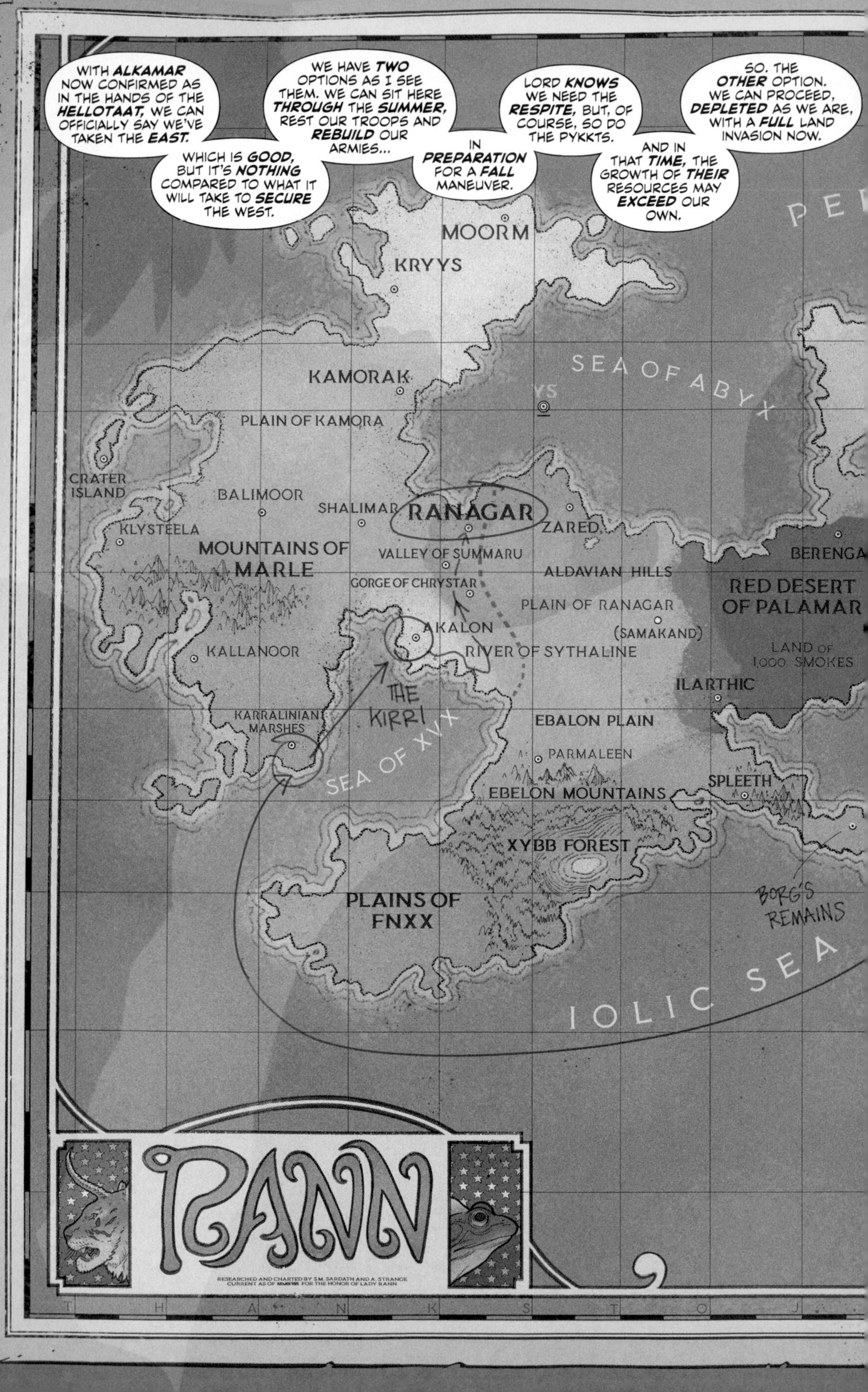
WITH ALKAMAR NOW CONFIRMED AS IN THE HANDS OF THE HELLOTAAT, WE CAN OFFICIALLY SAY WE'VE TAKEN THE EAST.
WHICH IS GOOD, BUT IT'S NOTHING COMPARED TO WHAT IT WILL TAKE TO SECURE THE WEST.
WE HAVE TWO OPTIONS AS I SEE THEM. WE CAN SIT HERE THROUGH THE SUMMER, REST OUR TROOPS AND REBUILD OUR ARMIES...
IN PREPARATION FOR A FALL MANEUVER.
LORD KNOWS WE NEED THE RESPITE, BUT, OF COURSE, SO DO THE PYKKTS.
AND IN THAT TIME, THE GROWTH OF THEIR RESOURCES MAY EXCEED OUR OWN.
SO. THE OTHER OPTION. WE CAN PROCEED, DEPLETED AS WE ARE, WITH A FULL LAND INVASION NOW.
MOORM
KRYYS
KAMORAK
SEA OF ABYX
YS
PLAIN OF KAMORA
CRATER ISLAND
BALIMOOR
SHALIMAR
RANAGAR
ZARED
KLYSTEELA
MOUNTAINS OF MARLE
VALLEY OF SUMMARU
BERENGA
ALDAVIAN HILLS
GORGE OF CHRYSTAR
RED DESERT OF PALAMAR
PLAIN OF RANAGAR
AKALON
(SAMAKAND)
LAND OF 1,000 SMOKES
KALLANOOR
RIVER OF SYTHALINE
THE KIRRI
ILARTHIC
KARRALINIAN MARSHES
SEA OF XVX
EBALON PLAIN
PARMALEEN
SPLEETH
EBELON MOUNTAINS
XYBB FOREST
PLAINS OF FNXX
BORG'S REMAINS
IOLIC SEA
RANN
RESEARCHED AND CHARTED BY S.M. SARDATH AND A. STRANGE
CURRENT AS OF MMXVII FOR THE HONOR OF LADY RANN
T H A N K S T O J

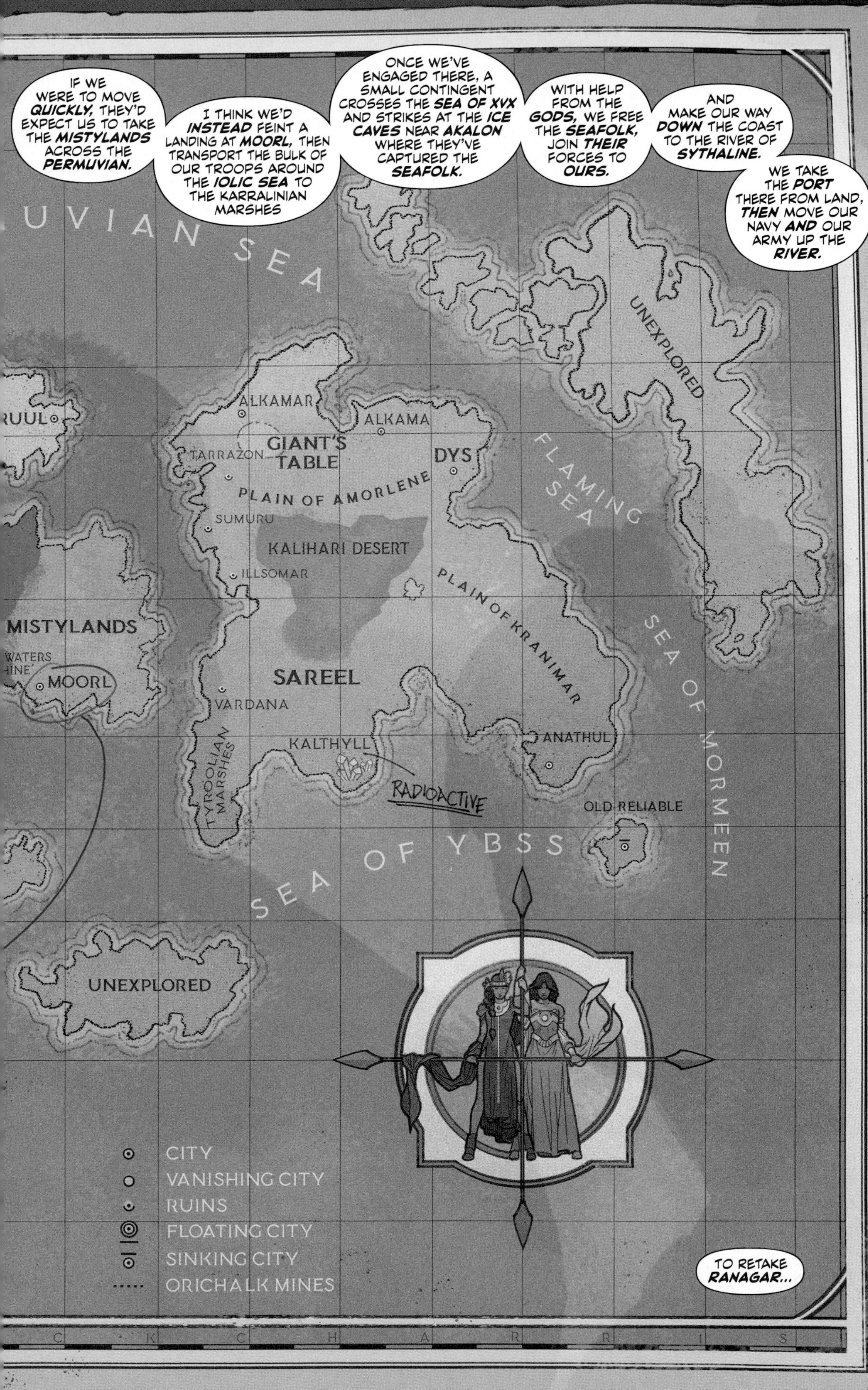
IF WE WERE TO MOVE QUICKLY, THEY'D EXPECT US TO TAKE THE MISTYLANDS ACROSS THE PERMUVIAN.
I THINK WE'D INSTEAD FEINT A LANDING AT MOORL, THEN TRANSPORT THE BULK OF OUR TROOPS AROUND THE IOLIC SEA TO THE KARRALINIAN MARSHES
ONCE WE'VE ENGAGED THERE, A SMALL CONTINGENT CROSSES THE SEA OF XVX AND STRIKES AT THE ICE CAVES NEAR AKALON WHERE THEY'VE CAPTURED THE SEAFOLK.
WITH HELP FROM THE GODS, WE FREE THE SEAFOLK, JOIN THEIR FORCES TO OURS.
AND MAKE OUR WAY DOWN THE COAST TO THE RIVER OF SYTHALINE.
WE TAKE THE PORT THERE FROM LAND, THEN MOVE OUR NAVY AND OUR ARMY UP THE RIVER.
TO RETAKE RANAGAR...
UVIAN SEA
UNEXPLORED
RUUL
ALKAMAR
ALKAMA
TARRAZON
GIANT'S TABLE
DYS
FLAMING SEA
PLAIN OF AMORLENE
SUMURU
KALIHARI DESERT
ILLSOMAR
PLAIN OF KRANIMAR
MISTYLANDS
WATERS
HINE
MOORL
SAREEL
SEA OF MORMEEN
VARDANA
TYROOLIAN MARSHES
KALTHYLL
ANATHUL
RADIOACTIVE
OLD RELIABLE
SEA OF YBSS
UNEXPLORED
CITY
VANISHING CITY
RUINS
FLOATING CITY
SINKING CITY
ORICHALK MINES

...AND DRIVE THESE BASTARDS OFF RANN.

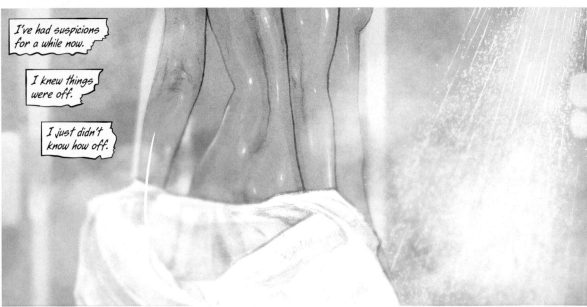

I've had suspicions for a while now.

I knew things were off.

I just didn't know how off.

I'd figured it had something to do with what you all had done.

Back there on Rann.

All the death you embraced.

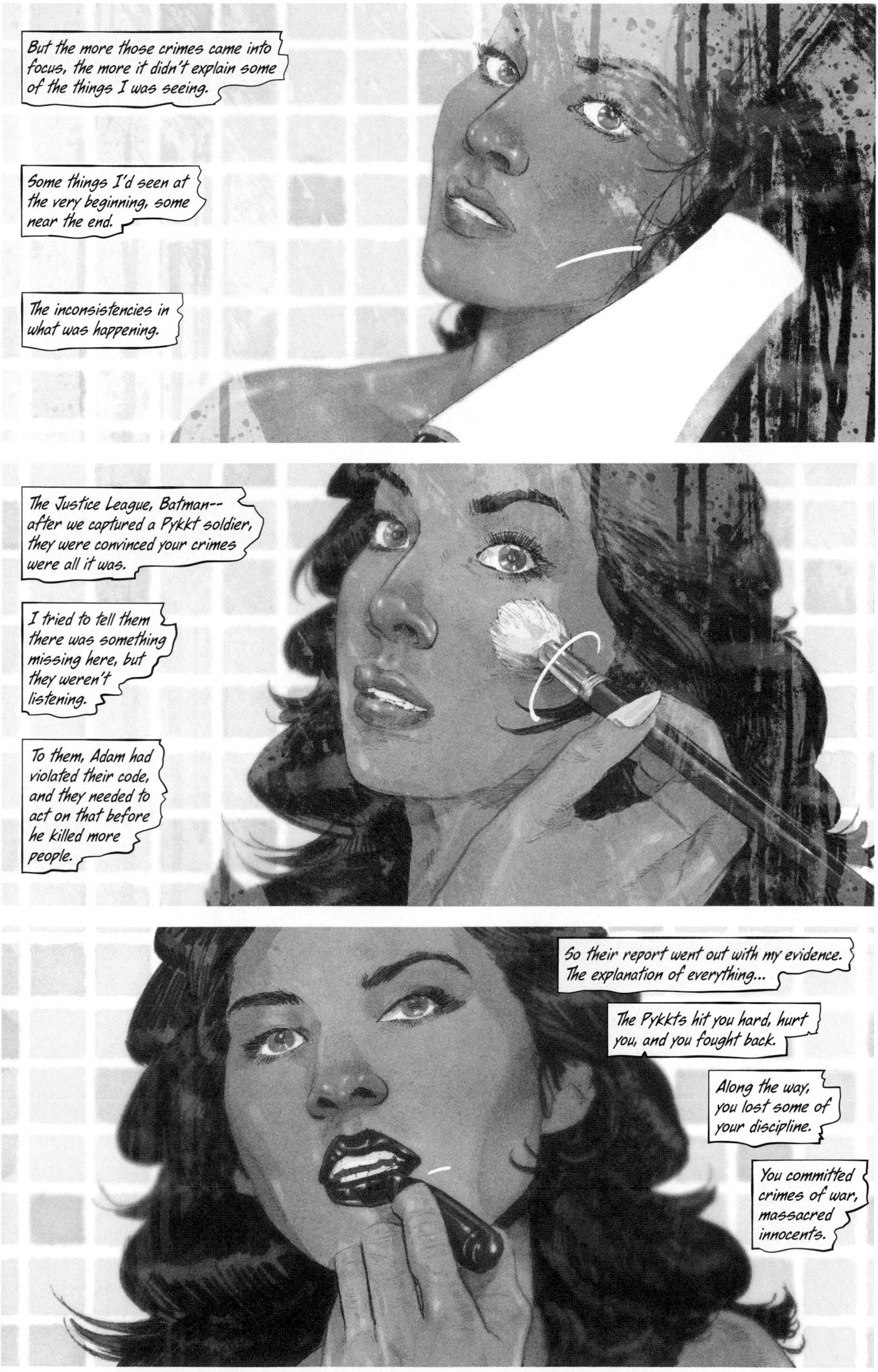
But the more those crimes came into focus, the more it didn't explain some of the things I was seeing.
Some things I'd seen at the very beginning, some near the end.
The inconsistencies in what was happening.
The Justice League, Batman-- after we captured a Pykkt soldier, they were convinced your crimes were all it was.
I tried to tell them there was something missing here, but they weren't listening.
To them, Adam had violated their code, and they needed to act on that before he killed more people.
So their report went out with my evidence. The explanation of everything...
The Pykkts hit you hard, hurt you, and you fought back.
Along the way, you lost some of your discipline.
You committed crimes of war, massacred innocents.

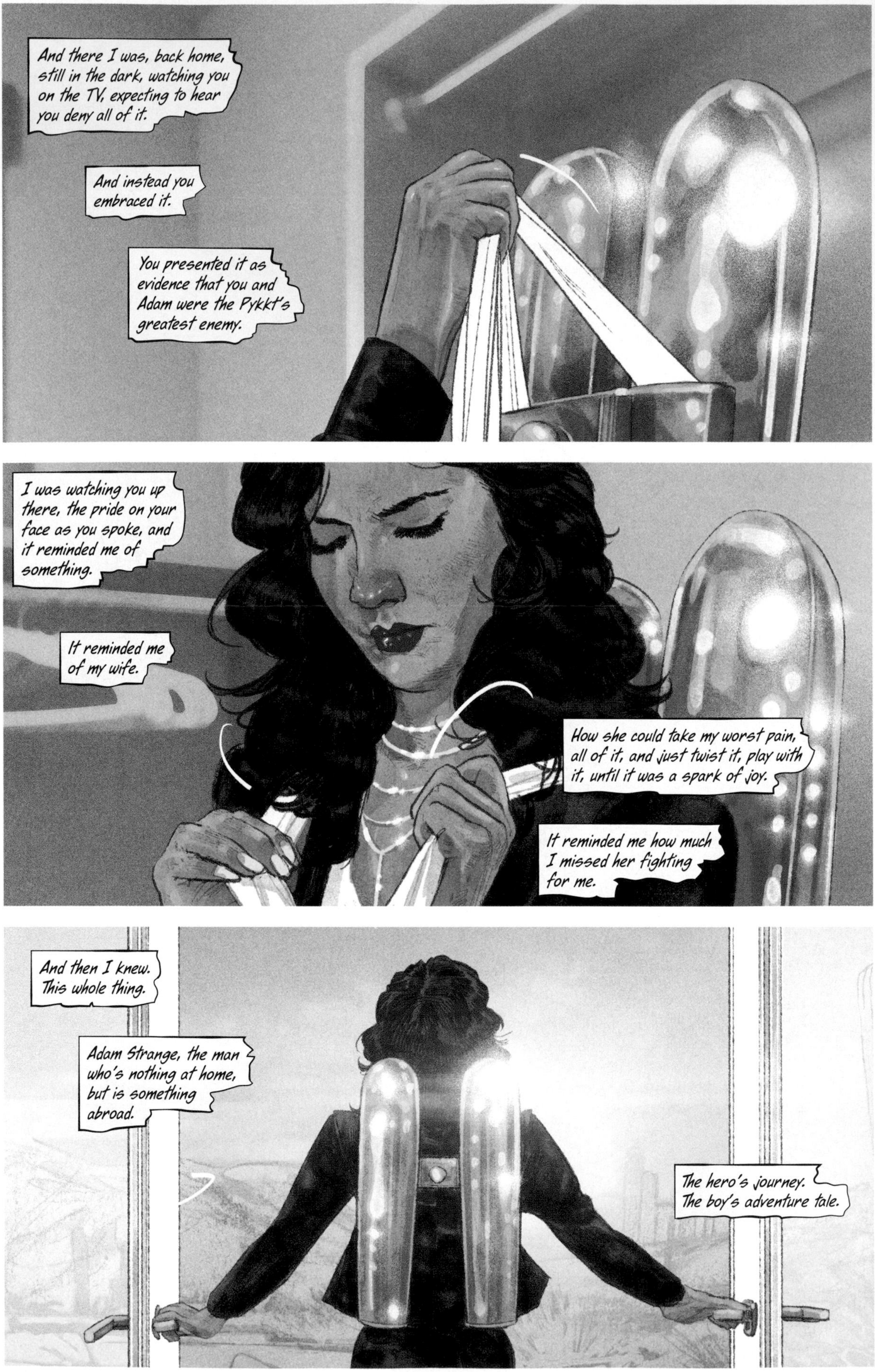
And there I was, back home, still in the dark, watching you on the TV, expecting to hear you deny all of it.
And instead you embraced it.
You presented it as evidence that you and Adam were the Pykkt's greatest enemy.
I was watching you up there, the pride on your face as you spoke, and it reminded me of something.
It reminded me of my wife.
How she could take my worst pain, all of it, and just twist it, play with it, until it was a spark of joy.
It reminded me how much I missed her fighting for me.
And then I knew. This whole thing.
Adam Strange, the man who's nothing at home, but is something abroad.
The hero's journey. The boy's adventure tale.

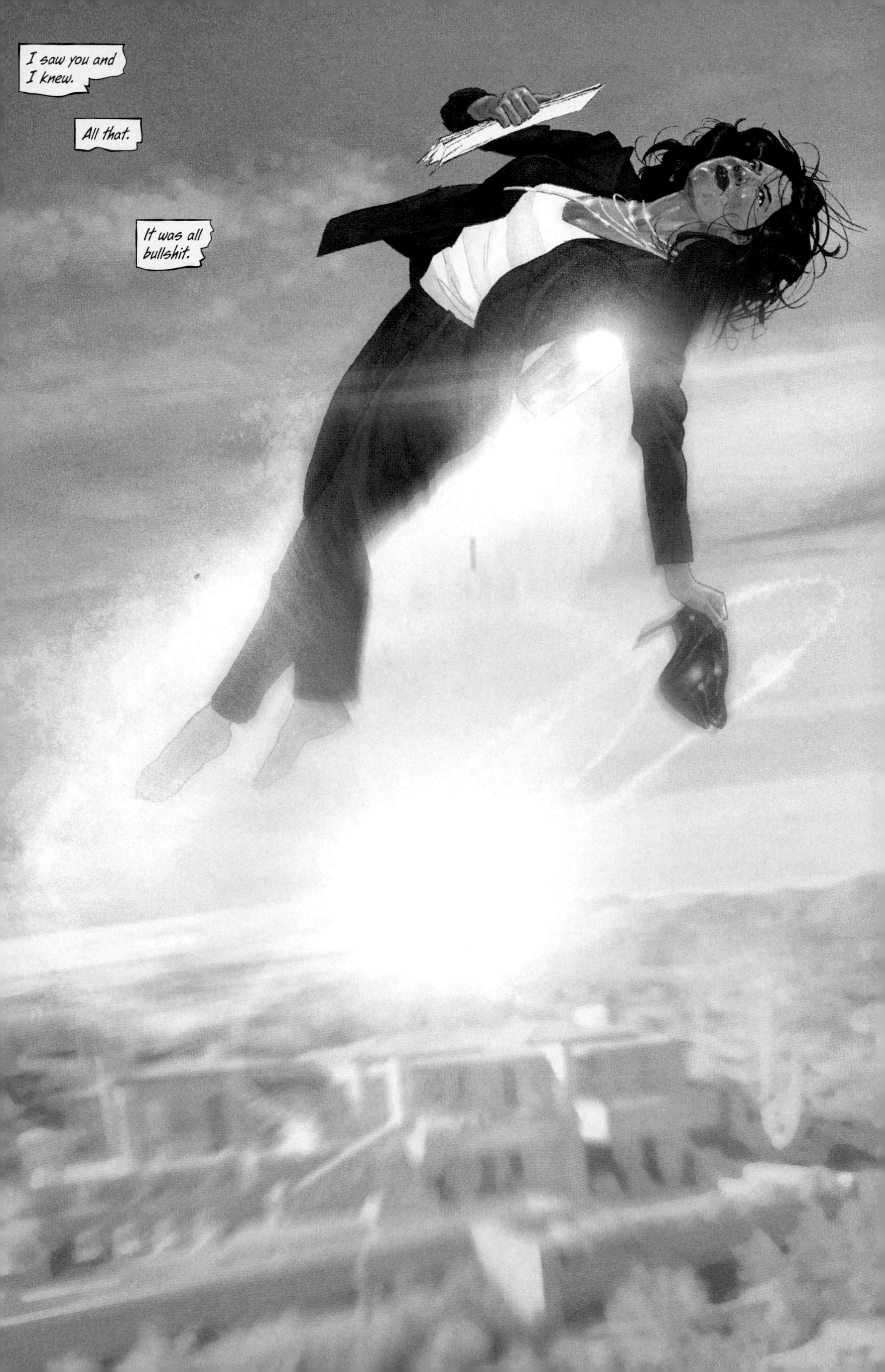
I saw you and I knew.
All that.
It was all bullshit.

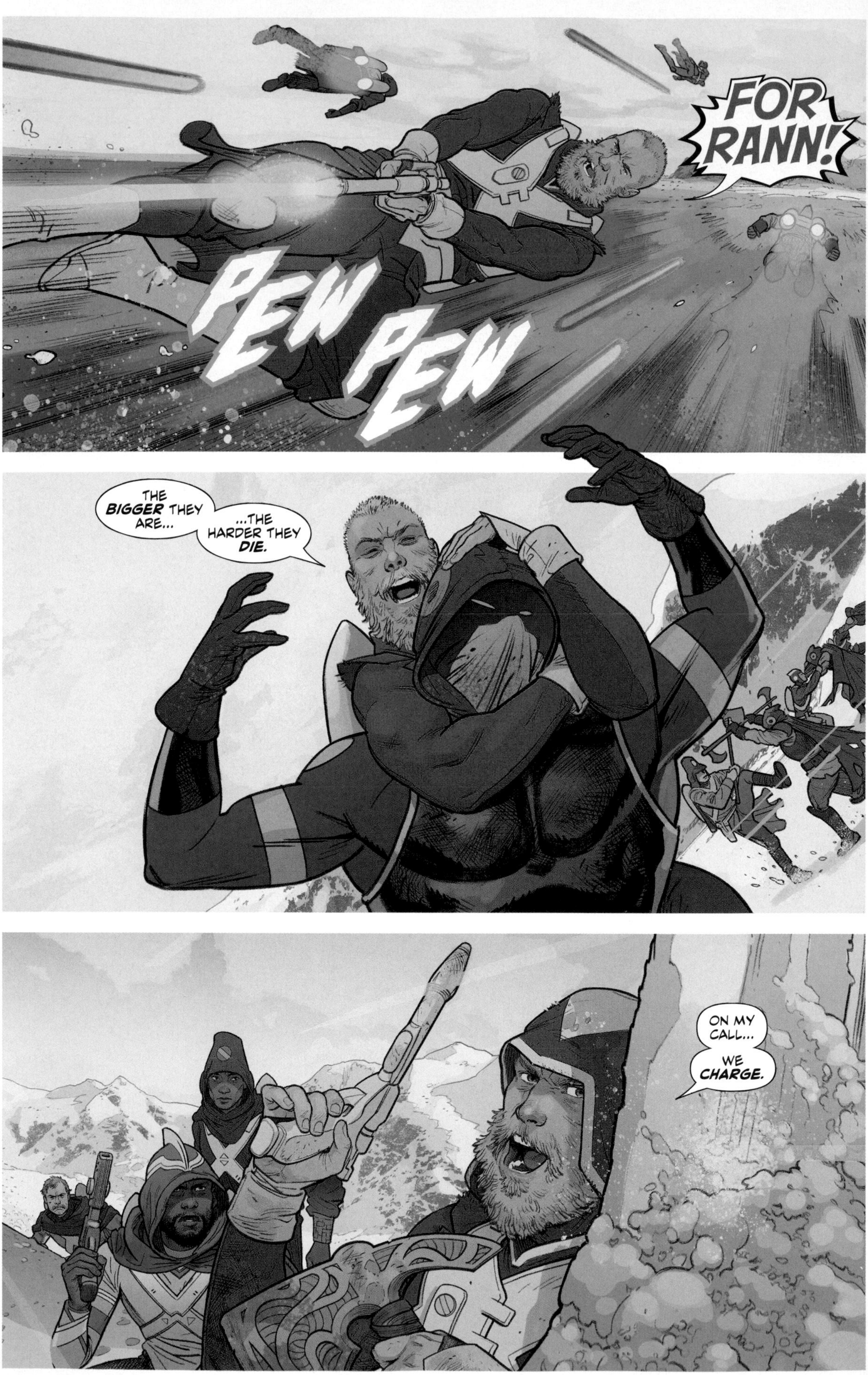
FOR RANN!
PEW PEW
THE BIGGER THEY ARE...
...THE HARDER THEY DIE.
ON MY CALL...
WE CHARGE.

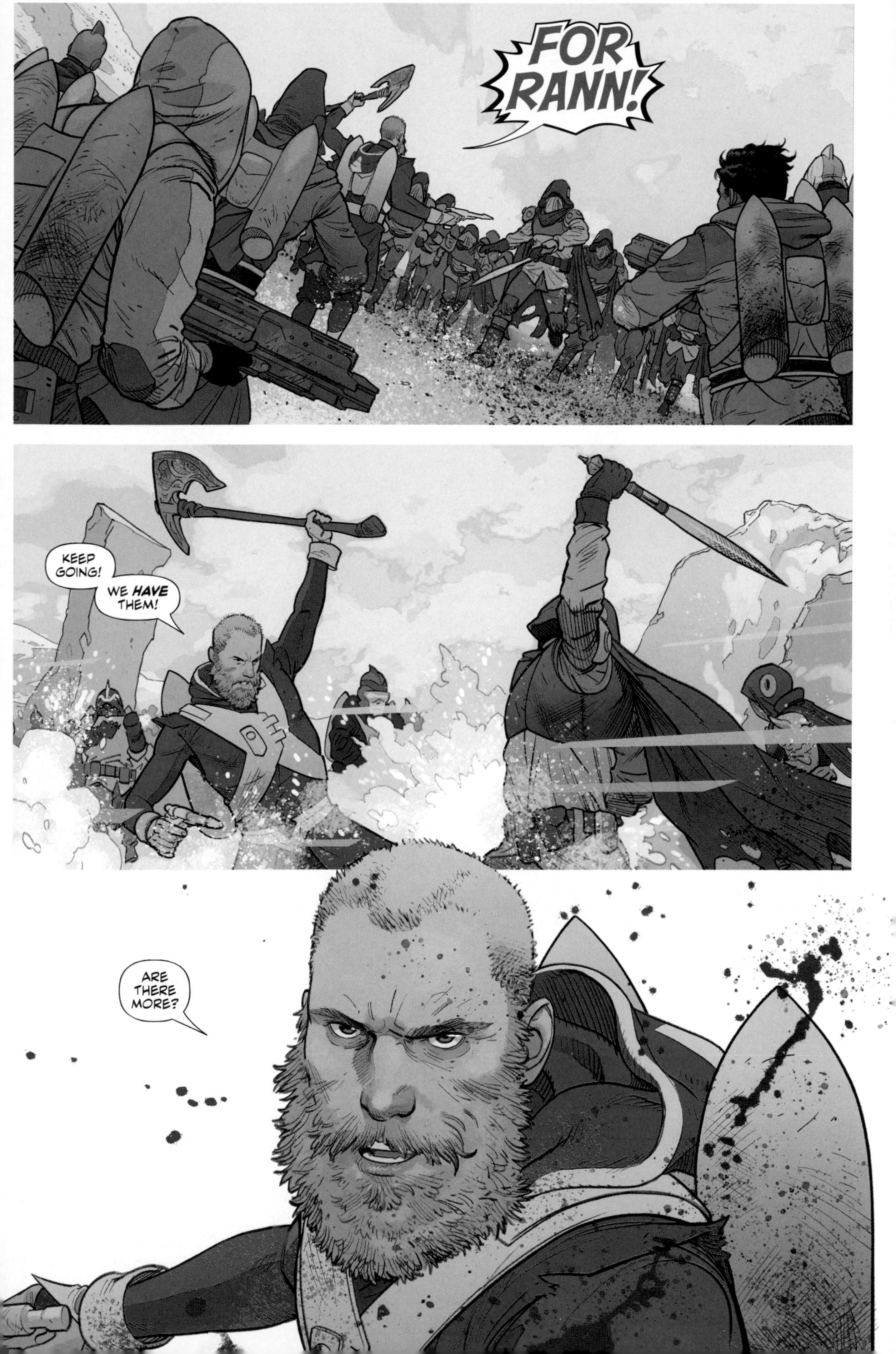
FOR RANN!
KEEP GOING!
WE *HAVE* THEM!
ARE THERE MORE?

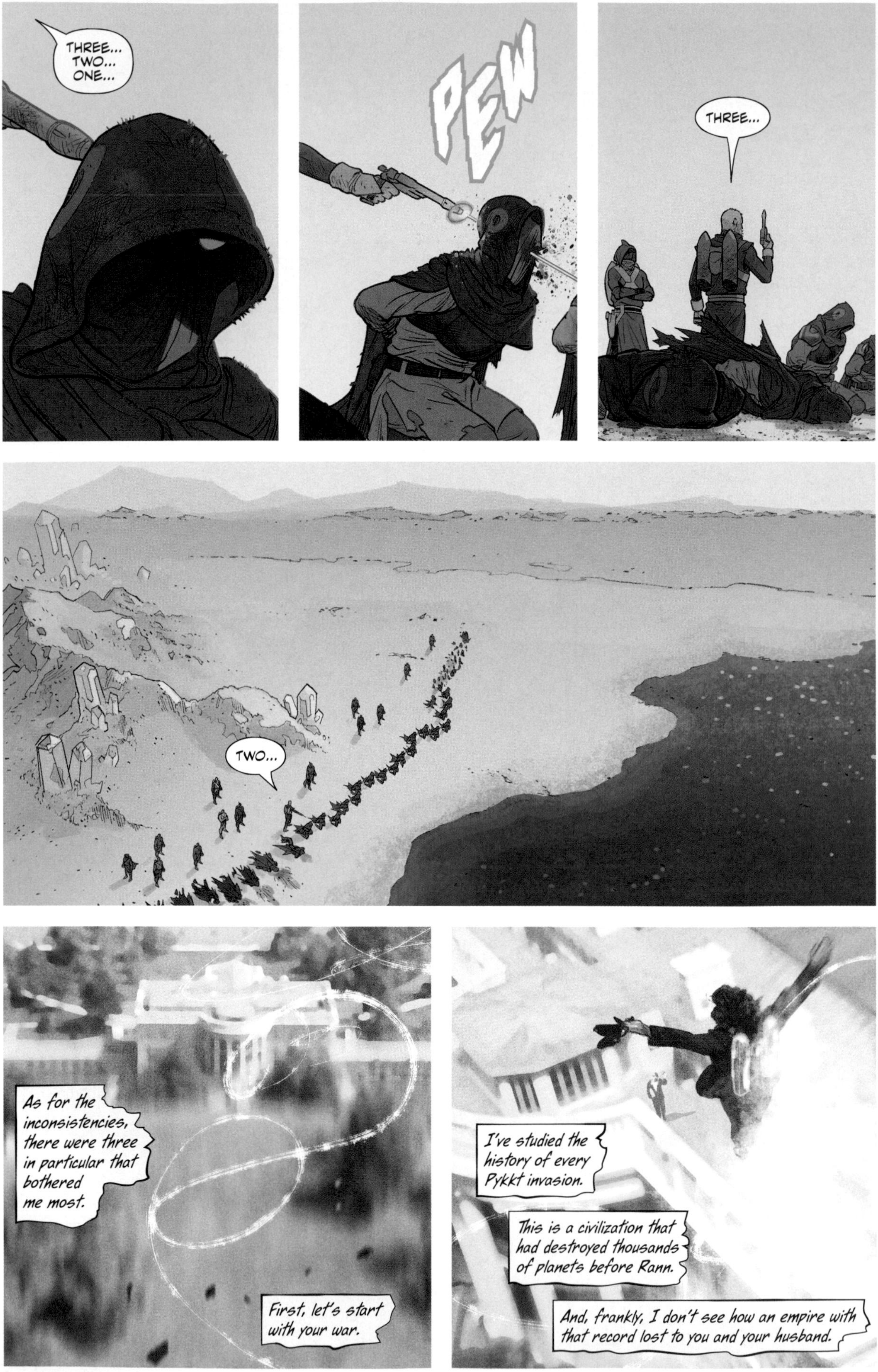
THREE... TWO... ONE...
PEW
THREE...
TWO...
As for the inconsistencies, there were three in particular that bothered me most.
First, let's start with your war.
I've studied the history of every Pykkt invasion.
This is a civilization that had destroyed thousands of planets before Rann.
And, frankly, I don't see how an empire with that record lost to you and your husband.

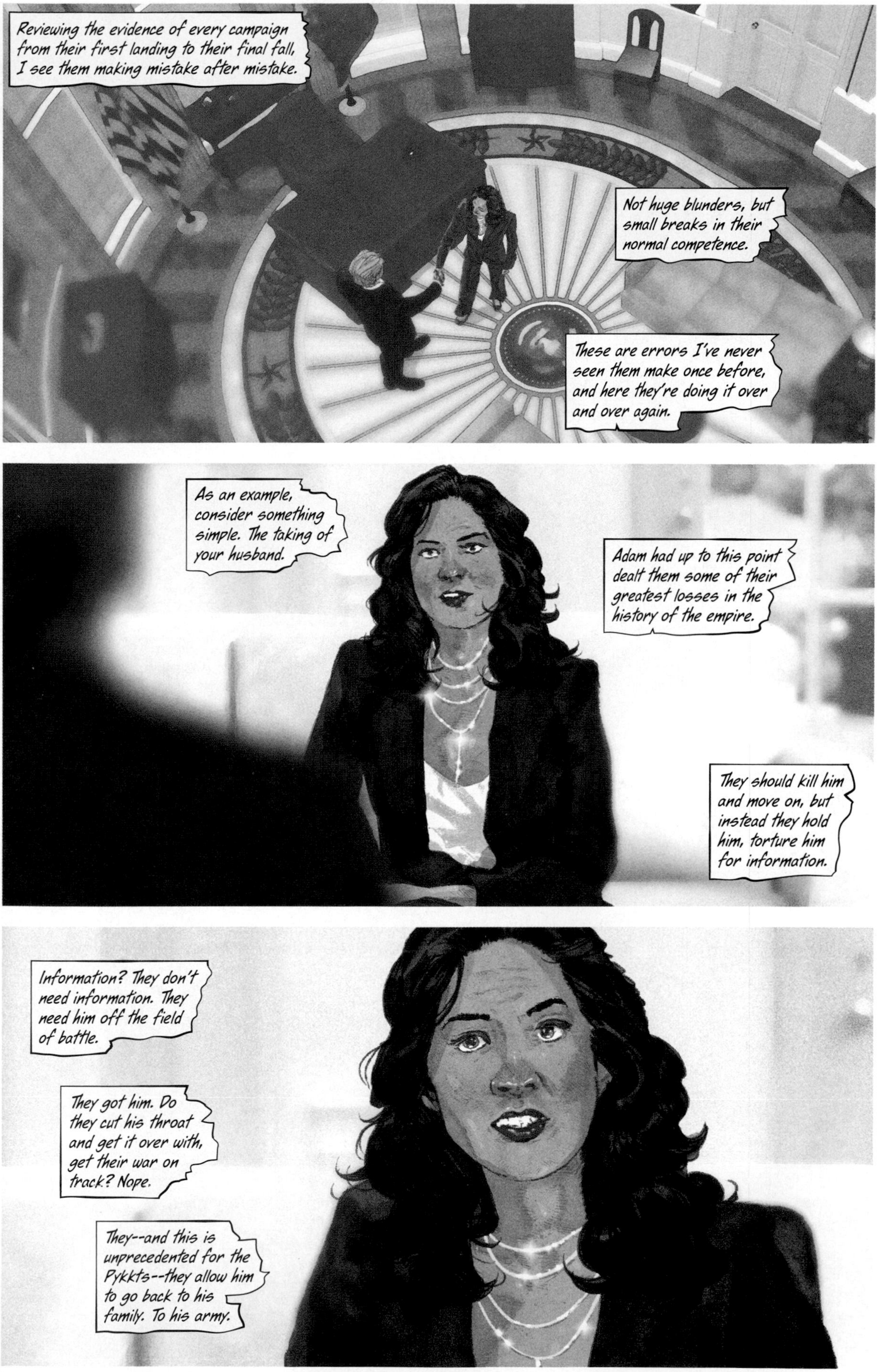

Reviewing the evidence of every campaign from their first landing to their final fall, I see them making mistake after mistake.
Not huge blunders, but small breaks in their normal competence.
These are errors I've never seen them make once before, and here they're doing it over and over again.
As an example, consider something simple. The taking of your husband.
Adam had up to this point dealt them some of their greatest losses in the history of the empire.
They should kill him and move on, but instead they hold him, torture him for information.
Information? They don't need information. They need him off the field of battle.
They got him. Do they cut his throat and get it over with, get their war on track? Nope.
They--and this is unprecedented for the Pykkts--they allow him to go back to his family. To his army.

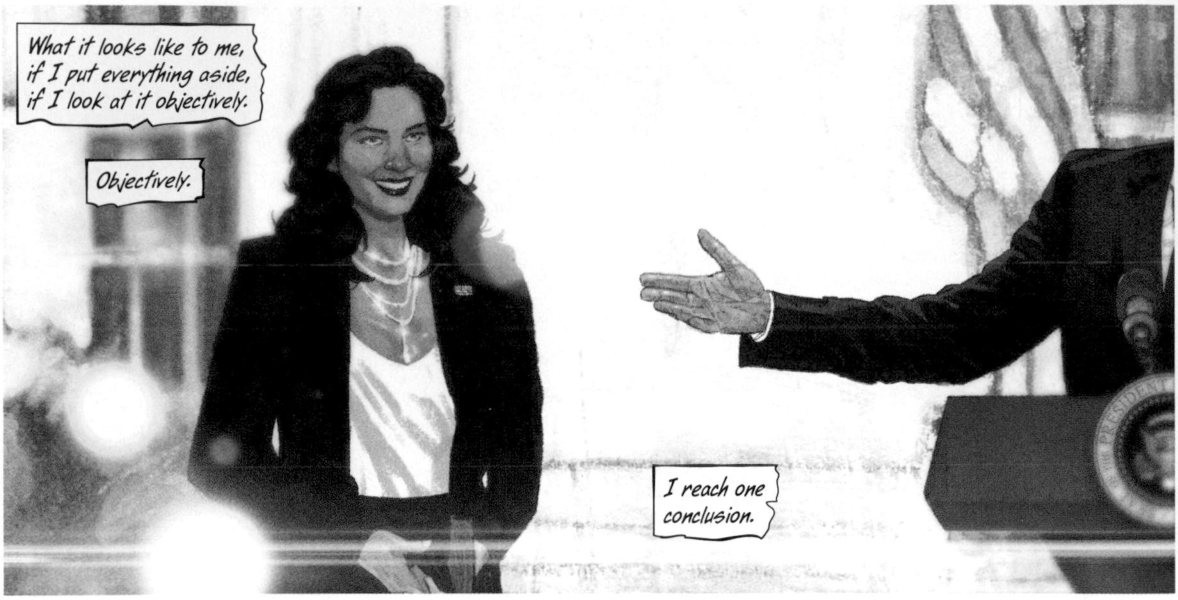
What it looks like to me, if I put everything aside, if I look at it objectively.
Objectively.
I reach one conclusion.
PRESIDENT

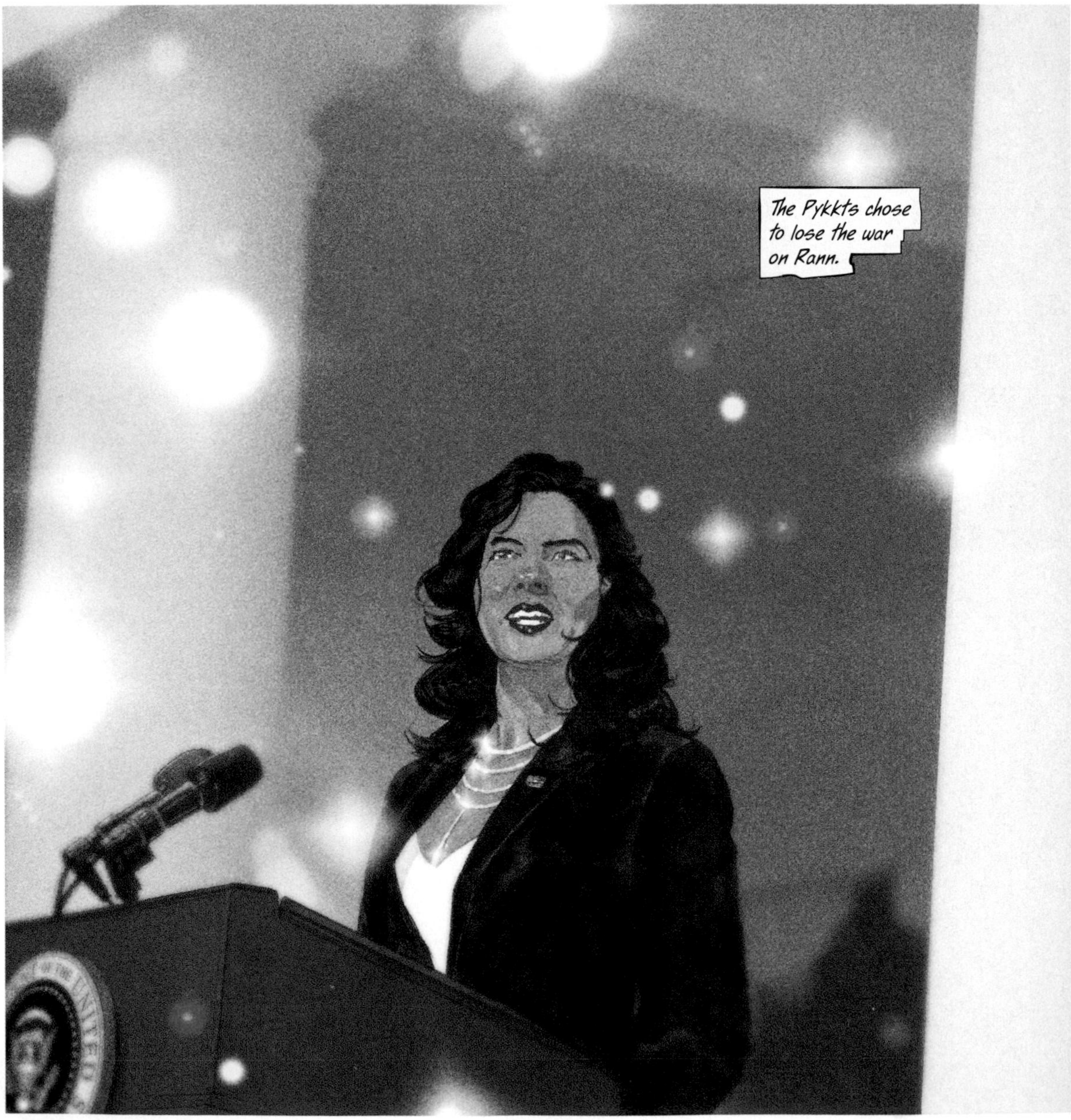
The Pykkts chose to lose the war on Rann.

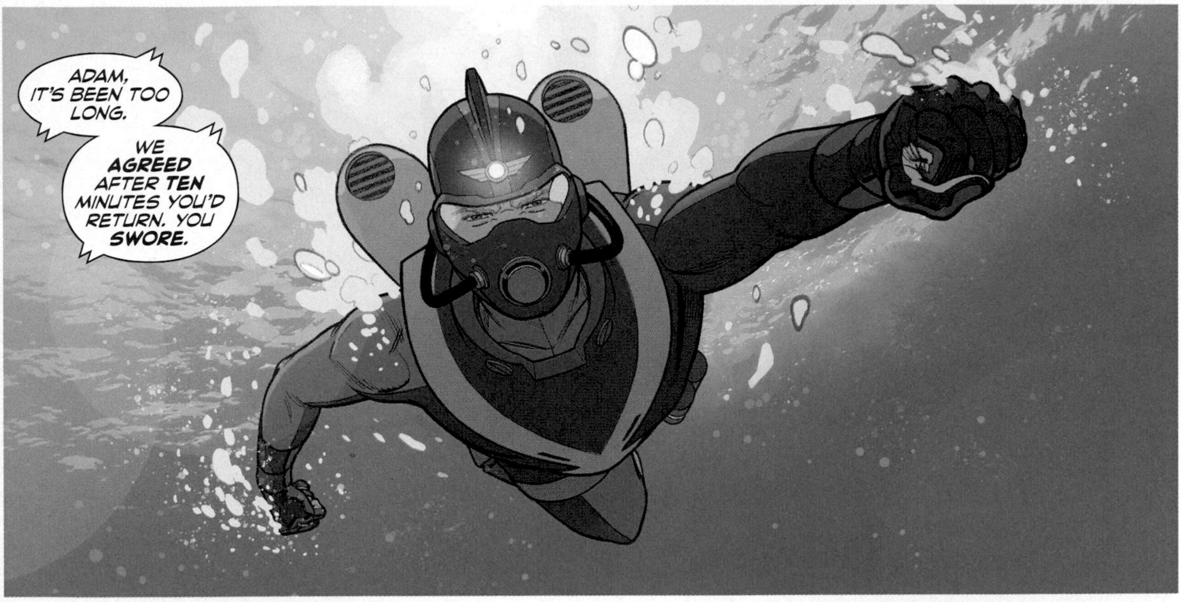
ADAM, IT'S BEEN TOO LONG.
WE **AGREED** AFTER **TEN** MINUTES YOU'D RETURN. YOU **SWORE.**

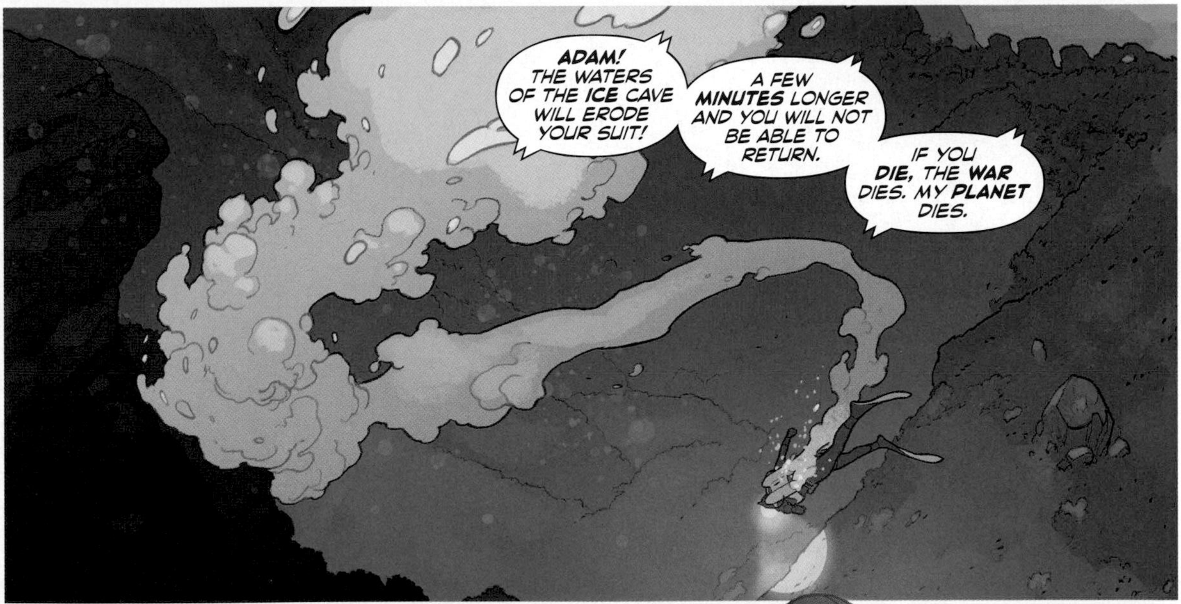
ADAM! THE WATERS OF THE **ICE** CAVE WILL ERODE YOUR SUIT!
A FEW **MINUTES** LONGER AND YOU WILL NOT BE ABLE TO RETURN.
IF YOU **DIE,** THE **WAR** DIES. MY **PLANET** DIES.

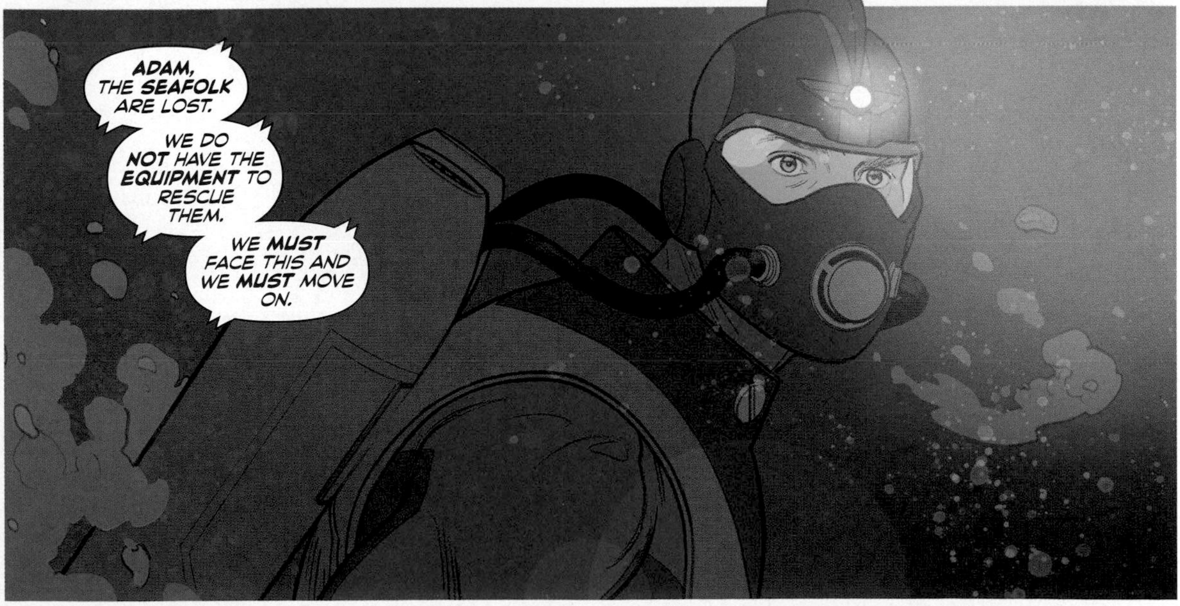
ADAM, THE **SEAFOLK** ARE LOST.
WE DO **NOT** HAVE THE **EQUIPMENT** TO RESCUE THEM.
WE **MUST** FACE THIS AND WE **MUST** MOVE ON.

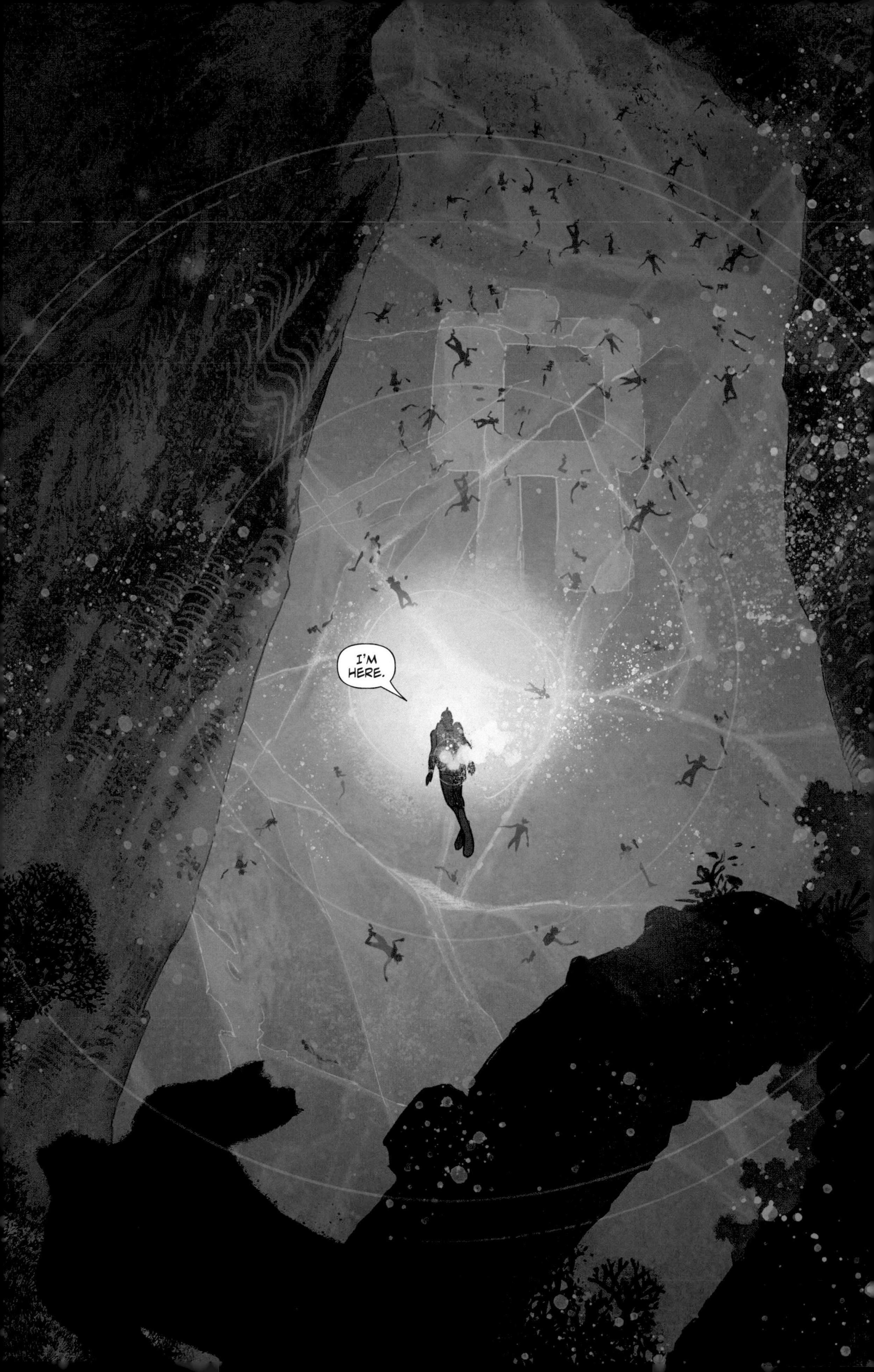
I'M HERE.

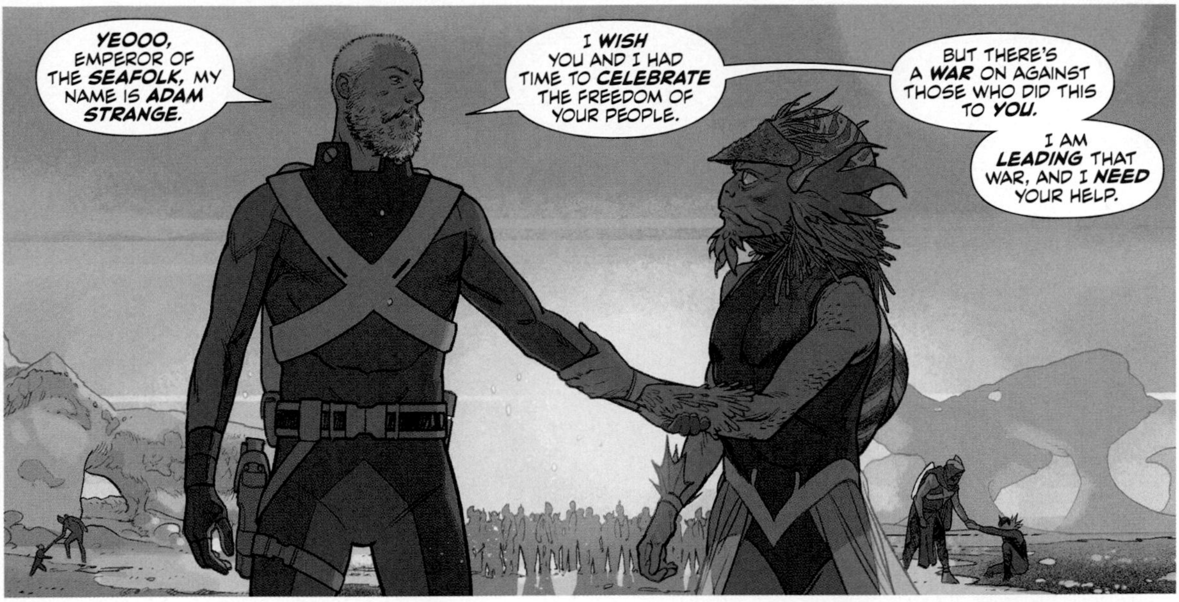
YEOOO, EMPEROR OF THE SEAFOLK, MY NAME IS ADAM STRANGE.
I WISH YOU AND I HAD TIME TO CELEBRATE THE FREEDOM OF YOUR PEOPLE.
BUT THERE'S A WAR ON AGAINST THOSE WHO DID THIS TO YOU.
I AM LEADING THAT WAR, AND I NEED YOUR HELP.

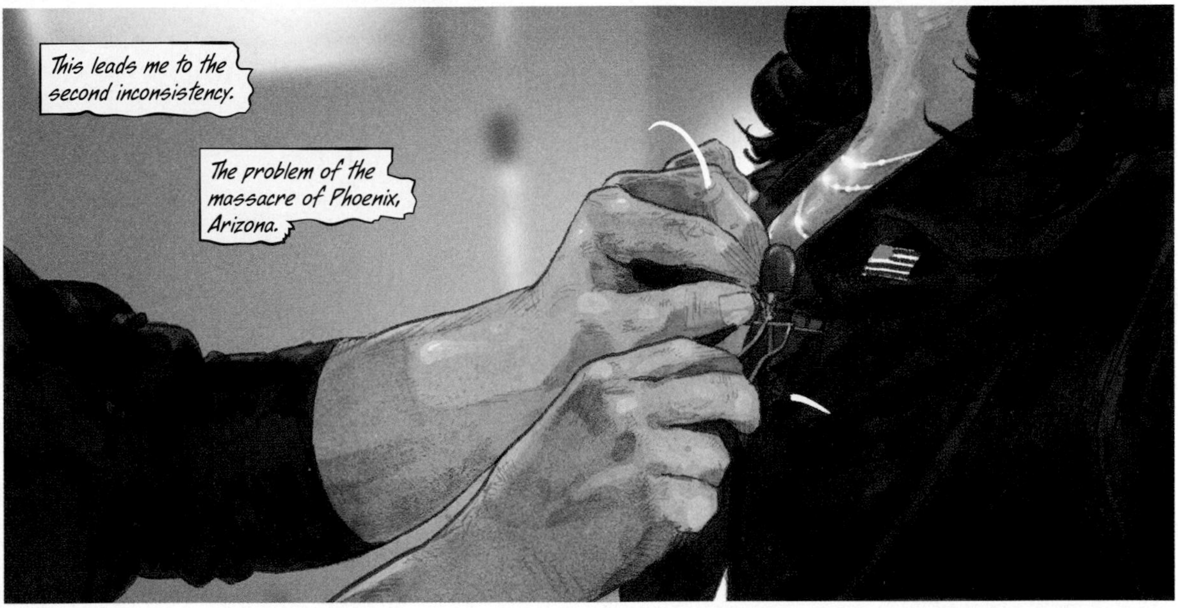
This leads me to the second inconsistency.
The problem of the massacre of Phoenix, Arizona.

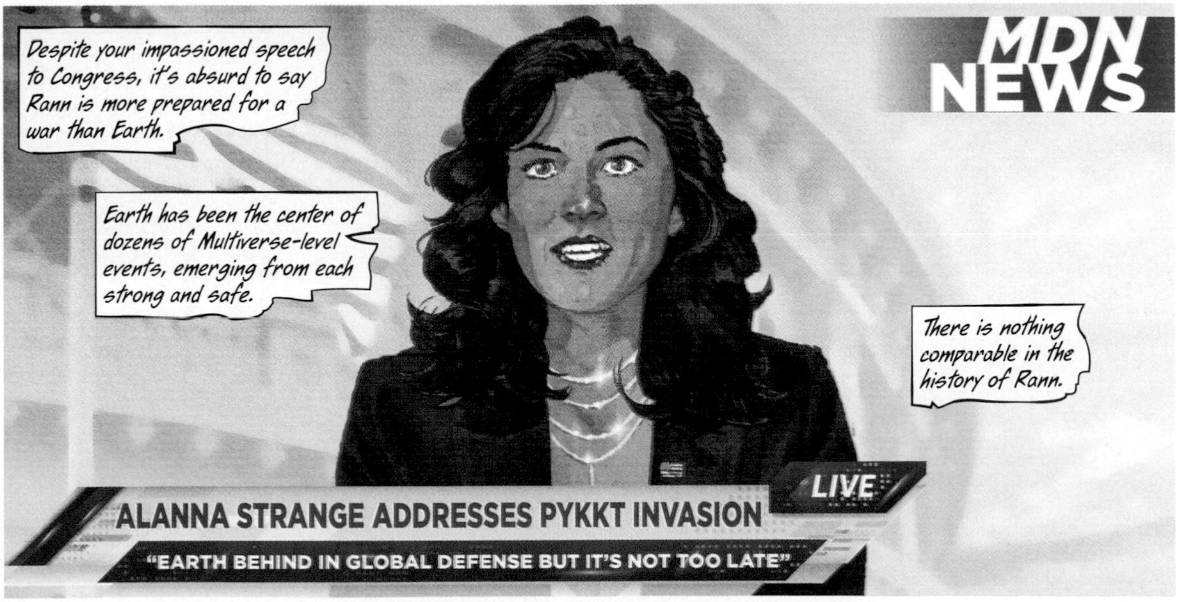
Despite your impassioned speech to Congress, it's absurd to say Rann is more prepared for a war than Earth.
MDN NEWS
Earth has been the center of dozens of Multiverse-level events, emerging from each strong and safe.
There is nothing comparable in the history of Rann.
LIVE
ALANNA STRANGE ADDRESSES PYKKT INVASION
"EARTH BEHIND IN GLOBAL DEFENSE BUT IT'S NOT TOO LATE"

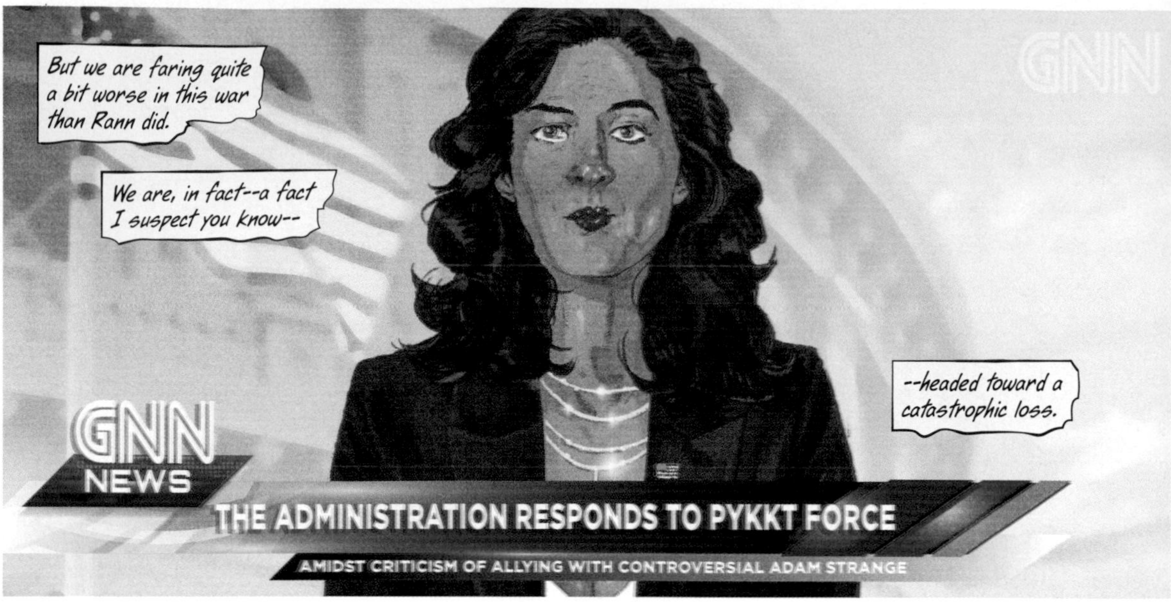
GNN
But we are faring quite a bit worse in this war than Rann did.
We are, in fact--a fact I suspect you know--
--headed toward a catastrophic loss.
GNN NEWS
THE ADMINISTRATION RESPONDS TO PYKKT FORCE
AMIDST CRITICISM OF ALLYING WITH CONTROVERSIAL ADAM STRANGE

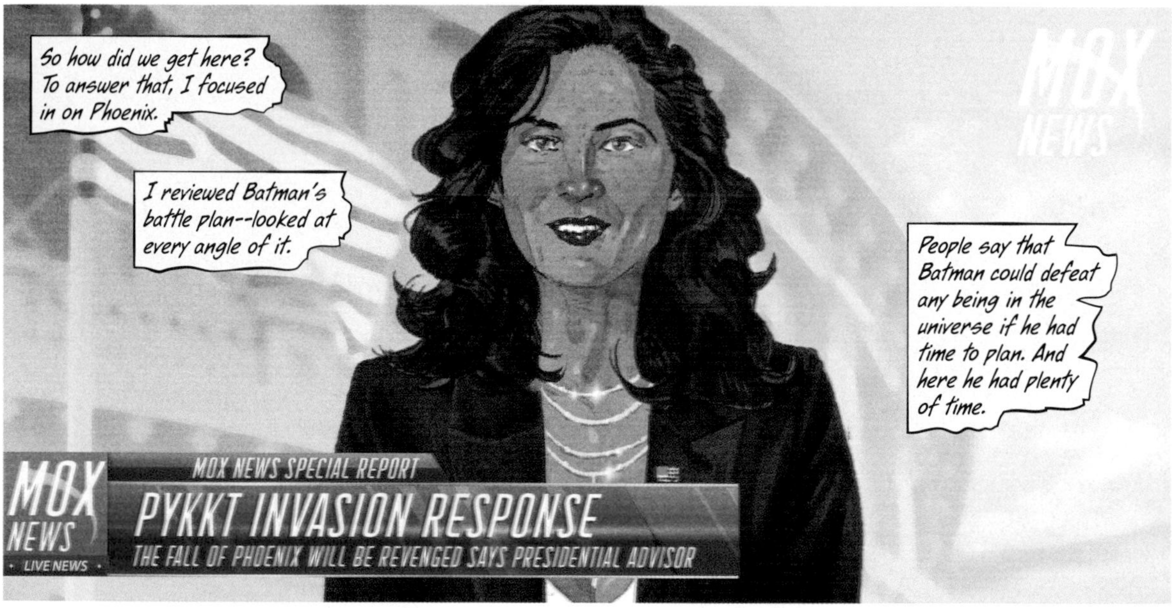
MOX NEWS
So how did we get here? To answer that, I focused in on Phoenix.
I reviewed Batman's battle plan--looked at every angle of it.
People say that Batman could defeat any being in the universe if he had time to plan. And here he had plenty of time.
MOX NEWS LIVE NEWS
MOX NEWS SPECIAL REPORT
PYKKT INVASION RESPONSE
THE FALL OF PHOENIX WILL BE REVENGED SAYS PRESIDENTIAL ADVISOR

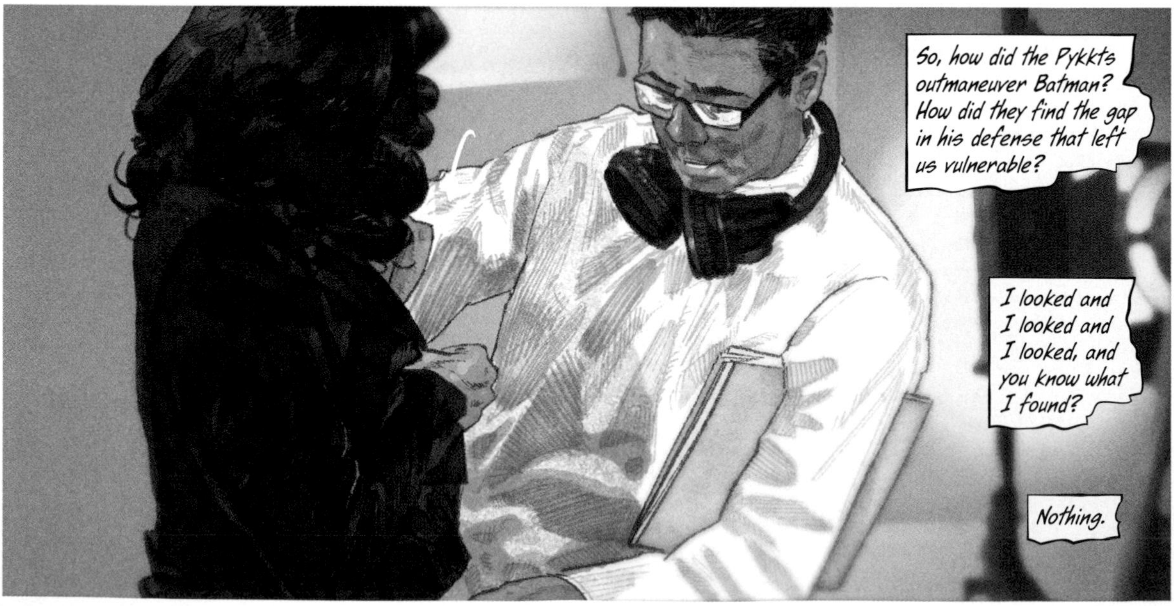
So, how did the Pykkts outmaneuver Batman? How did they find the gap in his defense that left us vulnerable?
I looked and I looked and I looked, and you know what I found?
Nothing.

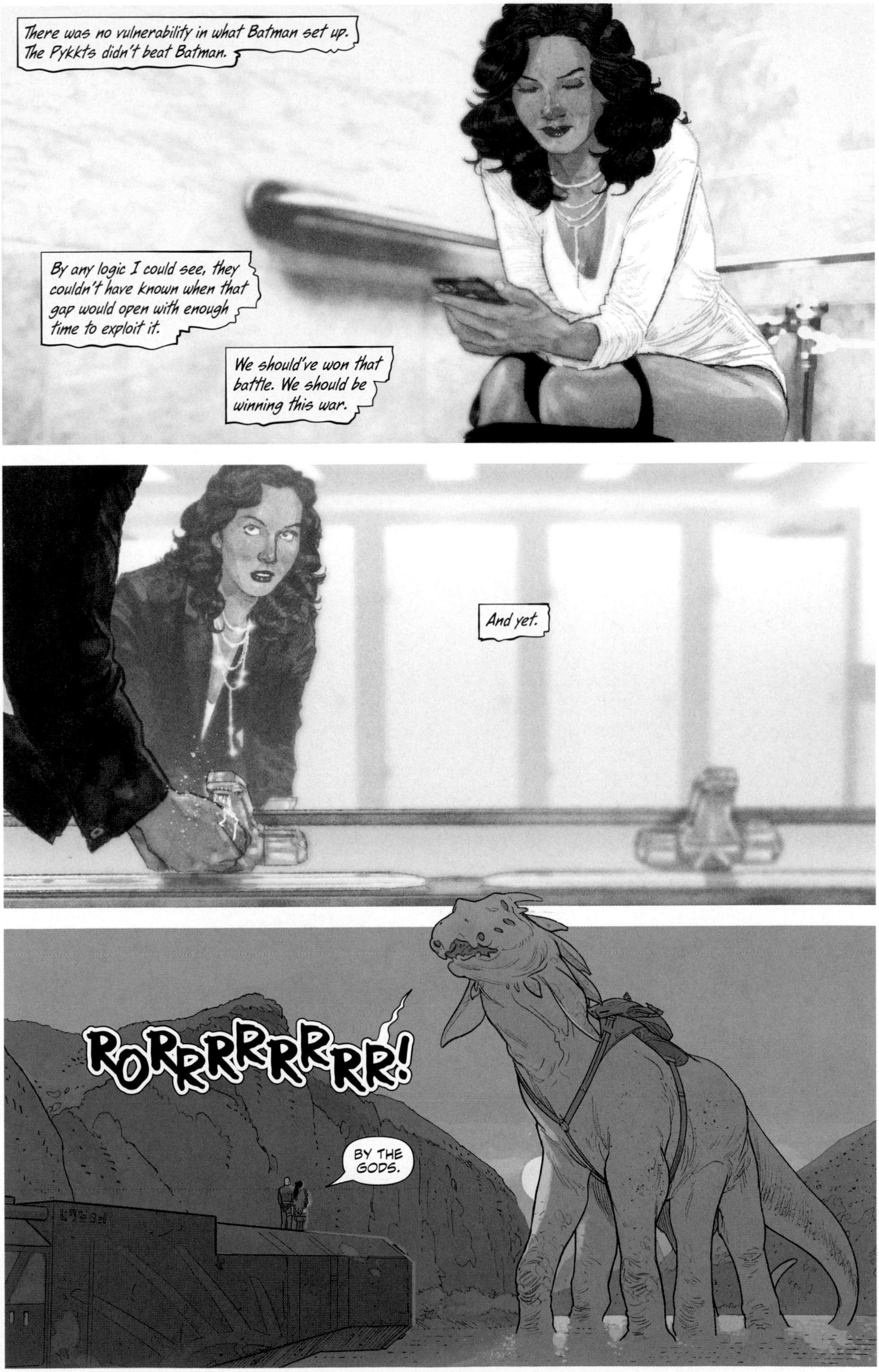
There was no vulnerability in what Batman set up. The Pykkts didn't beat Batman.
By any logic I could see, they couldn't have known when that gap would open with enough time to exploit it.
We should've won that battle. We should be winning this war.
And yet.
RORRRRRRRR!
BY THE GODS.

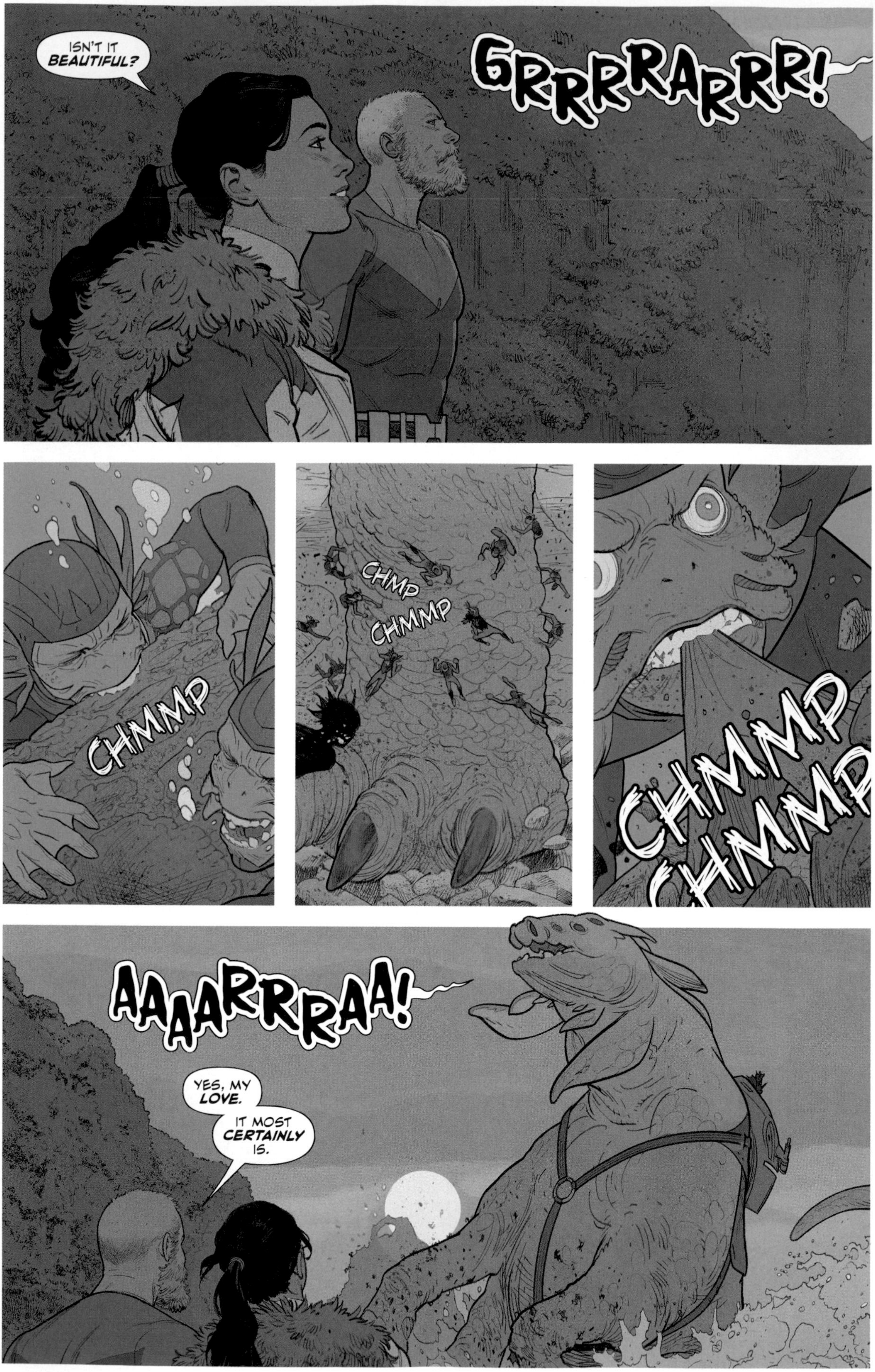
ISN'T IT BEAUTIFUL?
GRRRRARRR!
CHMMP
CHMP
CHMMP
CHMMP
CHMMP
AAAARRRAA!
YES, MY LOVE.
IT MOST CERTAINLY IS.

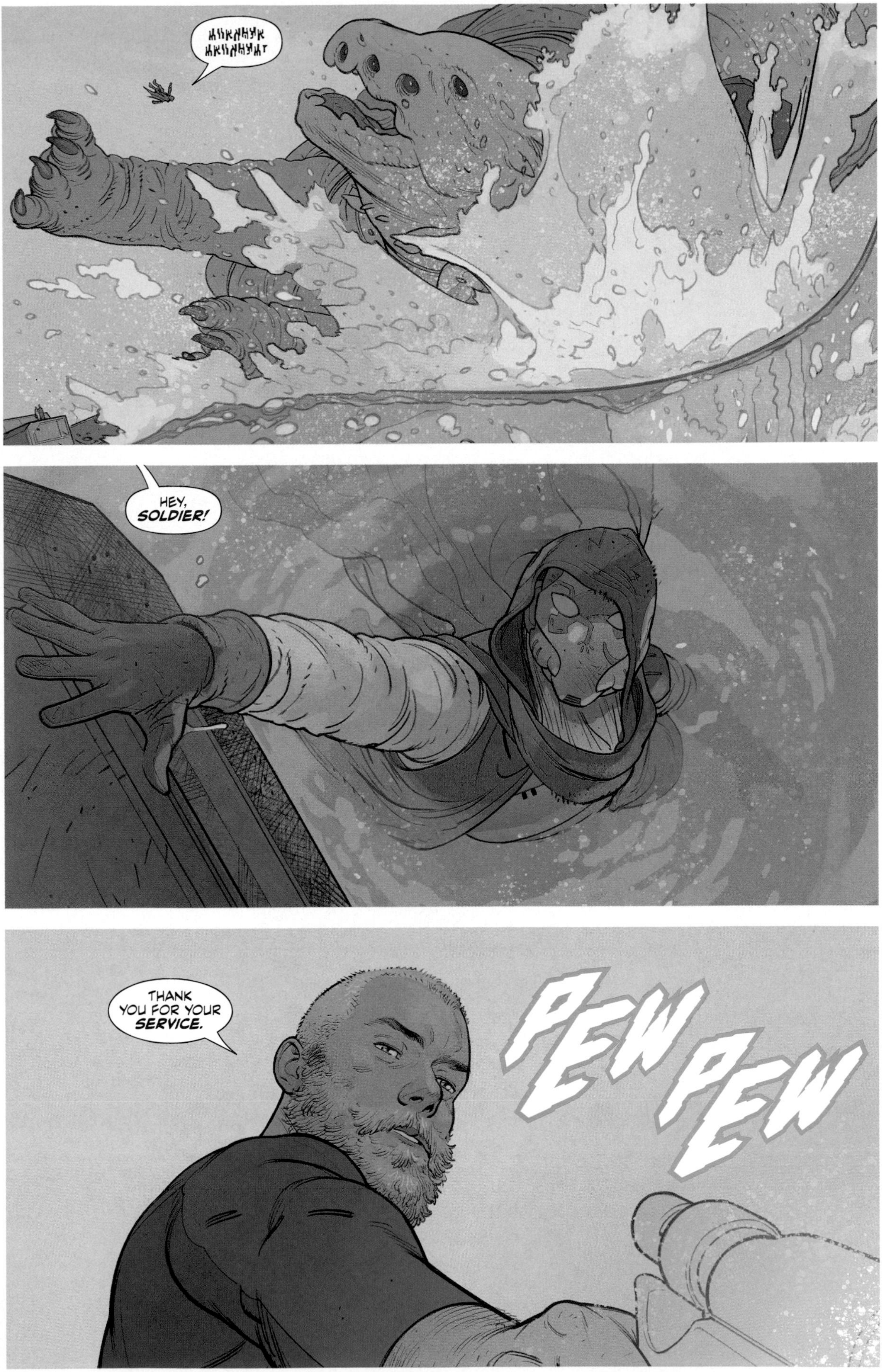
HEY, SOLDIER!
THANK YOU FOR YOUR SERVICE.
PEW PEW

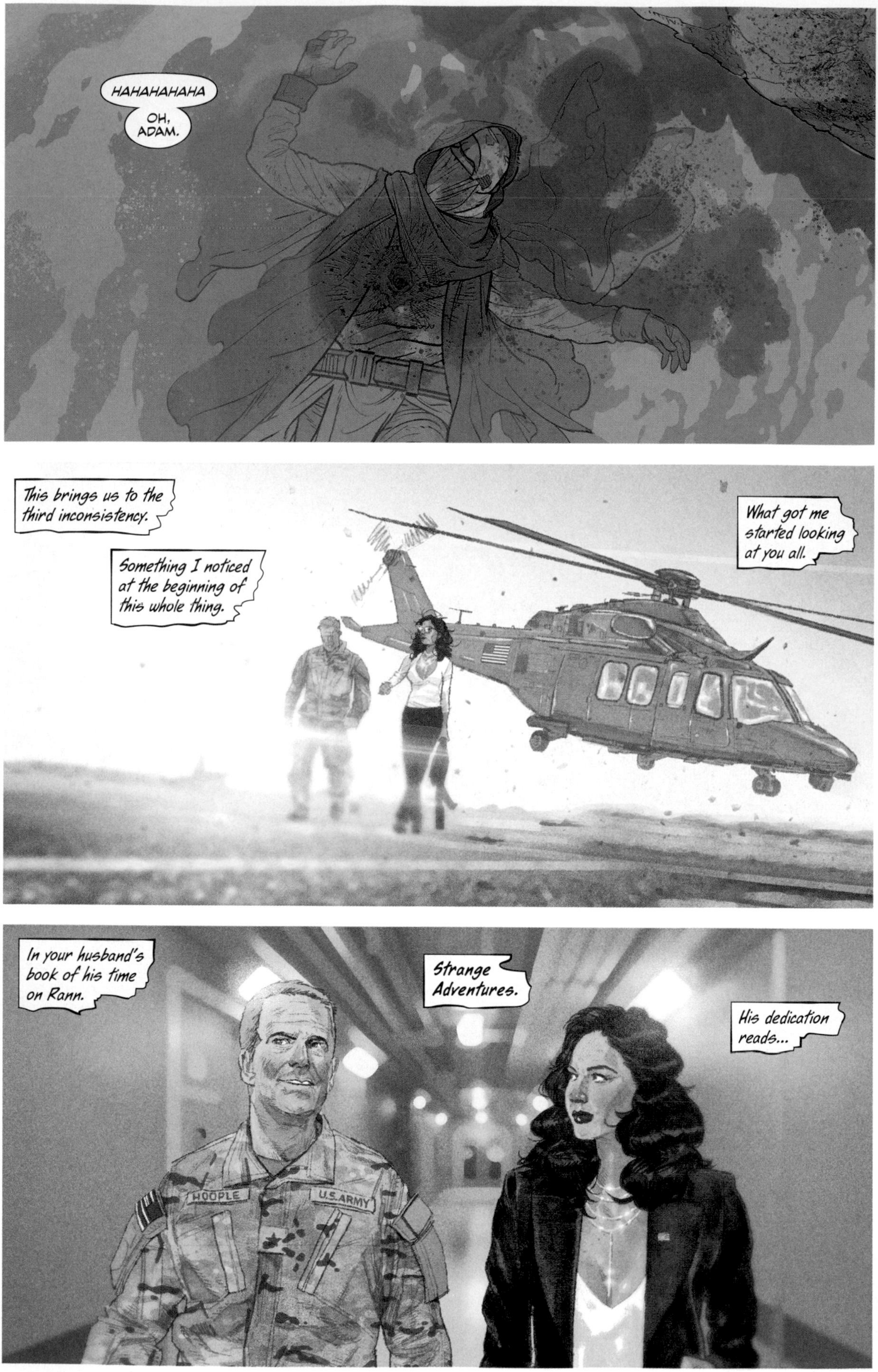
HAHAHAHAHA
OH, ADAM.
This brings us to the third inconsistency.
Something I noticed at the beginning of this whole thing.
What got me started looking at you all.
In your husband's book of his time on Rann.
Strange Adventures.
His dedication reads...
HOOPLE
U.S.ARMY

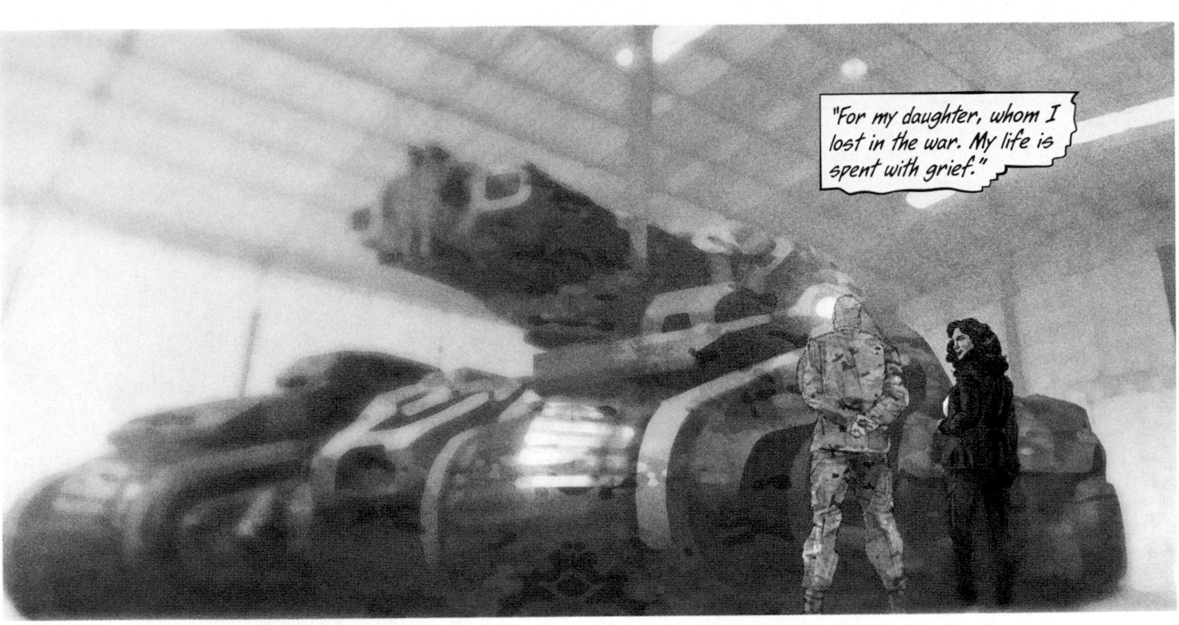
"For my daughter, whom I lost in the war. My life is spent with grief."

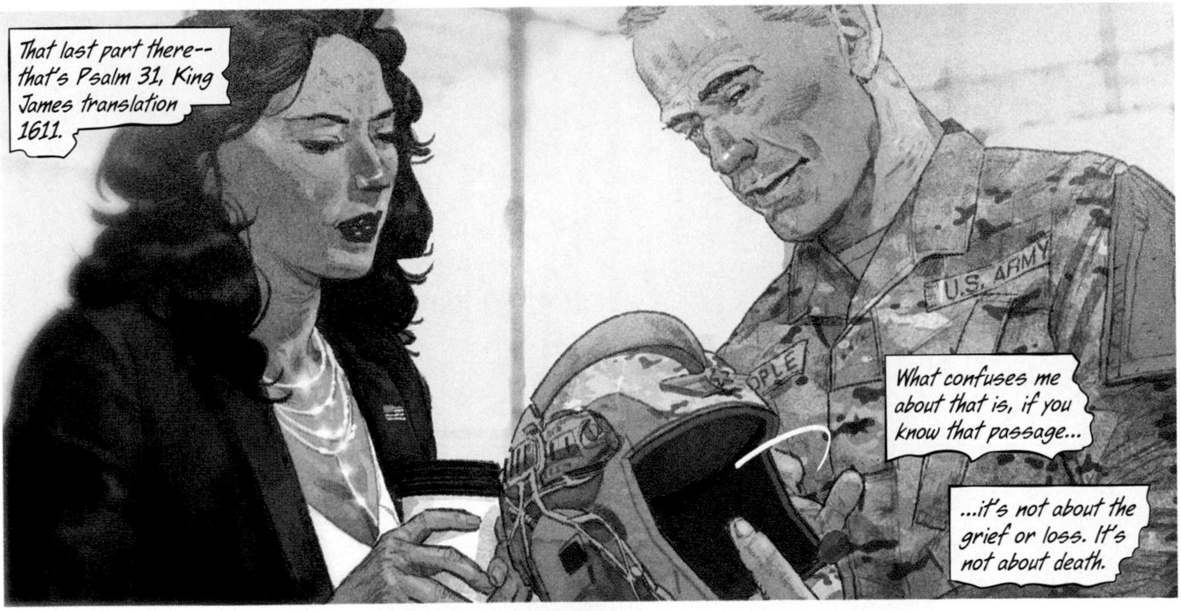
That last part there-- that's Psalm 31, King James translation 1611.
U.S. ARMY
What confuses me about that is, if you know that passage...
...it's not about the grief or loss. It's not about death.

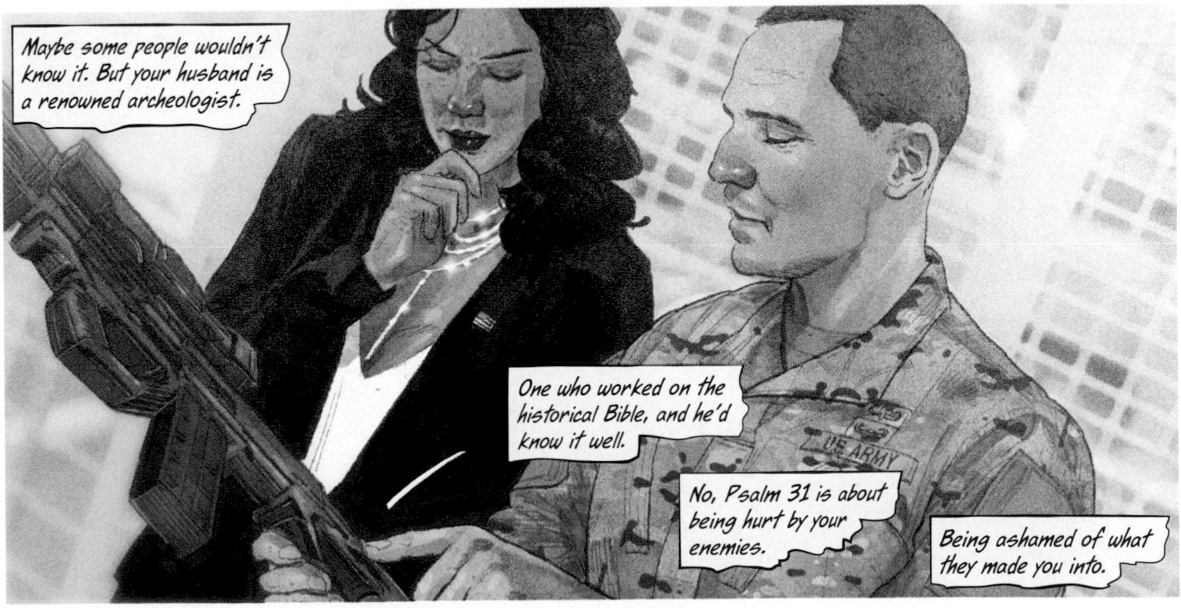
Maybe some people wouldn't know it. But your husband is a renowned archeologist.
One who worked on the historical Bible, and he'd know it well.
No, Psalm 31 is about being hurt by your enemies.
Being ashamed of what they made you into.

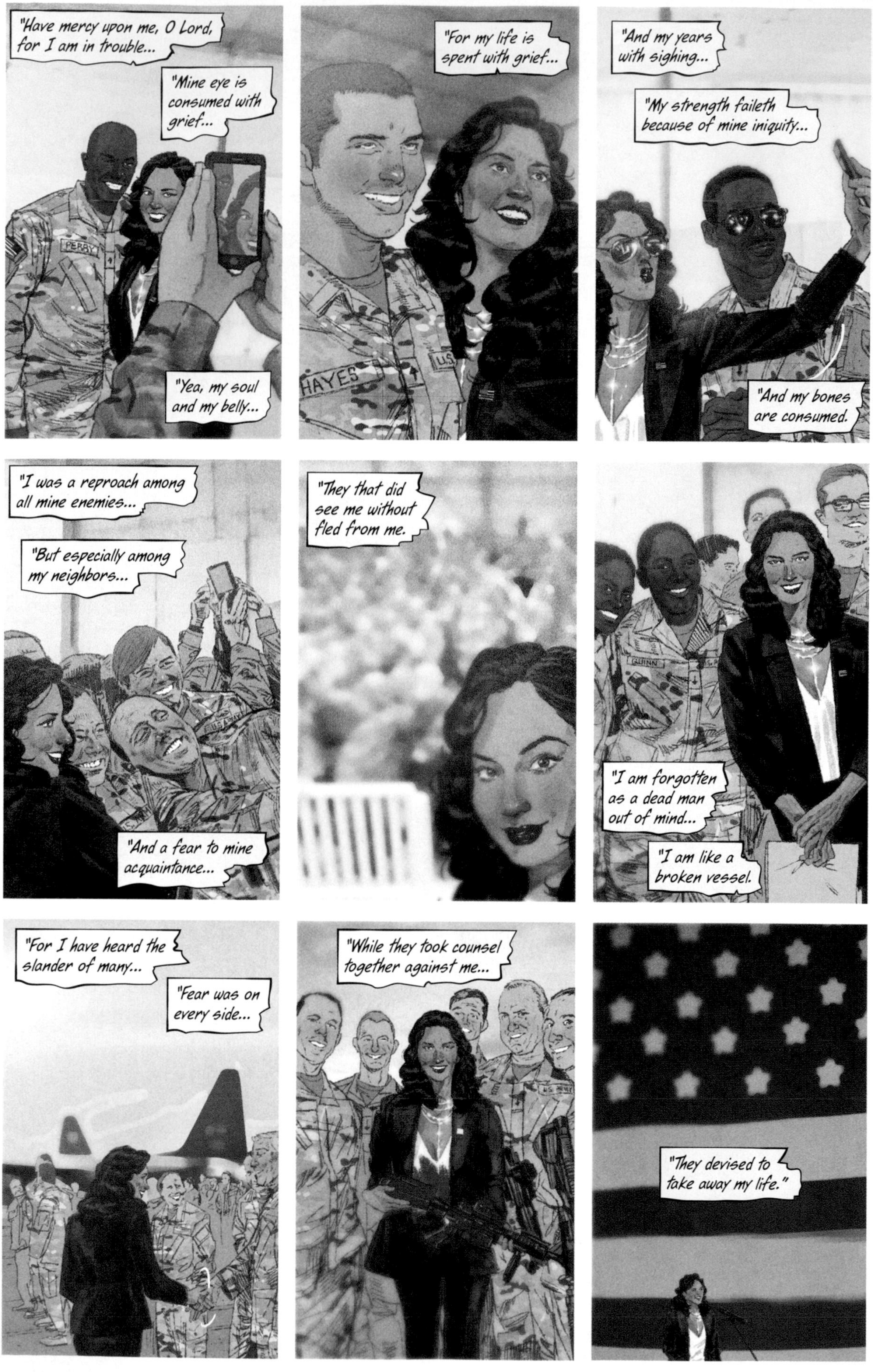
"Have mercy upon me, O Lord, for I am in trouble...
"Mine eye is consumed with grief...
PERRY
"Yea, my soul and my belly...
"For my life is spent with grief...
HAYES
"And my years with sighing...
"My strength faileth because of mine iniquity...
"And my bones are consumed.
"I was a reproach among all mine enemies...
"But especially among my neighbors...
"And a fear to mine acquaintance...
"They that did see me without fled from me.
QUINN
"I am forgotten as a dead man out of mind...
"I am like a broken vessel.
"For I have heard the slander of many...
"Fear was on every side...
"While they took counsel together against me...
"They devised to take away my life."

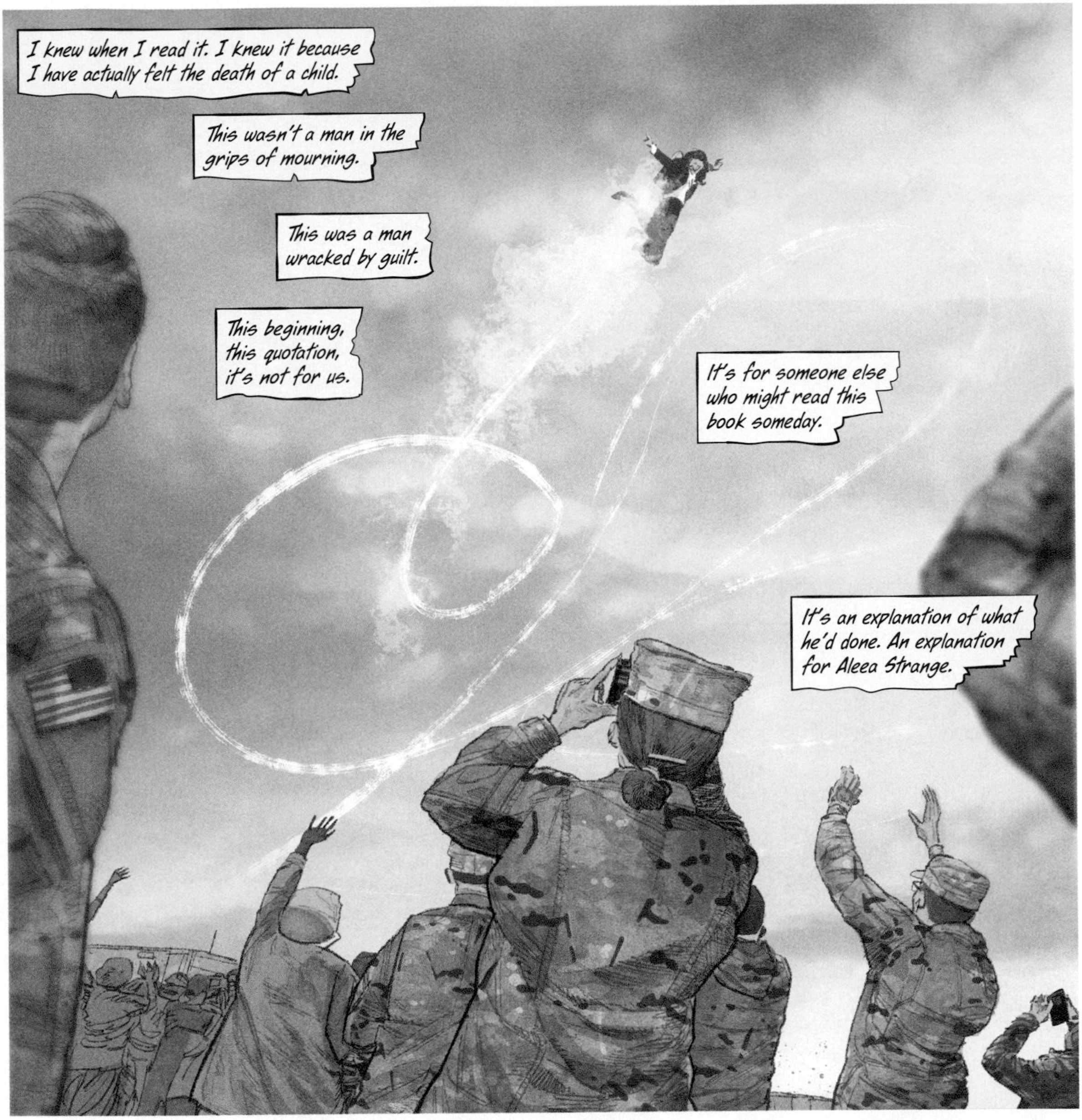
I knew when I read it. I knew it because I have actually felt the death of a child.
This wasn't a man in the grips of mourning.
This was a man wracked by guilt.
This beginning, this quotation, it's not for us.
It's for someone else who might read this book someday.
It's an explanation of what he'd done. An explanation for Aleea Strange.

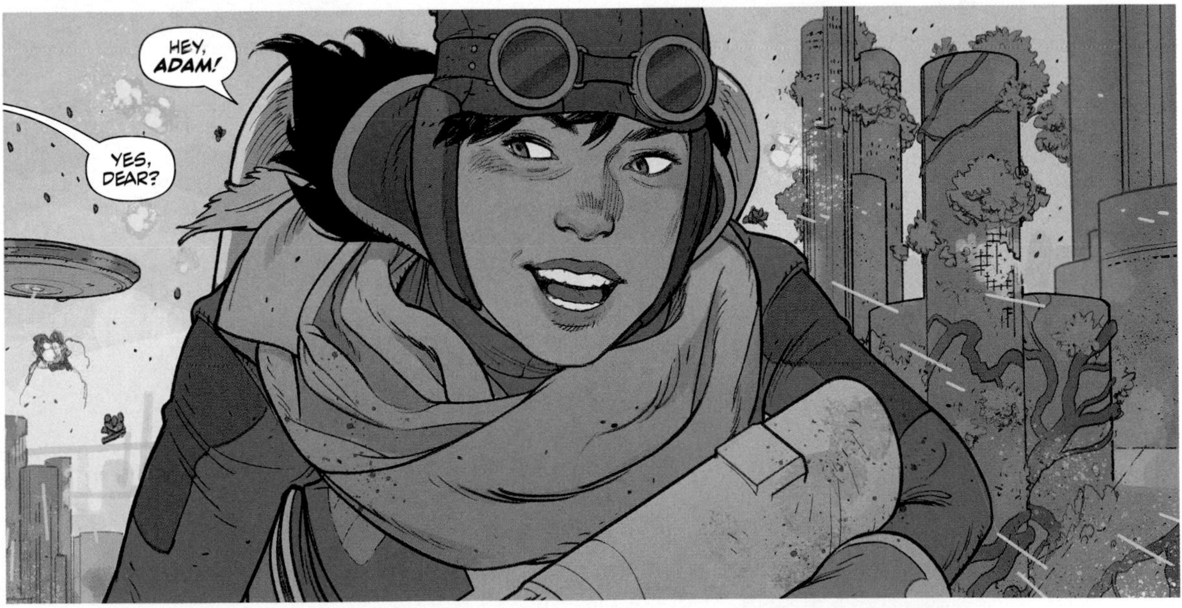
HEY, ADAM!
YES, DEAR?

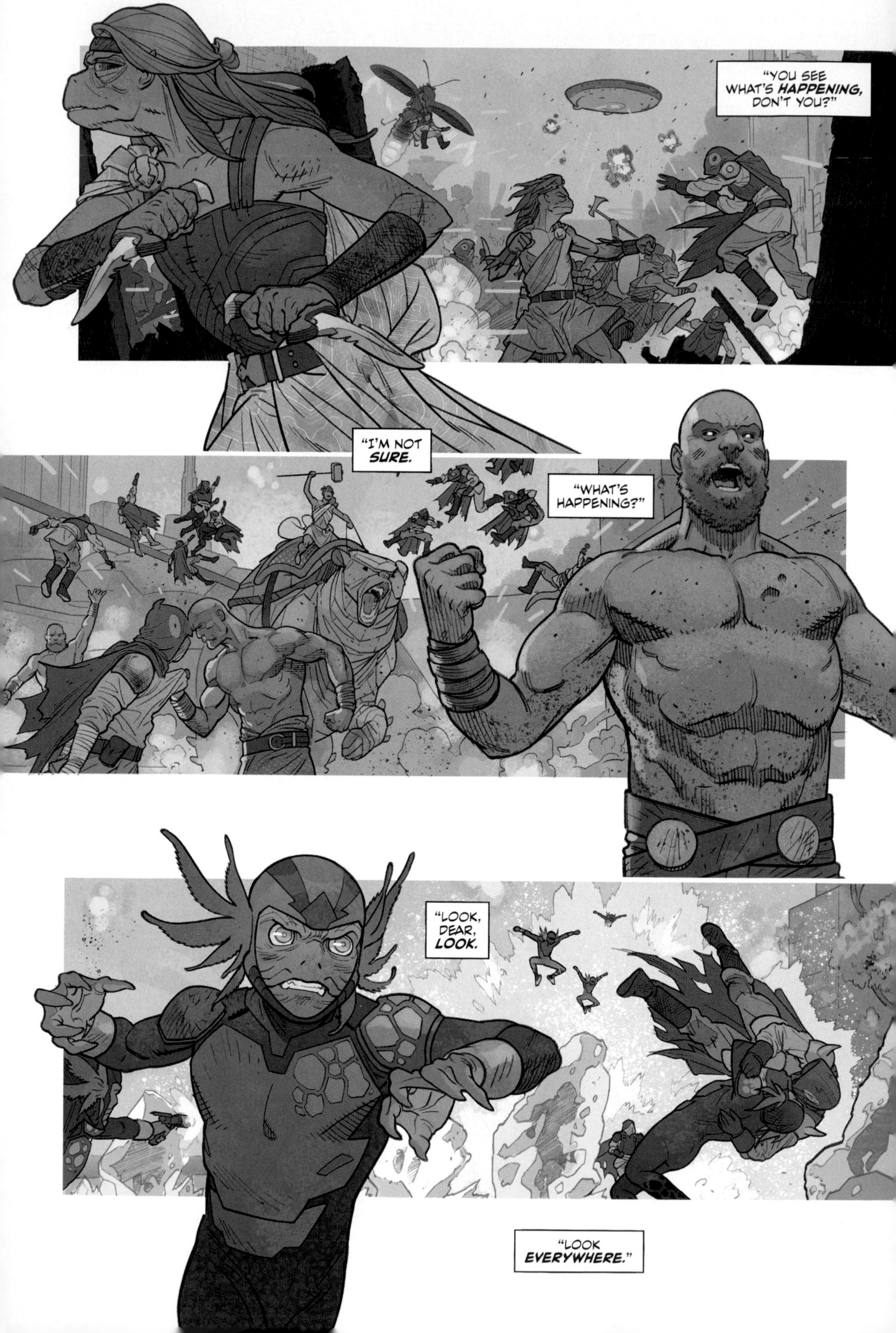
"YOU SEE WHAT'S HAPPENING, DON'T YOU?"
"I'M NOT SURE.
"WHAT'S HAPPENING?"
"LOOK, DEAR, LOOK.
"LOOK EVERYWHERE."

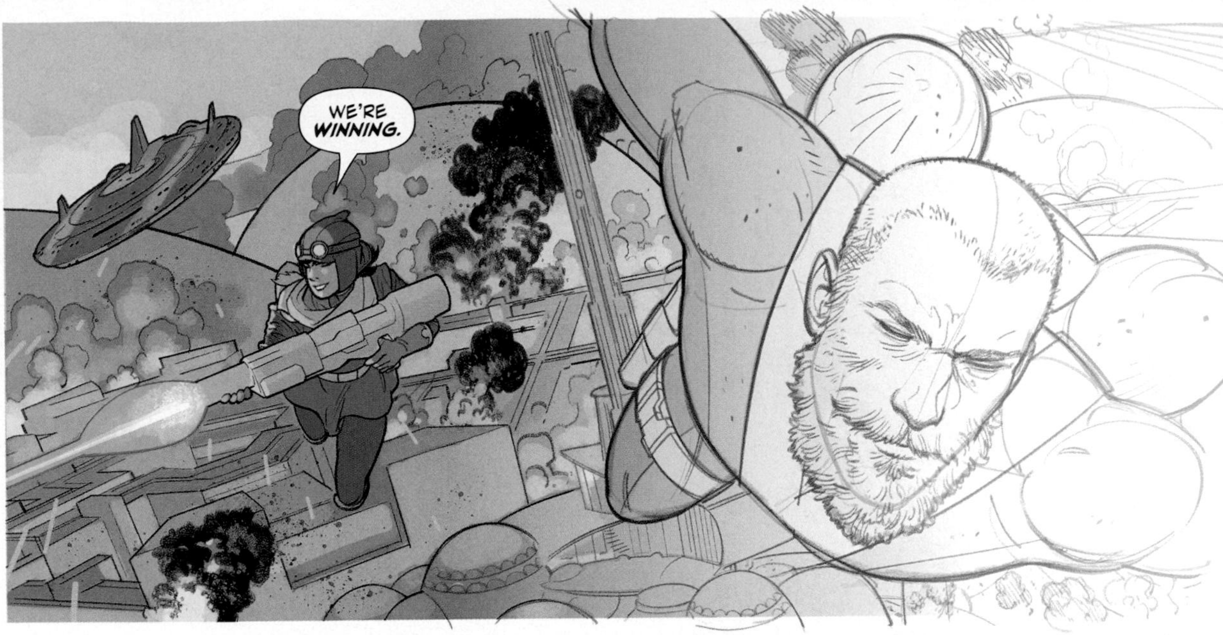
WE'RE WINNING.

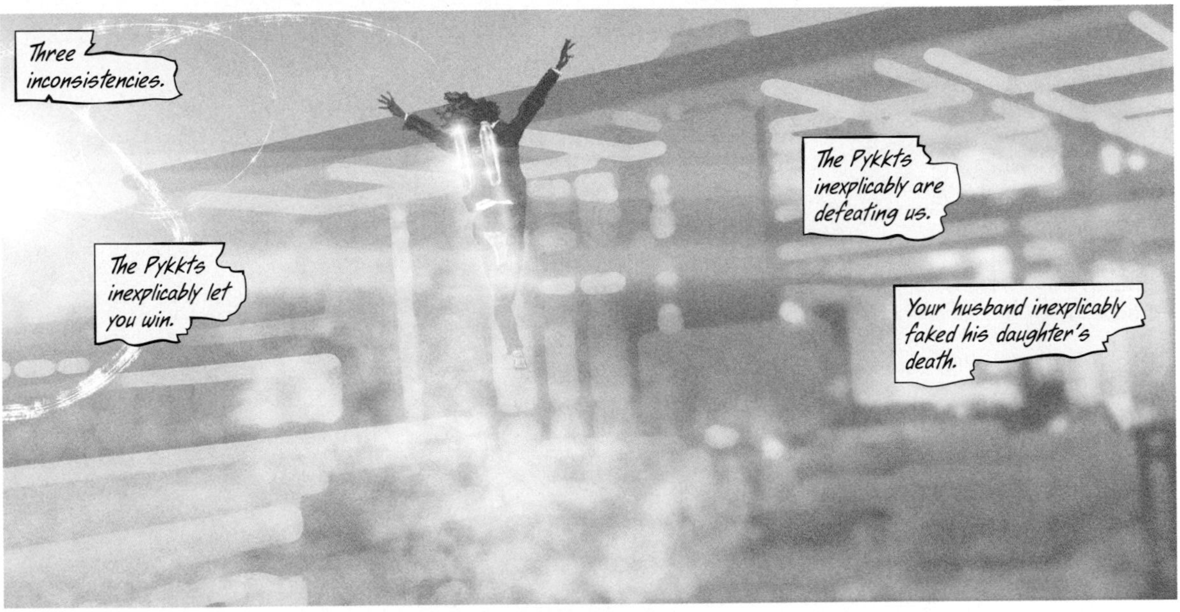
Three inconsistencies.
The Pykkts inexplicably let you win.
The Pykkts inexplicably are defeating us.
Your husband inexplicably faked his daughter's death.

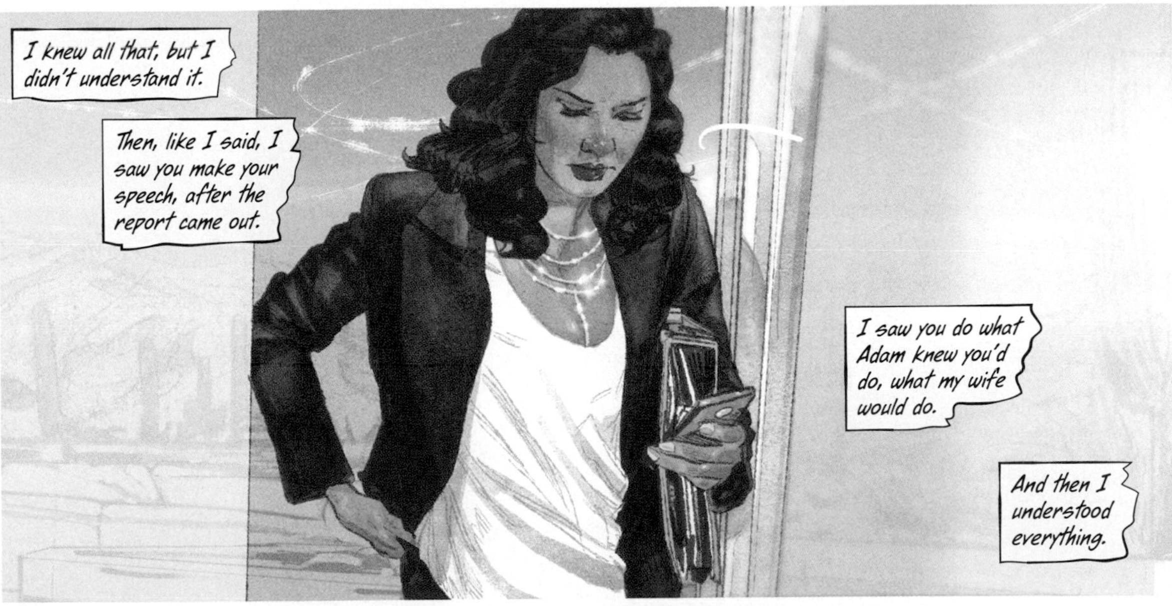
I knew all that, but I didn't understand it.
Then, like I said, I saw you make your speech, after the report came out.
I saw you do what Adam knew you'd do, what my wife would do.
And then I understood everything.

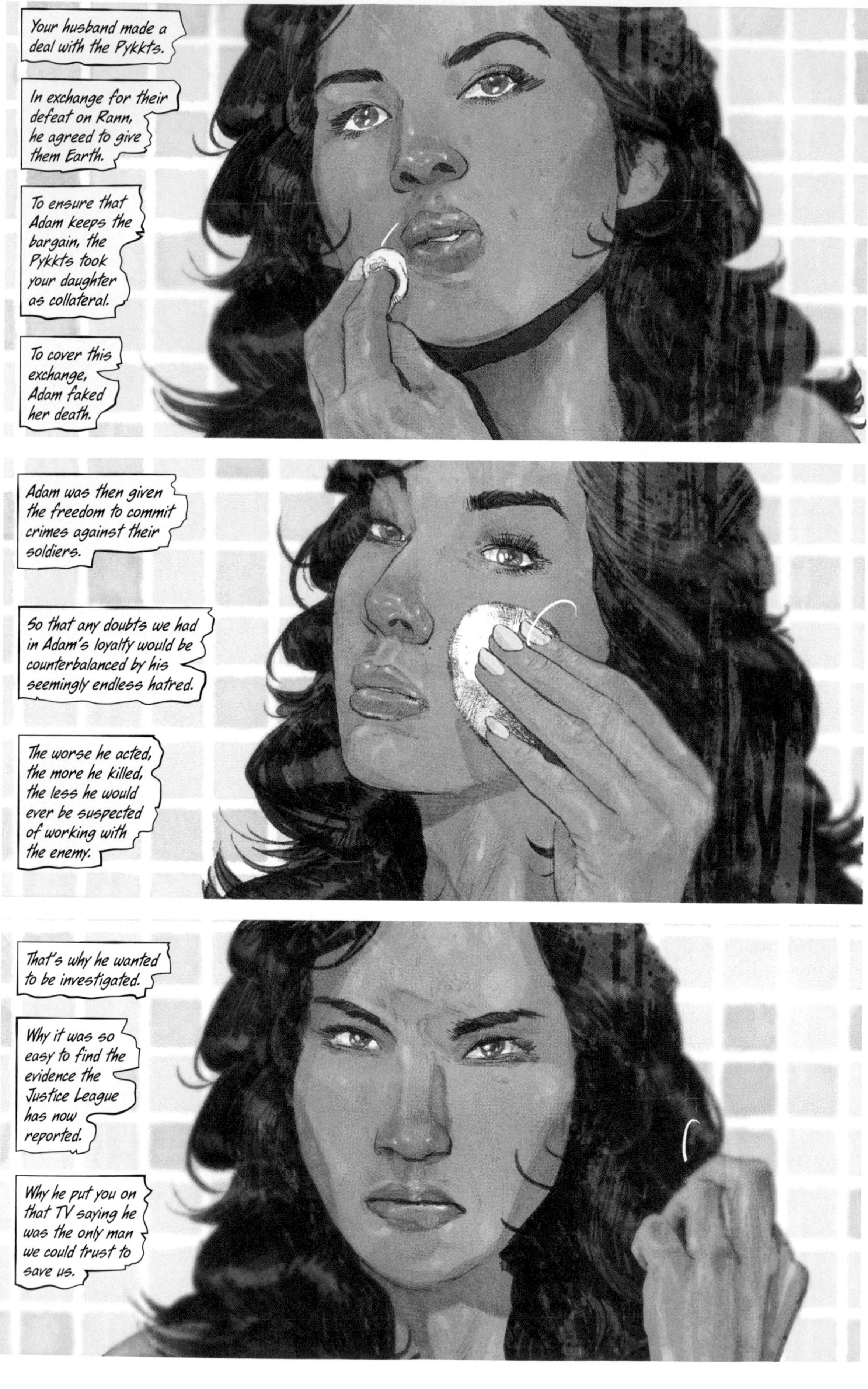
Your husband made a deal with the Pykkts.
In exchange for their defeat on Rann, he agreed to give them Earth.
To ensure that Adam keeps the bargain, the Pykkts took your daughter as collateral.
To cover this exchange, Adam faked her death.
Adam was then given the freedom to commit crimes against their soldiers.
So that any doubts we had in Adam's loyalty would be counterbalanced by his seemingly endless hatred.
The worse he acted, the more he killed, the less he would ever be suspected of working with the enemy.
That's why he wanted to be investigated.
Why it was so easy to find the evidence the Justice League has now reported.
Why he put you on that TV saying he was the only man we could trust to save us.

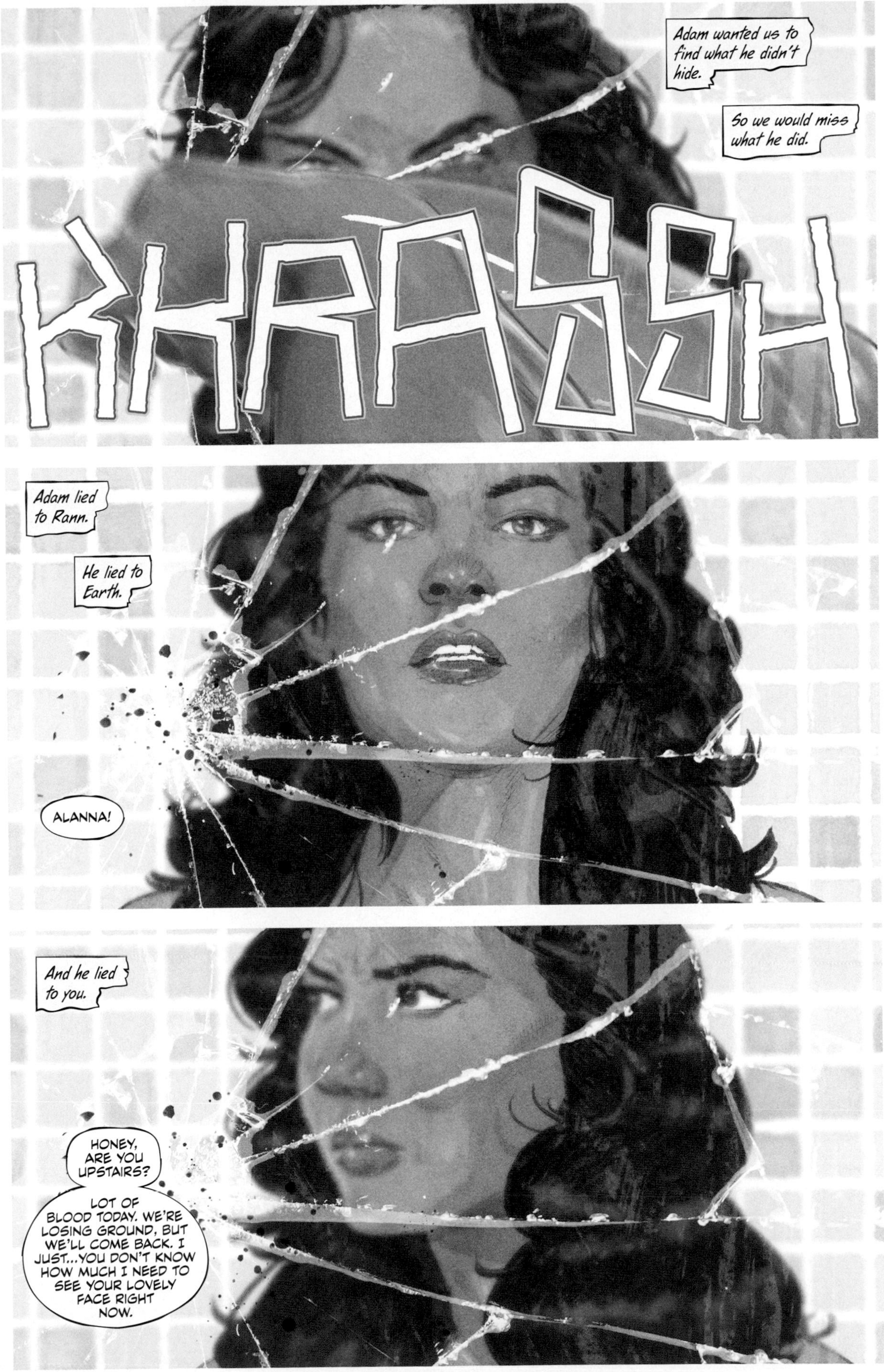
Adam wanted us to find what he didn't hide.
So we would miss what he did.
KKRASSH
Adam lied to Rann.
He lied to Earth.
ALANNA!
And he lied to you.
HONEY, ARE YOU UPSTAIRS?
LOT OF BLOOD TODAY. WE'RE LOSING GROUND, BUT WE'LL COME BACK. I JUST...YOU DON'T KNOW HOW MUCH I NEED TO SEE YOUR LOVELY FACE RIGHT NOW.

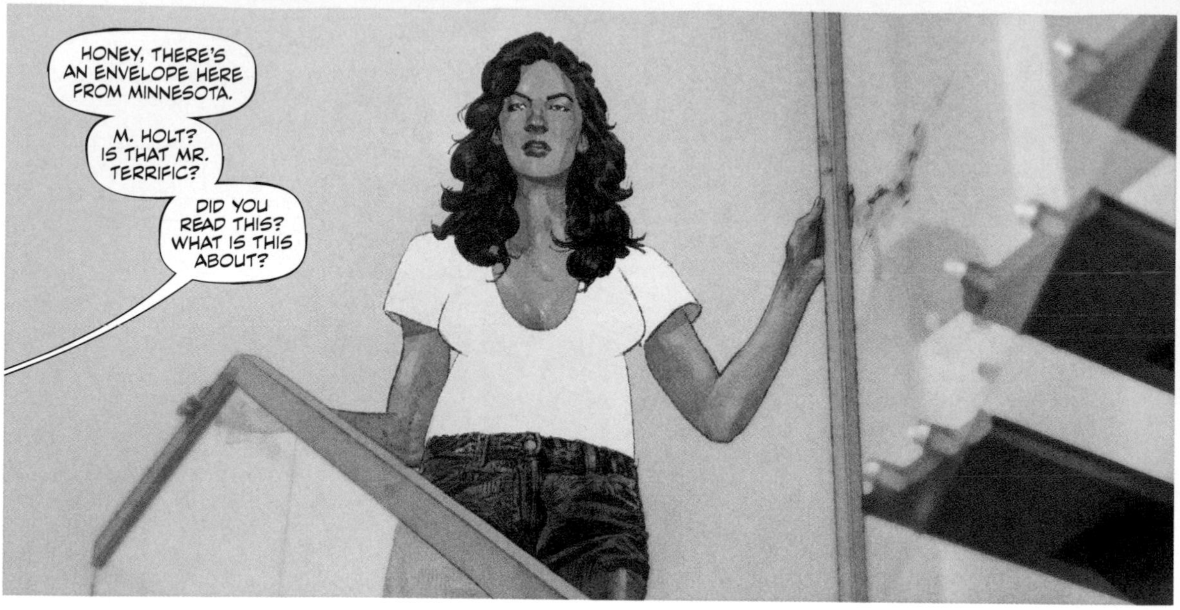
HONEY, THERE'S AN ENVELOPE HERE FROM MINNESOTA.
M. HOLT? IS THAT MR. TERRIFIC?
DID YOU READ THIS? WHAT IS THIS ABOUT?

Say you're doing an arm. You see the drapery crunch up to where the elbow breaks, and then the flare coming off the shoulder seam down. Once you tell somebody this is what happens, why it happens, you rule supreme.

—Jack Kamen

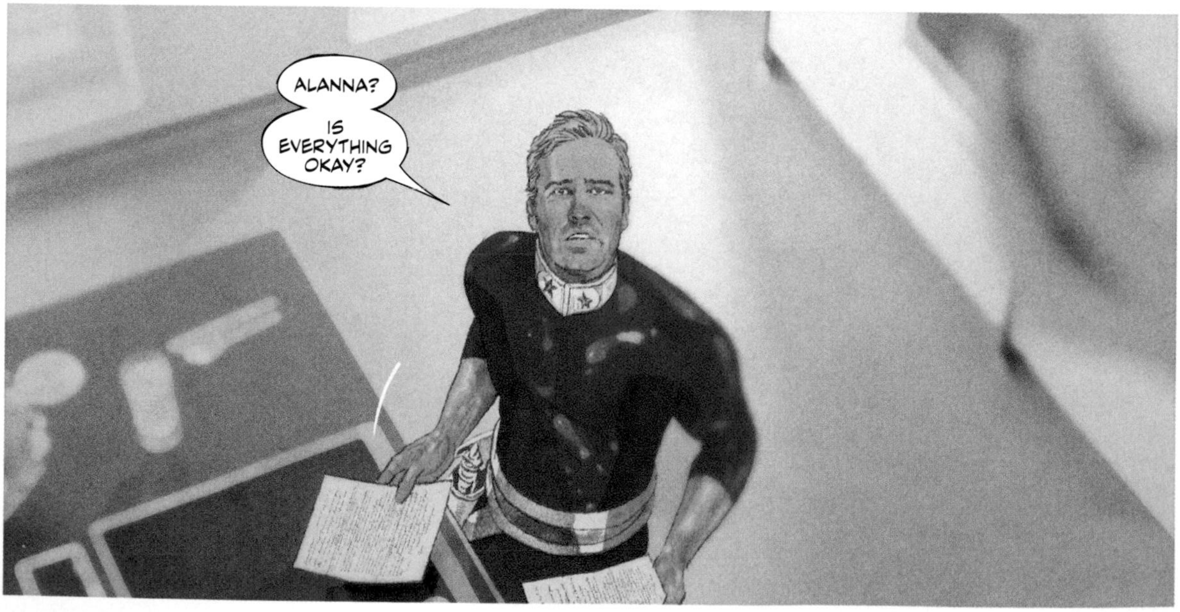
ALANNA?
IS EVERYTHING OKAY?

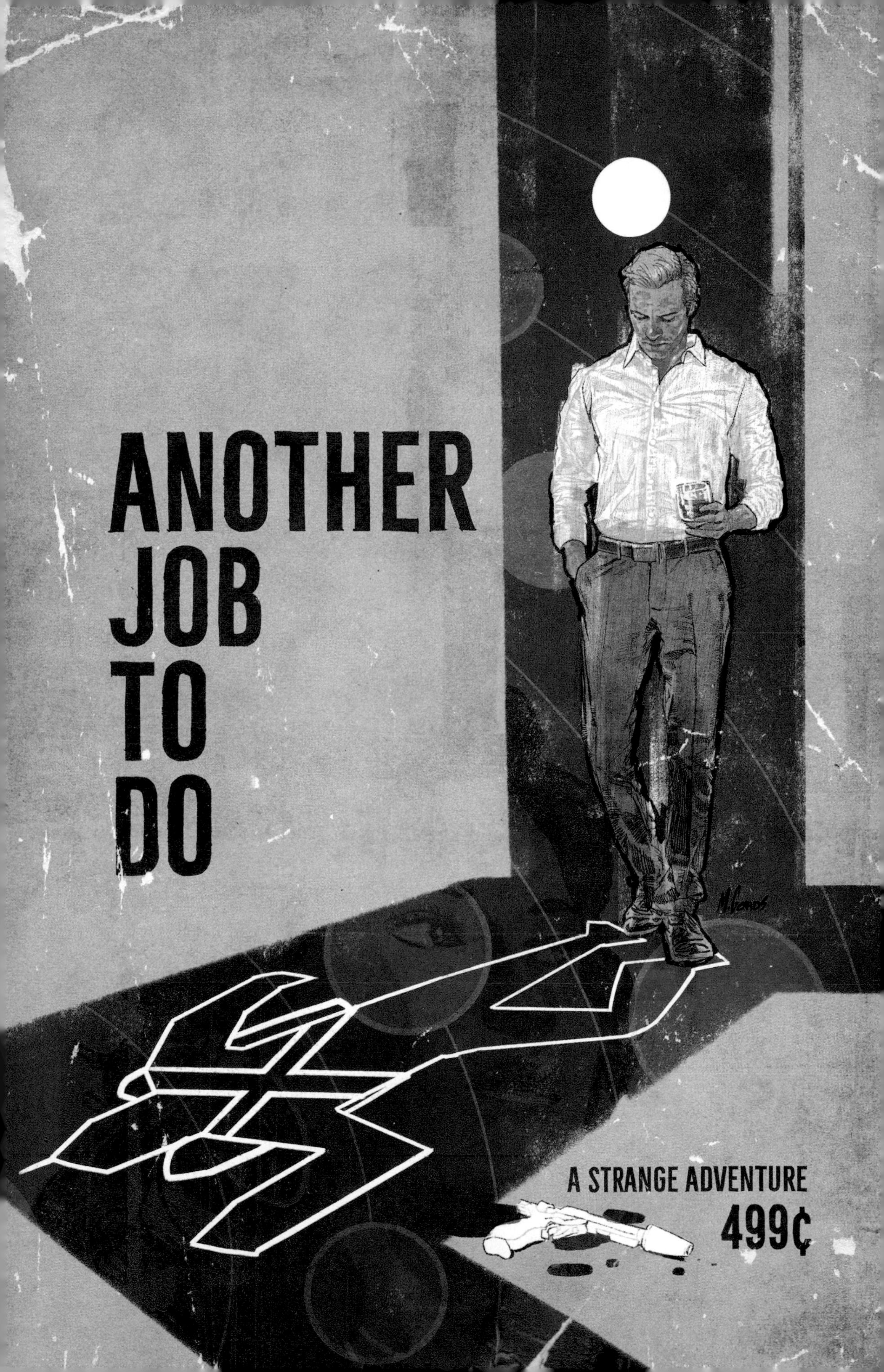
ANOTHER JOB TO DO
A STRANGE ADVENTURE
499¢

"TO SAVE ME, YOU KILLED ME."

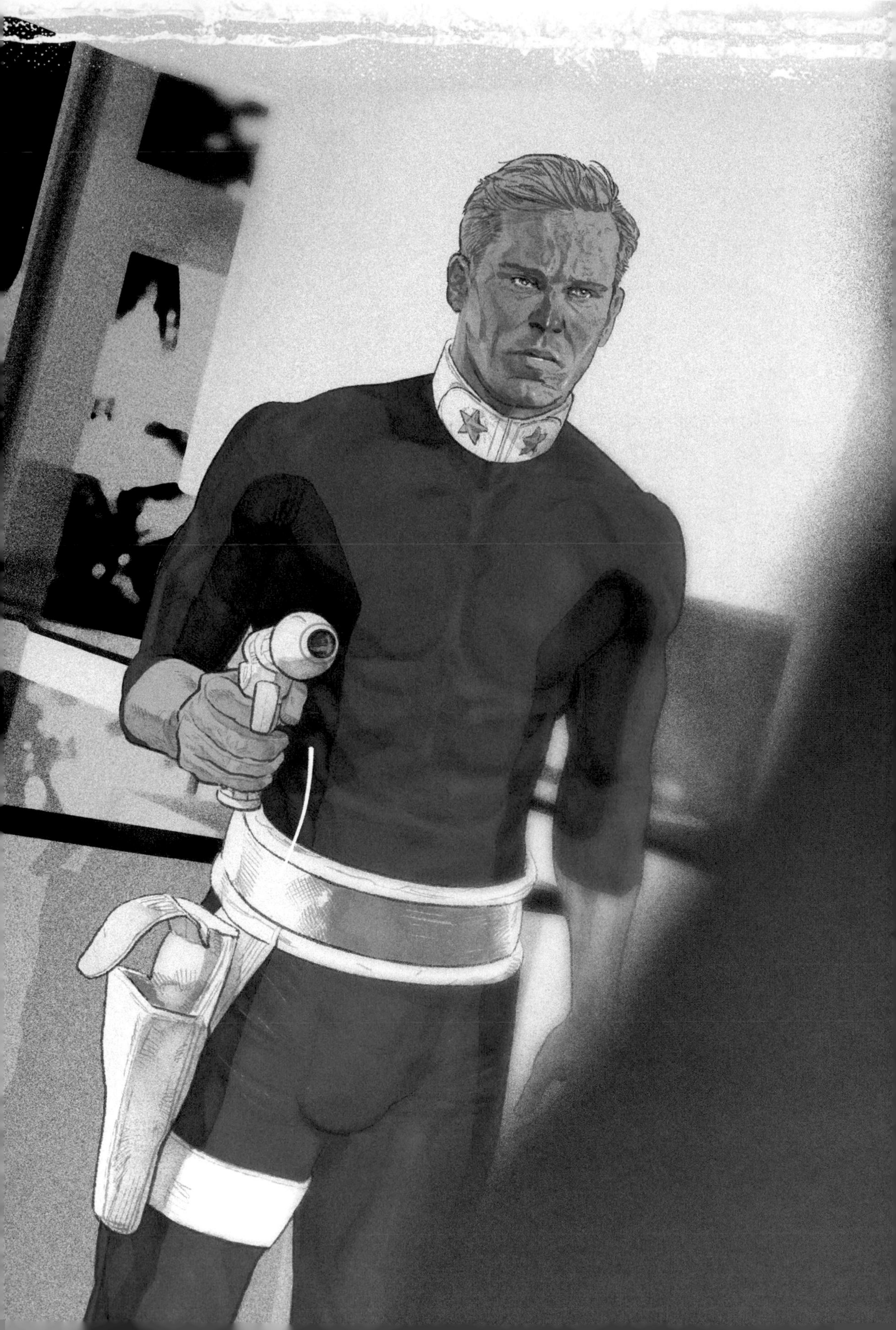

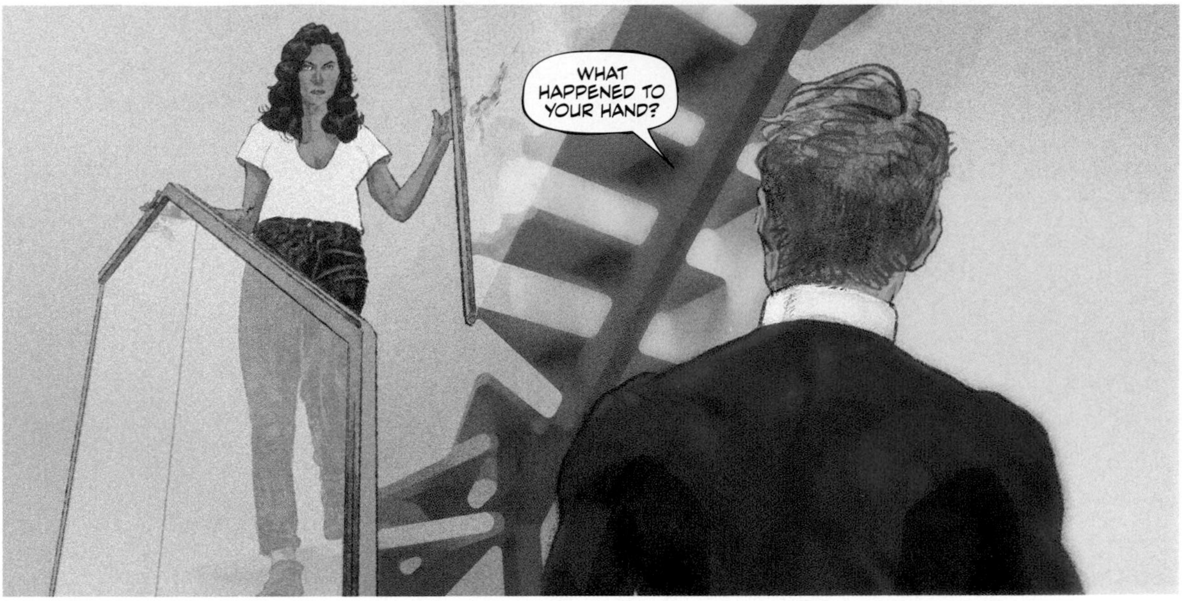
WHAT HAPPENED TO YOUR HAND?

Chapter 11

Another job to do

TOM KING	...Writer
MITCH GERADS EVAN "DOC" SHANER	...Interior & Cover Artists
CLAYTON COWLES	...Letterer
BIXIE MATHIEU	...Assistant Editor
BRITTANY HOLZHERR JAMIE S. RICH	...Editors

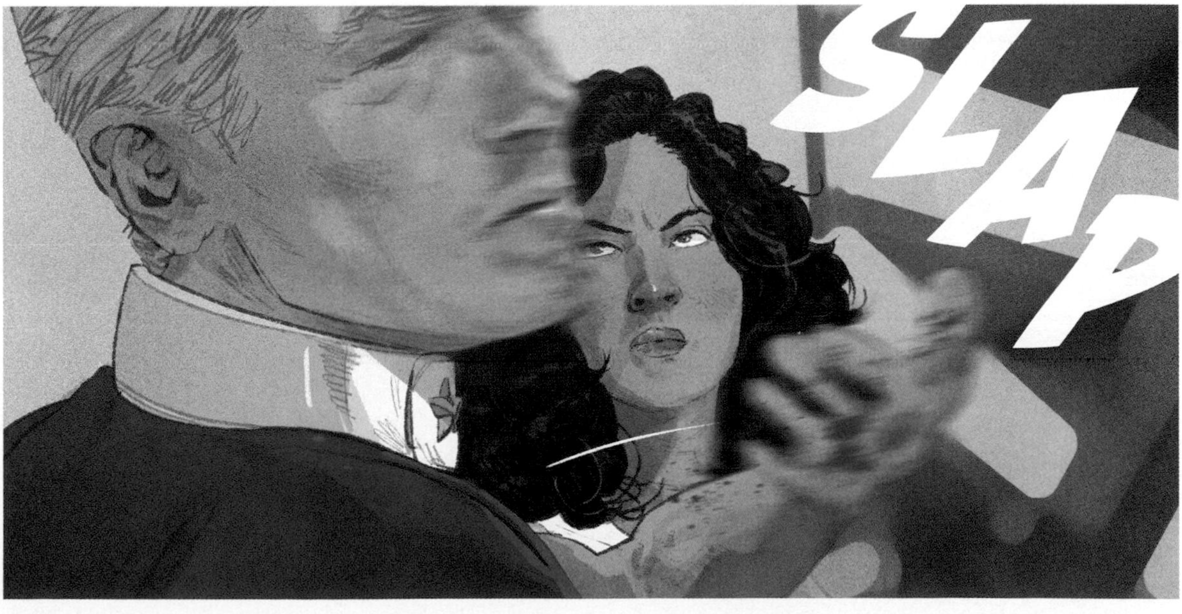
SLAP

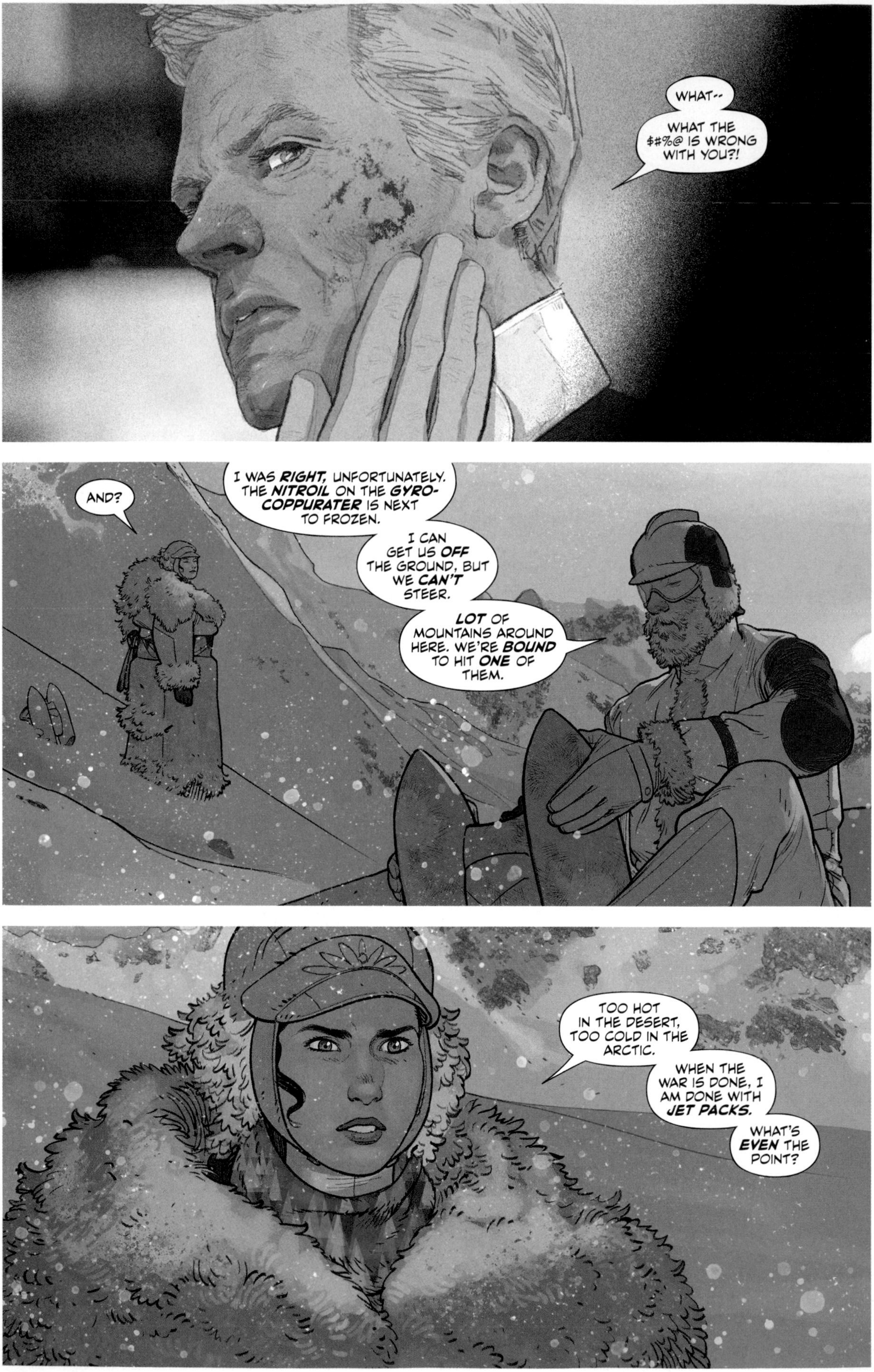
WHAT--
WHAT THE $#%@ IS WRONG WITH YOU?!
AND?
I WAS **RIGHT,** UNFORTUNATELY. THE **NITROIL** ON THE **GYRO-COPPURATER** IS NEXT TO FROZEN.
I CAN GET US **OFF** THE GROUND, BUT WE **CAN'T** STEER.
LOT OF MOUNTAINS AROUND HERE. WE'RE **BOUND** TO HIT **ONE** OF THEM.
TOO HOT IN THE DESERT, TOO COLD IN THE ARCTIC.
WHEN THE WAR IS DONE, I AM DONE WITH **JET PACKS.**
WHAT'S **EVEN** THE POINT?

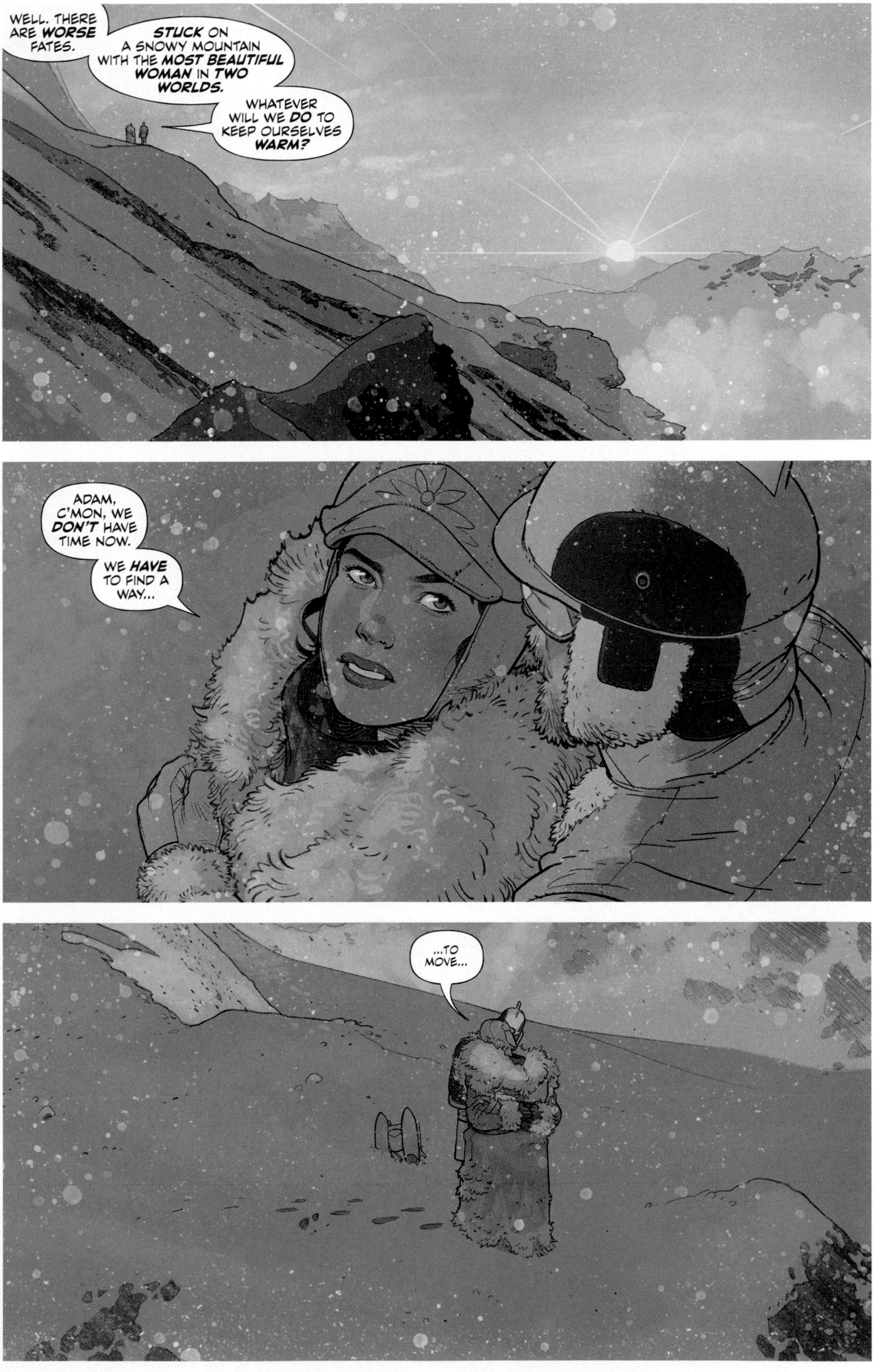
WELL. THERE ARE WORSE FATES.
STUCK ON A SNOWY MOUNTAIN WITH THE MOST BEAUTIFUL WOMAN IN TWO WORLDS.
WHATEVER WILL WE DO TO KEEP OURSELVES WARM?
ADAM, C'MON, WE DON'T HAVE TIME NOW.
WE HAVE TO FIND A WAY...
...TO MOVE...

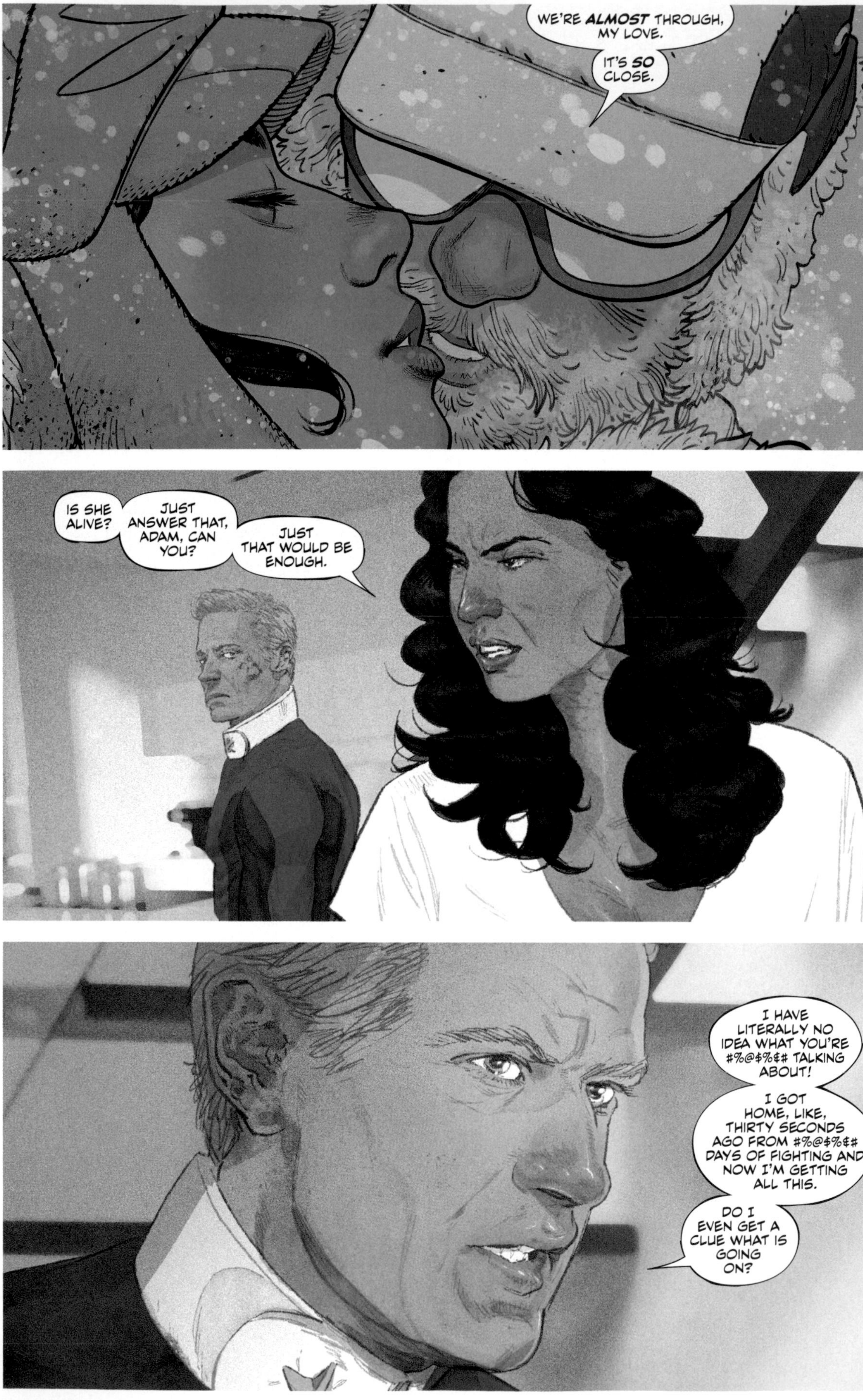
WE'RE **ALMOST** THROUGH, MY LOVE.
IT'S **SO** CLOSE.
IS SHE ALIVE?
JUST ANSWER THAT, ADAM, CAN YOU?
JUST THAT WOULD BE ENOUGH.
I HAVE LITERALLY NO IDEA WHAT YOU'RE #%@$%$# TALKING ABOUT!
I GOT HOME, LIKE, THIRTY SECONDS AGO FROM #%@$%$# DAYS OF FIGHTING AND NOW I'M GETTING ALL THIS.
DO I EVEN GET A CLUE WHAT IS GOING ON?

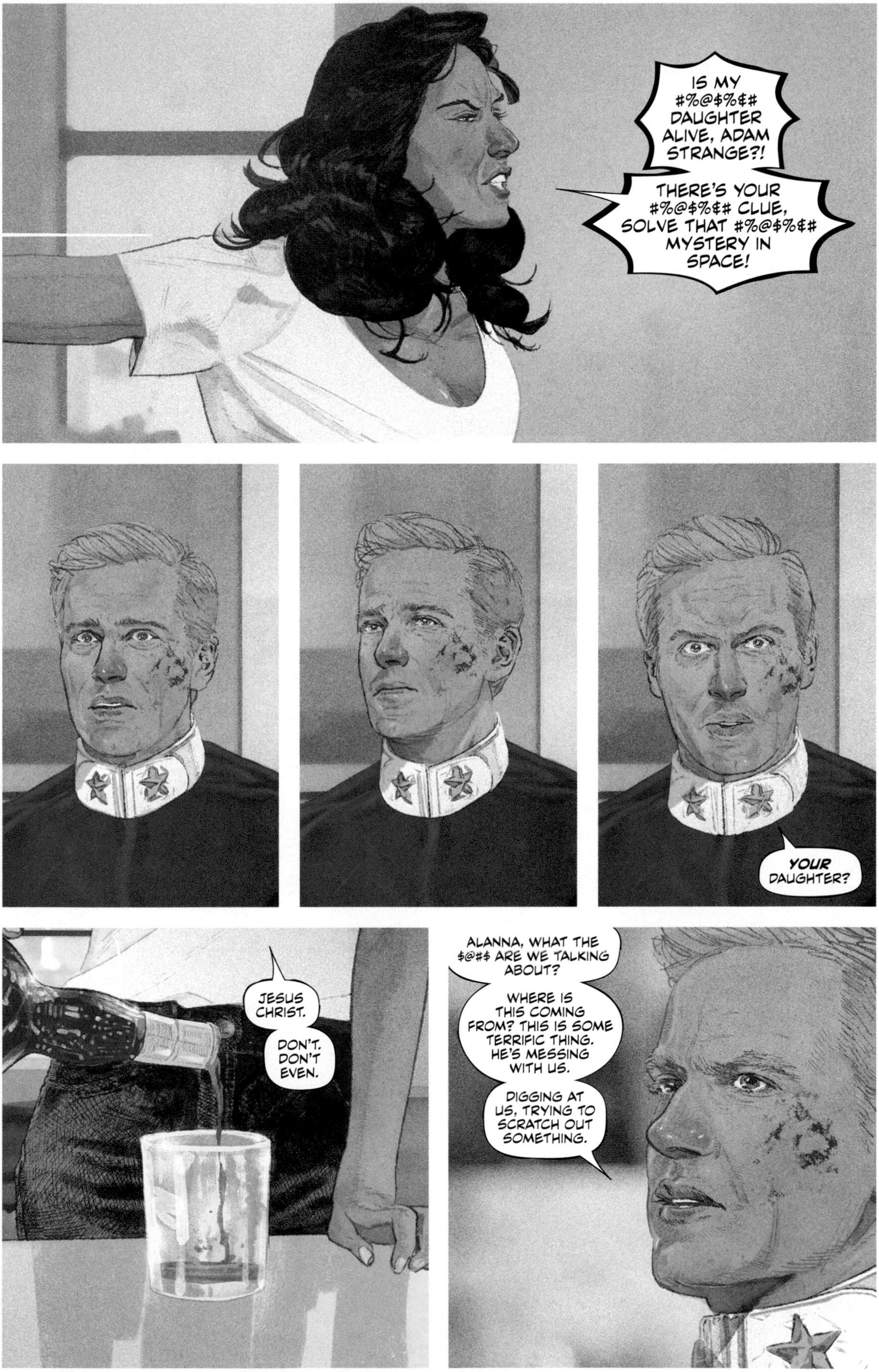
IS MY #%@$%$# DAUGHTER ALIVE, ADAM STRANGE?!
THERE'S YOUR #%@$%$# CLUE, SOLVE THAT #%@$%$# MYSTERY IN SPACE!
YOUR DAUGHTER?
JESUS CHRIST.
DON'T. DON'T EVEN.
ALANNA, WHAT THE $@#$ ARE WE TALKING ABOUT?
WHERE IS THIS COMING FROM? THIS IS SOME TERRIFIC THING. HE'S MESSING WITH US.
DIGGING AT US, TRYING TO SCRATCH OUT SOMETHING.

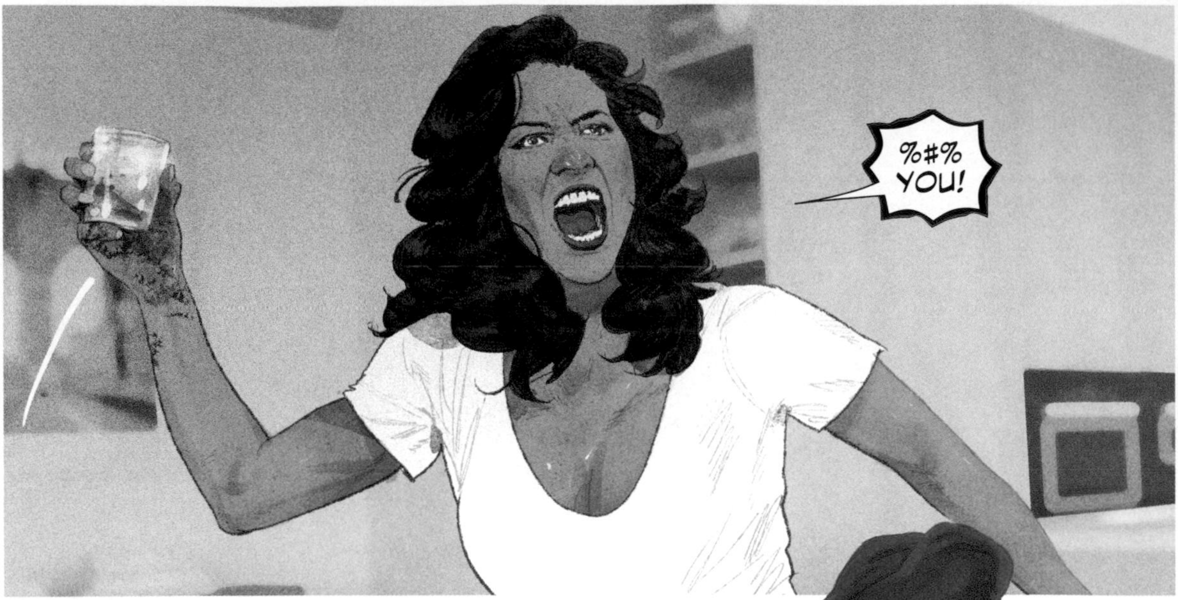
%#% YOU!

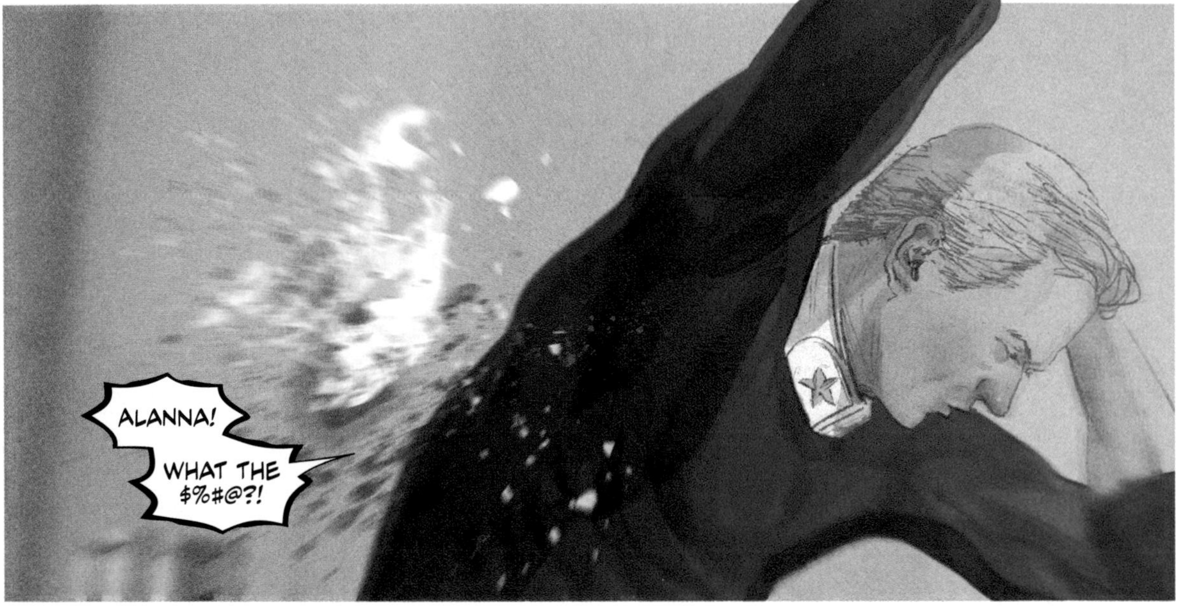
ALANNA!
WHAT THE $%#@?!

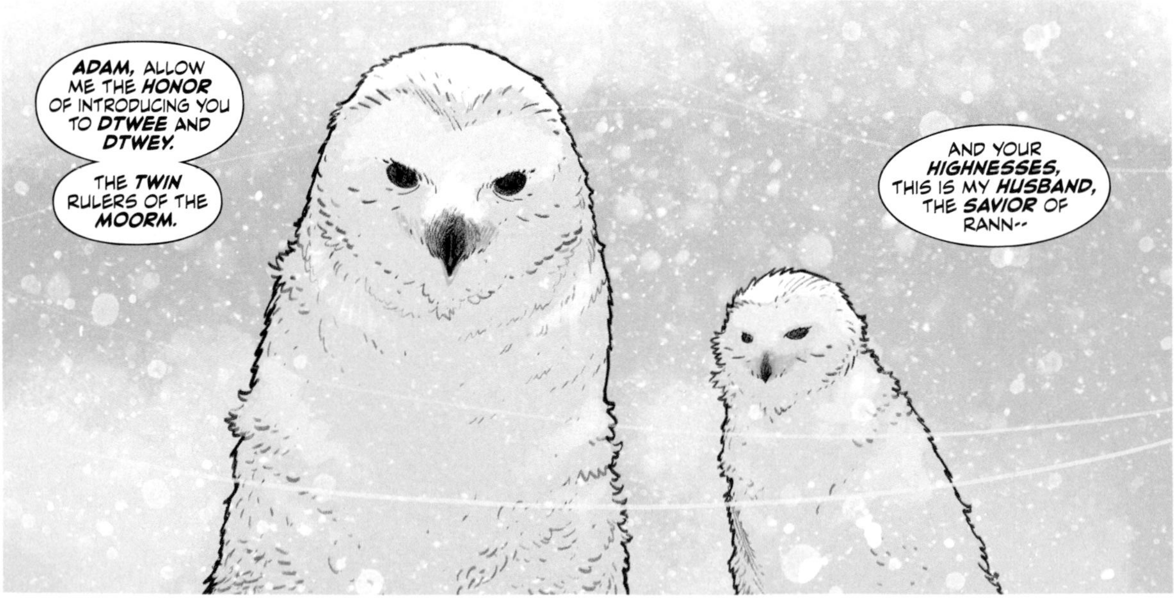
ADAM, ALLOW ME THE HONOR OF INTRODUCING YOU TO DTWEE AND DTWEY.
THE TWIN RULERS OF THE MOORM.
AND YOUR HIGHNESSES, THIS IS MY HUSBAND, THE SAVIOR OF RANN--

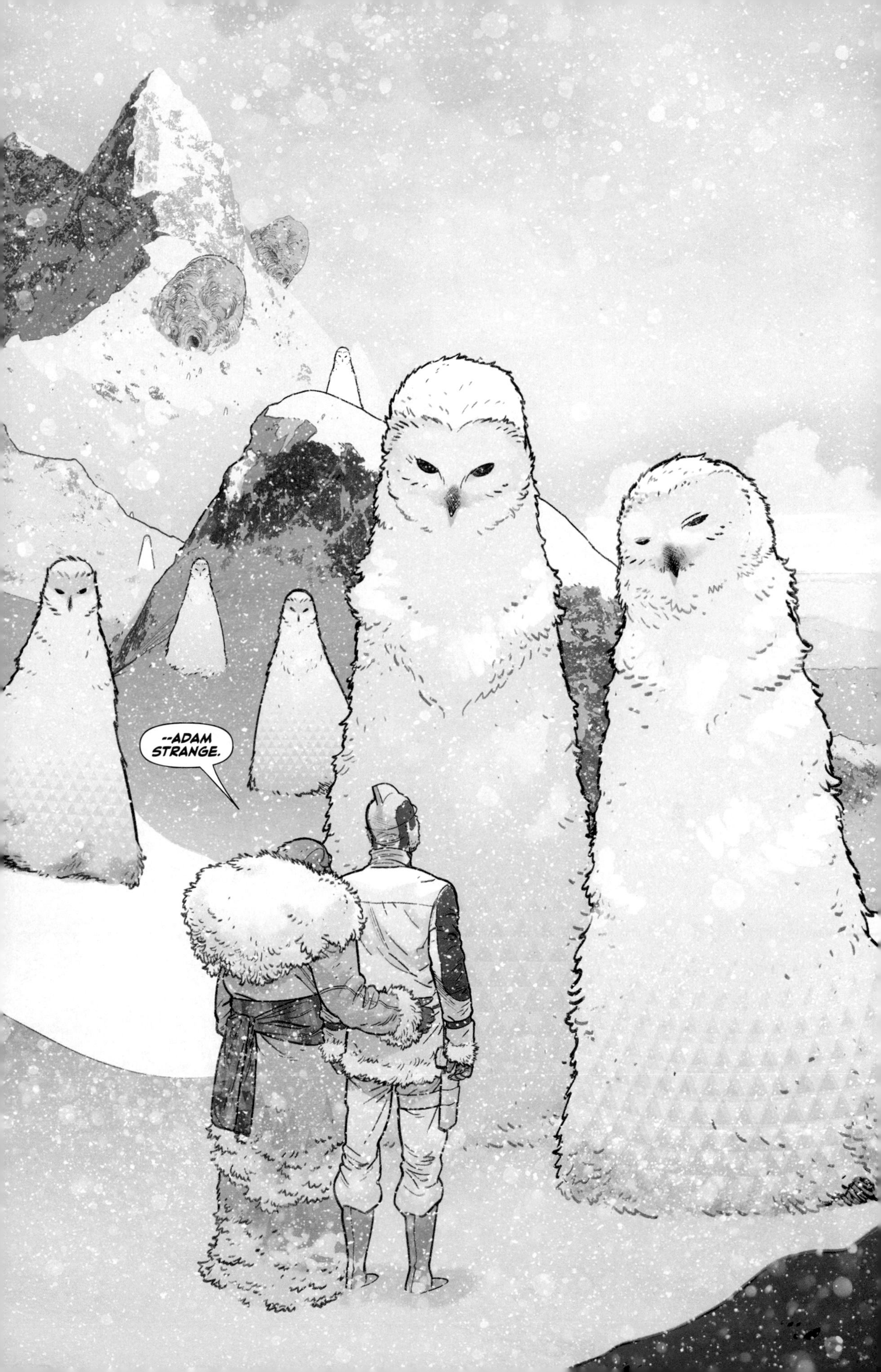
--ADAM STRANGE.

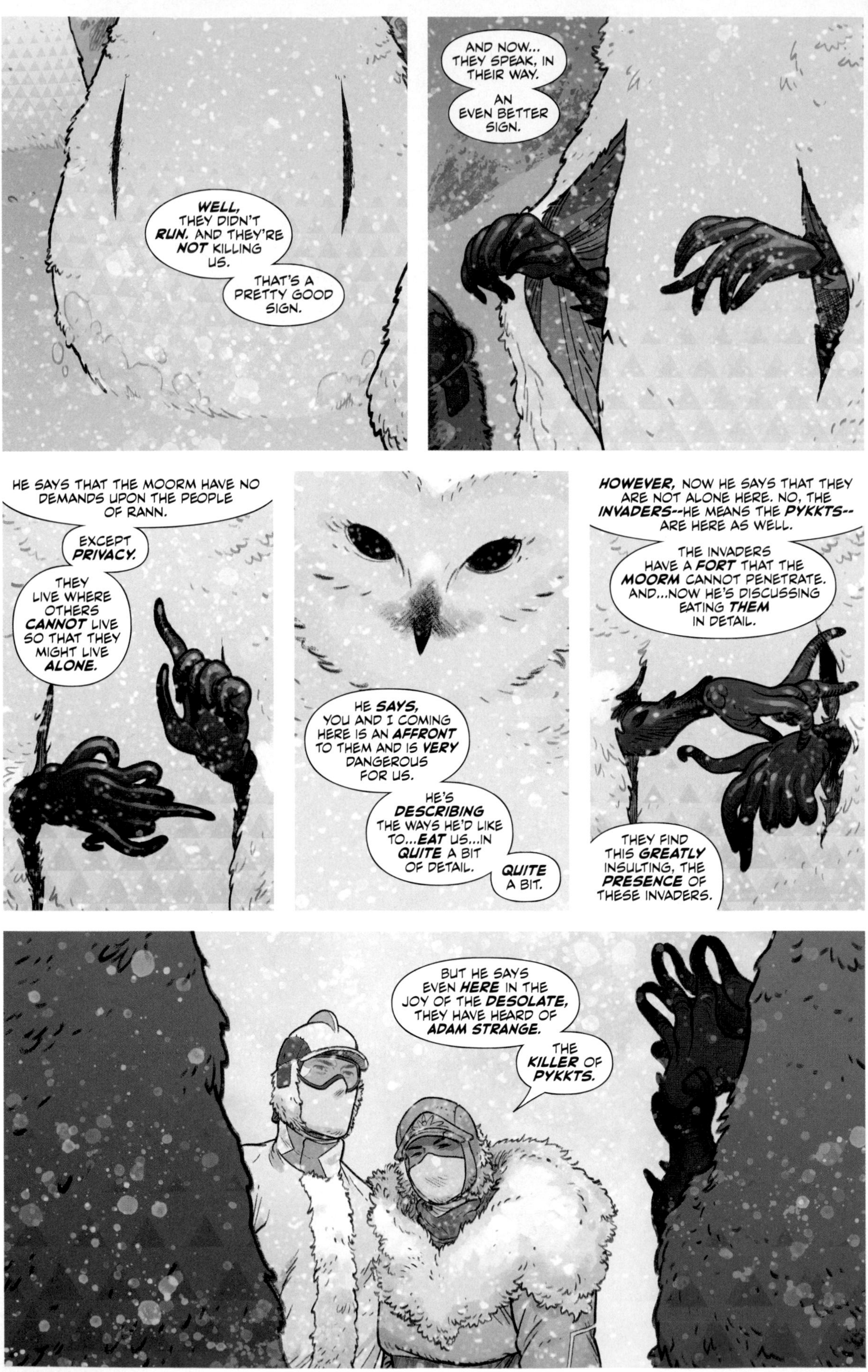
WELL, THEY DIDN'T RUN. AND THEY'RE NOT KILLING US.
THAT'S A PRETTY GOOD SIGN.
AND NOW... THEY SPEAK, IN THEIR WAY.
AN EVEN BETTER SIGN.
HE SAYS THAT THE MOORM HAVE NO DEMANDS UPON THE PEOPLE OF RANN.
EXCEPT PRIVACY.
THEY LIVE WHERE OTHERS CANNOT LIVE SO THAT THEY MIGHT LIVE ALONE.
HE SAYS, YOU AND I COMING HERE IS AN AFFRONT TO THEM AND IS VERY DANGEROUS FOR US.
HE'S DESCRIBING THE WAYS HE'D LIKE TO...EAT US...IN QUITE A BIT OF DETAIL.
QUITE A BIT.
HOWEVER, NOW HE SAYS THAT THEY ARE NOT ALONE HERE. NO, THE INVADERS--HE MEANS THE PYKKTS--ARE HERE AS WELL.
THE INVADERS HAVE A FORT THAT THE MOORM CANNOT PENETRATE. AND...NOW HE'S DISCUSSING EATING THEM IN DETAIL.
THEY FIND THIS GREATLY INSULTING, THE PRESENCE OF THESE INVADERS.
BUT HE SAYS EVEN HERE IN THE JOY OF THE DESOLATE, THEY HAVE HEARD OF ADAM STRANGE.
THE KILLER OF PYKKTS.

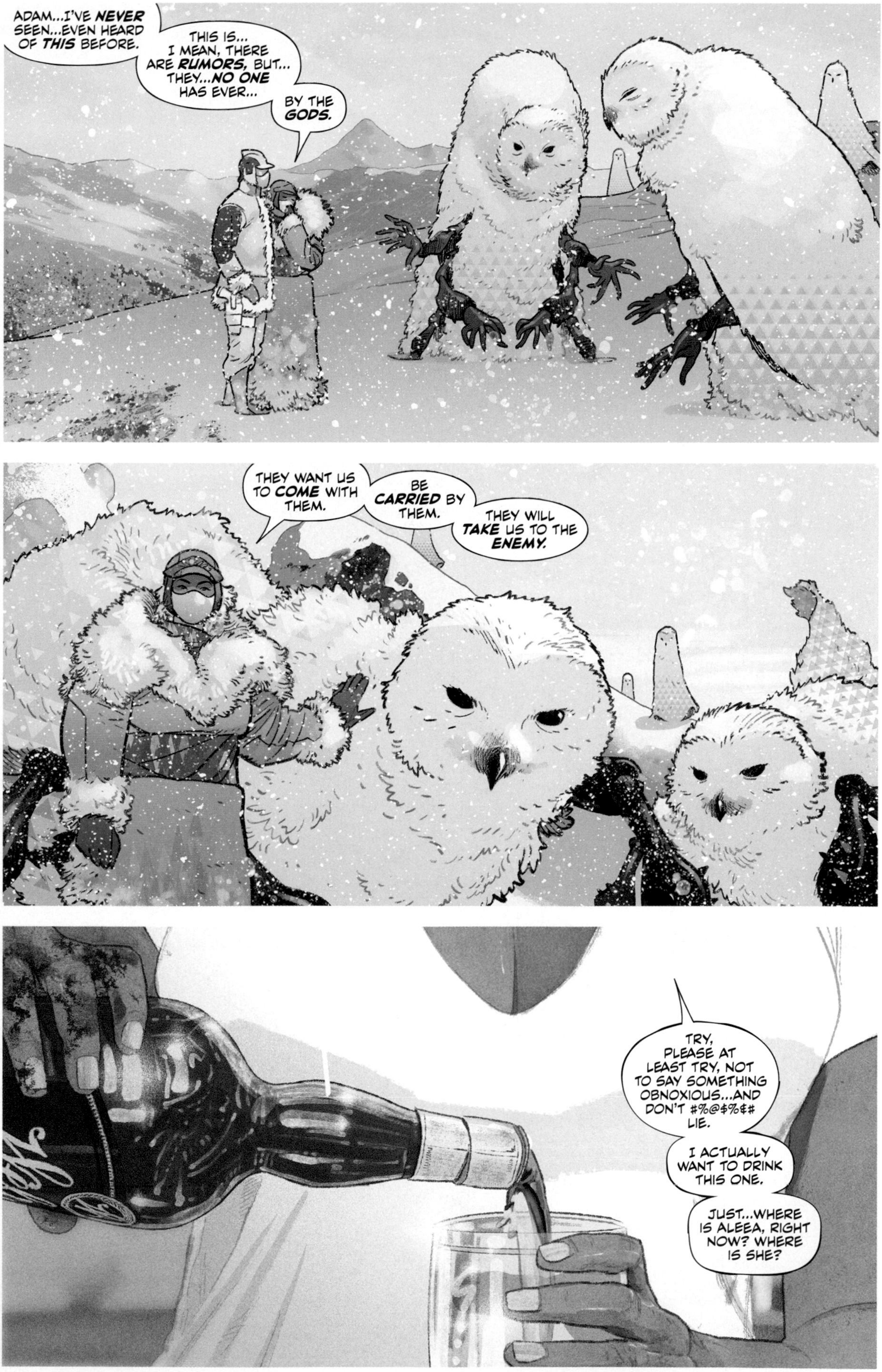
ADAM...I'VE NEVER SEEN...EVEN HEARD OF THIS BEFORE.
THIS IS... I MEAN, THERE ARE RUMORS, BUT... THEY...NO ONE HAS EVER...
BY THE GODS.
THEY WANT US TO COME WITH THEM.
BE CARRIED BY THEM.
THEY WILL TAKE US TO THE ENEMY.
TRY, PLEASE AT LEAST TRY, NOT TO SAY SOMETHING OBNOXIOUS...AND DON'T #%@$%$# LIE.
I ACTUALLY WANT TO DRINK THIS ONE.
JUST...WHERE IS ALEEA, RIGHT NOW? WHERE IS SHE?

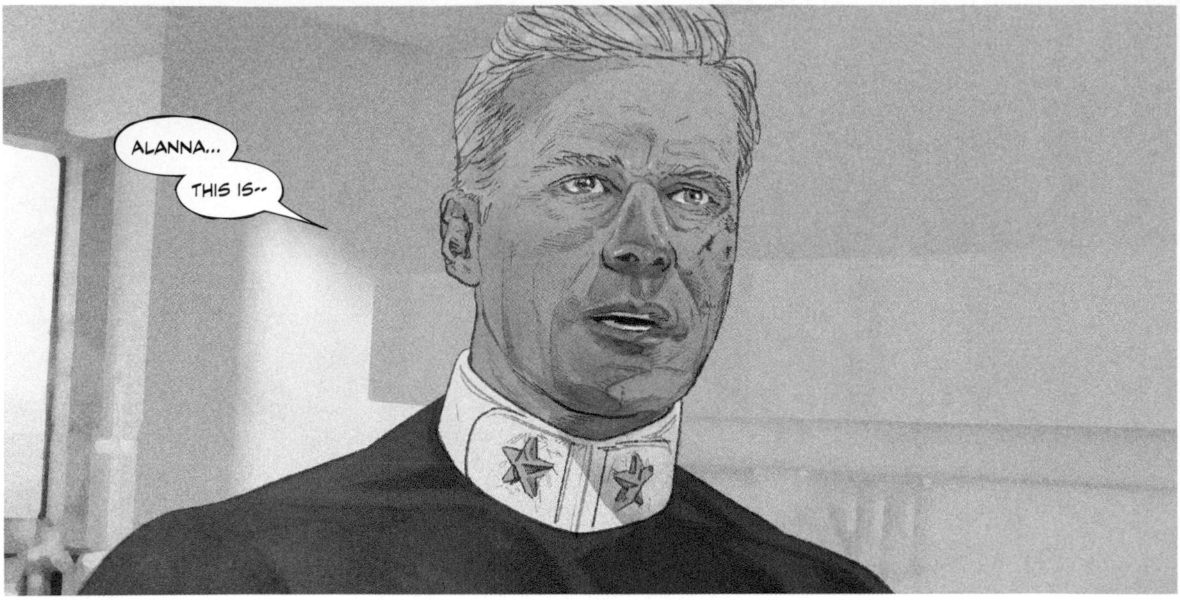
ALANNA...
THIS IS--

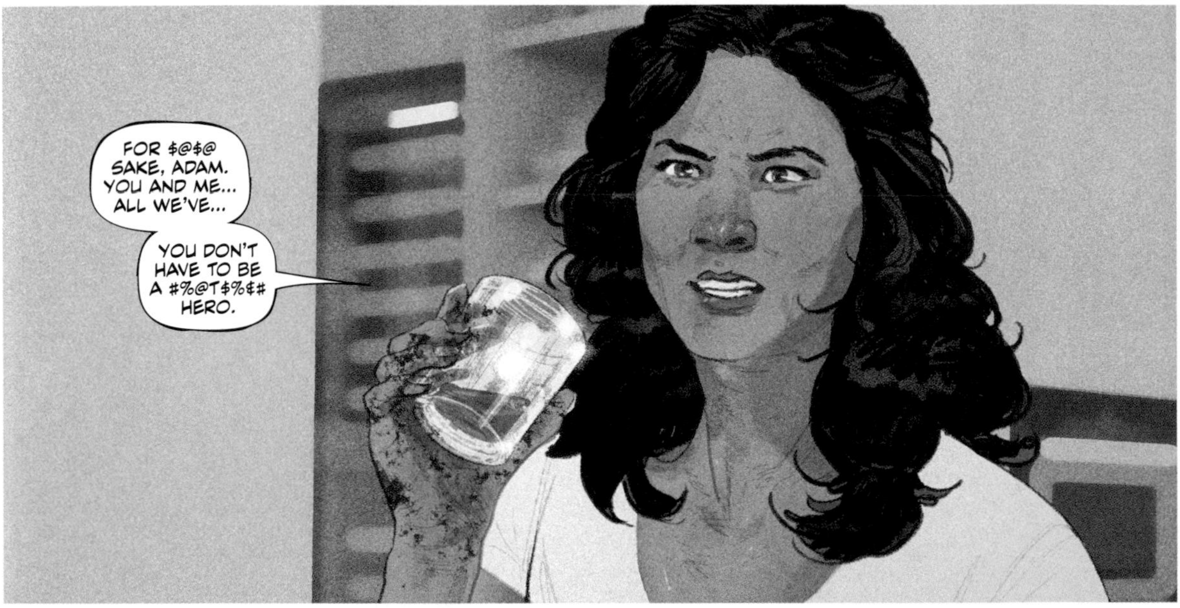
FOR $@$@ SAKE, ADAM. YOU AND ME... ALL WE'VE...
YOU DON'T HAVE TO BE A #%@T$%$# HERO.

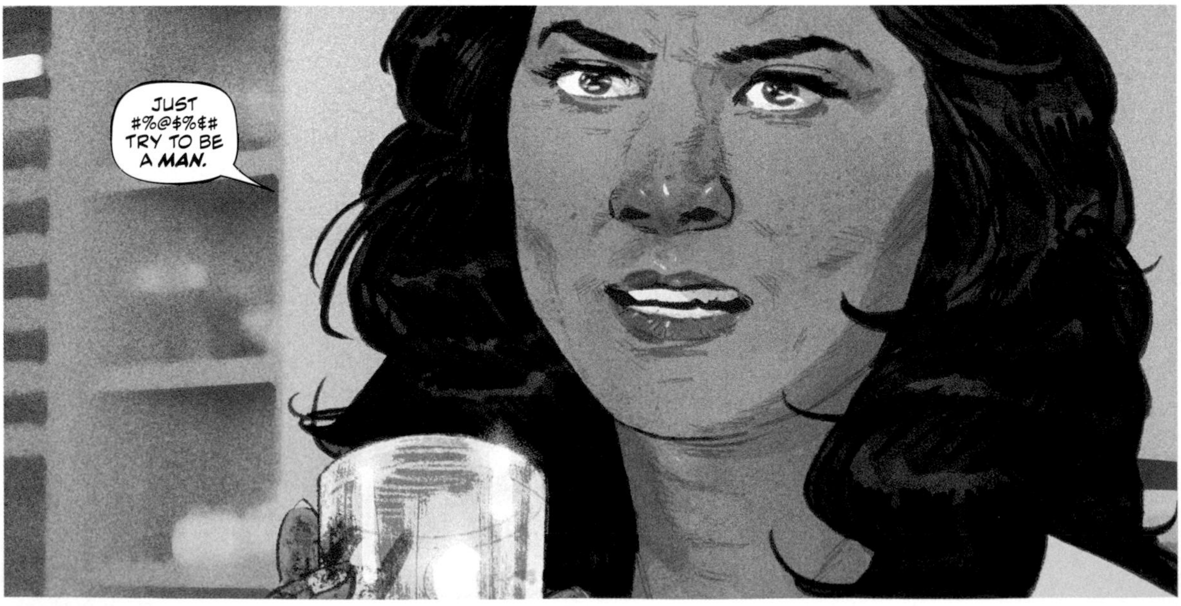
JUST #%@$%$# TRY TO BE A ***MAN.***

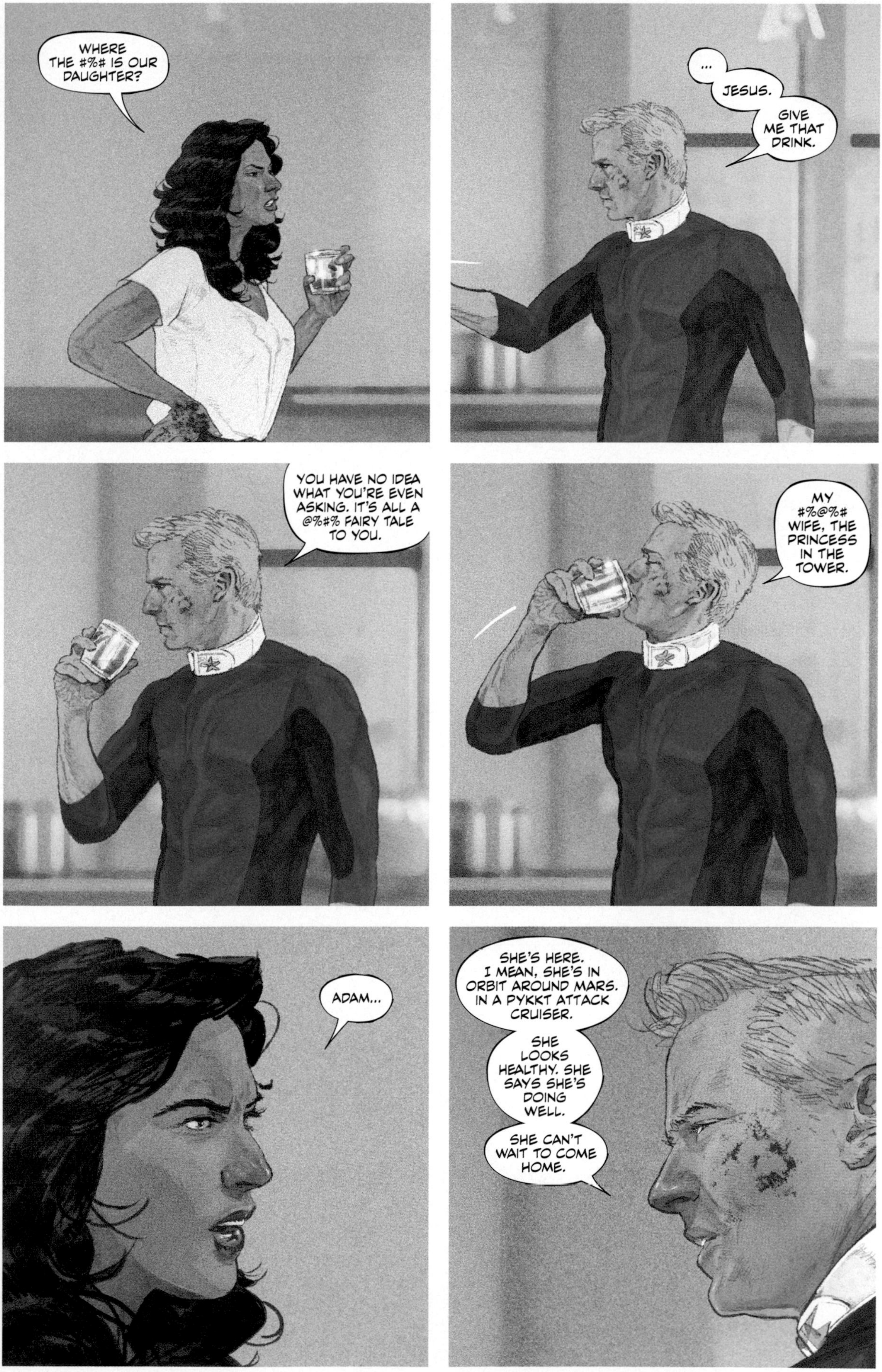

WHERE THE #%# IS OUR DAUGHTER?
...
JESUS.
GIVE ME THAT DRINK.
YOU HAVE NO IDEA WHAT YOU'RE EVEN ASKING. IT'S ALL A @%#% FAIRY TALE TO YOU.
MY #%@%# WIFE, THE PRINCESS IN THE TOWER.
ADAM...
SHE'S HERE. I MEAN, SHE'S IN ORBIT AROUND MARS. IN A PYKKT ATTACK CRUISER.
SHE LOOKS HEALTHY. SHE SAYS SHE'S DOING WELL.
SHE CAN'T WAIT TO COME HOME.

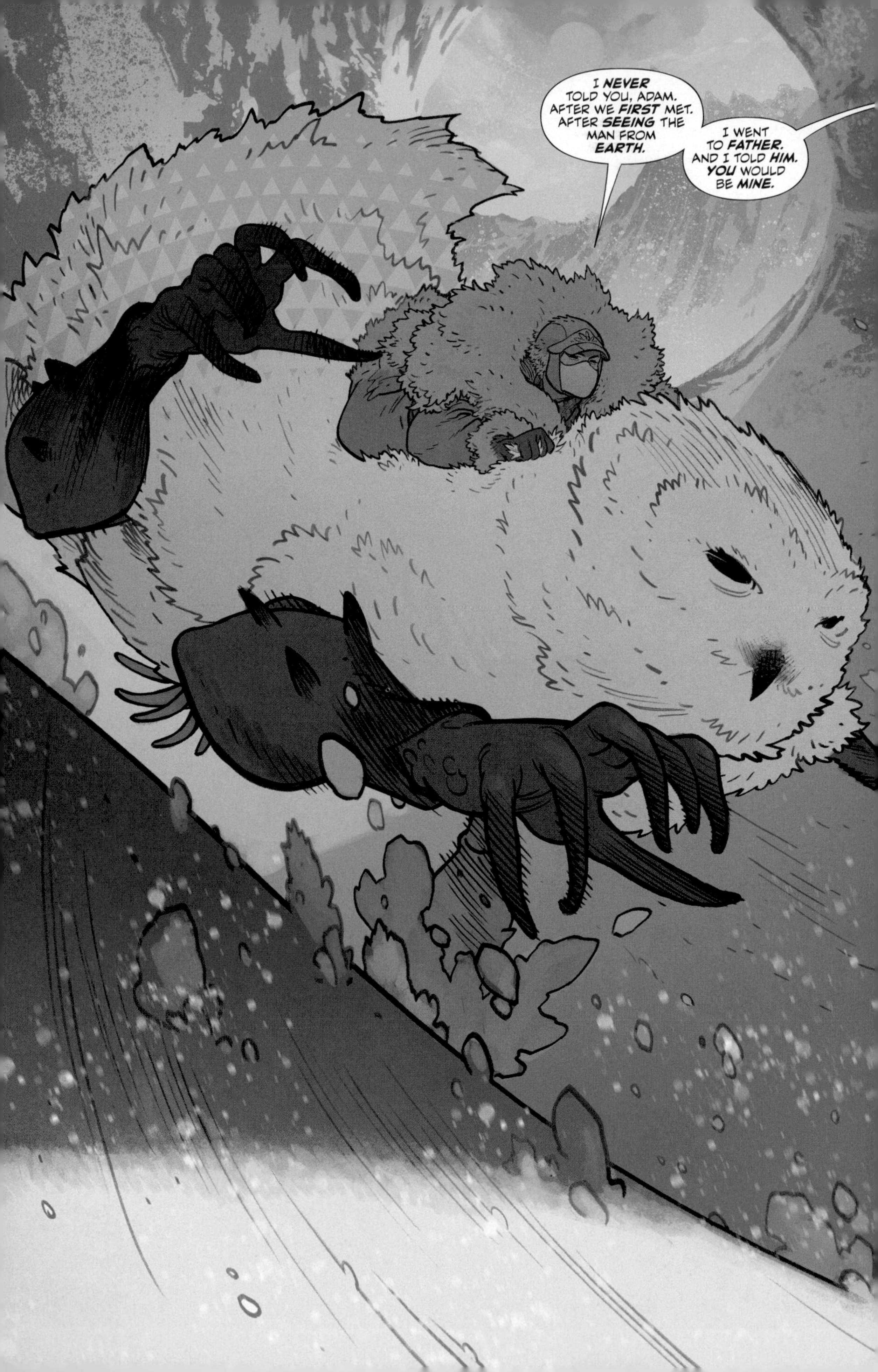
I NEVER TOLD YOU, ADAM. AFTER WE FIRST MET. AFTER SEEING THE MAN FROM EARTH.
I WENT TO FATHER. AND I TOLD HIM. YOU WOULD BE MINE.

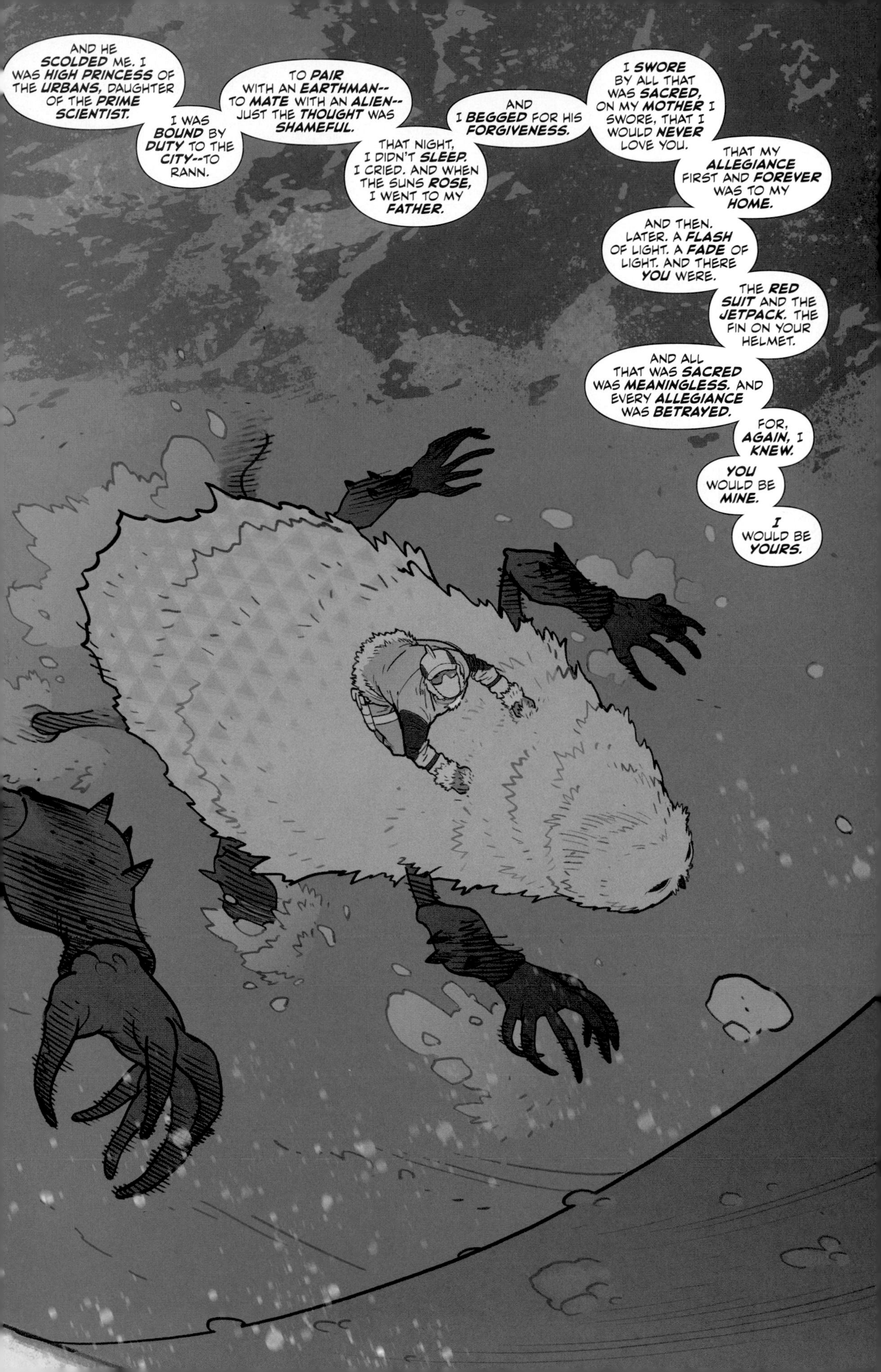
AND HE SCOLDED ME. I WAS HIGH PRINCESS OF THE URBANS, DAUGHTER OF THE PRIME SCIENTIST.
I WAS BOUND BY DUTY TO THE CITY--TO RANN.
TO PAIR WITH AN EARTHMAN-- TO MATE WITH AN ALIEN-- JUST THE THOUGHT WAS SHAMEFUL.
THAT NIGHT, I DIDN'T SLEEP. I CRIED. AND WHEN THE SUNS ROSE, I WENT TO MY FATHER.
AND I BEGGED FOR HIS FORGIVENESS.
I SWORE BY ALL THAT WAS SACRED, ON MY MOTHER I SWORE, THAT I WOULD NEVER LOVE YOU.
THAT MY ALLEGIANCE FIRST AND FOREVER WAS TO MY HOME.
AND THEN. LATER. A FLASH OF LIGHT. A FADE OF LIGHT. AND THERE YOU WERE.
THE RED SUIT AND THE JETPACK. THE FIN ON YOUR HELMET.
AND ALL THAT WAS SACRED WAS MEANINGLESS. AND EVERY ALLEGIANCE WAS BETRAYED.
FOR, AGAIN, I KNEW.
YOU WOULD BE MINE.
I WOULD BE YOURS.

SLAP
YOU LITTLE @%@$%.
DON'T.
YOU'RE SO STRONG NOW, AREN'T YOU?
YOU DO NOT--
I SAVED RANN. I SACRIFICED EVERYTHING I WAS TO SAVE YOU AND ALEEA.
AND YOU... YOU CANNOT TREAT ME LIKE I'M SOME SORT OF DEVIANT.
ADAM, IT HURTS.
I DID IT FOR YOU.
THEY WERE WINNING. THEY WERE GOING TO WIN. KILL YOU AND HER-- YOUR FATHER.
AND ME. OUR FAMILY. AND BILLIONS.
YOU AND YOUR PEOPLE. GONE.
I JUST DID WHAT I THOUGHT YOU WANTED ME TO DO.

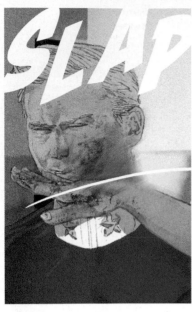

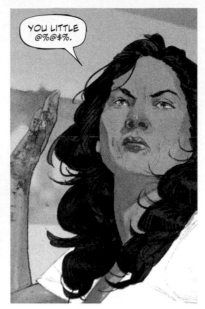

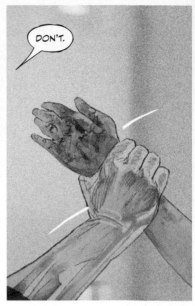

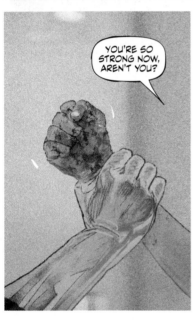

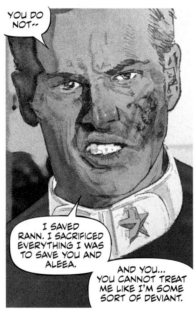

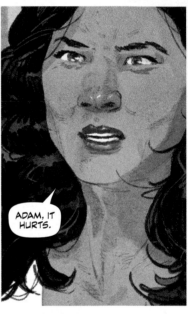

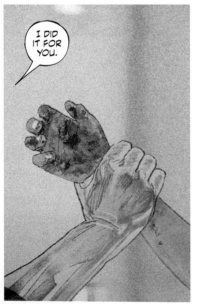

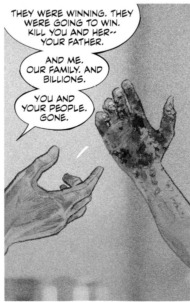

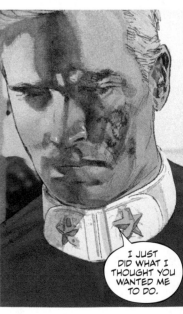

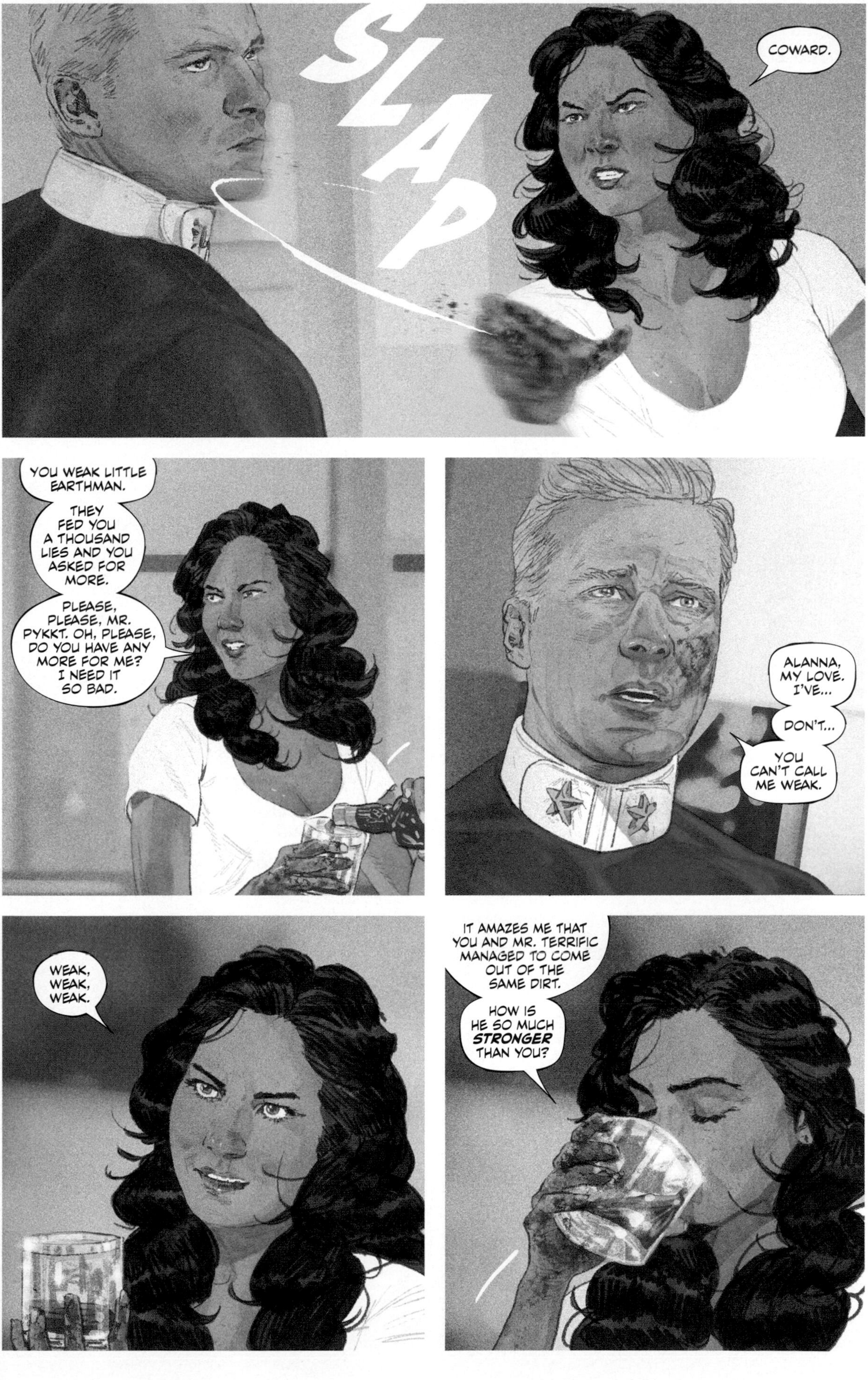
SLAP
COWARD.
YOU WEAK LITTLE EARTHMAN.
THEY FED YOU A THOUSAND LIES AND YOU ASKED FOR MORE.
PLEASE, PLEASE, MR. PYKKT. OH, PLEASE, DO YOU HAVE ANY MORE FOR ME? I NEED IT SO BAD.
ALANNA, MY LOVE. I'VE...
DON'T...
YOU CAN'T CALL ME WEAK.
WEAK, WEAK, WEAK.
IT AMAZES ME THAT YOU AND MR. TERRIFIC MANAGED TO COME OUT OF THE SAME DIRT.
HOW IS HE SO MUCH **STRONGER** THAN YOU?

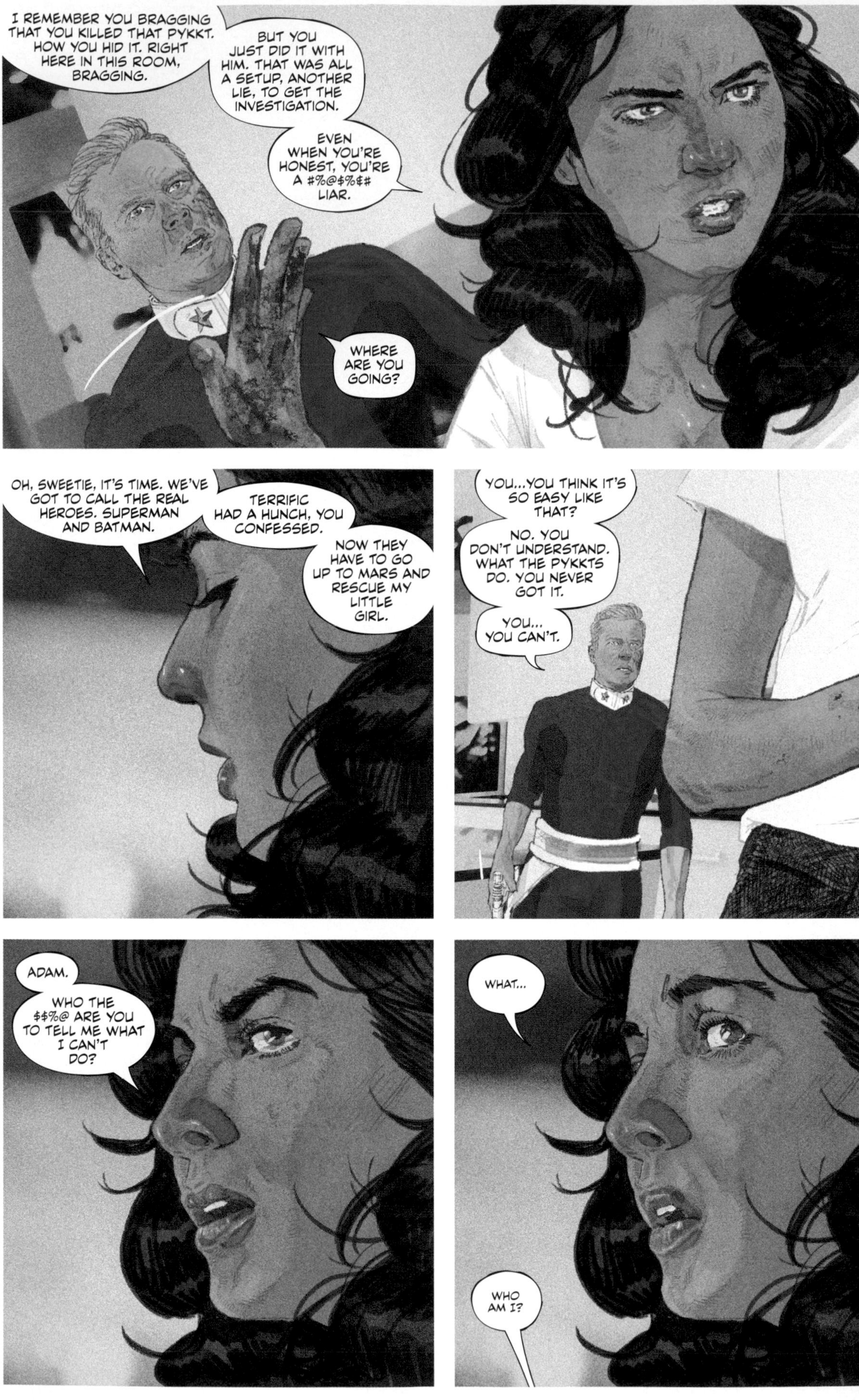

I REMEMBER YOU BRAGGING THAT YOU KILLED THAT PYKKT. HOW YOU HID IT. RIGHT HERE IN THIS ROOM, BRAGGING.
BUT YOU JUST DID IT WITH HIM. THAT WAS ALL A SETUP, ANOTHER LIE, TO GET THE INVESTIGATION.
EVEN WHEN YOU'RE HONEST, YOU'RE A #%@$%¢# LIAR.
WHERE ARE YOU GOING?
OH, SWEETIE, IT'S TIME. WE'VE GOT TO CALL THE REAL HEROES. SUPERMAN AND BATMAN.
TERRIFIC HAD A HUNCH, YOU CONFESSED.
NOW THEY HAVE TO GO UP TO MARS AND RESCUE MY LITTLE GIRL.
YOU...YOU THINK IT'S SO EASY LIKE THAT?
NO. YOU DON'T UNDERSTAND. WHAT THE PYKKTS DO. YOU NEVER GOT IT.
YOU... YOU CAN'T.
ADAM.
WHO THE $$%@ ARE YOU TO TELL ME WHAT I CAN'T DO?
WHAT...
WHO AM I?

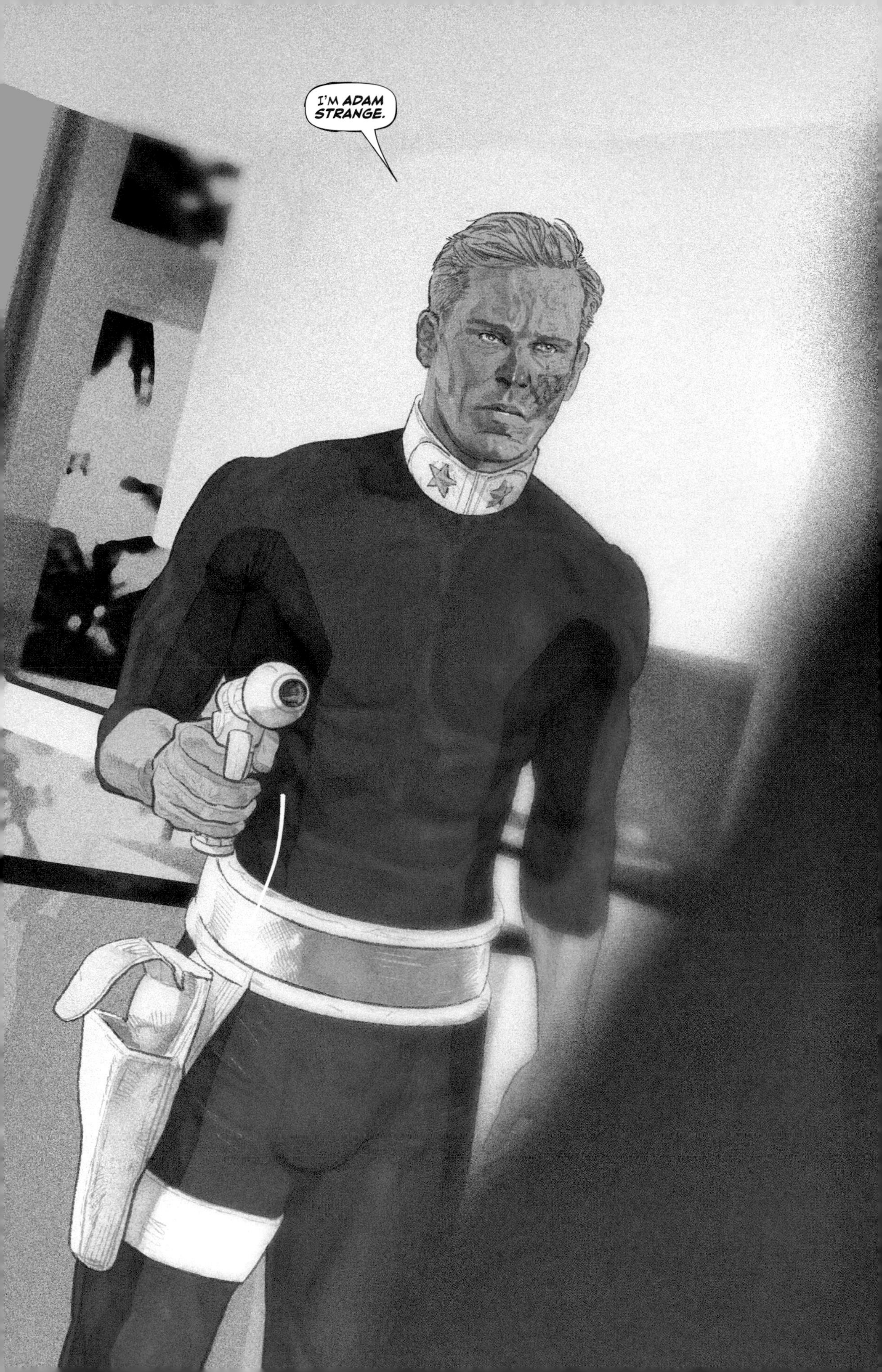
I'M ADAM STRANGE.

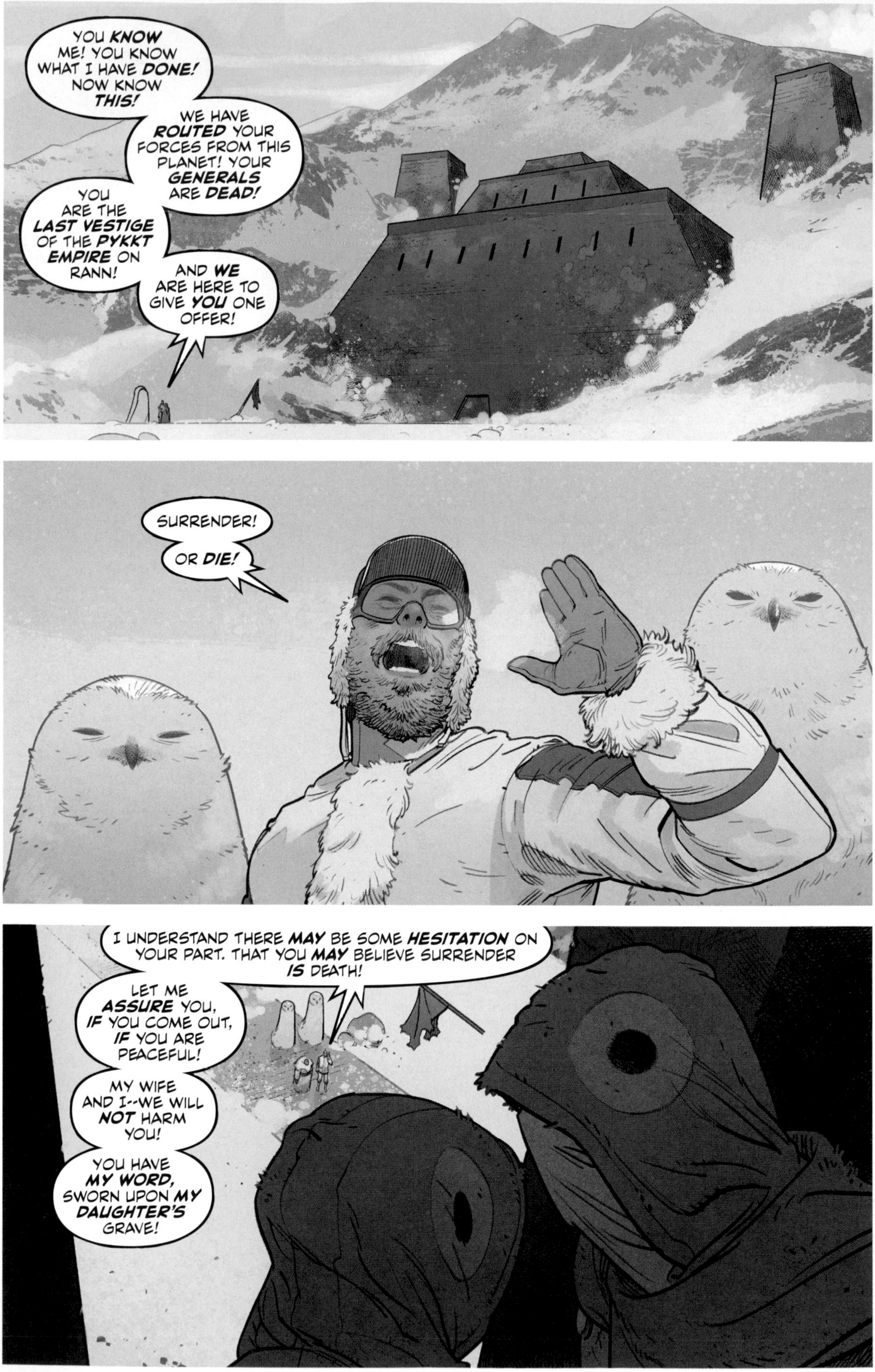
YOU KNOW ME! YOU KNOW WHAT I HAVE DONE! NOW KNOW THIS!
WE HAVE ROUTED YOUR FORCES FROM THIS PLANET! YOUR GENERALS ARE DEAD!
YOU ARE THE LAST VESTIGE OF THE PYKKT EMPIRE ON RANN!
AND WE ARE HERE TO GIVE YOU ONE OFFER!
SURRENDER!
OR DIE!
I UNDERSTAND THERE MAY BE SOME HESITATION ON YOUR PART. THAT YOU MAY BELIEVE SURRENDER IS DEATH!
LET ME ASSURE YOU, IF YOU COME OUT, IF YOU ARE PEACEFUL!
MY WIFE AND I--WE WILL NOT HARM YOU!
YOU HAVE MY WORD, SWORN UPON MY DAUGHTER'S GRAVE!

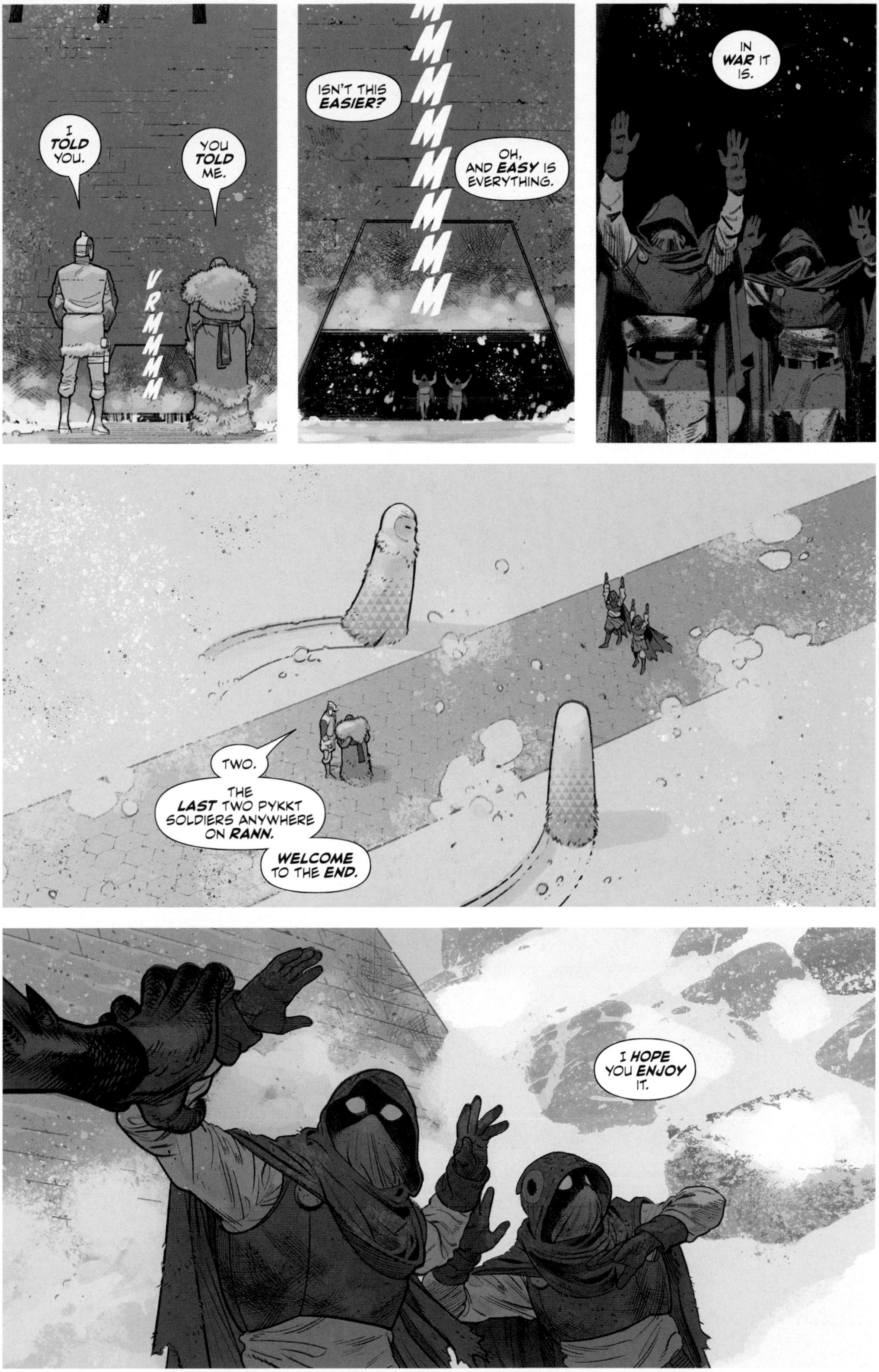
I TOLD YOU.
YOU TOLD ME.
VRMMMM
ISN'T THIS EASIER?
MMMMMMMMMM
OH, AND EASY IS EVERYTHING.
IN WAR IT IS.
TWO.
THE LAST TWO PYKKT SOLDIERS ANYWHERE ON RANN.
WELCOME TO THE END.
I HOPE YOU ENJOY IT.

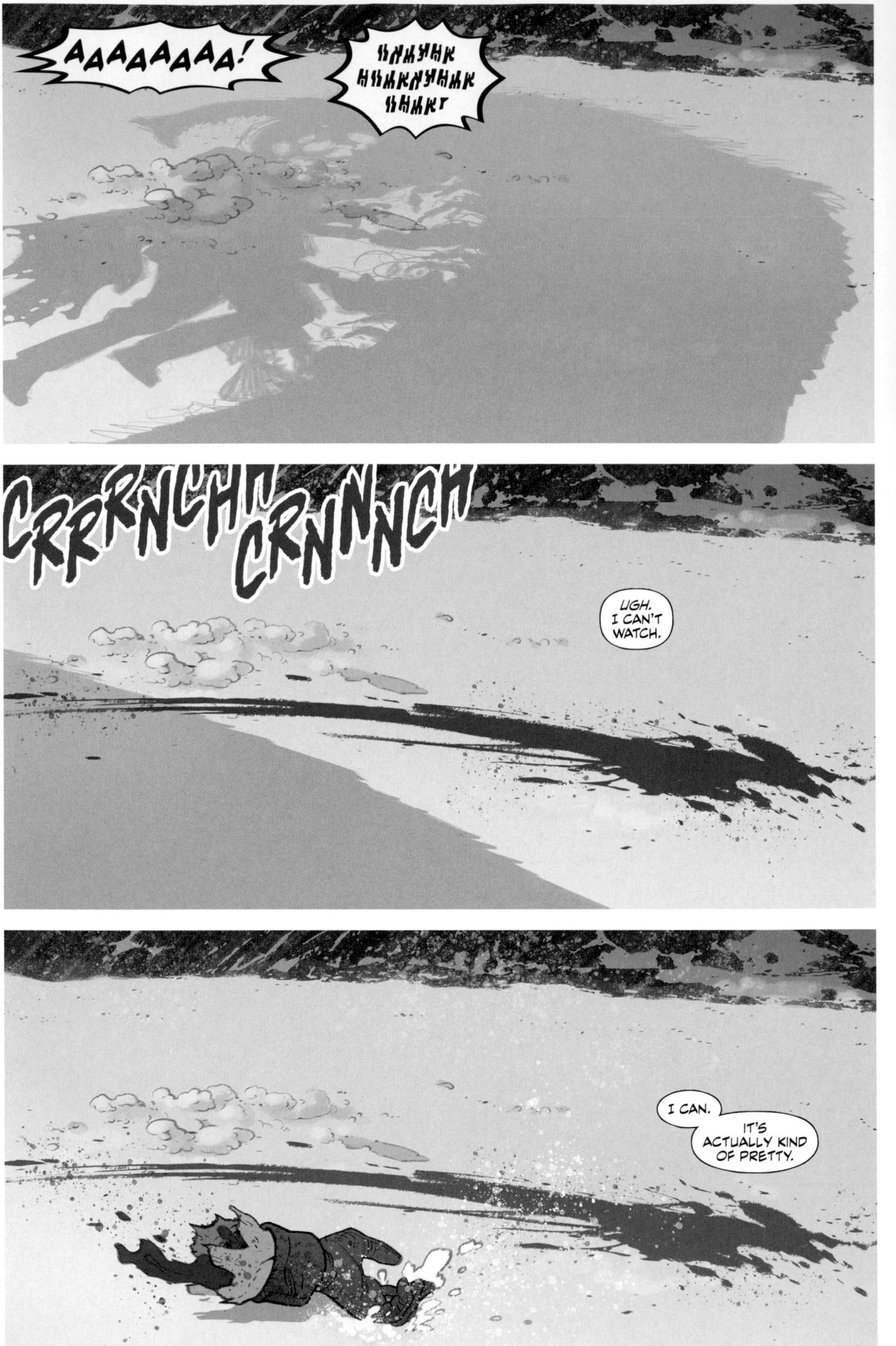
AAAAAAAA!
CRRRNCH
CRNNNCH
UGH. I CAN'T WATCH.
I CAN.
IT'S ACTUALLY KIND OF PRETTY.

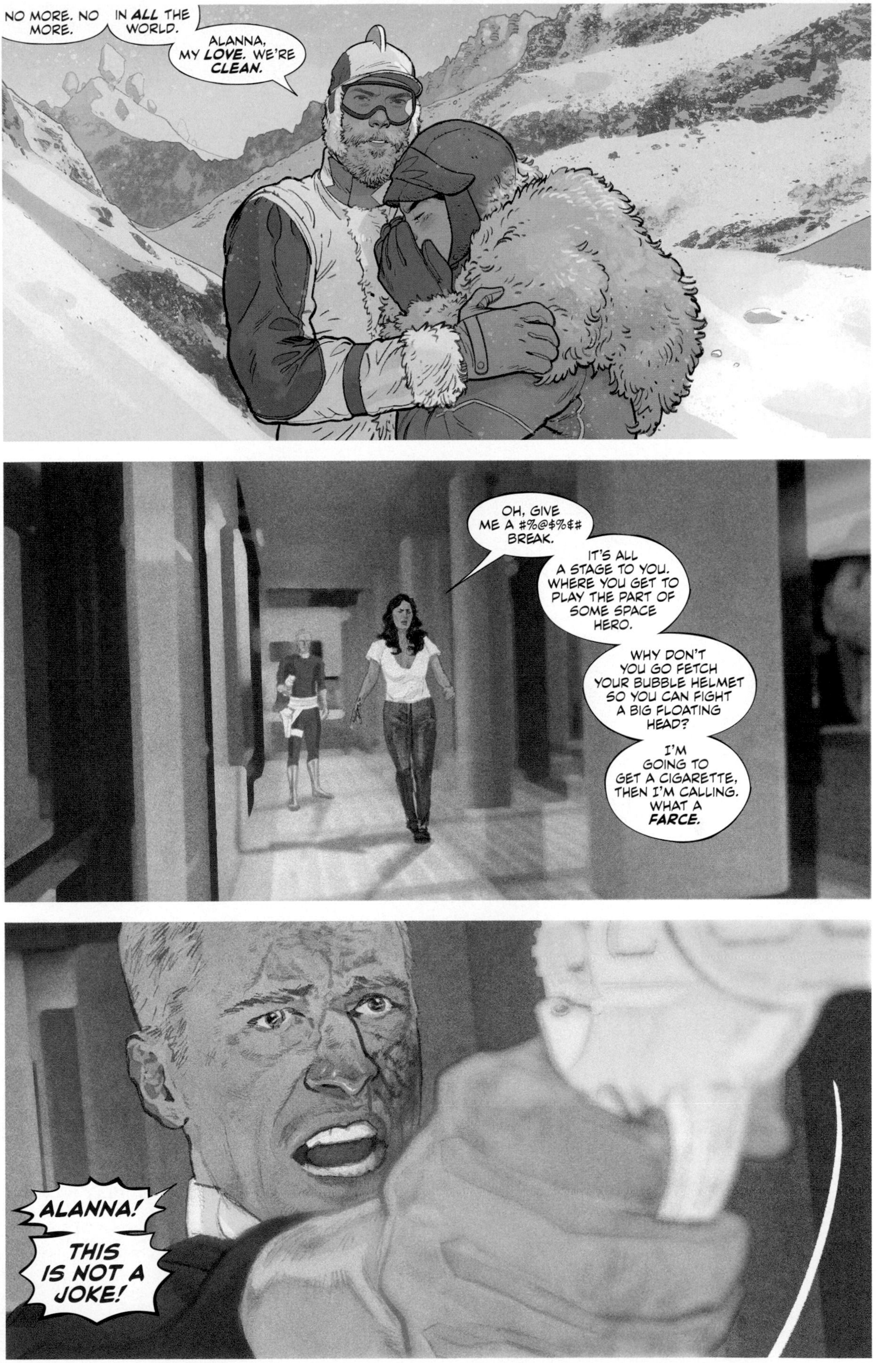
NO MORE. NO MORE.
IN ALL THE WORLD.
ALANNA, MY LOVE. WE'RE CLEAN.
OH, GIVE ME A #%@$%$# BREAK.
IT'S ALL A STAGE TO YOU. WHERE YOU GET TO PLAY THE PART OF SOME SPACE HERO.
WHY DON'T YOU GO FETCH YOUR BUBBLE HELMET SO YOU CAN FIGHT A BIG FLOATING HEAD?
I'M GOING TO GET A CIGARETTE, THEN I'M CALLING. WHAT A FARCE.
ALANNA!
THIS IS NOT A JOKE!

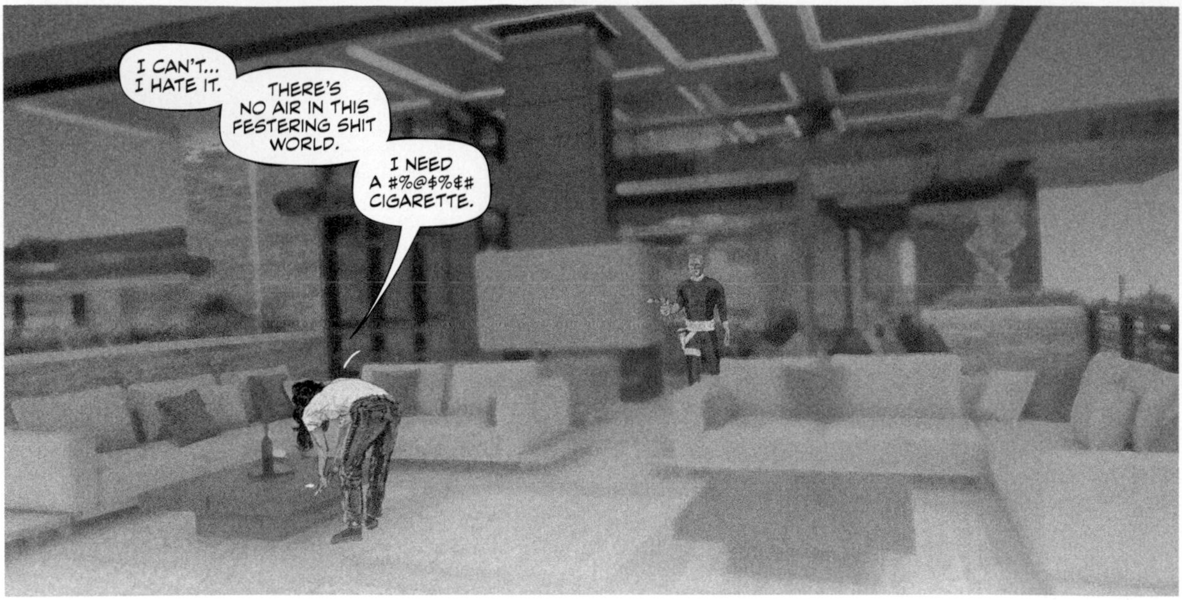
I CAN'T... I HATE IT.
THERE'S NO AIR IN THIS FESTERING SHIT WORLD.
I NEED A #%@$%$# CIGARETTE.

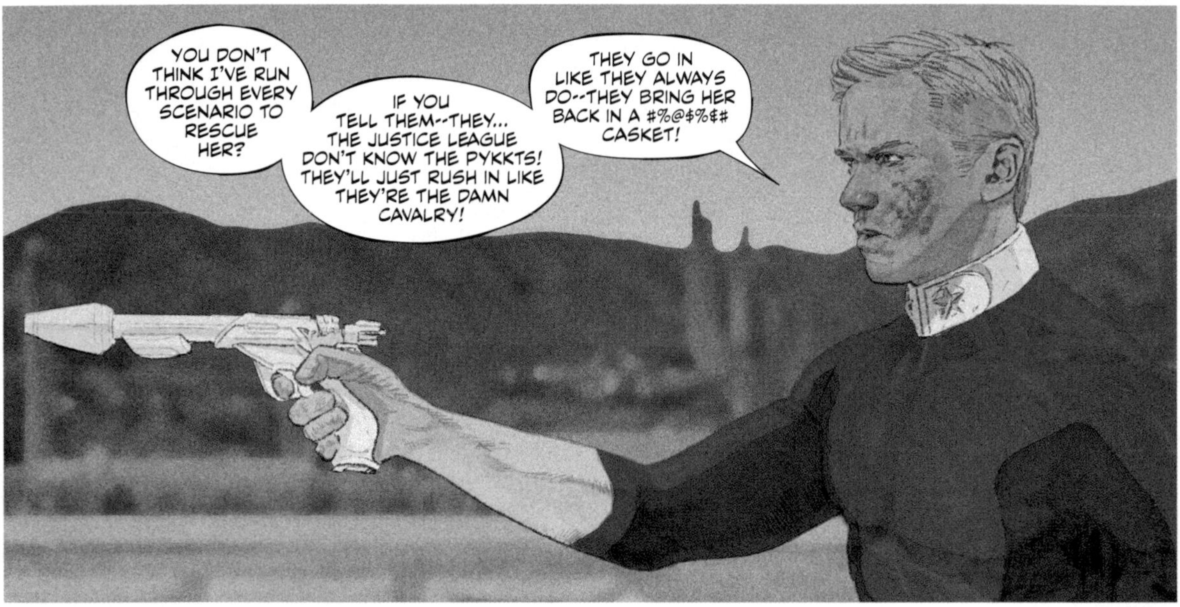
YOU DON'T THINK I'VE RUN THROUGH EVERY SCENARIO TO RESCUE HER?
IF YOU TELL THEM--THEY... THE JUSTICE LEAGUE DON'T KNOW THE PYKKTS! THEY'LL JUST RUSH IN LIKE THEY'RE THE DAMN CAVALRY!
THEY GO IN LIKE THEY ALWAYS DO--THEY BRING HER BACK IN A #%@$%$# CASKET!

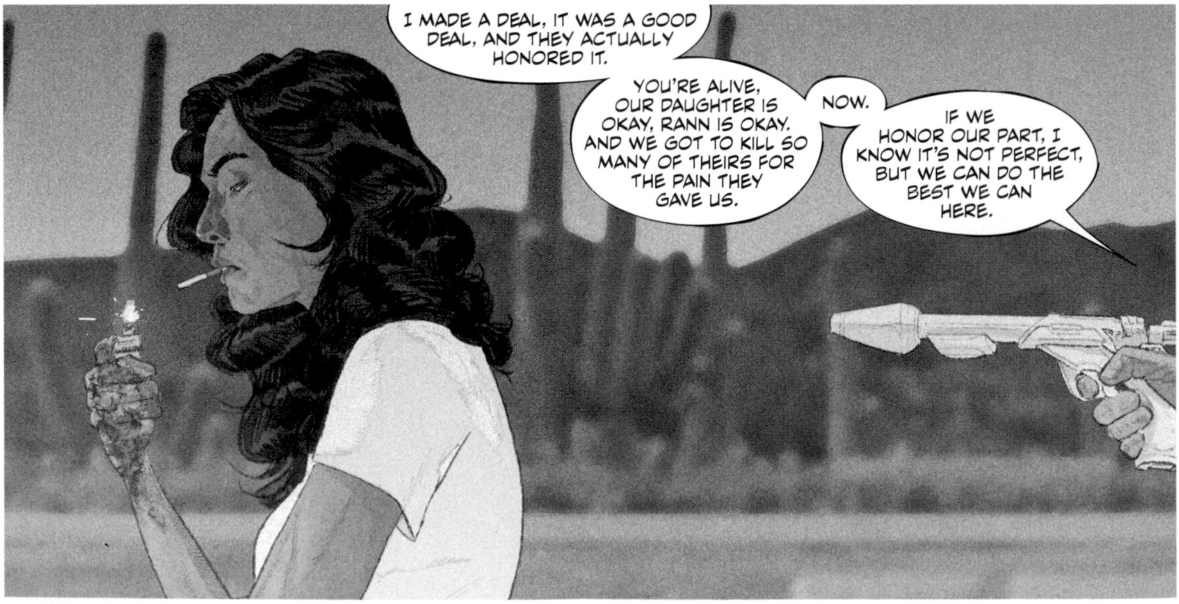
I MADE A DEAL, IT WAS A GOOD DEAL, AND THEY ACTUALLY HONORED IT.
YOU'RE ALIVE, OUR DAUGHTER IS OKAY, RANN IS OKAY. AND WE GOT TO KILL SO MANY OF THEIRS FOR THE PAIN THEY GAVE US.
NOW.
IF WE HONOR OUR PART, I KNOW IT'S NOT PERFECT, BUT WE CAN DO THE BEST WE CAN HERE.

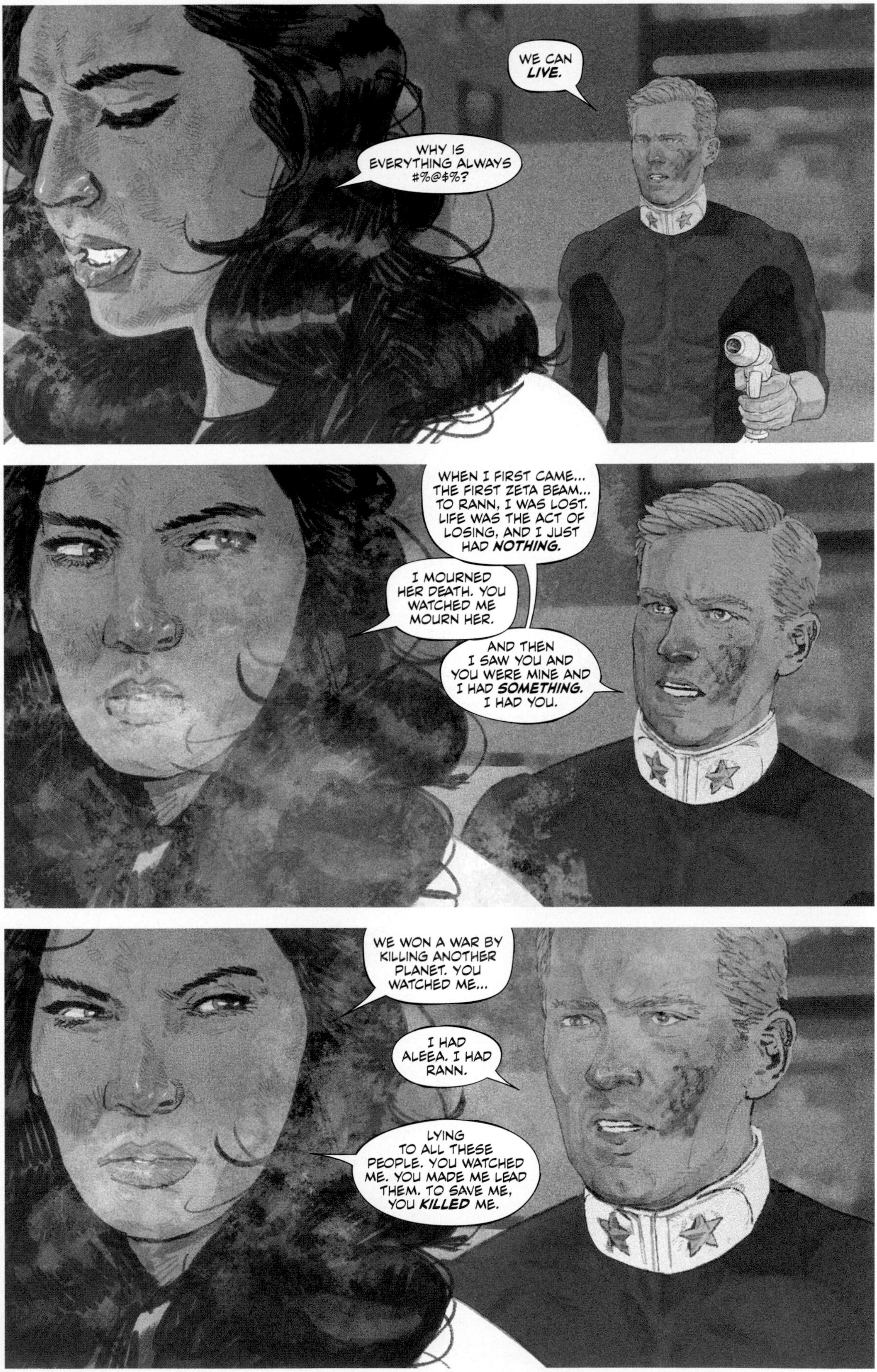
WE CAN LIVE.
WHY IS EVERYTHING ALWAYS #%@$%?
WHEN I FIRST CAME... THE FIRST ZETA BEAM... TO RANN, I WAS LOST. LIFE WAS THE ACT OF LOSING, AND I JUST HAD NOTHING.
I MOURNED HER DEATH. YOU WATCHED ME MOURN HER.
AND THEN I SAW YOU AND YOU WERE MINE AND I HAD SOMETHING. I HAD YOU.
WE WON A WAR BY KILLING ANOTHER PLANET. YOU WATCHED ME...
I HAD ALEEA. I HAD RANN.
LYING TO ALL THESE PEOPLE. YOU WATCHED ME. YOU MADE ME LEAD THEM. TO SAVE ME, YOU KILLED ME.

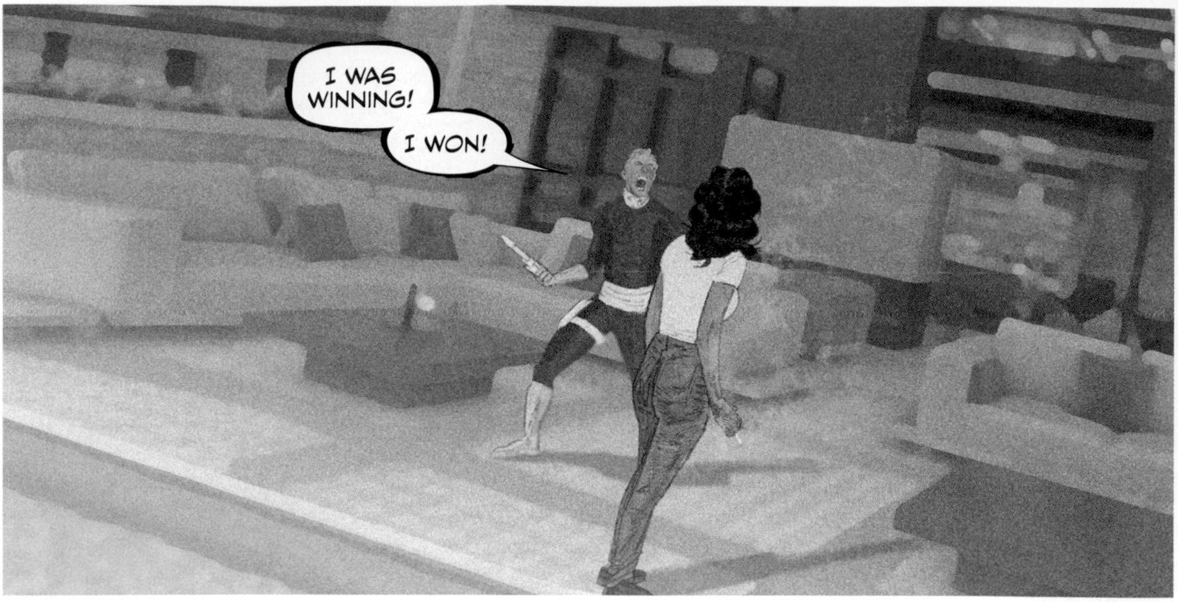
I WAS WINNING!
I WON!

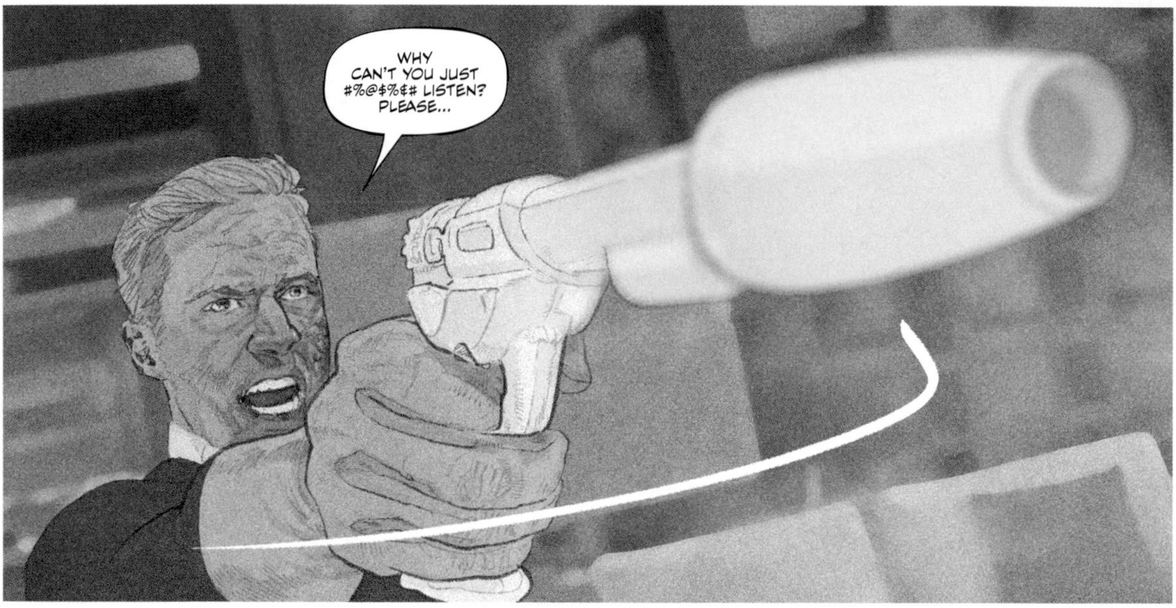
WHY CAN'T YOU JUST #%@$%¢# LISTEN? PLEASE...

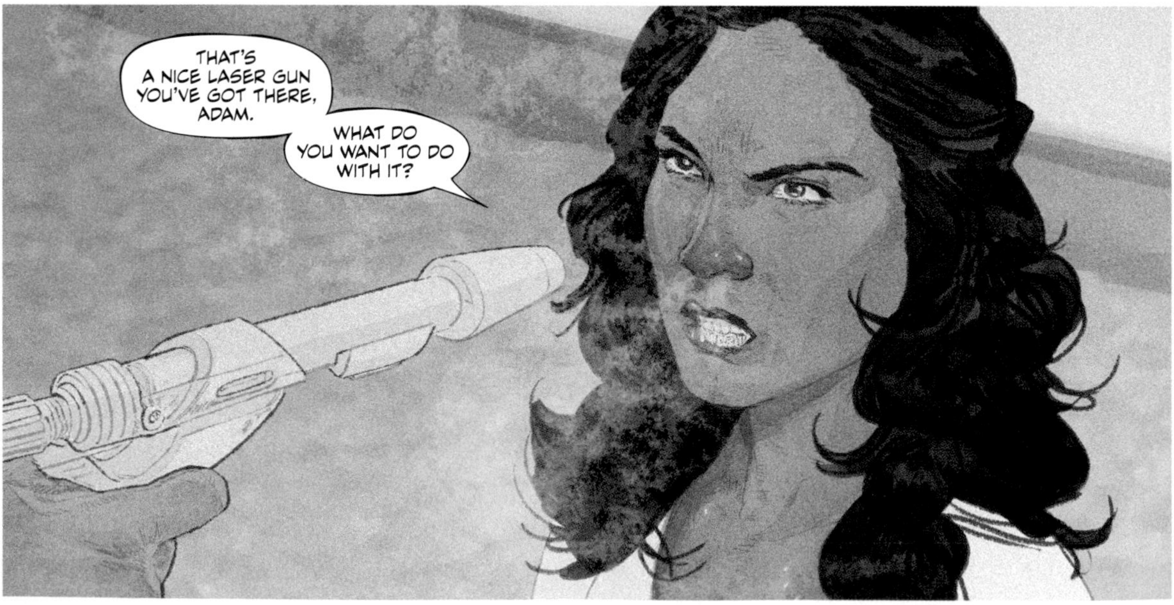
THAT'S A NICE LASER GUN YOU'VE GOT THERE, ADAM.
WHAT DO YOU WANT TO DO WITH IT?

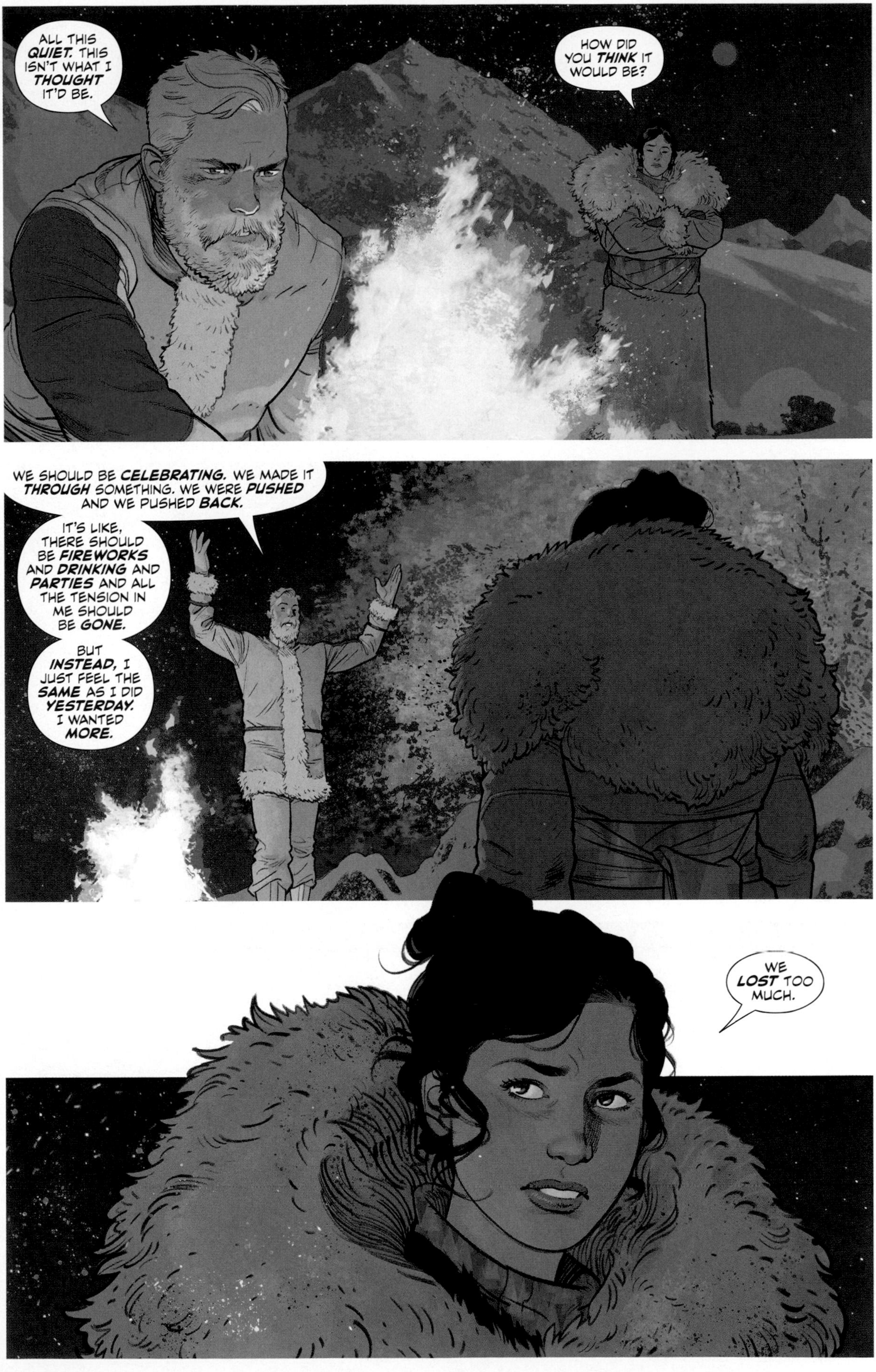
ALL THIS QUIET. THIS ISN'T WHAT I THOUGHT IT'D BE.
HOW DID YOU THINK IT WOULD BE?
WE SHOULD BE CELEBRATING. WE MADE IT THROUGH SOMETHING. WE WERE PUSHED AND WE PUSHED BACK.
IT'S LIKE, THERE SHOULD BE FIREWORKS AND DRINKING AND PARTIES AND ALL THE TENSION IN ME SHOULD BE GONE.
BUT INSTEAD, I JUST FEEL THE SAME AS I DID YESTERDAY. I WANTED MORE.
WE LOST TOO MUCH.

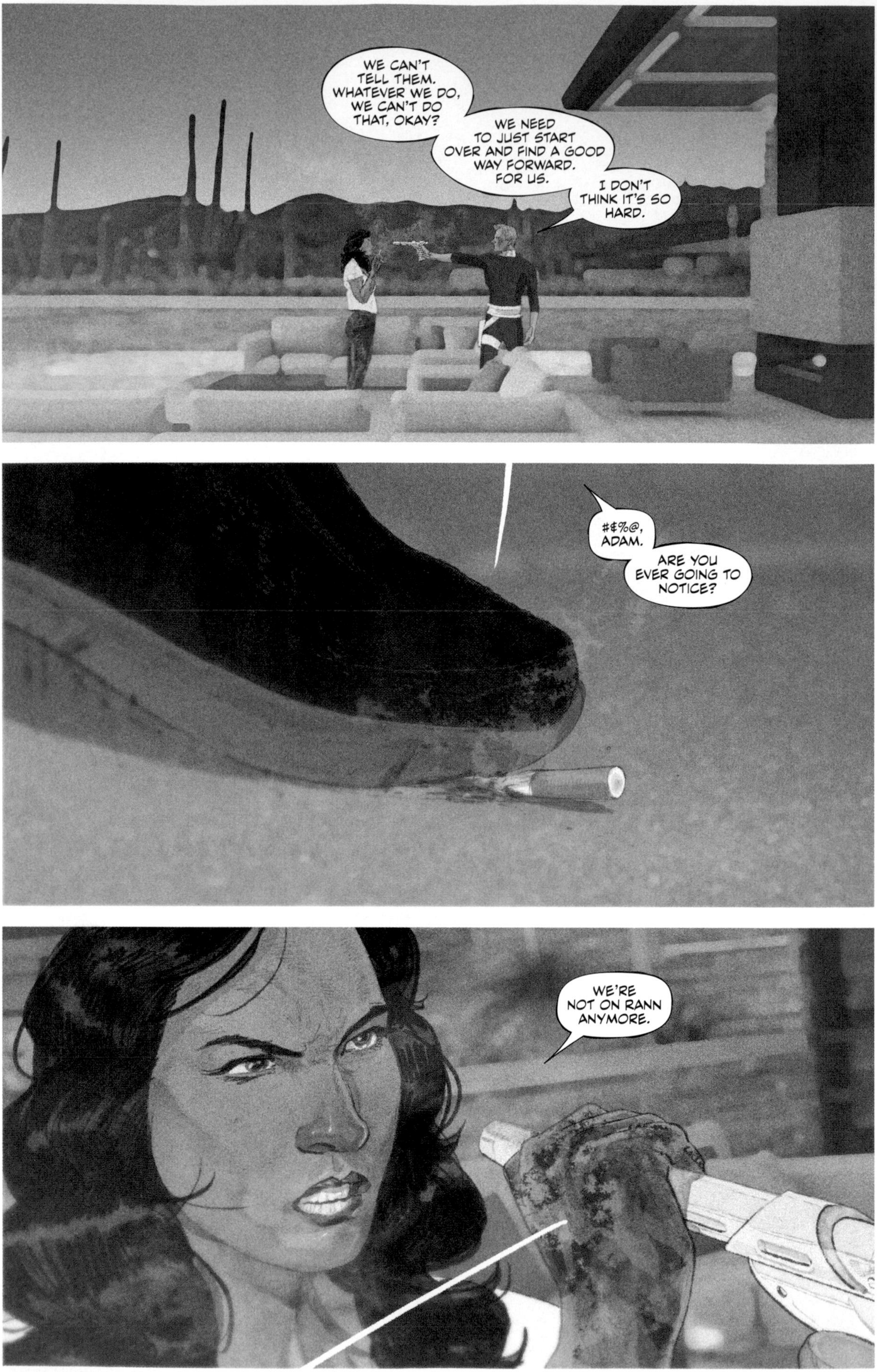
WE CAN'T TELL THEM. WHATEVER WE DO, WE CAN'T DO THAT, OKAY?
WE NEED TO JUST START OVER AND FIND A GOOD WAY FORWARD. FOR US.
I DON'T THINK IT'S SO HARD.
#$%@, ADAM.
ARE YOU EVER GOING TO NOTICE?
WE'RE NOT ON RANN ANYMORE.

I MISS HER. *EVERY* DAY, IT'S...

ALANNA, DON'T YOU...

I MISS HER *TOO*, BUT WE HAVE...

I'M NOT GOING TO LET YOU...

I *KNOW*, AND THAT'S THE *ONLY* THING THAT...

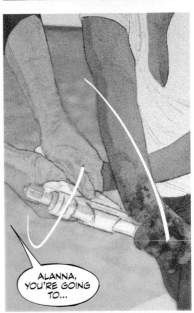

ALANNA, YOU'RE GOING TO...

I *LOVE* YOU, *ADAM*, NO MATTER...

I *LOVE* YOU, *ALANNA*. I ALWAYS WILL.

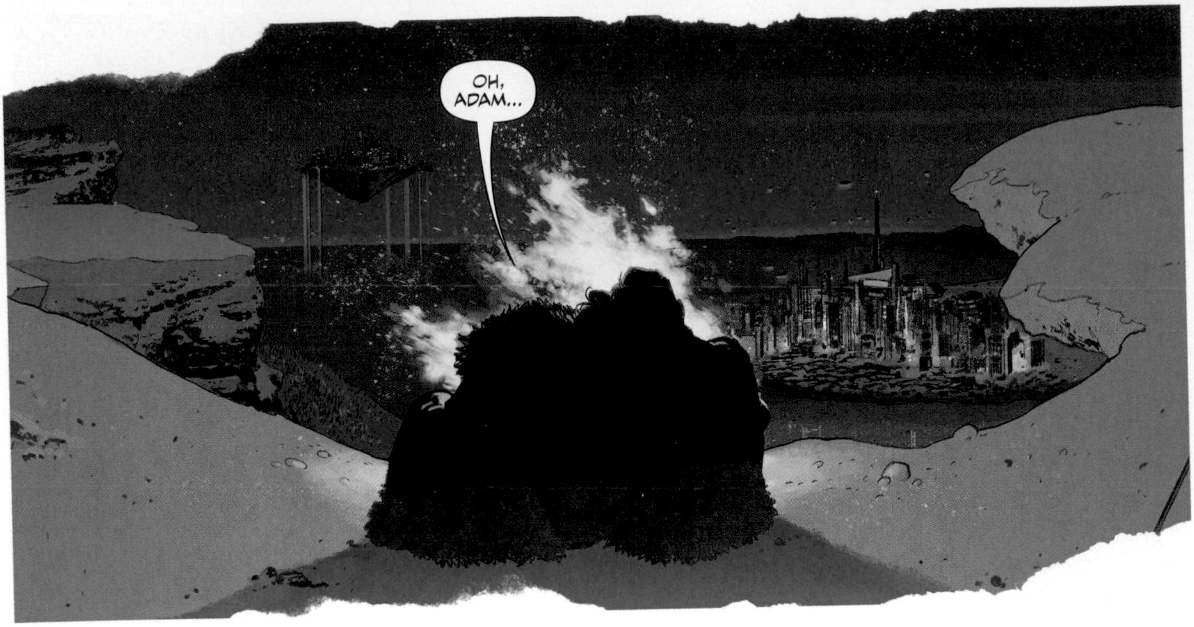
OH, ADAM...

"I was young and newly married, and I was trying to make a living. I had children, infants, and I was a freelance comic book artist-writer, and I had to make a living. Now what I had to do was to grind out the material, and really, this may disillusion a lot of people, but to me this was a job—this was another job to do."

—Al Feldstein

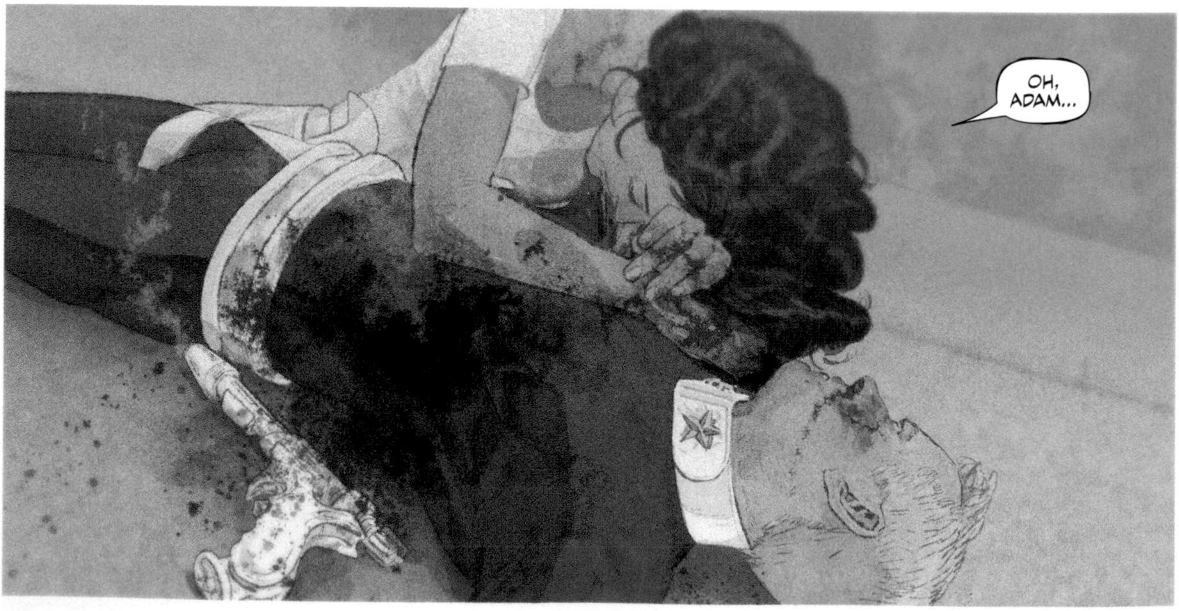
OH, ADAM...

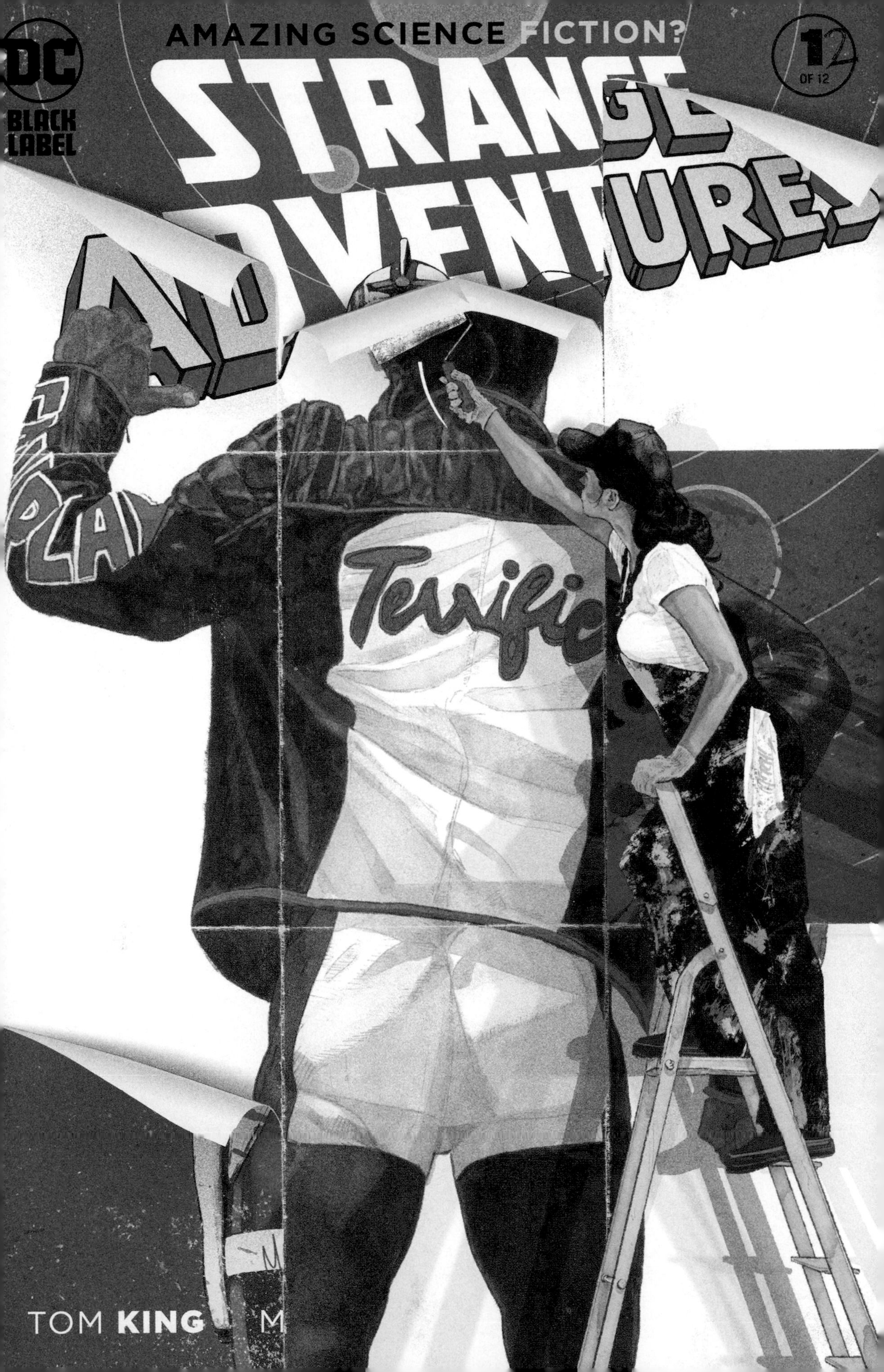
DC
BLACK LABEL
AMAZING SCIENCE FICTION?
STRANGE ADVENTURES
1 2
OF 12
Terrific
TOM KING M

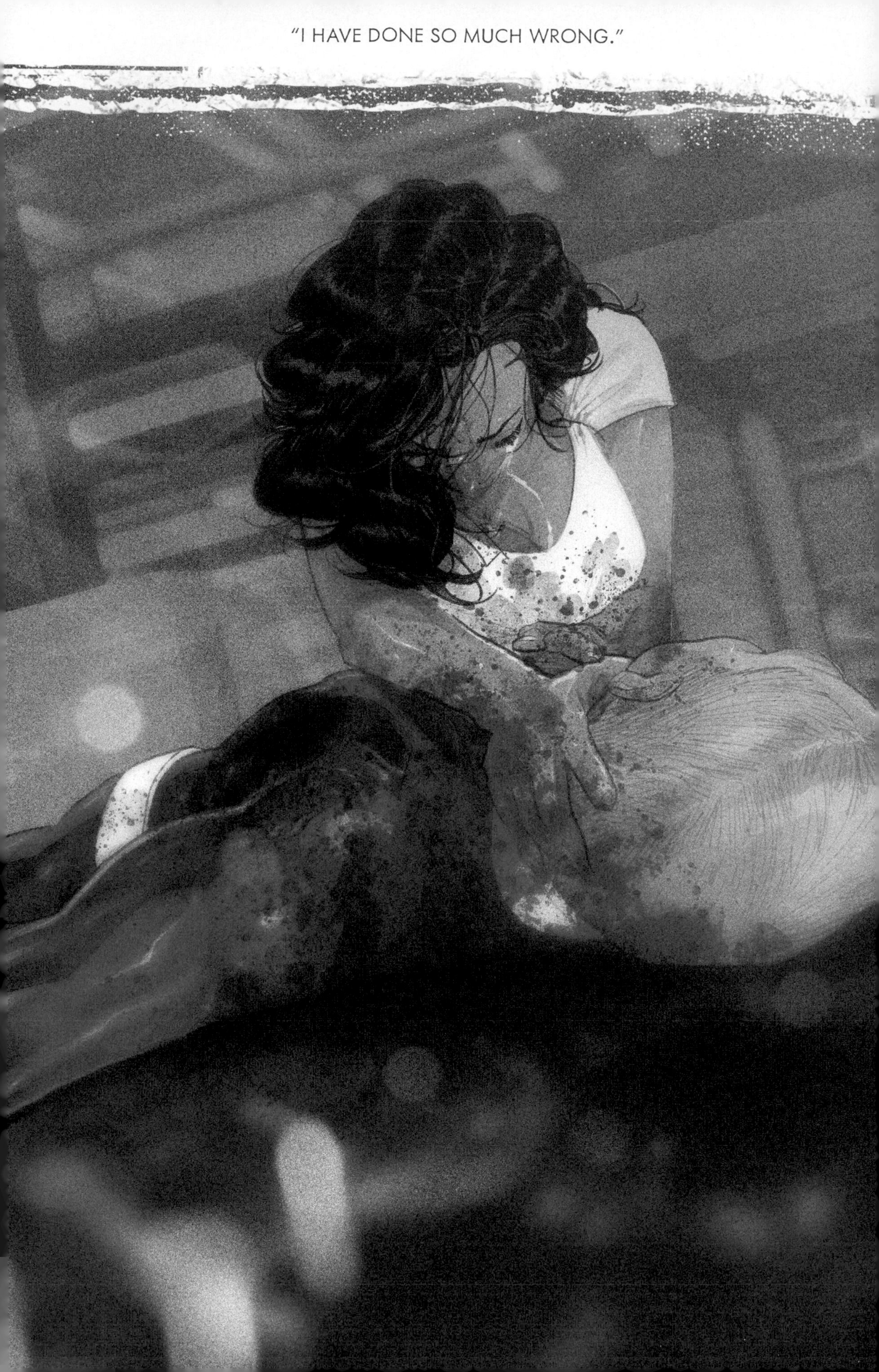
"I HAVE DONE SO MUCH WRONG."

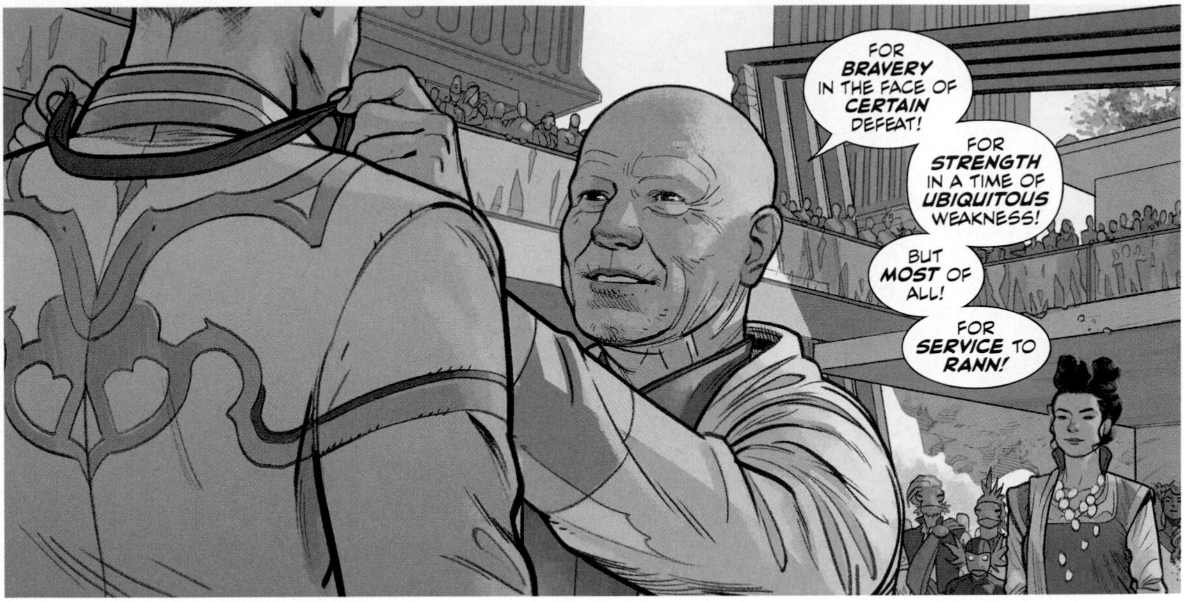
FOR BRAVERY IN THE FACE OF CERTAIN DEFEAT!
FOR STRENGTH IN A TIME OF UBIQUITOUS WEAKNESS!
BUT MOST OF ALL!
FOR SERVICE TO RANN!

Chapter 12

Dedication and fanaticism

TOM KING	...Writer
MITCH GERADS EVAN "DOC" SHANER	...Interior & Cover Artists
CLAYTON COWLES	...Letterer
BIXIE MATHIEU	...Assistant Editor
BRITTANY HOLZHERR JAMIE S. RICH	...Editors

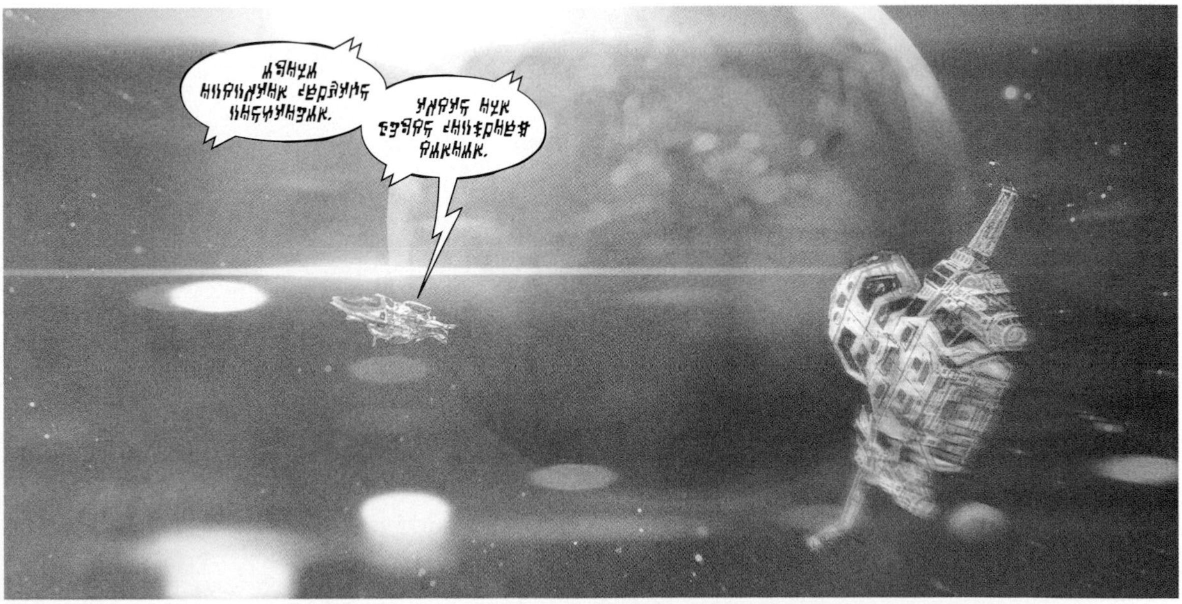

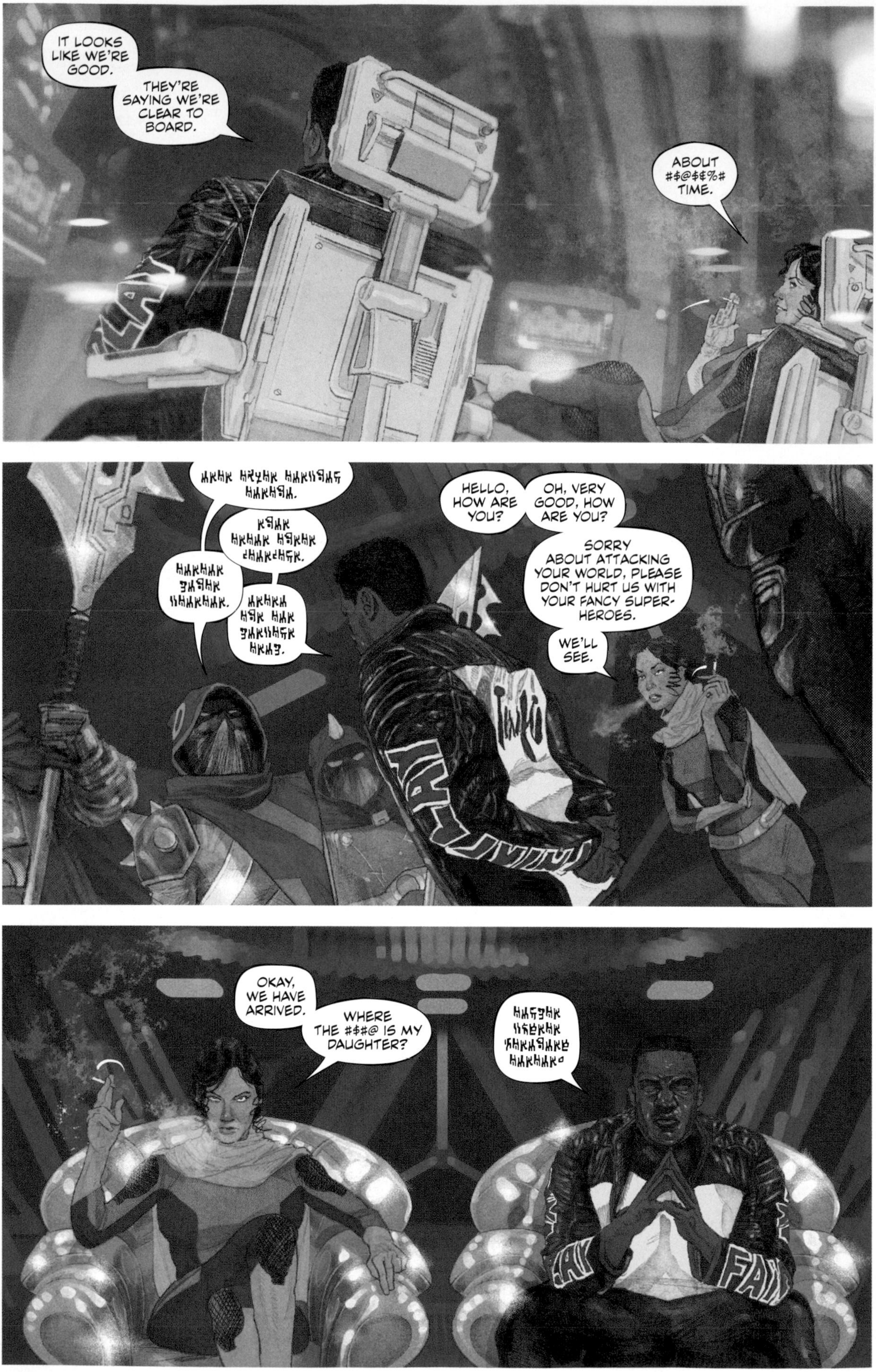
IT LOOKS LIKE WE'RE GOOD.
THEY'RE SAYING WE'RE CLEAR TO BOARD.
ABOUT #$@$&% # TIME.
HELLO, HOW ARE YOU?
OH, VERY GOOD, HOW ARE YOU?
SORRY ABOUT ATTACKING YOUR WORLD, PLEASE DON'T HURT US WITH YOUR FANCY SUPER-HEROES.
WE'LL SEE.
OKAY, WE HAVE ARRIVED.
WHERE THE #$#@ IS MY DAUGHTER?

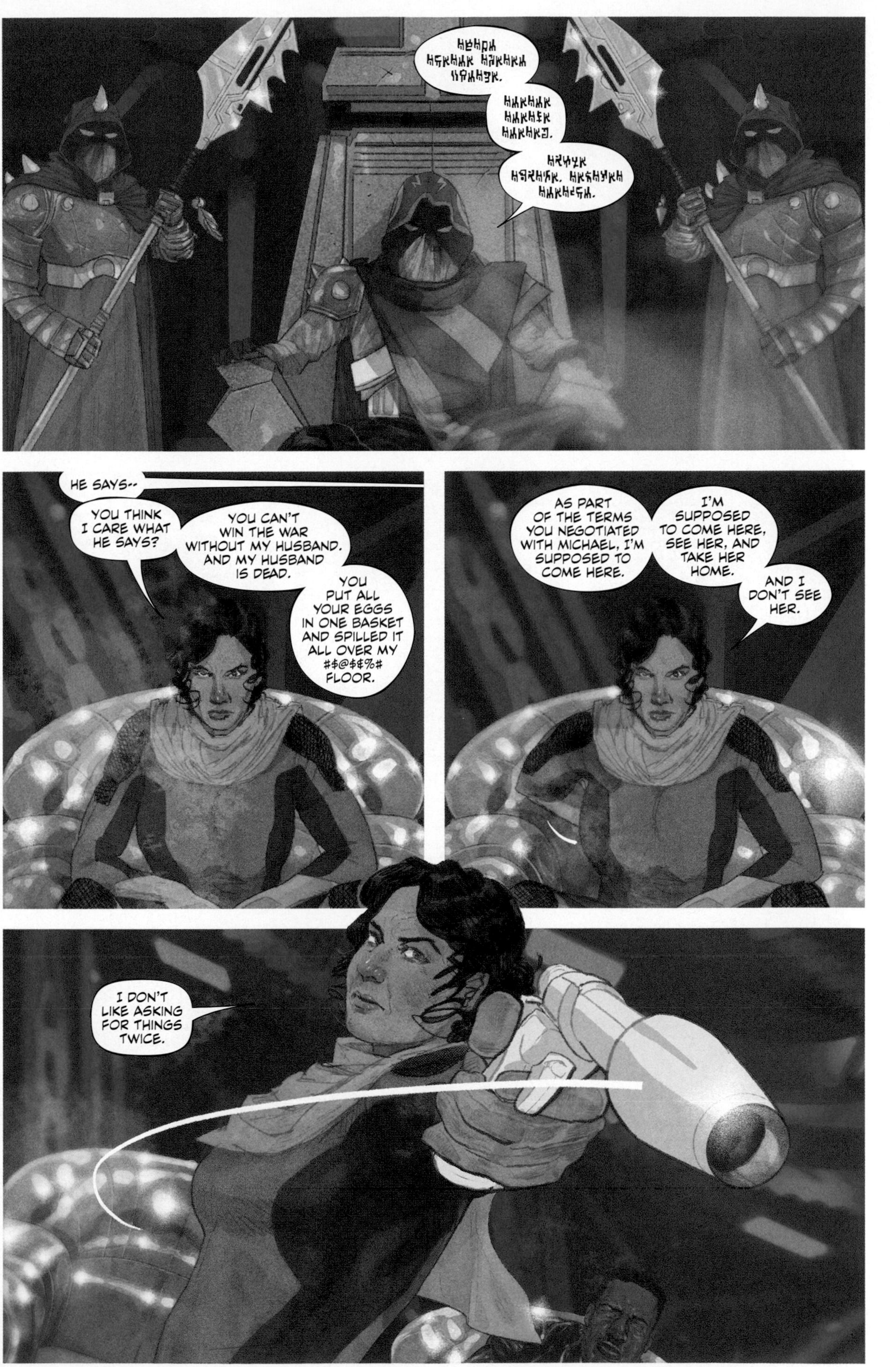
HE SAYS--
YOU THINK I CARE WHAT HE SAYS?
YOU CAN'T WIN THE WAR WITHOUT MY HUSBAND. AND MY HUSBAND IS DEAD.
YOU PUT ALL YOUR EGGS IN ONE BASKET AND SPILLED IT ALL OVER MY #$@$¢%# FLOOR.
AS PART OF THE TERMS YOU NEGOTIATED WITH MICHAEL, I'M SUPPOSED TO COME HERE.
I'M SUPPOSED TO COME HERE, SEE HER, AND TAKE HER HOME.
AND I DON'T SEE HER.
I DON'T LIKE ASKING FOR THINGS TWICE.

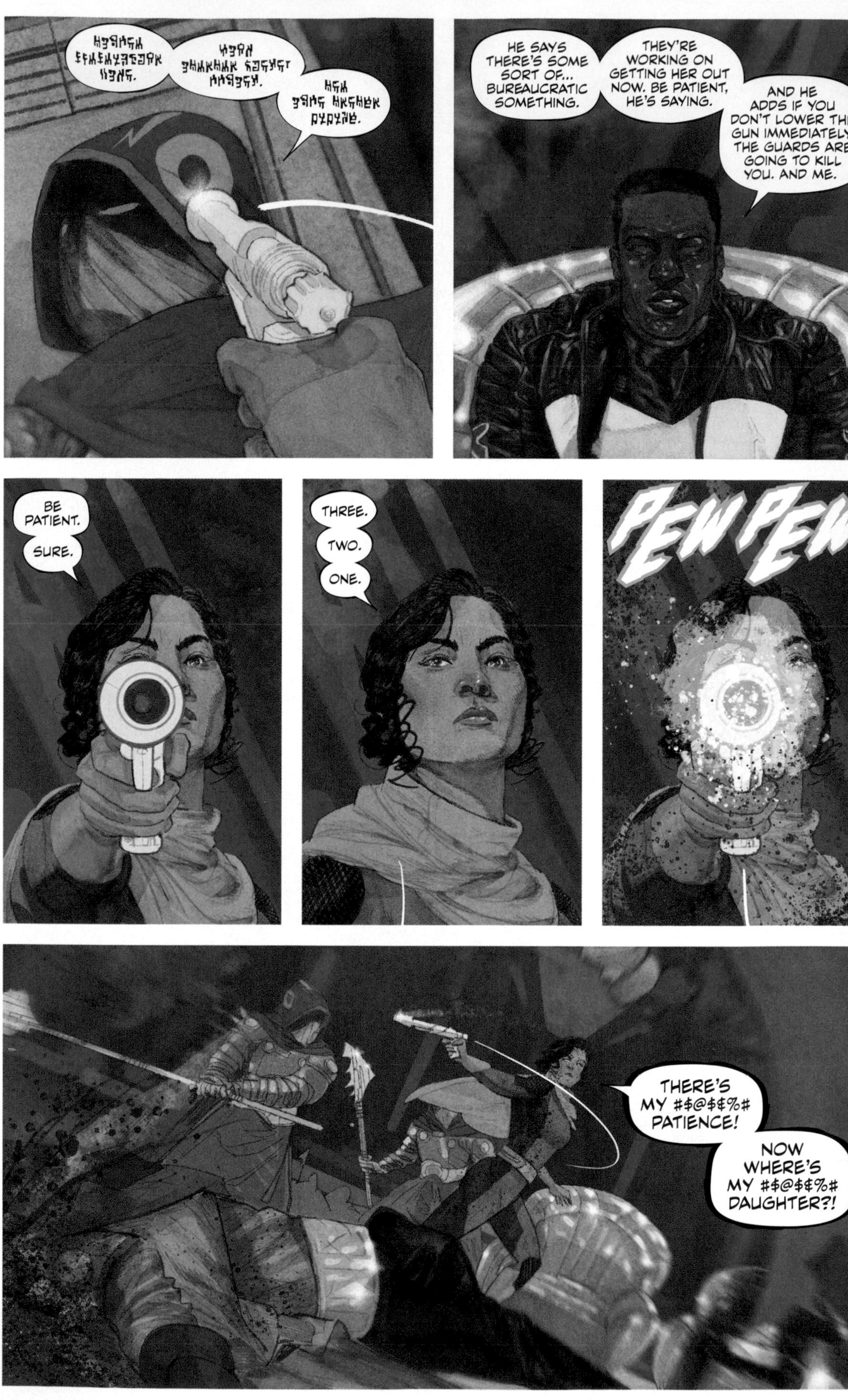

HE SAYS THERE'S SOME SORT OF... BUREAUCRATIC SOMETHING.
THEY'RE WORKING ON GETTING HER OUT NOW. BE PATIENT, HE'S SAYING.
AND HE ADDS IF YOU DON'T LOWER THE GUN IMMEDIATELY, THE GUARDS ARE GOING TO KILL YOU. AND ME.
BE PATIENT.
SURE.
THREE.
TWO.
ONE.
PEW PEW
THERE'S MY #$@$¢%# PATIENCE!
NOW WHERE'S MY #$@$¢%# DAUGHTER?!

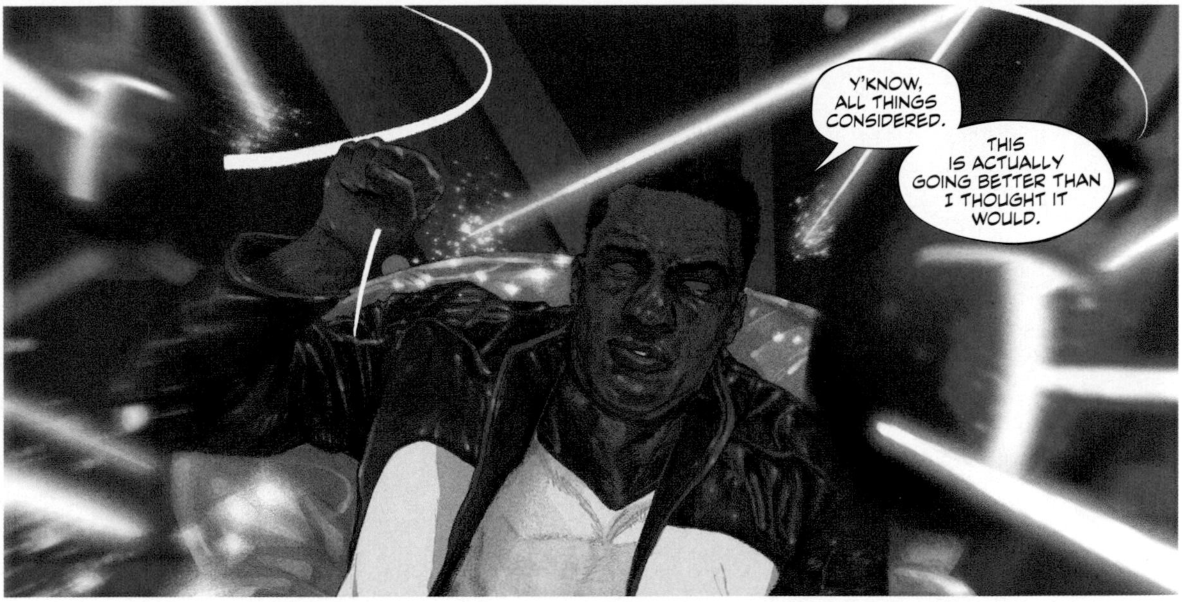
Y'KNOW, ALL THINGS CONSIDERED.
THIS IS ACTUALLY GOING BETTER THAN I THOUGHT IT WOULD.

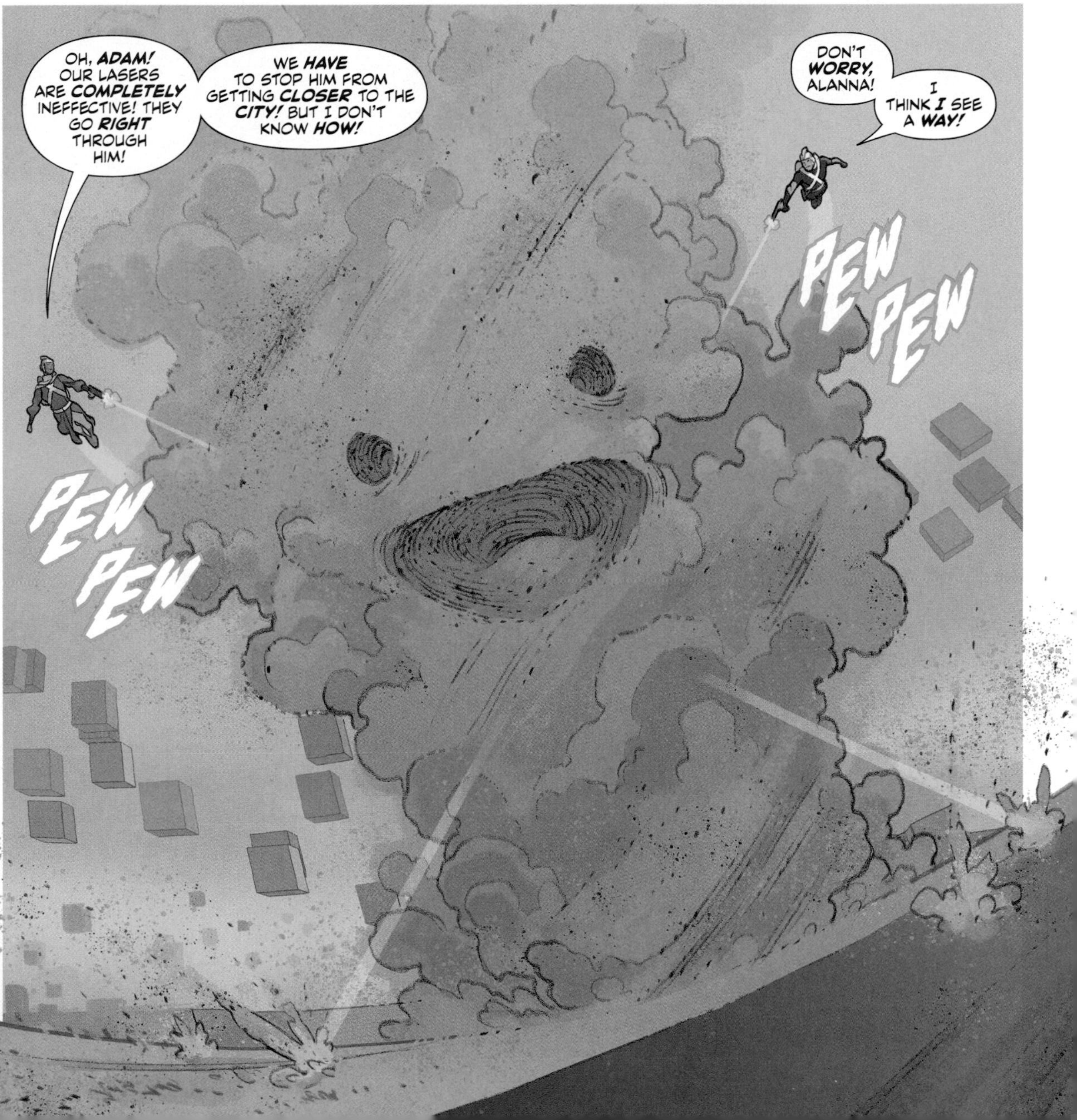
OH, ADAM! OUR LASERS ARE COMPLETELY INEFFECTIVE! THEY GO RIGHT THROUGH HIM!
WE HAVE TO STOP HIM FROM GETTING CLOSER TO THE CITY! BUT I DON'T KNOW HOW!
DON'T WORRY, ALANNA!
I THINK I SEE A WAY!
PEW PEW
PEW PEW

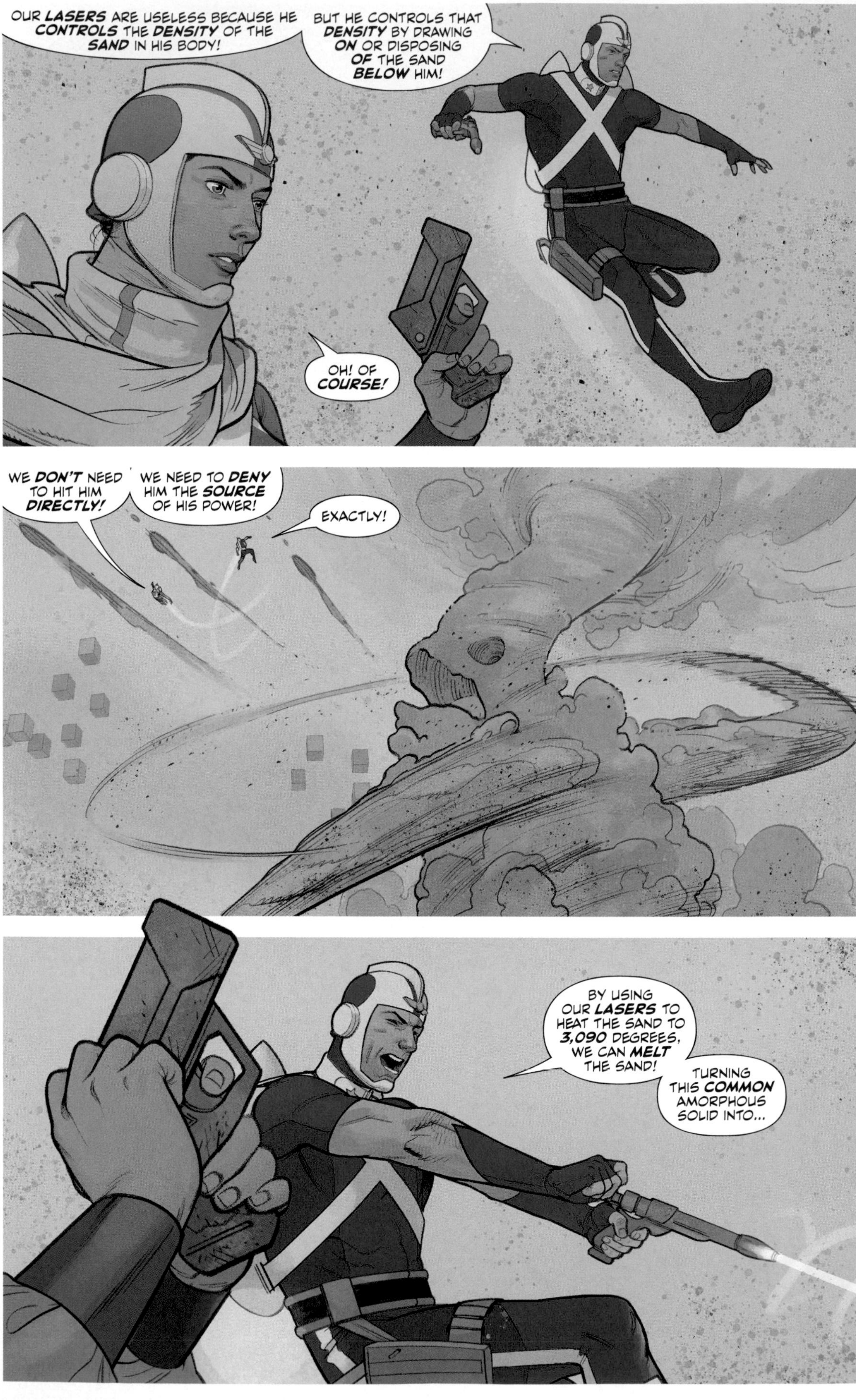
OUR LASERS ARE USELESS BECAUSE HE CONTROLS THE DENSITY OF THE SAND IN HIS BODY!
BUT HE CONTROLS THAT DENSITY BY DRAWING ON OR DISPOSING OF THE SAND BELOW HIM!
OH! OF COURSE!
WE DON'T NEED TO HIT HIM DIRECTLY!
WE NEED TO DENY HIM THE SOURCE OF HIS POWER!
EXACTLY!
BY USING OUR LASERS TO HEAT THE SAND TO 3,090 DEGREES, WE CAN MELT THE SAND!
TURNING THIS COMMON AMORPHOUS SOLID INTO...

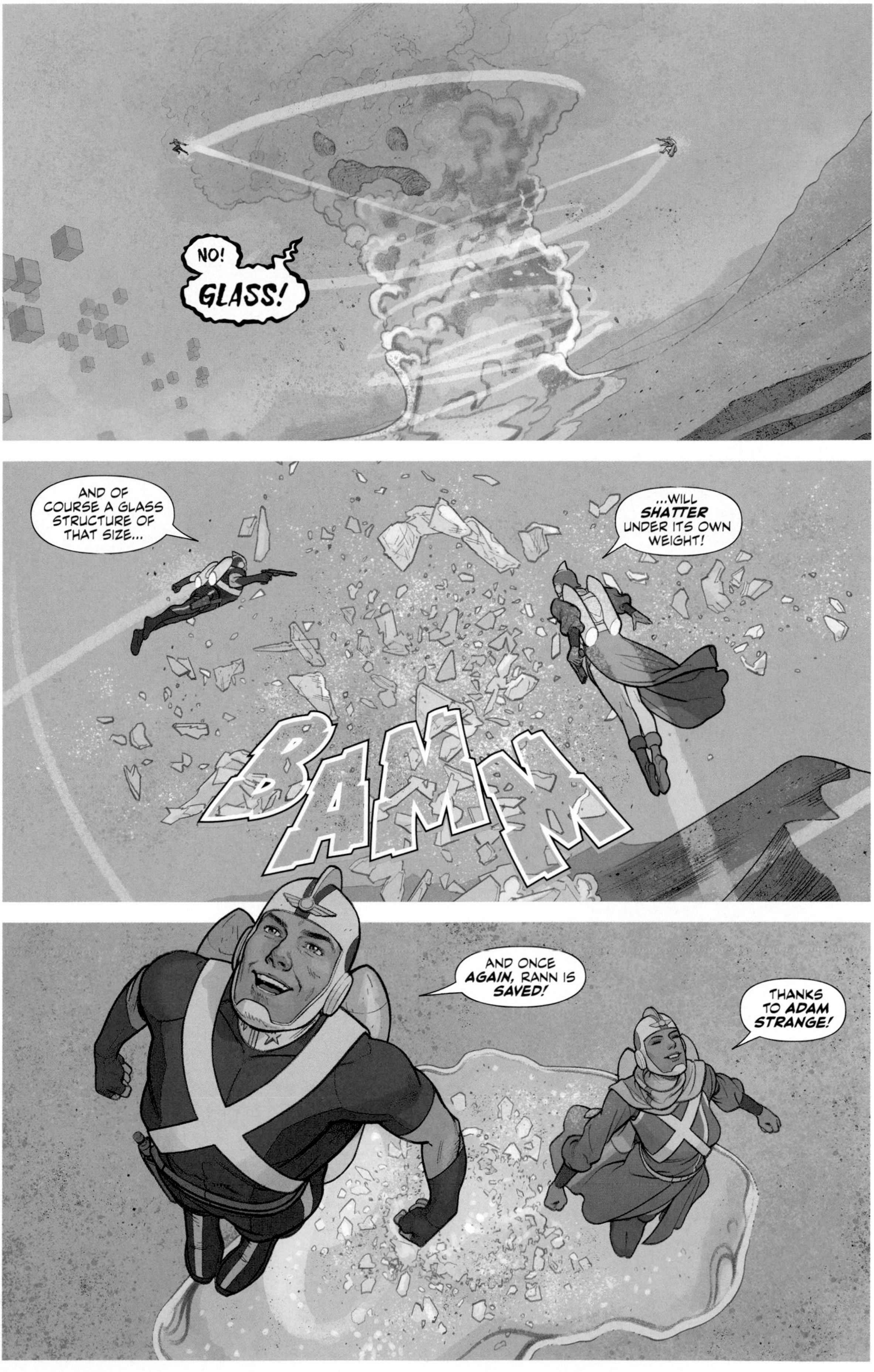
NO! GLASS!
AND OF COURSE A GLASS STRUCTURE OF THAT SIZE...
...WILL SHATTER UNDER ITS OWN WEIGHT!
BAMM
AND ONCE AGAIN, RANN IS SAVED!
THANKS TO ADAM STRANGE!

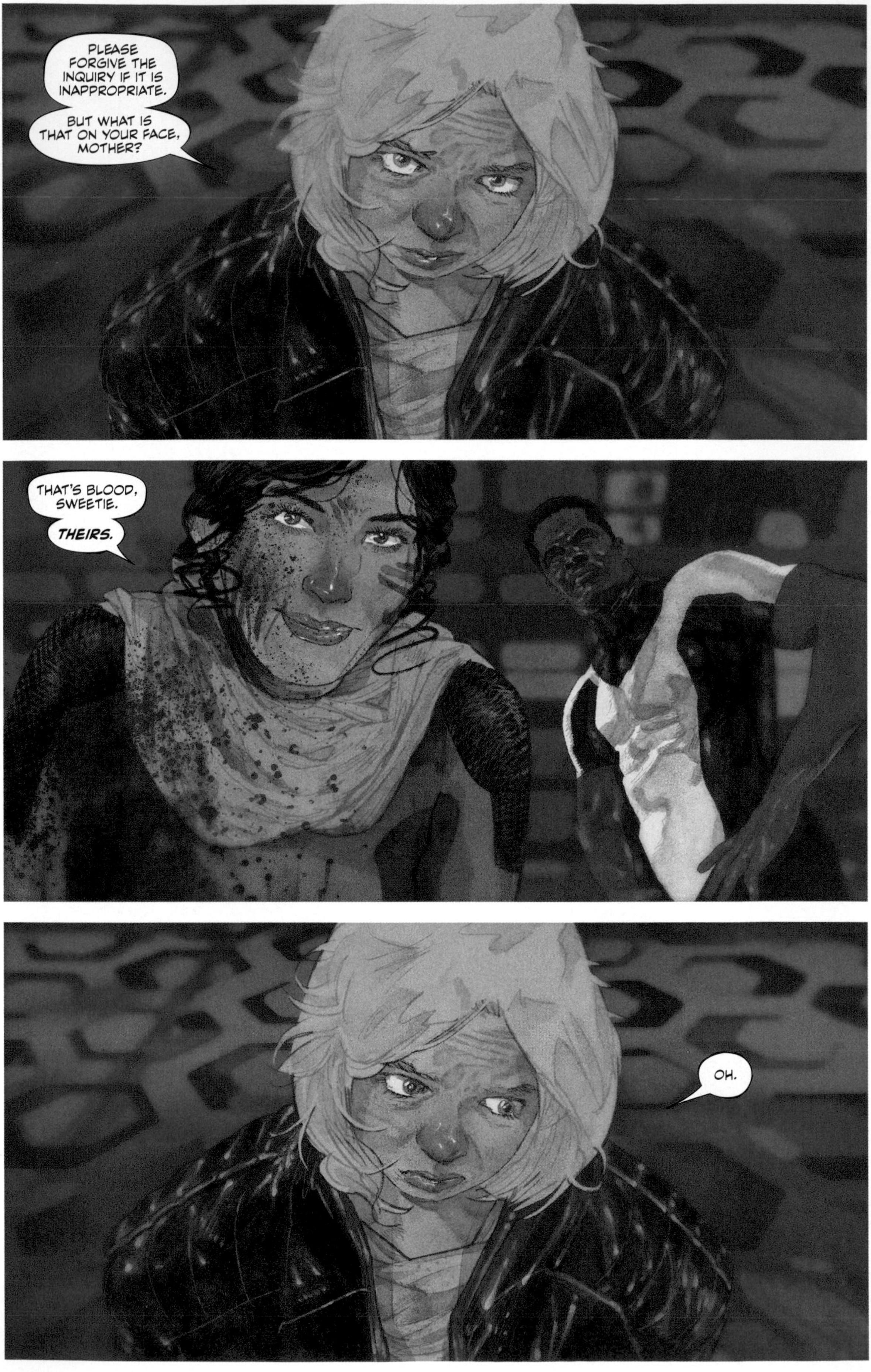
PLEASE FORGIVE THE INQUIRY IF IT IS INAPPROPRIATE.
BUT WHAT IS THAT ON YOUR FACE, MOTHER?
THAT'S BLOOD, SWEETIE.
THEIRS.
OH.

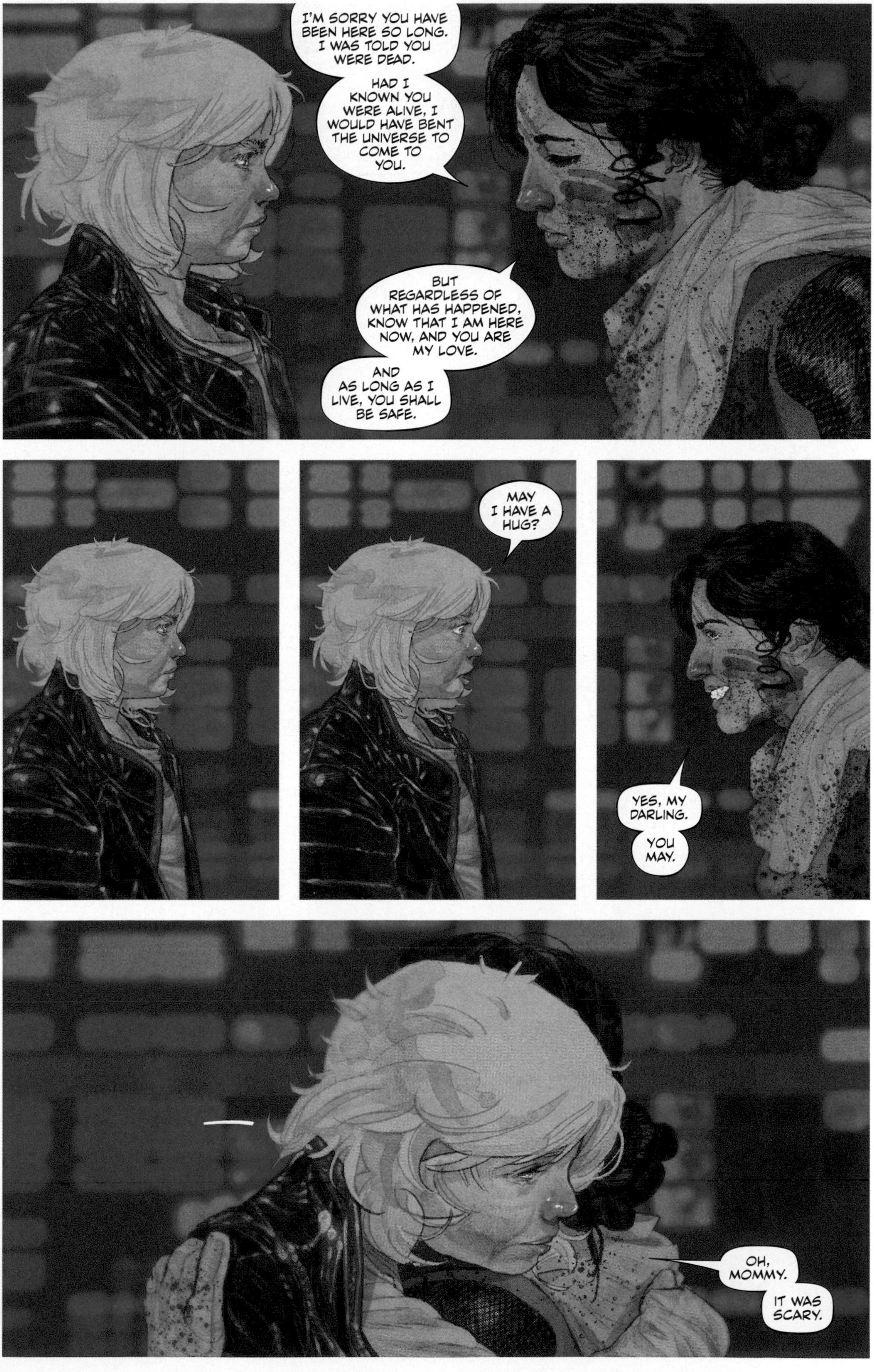
I'M SORRY YOU HAVE BEEN HERE SO LONG. I WAS TOLD YOU WERE DEAD.
HAD I KNOWN YOU WERE ALIVE, I WOULD HAVE BENT THE UNIVERSE TO COME TO YOU.
BUT REGARDLESS OF WHAT HAS HAPPENED, KNOW THAT I AM HERE NOW, AND YOU ARE MY LOVE.
AND AS LONG AS I LIVE, YOU SHALL BE SAFE.
MAY I HAVE A HUG?
YES, MY DARLING.
YOU MAY.
OH, MOMMY.
IT WAS SCARY.

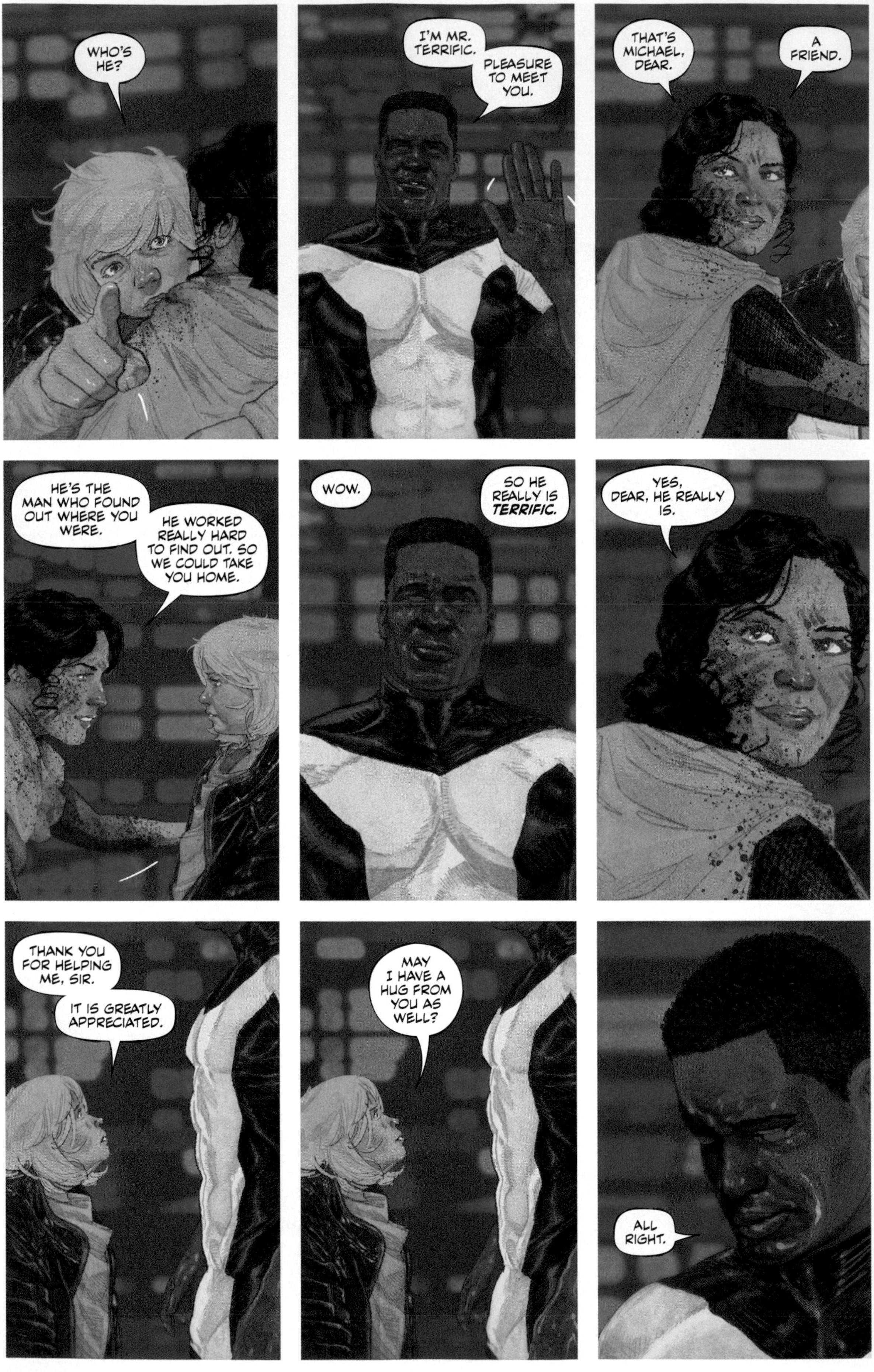
WHO'S HE?
I'M MR. TERRIFIC.
PLEASURE TO MEET YOU.
THAT'S MICHAEL, DEAR.
A FRIEND.
HE'S THE MAN WHO FOUND OUT WHERE YOU WERE.
HE WORKED REALLY HARD TO FIND OUT. SO WE COULD TAKE YOU HOME.
WOW.
SO HE REALLY IS *TERRIFIC.*
YES, DEAR, HE REALLY IS.
THANK YOU FOR HELPING ME, SIR.
IT IS GREATLY APPRECIATED.
MAY I HAVE A HUG FROM YOU AS WELL?
ALL RIGHT.

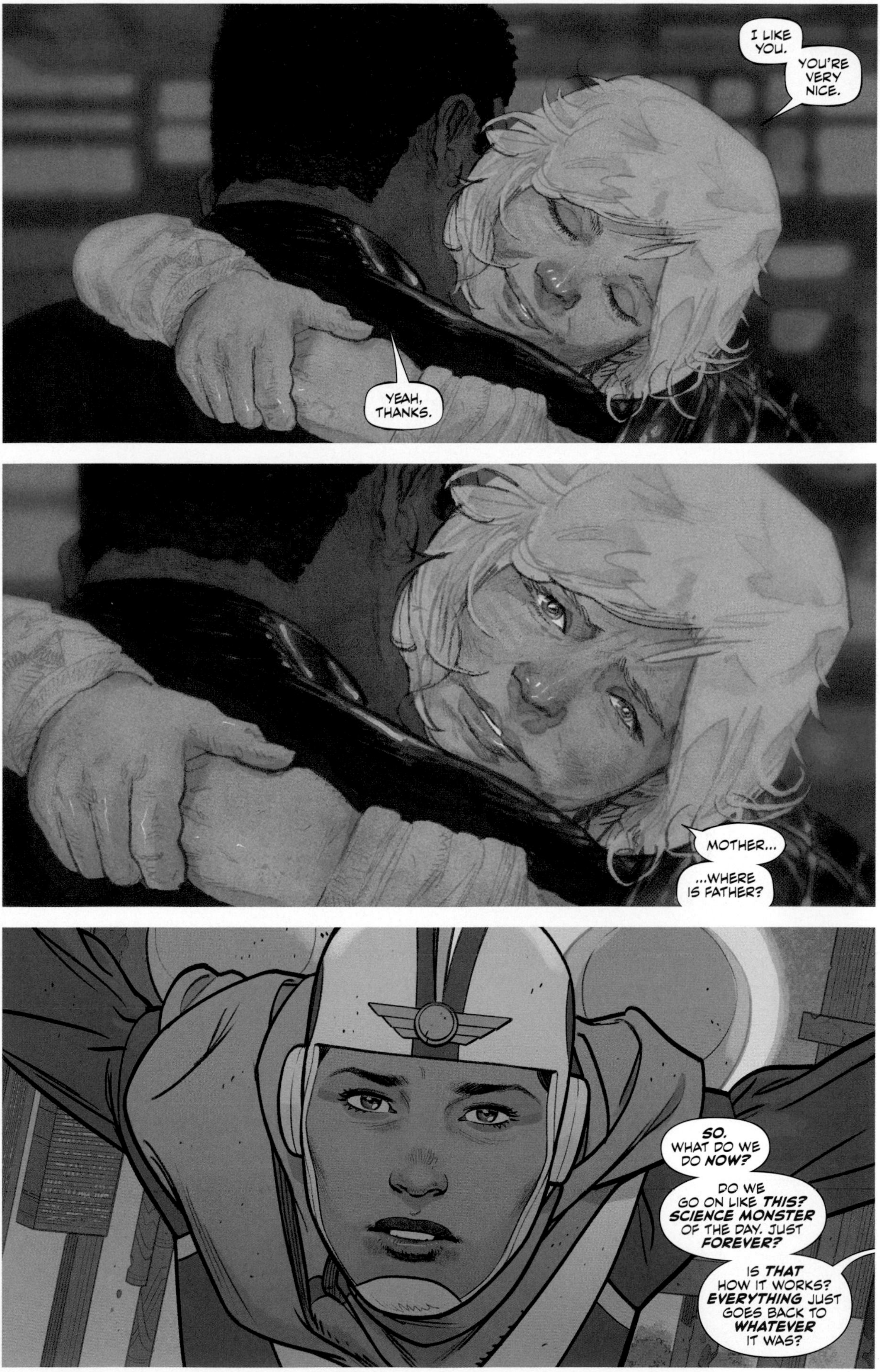
I LIKE YOU.
YOU'RE VERY NICE.
YEAH, THANKS.
MOTHER...
...WHERE IS FATHER?
SO. WHAT DO WE DO NOW?
DO WE GO ON LIKE THIS? SCIENCE MONSTER OF THE DAY. JUST FOREVER?
IS THAT HOW IT WORKS? EVERYTHING JUST GOES BACK TO WHATEVER IT WAS?

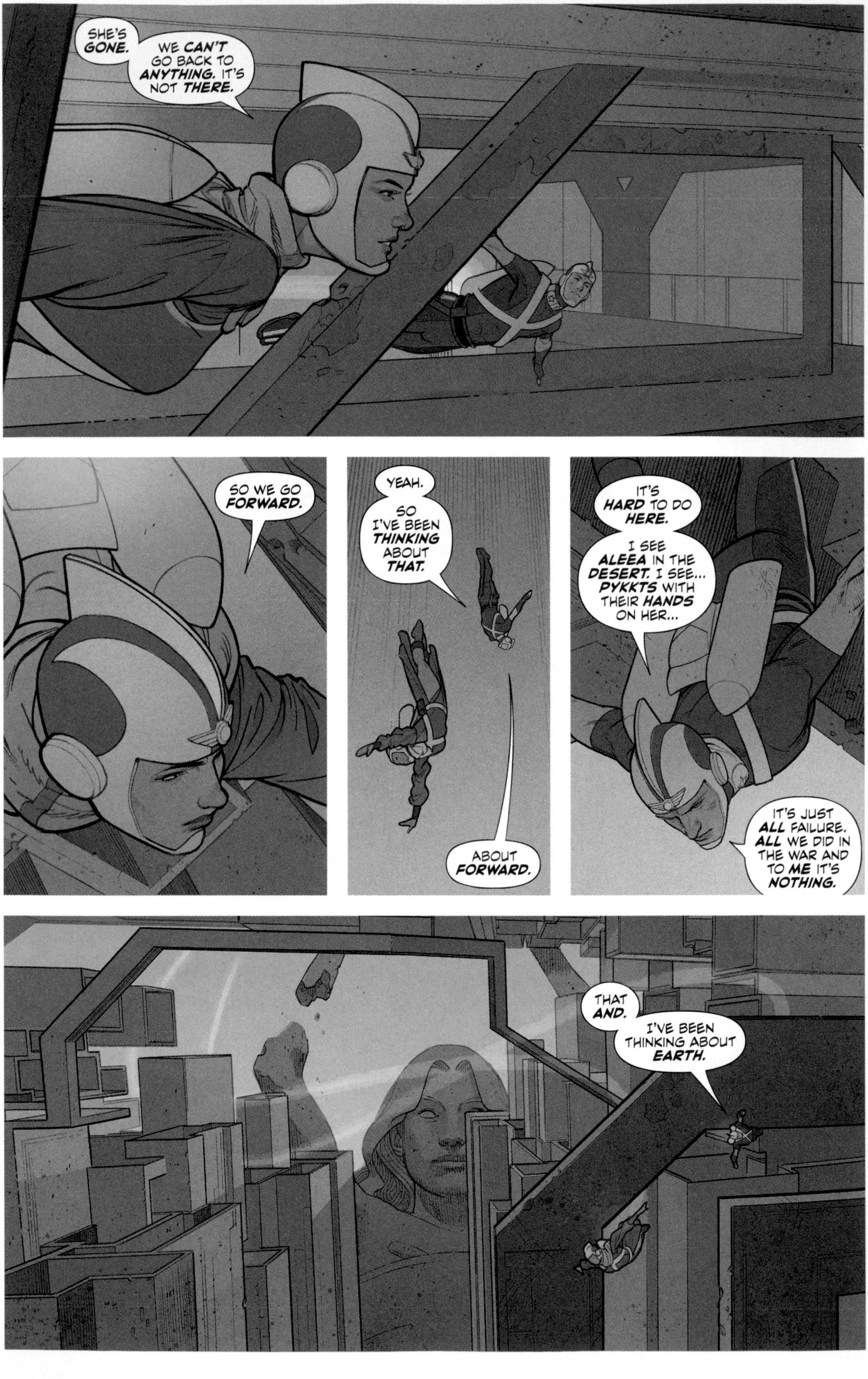
SHE'S GONE.
WE CAN'T GO BACK TO ANYTHING. IT'S NOT THERE.
SO WE GO FORWARD.
YEAH.
SO I'VE BEEN THINKING ABOUT THAT.
ABOUT FORWARD.
IT'S HARD TO DO HERE.
I SEE ALEEA IN THE DESERT. I SEE... PYKKTS WITH THEIR HANDS ON HER...
IT'S JUST ALL FAILURE. ALL WE DID IN THE WAR AND TO ME IT'S NOTHING.
THAT AND.
I'VE BEEN THINKING ABOUT EARTH.

I'VE...I'VE *GIVEN* ALL I CAN TO *THIS* WORLD AND I'M *GRATEFUL* FOR WHAT IT'S GIVEN *ME.*

BUT I DON'T *KNOW* IF I CAN GIVE IT *ANY MORE,* AND IF I *CAN'T...*

I DON'T KNOW, *MAYBE* IT'S TIME TO GO *HOME.*

BESIDES, THOSE *BASTARDS* ARE STILL OUT THERE *SOMEWHERE,* THEY WON'T COME FOR *RANN* AGAIN. *WE'VE* SEEN TO THAT.

BUT *EARTH.*

IF WE'RE *THERE...*AND *THEY* COME...WE... WE *COULD* HELP.

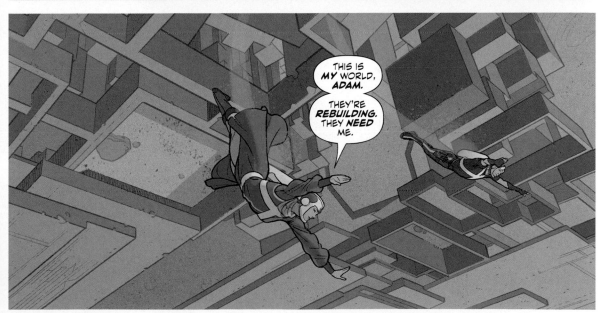

THIS IS *MY* WORLD, *ADAM.*

THEY'RE *REBUILDING.* THEY *NEED* ME.

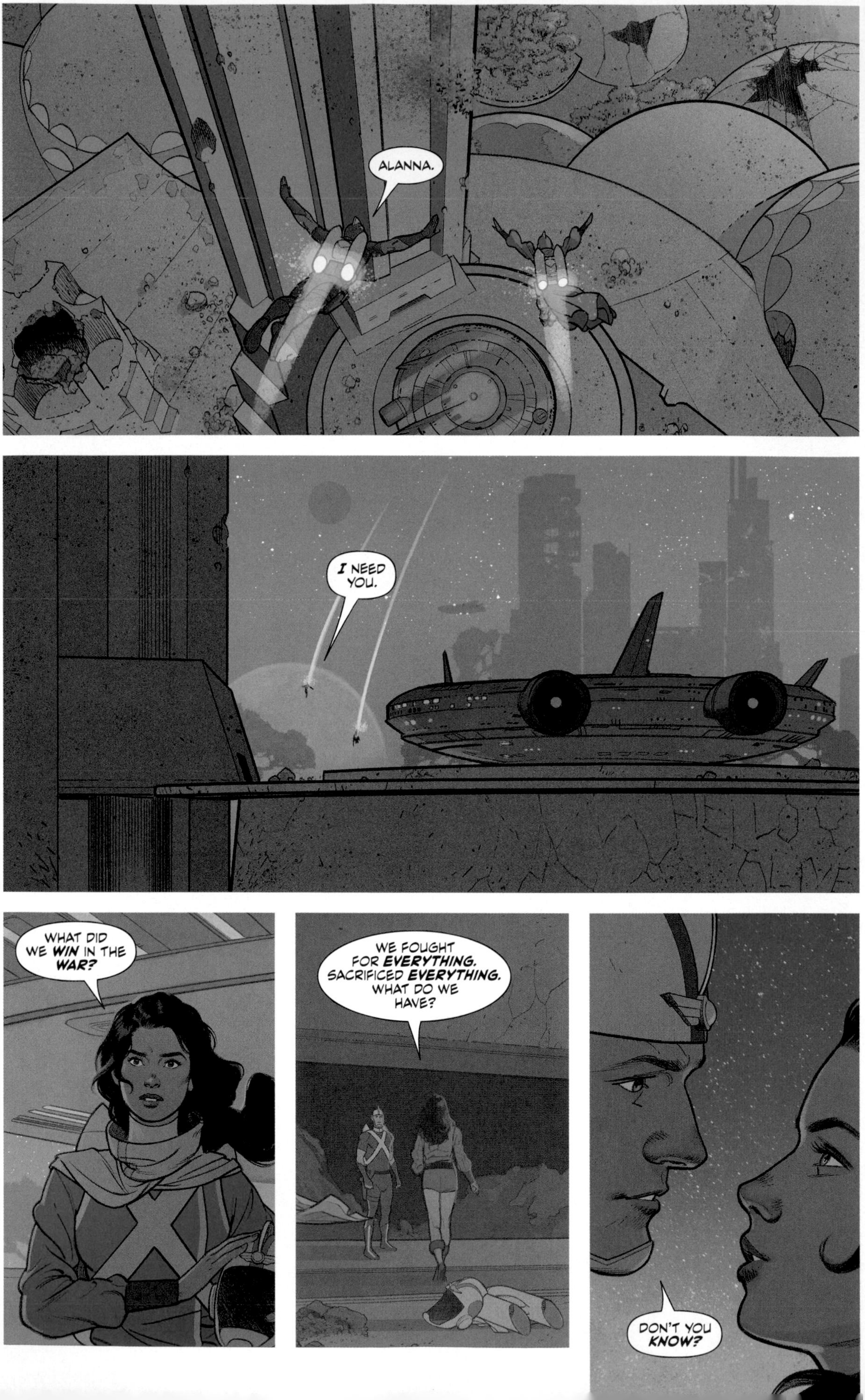
ALANNA.
I NEED YOU.
WHAT DID WE **WIN** IN THE **WAR?**
WE FOUGHT FOR **EVERYTHING.** SACRIFICED **EVERYTHING.** WHAT DO WE HAVE?
DON'T YOU **KNOW?**

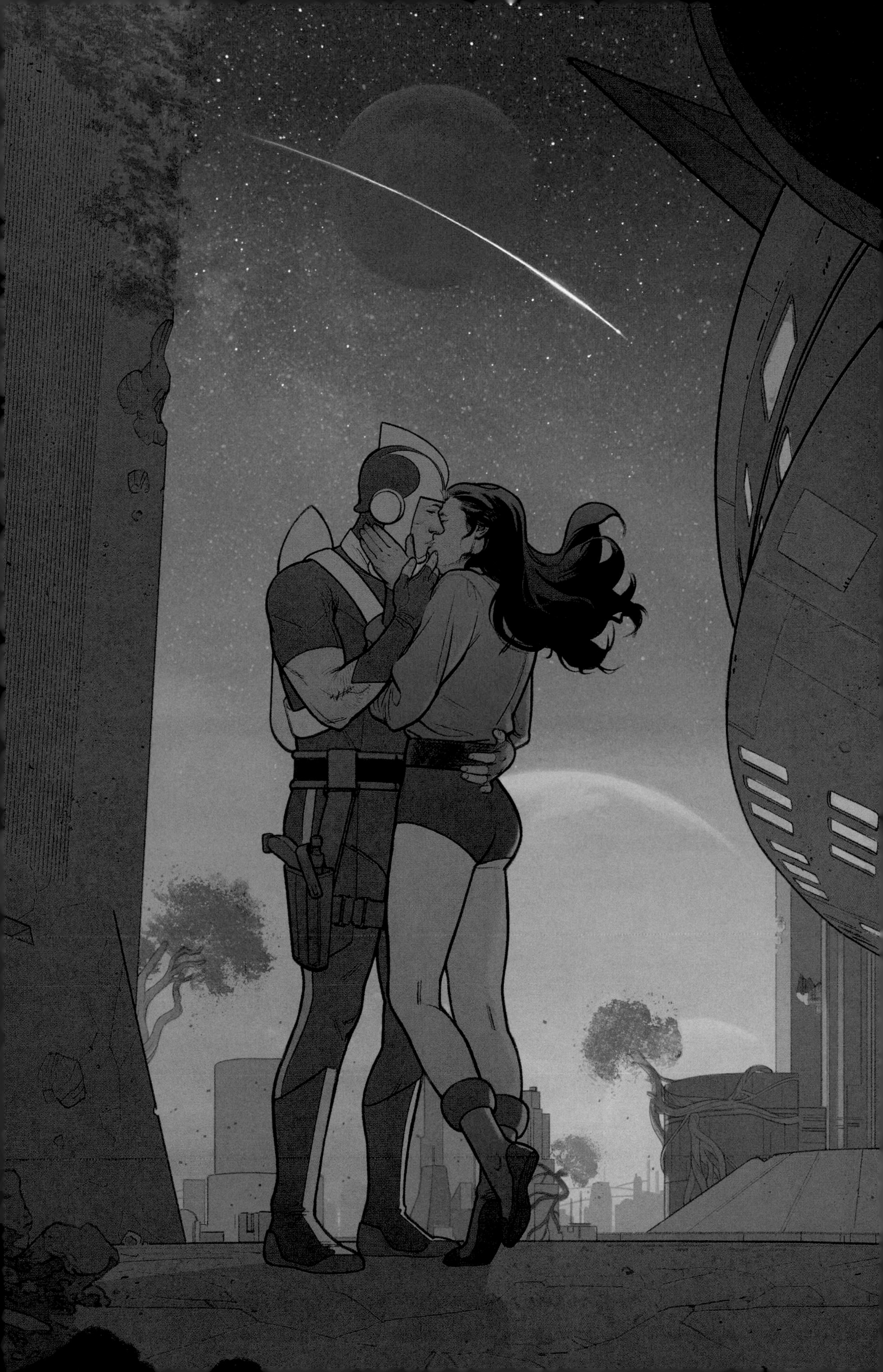

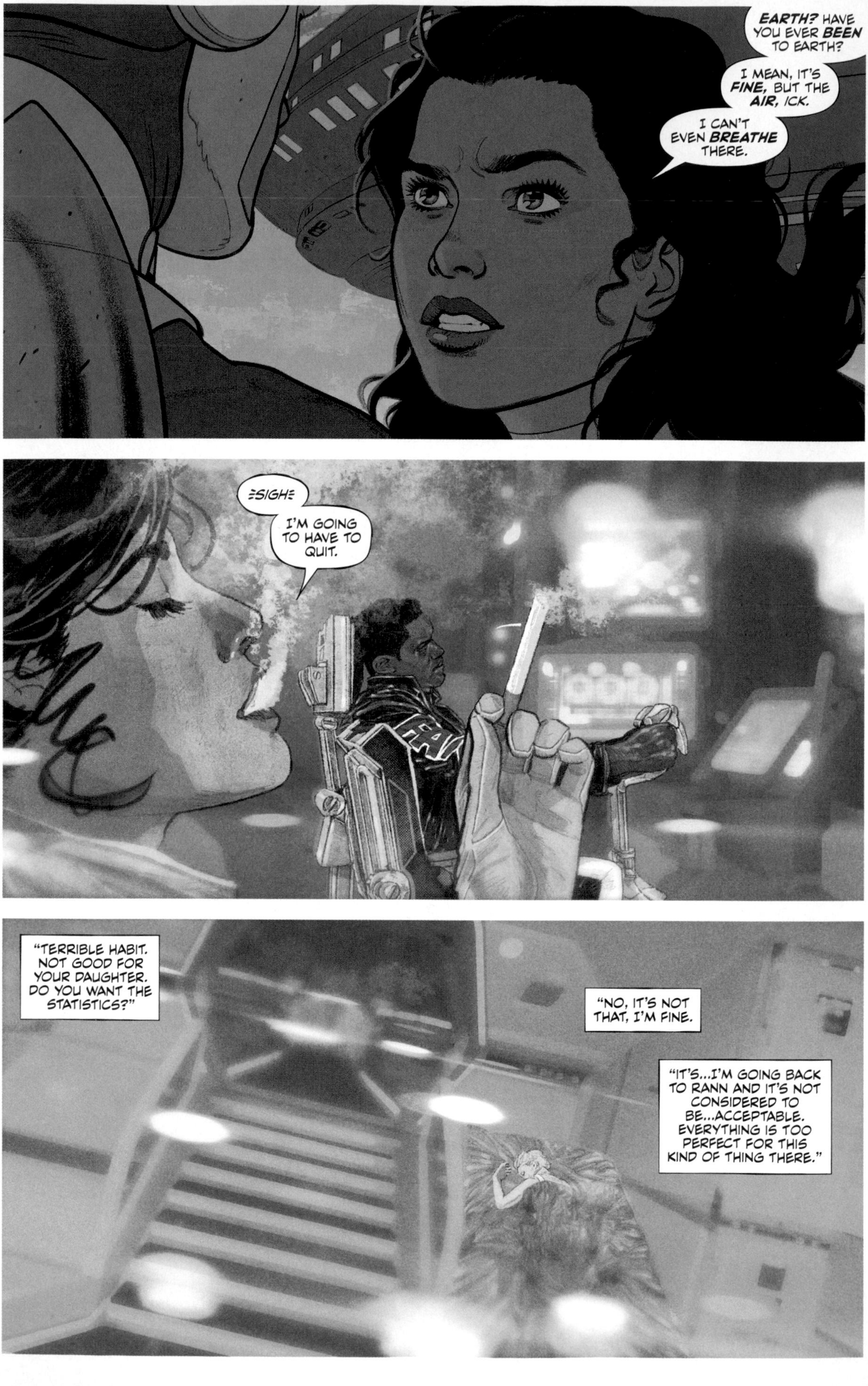
EARTH? HAVE YOU EVER BEEN TO EARTH?
I MEAN, IT'S FINE, BUT THE AIR, ICK.
I CAN'T EVEN BREATHE THERE.
=SIGH=
I'M GOING TO HAVE TO QUIT.
"TERRIBLE HABIT. NOT GOOD FOR YOUR DAUGHTER. DO YOU WANT THE STATISTICS?"
"NO, IT'S NOT THAT, I'M FINE.
"IT'S...I'M GOING BACK TO RANN AND IT'S NOT CONSIDERED TO BE...ACCEPTABLE. EVERYTHING IS TOO PERFECT FOR THIS KIND OF THING THERE."

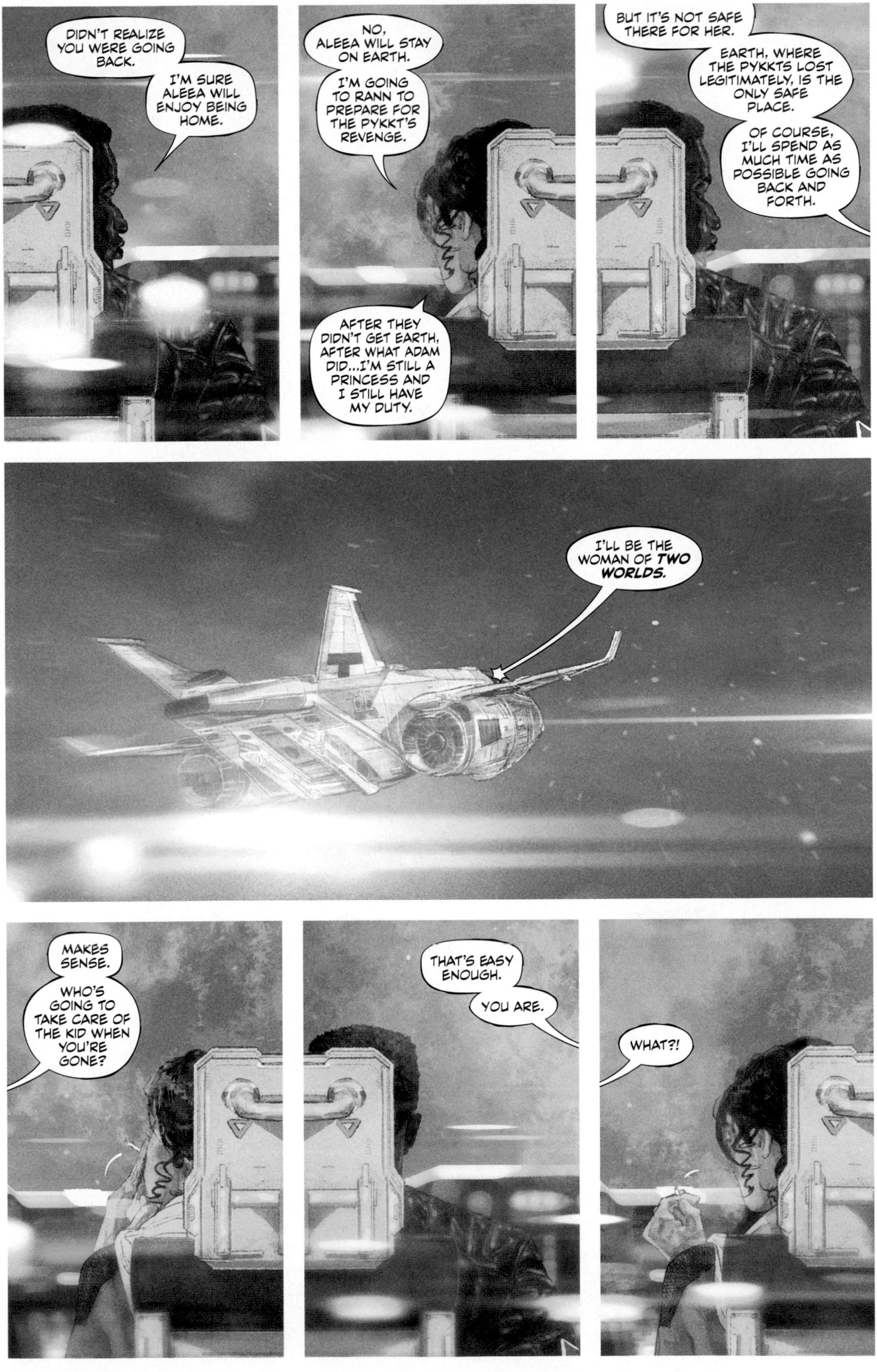
DIDN'T REALIZE YOU WERE GOING BACK.
I'M SURE ALEEA WILL ENJOY BEING HOME.
NO, ALEEA WILL STAY ON EARTH.
I'M GOING TO RANN TO PREPARE FOR THE PYKKT'S REVENGE.
AFTER THEY DIDN'T GET EARTH, AFTER WHAT ADAM DID...I'M STILL A PRINCESS AND I STILL HAVE MY DUTY.
BUT IT'S NOT SAFE THERE FOR HER.
EARTH, WHERE THE PYKKTS LOST LEGITIMATELY, IS THE ONLY SAFE PLACE.
OF COURSE, I'LL SPEND AS MUCH TIME AS POSSIBLE GOING BACK AND FORTH.
I'LL BE THE WOMAN OF ***TWO WORLDS.***
MAKES SENSE.
WHO'S GOING TO TAKE CARE OF THE KID WHEN YOU'RE GONE?
THAT'S EASY ENOUGH.
YOU ARE.
WHAT?!

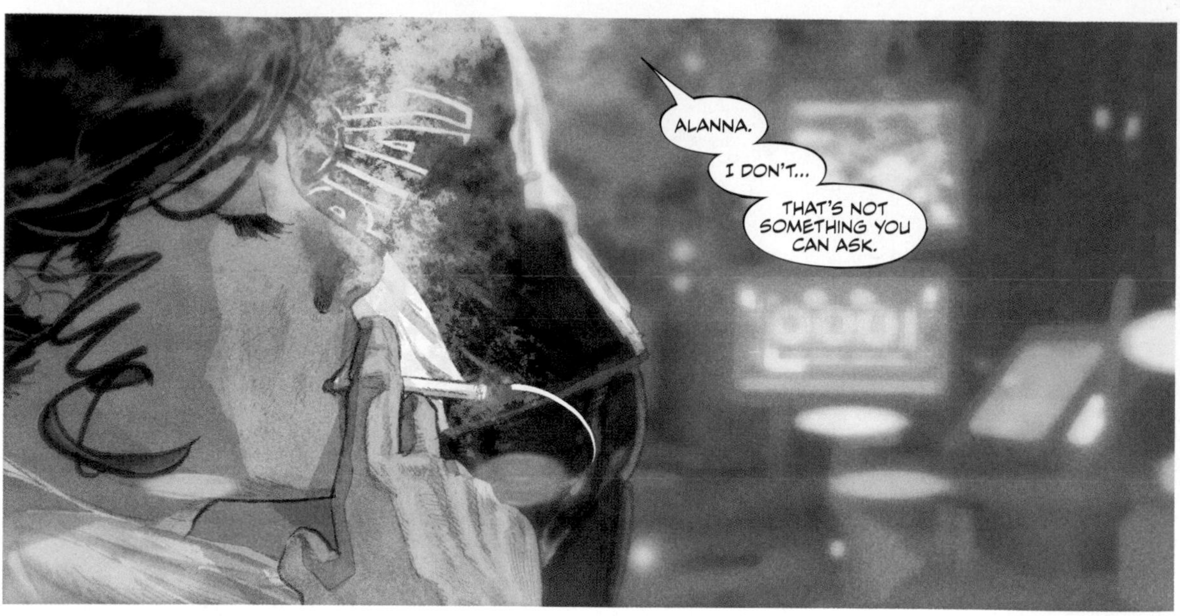
ALANNA.
I DON'T...
THAT'S NOT SOMETHING YOU CAN ASK.

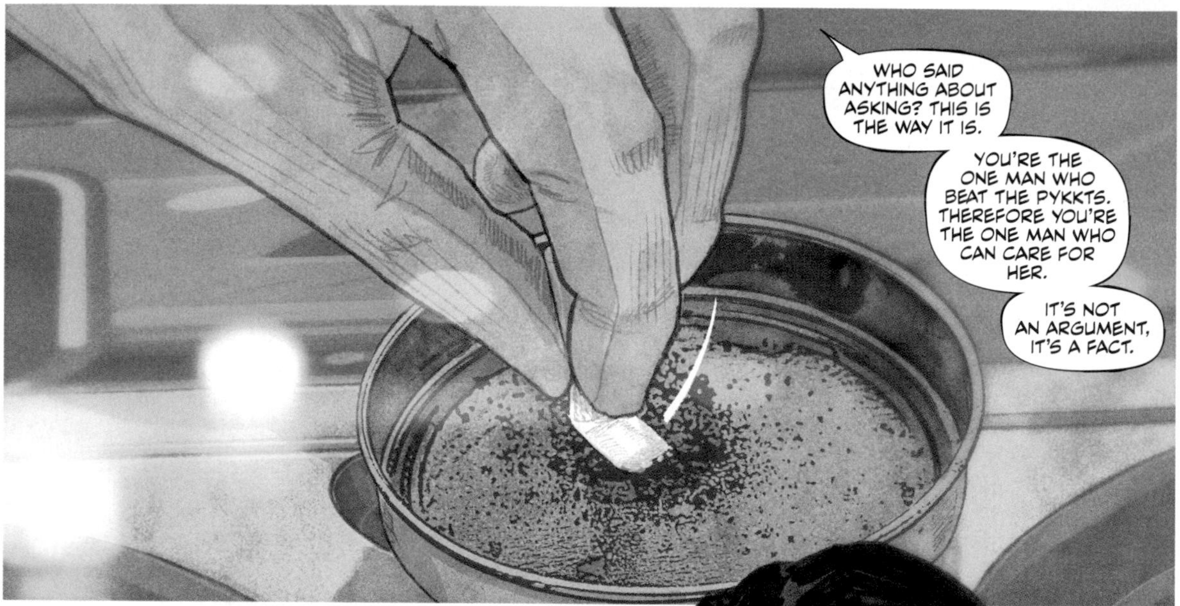
WHO SAID ANYTHING ABOUT ASKING? THIS IS THE WAY IT IS.
YOU'RE THE ONE MAN WHO BEAT THE PYKKTS. THEREFORE YOU'RE THE ONE MAN WHO CAN CARE FOR HER.
IT'S NOT AN ARGUMENT, IT'S A FACT.

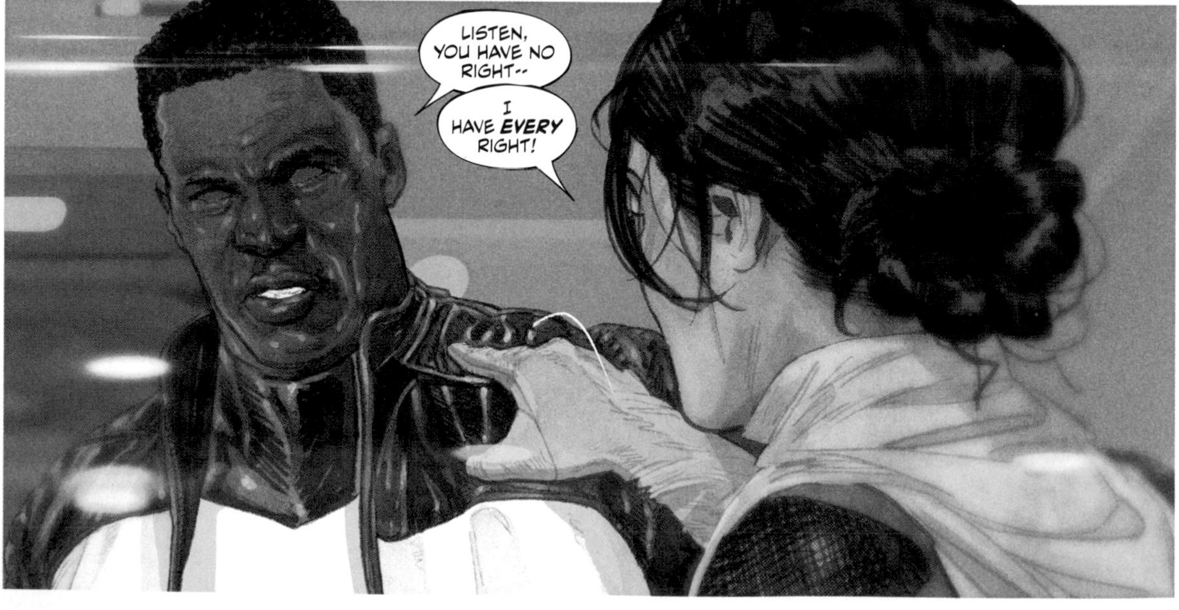
LISTEN, YOU HAVE NO RIGHT--
I HAVE ***EVERY*** RIGHT!

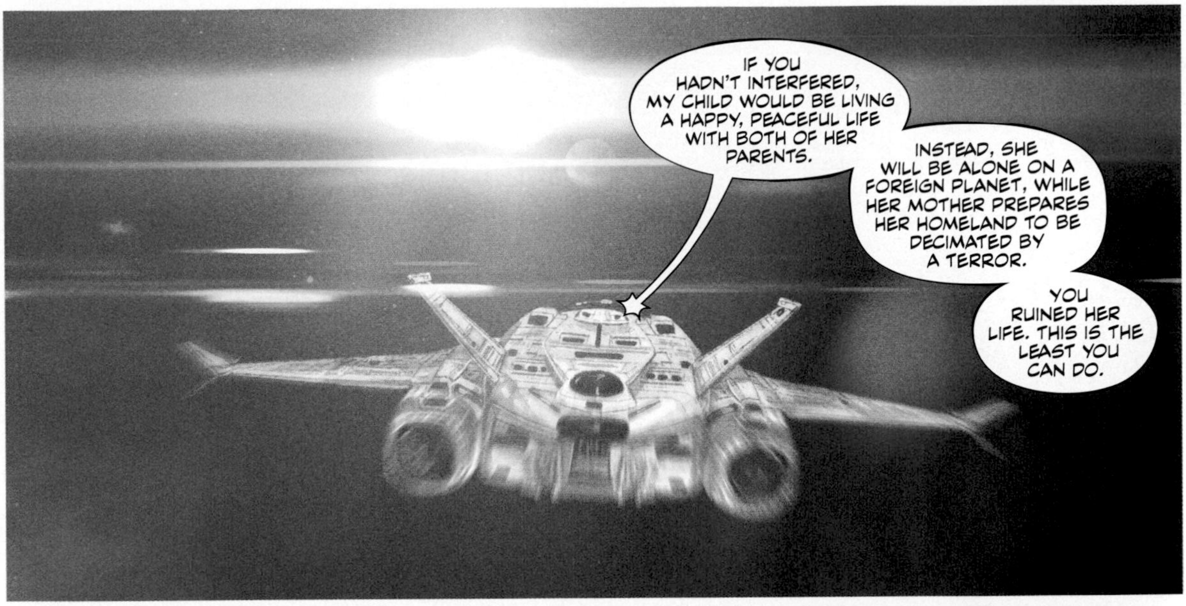
IF YOU HADN'T INTERFERED, MY CHILD WOULD BE LIVING A HAPPY, PEACEFUL LIFE WITH BOTH OF HER PARENTS.
INSTEAD, SHE WILL BE ALONE ON A FOREIGN PLANET, WHILE HER MOTHER PREPARES HER HOMELAND TO BE DECIMATED BY A TERROR.
YOU RUINED HER LIFE. THIS IS THE LEAST YOU CAN DO.

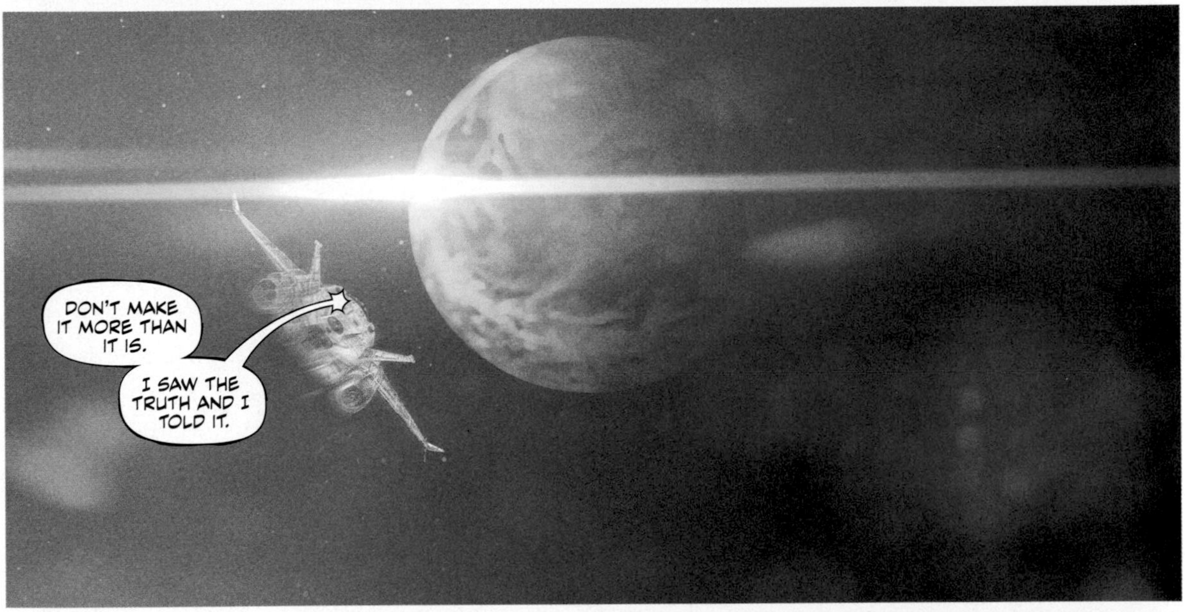
DON'T MAKE IT MORE THAN IT IS.
I SAW THE TRUTH AND I TOLD IT.

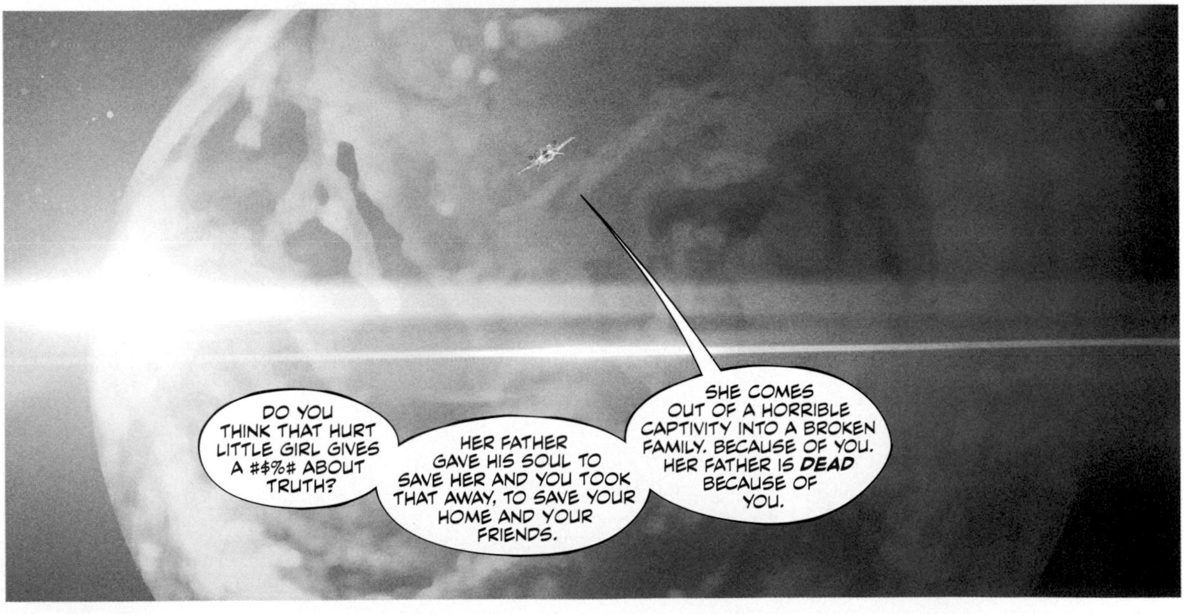
SHE COMES OUT OF A HORRIBLE CAPTIVITY INTO A BROKEN FAMILY. BECAUSE OF YOU. HER FATHER IS ***DEAD*** BECAUSE OF YOU.
HER FATHER GAVE HIS SOUL TO SAVE HER AND YOU TOOK THAT AWAY, TO SAVE YOUR HOME AND YOUR FRIENDS.
DO YOU THINK THAT HURT LITTLE GIRL GIVES A #$%# ABOUT TRUTH?

YOU OWE THIS TO HER.

MM.

IT'S A JOY WATCHING YOU WORK.

YOU SPIN IT ALL AROUND, ALANNA. I ADMIRE IT.

BUT IT'S STILL JUST A LIE.

AND... PERHAPS...

I OWE THIS TO YOU.

YOU NEED HER.

WE'RE APPROACHING EARTH ENTRY.

YOU SHOULD WAKE ALEEA.

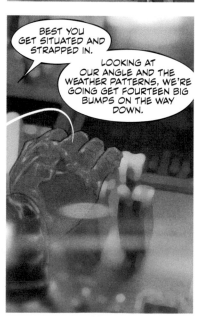

BEST YOU GET SITUATED AND STRAPPED IN.

LOOKING AT OUR ANGLE AND THE WEATHER PATTERNS, WE'RE GOING GET FOURTEEN BIG BUMPS ON THE WAY DOWN.

MICHAEL, LISTEN, I HAVE...

I HAVE DONE SO MUCH WRONG.

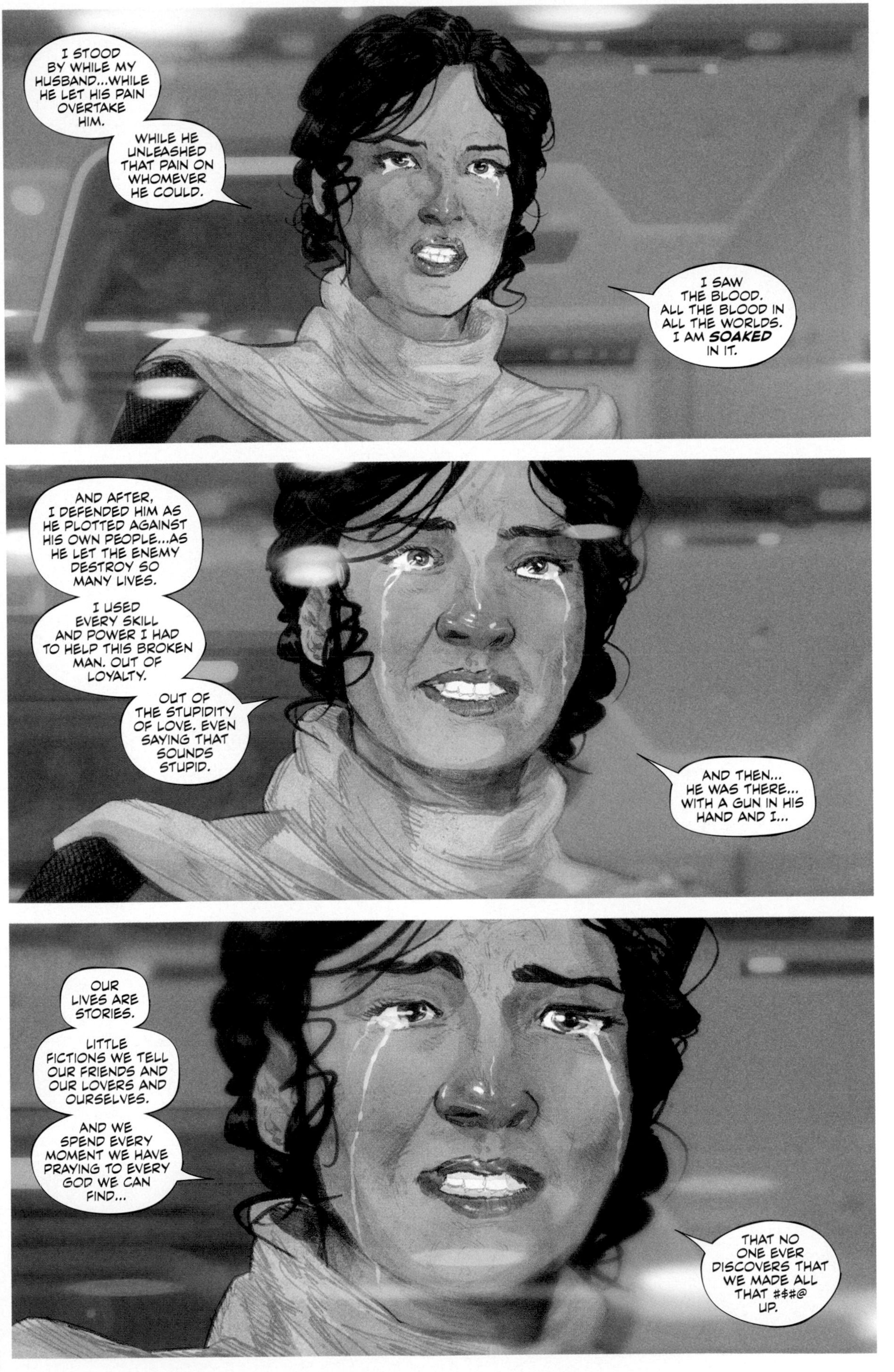
I STOOD BY WHILE MY HUSBAND...WHILE HE LET HIS PAIN OVERTAKE HIM.
WHILE HE UNLEASHED THAT PAIN ON WHOMEVER HE COULD.
I SAW THE BLOOD. ALL THE BLOOD IN ALL THE WORLDS. I AM **SOAKED** IN IT.
AND AFTER, I DEFENDED HIM AS HE PLOTTED AGAINST HIS OWN PEOPLE...AS HE LET THE ENEMY DESTROY SO MANY LIVES.
I USED EVERY SKILL AND POWER I HAD TO HELP THIS BROKEN MAN. OUT OF LOYALTY.
OUT OF THE STUPIDITY OF LOVE. EVEN SAYING THAT SOUNDS STUPID.
AND THEN... HE WAS THERE... WITH A GUN IN HIS HAND AND I...
OUR LIVES ARE STORIES.
LITTLE FICTIONS WE TELL OUR FRIENDS AND OUR LOVERS AND OURSELVES.
AND WE SPEND EVERY MOMENT WE HAVE PRAYING TO EVERY GOD WE CAN FIND...
THAT NO ONE EVER DISCOVERS THAT WE MADE ALL THAT #$#@ UP.

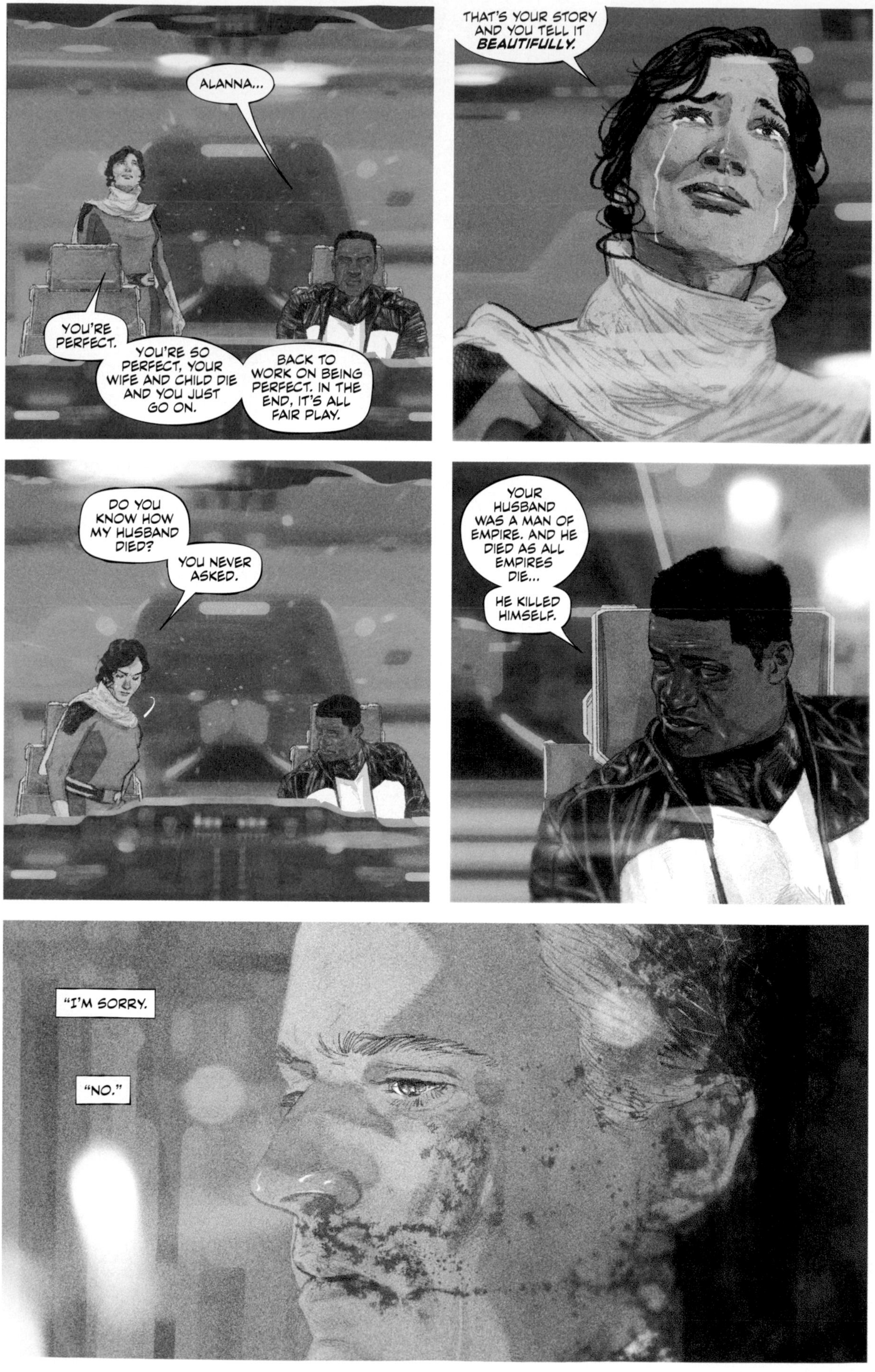

ALANNA...
YOU'RE PERFECT.
YOU'RE SO PERFECT, YOUR WIFE AND CHILD DIE AND YOU JUST GO ON.
BACK TO WORK ON BEING PERFECT. IN THE END, IT'S ALL FAIR PLAY.
THAT'S YOUR STORY AND YOU TELL IT BEAUTIFULLY.
DO YOU KNOW HOW MY HUSBAND DIED?
YOU NEVER ASKED.
YOUR HUSBAND WAS A MAN OF EMPIRE. AND HE DIED AS ALL EMPIRES DIE...
HE KILLED HIMSELF.
"I'M SORRY.
"NO."

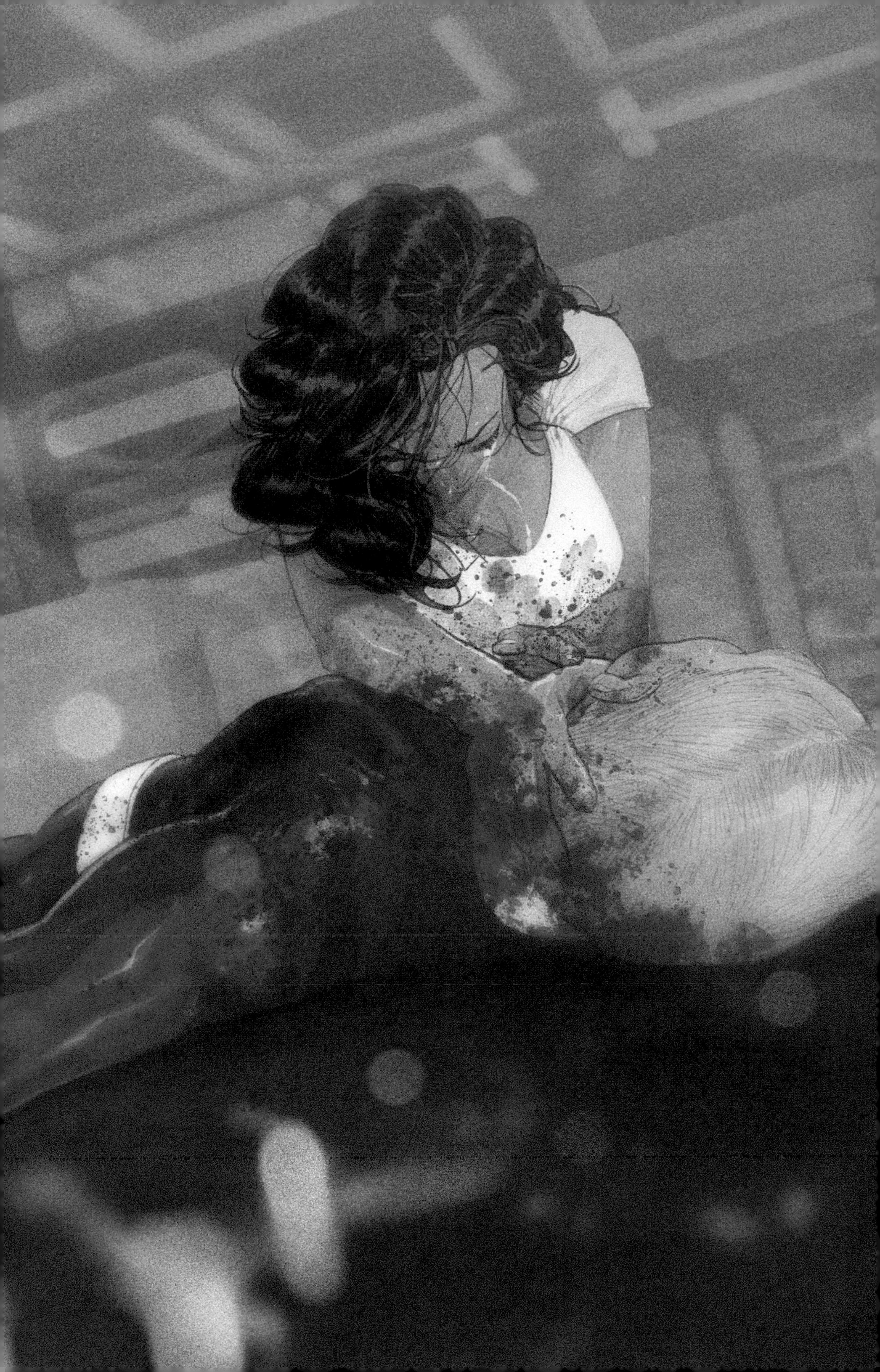

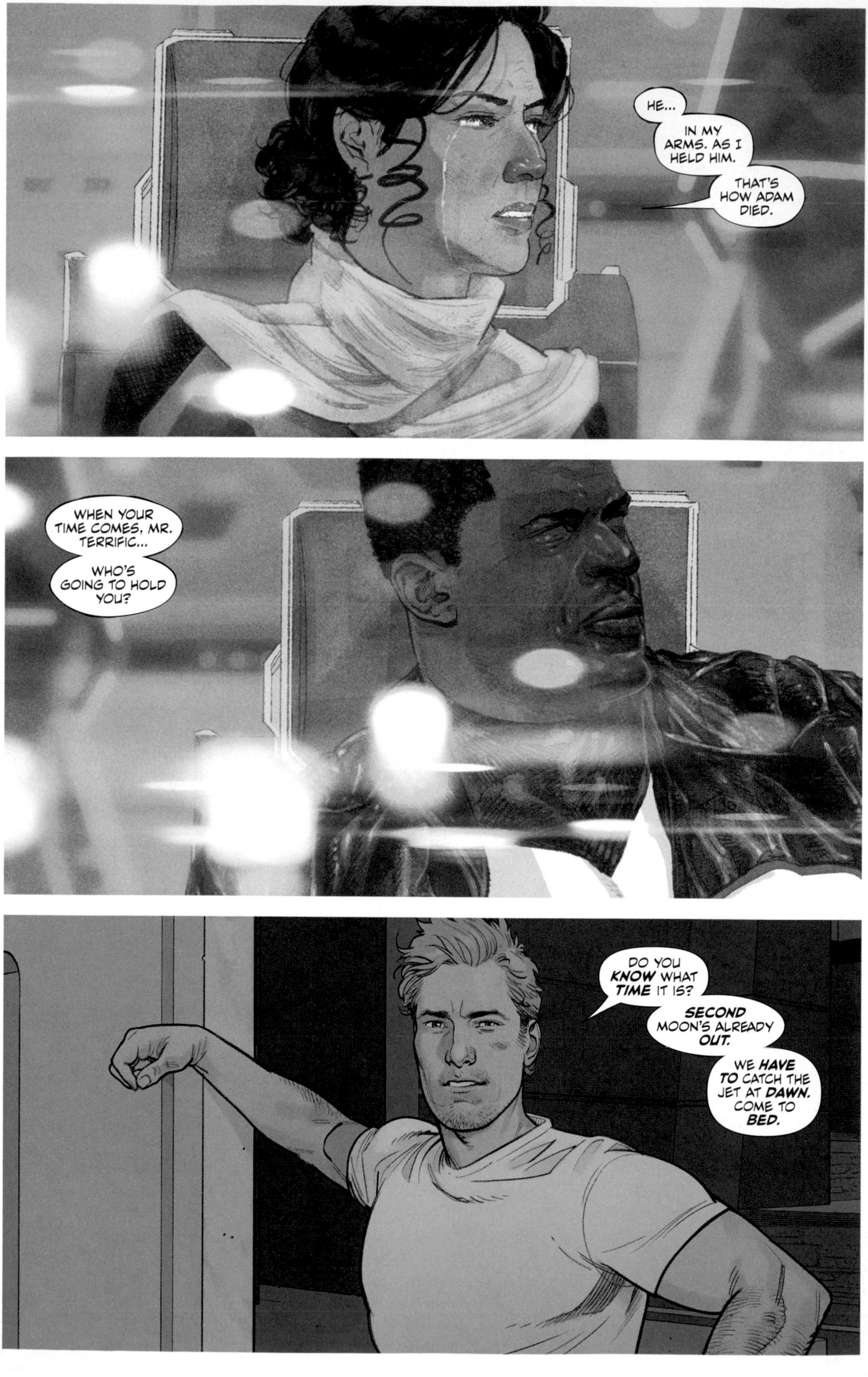
HE...
IN MY ARMS. AS I HELD HIM.
THAT'S HOW ADAM DIED.
WHEN YOUR TIME COMES, MR. TERRIFIC...
WHO'S GOING TO HOLD YOU?
DO YOU **KNOW** WHAT **TIME** IT IS?
SECOND MOON'S ALREADY **OUT.**
WE **HAVE TO** CATCH THE JET AT **DAWN.** COME TO **BED.**

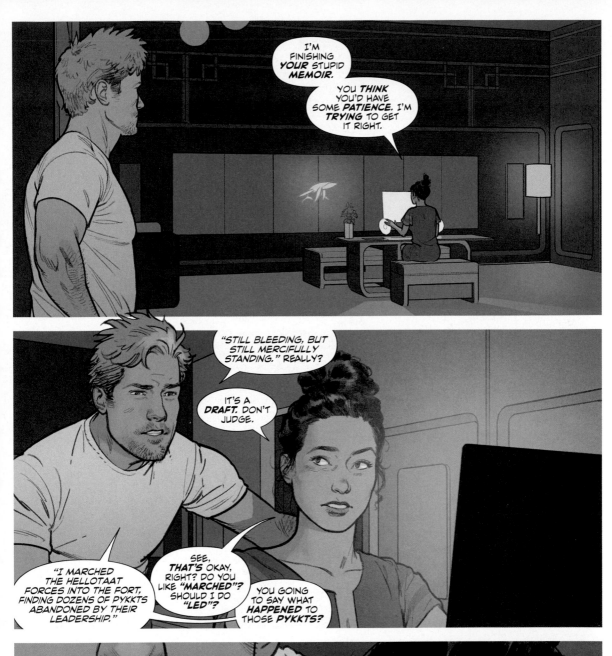

I'M FINISHING *YOUR* STUPID *MEMOIR.*

YOU *THINK* YOU'D HAVE SOME *PATIENCE.* I'M *TRYING* TO GET IT RIGHT.

"STILL BLEEDING, BUT STILL MERCIFULLY STANDING." REALLY?

IT'S A *DRAFT.* DON'T JUDGE.

"I MARCHED THE HELLOTAAT FORCES INTO THE FORT, FINDING DOZENS OF PYKKTS ABANDONED BY THEIR LEADERSHIP."

SEE, *THAT'S* OKAY, RIGHT? DO YOU LIKE *"MARCHED"*? SHOULD I DO *"LED"*?

YOU GOING TO SAY WHAT *HAPPENED* TO THOSE *PYKKTS?*

IT'S NOT *THAT* KIND OF BOOK.

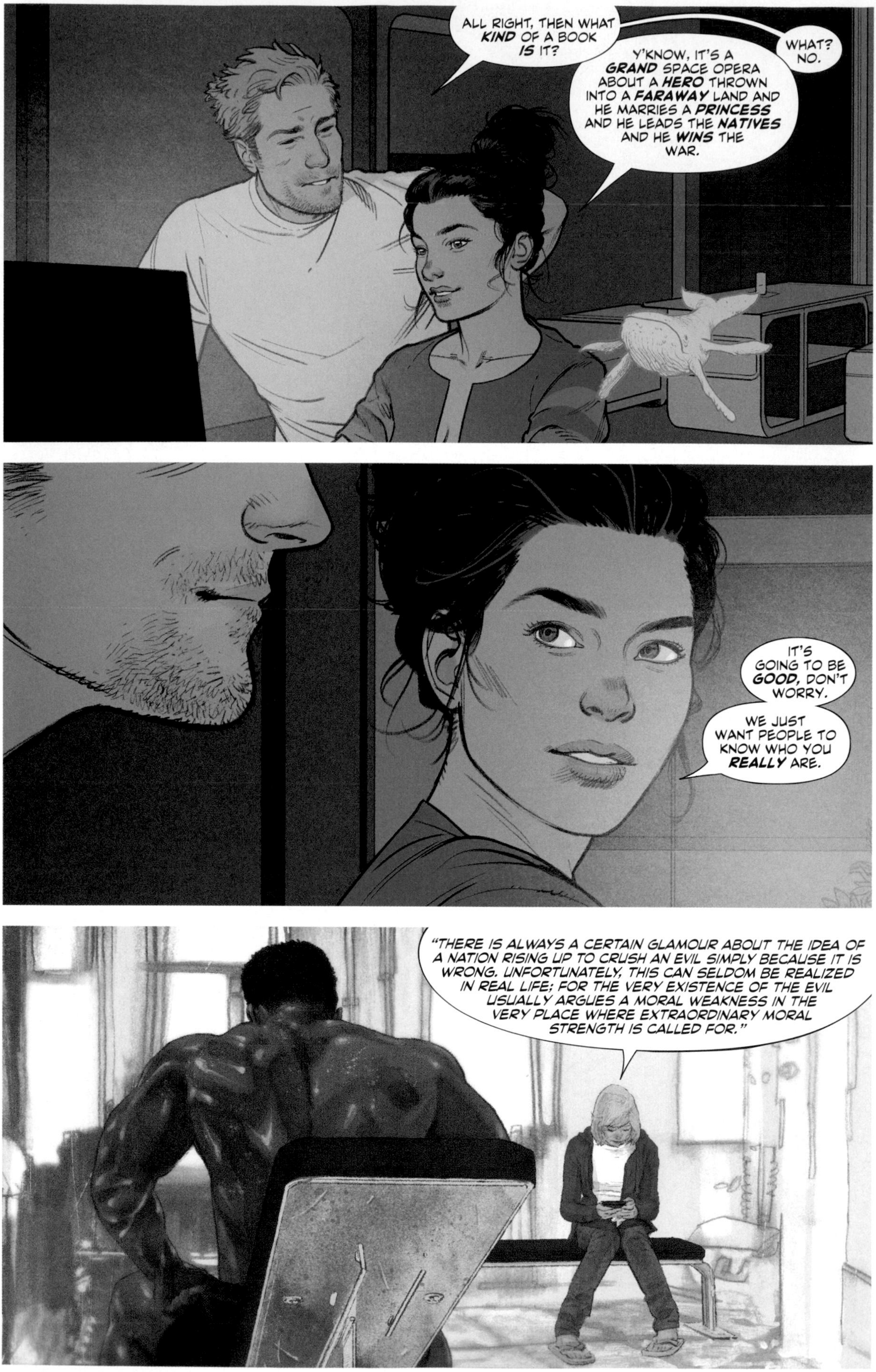
ALL RIGHT, THEN WHAT KIND OF A BOOK IS IT?
WHAT? NO.
Y'KNOW, IT'S A GRAND SPACE OPERA ABOUT A HERO THROWN INTO A FARAWAY LAND AND HE MARRIES A PRINCESS AND HE LEADS THE NATIVES AND HE WINS THE WAR.
IT'S GOING TO BE GOOD, DON'T WORRY.
WE JUST WANT PEOPLE TO KNOW WHO YOU REALLY ARE.
"THERE IS ALWAYS A CERTAIN GLAMOUR ABOUT THE IDEA OF A NATION RISING UP TO CRUSH AN EVIL SIMPLY BECAUSE IT IS WRONG. UNFORTUNATELY, THIS CAN SELDOM BE REALIZED IN REAL LIFE; FOR THE VERY EXISTENCE OF THE EVIL USUALLY ARGUES A MORAL WEAKNESS IN THE VERY PLACE WHERE EXTRAORDINARY MORAL STRENGTH IS CALLED FOR."

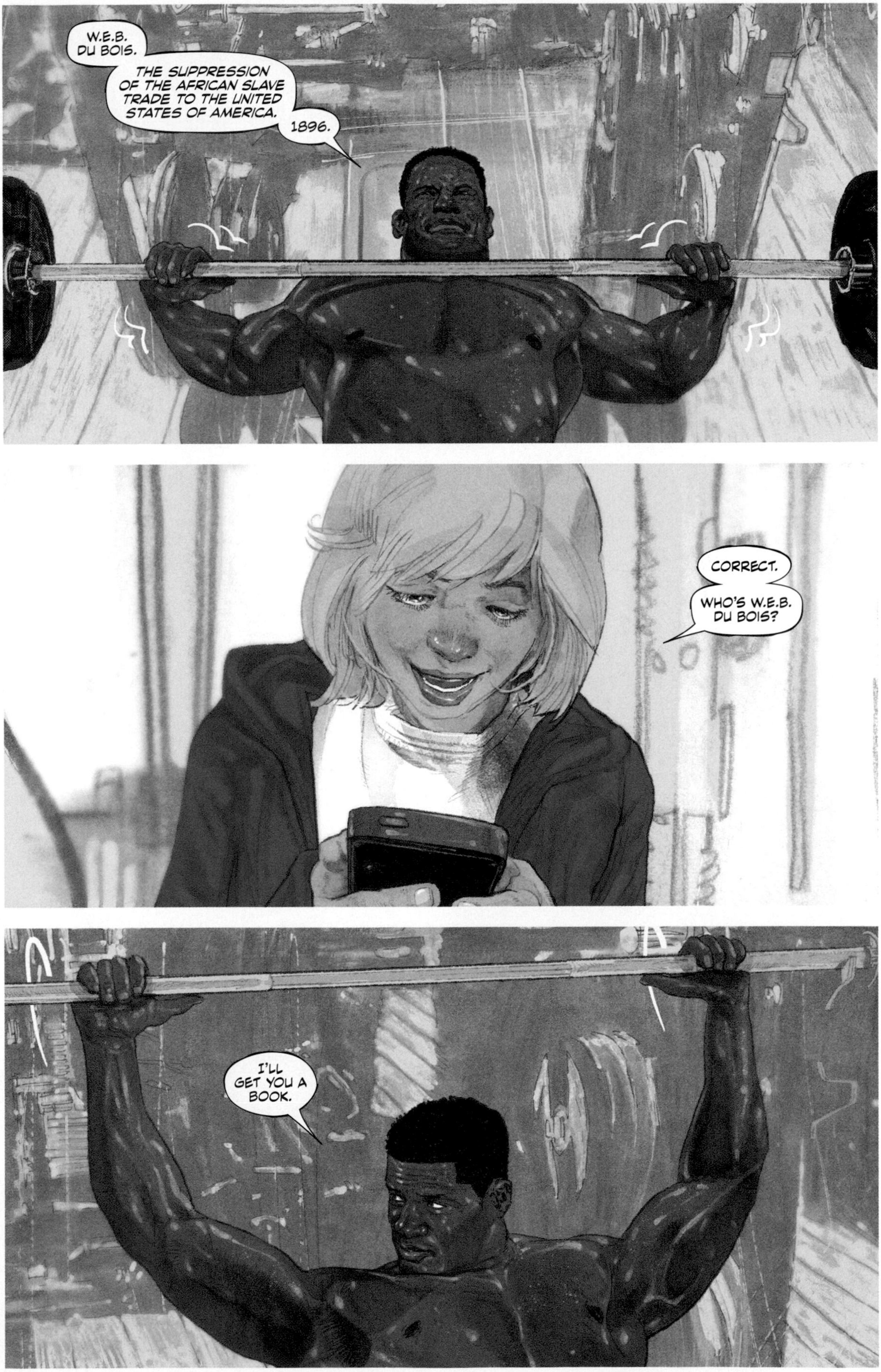
W.E.B. DU BOIS.
THE SUPPRESSION OF THE AFRICAN SLAVE TRADE TO THE UNITED STATES OF AMERICA.
1896.
CORRECT.
WHO'S W.E.B. DU BOIS?
I'LL GET YOU A BOOK.

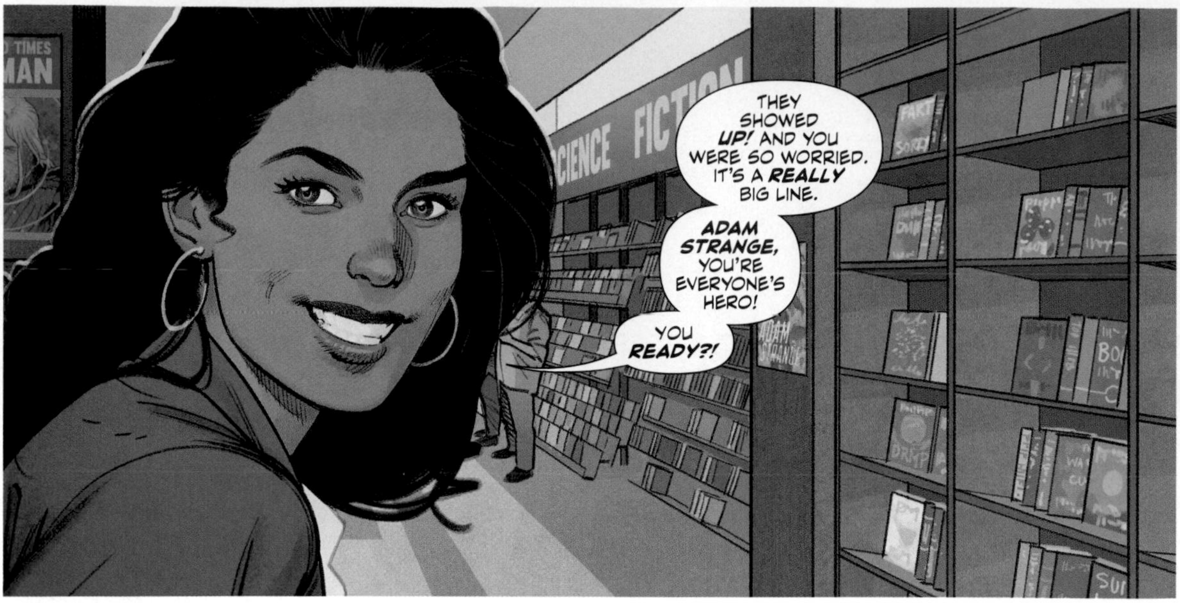
SCIENCE FICTION
THEY SHOWED UP! AND YOU WERE SO WORRIED. IT'S A REALLY BIG LINE.
ADAM STRANGE, YOU'RE EVERYONE'S HERO!
YOU READY?!

"One of the things that I found is that it is almost impossible to get somebody to make a cold turkey, dry, dispassionate decision to come into comics. It generally takes dedication and fanaticism."

—Gil Kane

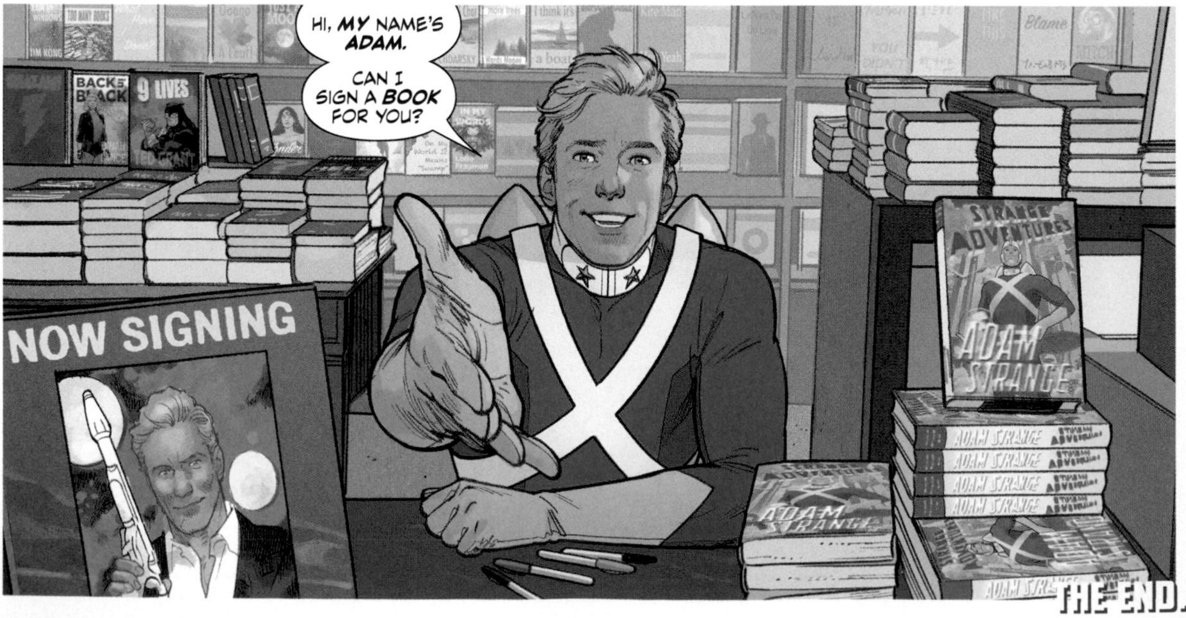
HI, MY NAME'S ADAM.
CAN I SIGN A BOOK FOR YOU?
NOW SIGNING
STRANGE ADVENTURES
ADAM STRANGE
THE END.

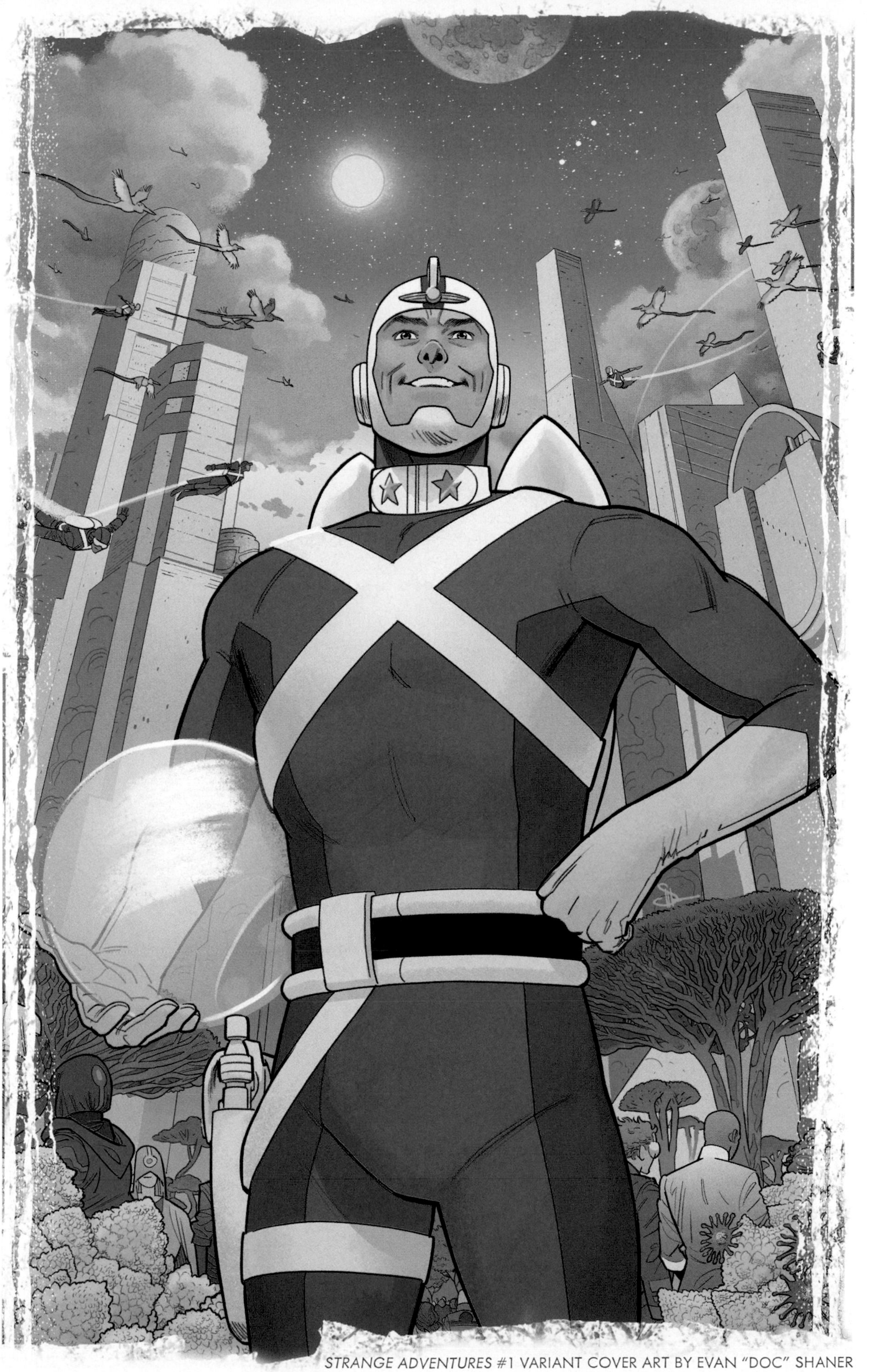

STRANGE ADVENTURES #1 VARIANT COVER ART BY EVAN "DOC" SHANER

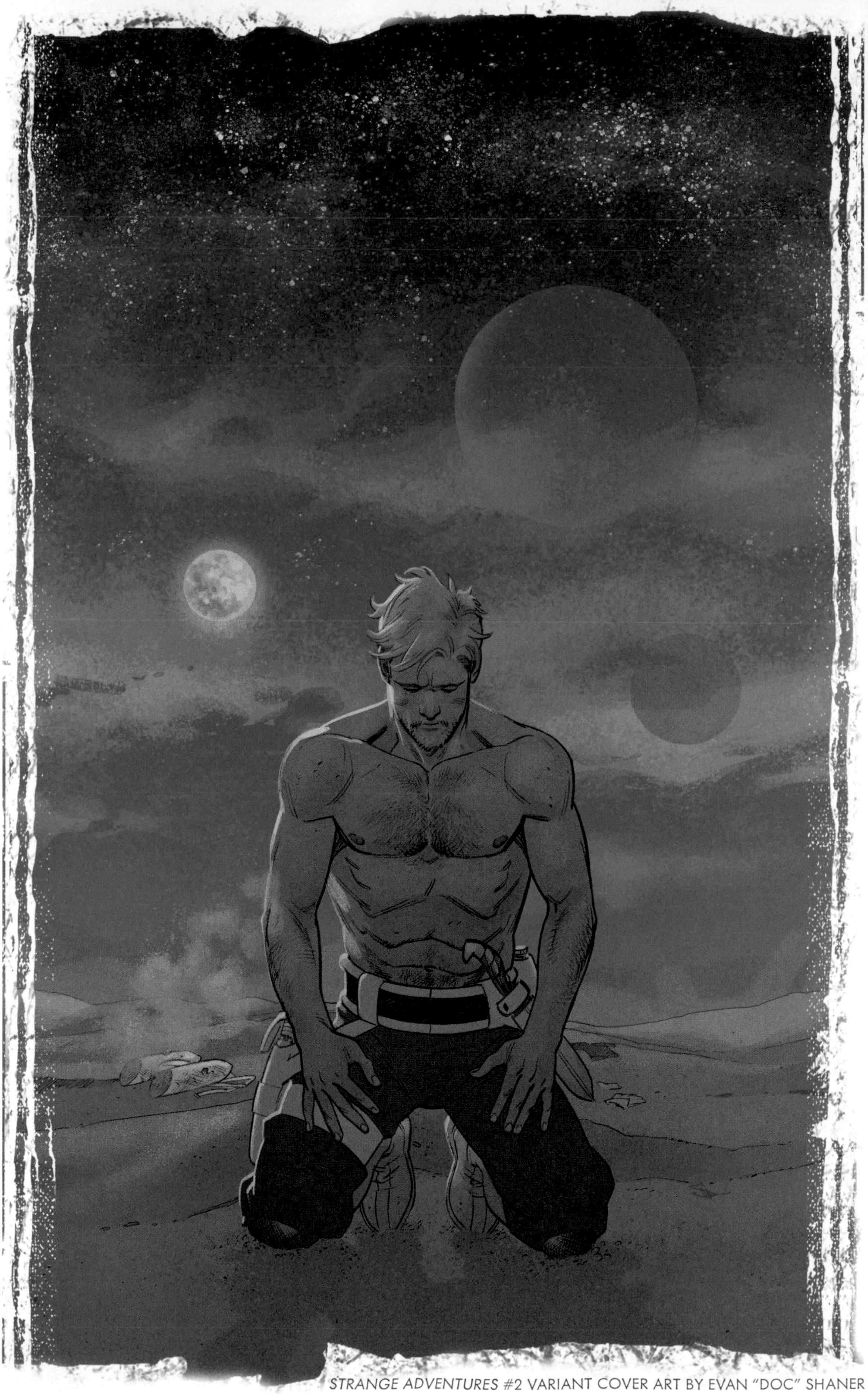

STRANGE ADVENTURES #2 VARIANT COVER ART BY EVAN "DOC" SHANER

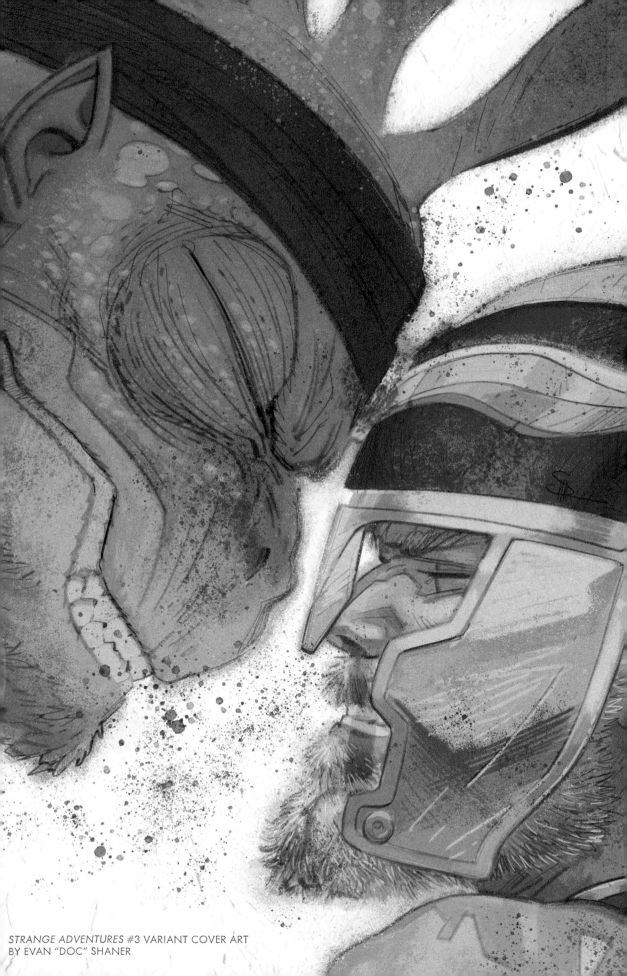

STRANGE ADVENTURES #3 VARIANT COVER ART
BY EVAN "DOC" SHANER

STRANGE ADVENTURES #4 VARIANT COVER ART BY EVAN "DOC" SHANER

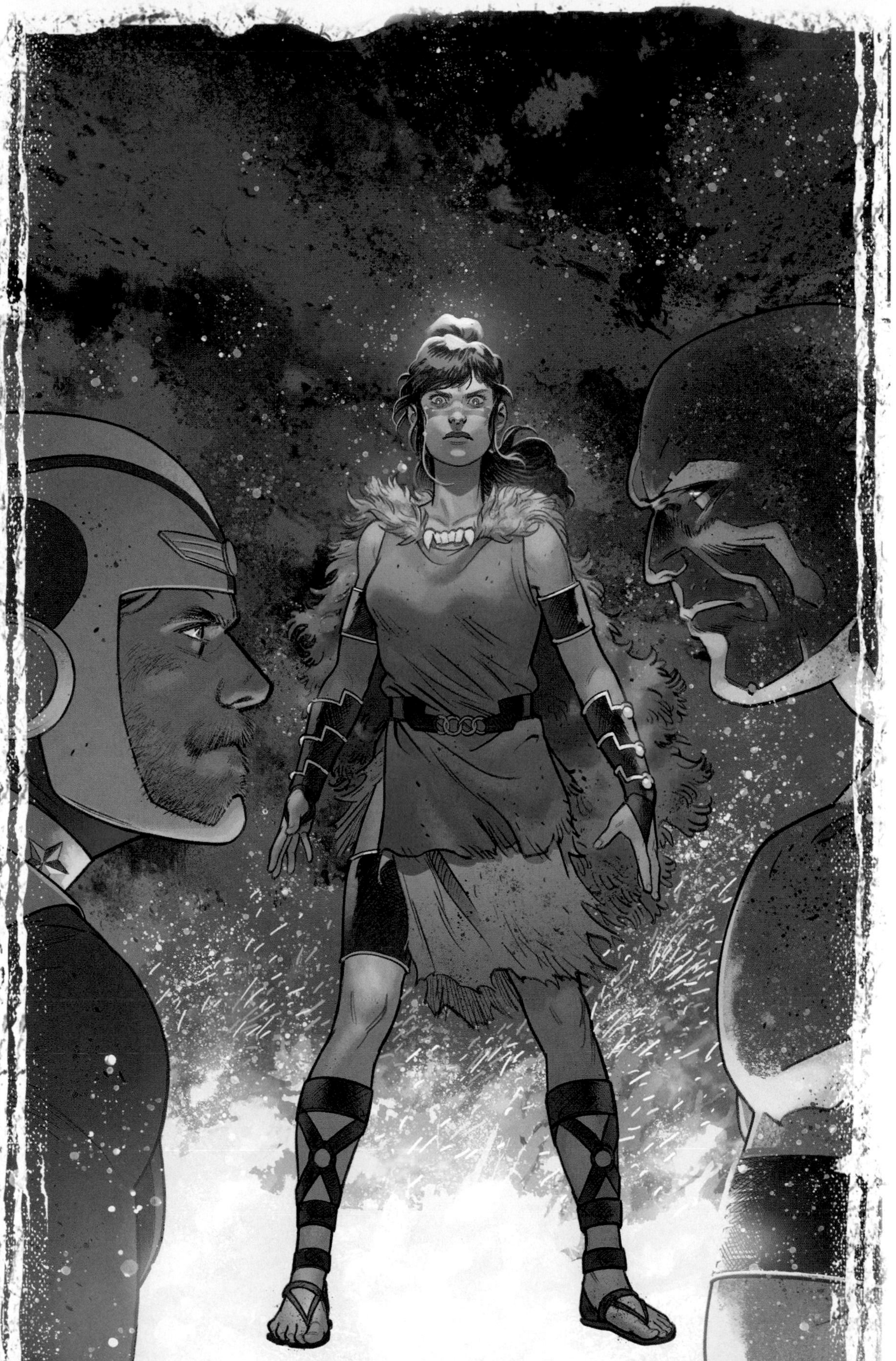

STRANGE ADVENTURES #5 VARIANT COVER ART BY EVAN "DOC" SHANER

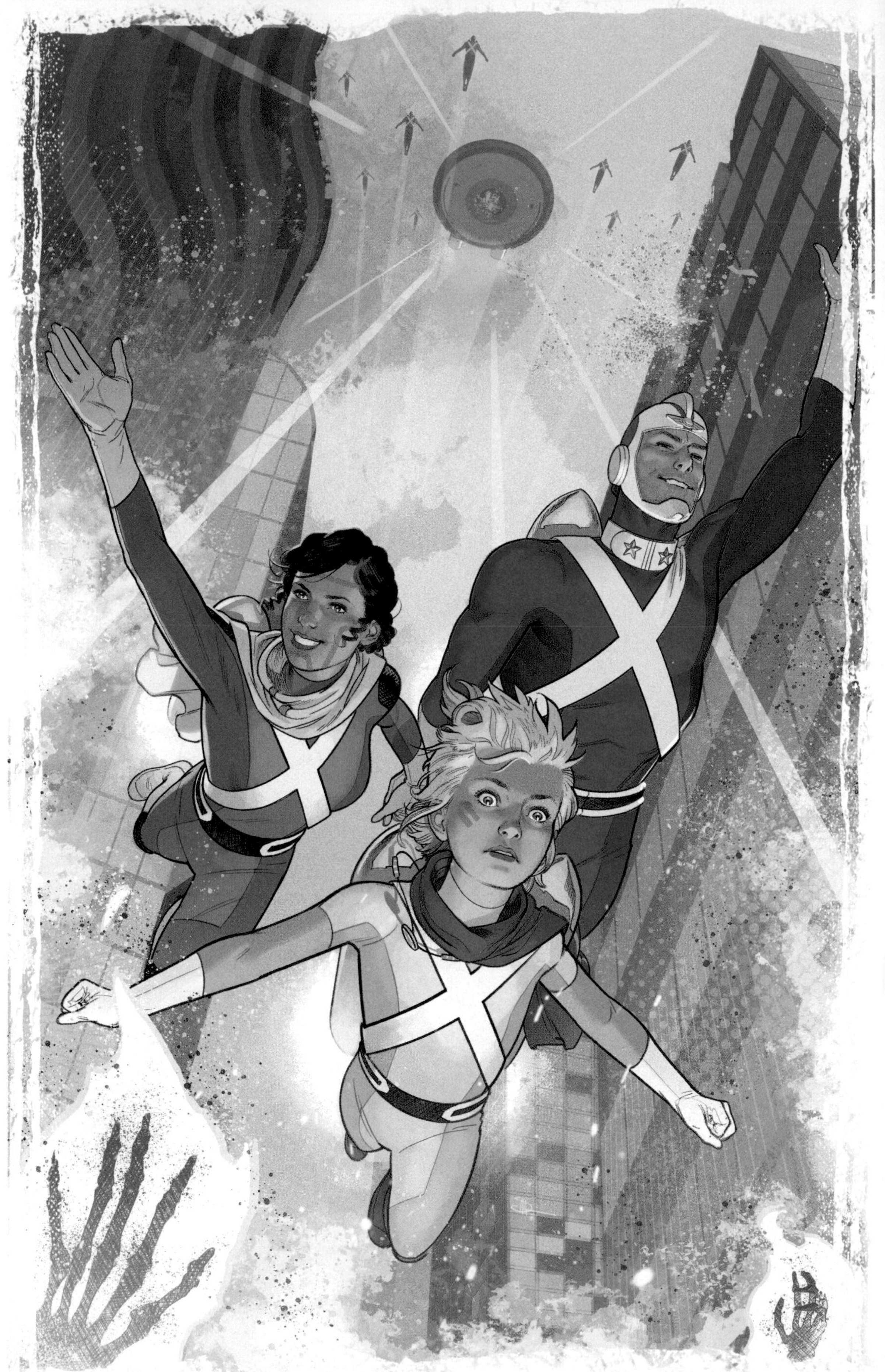

STRANGE ADVENTURES #6 VARIANT COVER ART BY EVAN "DOC" SHANER

STRANGE ADVENTURES #7 VARIANT COVER ART BY EVAN "DOC" SHANER

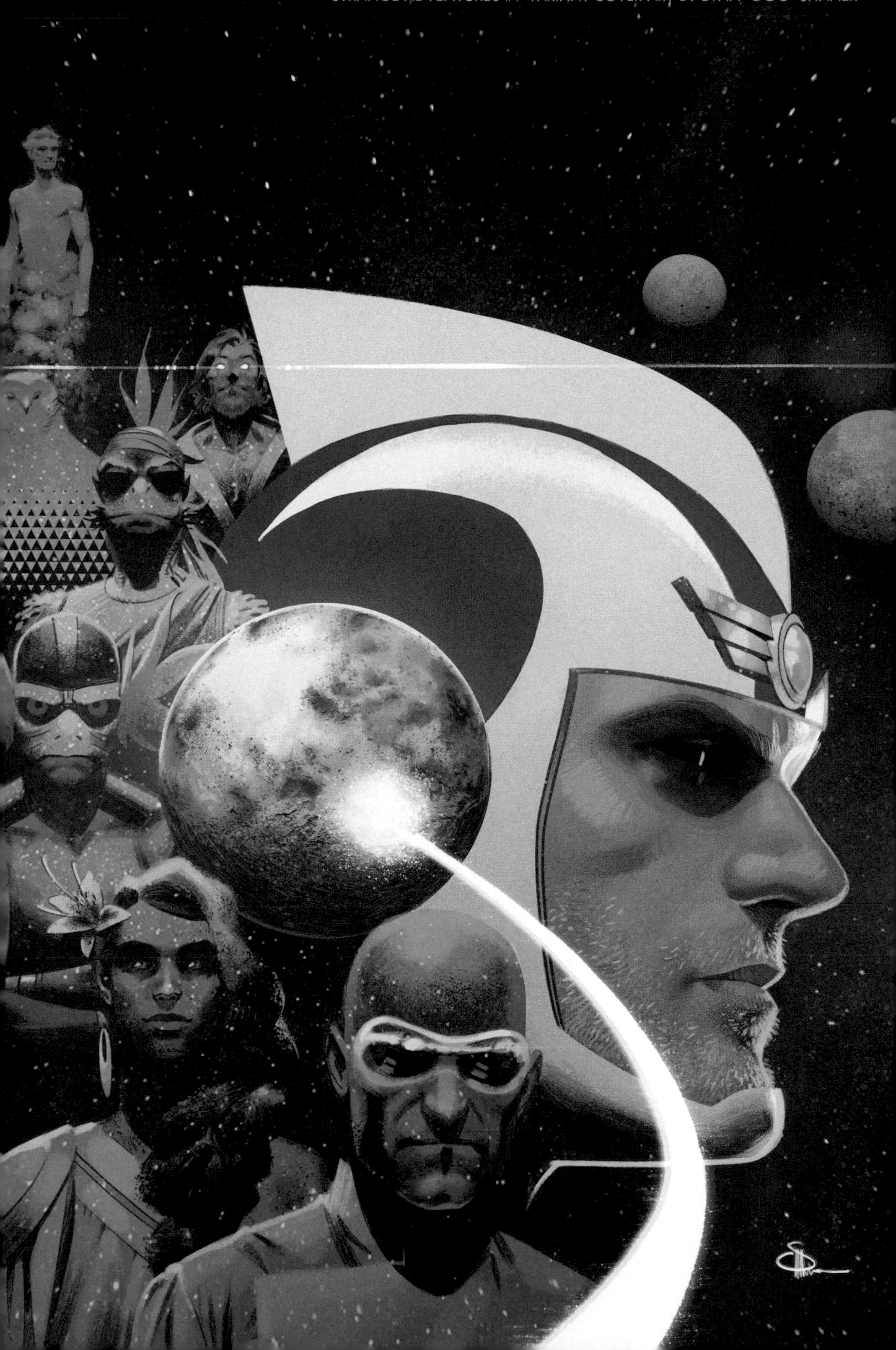

STRANGE ADVENTURES #8 VARIANT COVER ART
BY EVAN "DOC" SHANER

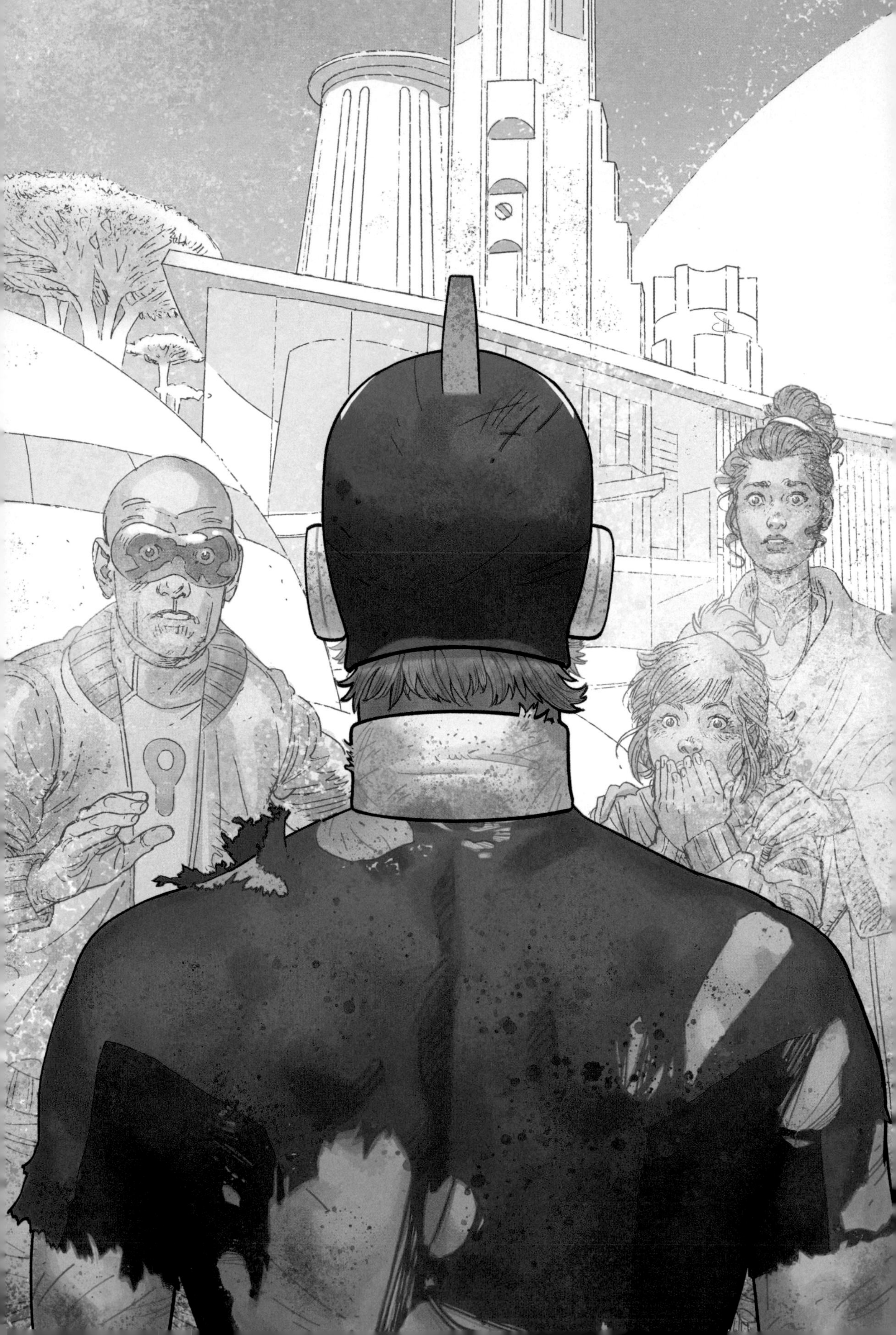

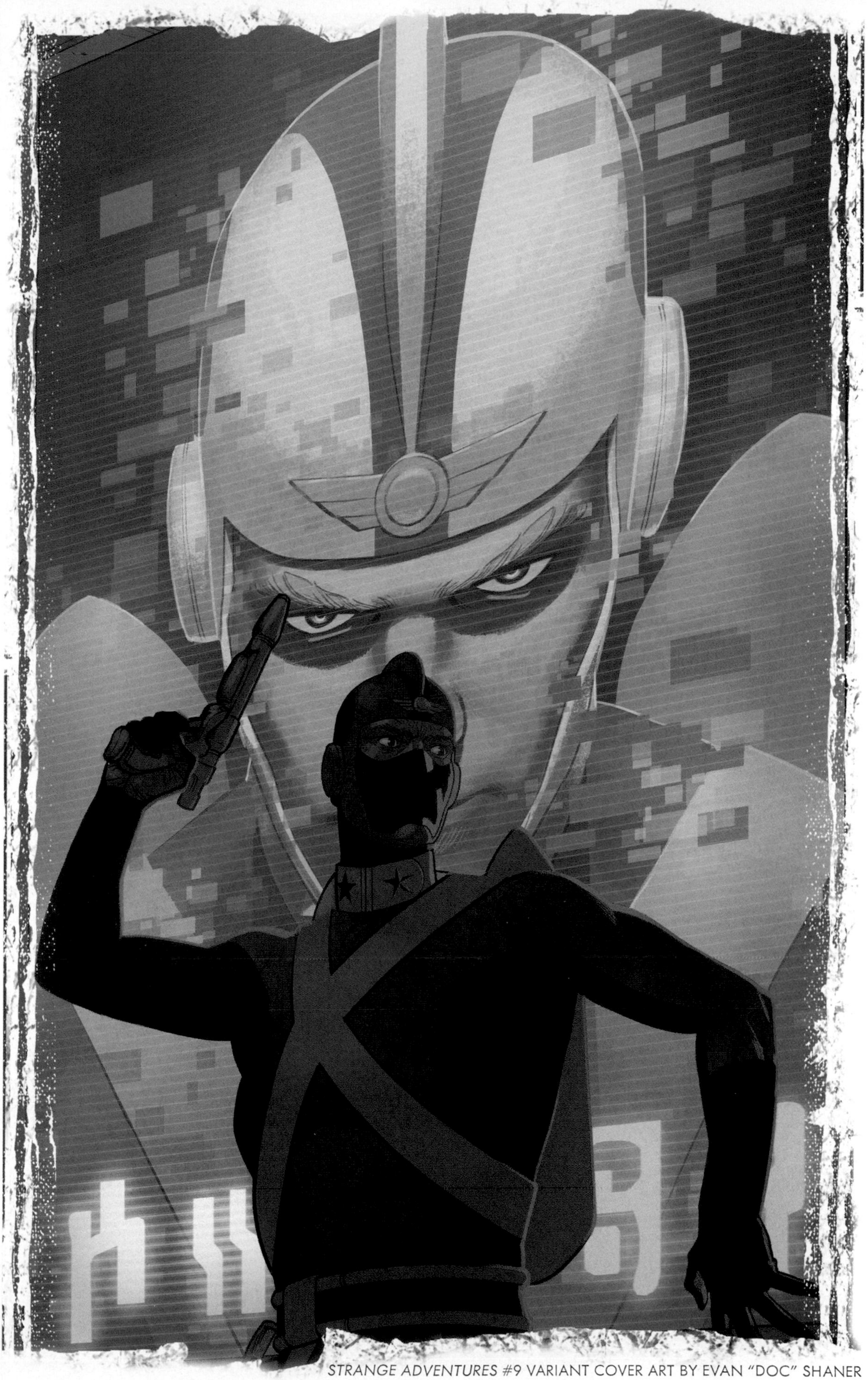

STRANGE ADVENTURES #9 VARIANT COVER ART BY EVAN "DOC" SHANER

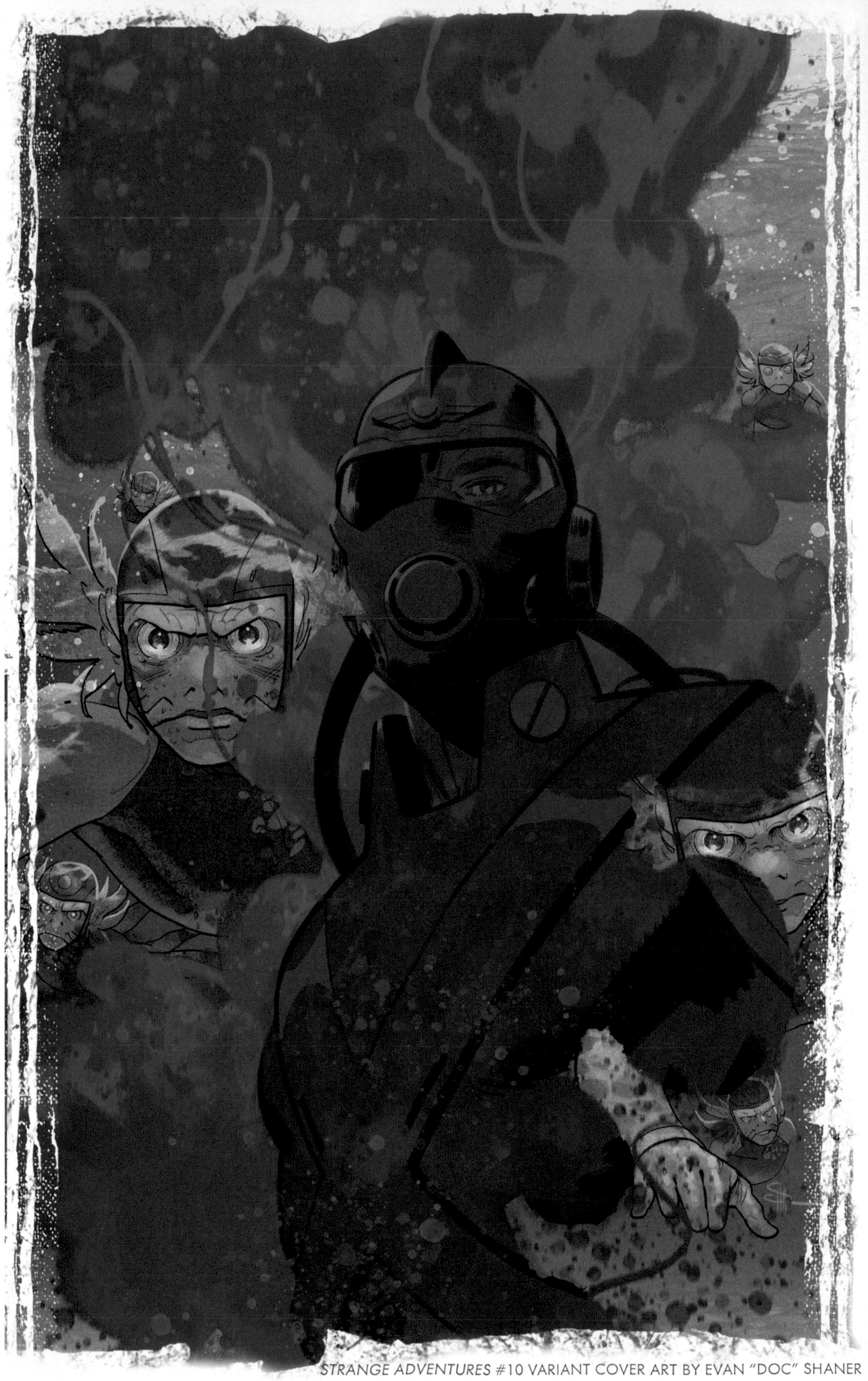

STRANGE ADVENTURES #10 VARIANT COVER ART BY EVAN "DOC" SHANER

STRANGE ADVENTURES #12 VARIANT COVER ART BY EVAN "DOC" SHANER

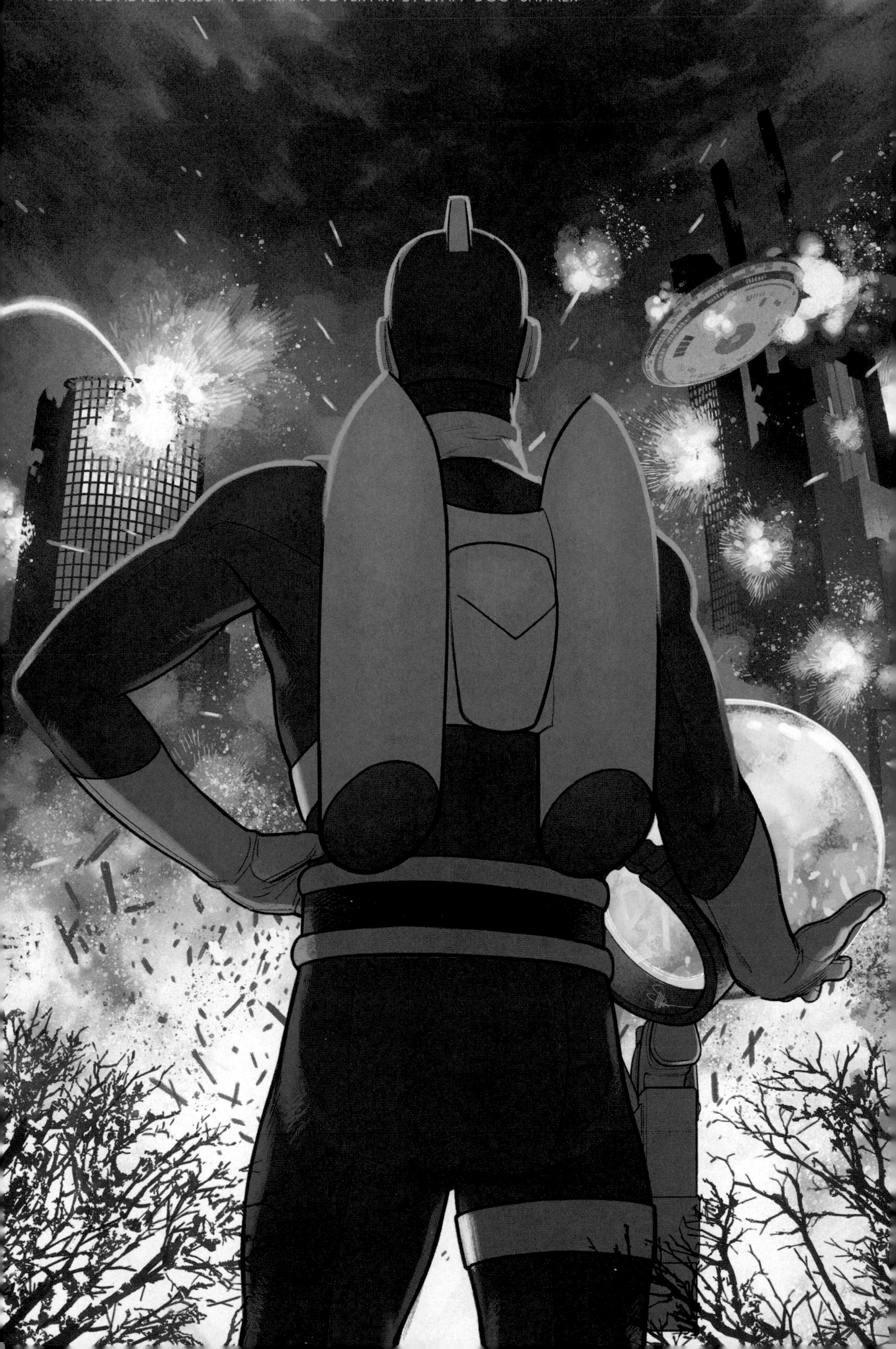

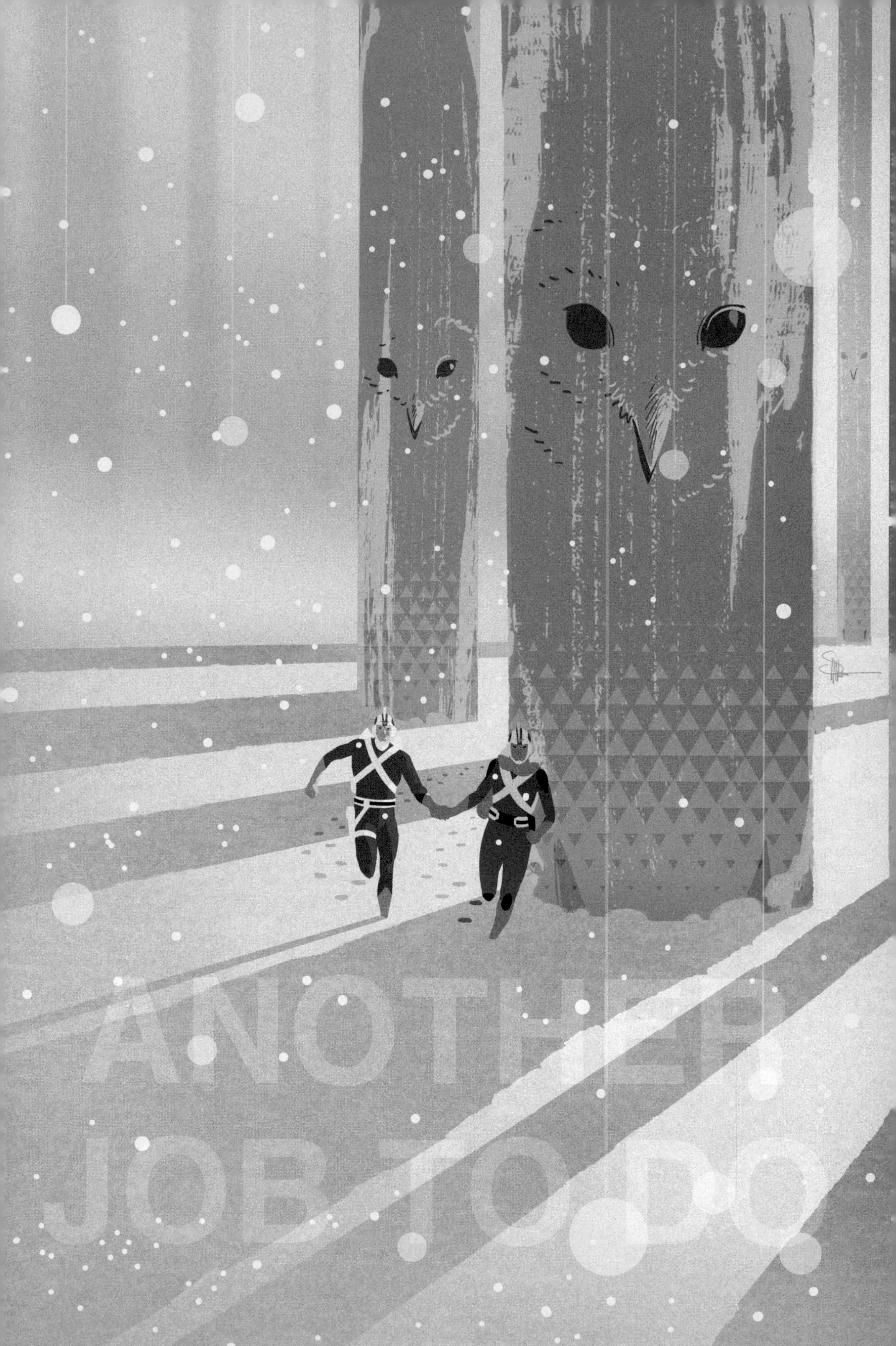
ANOTHER
JOB TO DO

STRANGE ADVENTURES #11 VARIANT COVER ART BY EVAN "DOC" SHANER